# Footprint Northern Spain

*Andy Symington*
3rd edition

*"My turning point was my pilgrimage to Santiago de Compostela.
It was then that I, who had dedicated most of my life to penetrate
the 'secrets' of the universe, realized that there are no secrets.
Life is and will always be a mystery."*

Paulo Coelho

# Northern Spain Highlights

See colour maps at back of book

**9** **Duero Valley**
Charming church-filled Soria and sumptuous Ribera del Duero wines, page 226.

**10** **Gormaz Castle**
One of the oldest Muslim citadels in Europe, with walls stretching for 1 km, page 227.

**11** **Bilbao** From urban wasteland to buzzy cultural capital, page 87.

**12** **Vizcayan Coast**
Plunging cliffs, a lush coastline and picturesque villages, page 79.

**13** **Laguardia and the wine country**
Catacomb-style bodegas beneath the medieval streets of Alava, page 115-117.

**14** **Dinosaur footprints**
120-million-year-old footprints harderened in the Mesozoic Riojan mud, page 206.

**15** **Tarazona** Hot and sleepy town that's a symphony of beautiful brick, page 165.

**16** **Fiesta de San Fermín**
Pamplona goes mad for its nine-day festival of bull running and wine swilling, page 128.

**17** **Jaca and the Aragonese Pyrenees**
The most dramatic area of the Pyrenees, page 179.

4

# Contents

*The traditional village of Alquézar in Huesca province is topped by a haughty castle. The surrounding zone is fabulous for canyoning.*

**Celtic dwelling**
*The traditional palloza can still be seen in Galicia. Dating back to Celtic times, it typically has a circular stone wall topped by a conical thatched roof.*

**Las Médulas**
This eerie and surreal area of mountains in the province of León has been sculpted into strange formations and criss-crossed by paths and tunnels.

# A foot in the door

Spain began in its north. Say that to the Asturians and they'll puff up with pride, for when the Moorish wave swept rapidly across the peninsula in the eighth century, the small mountain kingdom stood indomitable. It was from here that the long process of Christian reconquest began, laying the foundations of modern Spain. It wasn't necessarily subtle, and the culturally sophisticated Moors must have wondered where they had gone wrong, but the tide turned. The Asturians began to erect beautiful churches in the eighth century, León had 24 kings before Castilla had laws, and Castilla was a muscly European kingdom centuries before Madrid was heard of. Aragón ruled the western Mediterranean and half of Italy, and progressive Navarra briefly united the whole of Christian Spain in days when Vikings still prowled the seas.

Fascinatingly, these ancient kingdoms still exist, and not just in terms of modern administrative boundaries. Travel between the Basque country and neighbouring Burgos and you're crossing a sociocultural border that's immediately evident in every way: how people eat, dress, earn a living and even what language they speak. The same goes for Asturias, for Aragón, for Galicia; even the cities of the plain in Castilla seem like little autonomous kingdoms.

All this makes the region ripe for exploration. Apart from a few key areas, tourism in the north is is a world away from the crowded colonies of the southern coasts. It's the original Spain, or more accurately Spains, and whether you're admiring Gothic vaulting, nosing wine in the Rioja, surfing waves on the Basque coast or pacing the pilgrim road to Santiago, it's a vital, vivid and real place.

**Contemporary Northern Spain**

Although you'll still find rural villages seemingly unaffected by the passing of time, Northern Spain is a modern European society that has boomed in the 30-odd years since the death of Franco led to the end of dictatorship. The area, and the country as a whole, has flourished through the creation of semi-autonomous states; by celebrating rather than suppressing regional differences, the whole has been made stronger.

And these differences are vast. The Basque country is booming; it has one of the highest standards of literacy and living in the western world. By contrast, Galicia is one of the poorer regions in western Europe. Bilbao, transformed from a post-industrial anachronism to a byword for urban renewal, is ever-expanding, while tiny Soria administers one of the emptiest parts of the EU.

While you'll see many traditional aspects of life, such as the atmospheric fiestas in every hamlet and city – attend one if you can – don't let that fool you into thinking that there's anything 'quaint' about it.

**Modern styling**
*San Sebastián's Kursaal has brought architectural daring and film-star glamour to the formerly low-key district of Gros.*

The Spaniards have kept what they feel is valuable and relevant – socializing with friends, christening children, keeping close family ties – and discarded what they don't – attending church or having large families, for instance. Nevertheless, closer ties with Europe have ushered in some changes that would have been unthinkable a few years back. Smokers are being gradually marginalized, office workers in the cities are more likely to grab a quick sandwich than a three-course lunch, and the exigencies of work mean that on weekday nights people tend to be at home with a video rather than out on the town. These are relative, though, and there remains a refreshing unwillingness of the Spanish to be told what to do.

Without the year-round sunshine of the southern coasts, the regional governments have been active in promoting more diversified forms of tourism. The results are encouraging: the fabulous national parks and reserves of Asturias, the unspoiled mountainscapes of the Pyrenees and the green valleys of Euskadi or Galicia are backed by a network of excellent countryside accommodation.

**Romanesque ramparts**
*The Castillo do Loarre is one of the finest castles of Northern Spain and the setting for Ridley Scott's crusader film,* Kingdom of Heaven.

1  *Wine regions in northern Spain benefit from modern techniques but experiment with non-traditional varietals.* ▸▸ *See page 44.*

2  *The end of the road: pilgrims trudge for weeks to reach the magical cathedral of Santiago de Compostela.* ▸▸ *See page 386.*

3  *The coast of Asturias is popular with Spanish tourists in summer, but it's always possible to get away from the crowds.* ▸▸ *See page 365 and 373.*

4  *The Monasterio de San Juan de la Peña is decorated with the characteristic* ajedreazado jaqués *chessboard pattern that originated in these parts.* ▸▸ *See page 181.*

5  *Pamplona's nine-day Fiesta de San Fermín in July lays a serious claim to being the biggest party in Europe.* ▸▸ *See page 128.*

6  *Skiers enjoy the snow in the Canfranc Valley, one of several appealing winter-sports destinations in the Pyrenees.* ▸▸ *See page 182.*

7  *Wild bears and wolves still inhabit the forested parks of Asturias.* ▸▸ *See page 351.*

8  *Salamanca's architecturally perfect Plaza Mayor is a supreme spot to relax, as storks circle in the setting sun.* ▸▸ *See page 255.*

9  *The Picos de Europa would have been the first sight of land that weary Spanish sailors got on their return from the Americas.* ▸▸ *See page 329.*

10 *The 'coast of death' has an impressive history of shipwrecks and smugglers, but there are also excellent beaches and fishing towns.* ▸▸ *See page 410.*

11 *The two main pilgrim routes to Santiago converge near the beautiful Romanesque bridge at Puente La Reina.* ▸▸ *See page 143.*

12 *Mudéjar architecture, typified by the decorative use of brick and coloured tiles, was popular in Spain for several hundred years.* ▸▸ *See pages 166 and 460.*

**Highlights**

What you experience in Northern Spain depends in some ways on a choice between green and brown. Asturias has swathes of forested national park with the odd lurking bear, lively cities, seafood 'n' cider, pretty fishing ports, the sublime mountains of the Picos de Europa, terrific surf beaches and an ancient architecture all of its own. Many of the Pyrenees' best spots are in Aragón and Navarra; you can take your pick between lively centres for skiing and walking and find a hidden nook in a remote valley with only pasturing cows, soaring birds of prey and snow-capped summits for company. The Basque country is home to a very ancient people with a very ancient language; political goals aside, it's undeniably very different from the rest of the peninsula. The region's full of enticements – modern architecture, beaches, wine, walking and superb eating to name but a few – but the biggest drawcard are the Basques themselves. Convivial, opinionated, active, political, musical; they're the most welcoming folk in Northern Spain. The brown is Castilla, a wide expanse on the high, bare *meseta*. Studded with castles and fortified towns, it is at once noble, bleak, fierce and fascinating, mirroring the history of the empire it created and destroyed.

One common aspect is the region's immense architectural wealth. Even the most forgotten of villages may flaunt city walls, a majestic church and a handful of imposing stone *palacios* unchanged by the passage of time. All periods are represented; from the ancient and evocative Asturian royal constructions to the Gothic majesty of León or Burgos, from the

*One of the most enjoyable experiences in Bilbao is to stumble across the Guggenheim, perfectly framed, like some unearthly craft that's just landed.*

*Whether you're a serious climber, trekker or skier, or you just enjoy fresh air, the awe-inspiring mountainscapes of the Pyrenees live long in the memory.*

triumphant Plateresque of Salamanca to the Baroque flourishes of Santiago, the fine 19th-century lines of A Coruña, or modern tours de force in the Basque country. But many are the travellers who come to Northern Spain and leave seduced by the robust good looks and sensuous curves of the Romanesque. A large number of the region's most harmonious structures belong to this period; frequently built of golden stone and enlivened with imaginative stonework carved from the soul by outrageously talented masons. The style was diffused all along the Camino de Santiago, the great pilgrim route that crosses Northern Spain and is an unbeatable way to experience the region.

Spain always conjures up images of gastronomic pleasures; the north's passion for seafood is guaranteed to please anyone who casts hungry eyes at rockpools and goldfish bowls. Inland, hearty roasts and stews are perfect for banishing the winter chills. And the booze? Spain runs on it. While drinking cheap local wine in cafés and restaurants is an essential part of any visit, there are also several quality appellations that are worth seeking out. A jump in quality has put Rioja back among the best; Laguardia is a particularly atmospheric place to stay and do some tasting. While cruising the Galician coast, make sure you try some *albariño*, a deliciously aromatic white; inland the excellent reds of the Ribera del Duero and whites of Rueda perfume the air around Valladolid. The Basques make *txakolí*, a refreshing dry white with a slight fizz, and the reds of Navarra, Aragón, and León provinces are definitely something to be sniffed at too. *¡Salud!*

**Natural source**
The hilly landscape of western Navarra has many hidden treasures, such as the source of
the Urederra River, with its long waterfall and natural amphitheatre.

www.cyclingcenturies.com. Guided tours of the Camino de Santiago and Picos de Europa.
**Irish Cycling Safaris**, Belfield House, University College Dublin, Dublin 4, Ireland, T353 1 260 0749, www.cyclingsafaris.com. Irish set-up that runs tours to Northern Spain.
**Saddle Skedaddle**, T44 1912 651 110, www.skedaddle.co.uk. Mountain-biking and cycling trips in Northern Spain.

### Fiestas
**Travel Orb**, 4629 Cass St, San Diego CA 92109, T1 800 701 7826, www.travel orb.com. High-class tours to the San Fermín festival in Pamplona.

### Fishing
**GourmetFly**, 18 ave Edouard Vaillant, 92100 Boulogne, France, www.gourmetfly.com. Fly-fishing excursions to Northern Spain.

### Food and wine
**Epiculinary Tours**, www.epiculinary.com. Culinary tours and lessons that get into the heart of San Sebastián gastronomic societies.
**Euroadventures**, C Velásquez Moreno 9, Vigo, Spain, T34 986 221 399, www.euro adventures.net. Interesting tours and lessons, including culinary tours of the Basque region.

**Vintage Spain**, C Burgos 9, 4B, 09200 Miranda de Ebro, Spain, T34 699 2466 534, www.vintagespain.com. Tailor-made tours in Northern Spain, including wine tasting.

### Language
See also Language, page 22.
**Amerispan**, PO Box 58129 Philadelphia, PA 19102-8129, T215 751 1100 (worldwide), T800 879 6640 (North America), www.amerispan.com.
**Spanish Abroad**, 5112 N 40th St, Suite 103, Phoenix AZ 85253, T1 602 7786791, www.spanishabroad.com. 2-week immersion courses in Salamanca and San Sebastián.

### Motorcycling
**Ride Spain**, The Maltings, Knowle Hill, Hurley CV9 2JE, www.ridespain.com. Motorbike tours of the north, with flexible itineraries.

### Walking
See box, page 52, for Camino de Santiago.
**Pack and Pedal Europe**, RR # 1 Box 35A Springville, PA 18844-9578 USA, T1 570 965 2064, www.tripsite.com. Walking/cycling tours in the Pyrenees or Picos.
**Spain Adventures**, www.spainadventures. com. Hiking and biking in Northern Spain.

# Finding out more

The Spanish National Tourist Office produces a mass of information which you can obtain before you leave, from their offices abroad.

### Spanish tourist offices
See individual towns for local tourist offices.
**Belgium** Av des Arts 21, 1040 Bruxelles, T322 2801926.
**Canada** 2 Bloor St West, 34th floor, Toronto, Ont. M4W 3E2. T1 416 9613131.
**Denmark** Store Kogensgade,1-3, 1264 København, T45 33 151165.
**Finland** Mechelininkatu, 12-14, 00100 Helsinki, T358 0 441992.
**France** 43 Rue Decamps, 75784 Paris Cidex 16, T4503-8250.
**Germany** 180 Kurfürstendamm, 10707 Berlin, T49 308826543; Myliusstrasse 14, 60325 Frankfurt Main, T49 6972 5033.
**Italy** Via del Mortaro, 19-interno 5, Roma 00187, T39 66783106.

**Japan** Daini Toranomon Denki Bldg. 4F, 3-1-10 Toranomon. Minato-Ku; Tokio 105, T813 34326141/2.
**Netherlands** Laan Van Meerdervoort 8-8ª, 2517 Aj Den Haag, T31703465900.
**Norway** Ruselökkveien 26, 1251 Oslo – 2, T47 22834050.
**Sweden** Stureplan 6,114-35 Stockholm, T46 86114136.
**Switzerland** Seefeldstrasse 19, CH 8008 Zürich, T41 15257930.
**UK** 22-23 Manchester Sq, London W1M 5AP, T44 207 486 8077. 24-hr brochure request: T09063 640 630.
**USA** Water Tower Place, Suite 915 East 845, North Michigan Av, Chicago ILL 60611, T1 312 6421992; 8383 Wilshire Blvd, Suite 960, Beverley Hills, Los Angeles, CAL 90211, T1 213 658 7188; 1221; Brickell Av, Miami, Florida 33131, T1 305 3581992; 666 Fifth Av, New York NY 10103, T1 212 2658822.

**Useful websites**

**http://lacucaracha.info** Excellent site on the Spanish Civil War, with a humanist touch and strong Republican bias.

**soc.culture.spain** The busiest newsgroup on Spain. Multilingual, ranges from the political to the everyday, and is happily snobbery-free.

**www.alsa.es** Northern Spain's major bus operator. Book online.

**www.asturdata.es** *InfoAsturias*, the excellent Asturian government tourist site, with facilities for ordering brochures online.

**www.bilbao.net** The city's excellent website.

**www.ciudadhoy.com** Good Spanish-language site divided into cities with fresh information about bars, restaurants and nightclubs.

**www.elpais.es** Online edition of Spain's biggest-selling non-sports daily paper. English edition available.

**www.euskadi.net** The Basque government website. The tourism section is good if unwieldy; there's an accommodation search facility and you can order brochures online.

**www.feve.es** Website of the coastal FEVE train service.

**www.fordham.edu/halsall/sbook1p.html** A medieval sourcebook with lots of texts about the Middle Ages in Spain and plenty of handy links.

**www.idealspain.com** A good source of practical information.

**www.jcyl.es/jcyl/cict/dgt/svfit/turismo/** Castilla y León with lists of accommodation.

**www.okspain.org** Information about Spain, aimed at American viewers.

**www.paginasamarillas.es** Yellow Pages.

**www.paginasblancas.es** The White ones.

**www.paisvasco.com** A useful directory-style service with accommodation/restaurant section, as well as details of upcoming cultural activities.

**www.red2000.com** A good introduction to the geography and culture of Spain.

**www.renfe.es** Train timetables and tickets.

**www.spain.info** The official website of the Spanish tourist board.

**www.spain360vr.com** Cool 360° pictures of the Camino de Santiago route.

**www.staragon.com** Useful Aragonese site.

**www.tienda.com** Delivery of Spanish food products and handicrafts worldwide.

**www.tourspain.es** A good website run by the Spanish Tourist Board.

**www.turgalicia.es** The Galician Xunta's good tourist section.

**www.turismoaragon.com** About Aragón.

**www.turismo.cantabria.org** Cantabria's site.

**www.tuspain.com** A good selection of information about all aspects of Spain.

**www.vivirasturias.com** Comprehensive listing of tourist resources in Asturias.

# Language

For travelling purposes, everyone in Northern Spain speaks Spanish, known either as *castellano* or *español*, and it's a huge help to know some. Most young people know some English, and standards are rapidly rising, but don't assume that people aged 30 or over know any at all. While efforts to speak the language are appreciated, it's more or less expected, to the same degree as English is expected in Britain or the USA. Nobody will be rude if you don't speak any Spanish, but nobody will think to slow their rapid fire stream of the language for your benefit either, or pat you on the back when you say something in Spanish. While many visitor attractions have some sort of information available in English (and to a lesser extent French and German), many don't, or have English tours only in times of high demand. ◗◗ *See page 21 for language schools, and the Directory of individual towns. See Footnotes, page 478, for useful words and phrases.*

The other tongues you'll come across in Northern Spain are *Euskara/Euskera* (the Basque language), *Galego* (Galician), *Bable* (the Asturian dialect) and perhaps *Aragonés*. (Aragonese). *Euskara* is wholly unrelated to Spanish; if you're interested in Basque culture, by all means learn a few words (and make instant friends), but be aware that many people in Euskadi aren't Basque, and that it's quite a political issue. *Bable* and *Galego* are more similar (in descending order), and a limited knowledge of a couple of key words will be helpful for road signs, etc.

# Disabled travellers

Spain isn't the best-equipped of countries in terms of disabled travel, but things are improving rapidly. By law, all new public buildings have to have full disabled access and facilities (as do all hotels built since 1995), but disabled toilets are rare in other edifices. Facilities are significantly better in the touristed south than in Northern Spain. Most trains and stations are wheelchair friendly to some degree, as are many urban buses, but intercity buses are often not accessible for wheelchairs. **Hertz** offices in Madrid and Barcelona have a small range of cars set up for disabled drivers, but book them well in advance. Nearly all underground and municipal car parks have lifts and disabled spaces, as do many museums and castles. An invaluable resource for finding a bed are the regional accommodation lists, available from tourist offices. Most of these include a disabled-access criterion. Many *pensiones* are in buildings with ramps and lifts, but there are many that are not, and the lifts can be small. Nearly all *paradores* and modern chain hotels are fully wheelchair-accessible, but it's best to check. While major cities are quite straightforward, towns and villages often have uneven footpaths, steep streets (frequently cobbled) and little disabled infrastructure.

Blind visitors are comparatively well catered for in Spain as a result of the efforts of **ONCE**ⓘ *www.once.es (English-speaking)*, the national organization for the blind, which runs a lucrative daily lottery. Contact them for information and contacts.

**Useful organizations**
**Confederación Nacional de Sordos de España (CNSE)**, www.cnse.es. Links to local associations for the deaf.
**Federación ECOM**, T934 515 550, www.ecom.es. A helpful Barcelona-based organization that provides information on disabled-friendly tourist facilities in Spain.
**Global Access**, www.globalaccessnews.com. Reports from disabled travellers and links.

**Jubilee Sailing Trust**, Hazel Rd, Woolston, Southampton, SO19 7GB, T023 8044 9108, www.jst.org.uk. Tall ships running sailing journeys for disabled and able-bodied people, some around Northern Spain.
**RADAR**, T020 7250 3222, www.radar.org.uk. A British network for disabled people that can help members get information and contacts for disabled travel around Europe.

# Gay and lesbian travellers

Homosexuality is legal, and all ages of consent have been equalized (age 13; or 15 if an 18 year-old, or older is involved). Northern Spain has nothing to compare with the pink scene of Barcelona/Sitges, Madrid and Ibiza, but most middle-sized towns will have at least one venue; most have several.

Euskadi's political awareness and antipathy to Spanish conservatism means that the Basque cities are among the most tolerant in the peninsula. Gay tourism has increased dramatically in Bilbao since the opening of the Guggenheim, and it has the busiest scene. San Sebastián has plenty of life in summer, as do other places along the north coast, like Santander, Laredo and A Coruña. Overt displays of homophobia are rare and couples on the street shouldn't encounter any unpleasantness in the city; some of the smaller Castilian towns may be a different story. In rural areas amazed stares are the order of the day. It's very rare to see couples kissing in public.

*Black straws at the bar are often a discreet sign of a gay-friendly establishment, or bar de ambiente.*

**Useful organizations**
**Cogailes**, www.cogailes.org. A gay organization with a handy information service on e-ros@cogailes.org or a freephone hotline, T900 601 601 (daily T1800-2200).
**COLEGA**, www.colegaweb.net. A gay and lesbian association with offices in many cities.

**Shanguide** is a useful magazine with reviews, events, information and city-by-city listings for the whole country.

**Useful websites**
http://orbita.starmedia.com/~jordino/
   pagg.html  Links to organizations and sites.
www.chueca.com  Venues and listings.
www.corazongay.com  (Spanish).

www.damron.com  Listings and travel info.
www.es.gay.com  Contacts and chat.
www.gayinspain.com  Listings.
www.gay.com and www.gaywired.com
(English)  Listings and information about various Spanish cities.
www.guiagay.com  (Spanish).
www.mensual.com  Listings.
www.solodecontactos.com  Contacts.

## Student travellers

An **International Student Identity Card** (**ISIC**), available to full-time students, is valuable in Spain. You can get one where you study, or at many travel agencies both in and outside Spain. The cost varies from country to country, but is generally about €6-10 – a worthwhile investment, as it gets discounts of up to 20% on some plane fares, train tickets, museum entry, bus tickets and accommodation. A **Euro Under 26** card gives similar discounts, and is available to anyone aged 25 or under. In Spain, the most useful travel agencies for youth and student travel are **UsitUnlimited** and **TIVE**.

## Travelling with children

Kids are kings in Spain, and it's one of the easiest places to take them along on holiday. Children socialize with their parents from an early age here, and you'll see them eating in restaurants and out in bars well after midnight. The outdoor summer life and high pedestrianization of the cities is especially suitable and stress-free for both you and the kids to enjoy the experience.

Spaniards are very friendly and accommodating towards children, and you'll undoubtedly get treated better with them than without, except perhaps in the most expensive restaurants and hotels. Few places, however, are equipped with highchairs, unbreakable plates or baby-changing facilities. Children are expected to eat the same food as their parents, although you'll sometimes see a *menú infantil* at a restaurant, which typically has simpler dishes and smaller portions than the norm.

The cut-off age for children paying half or no admission/passage on public transport and in tourist attractions varies widely. **RENFE** trains let children under four travel for free, and its discount passage of around 50% applies up to the age of 12. Most car rental companies have child seats available, but it's wise to book these in advance, particularly in summer.

As for attractions, beaches are an obvious highlight, but many of the newer museums are attractively hands-on, and playgrounds and parks are common. Campsites cater to families and the larger ones often have child-minding facilities and activities.

## Women travellers

Northern Spain is a very safe destination for female travel; there's none of the harassment that you'll find in some parts of the south or elsewhere. While attitudes of the older generation are still prehistoric in some areas, this will rarely translate into anything less than perfect courtesy. Aggressive sexuality isn't part of the makeup of the northern Spanish male; if you go out on your own, you can expect to be chatted to, but it's very rarely going to be anything more than mild flirtation.

# Working in Spain

The most obvious paid work for English speakers is to teach the language. Even the smallest towns usually have an English college or two; it's taken off in a big way here. Rates of pay aren't great except in the large cities, but the cost of living is low, so you can live quite comfortably. The best way of finding work is by trawling around the schools, but there are dozens of useful internet sites; www.eslcafe.com, www.eslusa.org, or www.escapeartist.com. There's also a more casual scene of private teaching; noticeboards in universities and student cafés are the best way to find work of this sort, or to advertise your own services.

Bar work is also relatively easy to find, particularly in summer. Irish theme bars in the larger cities are an obvious choice, but smaller towns along the north coast also have plenty of seasonal work. Live-in English-speaking au pairs and childminders are also popular with wealthier city families wanting to give young children some exposure to the English language.

EU citizens are at an advantage when it comes to working in Spain; they can work without a permit for 90 days. In theory, you are supposed to apply for a *tarjeta de residencía* after 90 days – a time-consuming process, but in practice, with open borders, nobody really cares unless you give them a reason to. Non-EU citizens need a working visa, obtainable from Spanish embassies or consulates, but you'll need to have a firm offer of work to obtain it. Most English schools can organize this for you but make sure you arrange it before arriving in the country.

# Before you travel

## Visas and immigration

Entry requirements are subject to change, so always check with the Spanish tourist board or an embassy/consulate if you're not an EU citizen. EU citizens and those from countries within the Schengen agreement can enter Spain freely. UK/Irish citizens will need to carry a passport, while an identity card suffices for other EU/Schengen nationals. Citizens of Australia, the USA, Canada, New Zealand and Israel can enter without a visa for up to 90 days. Other citizens will require a visa, obtainable from Spanish consulates or embassies. These are usually issued very quickly and valid for all Schengen countries. The basic visa is valid for 90 days, and you'll need two passport photos, proof of funds covering your stay and possibly evidence of medical cover (ie insurance). For extensions of visas, apply to an *oficina de extranjeros* in a major city. These are also the places to go if, as an EU citizen, you are seeking residency (*tarjeta de residencia*). British citizens should get hold of a **European Health Insurance Card** (**EHIC**), available via www.dh.gov.uk or from post offices in the UK, before leaving home. This guarantees free medical care throughout the EU. Other citizens should seriously consider medical insurance, but check for reciprocal Spanish cover with your private or public health scheme first. Insurance is a good idea anyway to cover you for theft, etc. In the event of theft, you'll have to make a report at the local police station within 24 hours and obtain a report to show your insurers. (English levels at the police station are likely to be low, so try to take a Spanish speaker with you to help).

No **vaccinations** are needed to enter or travel around Spain. See Health, page 55, for further information.

## Spanish embassies and consulates

**Australia** 15 Arkana St, Yarralumla, Canberra 2600, T6273 35 55, ambespau@mail.mae.es.

**Canada** 74 Stanley Av, Ottawa, T747 2252, www.embaspain.ca.

**Denmark** Kristianiagade 21, 2100 Copenhagen, T31 42 47 00, embespdk@mail.mae.es.

**Finland** Kalliolinnantie 6, 00140 Helsinki, T687 7080, embespfi@mail.mae.es.

**France** 22 Av Marceau, 75381 Paris, Cedex 08, T44 43 18 00, ambespfr@mail.mae.es.

**Germany** Lichtensteinallee 1, D-10787, Berlin, T261 60 81, www.spanischebotschaft.de.

**Ireland** 17A Merlyn Park, Ballsbridge, Dublin 4. T269 16 40, embespie@mail.mae.es.

**Italy** Palacio Borghese, Largo Fontanella di Borghese 19, 00186 Rome, T684 0401, www.amba-spagna.com.

**Morocco** Av Président Habib Bourghiba 85, Tangier, T93 56 94, cgesp.tanger@ mail.mae.es.

**Netherlands** Lange Voorhout 50, 2514, The Hague, T302 4999, ambespnl@mail.mae.es.

**New Zealand** see Australia.

**Norway** Oscarsgate, 35, 0258 Oslo 2, T22 92 66 90, embespno@mail.mae.es.

**Portugal** Rua do Salitre 1, 1296 Lisbon, T213 472 381, embesppt@correo.mae.es.

**South Africa** 169 Pine St, Arcadia, Pretoria 0083, PO Box 1633, Pretoria 0001, T344 38 75, embespza@mail.mae.es.

**Sweden** Djurgardsvagen 21, Djugarden 11521 Stockholm, T667 94 30, embespse@mail.mae.es.

**UK** 39 Chesham Place, London SW1X 8SB, T020 7235 55 55, embespuk@mail.mae.es.

**USA** 2375 Pennsylvania Av, Washington DC 20037, T452 01 00, www.spainemb.org.

### Customs and duty free

Non-EU citizens are allowed to import 1 litre of spirits, 2 litres of wine, 200 cigarettes or 250 grams of tobacco or 50 cigars. EU citizens are limited to 'personal use' only.

# What to take

Spain is a modern European country, and you can buy almost everything you'll need here. If you don't know whether you'll need it or not, leave it at home and buy it here.

Be prepared for all weather; Northern Spain can be very cold outside summer, and the coast sees rain all year round. Take a small torch and a penknife (make sure it's in your check-in luggage if flying). Unless you're going to the beach or staying in hostels, you can leave the towel at home; even the most modest *pensión* will provide one with the room. Take an adaptor for electrical goods. See box, page 33, for voltage.

# Money

## Currency

At the beginning of 2002, Spain switched over to the euro, bidding farewell to the peseta in organized fashion. The euro (€) is divided into 100 centimos. Notes are standard across the whole zone, and come in denominations of 5, 10, 20, 50, 100, 200 and 500. Coins have one standard face and one national face; all coins are, however, acceptable in all countries. The coins can be difficult to tell apart when you're not accustomed to them. The coppers are 1, 2 and 5-cent pieces, the golds are 10, 20 and 50, and the silver/gold combinations are €1 and €2. You'll still see prices in pesetas occasionally, and some people will still use them verbally, especially when talking about high quantities. The exchange rate was approximately €6 to 1000 pesetas or 166 pesetas to the euro. So if someone says they paid 'cien mil' for something, they probably mean 100,000 pesetas; €600. ▶▶ *See the inside front cover for price code information.*

The best way to get money in Spain is by using plastic. ATMs are plentiful and just about all of them accept the major international debit and credit cards. The Spanish bank won't charge for the transaction, but beware of your own bank hitting you for a hefty fee: check with them before leaving home. Even if they do, it's likely to be a better deal than changing cash over a counter.

Banks are usually open from Monday to Friday 0830-1400 (plus Saturday in winter) and many change foreign money (sometimes only the central branch in a town will offer this service). Commission rates vary widely; it's usually best to change large amounts, as there's often a minimum commission of €6 or so. Nevertheless, banks nearly always give better rates than change offices (which are fewer by the day). If you're stuck, some large department stores such as the **Corte Inglés** change money at knavish rates. Traveller's cheques will be accepted in many shops, although they are becoming less and less frequent since the single currency was introduced.

> ‼ *To use a credit card in Spain, you'll need to show some photo ID (eg a passport), so remember to take it with you when leaving the hotel.*

*Essentials* Money

If you need to transfer money in a hurry, you're better off paying the premium charges at an agency like **Western Union**; a transfer from a British to a Spanish bank can still take more than a week.

## Taxes

Nearly all goods and services in Spain are subject to a value-added tax (IVA). This is only 7% for most items, but is as high as 16% on 'luxury' goods such as computer equipment. You're technically entitled to claim it back if you're a non-EU citizen, for purchases over €90. If you're buying something pricey, make sure you get a stamped receipt clearly showing the IVA component, as well as your name and passport number; you can claim the amount back at major airports on departure. Some shops will have a form to smooth the process.

## Cost of living and travelling

Spain is significantly cheaper than Britain, for example, but things aren't what they used to be. Prices have soared since the euro was introduced; some basics have risen by 50-80% in three years, and hotel and restaurant prices are rapidly approaching the Western European norm. Spain's average monthly salary of €1200 is low by EU standards, and the minimum monthly salary of €470 is very low indeed. You can still travel around cheaply. €50 per person per day is reasonable and achieved by nibbling on tapas, eating a lunchtime *menú del día* and taking public transport; €100 per day in a good *pensión* or *hostal* and you won't be counting pennies; €200 per day and you'll be very comfortable unless you're staying in four- or five-star lodgings.

Accommodation is more expensive in summer than in winter, particularly on the coast. The Basque lands are significantly more expensive year-round than the rest of Northern Spain, particularly for accommodation, eating and drinking. The news isn't great for the solo traveller; single rooms tend not to be particularly good value, and they are in short supply. Prices range from 60% to 80% of the double/twin price; some establishments even charge the full rate. Public transport is cheap; note that buses are nearly always cheaper and quicker than trains.

Two useful options for saving on hotels include the website www.laterooms.com, and the Bancotel scheme, www.bancotel.com, where you purchase vouchers for €50 that are valid for a double room in a wide number of Spanish hotels – good value for what is often four-star accommodation.

# Getting there

## Air

With the growth of budget airlines, it's easier than ever to get to Northern Spain. **Ryanair** fly to Santiago de Compostela, Valladolid, Santander, Vitoria, and Zaragoza from London, while **Easyjet** serve Bilbao and Asturias, and **Air Berlin** go to Bilbao from many German and Austrian airports. These airlines also run a couple of routes to other European cities. Other international airlines serve Bilbao (which is connected with London, Paris, Frankfurt, and several other European cities), Vigo, Santiago de Compostela, Zaragoza and Asturias. If you're not on the budget carriers, however, it's often cheaper to fly to Madrid and connect via a domestic flight or by land transport. Madrid is a major world airport and prices tend to be competitive.

Domestic connections via Madrid or Barcelona are frequent. **Iberia** connects Madrid with most cities of the north, while **Spanair** and **Air Europa** also operate some flights. Flights are fairly expensive, with a typical Madrid-Bilbao return costing €150. There are often some excellent specials on **Iberia's** website (see Airlines, below) that can bring the price down to as little as €50. If flying into Madrid from outside Spain, an onward domestic flight can often be added at little extra cost.

While budget carriers often offer excellent value (especially when booked well in advance), they offer very little flexibility in terms of changing flight times. It's hard to get close to the much-advertised ultra-low rates, and be aware that if you're only booking a week or so in advance, it may be cheaper on a standard airline.

The cheapest fares on standard airlines tend to involve a return flight and a Saturday night stay; maximum duration is often a month. Cheap fares will usually carry a heavy financial penalty for changing dates or cancellation; check the fineprint carefully before buying a ticket. Airlines don't like one-way tickets; it's often cheaper to buy a return. ➺ *For airline websites and online operators, see pages 29-30.*

### From the UK and Ireland

Competition between airlines serving Spain has benefited the traveller in recent years. Budget operators have taken a significant slice of the market and forced other airlines to compete. There are several options for flying to Northern Spain from the UK.

The cheapest direct flights are with the budget operators, whose fares can be as low as £20 return but are more usually £60-120. It's easier to get hold of a cheaper fare if you fly off-season or midweek, and if you book well in advance. The routes offered at time of writing were: **Ryanair** London Stansted to: Santiago de Compostela, Santander, Valladolid Vitoria, and Zaragoza. **Easyjet** London Stansted to: Bilbao, Asturias (Oviedo/Gijón/Avilés). **Ryanair** have a budget route from London Stansted to Biarritz, France. It can be easy to get cheap seats on this flight off season, although the taxes are fairly high. Biarritz is half an hour on the train to the Spanish border, from where it's another half-hour to San Sebastián. From Dublin, **Aer Lingus** fly to Bilbao, and **Ryanair** to Vitoria. The budget airline market is volatile and routes are added constantly. Check **www.whichbudget.com** to keep apace of the changes.

**Bilbao** is also served from London by **Iberia** and **British Airways**. These flights often end up cheaper than **Easyjet** if you are flying at a weekend with less than a month's notice. **APEX** fares tend to be about £110-140 return and can be more economical and flexible than the budget airline if you are connecting from another British city.

Direct flights from London to **Madrid** are operated by **Easyjet**, **Iberia**, **British Airways**, **BMI**, **Air Europa**, **Aerolíneas Argentinas**, **Lufthansa** and others. Expect to pay between £80 and £150 return, although flights on **Easyjet** can be even lower.

Iberia/British Airways also connect to Madrid directly from Manchester, Edinburgh, Glasgow and Birmingham, while Easyjet fly to Madrid from Liverpool. Prices from these destinations are slightly higher.

KLM, Lufthansa and Air France are also major carriers to Spain for those who don't mind changing at these airlines' hub airports. As well as Madrid and Barcelona these airlines all fly to Bilbao. Iberia and British Airways code share on direct flights between London and Santiago de Compostela and Oviedo/Gijón several times a week, but these flights tend to be a lot dearer; it's nearly always cheaper to connect via Madrid.

From Madrid airport (Barajas), it's very easy to hop in a taxi or the Metro to the bus station (Metro stop: Méndez Alvaro) and be in Northern Spain in a jiffy.

Iberia and Aer Lingus code share daily direct flights from Dublin to Madrid and Barcelona, while Aer Lingus runs budget flights from Dublin to Bilbao. Ryanair operate budget flights between Dublin and London if you can find a cheap flight from the UK.

## From North America and Canada
To reach Northern Spain from across the Atlantic, the best way is to fly in via Madrid. From the east coast, flights to Madrid can rise to about US$1500 in summer, but in winter or with advance purchase a return to Madrid can be as low as US$400. Prices from the west coast are usually only US$100 or so more. Iberia fly direct to Madrid from many US cities, such as Boston, New York, Washington, Atlanta, Chicago, Detroit, Los Angeles and Houston, while other airlines offering reasonable fares are American Airlines, Delta, Air Canada and US Airways. A domestic extension from Madrid won't necessarily add much to the fare. Flying in via other European hubs such as Paris or London is often less expensive, but adds a good few hours on to the journey.

## From Australia and New Zealand
There are no direct flights to Spain from Australia or New Zealand; the cheapest and quickest way is to connect via Frankfurt, Paris or London. The trip takes about 30 hours in total. It might be cheaper to book the Europe–Spain leg separately using a budget airline. Also consider a round-the-world option, which aren't that much more expensive.

## From Europe and Israel
There are many direct flights from Europe to Northern Spain, but most are overpriced apart from those on budget airlines. These routes include: Air Berlin from many German and Austrian cities to Bilbao; Ryanair from Milan Orio al Serio to Zaragoza, Berlin to Asturias, Valladolid to Charleroi, and Frankfurt Hahn and Roma Ciampino to Santander; and Vueling, www.vueling.com, from Bilbao to Roma Fiumicino. Check www.whichbudget.com for updated routes in this rapidly changing market.

On standard airlines, Bilbao is directly connected with several other European cities, including Frankfurt, Zürich, Brussels, Paris, Milan and Lisbon.

There are flights to Madrid from most European capitals. The budget airline Virgin Express is one of the most useful (www.virgin-express.com), connecting Madrid very cheaply with Brussels, Copenhagen, Geneva, Rome, Stockholm and more. Iberia/El Al fly directly from Tel Aviv to Madrid and Barcelona in about five hours.

## From South Africa
There are no direct flights from South Africa, the cheapest and quickest way is to connect via Europe: Zurich, Amsterdam, Frankfurt or London normally work out best.

**Airlines**

Aer Lingus  www.aerlingus.com
Aerolíneas Argentinas  www.aerolineas.com.ar
Air Berlin  www.airberlin.com
Air Canada  www.aircanada.ca

Air Europa  www.air-europa.co.uk
Air France  www.airfrance.com/uk, www.airfrance.fr
American Airlines  www.aa.com
BMI  www.flybmi.com

Essentials Getting there

**British Airways**  www.ba.com
**Delta**  www.delta.com
**Easyjet**  www.easyjet.com
**El Al**  www.elal.co.il
**Iberia**  www.iberia.com
**KLM**  www.klmuk.com
**Lufthansa**  www.lufthansa.co.uk
**Ryanair**  www.ryanair.com
**Spanair**  www.spanair.com/es
**US Airways**  www.usairways.com
**Virgin Express**  www.virgin-express.com

**Online operators**
www.avro.com
www.cheapflights.co.uk
www.easyvalue.com
www.ebookers.com
www.expedia.co.uk/www.expedia.com
www.kelkoo.com (price comparison)
www.opodo.com
www.travelcity.com
www.whichbudget.com (updated
budget flight information)

# Rail

Travelling from the UK to Northern Spain by train is unlikely to save either time or money; the only two advantages lie in the pleasure of the journey itself, and the chance to stop along the way. Using **Eurostar**, www.eurostar.com, T0870 160 6600, changing stations in Paris and boarding a TGV to Hendaye can have you in San Sebastián 10 hours after leaving Waterloo if the connections are kind. Once across the Channel, the trains are reasonably priced, but factor in £100-200 return on **Eurostar** and things don't look so rosy, unless you can take advantage of a special offer. Using the train/ferry combination will more or less halve the cost and double the time.

The main rail gateway from the rest of Europe is Paris (Austerlitz). There's a Paris-Madrid sleeper daily, which stops at Vitoria, Burgos and Valladolid. Standard tourist class fare is €119-125 in a reclining seat to Madrid one-way, and proportionally less depending on where you get off. Check www.elipsos.com for specials. The cheaper option is to take a **TGV** from Paris to Hendaye, on the border, from where you can catch a Spanish train to San Sebastián and beyond.

# Road

## Bus

**Eurolines** run several buses from major European cities to a variety of destinations in Northern Spain. From London, a bus that leaves London Victoria at 0800 on Monday and Saturday, and arrives in Bilbao at 0430 the next morning. The return leaves Bilbao at 0030 on Thursday and Saturday night, getting to London at 1945 the next evening. There's an extra bus in summer. A return fare costs about £100; it's marginally cheaper for pensioners and students, but overall isn't great value unless you're not a fan of flying. Bookings on T01582 404 511 or www.gobycoach.com.

## Car

The main route into Northern Spain is the E05/E70 motorway that runs down the southwest coast of France, crossing into Spain at Irún, near San Sebastián. More scenic but slower routes cross the Pyrenees at various points. The other motorway entrance is the E7 that runs down the east coast of Spain from France. At Barcelona you can turn inland for Lleida and Zaragoza. Both these motorways are fairly heavily tolled but worthwhile compared to the slow, traffic-plagued *rutas nacionales* on these sectors.

# Sea

**P&O** runs a ferry service from Portsmouth to Bilbao but in reality it's more of a cruise. The ship, the *Pride of Bilbao*, is the largest ferry operating out of the UK and has several restaurants, a cinema, pool, sauna and casino. None of this comes cheap at £400-500 return with a car. It's a two-night trip, and cabin accommodation is mandatory. Boats leave Portsmouth at 2045 every three days except during winter, when there are few crossings. The return ferry leaves Bilbao at 1315. Many passengers don't even get off. Check www.poferries.com for the timetable. Book online at www.poportsmouth.com or on T0870 242 4999. The ferry in Bilbao port is at Santurtzi, 13 km from the city centre.

A cheaper and faster option is the **Brittany Ferries** service from Plymouth to Santander, 100 km west of Bilbao. These leave the UK on Sunday and Wednesday mornings, taking a shade under 24 hours. Return ferries leave Santander on Monday and Thursday. Book at www.brittanyferries.co.uk, or T08705 561 600 (UK) or T942 360 611 (Spain). Prices are variable but can usually be had for about £70-90 each way in a reclining seat. A car adds about £140 each way, and cabins start from about £80 a twin. The service runs year-round, weather permitting. Cheaper offers are sometimes available from T0870 442 4223, www.ferrysavers.com.

---

# Touching down

## Airport information

**Madrid Barajas** is the main international airport of Spain, and, for non-European visitors, is the most convenient point of entry for the north. Situated 13 km northeast of the centre, it has two distinct parts, the new Terminal 4, used for all EU flights, and services run by **Iberia** and partner airlines, and the old terminals 1-3 (used by the rest). There are tourist information offices in Terminals 1, 2, and 4 and many multi-national car hire companies and banks with ATMs. There's also a hotel booking service.
▶▶ *Information on the smaller airports can be found in the Transport section of the relevant city.*

The most convenient way of getting into Madrid is to use the metro. There are entrances to it from Terminals 2 and 3. Until the Terminal 4 metro station is built, you'll have to take the free shuttle bus that runs between terminals. On the metro, you can be in central Madrid in as little as 20 minutes; a single ticket costs €1.15. If you're moving straight on to the north, change at Nuevos Ministerios (the end of the line). Jump on line 10 (Dirección Fuencarral) for four stops to reach Chamartin, the main northbound train station. Nine stops on Line 6 (Dirección Legazpi), on the other hand, will get you to Méndez Alvaro; which has a passage connecting to the main northerly bus station. There are also buses into town from outside Terminal 1, but these can take significantly longer, especially in traffic. A taxi to the centre of Madrid will cost about €15-20. Ignore any taxi-touts and go straight to the official taxi queue.

*‼ All departure and arrival taxes are now paid with the relevant plane ticket.*

Northern Spain's other principal air gateway is **Bilbao**. A small and manageable place, it's brand new and in Sondika, 10 km northeast of the centre. It's a beautiful building designed by Santiago Calatrava, seemingly in homage to the whale. A taxi to/from town costs about €18. There's an efficient bus service that runs to/from Plaza Moyúa in central Bilbao. It leaves from outside the terminal and takes 20-30 minutes and runs every half-hour; one-way €1.15. There are several car hire firms at the airport, as well as a tourist information office and banks with ATMs.

# Tourist information

The tourist information infrastructure in Northern Spain is organized by the regional governments and is generally excellent, with a wide range of information, often in English, German and French as well as Spanish. Offices within the region can provide maps of the area and towns, and lists of registered accommodation. If you're in a car, it's especially worth picking up the *turismo rural* booklet, listing farmstay and rural accommodation, which is starting to take off in a big way; hundreds are added yearly. Opening hours are longer in major cities; many rural offices are only open in summer. Average opening hours will be Monday to Saturday 1000-1400, 1600-1900. Offices are often closed on Sunday or Monday. Staff often speak English and other European languages and are well trained. The offices (*oficinas de turismo*) are often signposted to some degree within the town or city. Staff may ask where you are from; this is not nosiness but for statistical purposes.

Euskadi and Asturias have the best network of offices, while Navarra, Aragón, and Castilla y León also have a good system. Galicia and La Rioja have poorer ones. The city maps given out are often poor; ask for a *plano callejero* (street indexed) if you want a better one.

**Useful organizations**
**Asturias** Sociedad Regional de Turismo, www.infoasturias.com
**Cantabria** Consejería de Cultura, Turismo y Deporte, www.turismodecantabria.com

**Galicia** Turgalicia, www.turgalicia.es
**País Vasco** Departamento de Industria, Comercio y Turismo, Dirección de Promoción Turística, www.paisvascoturismo.net

# Local customs and laws

## Codes of conduct

Northern Spaniards are fairly reserved (except when on the dance floor), particularly towards foreigners, in whom they show little curiosity. They are usually polite and courteous, but cultural differences can give first-time visitors the opposite impression. Use of 'please' and 'thank you' is minimal, but it is usual to greet and bid farewell to shopkeepers or bartenders when entering/exiting. There's a different concept of personal space in Spain than in northern Europe or the USA; the idea doesn't really exist. People speak loudly as a matter of course; it doesn't mean they are shouting.

Most people go home for the long lunch break and often a *siesta*. Nearly all shops and sights are shut at this time (apart from large supermarkets), so you might as well tuck in to a big meal and have a nap yourself. Every evening, people take to the streets for the *paseo*, a slow stroll up and down town that might include a coffee or pre-dinner drink. It's a great time to observe Spanish society at work; the ritual is an integral part of Spanish culture. Especially in summer, the whole evening is spent outdoors; friends meet by design or chance.

'Spanish time' isn't as elastic as it used to be, but if you're told something will happen '*enseguida*' ('straight away') it may take 10 minutes, if you're told '*cinco minutos*' (five minutes), grab a seat and a book. Transport, especially buses, usually leaves promptly.

## Dress

Away from the beach and the *discoteca*, Northern Spaniards generally cover up, but no one in cities is going to be offended by brief clothing; things are a bit more

## ⁞ Touching down

**Business hours** Generally Mon-Fri
1000-1400, 1700-2000; Sat
1000-1400. **Banks**: Mon-Fri
0830-1400 plus Sat in winter.
**Emergencies** 112 is the general
emergency number throughout
Spain; **Police**: 092; **Ambulance**: 061.
**Official language** Spanish
(Euskara, Gallego).
**Official time** GMT +1.

**Telephone** IDD code: Dial 00
to call out from Spain. **Spain's
international code**: +34.
**Directory enquiries**: 11818
(national); 11825 (international).
**Voltage** 220V (the same as the rest
of Europe). A round two-pin plug is
used (Standard European).
**Weights and measures**
All metric.

conservative in the countryside, however. Always consider wearing long trousers, taking off hats and covering shoulders if you're going in to a church or monastery. Spaniards seldom wear shorts except when on holiday. Topless sunbathing is acceptable on most Spanish beaches and there are many nudist areas along the north coast. Nudism on beaches is very mainstream in Spain.

## Eating

Spaniards eat little for breakfast, usually just a coffee and maybe a croissant or pastry. The mid-morning coffee and piece of tortilla is a ritual, especially for office workers, and then there might be a quick bite and a drink in a café or bar before lunch, which is usually between 1400-1530 or thereabouts. This is the main meal of the day and the cheapest time to eat, as most restaurants offer a cheap set menu. Lunch (and dinner) is extended at weekends, particularly on Sundays, when the *sobremesa* (chatting over the remains of the meal) can go on for hours. It's common to have an evening drink or *tapa* in a bar after the *paseo*, if this is extended into a food crawl it's called a *txikiteo* (Basque country) or *tapeo*. Dinner (*cena*) is normally eaten from about 2200 onwards, although sitting down to dinner at midnight at weekends isn't unusual. In smaller towns and midweek you might not get fed after 2230. Most restaurants are closed Sunday nights, and usually take a day off either Monday or Tuesday. If you don't want to adapt to Spanish dining hours, be aware that any restaurant open for dinner before 2000 could well be a tourist trap. ▸▸ *See also Eating and drinking, page 40, for further details.*

## Tipping

Tipping in Spain is far from compulsory, but much practised. Ten per cent is considered very generous in a restaurant; five percent is more usual. It's rare for a service charge to be added to a bill. Waiters do not normally expect tips for lunchtime set meals or tapas, but here and in bars and cafés people will often leave small change, especially for table service. Taxi drivers don't expect a tip, but will be pleased to receive one. In rural areas, churches will often have a local keyholder who will open it up for you; if there's no admission charge, a tip or donation is appropriate (say €1 per head; more if they've given a detailed tour).

## Religion

A huge percentage of Spaniards are Catholics, but only a third of them trouble the priest regularly (see Religion, page 471). Don't wander around churches if there's a Mass on, and dress appropriately. Sunday is a family day, and very few shops are open; transport services are also much reduced.

**Prohibitions and drugs**

The laws in Spain are broadly similar to any western European country. One point to be aware of is that you are legally required to carry a passport or ID card at all times (although this is rarely an issue; hotels often hang on to them until you've paid). Smoking *porros* (joints) is widespread, although far more common in Euskadi than anywhere else (locals say the Spanish government ships the hash in to keep the Basques placid). It is technically illegal, but has been considered legal in the recent past. Police aren't too concerned about personal use, but don't be foolish. You'll soon work out which bars are smoker-friendly – the rolling papers on the bar are a handy sign. Use of cocaine, speed and ecstasy is widespread (expect long queues to use the toilets in *discotecas*) but means serious trouble if caught.

# Responsible tourism

Responsible tourism comes down to respect for local people, their culture, the environment and other travellers. While certain aspects of Spanish society may frustrate on occasion, take them in their cultural context; they're not going to change, and abusing a slow waiter in a stream of English isn't going to get you anywhere. Talking loudly about locals in English (or any other language) is a sure way to be instantly disliked, and won't do the next passing traveller any favours either. Treat people with courtesy and patience; it's very common to sit through a meal in Spain thinking the waiter is rude or ignoring you only to find he/she throws in a free coffee and liqueur at the end of dinner because he/she actually likes you.

When in the country, be aware of the environment. Stick to walking trails and carry rubbish with you, even if locals don't. If you're striking off on a seldom-used trail in the mountains, let someone know where you're going and when you expect to be back – it might save your life if the weather closes in or you have an accident. Don't camp where you're not allowed to; the prohibitions are usually in force for a very good reason.

# Safety

Northern Spain is generally a very safe place indeed. While port cities like Bilbao, Vigo and Santander have some dodgy areas, tourist crime is very low in this region, and you're more likely to have something returned (that you left on that train) than something stolen. That said, don't invite crime by leaving luggage or cash in cars. If parking in a city or, particularly, a popular hiking zone, try to make it clear there's nothing to nick inside by opening the glovebox, etc. Muggings are very rare, but don't leave bags unattended.

There are several types of police, helpful enough in normal circumstances but not the friendliest if you've done something wrong, or they think you have. The paramilitary **Guardia Civil** are hated by the Basques for their Francoist associations, frequent repressionist tactics and torture of prisoners. This national force dress in green and are responsible for the roads (including speed traps and the like), borders and law enforcement away from towns. They're not a bunch to get the wrong side of but are polite to tourists and have thankfully lost the bizarre winged hats they used to sport. The **Policía Nacional** are responsible for most urban crimefighting. Brown-shirted folk, these are the ones to go to if you need to report anything stolen, etc. **Policía Local/Municipal** are present in large towns and cities and are responsible for some urban crime, as well as traffic control and parking. The **Ertzaintza** are the most dashing force in Spain, with cocky red berets. They are a Basque force who deal with the day-to-day beat and some crime. There's a similar corps in Navarra.

# Getting around

Public transport between the larger towns in Northern Spain is good; you can expect several buses a day between adjacent provincial capitals; these services are quick, efficient, and nearly always beat the train in price, speed and efficiency. Once off the main routes, however, it's a different story. Don't expect to get to those picturesque rural monasteries if you're not prepared to hitch, walk or hire a car.

## Air

Most provincial capitals in Northern Spain have an airport that is serviced from Barcelona and Madrid at least once daily. The drawback is the cost; a full fare return from Madrid to Oviedo, for example, costs around €280. If you are fairly flexible about when you fly, **Iberia**'s website specials are good. Otherwise, by far the best way is to go to a local travel agent, who can often find excellent deals on domestic flights. Flying within Northern Spain itself is less attractive, as you usually have to go via Madrid, although there are connections to Bilbao from Vigo, A Coruña and Santiago.

Most internal flights in Spain are operated by **Iberia**; **Spanair** and **Air Europa** also run some routes. If you're flying into Spain from overseas, a domestic leg can often be added at comparatively little cost.

If you're flying into Spain from anywhere else in the world, **Iberia** have an airpass available, that has to be purchased with your international ticket. It includes two or more flight vouchers for travel anywhere within Spain. Depending on season, they cost €60-100 per flight; more if the Canaries are included. **Spanair** have a *Spanair Pass*, but you have to buy 10 vouchers and it's not very good value.

## Rail

The Spanish national rail network, **RENFE** ① *T902 240 202, www.renfe.es*, only achieves partial coverage in Northern Spain and is beaten by bus services on most routes. There's a bewildering variety of services, but unless you're on the main rail arteries, the choice will be limited. Even a large city like Bilbao only has a handful of services a day on mainline routes. The **RENFE** website has timetables and ticketing.

Prices vary significantly according to the type of service you are using. The super-fast **AVE** service currently runs from Madrid to Zaragoza, and the network is being rapidly extended across the north. The standard high-speed intercity service is called *Talgo*, while other intercity services are labelled *Arco*, *Intercity*, *Diurno* and *Estrella* (overnight). Slower local trains are called *regionales*.

It's always worth buying a ticket in advance for long-distance travel, as trains are often full. Allow plenty of time to queue for tickets at the station. Ticket windows are labelled *venta anticipada* (in advance) and *venta inmediata* (immediate, ie six hours or less before the journey). A better option can be to use a travel agent; the ones in town that sell tickets will display a **RENFE** sign, but you'll have to purchase them a day in advance. Commission is minimal.

All Spanish trains are non-smoking. The faster trains will have a first-class (*preferente*) and second-class sections as well as a *cafetería*. First class costs about 30% more than standard and can be a worthwhile deal on a crowded long journey. Other pricing is bewilderingly complex. Night trains are more expensive, even if you don't take a *couchette*, and there's a system of peak/off-peak days that makes little difference in practice. Buying a return ticket is about 20% cheaper than two singles, but you qualify for this discount even if you buy the return leg later (but not on every service). A useful tip: if the train is 'full' for your particular destination, buy a ticket half-way (or even one stop) and let the ticket inspector know where you want to get to. You may have to shuffle seats a couple of times, but most are fairly helpful – you can pay the excess fare on board.

The other important Northern Spanish network is **FEVE** ⓘ *www.feve.es*, whose principal line runs along the north coast from Bilbao west to Santander, Asturias and as far as Ferrol in Galicia; there's another line from Bilbao to León. It's a slow, narrow-gauge line, but very picturesque. It stops at many small villages and is very handy for exploring the coast. A third handy network is **Eusko Trenbideak**, a short-haul train service in the Basque country. It's an excellent service with good coverage of the inland towns in that region.

Both **FEVE** and **RENFE** operate short-distance *cercanías* (commuter trains) in some areas, essentially suburban train services. These are particularly helpful in Asturias and Bilbao.

## Discounts and rail passes

An ISIC student card or under-26 card grants a discount of between 10-20% on most train services. It's worth getting the Spanish version, the *Tarjeta Joven*, which increases the discount to 50% if you're travelling on off-peak 'blue days'. If you're using a European railpass, be aware that you'll still have to make a reservation on Spanish trains and pay the small reservation fee (which covers your insurance). The *tarjeta turística* is a Spanish rail pass available to non-residents for period of three, five, 10, 15 or 22 days. Valid on all **RENFE** trains, it's expensive, and unless you plan to travel a long distance every day, forget it. ▸▸ *See also Student travellers, page 24.*

---

# Road

## Bus

Buses are the staple of Spanish public transport. Services between major cities are fast, frequent, reliable and fairly cheap; the four-hour trip from Madrid to León, for example, costs €19. On some routes, some journeys will be on more expensive, but faster and on more luxurious buses. When buying a ticket, always check how long the journey will take; some buses will be an 'all-stations-to' job, calling in at villages that seem surprised to even see it. Tourist offices never know how long a route takes; you must ask the bus company themselves.

While some cities have several departure points for buses, most have a single terminal, the *estación de autobuses*, which is where all short- and long-haul services leave from. Buy your tickets at the relevant window; if there isn't one, buy it from the driver. Many companies don't allow any baggage at all in the cabin of the bus, but security is pretty good. Most tickets will have a seat number (*asiento*) on them; ask when buying the ticket if you prefer a window (*ventana*) or aisle (*pasillo*) seat. If you're travelling at busy times (particularly a fiesta or national holiday) always book the bus ticket ahead. If the bus station is out of town, there are usually travel agents in the centre who can do this for you for no extra charge.

There's a huge number of intercity bus companies; the most useful in Northern Spain is **ALSA**, T902 422 242 (with a scary robot operator), www.alsa.es, which is based in Asturias and runs many routes. Another big operator is **Continental**, www.continental-auto.es.

Rural bus services are slower, less frequent and more difficult to co-ordinate. They typically run early in the morning and late in the evening; they're designed for villagers who visit the 'big smoke' once a month or so to shop. If you're trying to catch a bus from a small stop, you'll often need to almost jump out under the wheels to get the driver to you know when your stop comes up, keep an eye out as they tend to forget.

All bus services are reduced on Sundays, and many on Saturdays too; some services don't run at all on weekends. Many local newspapers publish a comprehensive list of departures. While most large villages will have at least some bus service to their provincial capital, the same doesn't apply for many touristed spots; it's assumed that all tourists have cars.

Most Spanish cities have their sights closely packed into the centre, so you won't find local buses particularly necessary. There's a fairly comprehensive network in most towns, though; the Ins and outs and Transport sections indicate where they come in handy.

To reach those far-flung monasteries, beaches and mountains without transport, a combination of walking and hitching usually works pretty well. The scarcity of bus services means that's what many locals do and you'll commonly be offered a lift on remote country roads even if you don't have your thumb out.

## Car

The roads in Northern Spain are good, excellent in many parts. While driving isn't as sedate as in parts of northern Europe, it's generally of a very high standard, and you'll have few problems. To drive in Spain, you'll need a full driving licence from your home country. This applies to virtually all foreign nationals, but in practice, if you're from an 'unusual' country, consider an International Driving Licence or official translation of your licence into Spanish. ▸▸ *See individual town and city Transport sections for details of car hire; all airports in Northern Spain have offices for the main multi-nationals.*

There are two types of motorway in Spain, *autovías* and *autopistas*; for drivers, they are little different. They are signposted in blue and may have tolls payable, in which case there'll be a red warning circle on the blue sign when you're entering the motorway. Tolls are generally reasonable, except in Euskadi, where they are extortionate. The quality of motorway is generally excellent. The speed limit on motorways is 120 kph.

*Rutas Nacionales* form the backbone of Spain's road network. Centrally administered, they vary wildly in quality. Typically, they are choked with traffic backed up behind trucks, and there are few stretches of dual carriageway. Driving at *siesta* time is a good idea if you're going to be on a busy stretch. *Rutas Nacionales* are marked with a red 'N' number. The speed limit is 100 kph outside built-up areas, as it is for secondary roads, which are numbered with a provincial prefix (eg BU-552 in Burgos province), although some are demarcated 'B' and 'C' instead.

In urban areas, the speed limit is 50 kph. Many towns and villages have sensors that will turn traffic lights red if you're over the limit on approach. City driving can be confusing, with signposting generally poor and traffic heavy. While not overly concerned about rural speed limits, police enforce the urban limits quite thoroughly (particularly in small villages on main roads); foreign drivers are liable to a large on-the-spot fine. Drivers can also be punished for not carrying two red warning triangles to place on the road in case of breakdown, a bulb-replacement kit and a bright green waistcoat to wear if you break down by the side of the road. Drink driving is being cracked down on more than was once the case; the limit is 0.25 mg/l in breathed air, slightly less than the equivalent in the UK, for example.

**Parking** is a problem in nearly every town and city in Northern Spain. Red or yellow lines on the side of the street mean no parking. Blue lines indicate a metered zone, while white lines mean that some restriction is in place; a sign will give details. Parking meters can usually only be dosed up for a maximum of two hours, but they take a *siesta* at lunchtime too. Print the ticket off and display it in the car. Once the day's period has expired, you can charge it up for the next morning to avoid an early start. If you get a ticket, you can pay a minimal fine at the machine within the first half

## A bed for the night

The price codes, see inside front cover, refer to a standard double/twin room, inclusive of the 7% IVA (value-added tax). The rates are generally for high season (usually June-August). Occasionally, an area or town will have a short period when prices are hugely exaggerated; this normally corresponds to a fiesta or similar event. Low-season prices can be significantly lower; up to half in some areas such as the seaside.

Many mid- to top-range hotels in cities cater for business travellers during the week and so keep prices high. The flipside is that they have special weekend rates, which can be very good value. Typically, these involve staying on the Friday and Saturday night and pre-booking. Breakfast will often be thrown in gratis and the whole deal can save you more than 50% on the quoted price. Contact the hotel for these deals.

hour or hour instead of the full whack. Underground car parks are common and always well signposted, but fairly pricey; €10-15 a day is normal. However, this is the safest option if you are going to leave any valuables in your car.

Liability **insurance** is required for every car driven in Spain and you must carry proof of it. If bringing your own car, check carefully with your insurers that you're covered, and get a certificate (green card). If your insurer doesn't cover you for breakdowns, consider joining the **RACE** ① *T902 120 441, www.race.es*, Spain's automobile association, which provides good breakdown cover.

**Hiring a car** in Spain is easy but not especially cheap. The major multinationals have offices at all large towns and airports; a Spanish operator with an excellent network is **ATESA** ① *www.atesa.es*, a cheaper company is **Holiday Autos**. Prices start at around €150 per week for a small car with unlimited mileage. You'll need a credit card and most agencies will either not accept under 25s or demand a surcharge. Rates from the airports tend to be cheaper than from towns; with the big companies, it's usually cheaper to book over the internet.

## Cycling

Cycling presents a curious contrast; Spaniards are mad for the competitive sport, but comparatively uninterested in cycling as a means of transport. Thus there are plenty of cycling shops (although beware; it can be time-consuming to find replacement parts for non-standard cycles) but very few bike lanes. By far the best places to cycle are the north coast and the Pyrenees; these are where interest in cycling is high also. Trying to enjoy a Castilian highway in 40°C heat with trucks zipping past your ears is another matter, although many cyclists follow the Camino de Santiago route. Contact the **Real Federación de Ciclismo en España** ① *www.rfec.com*, for more links and assistance.

## Motorcycling

Motorcycling is a good way to enjoy Spain and there are few difficulties to trouble the biker; bike shops and mechanics are relatively common. Hiring a motorbike, however, is difficult; there are few outlets in Northern Spain. The **Real Federación Motociclista Española** ① *www.rfme.com*, can help with links and advice.

## Taxis

Taxis are a good option; flagfall is €2-2.50 in most places (it increases slightly at night and on Sundays) and it gets you a good distance. A taxi is available if its green light is lit; hail one on the street or ask for the nearest rank (*parada de taxis*). All towns have their own taxi company; phone numbers are given in the text.

# Maps

The **Michelin** series of road maps are by far the most accurate for general navigation, although if you're getting off the beaten track you'll often find a local map handy. Tourist offices provide these, which vary in quality from province to province. The **Everest** series of maps cover provinces and their main towns; they're not bad, although tend to be a bit out of date.

# Sleeping

There are a reasonable number of well-equipped but characterless places on the edges or in the newer parts of towns in Spain. This guide has expressly minimized these in the listings, preferring to concentrate on more atmospheric options. If booking accommodation without this guide, always be sure to check the location if that's important to you – it's easy to find yourself a 15-minute cab ride from the town you want to be in. Having said this, the standard of accommodation in Northern Spain is very high; even the most modest of *pensiones* are usually very clean and respectable. Places to stay (*alojamientos*) are divided into three main categories; the distinctions between them follow an arcane series of regulations devised by the government.

All registered accommodations charge a 7% value-added tax (IVA); this is often included in the price at cheaper places and may be waived if you pay cash (tut tut). If you have any problems, a last resort is to ask for the *libro de reclamaciones* (complaints book), an official document that, like stepping on cracks in the pavement, means uncertain but definitely horrible consequences for the hotel if anything is written in it. If you do write something in it, you have to go to the police within 24 hours and report the fact.

## Hoteles, hostales and pensiones

*Hoteles* (marked H or HR) are graded from one to five stars and usually occupy their own building, which distinguishes them from *hostales* (Hs or HsR), which go from one to three stars. *Pensiones* (P) are the standard budget option, and are usually family-run flats in an apartment block. Although it's worth looking at a room before taking it, the majority are very acceptable. *Fondas* (F) are in short supply these days, but are generally restaurants with cheap rooms available; a continuation of the old travellers' inn. The Spanish traditions of hospitality are alive and well; even the simplest of *pensiones* will generally provide a towel and soap, and check-out time is almost uniformly a very civilized midday. Most *pensiones* will give you keys to the exterior door; if they don't, be sure to mention the fact if you plan to stay out late.

## Agroturismos and casas rurales

An excellent option if you've got transport are the networks of rural homes, called a variety of things from *agroturismos* to *casas rurales*. Although these are under a different classification system, the standard is often as high as any country hotel. The best of them are traditional farmhouses or old village cottages. Some are available only to rent out whole, while others operate more or less as hotels. Rates tend to be excellent compared to hotels, and many offer kitchen facilities and home-cooked meals. While many are listed in the text, there are huge numbers, especially in the coastal and mountain areas. Each regional government publishes its own listings

*For an explanation of the sleeping and eating price codes used in this guide, see inside the front cover.*

booklet, which is available at any tourist office in the area. The website www.toprural.com is another good place to find them. If you've got a car, this can be a hugely relaxing form of holiday accommodation.

## Albergues and refugios

There are a few youth hostels (*albergues*) around, but the price of *pensiones* rarely makes it worth the trouble except for solo travellers. Spanish youth hostels are frequently populated by noisy schoolkids and have curfews and check-out times unsuitable for the late hours the locals keep. The exception is in mountain regions, where there are excellent *refugios*; basically simple hostels for walkers and climbers along the lines of a Scottish bothy, see box, page 184.

## Campsites

Most campsites are set up as well-equipped holiday villages for families; many are open only in summer. While the facilities are good, they get extremely busy in peak season; the social scene is good, but sleep can be tough. In other areas, camping, unless specifically prohibited, is a matter of common sense: in the country most locals will either know of or offer a place where you can pitch a tent (*tienda de campaña*) without problem.

# Eating and drinking

Nothing in Spain illustrates its differences from the rest of Europe more than its eating and drinking culture. Whether you're halfway through Sunday lunch at 1800, ordering a plate of octopus some time after midnight, snacking on *pintxos* in the street with the entire population of Bilbao doing the same around you, or watching a businessman down a hefty brandy with his morning coffee, it hits you at some point that the whole of Spanish society more or less revolves around food and drink. ▸▸ *See Food glossary, page 483, for further details.*

Eating hours are the first point of difference. Spaniards don't have much more than a coffee and a pastry for breakfast most of the time, a habit described indignantly by HV Morton as "deplorable". People might sidle out from work at some point for a pre-lunch drink and *tapa* before the main event. Lunchtime (*la hora de comer*) varies slightly across Northern Spain but is normally eaten around 1400-1530, often later at weekends. Most folk head home for the meal during the working week and get back to work about 1700; some people have a nap (the famous *siesta*), some don't.

People take to the streets from about 1930 for the *paseo*, a stroll around the town often rounded off with a coffee or a drink and a tapa. This can turn into a *tapeo* or *txikiteo*, a crawl around various tapas bars, which are usually busiest from about 2100-2300. If people are going to eat dinner (*cenar*), they'll do it from about 2200, although it's not unusual to sit down to a meal at midnight or later. After eating, *la marcha* (literally 'the march') hits drinking bars (*bares de copas*) and then nightclubs (*discotecas*; a *club* is a brothel). Many of these places only open at weekends and are usually busiest from about 0300 onwards. Some don't even bother opening until 0400.

Eating and drinking hours vary from region to region. Week nights are always quieter but particularly so in the Basque country and in rural areas, where many restaurants close their kitchens at 2200. The nature of bar food changes across the area too. In the Basque country, *pintxos* (bar-top snacks) are the way forward; in León a free small plate of food accompanies even the smallest drink; while in some other places you'll have to order *raciones* (full plates of tapas).

# Cycling

Many organizations run cycling trips around Northern Spain; see page 20, for details. Apart from the dusty Castilian plains, the region is very good cycling, and it's a popular weekend activity in Navarra and Euskadi. Contact the **Real Federación de Ciclismo en España** ⓘ *www.rfec.com*.

# Fishing

Northern Spain has some superb trout and salmon fishing, as immortalized by Hemingway in *Fiesta/The Sun Also Rises*. It's all regulated, and you'll need a permit (*permiso de pesca*), usually obtainable from the local *ayuntamiento* and valid for two weeks. The **Federación Española de Pesca** ⓘ *T915 328 353, www.fepyc.es, C Navas de Tolosa 3, Madrid*, is a good starting point for information.

# Gastronomy

With Spain's best food in Euskadi and Galicia, as well as most of the country's best wine regions, Northern Spain has much to offer the taste-buds. The culinary scene in Euskadi includes some fine gourmet restaurants, superb bartop *pintxos*, the strange all-male cooking societies (*txokos*) and hearty meals in *sagardotegiak* (cider houses) washed down by as much fresh cider as you can manage. In Galicia, the sheer quality and quantity of seafood available is an obvious attraction. Any wine-oriented visit should take in the Rioja, while the Ribera del Duero is also a good option, less tourist-oriented. Nearly all winery visits need to be organized beforehand by telephone.

▸▸ *See also page 18, for specialist tour operators.*

# Skiing

There are 13 ski resorts in the area covered by this guide, the best and most popular of which are in the Aragonese Pyrenees. Candanchú and Formigal offer the greatest variety of runs. The resorts are fairly priced by European standards but the snow quality is variable. The season runs from Christmas to April, with February likely to be the best month. Skiing packages are on offer in travel agents, but don't necessarily save a great deal of money. Most resorts have a ski-school and a range of accommodation, although budget options should be booked well in advance. Get in touch with **ATUDEM** ⓘ *T913 591 557, www.ski-spain.com*, the Spanish ski-tourism agency.

> ‼ *For snow conditions, call T913 502 020.*

# Walking and climbing

As well as the Camino de Santiago, Northern Spain offers some fantastic walking, mostly in its mountainous and coastal areas. The first thing for the walker to be aware of is Spain's excellent network of marked walking trails. These are divided into *pequeño recorrido* (PR), short trails marked with yellow and white signs, and *gran recorrido* (GR), longer distance walks marked in red and white. These take in places often inaccessible by car; the GR trails are planned so that nights can be spent at *refugios* (walkers' hostels) or in villages with places to stay. Detailed maps and descriptions of these routes can be found in good bookshops or outdoor equipment shops.

> ‼ *See page 21 for walking-based tour operators. Tourist offices have details of local routes and refugios.*

Climbers, too, will have a good time of it in the Pyrenees and Picos. There are many peaks offering varying degrees of challenge; some of these are mentioned in the text, but for further details contact the **Federación Española de Deportes de Montaña y Escalada** ⓘ *T914 451 382, www.fedme.es*.

Walkers and climbers in these areas should take every precaution, even in the height of summer. Get a weather forecast if you're heading into the mountains, and watch what's going on, as mists can roll in pretty fast. A compass is invaluable, as is a decent map and protective clothing (including good boots). If you're not on a well-used trail, let someone know where you're going and when you expect to be back.

## Walking the Camino de Santiago

An ever-increasing number of pilgrims walk and ride to Santiago every year. Today's *peregrines* come from all backgrounds; many are not even Christians. It's a fantastic way to see Northern Spain; the route crosses the whole region, taking in the Pyrenees, green Galicia, historic Castilla and many of the area's most picturesque villages and most interesting towns. There's a huge variety of routes, and which you take should depend on what you want to see. The main route, and the one with the most pilgrim facilities, is the **Camino Francés**, which enters Spain above Roncesvalles in the Pyrenees. The **Camino Aragonés** is also popular, entering the country in the Aragonese mountains above Jaca. These two join up at Puente La Reina in Navarra. A less-used route, the **Camino del Norte**, follows the north coast and is the most attractive of the routes, avoiding the hard trudges across the dusty *meseta*. The full route from Roncesvalles to Santiago is some 800 km, which translates to a walk of four to five weeks or a pedal of a fortnight. Many pilgrims do the journey in stages, a week each year, or just do the last bit, starting from León or Ponferrada.

To use the network of *albergues* and *refugios*, dedicated pilgrim hostels with dormitory accommodation, you'll need to be an accredited pilgrim. This status comes in the form of a Pilgrim Passport or *credencial*, issued by a number of organizations outside Spain and obtainable from several places on the route itself; these include **Accueil St Jacques**, 39 Rue de la Citadelle, St Jean Pied-de-Port (many pilgrims start from this French town, a day's walk from Roncesvalles), the monastery in **Roncesvalles**, and the *refugios* in main towns along the route. This document should be stamped daily at the *refugios* or at churches or *ayuntamientos* to help prove you've actually travelled the route without a motor. Once you reach Santiago, presenting a completed pilgrim passport at the Pilgrim Office near the cathedral entitles you to a *compostela*, a Latin certificate of completion of the pilgrimage. To be eligible for this, you have to have walked at least the last 100 km, or cycled the last 200 km If you are only doing the last section of the pilgrimage, it is recommended to get at least two stamps a day in the credencial. Presenting a photocopy of the document at Santiago's *parador* entitles the pilgrim to three days of free meals (in a canteen, not in the restaurant). Religion is not a requirement either to obtain the credencial or the *compostela*, but a suitable attitude and respect for the journey is expected.

There are many *albergues* along the *camino*; these are typically simple places that ask for a small fee or donation (€4-8) for lodging in dormitory accommodation. Most also serve cheap (or free) meals and have cooking facilities and hot water. As most pilgrims set off early to avoid the fierce afternoon sun, the *albergues* generally have a curfew of 2200-2230, and a checkout of 0600-0700. They may not open their doors until 1500 or so in the afternoon. The curfews are a handicap, as you'll miss much of Spanish life, so many pilgrims alternate with nights in cheap *pensiones* or the odd nice hotel to rest weary feet. You'll need your own sleeping bag for many *albergues*; a sleeping mat is also advisable if you need to kip on the floor if there are no bunks left. At present, *albergues* are struggling to cope with the ever-increasing numbers of pilgrims, and there's a sort of race for beds in the next town, with pilgrims getting up ever-earlier.

To look like an authentic medieval pilgrim, many people don the traditional garb. A long staff is a sensible option anyway, a gourd for water, a broad-brimmed hat to keep out sun and rain and a scallop shell as badge of Santiago. In former times, it was forbidden to sell scallops except in Santiago itself, so arriving pilgrims would quickly chow one down and take the shell as proof of completion of the journey. More practically, sturdy walking boots, a weatherproof jacket, sun protection, first aid kit and a reasonable level of fitness are essential to the modern pilgrim. Be prepared to encounter all weathers, as the route crosses high mountain passes as well as scorching plains.

It's difficult to decide the best time to do the route; spring and autumn avoid the worst of the *meseta* heat, but will be cold at nights on the plains and wet in the more mountainous parts. In summer Galicia and Navarra are pleasant, but the haul across the plains from Logroño to León will be gruelling. The best compromise is May or September.

While the text of this guide contains much information about the places along the various *caminos*, lists of pilgrim hostels (*albergues de peregrinos*) have not been included; there are many such guides. The **Confraternity of Saint James**, www.csj.org.uk, is a useful organization wich issues pilgrim passports to members, and also sells a good range of practical guides to the pilgrim routes online. The website is also helpful for further information on the *camino*. www.caminosantiago.org (in Spanish) also has heaps of up-to-date information and good route descriptions and maps.

**Camino Francés** This is the classic route and the one travelled by the majority of pilgrims; it also has the most facilities along the way. Originating in the French town of St Jean Pied-de-Port in the Pyrenees, it crosses the Ibañeta pass to Roncesvalles, then descends the Navarran valley to Pamplona. Heading southwest, it then passes through Puente la Reina, and Estella, near which is a fine thirstquencher – a tap dispensing red wine! Then through Viana to Logroño, capital of the Rioja region. The next stages take in Nájera and Santo Domingo de la Calzada, where the chickens in the

church are part of the *camino*'s rich folk history.

Once out of La Rioja, the *meseta* plain really kicks in. The next major stop is Burgos, then it's more villages of the plain in Castrojeriz, Frómista, Villalcázar and Carrión, all bursting with the Romanesque architecture from the early days of the pilgrimage.

Next, it's León province, through Sahagún, Mansilla and to the capital itself, a good rest stop normally reached by walkers 17-20 days into the journey. On to Astorga, then Ponferrada via the enchanting village of Molinaseca.

From Ponferrada, the last, long, climb begins into the Galician mountains. This is one of the prettiest sections of the route, taking in Villafranca, before ascending to the Piedrafita pass and the hamlet of O Cebreiro.

From here, it's downhill all the way through Sarria, Portomarín and Melide before winding up gazing up at the granite towers of the cathedral in Santiago itself. Some pilgrims choose to continue on to Finisterre – there are *albergues* on the way, but remember to take a photocopy of your credencial, which you've likely handed over in Santiago.

**Camino Aragonés** This route differs only in its initial phase, which crosses into Spain in a more spectacular section of the Pyrenees, and descends the Canfranc Valley to the lively town of Jaca. It then heads westwards to the town of Sangüesa, with optional, worthwhile detours to the monastery of Leyre and the Foz de Lumbier. It then continues to Puente la Reina, where it joins the *Camino Francés*.

**Other routes** There are as many pilgrim routes as there were points of origin; another worthwhile route is the **Camino del Norte** along the coast of Asturias and Galicia, while the **Ruta de la Plata**, taken by people coming from the south of Spain, passes through Salamanca and Zamora.

In summer trails can become conga lines at weekends, so if you're after a bit of peace and solitude, use the lesser-known trails or go at different times.

## Watersports

The north coast is the obvious choice for watersports, with many companies arranging activities in Euskadi, Cantabria and Asturias. The Río Sella in Asturias is a popular choice for canoeing and rafting, while windsurfers generally head for the Rías Baixas in Galicia. There are good surf beaches right along the coast; the biggest scene is at Zarautz and Mundaka in Euskadi, while the beaches of Asturias and Galicia offer more solitude. There's some reasonable diving on the Guipúzcoan Coast too.

# Spectator sports

The sports daily, *Marca*, is a thick publication dedicated mostly to football, and it's the most widely read paper in Spain. *As*, a similar publication, is also well into the top 10. The conclusion to be drawn is that Spaniards are big on sport, and **football** is king.

While none of Spain's biggest clubs are in Northern Spain, the region has held its own: *Athletic Bilbao*, *Real Sociedad* and *Deportivo La Coruña* have all won the championship, while *Real Zaragoza* have won two European titles and *Celta Vigo* and *Alavés* have raised eyebrows in Europe in recent times. Going to a game is an excellent experience; crowds are enthusiastic but well behaved, and it's much more of a family affair than in the UK, for example. Games usually take place on a Sunday evening (most at 1700) although there are a couple of Saturday fixtures, and tickets are relatively easy to come by for most games. The *taquillas* (ticket booths) are normally open at the ground for two days before the match and for the couple of hours before kick-off. Watching the game in a bar is a Sunday ritual for many people, and also good fun. Regional rivalries add to the tension; every game for *Athletic Bilbao* is like an international, and Galician and Asturian teams have no love for *Real Madrid* either. At the time of writing, seven of the 20 teams in the Primera Division were from the north.

The best-known Basque sport, however, is **pelota** ① www.euskalpilota.com, sometimes known as *jai alai*, played on a three-sided court. In the most common version, two teams of two hit the ball with their hands against the walls seeking, like squash, to prevent the other team from returning it. The ball is far from soft; after a long career players' hands resemble winning entries in a root-vegetable show. Variations of the game are *pelota a pala*, using bats, and *cesta punta*, using a wickerwork glove that can propel the ball at frightening speeds. Most courts have matches on Saturday and Sunday evenings. Confusingly, the seasons vary from town to town, but there's always something on somewhere. **Road cycling**, **handball** and **basketball** are also popular spectator sports.

In the Basque country, traditional sports tend to be unreconstructed tests of strength, such as **wood-chopping**, or the alarming **stone-lifting**, in which stocky *harrijasotzaileak* dead- lift weights in excess of 300 kg. The best places to see these sports are at village fiestas.

**Bullfighting** is the most controversial of activities but popular in Northern Spain (see box page 50). Each town usually only has a few a year, normally all during its main summer *fiesta*. Tickets are generally pretty easy to get; just turn up at the *taquilla* at the bullring (*plaza de toros*) the previous day, or a few hours before. The pageantry doesn't come cheap, however; count on at least €25 a ticket at the bigger venues. Tickets in the sun (*sol*) are the cheapest, followed by *sol y sombra* and *sombra* (shade). Within the sections, ringside seats (*barreras*) are the most expensive.

# Health

Health for travellers in Spain is rarely a problem. Medical facilities are good, and the worst most travellers experience is an upset stomach, usually merely a result of the different diet rather than any bug.

If you are a UK resident you are entitled to free, or reduced cost, state-provided healthcare when visiting a European Union (EU) country, Iceland, Liechtenstein, Norway or Switzerland. However, to be covered you will need to take a new **European Health Insurance Card** (**EHIC**) with you. These are available free of charge in the UK from www.dh.gov.uk or post offices. Other EU nationals should contact the Department of Health in their own country.

**Non-EU citizens** should consider travel insurance to cover emergency and routine medical needs; be sure that it covers any sports or activities you may get involved in.

The water is safe to drink, but isn't always that pleasant, so many travellers (and locals) stick to bottled water. The sun in Spain can be harsh, so take adequate precautions to prevent heat exhaustion/sunburn. Many medications that require a prescription in other countries are available over the counter at pharmacies in Spain. Pharmacists are highly trained but don't necessarily speak English. In all medium-sized towns and cities, at least one pharmacy is open 24 hours; this is performed on a rota system; details are posted in the window of all pharmacies and in local newspapers.

# Keeping in touch

## Communications

### Internet
While all the provincial capitals have cybercafés, internet access can still be a problem in smaller towns, even fairly touristy ones, although this will surely change in the very near future. The areas with the worst availability are currently Navarra and Aragón; even the flood of tourists visiting the Pyrenees are web-less in most areas.

Where there is internet access, it's normally pretty good; even the coin-operated terminals seem to have a reasonable connection. Access normally costs from €1.50-€3 per hour, and many cybercafés are open late, although you'll have to cope with the shellbursts and automatic weaponfire from online games, which are very popular. Most modern hotels above a certain standard have walljacks where you can connect a laptop, and a number of restaurants and hotels now offer free wireless facilities. While we have listed internet places throughout the guide, these tend to appear and disappear rapidly, so ask at the tourist information office for the latest advice.

### Post offices
The Spanish post is still notoriously inefficient and slow by European standards. Post offices (*correos*) generally open Monday to Friday 0800-1300, 1700-2000; Saturday 0800-1300, although main offices in large towns will stay open all day. Stamps can be bought here or at tobacconists (look for the *TABACOS* sign or wafting aroma of cigars), who will carefully wrap them in paper. A letter or postcard within Spain costs €0.28, within Europe s €0.53, and elsewhere €0.78.

There's a public telephone in many bars, but hearing the conversation over the ambient noise can be a hard task and rates are slightly higher than on the street. Phone booths on the street are mostly operated by **Telefónica**, and all have international direct dialling (oo is the prefix for international calls). They accept coins from €0.05 upwards and phone cards, which can be bought from *estancos* (newspaper kiosks). For calls within the EU, you need to insert a minimum of €0.60, which doesn't last long. All calls are generally cheaper after 2000 and at weekends. Short local calls cost about €0.20.

Directory enquiries can be reached on 11818 (11825 international), a local operator on 1009; while 112 is the universal emergency number. For international reverse-charge calls, dial 900 99 00 followed by 44 for the UK, 15 for the USA and Canada, 61 for Australia or 64 for New Zealand; you'll be put straight through to an operator in the relevant country. Dialling 1008 will get you an international operator.

Domestic landlines have nine-digit numbers beginning with 9. Although the first three digits indicate the province, you have to dial the full number from wherever you are calling, including abroad. Spain's international code is 34.

Mobile (*móviles*) coverage is very good. Most foreign mobiles will work (with the exception of North America); check with your service provider about call costs. Many mobile networks require you to call up before leaving your home country to activate overseas service. Spanish recharge cards for multinational companies such as Vodafone will work on foreign mobiles. If you're staying a while, it may be cheaper to buy a Spanish mobile or SIM card, as there are always numerous offers and discounts.

# Media

## Newspapers and magazines

The Spanish press is generally of a high journalistic standard. The national dailies *El País* (still a qualitative leap ahead), *El Mundo* and the rightist *ABC* are read throughout the country, but regional papers often eclipse these in readership. In the Basque lands, there is *El Correo*, a quality Bilbao-based syndicated chain. *El Diario Vasco* is another Basque daily, while there's also *El Norte de Castilla*, *El Diario de León*, *El Heraldo de Aragón*, *El Comercio* (Asturian) and *El Correo Gallego* (Galician). Overall circulation is low, partly because many people read the newspapers provided in cafés and bars.

The terribly Real Madrid-biased sports dailies *Marca* and *As*, dedicated mostly to football, have an extremely large readership that rivals any of the broadsheets. There's no tabloid press as such; the closest equivalent is the *prensa de corazón*, the gossip magazines such as *¡Hola!* (forerunner of Britain's *Hello!*). English-language newspapers are widely available in kiosks in the larger towns.

## Radio

Radio is big in Spain, with audience figures relatively higher than most of Europe. There's a huge range of stations, mainly on FM wavelengths, many of them broadcasting to a fairly small regional area. You'll be unlikely to get much exposure to it unless you're in a car or take your own set, however.

## Television

TV is the dominant medium in Spain, with audience figures well above most of the EU, and second only to Britain's. The main television channels are the state-run *TVE1*, with standard programming, and *TVE2*, with a more cultural/sporting bent alongside the private *Antena 3*, *Tele 5* and *Canal Plus*. Regional stations such as *ETB1* and *ETB2* in the Basque country also draw audiences. Overall quality is low, with reality shows and lowest-common-denominator kitsch as popular here as anywhere. Cable TV is widespread, and satellite and digital are beginning to spread.

## ⚇ Footprint features

# Introduction

It's official: Europe's oldest people have been reborn, and everywhere the visitor looks there's some celebration or affirmation that it's good to be Basque again. Euskadi is back with a bang, and the old feeling that Bilbao is the centre of the world has rapidly returned.

Whatever your views on independence movements, global villages, or the single European currency, Euskadi (the Basque name for this part of the world) doesn't feel very Spanish. Even the most imperialistic of the Madrid establishment refer to it as 'El País Vasco', the Basque country. The name for the region in Euskara is either Euskadi or Euskal Herría. Things are certainly different here; there's a strange language on road signs, weird sports are played to packed houses, it rains an awful lot and there's a subtle vibrancy that infects even the most mundane of daily tasks.

Bilbao, has managed superbly to reinvent itself from declining industrial dinosaur to optimistic European city. The Guggenheim museum is a powerful symbol of this, but it's the vision and spirit that put it there that are even more invigorating. San Sebastián, meanwhile, is perennially popular for its superb natural setting, and Vitoria, the peaceful Basque capital, is also very appealing.

Euskadi isn't very large, which means that most of the rural areas are within easy reach of the three cities. The rugged coast has a few excellent beaches and some very personable fishing towns. Inland, medieval towns still preserve an excellent architectural heritage, while Laguardia, by happy coincidence, is both one of the most attractive walled towns in Northern Spain and an important centre of the Rioja wine region. Outside the towns, the green hills and rocky peaks of this corner of the peninsula are an invitation into the open air.

Goya in the art of portrait painting, one of the best examples here is his Columbus, who is deep and soulful (and suspiciously Basque-looking). There's also a small memorial to Zuloaga in the plaza outside. Upstairs, the gallery of Basque painting is a good place to get an idea of how different the local landscapes and physiques are to those of Spain; the quality is good, although there's not a sniff of the controversial, political or avant-garde.

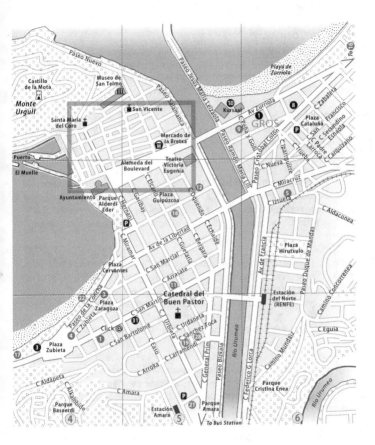

Pensión Aída **5** *B6*
Pensión Amaiur **6** *detail*
Pensión Anne **7** *detail*
Pensión Edorta **8** *detail*
Pensión Gran Bahía
  **13** *detail*
Pensión Kursaal **9** *A5*
Pensión San Jerónimo
  **15** *detail*
Pensión San Lorenzo
  **10** *detail*
Pensión San Martín **11** *B5*
Villa Soro **16** *A6*
La Sirena **17** *C1*

**Eating** 🍴
Altuna Berri **31** *C5*
Barbarin **2** *detail*
Bar Garriti **9** *detail*
Bar Ondarra **1** *A6*
Bodegón Alejandro
  **23** *detail*
Café de la Concha **3** *C4*
Casa Gandarias **4** *detail*
Casa Nicolasa **6** *detail*
Casa Urola **25** *detail*
Casa Vergara **27** *detail*
Ganbara **7** *detail*
Garbola **8** *A6*

Kursaal **10** *A5*
La Cepa **11** *detail*
La Cuchara de
  San Telmo **12** *detail*
Munto **30** *detail*
Oquendo **13** *detail*
Panier Fleuri **14** *detail*
Portaletas **26** *detail*
San Martín **24** *B1*
Urapel **14** *detail*

**Bars & clubs** 🍷
Altxerri **15** *detail*
Bataplán **17** *C4*

Be Bop **29** *detail*
Bideluze **18** *B5*
El Nido **19** *C5*
Garagar **20** *detail*
Komplot **21** *C5*
Rotonda **22** *C4*
Soma 107 **28** *C5*

**Iglesia de San Vicente**

The most interesting of San Sebastián's churches, San Vicente is a castle-like sandstone building that squats in the northeast of Parte Vieja. Started in the early 16th century, it features a massive *retablo* with various biblical scenes, and a gallery with an impressive organ. Jorge Oteiza's fluid, modern *Pietá* stands graciously outside the southern door.

# Centro and New Town

## Playa de la Concha

This beautiful curving strip of sand, has made San Sebastián what it is. Named *La Concha* (shell) for its shape, it gets seriously crowded in summer but is relatively quiet at other times, when the chilly water makes swimming a matter of bravado. Behind the beach, and even more emblematic, is the **Paseo**, a promenade barely changed from the golden age of seaside resorts. It's still the place to take the sea air (so good for one's constitution) and is backed by gardens, a lovely old merry-go-round, and a row of desirable beachfront hotels and residences that still yearn for the days when royalty strolled the shore every summer season.

## Isla Santa Clara

Out in the bay this is a pretty rocky island that could have been placed there purposely as a feature. There's nothing on it but a lighthouse and a jetty, but it's prime picnic territory and the setting is unbeatable. It's only accessible by public transport during the summer, when a motorboat leaves from the harbour close to the end of the beach.

## Ondarreta

Where the beach of La Concha graciously concedes defeat at a small rocky outcrop, the beach of Ondarreta begins. Atop the rock sits the **Palacio de Miramar**; commissioned by the regent María Cristina in the late 19th century, it would not look out of place offering selective bed and breakfast in an English village.

*♟ A good place to stay in summer, with less hustle and bustle.*

The **beach** of Ondarreta gazes serenely across at the rest of San Sebastián from beyond the Palacio de Miramar. It's a fairly exclusive and genteel part of town, appropriately watched over by a statue of a very regal Queen María Cristina. The beach itself feels somewhat more spacious than La Concha and, at the end the town, gives way to the jagged rocky coastline of Guipúzcoa. Integrating the two is **El Peine del Viento**, the comb of the wind, one of sculptor Eduardo Chillida's (see box, page 66) signature works. It consists of three twisted rusty iron whirls, which, at times, seem to be struggling to tame the ragged breezes that can sweep the bay. Chillida asked to borrow helicopters from the US embassy to help place the sculptures. They refused, and the sculptures were finally erected using a specially designed floating bridge.

## Monte Igueldo

Above Ondarreta rises the steep Monte Igueldo, which commands excellent views of all that is San Sebastián. It's not a place to meditate serenely over the panorama – the summit of the hill is capped by a luxury hotel and a slightly tacky **amusement park** ① €1.10. The view makes it special though, and is unforgettable in the evening, when the city's lights spread out like a breaking wave below.

There's a **funicular** ① 1100-2000, €0.80/1.50 return, running up and down from a station behind the tennis club at the end of the beach. Otherwise it's a walk up the winding road beside it, which gives occasional views both ways along the coast. To reach Ondarreta and the funicular, walk or take bus No 16 from Plaza Guipúzcoa (hourly/half-hourly in summer; €0.90).

## Catedral del Buen Pastor

The simple and elegant neo-Gothic Catedral del Buen Pastor is light and airy with an array of geometric stained glass, but in reality, there's little to detain the visitor – it's more impressive outside than in. Lovers of kitsch art will, however, have a field day – the Christ with sheep above the altar is upstaged by the painted choirboy with donation box in hand.

# Gros

A bit more down-to-earth and relaxed than the rest of San Sebastián, Gros lies across the river and backs a good beach, which sees some decent surf. It's dominated by the Kursaal, but is also worth exploring for its *pintxos* (see box, page 101).

## Kursaal

① *Av Zurriola 1, T943 003 000, www.kursaal.org, guided tours Mon-Fri 1330, Sat and Sun 1130, 1230, 1330, €2.*

In a space that was derelict for three decades since the old Kursaal was demolished, these two stunning glass prisms opened their doors in 1999. Designed by Navarran architect Rafael Moneo to harmonize with the rivermouth, the sea and 'communicate' with the hills of Uría and Urgull to either side, the concert hall has inspired much comment. The architect fondly refers to his building as 'two stranded rocks' – critics might agree – but the overall reaction has been very positive, and in 2001 the building won the European Union prize for contemporary architecture. The main building hosts concerts and conventions, while its smaller

❖ *The Kursaal looks at its most impressive when reflecting the setting sun, or when lit up eerily at night.*

sidekick is an attractive exhibition centre. It's also the new home of the San Sebastián Film Festival and it houses a café and an upmarket modern restaurant as well.

# Around San Sebastián

## Museo Chillida-Leku

① *Barrio Jauregui 66, T943 336 006, Sep-Jun Wed-Mon 1030-1500 (Jul/Aug to 1900), €7.*

The Museo Chillida-Leku is a very relaxing place to spend a few hours out of the city. The late Basque sculptor Eduardo Chillida (see box page 66) gracefully restored a 16th-century farmhouse with his own concepts of angles and open interior space. The lower floor, lit by a huge window, has a selection of large pieces; upstairs is some of his smaller, earlier work, as well as preparatory drawings. Around the house is a large park, which has about 40 of his larger sculptures (these are changeable depending on exhibition commitments). It's a very peaceful and shady place to stroll; the organized should pack a picnic. Bus No 92 from Calle Oquendo runs to the museum every 30 minutes on the half-hour.

## Cider houses

① *The tourist office in San Sebastián has a map and list of the cider houses; several are in very picturesque locations with walking trails through the hills and valleys from Astigarraga and Hernani, a 15-min bus ride from Plaza Guipúzcoa in the centre.*

In the hills around Hernani and Astigarraga a short way south of town, apples are grown among stunning green hills. Although it's not hugely popular as a day-to-day drink in San Sebastián these days, cider has an important place in Guipúzcoan history. It's nothing like your mass-produced commercial ciders, being sharpish, yeasty and not very fizzy. It's best drunk fresh, poured from a height to give it some bounce after hitting the glass. The cider is mostly made in the hills near San Sebastián in the many small

# ❗ Bitter and twisted

You can't go far in the Basque lands without coming across a hauntingly contorted figure or sweep of rusted iron that signals a creation of Jorge de Oteiza or Eduardo Chillida. The powerful and original work of these two Basque sculptors is emblematic of the region.

**Jorge de Oteiza**, forthright and uncompromising well into his 90s, was born in Orio in 1908. After ditching a medical career in favour of sculpture he taught in South America before his big breakthrough came when commissioned to create pieces for the façade of the visionary new monastery at Arantzazu in the early 1950s. With his grey beard, leather jacket, beret and thick glasses, Oteiza cut quite a figure on site, but the anguish and power he managed to channel into his *Apostles* and *Pietá* was quite extraordinary. The Vatican prevented the erection of the 14 apostles for 18 years. Oteiza was always preoccupied with relevance, famously saying that "a monument will be no more than a pile of stones or a coil of wire if it does not contribute to the making of a better human being, if it is not…the moulded key to a new kind of man".

**Eduardo Chillida** was born in 1924 in San Sebastián and in his youth (and before a knee injury) appeared between the sticks for Real Sociedad. A sculptor of huge world renown, the spaces he created within his work are as important as the materials that comprise it. The *Peine de los Vientos* at San Sebastián and the *Plaza de los Fueros* in Vitoria are designed to interact dynamically with their setting, while his exploration of oxidized iron as a medium was particularly appropriate for Euskadi, built on the glories of a now-faded iron industry. Softer work in alabaster and wood is less confronting, but evokes the same theme of space. Chillida-Leku museum outside San Sebastián houses a large cross-section of his massive output.

The two sculptors were on bitter terms for many years: Oteiza, perhaps jealous of Chillida's rising profile, held the view that he had 'sold out', refused to use his name, and criticized him bitterly in public. Over the years there were accusations of plagiarism from both sides. Oteiza eventually had a change of heart and after many peaceful overtures were rejected, they finally buried the hatchet in 1997 with the 'Zabalaga embrace'. In fact, it seems that before Chillida's death in August 2002, aged 78, they had become firm friends. Oteiza died only months later, in April 2003, aged 94.

*sagardotegiak*, or *sidrerías*. When it's ready, in early January, cider houses stoke up their kitchens, dust down the tables and fling the doors open to the Donostian hordes, who spend whole afternoons eating massive traditional cider house meals and serving themselves freely from taps on the side of the vats. It's an excellent experience even if you're not sold on the cider itself. Tradition has it that this lasts until late April or so, although several are now open year-round.

The typical meal served starts with *tortilla de bacalao* (salt-cod omelette), continues with a massive slab of grilled ox, and concludes with cheese, walnuts, and *membrillo* (quince jelly, delicious with the cheese). The best of the places are the simpler rustic affairs with long, shared, rowdy wooden tables and floors awash with the apple brew, but these tend to be harder to get to. Expect to pay from €15-30 for the *menú sidrería*, which includes as much cider as you feel like sinking.

# Inland from San Sebastián ⬣🍴🏃🎵🏨 ›› *p68-73.*

Guipúzcoa is criss-crossed by valleys that are lush from rainfall and dotted with small towns, some agricultural centres for the surrounding farmland, some seats of heavier Basque industry such as cement or paper manufacture.

In many ways this is the 'real' Basqueland and the smaller, poorer communities are still where separatism flourishes most strongly. The valleys also conceal beautiful churches (as well as the massive Loiola basilica), and plenty of walks and picnic spots. Due to Euskadi's good transport connections, many of these places are within easy day-trip range of both San Sebastián and Bilbao. However, there are good accommodation options, especially in *casas rurales* or *agroturismos*, usually Basque farmhouses with good welcoming accommodation in the heart of the countryside.

## Santuario de Loiola → *Colour map 3, B3.*

Now here's a strange one. A massive **basilica** ① *daily 1000-1300, 1500-1900*, not quite St Peter's or St Paul's but not very far off, standing in the middle of Guipúzcoan pasture land. All is explained by the fact that St Ignatius, founder of the Jesuits (see page 75) was born here. The house where he first saw daylight has bizarrely had the basilica complex built around it; it's now a museum.

The most arresting feature of the basilica from a distance is the massive dome, which stands 65 m high. Designed by Carlo Fontana, an Italian architect from Bernini's school, it's topped by an ornate cupola. Lavish is the word to describe the rest of the decoration of the church; minimalist gurus will probably drop dead on the spot. The building is designed to be viewed from a distance – this is the function of the formal promenade in front of it – and what first strikes the visitor are the harmonious proportions. On closer inspection, the intricacy of the decoration becomes apparent. Inside, the Baroque style is grandiose (almost to the point of pomposity), with a silver-plated statue of Ignatius himself gazing serenely at some very elaborate stonework and massive slabs of marble.

> ❗ The best time to visit is during the week, at weekends it's overcrowded with elderly pilgrims paying their respects to the saint.

Those with a keen interest in the saint might want to take themselves down to nearby **Azpeitia** to see the font where he was baptized, in the church of San Sebastián.

## Oñati → *Colour map 3, B2.*

The town of Oñati is one of the most attractive in the region and has a proud history as a university town and, until the mid-19th century, as a semi-independent fief of the local lord. The university, **Universidad de Sancti Spiritus**, was established in 1540 and is a beautiful example of cultured Renaissance architecture with an attractive colonnaded quadrangle. The stately red-balconied **Casa Consistorial** overlooks the main square where the two principal pedestrian streets, Calle Zaharra and Calle Barria, meet. These streets are the centre of the lively weekend nightlife as well as being the town's major axes. Oñati's **tourist office** is on Plaza de los Fueros.

## Santuario de Arantzazu

Some 9 km south of Oñati is the Franciscan Santuario de Arantzazu, perching on a rock in a valley of great natural beauty. The basilica, built in the 1950s, is one of the most remarkable buildings in Euskadi. Incredibly avant-garde for the time, its spiky stone exterior is a reference to the hawthorn bush: according to tradition, a statue of Mary was found by a shepherd in 1468 on the spines of a hawthorn. A tinkling cowbell had led him to the spot, and the discovery ended years of war and famine in the area. The statue now sits above the altar, surrounded by the

> ❗ There are some excellent opportunities for walking in the area, which is one of the most beautiful parts of Euskadi.

visionary abstract altarpiece of Luzio Muñoz. Although it appears to be made of stone, it's actually treated wood, and 600 sq m of it at that. Above the iron doors, sculpted by Eduardo Chillida, are Jorge Oteiza's fluid apostles and *Pietá*. He created great controversy by sculpting 14 apostles; for years they lay idle near the basilica as the Vatican wouldn't permit them to be erected. In the crypt, the impressive paintings of Néstor Basterretxea also caused problems with the church hierarchy. He originally painted the crucifixion backwards; when this was censured, he agreed to repaint it but with an angry Jesus. He succeeded – his powerful red Christ is an imposing figure. See box, page 66, for further information on Oteiza and Chillida.

---

## 🛏 Sleeping

**San Sebastián** *p60, map p62*
The Parte Vieja is the best spot for budget accommodation; there's also plenty near the cathedral around C San Martín. All accommodation in San Sebastián is overpriced; there is no getting away from the fact. High season is Jun-Sep; prices are at least 30% lower in most places outside this period.
**LL Hotel María Cristina**, C Oquendo 1, T943 437 600, www.westin.com/mariacristina. Taking up an entire block, its elegant sandstone bulk has cradled more celebrities than you could drop a fork at. It has all the services, luxury, and style you would expect, including a childminding service and a proper concierge, as well as prices that boot other Basque hotels into the campsite class. A double costs about €400 in season.
**LL Villa Soro**, Av de Ategorrieta 61, T943 297 970, www.villasoro.com. To the east of Gros, this sumptuous 19th-century villa is something of an oasis, set in large grounds with manicured gardens. It really feels like a rural hotel, with discreet service, a refined, relaxing feel, and seriously comfortable rooms, some in an annexe. No restaurant.
**L Hotel de Londres y de Inglaterra**, C Zubieta 2, T943 440 770, www.hlondres.com. Grand old beachfront hotel that is an emblem of the city's glory days. Great location and good service – if royalty don't drop by as often as they once did, no one's letting on.
**L Hotel Monte Igueldo**, Paseo del Faro 134, T943 210 211, www.monteigueldo.com. It's all about location here. At the top of Monte Igueldo, most of the rooms offer a spectacular view one way or another. It's hardly a peaceful retreat though, as the summit of the hill is shared with an amusement park.
**AL Hotel Niza**, C Zubieta 56, T943 426 663, www.hotelniza.com. Slap bang on the beach, this hotel is an odd mixture of casual seaside and starchy formality. About half the rooms

have views – some are better than others – and some are noisy. The singles are a little dark but offer very good value.
**AL-A Hotel Ezeiza**, Av Satrustegui 13, Ondarreta, T943 214 311, www.hotel ezeiza.com. Well situated at the peaceful western end of Ondarreta beach, this is a welcoming place with the added attraction of an excellent terrace bar.
**B Hostal Alemana**, C San Martín 53, T943 462 544, www.hostalalemana.com. An efficient modern hotel with warm personal service. Despite its *hostal* category it is effectively a hotel, with all the conveniences, plus some nice views and a pretty breakfast room. Minimum 5-night stay in Aug.
**B Pensión Aída**, C Iztueta 9, Gros, T943 327 800, www.pensionesconencanto.com. A very good place to stay in Gros, and convenient for the station. The gleaming rooms are appealing, and the breakfast in bed is a great way to start the day.
**B Pensión Gran Bahía**, C Embeltrán 16, T943 420 216, www.paisvasco.com/granbahia. This attractive and upmarket *pensión* is convenient for both the beach and Parte Vieja. Recently renovated, the beds are very comfortable, and the rooms well-equipped and quiet. All have bathroom and a/c. **D** off-season.
**B Pensión Kursaal**, C Peña y Goñi 2, T943 292 666, www.pensionesconencanto.com. A good place to stay just across the river in Gros, and very near the beach. The attractive rooms have large windows, bathrooms and TV. As in many of these old buildings, the plumbing and heating can make a racket. Internet access in the lobby. Parking available under the Kursaal for €9 a day – a good deal. Recommended.
**B-C Pensión Edorta**, C Puerto 15, T943 423 773, www.pensionedorta.com. Overpriced but charming, this beautiful *pensión* is right in the old town near the fishing harbour. Only

recently opened, the rooms are beautiful, with rough stone-faced walls, polished floorboards and elegant iron-headed beds. The bathrooms are also very elegant, but some of them are shared.

**C Pensión Anne**, C Esterlines 15, T943 421 438, www.pensionanne.com. Behind an imposing wooden door is a spotlessly bright, welcoming *pensión*. All rooms are exterior, with heating, TV, and optional bathroom. It has an arty, homely feel, and is particularly good value off season (**E**). Recommended.

**C Pensión San Jerónimo**, C San Jerónimo 25, T943 427 525, www.pensionsan jeronimo.com. This spick and span place is ideally situated right in the heart of the old town and offers better value than many. The rooms have shiny wooden floors and the beds, if on the small side, are new and firm. All rooms have a small bathroom. **E** off-season.

**C-D Pensión San Martín**, C San Martín 10, T943 428 714. One of the better of the host of choices on this street. The rooms are good and comfy, and have bathrooms and TV. Very handy for the train station.

**D Pensión San Lorenzo**, C San Lorenzo 2, T943 425 516, www.pensionsanlorenzo.com. A friendly star of the old town near the Bretxa market. The 5 well-priced rooms are brightly decorated and come with full bathroom, TV, fridge, kettle and piped radio. Internet access for €2/hr with 15 mins free. It's a quiet place and highly recommended, but fills very fast. **F** off-season.

**D-E Pensión Amaiur**, C 31 de Agosto 44, T943 429 654, www.pensionamaiur.com. Situated in the oldest house in the Parte Vieja (few others survived the 1813 fire), this is one of the best budget options in town. Lovingly decorated and sympathetically run, there is a variety of smallish but homely rooms, most with satellite TV and some with balconies. Guests have free use of the pretty (stoveless) kitchen, and there's coin-operated high-speed internet access. Highly recommended.

**E La Sirena**, Paseo de Igueldo 25, T943 310 268, www.inturjoven.com. Although it's far from central, San Sebastián's HI hostel is close to Ondarreta beach, and easily accessible by bus No 24 from town. Curfews, early check-outs, and school groups are the drawbacks, but the facilities are good, and there's internet access and breakfast included.

**Camping Igueldo**, Paseo Padre Orkolaga 69, T943 214 502, www.campingigueldo.com. Open all year, this big San Sebastián campsite is back from Ondarreta beach behind Monte Igueldo.

### Santuario de Loiola *p67*

**B Hotel Loiola**, Av de Loiola s/n, Loiola, T943 151 616, www.hotelloiola.com. Although the building itself won't win many prizes for harmonious rural architecture, it's handy for the basilica, and reasonable value. The rooms are a touch dull but don't lack conveniences.

**E Laja Barrio**, Santa Cruz, Azkoitia, T943 853 075. A good choice on the edges of Azkoitia in a traditional-looking *baserri* farmhouse that offers home-cooked meals and very good-value rooms in striking distance of the basilica.

### Oñati *p67*

The cheaper beds in Oñati fill up quickly at weekends.

**C Ongi Etorri**, C Zaharra 19, T943 718 285, F943 718 284. This family-run hotel is well located on the main pedestrian street. The rooms are thoughtfully decorated, a touch small, but snug with heating and a/c.

**E Arregi**, Ctra Garagaltza-Auzoa 21, T943 780 824. An excellent *agroturismo* a couple of kilometres from Oñati. A big farmhouse in a green valley with beautiful dark-wood rooms, a ping-pong table, and pleasant owners. You can use the kitchen, or they can provide dinner with advance notice. Recommended.

**F Etxebarría**, C Barria 15, T943 780 460. A cheap *pensión* not far from the main square. Rooms and clean and good value but it's definitely worth ringing ahead. It can get a little noisy at weekends.

### Santuario de Arantzazu *p67*

There are a couple of hotels and bars in Arantzazu but, happily, nothing else.

**E Hospedería de Arantzazu**, Arantzazu 29, T943 781 313, ostatua@arantzazu.org. Right next to the basilica, this guesthouse offers simple comfort run by monks. There are different grades of room, but no great price differential, so grab the ones with a balcony. There's a room equipped for the disabled.

## ❶ Eating

### San Sebastián p60, map p62

San Sebastián has a strong claim to the title of gourmet capital of Spain, with some seriously classy restaurants dotting the city and the hills around. It's also a great place for crawling around bars eating *pintxos*; the best zone for this is the Parte Vieja, where 'eat street' is **C Fermín Calbetón**, with several excellent places. Gros is a quieter but equally tasty option. Eating in the city is far from cheap by Spanish standards.

**Casa Nicolasa**, C Aldamar 4, T943 421 762. This simple and gracious 2nd-floor dining room is one of the city's best restaurants. The emphasis is on seafood – the *almejas* (small clams) with trout roe are superb – and the service is restrained and attentive.

**Kursaal Restaurant**, Av Zurriola 1, T943 003 162. One of several restaurants overseen by top local chef Martín Berasategui, this is attractively set in the Kursaal and features the most modern of Basque *nouvelle cuisine*. For the quality on offer it's not too dear; you can eat well for about €50 a head, and there are various *menús de degustación*.

**Zuberoa**, Barrio Iturriotz 8, T943 491 228. Closed Sun night and Mon. Outside San Sebastián, near the town of Oiartzun/Oyarzun is the lair of top chef Hilario Arbelaitz and his brothers, in an attractive stone farmhouse with a wooden porch and terrace. Arbelaitz combines an essential Basqueness with a treatment inspired by the very best of French and Mediterranean cuisine. Everything is delicious, from a typical fish soup to the untypical grapefruit, spider crab and trout roe jelly with potato and olive oil cream. For a real gastronomic experience, order the €96 *menú de degustación*, a once-in-a-lifetime 11-course sonata of a meal (drinks not included).

**Altuna Berri**, C San Martín 43, T943 451 350. This compact bar is run by very decent people, and has a short but excellent *menú* for €11.90, as well as tasty *raciones* – the eggs have a high reputation. An excellent spot for lunch, and not far back from the beach.

**Barbarin**, C Puerto 21, T943 421 886. A friendly, comfortable and spacious restaurant specializing in well-priced local seafood. The *rollitos de txangurro* (fried crab rolls) are especially tempting; they also do a good paella and cheap steaks.

**Bodegón Alejandro**, C Fermín Calbetón 4, T943 427 158. This popular spot is overseen by celebrated chef Martín Berasategui and has become very popular. With a homely, unpretentious interior, the focus is on the quality cuisine, which is French in style. There's a daily *menú* for €11.50 and an excellent evening bistro menu for €29.50.

**Casa Urola**, C Fermín Calbetón 20, T943 423 424. An enticing choice whether for *pintxos* or a full meal, this small and busy bar has exquisite gourmet snacks on the counter. There are 2 dining areas; upstairs is more peaceful. The fish dishes are excellent and the *solomillo*'s tasty too. Recommended.

**Garbola**, Paseo Colon 11, T943 285 019. Legendery for its scrumptious mushroom creations and *caipirinhas*, this Gros bar also offers more unusual snacks, such as kangaroo and shark. It's very plush and upmarket, and the owner will keep tempting you with further delights.

**Munto**, C Fermín Calbeton 17, T943 426 088. This thoroughly worthwhile place is one of many good choices on this street. The downstairs *comedor* is very attractively lit and decorated, the service is attentive, and the food – tasty steaks and delicately-treated seafood – is of excellent quality for the price.

**Oquendo**, C Oquendo 8, T943 420 932. A good, fairly formal restaurant near the **Hotel María Cristina**, serving a range of fresh fish around €18 a plate. The front's got some good bar-top eating, and the photo wall from the San Sebastián Film Festival is great for testing your silver-screen knowledge.

**Panier Fleuri**, Paseo Salamanca 2, T943 424 205. A bright and airy split-level restaurant with a French-inspired menu and an emphasis on fresh market produce and char-grilled meats.

**Restaurante San Martín**, Plazoleta Funicular, T943 214 084. Next to the Igueldo funicular, this pretty house-on-a-hill is a restaurant specializing in fish and the occasional game-bird. Outdoor eating and some great views from the dining room.

**Sansonategi**, Barrio Martindegi s/n, T943 553 260. One of the few cider-houses to be open for meals year-round. Rates about midway on the authentic scale, and offers the traditional *menú sidrería* for €27, as well as good à la carte choices.

**Urepel**, Paseo Salamanca 3, T943 424 040. A long and brooding restaurant with a fairly

Spanish feel. The food is lighter, and the highlight is an elegantly treated shellfish. A good wine list accompanies the classy nosh.

† **Bar Garriti**, C San Juán 8. An unglamorous bar that's been going for years. Somewhat surprisingly, on entering you are confronted with a mighty impressive spread of *pintxos* during the day and early evening. You could spend all day in here if you weren't careful.

† **Bar Ondarra**, Av de la Zurriola 16, T943 326 033. Opposite the Kursaal exhibition centre in Gros, this is a decent tapas bar with a small street level and an underground den featuring regular live jazz and soul. Good *pintxos*.

† **Casa Gandarias**, C 31 de Agosto 25, T943 428 106. This busy tapas bar is near the Santa María church and has an adjoining restaurant. The *pintxos* are excellent and are served by efficient and cordial staff. The *solomillo* or the grilled *foie* are particularly recommended. Good whisky selection, too.

† **Casa Vergara**, C Mayor 21, T943 431 073. This highly recommendable tapas bar is on the corner of the ever-popular 31 de Agosto. While it's worth sitting down in the simple but comfortable *comedor* to try *raciones* of stews like *callos* (tripe), *chipirones* (squid) or *pulpo* (octopus), the *pintxos* at the bar are delightful. Try the *gulas* wrapped in smoked salmon if they're about. It's well priced too.

† **Ganbara**, C San Jerónimo 21, T943 422 575. This is a fairly upmarket tapas bar and *asador* with a worthwhile array of *pintxos* to accompany the cheerfully poured wine. The *raciones* are delicious, with such delicacies as *trufas* (truffles) and *percebes* (goose barnacles) making an appearance.

† **La Cepa**, C 31 de Agosto 7, T943 426 394. Perennially and deservedly popular tapas bar lined with hams and featuring the head of a particularly large *toro* on the wall. Good atmosphere and *pintxos* and *raciones* to match.

† **La Cuchara de San Telmo**, C 31 de Agosto 28 (back), T943 420 840. An extraordinary bar up the side of the museum. The kitchen serves made-to-order gourmet dishes in miniature, which cost €2-2.50. It's original and inspiring. Recommended.

† **Portaletas**, C Puerto 8, T943 423 888. This welcoming establishment offers unpretentious hospitality, with its stone-faced walls and wooden beams. There are appetizing *pintxos*, mostly on slices of bread. There's also a cheap *menú del día* and good value *raciones* (€5-10).

## Cafés

**Café de la Concha**, Paseo de la Concha s/n, T943 473 600. A pretty place to stop for a coffee or a glass of wine during a stroll along the beach. It's also got a decent restaurant with good views and a terrace. €10 *menú del día*.
**Kursaal Café**, Av Zurriola 1, T943 003 162. The café is an excellent spot for an early evening *pintxo* and drink, with superb views over the rivermouth and sea.

### Santuario de Loiola *p67*

†† **Kiruri**, Loiola Auzoa 24, T943 815 608. The best option in the area, directly opposite the basilica. It does some good traditional dishes and is popular for its *rabas* (calamari strips). Service can be slow if there's a coachload of pilgrims in. There's a good terrace outside.

### Oñati *p67*

The **Etxebarría** (see Sleeping, above) runs a good cheap restaurant a couple of doors down the street.

† **Arkupe**, Plaza del los Fueros 9, T943 781 699. A good bar/restaurant on the main square, with a variety of cheap *raciones* and *platos*. Also a focus of the early evening outdoor drinking scene.

## ⊕ Bars and clubs

### San Sebastián *p60, map p62*

The Parte Vieja has many options and the crossroads of C **Larramendi** and C **Reyes Católicos** near the cathedral is full of bars. There's studenty nightlife around C **San Bartolomé**, just back from the beach.

**Altxerri Bar**, C Reina Regenta 2. An atmospheric cellar bar by the tourist office that regularly showcases live jazz and other acts. Draws an interesting crowd and is worthwhile even if there's nothing on.

**Bataplán**, Playa de la Concha s/n, T943 460 439. San Sebastián's most famous *discoteca*, right on La Concha beach. Open Thu-Sat from 2400 and attracts a smart young crowd. The music is mostly club anthems and pop crowd pleasers. Rises to prominence during the film festival when it hosts various after-parties. €7-15 entry.

**Be Bop**, Paseo de Salamanca 3. This well-visited bar by the rivermouth is quiet and relaxing and has regular live jazz music playing; entry is usually about €5.

**Bideluze**, Plaza Guipúzcoa 14, T943 422 880. A lively and interesting bar, with 2 floors of eccentric furniture, on the south side of Plaza Guipúzcoa. Simple food is served downstairs and *pintxos* upstairs. It's popular with young and old; you may be addressed in Euskara.
**El Nido**, C Larramendi 13. A sizeable pub that fills after work and doesn't empty again until late. Friendly crowd and board games.
**Garagar**, Alameda del Boulevard 22, T943 422 840. Slightly overpriced pub at the edge of the Parte Vieja with some comfy booths. Busy till 0200 most nights (0400 at weekends), and more relaxed than some of the other late-openers. There's a DJ upstairs at weekends.
**Kandela**, C Escolta Real 20, Antiguo. This bar in the suburb of Antiguo usually features live bands from Thu-Sun. It ranges from rock to pop and usually kicks off at about 2300. The €6 entry includes a drink.
**Komplot**, C Pedro Egaña 5, T943 472 109. Small and *à la mode* club featuring probably the best house music in San Sebastián.
**Ku**, Monte Igueldo s/n. Atop the Igueldo hill at the end of Ondarreta beach is one of the city's more glamorous discos, with a smart mixed crowd. Usually goes later than anywhere.
**Rotonda**, Playa de la Concha 6, T943 429 095. Another club on La Concha beach and open very late weekend nights. The music hovers around popular dance, with some salsa and reggae thrown in as required.
**Soma 107**, C Larramendi 4, T943 468 810. Every facet of this unusual bar is devoted to making the smoking of *porros* (joints) as comfortable as possible. It's almost a dope centre rather than a bar, with internet, books, food and 2 levels of seating decorated with murals, graffiti and paintings.

**Oñati** *p67*
For later action, head for one of the bars on C Zaharri, such as **Bar Irritz**, which is friendly and has a popular techno scene at weekends.

## ⊕ Entertainment

**San Sebastián** *p60, map p62*
**Bullfighting**
Near the stadium is the new bullring, **Illumbe**, which was inaugurated in 1998 and includes a massive cinema complex. The city had been without a bullring since 1973, when the famous **El Chofe**, in Gros, was demolished.

**Football club**
**Estadio de Anoeta**, Paseo de Anoeta 1, T943 462 833, www.real-sociedad-sad.es. This is the home of **Real Sociedad**, the city's football team. Given the title 'Real' (Royal) in 1910 by the king, who spent much time in the city, the club is one of comparatively few to have won the Spanish league title, which it managed twice in 1981 and 1982. Tickets €25-40 (sold at the stadium from the Thu afternoon before a game to the Sat evening, then 2 hrs before kick-off, usually 1700 on Sun).

**Theatre**
The beautiful Teatro Victoria Eugenia is a sparklingly atmospheric place to catch a show, but it is currently still under renovation.

## ⊕ Festivals and events

**San Sebastián** *p60, map p62*
**19-20 Jan** Tamborrada, the feast day of San Sebastián, is celebrated with a deafening parade of drummers through the streets from midnight on the 19th.
**Week before 15 Aug** The Aste Nagusia or 'big week', the city's major fiesta, kicks off in San Sebastián with world-renowned fireworks exhibitions.
**3rd week of Sep** International Film Festival.

## ○ Shopping

**San Sebastián** *p60, map p62*
**Graphos**, C Mayor 1, T943 426 377. On the edge of the old town, this has an excellent selection of maps of the region.
**La Bretxa**, Plaza de Bretxa, Market complex in the old town.
**Solbes**, C Aldamar 4, T943 421 724, San Sebastián. A delicatessan and wine shop with a high-quality line-up that isn't particularly cheap.

## ▲ Activities and tours

**San Sebastián** *p60, map 62*
**Tour operators**
The tourist office hire out multilingual audio guides for the city; these cover the old town and cost €10 for a day. There's a hop-on, hop-off bus that runs Oct-Jun daily except Tue (mornings only in winter months), and daily Jul-Sep. Ticket (€10) valid for 24 hrs;

another service goes to the Chillida museum. There's also a small tourist **train** running around the streets. It leaves every hour from Teatro Victoria Eugenia.

**Barco de Ocio**, runs 1½-hr trips around the bay, Sat and Sun am and pm hourly departures, daily in summer, €6 (leaves from half-way along aquarium wharf).

---

## ☺ Transport

**San Sebastián** *p60, map p62*
**Bicycle hire** Bici Rent Donosti, Av de la Zurriola 22, T943 290 854, T655 724 458. Open daily 0900-2100, this shop on Gros beach rents bikes by the hour and by the day. They're not cheap at €18 per day, but there's a decent range, and the staff will help with planning trips.

**Bus** The main bus station is an inconvenient 20-min walk from the old town; buses No 26 and No 28 run there regularly from the Alameda del Boulevard. For the tickets, you have to go to the company offices, situated on Paseo Vizcaya and Av Sancho el Sabio on either side of the bus bays.

Bilbao (1 hr 20 mins, €8) is served at least hourly, and **Vitoria** (1 hr 45 mins, €6.73) 7 or more times a day.

Other destinations include **Pamplona** (4 daily, 1 hr 45 mins, €5.61), **Madrid** (8 daily, 5 hrs 45 mins, €27.37), **Burgos** (7 daily, 3-4 hrs, €13.33), and **Santander** (9 daily, 3 hrs, €11.72). There are also buses to **Bayonne** and **Biarritz** in France.

Shorter-haul buses to Guipúzcoan destinations leave from the central Plaza Guipúzcoa. Destinations include **Zumaia**, **Zarautz**, **Azkoitia** and **Loiola** (the exception; this leaves from the bus station, €3.55), **Tolosa**, **Oiartzun**, **Hernani**, **Astigarraga**, all with very frequent departures.

**Train** There are several mainline train departures to **Madrid** (3 daily, 6 hrs 30 mins, from €33) and other Spanish cities.

There are 11 trains a day for **Vitoria** (1 hr 40 mins, from €7.20). Euskotren connects the city with other Basque destinations on the coast and inland: its hub is Amara, on Plaza Easo in the south part of the new town. **Bilbao** is served hourly via the coast

(2 hrs 40 mins, €5.50). **El Topo** (the Mole) is a train service running from Amara to **Hendaye** in France, it runs every 10-15mins and takes 35 mins. At Hendaye you can change to mainline **SNCF** train services.

**Santuario de Loiola** *p67*
**Bus** You can reach Azkoitia and Loiola by bus from **Bilbao's** bus station (3 a day), and from **San Sebastián** (hourly, 1 hr, €3.55) (destination may be marked Azpeitia).

**Oñati** *p67*
**Bus** Oñati is accessed by bus from **Bilbao's** bus station with **Pesa** once daily Mon-Fri, otherwise connect with local bus from **Bergara**. There's no public transport from Oñati to Arantzazu; a taxi costs about €10 each way. Walking from Oñati takes about 2 hrs, but the return trip downhill is significantly quicker. There's plenty of traffic, and it's easy to hitch a ride.

---

## ☺ Directory

**San Sebastián** *p60, map p62*
**Internet** Ciber Sare, C Aldamar 3, San Sebastián, T943 430 887, is a good option with heaps of terminals, €0.05 per min; **Click in D@ House**, C San Martín 47, €3 per hr; **Donosti-Net**, C Embeltrán 2 and C San Jerónimo 8, T943 429 497, in the heart of the old town, also offers a left-luggage service, €3 per hr; **Zarranet**, C San Lorenzo 6, T943 433 381, with a fast connection, €3 per hr.
**Laundry** Lavomatique, C Iñio 4, self-service laundry in the Parte Vieja, Mon-Fri 0930-1300, 1600-1930, Sat 1000-1400; also does a drop-off service. Wash'n Dry, C Iparragirre 6, San Sebastián, T943 293 150, is an Aussie laundromat across the river in Gros offering self-serve and drop-off facilities. The friendly owner is a mine of information about the city. Typical wash 'n' dry €10, service wash €14. **Medical services** Hospital Nuestra Señora de Arantzazu, Av Doctor Begiristain 115, T943 007 000. **Police and emergencies** The emergency number for all necessities is 112, while 091 will take you to the local police. **Policia Municipal San Sebastián**, C Larramendi 10, T943 450 000, is the main police station. **Post office** Paseo de Francia s/n.

# Guipúzcoan Coast

*Crossing the French border, the first stretches of Spain are well worth investigating, starting with the very first town. Hondarribia is a very beautiful walled place completely free of the malaise that seems to afflict most border towns; if you don't mind a few day-trippers, this is one of the most beautiful towns in Euskadi. It's a good place to stay, but is easily reached as an excursion from San Sebastián too.*

*The coast west of San Sebastián is characterized by some fairly muscular cliffs placated by a few excellent beaches, a popular summer playground. As with Vizcaya, the area's history is solidly based on the fishing of anything and everything from anchovies to whales. While Zarautz's aim in life seems to be to try and emulate its big brother San Sebastián just along the coast, Getaria is a particularly attractive little port. Some 5 km further along, Zumaia may lack the charm of its neighbour, but is home to the Museo Ignacio Zuloaga.* ▸▸ *For Sleeping, Eating and other listings, see pages 77-78.*

## East of San Sebastián 🚌🍴🛏 ▸▸ *pp77-78.*

### Hondarribia/Fuenterrabia → *Colour map 3, B4.*
This old fishing port sits at the mouth of the Río Bidasoa looking directly across at France, a good deal more amicably now than for much of its history. The well-preserved 15th-century walls weren't erected just for decoration, and the city has been besieged more times than it cares to remember.

Although there's a fishing port and a decent beach, the most charming area of Hondarribia is the walled part, a hilly grid of cobbled streets entered through arched gates. The stone used for many of the venerable old buildings seems to be almost luminous in the evening sun. The hill is topped by a plaza and a 16th-century **palace of Carlos V**, now a *parador*; its imposing bulk is offset by a very pretty courtyard.

❖ *Hondarribia is the birthplace of double Masters champion golfer José María Olazábal.*

Nearby, the **Iglesia de Santa María de Manzano** is topped by a belltower and an impressive coat-of-arms. It was here in 1660 that María Teresa, daughter of Felipe IV, married Louis XIV of France, the Sun King.

**Plaza Guipúzcoa** is even nicer than the main square, with cobbles and small but ornate buildings overhanging a wooden colonnade. Outside the walls, there are two ports, an old and a new. Near the new one is the **cala asturiaga**, where there are remnants of a Roman ship and anchorage. Information is available from Hondarribia's **tourist office** ① *C Ugarte 6, www.bidasoaturismo.com.*

### Pasaia/Pasajes
West of Hondarribia, the GI-3440 rises steeply towards the east, affording some fantastic views over a long stretch of coastline. Before reaching San Sebastián, it's worth stopping at Pasaia/Pasajes, the name given to a group of towns clustering around a superb natural harbour 6 km east of San Sebastián. **Pasajes San Juán** (Pasai Donibane), distinct from the other parts that are devoted to large-scale shipbuilding, is a very charming town that literally only has one street, which wends its way along the water, winding around some buildings and simply going through others. While now dwarfed by the industry across the water, this was for periods in history the most important Basque port. The Romans made use of it to export mining products; whaling expeditions boldly set off for some very far-flung destinations indeed; and a good part of the Spanish Armada was built and crewed from this area. A later boost was given to the town as a result of the chocolate trade with Venezuela but by the time Victor Hugo came to live here for a spell, it was no longer the shipping centre it had been.

# The army of Christ

There can be few organizations that have had such an impact on all levels of world history than the Society of Jesus, or Jesuits. Their incident-filled five centuries of existence matches the strange life of their founder, Iñigo de Loiola (see page 67), a Basque from a small town in the valleys of Guipúzcoa.

Born in 1491 to a wealthy family, Iñigo was the youngest of 13 children. Sent as a pageboy to the court of Castilla, he embarked on a life of gambling, womanizing and duelling. He fought alongside his brother in attempting to relieve the French siege of Pamplona and was badly wounded in the legs by a cannonball. After being taken prisoner and operated on, he was sent home on a stretcher by the French, who admired his courage. His leg didn't mend, however, and it had to be rebroken and set. Although near to death several times, the bones eventually healed, but the vain Iñigo realized to his horror that a knob of bone still protruded from his leg, which had become shorter than the other. Desperate to strut his stuff as a dashing courtier again and despite anasthetics not being available, he ordered the doctors to saw the bone off and lengthen the leg by repeated stretching.

During his boredom and pain, he began to read the only books at hand, the lives of the saints and a book on Jesus. Finally recovered in 1522, he set off on a journey, hoping to reach Jerusalem. Not far from home, riding muleback, he came across a Moor, with whom he argued about the virginity of Mary in her later life. When they parted company at a fork in the road, Iñigo decided that if his mule followed the Moor, he would kill him, and if it went the other way, he would spare him. Luckily the mule went the other way.

After further enlightening experiences, and a spell in jail courtesy of the Inquisition, Iñigo ended up in Paris, meditating on what later became his Spiritual Exercises. His sceptical roommate was Francis Xavier, another Basque, whom Iñigo eventually won over. He and some companions travelled to Rome and, with the Pope's blessing, formed the Society of Jesus.

Iñigo died in 1556 and was canonized along with Francis Xavier in 1609. Since then the Jesuits, 41 saints on, have shared his passion for getting their hands dirty, being involved in education, charity and, more ominously, politics. They are a favoured target of conspiracy theorists, who see them as the real power behind the Vatican – the top Jesuit, the Superior General, is often called the 'Black Pope.'

For many centuries, however, the Jesuits were the prime educational force in western Europe and the New World: they have been called the 'schoolmasters of Europe'. The *reducciones*, communities of native Amerindians that they set up in Paraguay and Argentina were a brave and enlightened attempt to counteract slavery. These efforts, made famous by the film *The Mission*, were lauded by Voltaire (an unlikely source of praise) as "a triumph of humanity which seems to expiate the cruelties of the first conquerors". As a direct result of these works they were expelled from South America and Spain. In more recent times, the Jesuits have again courted the displeasure of western powers by advocating human rights in South America, a so-called liberation theology seen as a grave danger to US musclepower in the region.

Pasajes gets a fair number of French tourists strolling through, which means that there are several restaurants (although, at time of writing, no accommodation). Apart from eating and strolling, there's not much going on, although you might want to investigate **Ontziola** (T943 494 521), an organization that builds traditional Basque boats, such as were used in Pasajes' heyday. There's a **tourist office** ① *daily 1100-1400, 1600-1800*, in Victor Hugo's old pad.

---

# West of San Sebastián ●●❷▲● ➤➤ *pp77-78.*

## Zarautz → *Colour map 3, B3.*
While similarly blessed with a beautiful stretch of sandy beach and a characterful old town, like its neighbour San Sebastián, Zarautz has suffered from quick-buck beachfront high-rise development, which seems to appeal to the moneyed set who descend here by the thousand during the summer months. Nevertheless, despite the rows of bronzed bodies and the prudish but colourful changing tents, it can be quite a fun place. There's a good long break for surfing – one of the rounds of the world championship is often held here – and there's scope for more unusual watersports such as windboarding.

The old town is separated from the beach by the main road, giving Zarautz a slightly disjointed feel. There are a few well-preserved medieval structures, such as the **Torre Luzea**, and a handful of decent bars. Zarautz is known for its classy restaurants; after all, there's more to a Basque beach holiday than fish 'n chips. The **tourist office** is on the main street through town.

## Getaria/Guetaria → *Colour map 3, B3.*
Improbably perched on a hunk of angled slate, Getaria is well worth a stop en route between Bilbao and San Sebastián. Despite being a large-scale fish cannery, the town is picturesque with cobbled streets winding their way to the harbour and, bizarrely, through an arch in the side of the church.

Getaria gets its fair share of passing tourists, which is reflected in the number of *asadores* that line its harbour and old centre. For an unbeatable authentic feed, grab a bottle of sprightly local *txakoli* and wash it down with a plate of grilled sardines – you'll turn your nose up at the canned variety for ever more.

The **Iglesia de San Salvador** is intriguing, even without the road that passes under it. The wooden floor lists at an alarming angle; to the faithful in the pews the priest seems to be saying mass from on high.

You won't stay long without coming across a statue of **Juan Sebastián Elkano**, winner of Getaria's most famous citizen award for 480 years running, although fashion designer Cristóbal Balenciaga has come close in more recent times. Elkano, who set sail in 1519 on an expedition captained by Magellan, took command after the skipper was murdered in the Philippines. Sailing into Sevilla with the scant remnants of the expedition's crew, he thus became the first to circumnavigate the world. Not a bad finish for someone who had mutinied against the captain only a few months after leaving port.

Beyond the harbour, the wooded hump of San Antón is better known as **El Ratón** (the mouse), and it certainly does resemble that rodent. There are good views from the lighthouse at its tip; if the weather is clear you can see the coast of France arching northwards on the horizon.

## Zumaia/Zumaya
Some 5 km further along, Zumaia is not as attractive, but has the worthwhile **Museo Zuloaga** ① *Ctra San Sebastián-Bilbao, T943 862 341, Wed-Sun 1600-2000 Apr-Sep only*. Ignacio Zuloaga, born in 1870, was a prominent Basque painter and a member

of the so-called 'Generation of 98', a group of artists and thinkers who symbolized Spain's intellectual revival in the wake of the loss of the Spanish-American War, known as 'the disaster'. Zuloaga lived in this pretty house and garden, which now contains a good portion of his work as well as other paintings he owned, including some Goyas, El Grecos and Zurbaráns. Zuloaga himself is most admired for his expressive portraiture, with subjects frequently depicted against a typically bleak Spanish landscape. In the best of his work, the faces of the painted have a deep wisdom and a deep sadness that seems to convey both the artist's love and hatred for his country. The museum is a 15-minute walk on the Getaria/San Sebastián road from the centre of Zumaia.

## ⦿ Sleeping

### Hondarribia *p74*
L **Parador de Hondarribia**, Plaza de Armas 14, T943 645 500, www.parador.es. This fortress was originally constructed in the 10th century, then reinforced by Carlos V to resist French attacks. Behind the beautiful martial façade is a hotel of considerable comfort and delicacy, although the rooms don't reach the ornate standard set by the public areas, which are bristling with reminders of the military function of the fortress. A pretty courtyard and terrace are the highlights of this relaxing hotel.

AL **Hotel Obispo**, Plaza del Obispo s/n, T943 645 400, www.hotelobispo.com. The former archbishop's palace is also overflowing with character; it's a beautiful building and features some pleasant views across the Bidasoa. The rooms are delightful, particularly those on the top floor. There's free internet access for guests and frequent special offers.

B **Hotel San Nikolas**, Plaza de Armas 6, T943 644 278. Also attractively set on the main square, this hotel offers reasonable and colourful rooms with TV and bathroom. Slightly overpriced, but it aint a cheap town.

C **Hostal Alvarez Quintero**, C Bernat Etxepare 2, T943 642 299. A tranquil little place with a distinctly old-fashioned air. The rooms are simple but not bad for this price in this town. It's a little difficult to find: the entrance is through an arch on the roundabout by the tourist office.

D **Hostal Txoko-Goxoa**, C Murrua 22, T943 644 658. A pretty little place on a peaceful, sunny street by the town walls. The bedrooms are on the small side but homely, with flowers in the window boxes, and spotlessly clean.

### Camping
**Faro de Higuer**, Paseo del Faro 58, T943 641 008, F640 150. One of 2 decent campsites, slightly closer to town on the way to the lighthouse.

### Zarautz *p76*
D **Pensión Txikipolit**, Plaza Musica s/n, T943 835 357, www.euskalnet.net/txikipolit. One of the nicest budget options. Very well located in a square in the old part of town, with comfy and characterful rooms with plenty of facilities. There are some cheaper rooms without bathroom.

### Camping
**Gran Camping Zarautz**, T943 831 238. A massive campsite with the lot, open all year round but depressingly packed in summer's dog days.

### Getaria *p76*
D **Gure Ametsa**, Orrua s/n, T943 140 077. Off a backroad between Zumaia and Getaria, this friendly farmhouse is in a superb location with hilly views over the sea. There are also cheaper rooms without en suite.

D **Pensión Iribar**, C Nagusia 34, T943 140 406, iribarjatetxea@yahoo.com. Clean and comfy little rooms with bathroom around the back of the restaurant of the same name, right in the narrow heart of the old town.

E **Hostal Itxas Gain**, C San Roque 1, T943 141 033. Lovely place overlooking the sea (that's what the name means). This warm-hearted and open place has some lovely rooms with impressionist pictures on the walls. On the top floor there's a suite with a spa-bath. There's also a garden, which is a top place to chill in hot weather, and a friendly dog. Open Easter-Sep.

# 🍴 Eating

**Hondarribia** *p74*

The town is notable for its excellent restaurants; the standard no doubt kept high by the visiting French!

🍴🍴🍴 **Sebastián**, C Mayor 9, T943 640 167. This excellent restaurant is attractively set in a dingy old grocery packed with interesting aromas. The food goes far beyond the humble decor: this is known as one of the better restaurants in Euskadi. There's a good value *menú de degustación*; the foie-gras is excellent too. Closed during Nov and on Mon.

🍴 **Medievo**, Plaza Guipúzcoa 8, T943 644 509. An intriguing restaurant decorated in 21st-century medieval style. It may sound debatable, but it works, and so does the imaginatively prepared food. Try the venison with prunes. There's a *menú del día* for €11. À la carte, €30 a head.

🍴 **Bar Itxaropena**, C San Pedro 67, T943 641 197. A good bar in the new town offering a variety of cheap foodstuffs and plenty of company at weekends.

**Zarautz** *p76*

🍴🍴🍴 **Kulixka**, C Bixkonde 1, T943 134 604. This is a welcoming waterfront restaurant with an unbeatable view of the beach. There's good seafood as you'd expect, roast meats and a decent *menú del día*.

**Getaria** *p76*

🍴🍴🍴 **Kaia**, C Katrapona Aundia 10, T943 140 500. The best and priciest of Getaria's restaurants with a sweeping view over the harbour and high standard of food and service. Whole fish grilled over the coals outside are a highlight, as is the exceptional and reasonable wine list. Try some of the local *txakolí*, the best around.

🍴 **Asador Mayflower**, C Katrapona 4, T943 140 658. One of a number of *asadores* in this attractive harbour town, with the bonus of an excellent *menú del día*. Grilled sardines are a tasty speciality.

🍴 **Politena**, Kale Nagusia 9, T943 140 113. A bar oriented towards weekend visitors from Bilbao and San Sebastián. There's a

very enticing selection of *pintxos*, and a €12.50 'weekend' *menú*, which isn't bad either.

🍴 **Txalupa**, C Herrerieta 1, T943 140 592. A great place to buy or taste the local fish and *txakolí* in a hospitable bar, which offers *pintxos* as well as *cazuelitas*, small portions of bubbling stews or seafood in sauce.

# 🏔 Activities and tours

**Getaria** *p76*
**Diving**

**K-Sub**, C Txoritonpe 34, T/F943 140 185, www.ksub.net. Offers PADI scuba courses, and hires out diving equipment. Also gives advice on good locations.

# ⊖ Transport

**Hondarribia** *p74*

**Bus** There are buses to and from Plaza Guipúzcoa in **San Sebastián** every 20 mins. A few buses cross the border into France. There are frequent buses linking Hondarribia with **Irún**, just a few kilometres down the road.

**Boat** Boats run across the river to the French town of **Hendaye**.

**Train** The most common way of crossing the border is by the *topo* train that burrows through the mountain from between **San Sebastián** or ugly **Irún** and **Hendaye**.

**Zarautz** *p76*

**Bus** Buses run regularly to/from **San Sebastián** bus station.

**Train** Zarautz is serviced by Euskotren hourly from **Bilbao's** Atxuri station and **San Sebastián's** Amara station.

**Getaria** *p76*

**Bus** Getaria is serviced by bus from **San Sebastián** bus station regularly.

**Train** Zumaia is serviced by Euskotren trains hourly from **Bilbao's** Atxuri station and **San Sebastián's** Amara station. Regular buses connect the 2 towns.

# Vizcayan Coast

*The Vizcayan section of the Basque coastline is some of the most attractive and dramatic of Northern Spain: cliffs plunge into the water around tiny fishing villages, surfers ride impossibly long breaks, and the towns, like spirited Ondarroa, are home to a convivial and quintessentially Basque social scene. The eastern section is the most rough-edged, with stirring cliffs and startling geological folding contrasting with the green foliage. Fishing is god around here; some of the small villages are far more accessible by sea than by land. The main town of this stretch is Lekeitio, one of Euskadi's highlights.* ➤ *For Sleeping, Eating and other listings, see pages 84-86.*

## Ondarroa 🚌🅿🛏🚻 ➤➤ *pp84-86.*

➔ *Colour map 3, B2.*

The friendliest of towns, Ondarroa marks the border of Vizcaya and Guipúzcoa. Situated at the mouth of the Río Artibai, the town is straddled by two bridges, one the harmonious stone **Puente Viejo**, the other a recent work by Santiago Calatrava, which sweeps across with unmistakable panache. Although low on glamour and short on places to stay, Ondarroa could be worth a stop if you're exploring the coast, particularly on a Friday or Saturday night, when the nightlife rivals anywhere in Euskal Herría.

Music has long been a powerful vehicle of Basque expression, and here the bars pump not with salsa or *bacalao* but nationalist rock. "*Bacalao* (salt cod) is for eating, not for listening to", said one group of locals.

### Markina ➔ *Colour map 3, B2.*

This village in the Vizcayan hills, a short distance inland from Ondarroa, is set around a long leafy plaza. Not a great deal goes on here but what does is motivated by one thing and one thing only: *pelota* (see Spectator sports, page 54). Many 'sons of Markina' have achieved star status in the sport, and the *frontón* is proudly dubbed the 'university of pelota'. As well as the more common *pelota a mano*, there are regular games of *cesta punta*, in which a long wicker scoop is worn like a glove, adding some serious velocity to the game. Games are usually on a Sunday evening, but it's worth ringing the tourist office for details, or checking the website, www.euskalpilota.com.

The hexagonal chapel of **San Miguel de Arretxmago** is a 10-minute stroll from the plaza on the other side of the small river. The building itself is unremarkable but inside, surprisingly, are three enormous rocks, naturally balanced, with an altar to the saint underneath that far predates the building. According to local tradition, St Michael buried the devil here; a lingering odour of brimstone would tend to confirm this. This is the place to be at midnight on 29 September, when the village gathers to perform two traditional dances, the *aurresku*, and the *mahai gaineko*. There's a summer **tourist office** in a palace across the iron footbridge over the river.

## Lekeitio 🚌🅿🛏❄🚻🅿 ➤➤ *pp84-86.*

➔ *Colour map 3, B2.*

Along the Basque coastline, Lekeitio stands out as one of the best places to visit and stay. Its fully functioning fishing harbour is full of cheerfully painted boats, and the tall old houses seem to be jostling and squeezing each other for a front-row seat. Once a favourite of holidaying royalty, the town is lively at weekends and in summer, when it's a popular destination for Bilbao and San Sebastián families. There are two **beaches** – the one a bit further from town, across the bridge, is better. Both look across to the pretty rocky islet of the **Isla de San Nicolás** in the middle of the bay, covered in trees and home only to goats. The countryside around Lekeitio is beautiful, with rolling hills and jagged cliffs. The emerald green colour unfortunately doesn't come for nothing though – the town gets its fair share of rainy days.

The narrow streets backing the harbour conceal a few well-preserved medieval buildings, while the harbour itself is lined with bars. The **Iglesia de Santa María de la Asunción** is worth a visit. Lauded as one of the best examples of Basque Gothic architecture, it seems to change colour completely from dull grey to warm orange depending on the light. The *retablo* is an ornate piece of Flemish work, while the exterior has extravagant flying buttresses. The helpful **tourist information office** ① *C Independencia s/n, T946 844 017, turismo@learjai.com, Mon-Sat 1000-1400, 1600-1900. Sun 1030-1400,* has a good range of information.

### Elantxobe → *Colour map 3, B2.*

If tiny fishing villages are your thing, Elantxobe, west of Lekeitio, might be worth adding to your itinerary. With amazingly steep and narrow streets leading down to a small harbour, it seems a forgotten place, tucked away at the bottom of a sheer escarpment. It's authentic without being overly picturesque. There's now a road that winds around the hill down to the port, but the bus still gets spun around on a turntable in the tiny square up above. There are a few places to try the catch of the day, and a *hostal*. **Bizkaibus** A3513 between Bilbao and Lekeitio stops here. It leaves Bilbao every two hours from Calle Hurtado Amezaga by Abando train station.

Beyond Elantxobe, the coast is broken by the **Urdabai estuary**, home to many waterbirds. The good beach of **Laia** looks across at the surfing village of **Mundaka**, but the road heads a fair way inland, crossing the river at the area's main town, Gernika.

---

# Gernika/Guernica ⬛🚻👪🏨🍴 ⟫ *pp84-86.*

→ *Colour map 3, B2.*

A name that weighs heavy on the tongue, heavy with blood and atrocity, is Gernika. The symbol of Basque pride and nationalism, this thriving town has moved on from its tragic past, and provides the visitor with a great opportunity to experience Basque culture.

Today, Gernika is anything but a sombre memorial to the devastation it suffered (see box, page 81). While it understandably lacks much of its original architecture, it's a happy and friendly place that merits a visit. The Monday morning market is still very much in business and entertaining to check out. The **Casa de Juntas** ① *1000-1400, 1600-1800 (till 1900 in summer), free,* symbolically placed next to the famous oak tree, is once again the seat of the Vizcayan parliament. The highlight of the building itself is the room with a massive stained-glass roof depicting the oak tree. The tree itself is outside by the porch, while part of the trunk of an older one is enshrined in a slightly silly little pavilion. Behind the building is the **Parque de los Pueblos de Europa** ① *1000-1900 (2100 summer),* which contains sculptures by Henry Moore and Eduardo Chillida. Both recall the devastated buildings of the town and are dedicated to peace.

## Museo de la Paz

① *Plaza Foru 1, T946 270 213, www.museodelapaz.org. Tue-Sat 1000-1400, 1600-1900; Sun 1000-1400. No lunchtime closing in summer. €4. The tourist office sells a discount voucher, the Billete Unico. It costs €3 and covers 4 attractions; 3 of these are free anyway, so it effectively saves you €1 on your visit.*

● "...*the concentrated attack on Guernica was the greatest success*" *(from a secret memo to Hitler written by Wolfgang von Richthofen, commander of the Condor Legion and cousin of the Red Baron First World War flying ace).*

## ⁞ The bombing of Gernika

During the Spanish Civil War, in one of the most despicable planned acts of modern warfare there has ever been, 59 German and Italian planes destroyed the town in a bombardment that lasted three gruelling hours. It was 26 April, 1937, and market day in Gernika and thousands of villagers from the surrounding area were in the town, which had no air defences to call on. Three days earlier a similar bombardment had killed over 250 in the town of Durango, but the toll here was worse. Splinter and incendiary bombs were used for maximum impact, and fighters strafed fleeing people with machine guns. The attack resulted in about 1650 deaths.

Franco, the head of the Nationalist forces, simply denied the event had occurred; he claimed that any damage had been caused by Basque propagandists. In 1999 Germany formally apologized for the event, making the Spanish conspicuous by their silence. Apart from a general wish to terrorize and subdue the Basque population, who were resisting the Nationalist advance on Bilbao, Gernika's symbolic value was important. For many centuries Basque assemblies had met here under an oak tree – this was common to many Vizcayan towns but the Gernika meetings became dominant. They were attended by the monarch or a representative, who would solemnly swear to respect Basque rights and laws – the *fueros*. Thus the town became a powerful symbol of Basque liberty and nationhood. The first modern Basque government, a product of the civil war, was sworn in under the oak only six months before the bombing.

One of the most famous results of the bombing was Picasso's painting, named after the town. He had been commissioned by the Republican government to paint a mural for the upcoming World Fair, and this was the result. It currently sits in the *Reina Sofia* gallery in Madrid although constant Basque lobbying may yet bring it to Bilbao. A ceramic copy has been made on a wall on Calle Allende Salazar. Picasso commented on his painting: "By means of it, I express my abhorrence of the race that sunk Spain in an ocean of pain and death".

Gernika's showpiece, the recently reformed Museo de la Paz (Museum of Peace), is an excellent, and moving, museum. It focuses on peace as a concept and as a goal to strive for, and then examines the Gernika bombing, and, crucially, the importance of reconciliation and an optimistic outlook. Two excellent audiovisual presentations are included; the staff cleverly put these in the right language as they monitor your progress through the museum. A visit to Gernika is highly recommended for this museum alone.

Gernika has a **tourist office** ① *Artekale 8, T946 255 892, turismo@gernika-lumo.net, Mon-Fri 1000-1330, 1600-1900, Sat and Sun 1100-1400; guided tours of the town leave here daily at 1100*, with English-speaking staff.

The **Euskal Herria Museoa** ① *C Allendesalazar 5, Tue-Sat 1000-1400, 1600-1900, Sun 1100-1430, 1600-2000, free*, is housed in a strikingly beautiful 18th-century *palacio* and is the repository for a sizeable collection of artefacts relating to the history and ethnography of the Basque country.

## Around Gernika 🏨🍴 ▸▸ *pp84-86.*

Gernika sits at the head of the estuary of the Río Oka, the **Urdaibai Reserve**, a varied area of tidal sandflats and riverbank ecology that is home to a huge amount of wildlife. UNESCO declared it a Biosphere Reserve in 1984. It's a great spot for birdwatching, but mammals such as the badger, marten and wild boar are also present. The **park headquarters** ① *T946 257 125*, are just outside the town centre of Gernika in the Palacio de Udetxea on the road to Lumo. Vistas of the estuary can be had from either side of the estuary, but to really appreciate the area, you might be better off taking a tour.

## Cueva de Santimamiñe
① *Tours are free but limited to 15 people on a first-come, first-served basis. They run Mon-Fri at 1000, 1115, 1230, 1630 and 1715.*

The cave of Santimamiñe is well worth a visit. It was an elegant and spacious home for thousands of generations of prehistoric folk, who decorated it with an important series of paintings depicting bison, among other animals. The chamber with the paintings is now closed to protect the 12,000-year-old art from further deterioration. The cave itself is fascinating, nonetheless, winding deep into the hillside and full of eerily beautiful rock formations. The cave is a short climb up stairs from the car park. The bus from Gernika to Lekeitio (approximately every two hours) can drop you at the turn-off just before the town of Kortezubi. From there it's a half-hour walk. Hitching is easy.

## Bosque Pintado de Oma
① *Free.*

Near the caves is an unusual artwork: the Bosque Pintado de Oma. In a peaceful pine forest on a ridge, Agustín Ibarrola has painted eyes, people and geometric figures on the tree trunks in bright, bold colours. Some of the trees combine to form larger pictures – these can be difficult to make out, and it doesn't help that most of the display panels have been erased. Overall, it's a tranquil place with the wind whispering through the pines, and there's a strangely primal quality about the work. It's hard not to feel that more could have been made of the original concept though. A dirt road climbs 3 km to the wood from opposite the **Lezika** restaurant next to the Santimamiñe caves. The forest is accessible by car, but it's a pleasant walk. If on foot, it's worth returning another way. Take the path down the hill at the other end of the Bosque from the entrance. After crossing a couple of fields, you'll find yourself in the tiny hamlet of **Oma**, with attractive Basque farmhouses. Turning left along the road will lead you back to the caves.

# Mundaka and Bermeo ●🏛🎭🎵 »» *pp84-86.*

→ *Colour map 3, B2*

From Gernika, following the west bank of the estuary takes you back to the coast. A brisk half-hour's walk is all that separates the fishing towns of Bermeo and Mundaka, but they couldn't be more different. Mundaka is petite and slightly upmarket as visitors come to admire its beautiful harbour. Bermeo puts it in the shade in fishing terms: as one of the most important ports on this coast some of its boats seem bigger than Mundaka's harbour. There's a good atmosphere though, and an attractive old town.

## Mundaka
While Mundaka still has its small fishing fleet, it's better known as a surfing village. Until recently, that is. For many years, it was a Mecca of the global surf community, with its magnificent left-break ((a wave that breaks from right to left, looking towards the beach). When the wind blew and the big waves rolled in, a top surfer could jump in off the rocks by Mundaka harbour and ride a wave right across the estuary mouth to Laida beach, a couple of kilometres away. But, in 2003, dredging operations in the estuary, undertaken to allow transit of larger boats to a shipyard, severely affected the wave, and it hasn't really come back. Environmentalists are demanding that the situation be

## Cod, whales and America

In former times whales were a common species off the northern coast of Spain. The Basques were among the first to hunt the giant mammals, which they were doing as far back as the seventh century. It became a major enterprise and, as the whales grew scarcer, they had to go further afield, venturing far into the North Atlantic. It's a good bet they reached America in the 14th century at the latest, signing the native Americans' visitors book under the Vikings and the shadowy, debatable scrawl of St Brendan.

The whaling expeditions provisioned themselves by fishing and preserving cod during the trip. The folk back home got a taste for this *bacalao*, and they still love it, to the bemusement of many tourists. Meanwhile, Elkano added to the Basques' seafaring CV by becoming the first man to circumnavigate the globe, after the expedition leader, Magellan, was killed in the Philippines. Basque whalers established many a settlement along the coast of Labrador during the 16th century and, later, Basques left their homes in droves for the promise of the New World; Basque culture has been significant in the development of the USA, particularly in some of the western states, as well as in Argentina and Chile.

rectified (the Urdabai estuary is, after all, a Biosphere Reserve), and locals have their fingers crossed. Mundaka is well worth visiting anyway, with a beautiful bonsai harbour and relaxed ambience. The village is a small maze of winding streets and an oversized church. There are some good places to stay or camp, and it's within striking distance of several highlights of the Basque coast. In summer, boats run across to **Laida beach**, which is the best in the area. It's almost worth the trip merely to taste the *tigres* at the small bar on the estuary. There's a small **tourist office** by the harbour.

## Bermeo

Bermeo is a bigger and more typical Basque fishing town with a more self-sufficient feel. One of the whaling towns that more or less pioneered the activity, Bermeo has a proud maritime history documented in its museum. The ships for Columbus' second voyage were built and largely crewed from here. There's much more action in the fishing harbour here than in peaceful Mundaka.

The old town is worth a visit. There's a cobbled square across which the church and the Ayuntamiento vie for power; the latter has a sundial on its face. There's a small chunk of the old town wall preserved, with a symbolic footprint of John the Baptist, who is said to have made Jonathan Edwards weep by jumping from here to the sanctuary of Gaztelugatxe in three steps. The **Museo del Pescador** ① *Plaza Torrontero 1, T946 881 171, F946 186 454, Tue-Sat 1000-1330, 1600-1930, Sun 1000-1330, free*, is set in a 15th-century tower and is devoted to the Basque fishing industry and the various members of the finny tribes. The **tourist office** is opposite the station.

## Santuario de San Juan de Gaztelugatxe and around

West of Bermeo, some 6 km from town, is the spectacular sanctuary of San Juan de Gaztelugatxe. In the early 11th century, Sancho the Great, King of Navarra, was in Aquitaine, in France, when a surprising gift was presented to the local church hierarchy: the head of John the Baptist, which had mysteriously turned up a short while before. As a result, the cult of the Baptist received an understandable boost and many monasteries and sanctuaries were built in his

*While you're here, have lunch at the Ereperi, overlooking the sanctuary with a superb terrace and a cheap lunch menu.*

name, including several in northeastern Spain, with the express encouragement of the impressed Sancho.

San Juan de Gaztelugatxe is one of these (although the church dates from much later). A rocky island frequently rendered impressively bleak by the coastal squalls, is connected by a bridge to the mainland, from where it's 231 steps to the top. Apart from the view, there's not a great deal to see, but the setting is spectacular. The island is a pilgrimage spot, particularly for the feast of St John on 24 June, and also on 31 July. To get there from Bermeo, take a bus (about every two hours) along the coast road towards Bakio; you can get off opposite the sanctuary.

## ● Sleeping

### Ondarroa *p79*
**C-E Arrigorri**, Arrigorri 3, T946 134 045, www.arrigorri.net. A good choice across the river from the centre, right on the beach. The best rooms have a bathroom and views over the sea; in low season they are only €7 more than the cheapest rooms. It's colourful, friendly and comfortable. Breakfast included.
**F Patxi**, Arta Bide 21, T609 986 446. On the sloping street heading down into the town when coming from the west, this is an exceedingly good value *pensión* with comfortable rooms and a shared bathroom.

### Markina *p79*
**D-E Hotel Vega**, C Abasua 2, T946 166 015. A sleepy place on the square that makes a relaxing base and has rooms both with and without bathroom. There's a popular café with a terrace downstairs.

### Lekeitio *p79*
Lekeitio has some very inviting options, but none are really in the budget category.
**A Emperatriz Zita**, Santa Elena Etorbidea s/n, T946 842 655, www.aisiahoteles.com. This slightly odd-looking hotel was built on the site of a palace where Empress Zita had lived in the 1920s. Married to the last Austro-Hungarian emperor, who unluckily acceded to the throne in a losing position in WW1; she was left with 8 children when he died of pneumonia on Madeira in 1922. The hotel is furnished in appropriately elegant style and is also a thalassotherapy (sea water) and health centre. The rooms are very pleasant and well priced for the location, as is the restaurant.
**B Hotel Zubieta**, Portal de Atea, T946 843 030, www.hotelzubieta.com. A superbly converted coachhouse in the grounds of a *palacio*. Considering its surprisingly low prices, this is one of the best places to stay, with friendly

management, a lively bar, and cosy rooms with sloping wooden ceilings. Light sleepers, however, will enjoy it more at weekends, for the woodyard next-door can be noisy on weekday mornings. Recommended. Also has reasonably priced apartments for 2-4.
**D Piñupe Hotela**, Av Pascual Abaroa 10, T946 842 984, F946 840 772. The cheapest place in town and a sound choice. The rooms have en suite, phone and TV and are plenty more comfortable than the bar downstairs would indicate.

### Gernika *p80*
**A Hotel Katxi**, Morga/Andra Mari s/n, T946 270 740, www.katxi.com. A few kilometres west of Gernika in the hamlet of Morga is this excellent rural hotel. The rooms, some much larger than others, are extremely comfortable, and there's a friendly lounge area. It's a great place to get away from things, with a warm atmosphere, and plenty of opportunity for relaxing on the terrace or in the garden. The owners run a good *asador* next door.
**B Hotel Gernika**, C Carlos Gangoiti 17, T946 254 948, www.hotel-gernika.com. Gernika's best hotel is nothing exceptional, with uninteresting rooms in an ugly brick building on the edge of town. However, there's a bar and café, and the service is helpful.
**C Pensión Akelarre**, C Barrenkale 5, T946 270 197, www.hotelakelarre.com. This enjoyable place has funky little rooms with TV and varnished floorboards. There's a terrace to take some sun and it's in the heart of the pedestrian area. There's free wireless internet access. There are discounts if you stay more than one night, and it's significantly cheaper off-season.
**D Hotel Boliña**, C Barrenkale 3, T946 250 300, F946 250 304. In the centre of Gernika, this hotel has some good-value doubles

with TV and telephone. It's well run and makes a good choice, although it can be stuffy in the height of summer.
**E Pensión Madariaga**, C Industria 10, T946 256 035. Very attractively furnished rooms with TV, bathroom and heating. Good value.

### Bosque Pintado de Oma *p82*
**E Bizketxe**, Oma 8, T946 254 906, anidketxe@ terra.es. Excellent if you've got transport. Lovely rooms in a traditional farmhouse, with or without bath. Recommended.

### Mundaka *p82*
Accommodation in Mundaka isn't cheap.
**A Hotel Atalaya**, C Itxaropen 1, T946 177 000, www.hotel-atalaya-mundaka.com. The classier of the town's options, with a summery feel to its rooms and café. Garden and parking adjoin the stately building. Very nice breakfasts (not included).
**B Hotel El Puerto**, Portu Kalea 1, T946 876 725, www.hotelelpuerto.com. The best value of Mundaka's 3 hotels, set right by the tiny fishing harbour. Delightful rooms, very cosy and some overlooking the harbour (worth paying the few extra euros). The bar below is one of Mundaka's best. Recommended.
**C Hotel Mundaka**, C Florentino Larrinaga 9, T946 876 700, www.hotelmundaka.com. Decent option with a garden and a bar. Irreproachable, but lacks some of the charm of the others. Internet €3/hr.

### Camping
**Portuondo**, 1 km out of Mundaka on the road to Gernika, T/F946 877 701, www.camping portuondo.com. Sardined during the summer months, this is a well-equipped campsite with a swimming pool, cafés and laundry. There are several bungalows that sleep up to 4, but are not significantly cheaper than the hotels in town with only 1 or 2. They do come with kitchen, fridge, and television though.

### Bermeo *p83*
**C Hostal Torre Ercilla**, C Talaranzko 14, T946 187 598, barrota@piramidal.com. A lovely place to stay in Bermeo's old town, between the museum and church. Rooms are designed for relaxation, with small balconies, reading nooks and soft carpet. There's also a lounge, terrace, chessboard and barbecue among other comforts. Recommended.

## ❼ Eating

### Ondarroa *p79*
**❛❛❛ Eretegia Joxe Manuel**, C Sabino Arana 23, T946 830 104. Although it does a range of other appetizing dishes, the big charcoal grill outside this restaurant caters to carnivores with large appetites. Forget quarter-pounders; here the steaks approach the kilogram mark and are very juicy and tasty. Go for the *buey* (ox) for extra flavour.
**❛❛❛ Sutargi**, Nasa Kalea 11, T946 832 258. A popular bar with a good-value restaurant upstairs with main dishes around €10-14. It's difficult to get a table at weekends.

### Lekeitio *p79*
Despite the busy summer scene, there are lots of fairly traditional places to eat and drink. The Irish pub isn't one of them; although it's ok for a Guinness, readers have reported being ripped off on their food.
**❛❛❛❛ Oxangoiti Jauregia**, C Gamarra 2, T946 843 151. A fairly expensive restaurant in a historic building next to the *ayuntamiento*. Smart wooden interior, a craft shop and tasty seafood at fairly stiff prices.
**❛❛❛ Emperatriz Zita**, Santa Elena Etorbidea s/n, T946 842 655. The restaurant in this seafront hotel is well priced and of good quality in a rather grand dining room.
**❛❛❛ Kaia**, Txatxo kaia 5, T946 840 284. One of the many harbourside restaurants and bars, this serves fairly upmarket but tasty fish.

### Gernika *p80*
**❛❛❛ Arrien**, C Eriabarrena 1, T946 258 551. Overlooking the flowery Jardines de El Ferial, this terraced restaurant/bar has a good *menú del día* for €8.50 and various other set meals from €10 as well as à la carte selections.
**❛ Foruria**, C Industria 10, T946 251 020. A good option for a cheapish meal, with a selection of hot dishes around the €9 mark as well as a wide selection of *jamón*, *chorizo* and cheese for cold platters.

### Around Gernika *p81*
**❛❛❛ Lezika**, Cuevas de Santimamiñe, Kortezubi. The whole of Vizcaya seems to descend on the beer garden here at weekends with kids and dogs in tow; the restaurant is worthwhile as well and better value than the meagre *raciones* on offer at the bar.

**Mundaka** *p82*

🍴 **Asador Bodegón**, Kepa Deuna 1, T946 876 353. Mundaka's best restaurant, despite a slight air of 'we know what the tourists want'. Meat and especially fresh fish are grilled to perfection over the coals. Try the home-made *patxarán*, a liqueur made from sloe berries. Upstairs is **Casino**, a traditional members' club that's also a high-quality restaurant with a very old-fashioned feel and great views from the gallery. Fish is the thing to try here.

## 🎵 Bars and clubs

**Ondarroa** *p79*

Ondarroa's nightlife scene revolves around the main streets of the old centre. **Nasa Kalea** is well-stocked with bars, many of which are temples to Basque rock, which is heavily identified with the Independence movement. **Apallu**, Nasa Kalea 30. Worth dropping in on. **Ku-Kua**, Kanttoipe Kalea s/n. A very lively bar that gets very full and goes on very late. **Music school**, corner of Iñaki Deunaren and Sabino Arana (Arana'tar Sabin). Often has live Basque alternative rock on Fri or Sat nights – it's usually free. **Sansonategi**. Nasa Kalea. Another worthwhile bar on this street.

**Lekeitio** *p79*

**Hotel Zubieta**, Portal de Atea, T946 843 030. The lively café bar in this beautifully restored coachhouse is an excellent spot for a chat and a beverage in uplifting surroundings. **Talako Bar**, above the fisherman's co-operative on the harbour, is a great spot for one of Lekeitio's rainy days, with a pool table, board games and a 180-degree view of the harbour, town and beaches. **Txalupa**, Txatxo kaia 7. While Lekeitio isn't as out-and-out Basque as Ondarroa, this bar on the harbourside keeps the Basque rock pumping, and does a range of simple snacks.

**Gernika** *p80*

**Arrana**, C Juan Calzada 6. A vibrant Basque bar with a lively young crowd spilling outside at weekends. **Metropol**, corner of C Unamuno and Iparragirre. A cavernous and comradely bar, open later than anywhere else.

## ❀ Festivals and events

**Lekeitio** *p79*

**5 Sep** Fiesta de San Antolín. In a land of strange festivals, this is one of the strangest. It involves a long rope, a few rowing boats, plenty of able-bodied young folk and a goose. Thankfully these days the goose is already dead. The hapless bird is tied in the middle of the rope, which is stretched across the harbour and held at both ends. Competitors take turns from rowing boats to grab the goose's head (which has been liberally greased up) under their arm. The rope is then tightened, lifting the grabber into the air, and then slackened. This is repeated until either the goose's head comes off, or the person falls into the water.

## ⊖ Transport

**Ondarroa** *p79*

Ondarroa is served by Bizkaibus from **Bilbao** bus station (hourly, €2.75) via **Markina** and Pesa from **San Sebastián** bus station (€4.15, 50 mins) 4 times a day (twice at weekends).

**Lekeitio** *p79*

Bizkaibus hourly from the bus station in **Bilbao** (30 mins, €2.75); Pesa 4 times daily from the bus station in **San Sebastián** (2 at weekends, 1 hr 25 mins, €5.05) .

**Gernika** *p80*

There are hourly trains to Gernika from **Bilbao**'s Atxuri station, and buses ½ hourly (hourly at weekends) from C Hurtado de Amezaga next to Abando station (€2, 30 mins).

**Mundaka and Bermeo** *p82*

Hourly trains run to both towns from **Bilbao**'s Atxuri station, and ½-hourly buses from C Hurtado de Amezaga next to Abando station (€2).

## ⓓ Directory

**Lekeitio** *p79*

**Internet** Ziber Jaure, C Agirre Solarte 17, €2.40 per hr; **Gozamen**, C Gamarra 10, T946 841 448.

**Gernika** *p80*

**Internet** Aramu Sarea, C Miguel Unamuno 1, T946 258 522. €2.50.

# Bilbao/Bilbo

→ *Phone code: 944. Colour map 3, B1. Population: 353,173, although there are many more in the total urban area.*

*In an amazingly short time, and without losing sight of its roots, Bilbao, the dirty industrial city, has successfully transformed itself into a buzzing cultural capital. The Guggenheim museum is the undoubted flagship of this triumphant progress, a sinuous fantasy of a building that literally takes the breath away. It inspires because of what it is, but also because the city had the vision to put it there. While the museum has led the turnaround, much of what is enjoyable about modern Bilbao was already there. Bustling bar-life, harmonious old and new architecture, a superb eating culture, and a tangible sense of pride in being a working city are still things that make Bilbao a little bit special, and the exciting new developments can only add to those qualities.*

*The Casco Viejo, the old town, still evokes a cramped medieval past. Along its web of attractive streets, designer clothing stores occupy the ground floors where families perhaps once huddled behind the city walls. El Ensanche, the new town, has an elegant European feel to it. The wealth of the city is more evident here, with stately banks and classy shops lining the planned avenues. The riverbank is the most obvious beneficiary of Bilbao's leap into the 21st century: Calatrava's eerily skeletal bridge, designer promenades and Gehry's exuberant Guggenheim bring art and architecture together and make the Río Nervión the city's axis once more. It doesn't stop there, as ongoing work aims to further soften the remaining industrial edges.*

*The seaside suburbs, once reached by hours of painstaking river navigation, are now a nonchalant 20 minutes away by Metro. Fashionable Getxo has a relaxed beach atmosphere, while, across the estuary, Portugalete still seems to be wondering how Bilbao gets all the credit these days: for hundreds of years it was a far more important port.* ▸▸ *For Sleeping, Eating and other listings, see pages 97-107.*

## Ins and outs

**Getting there** Bilbao's airport is one of two international ones in Euskadi, and is a good gateway to Northern Spain with connections to several European destinations. There's also a ferry service from Portsmouth, which is cruise-like in style and pricing. The city is well served by buses from the rest of the nation and is exceedingly well connected with Vitoria, San Sebastián and smaller destinations in Euskadi. There are a few train services to other Spanish cities and a narrow-gauge line along the coast to Santander, Oviedo and Galicia. ▸▸ *For further details, see Transport, page 106.*

**Getting around** Bilbao isn't large and is reasonably walkable. The Guggenheim museum, as far afield as many people get, is about 20 minutes' walk from the old town along the river. For further-flung parts of Bilbao, such as the beach or the bus station, the metro is excellent. Sir Norman Foster's design is simple, attractive and, above all, spacious. Although there's a reasonable network of local bus services in Bilbao, they are only generally useful for a handful of destinations; these are indicated in the text. The newly re-established tram network is handy, particularly for reaching the Guggenheim from the old town. There's just one line so far; a scenic one, running from Atxuri station along the river, skirting the Casco Viejo (stopping behind the Teatro Arriaga), then continuing on the other side of the Nervión, stopping at the Guggenheim and the bus station among other places.

**Best time to visit** Bilbao's summers are warm but not baking. This is the best time to visit, but be sure to book ahead during the boisterous August fiesta (see Festivals and events, page 105). At other times of year, Bilbao is a fairly wet place, but never gets especially cold. The bar life and museums provide ample distraction from the drizzle.

88 **Tourist information** Bilbao's main **tourist office** ① *Plaza Arriaga s/n, T944 795 760, bit@ayto.bilbao.net, Mon-Sat 0930-1400, 1600-1930, Sun 0930-1400*, has temporarily moved to the Teatro Arriaga on the edge of the old town. There's another in the **new town** ① *Plaza Ensanche 11, Mon-Fri 0900-1400, 1600-1930*. There is also a smaller office by the **Guggenheim museum** ① *Abandoibarra Etorbidea 2, Tue-Fri 1100-1430, 1530-1800, Sat 1100-1500, 1600-1900, Sun 1100-1400, Jul and Aug Mon-Sat 1000-1500, 1600-1900, Sun 1000-1500*, and an office at the airport. These offices can provide a good free map of the city; they can also sell you the **Bilbao Card**, which allows free transport on local buses, metro, tram and the Artxanda funicular, as well as providing discounts in several shops and museums. It costs €6 for a day or €12 for three days. The city's website, www.bilbao.net, is also a good source of information.

## Background

In 1300 the lord of the province of Vizcaya, Don Diego López de Haro V, saw the potential of the riverside fishing village of Bilbao and granted it permission to become a town. The people graciously accepted, and by the end of the 14th century history records that the town had three parallel streets: Somera, Artekale and Tendería. These were soon added to: Belostikale, Carnicería Vieja, Barrenkale and Barrenkale Barrena, forming the Siete Calles – the seven original streets of the city. It was a time of much strife and the fledgling town was walled, but at the end of the 15th century these original fortifications came down and the city began to grow.

Bilbao suffered during the first Carlist war in the 19th century, when the liberal city was besieged (ultimately unsuccessfully) by the reactionary Carlist forces. The one bright spot to emerge was the invention of *bacalao al pil-pil*, now the city's signature dish, but originally devised due to lack of any fresh produce to eat. Not long after the war, Bilbao's boom started. The Vizcayan hills harboured huge reserves of haematite, the ore from which the city's iron was produced. By the middle of the century, it had become evident that this was by far the best ore for the new process of steelmaking. Massive foreign investment followed, particularly from Britain, and the city expanded rapidly as workers flooded in from all parts of the peninsula. The good times didn't last, however, and by the early 20th century things were looking grimmer. Output declined and dissatisfied workers sank into poverty. The Civil War hit the city hard too; after the Republican surrender, Franco made it clear he wasn't prepared to forgive the Basques for siding against him. Repressed and impoverished, the great industrial success story of the late 19th century fell into gloom. The dictator's death sparked a massive reflowering of Basque culture, symbolized by the bold steps taken to revitalize the city. The Guggenheim's opening in 1997 has confirmed Bilbao's newly won status as a cultural capital of Northern Spain, and ongoing regeneration works proceed apace.

*The city's coat of arms features two wolves; these were the family symbol of Don Diego – his surname López derives from the Latin word lupus, wolf.*

# Casco Viejo

Bilbao's old town is a good place to start exploring the city. This is where most of the budget accommodation and bar life is based. Tucked into a bend in the river, it's the most charming part of town, a lively jumble of pedestrian streets that has always been the city's social focus. There's something of the medina about it; on your first few forays you surely won't end up where you might have thought you were going.

### Siete Calles

The parallel Siete Calles (seven streets) are the oldest part of town, and even locals struggle to sort out which bar is on which street. While there aren't a huge number of sights per se, there are dozens of quirky shops and some very attractive architecture;

leisurely wandering is in order. The true soul of the Casco emerges from early evening
on, however, when Bilbaínos descend like bees returning to the hive, strolling the
streets, listening to buskers, debating the quality of the *pintxos* in the myriad bars and
sipping wine in the setting sun.

## Catedral de Santiago

In the centre of the market area is the **Catedral de Santiago** ① *Tue-Sat 1000-1300,
1600-1900, Sun 1030-1330, free*, whose slender spire rises high above the tight streets.
A graceful Gothic affair, it was mostly built in the late 14th century on the site of a
previous church, but was devastated by fire in the 1500s and lost much of its original
character. Two of its best features are later additions: an arched southern porch and a
small but harmonious cloister (if it's locked, ask an attendant). The interior is small and
has an inclusive, democratic air. Also worth spotting is a beautifully worked Gothic tomb
in the chapel of San Antón. Promoted to cathedral in 1950, the building has benefited
from recent restoration work. A few shops are charmingly nestled into its flank.

## Plaza Nueva

The 'New Square', one of a series of similar cloister-like squares in Euskadi, was
finished in 1849. Described by Unamuno (see box, page 96) as "my cold and uniform
Plaza Nueva", it will particularly appeal to lovers of geometry and symmetry with its
courtly neoclassical arches, which conceal an excellent selection of restaurants and
bars, offering some of the best *pintxos* in town. In good weather, most have seating
outside in the square.

## Museo Vasco

Near the Plaza Nueva, the **Museo Arqueológico, Etnológico e Histórico Vasco** ① *Plaza
Miguel de Unamuno 4, T944 155 423, www.euskal-museoa.org, Tue-Sat 1100-1700,
Sun 1100-1400, €3 (free on Thu)*, is attractively set around an old Jesuit college and
houses an interesting if higgledy-piggledy series of Basque artefacts and exhibits
covering thousands of years. There's a fascinating room-sized relief model of Vizcaya
on the top floor, a piece of one of the Gernika oak trees and some good displays on
Basque fishing, as well as a decent but poorly presented series of prehistoric finds.

## Arenal and around

Formerly an area of marshy sand, the Arenal was drained in the 18th century. There's a
bandstand with frequent performances, often of folk dancing. Next to it is the
18th-century Baroque façade of **San Nicolás de Bari**. Opposite,
the **Teatro Arriaga** seems very sure of itself, but was only
reopened comparatively recently (in 1986) after decades of
neglect. It's very much in plush *fin de siècle* theatre style, with
chandeliers, soft carpet and sweeping staircases, but at times

❖ *The Arenal by the river is
a busy nexus point for
strollers, lovers, demon-
strators and dog-walkers.*

presents some fairly cutting-edge art, usually of a strong standard and fairly priced.

## Basílica de Begoña

Atop a steep hill above the Casco Viejo, the Basílica de Begoña is Bilbao's most
important church, home of the Virgin of Begoña, the patron of Vizcaya. It's built in
Gothic style on the site of a chapel where the Virgin is said to have appeared in former
times. The cloister is a later addition, as is the flamboyant tower, which gives a slightly
unbalanced feel to the building. To get there from the Casco Viejo, take the lift from
Calle Esperanza or leave the Metro station by the 'Begoña/Mallona' exit. From there,
walk up the hill to the basilica. Buses No 3 and No 30 come here from Plaza Circular, or
bus No 41 from Gran Vía. On your way back down, rather than taking the Mallona lift,
head down the flight of stairs next to it; a charming descent into the Casco Viejo warren,
emerging on Plaza Unamuno.

País Vasco Bilbao/Bilbo

# Along the riverbank

*"You are, Nervión, the history of the town, you are her past and her future, you are memory always becoming hope." Miguel de Unamuno*

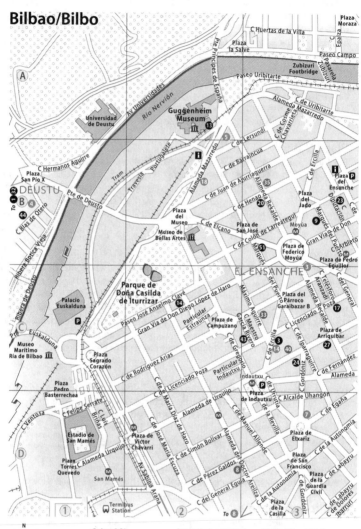

Bilbao/Bilbo

N

0 metres    100
0 yards     100

**Sleeping** 🛌
Albergue Bilbao
  Aterpetxea **8** *D2*
Arriaga **1** *detail*
Bilbao Jardines **19** *detail*

Carlton **3** *B3*
Deusto **4** *B1*
Ercilla **14** *C3*
Gran Domine Bilbao **5** *A2*
Hostal Begoña **2** *B4*
Hostal Gurea **6** *detail*
Hostal Mardones **10** *detail*
Hostal Méndez **11** *detail*
Indautxu **7** *D3*
Iturrienea Ostatua **17** *detail*
Miróhotel Bilbao **18** *B2*

Pensión Ladero **16** *detail*
Pensión Manoli **9** *detail*
Petit Palace Arana **13** *detail*
Sirimiri **12** *B6*

**Eating** 🍴
Artajo **2** *B4*
Bar Irintzi **15** *detail*
Bermeo **3** *C3*
Berton **4** *detail*
Buda **5** *B4*

Café-Bar Bilbao **6** *detail*
Café Boulevard **7** *detail*
Café Iruña **16** *B4*
Café La Granja **52** *B4*
Café Lamiak **22** *detail*
Cappuccino **24** *C3*
Casa Vasca **32** *B1*
Egiluz **25** *detail*
El Kiosko del Arenal **10** *A5*
Garibolo **11** *C4*
Gatz **12** *detail*

The **Nervión** made Bilbao and Bilbao almost killed the Nervión; until recently pollution levels were sky-high. Although your immune system would still have words to say about taking a dip, the change is noticeable. The riverbank has been and continues to be the focus of most of Bilbao's beautification schemes; if you only take one stroll in Bilbao, an evening *paseo* from the Casco Viejo along the river to the Guggenheim should be it.

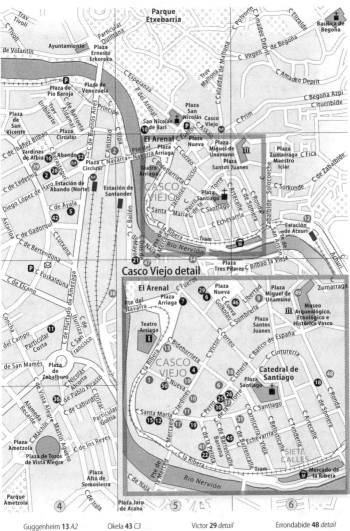

Cross the river at the **Zubizuri** footbridge, one of the most graceful of the acclaimed bridges of Santiago Calatrava. After crossing the footbridge, you are on the **Paseo Uribitarte**; this riverside walk leading to the Guggenheim museum is where plenty of Bilbaínos gather for the evening stroll.

## Museo Guggenheim

ⓘ *Abandoibarra Etorbidea 2, T944 359 000, www.guggenheim-bilbao.es, Tue-Sun 1000-2000 (Jul and Aug daily 1000-2000), €10, students/pensioners €6, children under 12 free, €11 including Museo de Bellas Artes; audio tour €3.50, guided tours free at 1130, 1230, 1630, 1830 (Spanish, English and Euskara).*

Daring in concept and brilliant in execution, the Guggenheim museum has driven a massive boom in the local confidence as well as, more prosaically, the economy; its success has given the green light to further ambitious transformations of the formerly industrialized parts of the city.

It all started when the Guggenheim Foundation, strapped for cash (or something like that...), decided to build a new museum to enable more of their collection to be exhibited. Many cities around the globe were considered, but Bilbao was keenest and the Basque government were prepared to foot the US$100 million bill for its construction.

Frank Gehry was the man who won the design competition and the rest is the reality of what confronts visitors to Bilbao today: a shining temple of a building that completely fulfils the maxim of 'architecture as art'. Gehry's masterstroke was to use titanium, an expensive soft metal normally reserved for Boeing aircraft and the like. He was intrigued by its futuristic sheen and malleable qualities; the panels are literally paper-thin. The titanium makes the building shimmer: it seems that the architect has managed to capture motion.

One of the most impressive features of the design is the way it interacts with the city. One of Bilbao's enjoyable and surprising experiences is to look up when crossing a street in the centre of town and see the Guggenheim perfectly framed, like some unearthly craft that's just landed. Gehry had to contend with the ugly bulk of the Puente de la Salve running through the middle of his site, yet managed to incorporate the bridge fluidly into his plans. The raised tower at the museum's eastern end has no architectural purpose other than to link the building more effectively with the town upriver; it works.

The building also interacts fluidly with the river itself; the pool at the museum's feet almost seems part of the Nervión, and Fuyiko Nakaya's mist sculpture, when turned on, further blurs things. It's entitled *FOG*, which also happen to be the architect's initials...

A couple of creatures have escaped the confines of the gallery and sit in the open air. Jeff Koons's giant floral sculpture, *Puppy*, sits eagerly greeting visitors. Formerly a touring attraction visiting the city for the opening of the museum in 1997, he couldn't escape the clutches of the kitsch-hungry Bilbaínos, who demanded that he stayed put. On the other side of the building, a sinister spider-like creature guards the waterside approach. Entitled *Maman*, we can only be thankful that sculptor Louise Bourgeois's mother had long since passed away when it was created. It's a striking piece of work, and makes a bizarre sight if approached when the mist is on.

On the western side of the building is *Quantum Field-X*, two huge cube-like structures covered in panels onto which are projected coloured laser beams.

So much for the exterior, which has met with worldwide acclaim. What about the inside? It is, after all, an art museum.

Gehry's idea was that there would be two types of gallery within the building: "galleries for dead artists, which have classical square or rectangular shapes, and galleries for living artists, which have funny shapes, because they can fight back".

● *There's a spot in the museum permanently reserved for Picasso's* Gernika, *which the*
● *Basque government persistently try and prise away from the Reina Sofia gallery in Madrid.*

# 66 99 The exuberant curves recall the fish, one of Gehry's favourite motifs; the structure could almost be a writhing school of herring or salmon.

The embodiment of the latter is the massive Gallery 104, built with the realization that many modern artworks are too big for traditional museums. Central to this space is Richard Serra's *Snake*, whose curved iron sheets will carry whispers from one end to another. A hundred feet long, and weighing 180 tons, it's meant to be interactive – walk through it, talk through it, touch it.

This, however, is one of only a few pieces that live in the museum; the rest are temporary visitors, some taken from the permanent collection of the Guggenheim Foundation, others appearing in a range of exhibitions. This, of course, means that the overall quality varies according to what's on show.

Architecturally, the interior is a very soothing space, with natural light flooding into the atrium. It's a relief to realize that this isn't one of those galleries that makes you feel you'll never be able to see everything unless you rush about; it's very uncluttered and manageable. In the atrium is Jenny Holzer's accurately titled *Installation for Bilbao*, an arresting nine-column LED display that unites the different levels of the building. The effect created is a torrent of primal human sentiment expressed simply in three languages.

There are three floors of galleries radiating off the central space. For a look at some smaller-scale Frank Gehry work, drop into the reading room on the ground floor, furnished with his unusual cardboard chairs and tables, which are surprisingly comfortable and solid. The cafés also feature chairs designed by him. As well as the usual gallery shop, the museum also has an excellent modern art bookshop.

The closest Metro stop to the museum is Moyúa, but it's a few blocks away; better is the tram, which stops just outside.

*The tram is a good way to see the river, running more or less along it from Atxuri station to the Guggenheim and Euskalduna palace.*

## Palacio Euskalduna
Beyond the Guggenheim, the Euskalduna Palace is a bizarre modern building that echoes both the shipbuilding industry and Vizcaya's iron trade. It's now a major venue for conferences and concerts, particularly classical. More *simpático* is the covered Euskalduna bridge nearby, which sweeps into Deustu in a confident curve.

## Museo Marítimo Ría de Bilbao
ⓘ *Muelle Ramón de la Sota 1, T902 131 000, www.museomaritimobilbao.org, Tue-Fri 1000-1400, 1600-1800, Sat and Sun 1000-1400, 1600-2000; €4 (extra applies for special exhibitions).*

This new museum nestles under the Euskalduna bridge and examines the maritime history of this proud city. It's on the site of what was once an important shipbuilding and cargo area; a massive derrick and various ships in dry dock are part of the exterior exhibition. Inside, the focus is on the Bilbao estuary and Vizcayan shipping in general. It's dry but fascinating, with a couple of good AV presentations in English (other displays have translation sheets). One of the highlights is the aerial photograph of Bilbao and its *ría*. There are often excellent temporary exhibitions, which have included visiting 'guest ships' that moor outside.

País Vasco Bilbao/Bilbo

# Deustu

Across from the Guggenheim is Deusto (recently officially renamed Deustu), a bohemian university district buzzing with purpose. Sometimes described as a republic, it developed separately from Bilbao for much of its history and still has a different vibe. Traditionally frequented by artists, students and agitators, the cafés and bars hum with political discussion.

❗ *If you want that perfect snap of Frank Gehry's masterpiece, this is the place to come, particularly in the evening light.*

The Universidad de Deustu, Bilbao's main university, was founded in 1886 by the Jesuits. It now counts over 20,000 students and staff among its several buildings. While the academic standard of the university has traditionally been very high, it was an important centre of radical opposition to the Franco dictatorship, and has also played an important role in Basque nationalism.

On Deustu's waterfront, a large stone lion defies the sky. This building was originally a pavilion to house the small workshops of local tradespeople but has now been converted into luxury apartments. Bilbaínos perversely name it **El Tigre** (the tiger), which it does somewhat resemble.

# El Ensanche

The residents of old Bilbao had long been crammed into the small Casco Viejo area when the boom came and the population began to surge. In 1876 the Plan de Ensanche (expansion) de Bilbao was approved, and the area across the river was drawn up into segments governed by the curve of the Nervión. The Ensanche quickly became Bilbao's business district, and it remains so today, its graceful avenues lined with stately buildings, prestige shops and numerous bars.

## Museo de Bellas Artes

ⓘ *Plaza del Museo 2, T944 396 060, www.museobilbao.com, Metro Moyúa, Tue-Sat 1000-2000, Sun 1000-1400, €4.50, €11 with Guggenheim, €2 audio guide.*
Not to be outdone by its titanium colleague, the fine arts museum has tried to keep up with the times by adding a modern building of its own on to the existing museum. The result is a harmonious credit to its architect, Luis Uriarte, who seamlessly and attractively fused new to old. Similarly, the collection is a medley of modern (mostly Basque) art and older works – there's also a new space for temporary exhibitions.

The Basque sculptors Eduardo Chillida and Jorge de Oteiza (see box, page 66) are both well represented, but the museum confidently displays more avant-garde multimedia work by young artists too. Among the portraits, the jutting jaw of the Habsburg kings is visible in two famous works. The first, of a young Felipe II, is by the Dutchman Moro, while the Felipe IV, attributed to Velásquez, and similar to his portrait of the same king in the Prado, is a master work. The decline of Spain can be seen in the sad king's haunted but intelligent eyes, which seem to follow the viewer around the room. A lighter note is perhaps unintentionally struck by the anonymous *Temptations of St Anthony*, who is pestered by a trio of colourful demons. Among other items of interest is a painting of Bilbao by Paret y Alcázar. Dating from 1793 and painted from the Arenal, it looks like a sleepy riverside village.

## Plaza de Toros de Vista Alegre

ⓘ *Check the website, www.torosbilbao.com, for details of* corridas *and ticketing.*
Bilbao's temple of bullfighting sees most action during *Semana Grande* in August, when there are *corridas* all week. The locals are knowledgeable and demanding of their matadors, and the bulls they face are acknowledged to be among the most *bravo* in

## ❧ Athletic Bilbao

So this Bilbaíno is in a bar chatting with a friend and asks him:
-Did you hear that they've spent 100 million on El Guggenheim? The friend thinks for a while:
-Well, as long as he bangs in a few goals that's not too bad…

Rarely is a football team loved quite as deeply as Athletic Club are by Bilbao. A Basque symbol in the same league as the *ikurriña* or the Gernika oak, the team, as a matter of principle, only fields Basque players. Astonishingly they have remained very competitive in one of the strongest leagues in the world and have never been relegated. To date, they have won the championship eight times (more than any other club bar the two Madrid giants and Barcelona) and have won 24 Spanish Cups.

Athletic Club grew out of the cultural exchange that was taking place in the late 19th century between Bilbao and the UK. British workers brought football to Bilbao, and Basques went to Britain to study engineering. In the early years, Athletic fielded many British players, and their strip was modelled on that of Sunderland, where many of the miners were from. José Antonio Aguirre, who led the Civil War Basque government so nobly, had been a popular player up front for the club.

San Mamés (see below) is one of the country's most atmospheric places to watch football, as every game is a sort of international for the Basque nation. Games are usually on Sundays at 1700.

País Vasco Bilbao/Bilbo

Spain. Tickets to the spectacles don't come cheap, starting at about €30. The bullring is also home to a **museum** ① *C Martín Agüero 1, T944 448 698, Metro Indautxu, Mon-Fri 1030-1300, 1600-1800, €1.50*, dedicated to tauromachy. There are displays on the history of the practice, as well as memorabilia of famous matadors and bulls.

### Estadio de San Mamés

① *C Felipe Serrate s/n, Metro San Mamés, T944 411 445, www.athletic-club.es. Tours Tue-Fri 1030-1330, 1600-1900, Sat 1000-1400, 1600-1900, Sun 1000-1400, hourly, €6.*
The Estadio de San Mamés is at the far end of the new town. Few in the world are the football teams with the social and political significance of Athletic Bilbao (see box above); support of the team is a religion, and this, their home stadium, is known as the Cathedral of Football. Services are held fortnightly, usually on Sundays at 1700. The Basque crowd are fervent but good-natured. It's well worth going to a game; it's a far more friendly and social scene than the average match in the rest of Europe. The Monday papers frequently devote ten pages or more to Athletic's game. Tickets usually go on sale at the ground two days before the game. On match days, the ticket office opens two hours before kick-off. Tickets range from €25-50 depending on the area of the ground. The ground also holds a small **museum** ① *Mon-Fri 1030-1330, 1600-1900, Sat 1000-1400, 1600-1900, Sun 1000-1400, €6*, displaying trophies and other memorabilia of 'Los Leones'. Entry includes a guided tour of the stadium.

## Bilbao's seafront ⊜❼▲❸❶ ➨ *pp97-107.*

At the mouth of the estuary of the Nervión, around 20 km from Bilbao, the fashionable barrio of Getxo is linked by the improbably massive Puente Vizcaya with the grittier town of Portugalete, in its day a flourishing medieval port. It's a great day trip from Bilbao; the fresh air here is a treat for tired lungs, and not far from Getxo stretch the languid beach suburbs of Sopelana, Plentzia and Gorliz.

## The philosopher's last stand

One of Bilbao's most famous sons was Miguel de Unamuno, poet, philosopher and academic, born in 1864 on Calle Ronda. A member of the 'Generation of '98' – a new wave of artists and thinkers emerging in the wake of the Spanish-American war of 1898 – Unamuno, who spoke 15 languages, was a humanist and a Catholic with an idealistic love of truth. This made him enemies in a Spain where political beliefs tended to come first. To this day, many Basques have mixed feelings about 'Don Miguel', who, although proud of being Basque, wasn't pro-independence and deplored some of the myths created in the name of nationalism.

Unamuno became rector of the university at Salamanca but after criticizing the dictatorship of Primo de Rivera, he was imprisoned in the Canary Islands, from where his rescue was organized by the editor of the French newspaper *Le Quotidien*.

In Salamanca when the Civil War broke out, Unamuno, previously a deputy in the Republic, had supported the rising, but grew more and more alarmed with the nature of the Nationalist movement and the character of the war.

On October 12, 1936 he was presiding over the Columbus day ceremony at the university. The gathering rapidly degenerated into a fascist propaganda session. Catalan nationalism was denounced as a cancer that fascism would cut out, and General Millán Astray, a war veteran, continued with more empty rhetoric; the hall resounded to the popular Falangist slogan "long live death".

Unamuno rose to close the meeting: "At times to be silent is to lie", he said, and went on to criticize harshly what had been said. The general responded by crying "Death to intellectuals". Guns were pointed at the 72-year-old, who continued: "You will win, because you have the brute force. But you will not convince. For to convince, you would need what you lack: reason and right in the struggle". At the end of his speech, he was ushered out of the hall by Franco's wife to safety. Under house arrest, he died a couple of months later, it was said, of a broken heart. On the day of his death, his two sons enlisted in the anti-fascist militia.

## Getxo

Very much a separate town rather than a suburb of Bilbao, Getxo is a wealthy, sprawling district encompassing the eastern side of the rivermouth, a couple of beaches, a modern marina, and a petite old harbour. It's home to a good set of attractive stately mansions as well as a tiny but oh-so-pretty whitewashed old village around the now disused fishing port-ette. There's a very relaxed feel about the place, perhaps born from a combination of the seaside air and a lack of anxiety about where the next meal is coming from.

The **Playa de Ereaga** is Getxo's principal stretch of sand, and location of its **tourist office** ① *T944 910 800*, and finer hotels. Near it, the **Puerto Viejo** is a tiny harbour, now silted up, and a reminder of the days when Getxo made its living from fish. The solemn statues of a fisherman and a *sardinera* stand on the stairs that look over it, perhaps mystified at the lack of boats. Perching above, a densely packed knot of white houses and narrow lanes gives the little village a very Mediterranean feel – unless the *sirimiri*, the Bilbao drizzle, has put in an appearance. There are a couple of restaurants and bars to soak up the ambience of this area, which is Getxo's prettiest quarter.

Further around, the **Playa de Arrigunaga** is a better beach flanked by crumbly cliffs, one topped by a windmill, which some days has a better time of it than the shivering bathers. A pleasant, if longish, walk leads downhill to the estuary end of

Getxo, past the marina, and an ostentatious series of 20th-century *palacios* on the waterfront, and a monument to Churruca, whose engineering made the estuary navigable, making Bilbao accessible to large vessels; a vital step in its growth.

Passing the hulking modern **Iglesia de Nuestra Señora de las Mercedes** (which contains some highly regarded frescoes) will bring you to the unmistakable form of the Puente Vizcaya and the trendy shopping area of **Las Arenas** (Areeta).

## Puente Vizcaya

*① 1000-2200; crossings €0.25 per person, €1.05 per car; walkway €3. Metro Areeta.*
A bizarre cross between a bridge and a ferry, the Puente Vizcaya was opened in 1893, a time when large steel structures were à la mode in Europe. Wanting to connect the estuary towns of Getxo and Portugalete by road, but not wanting a bridge that would block the *ría* to shipping, the solution taken was to use a 'gondola' suspended by cables from a high steel span. It's a fascinating piece of engineering: the modern gondola fairly zooms back and forth with six cars plus foot passengers aboard. You can also ascend to the walkway 50 m above. You'll often see the bridge referred to as the **Puente Colgante** (hanging bridge).

## Portugalete

On the other side of the Puente Vizcaya from Getxo is Portugalete, a solid working-class seamen's town with a significant seafaring history. In former times, before Churruca did his channelling work, the Nervión estuary was a silty minefield of shoals, meanders and sandbars – a nightmare to navigate in anything larger than a rowing boat. Thus Bilbao was still a good few hours' journey by boat, and Portugalete's situation at the mouth of the *ría* gave it great importance as a port. Nowadays, although from across the water it looks thoroughly functional, it preserves a characterful old town and attractive waterfront promenade.

Above the waterside the old Casco is dominated by the **Iglesia de Santa María**, commissioned by Doña María the Kind at the time of the town's beginnings, although the current building, in Gothic style, dates from the early 16th century. There's a small museum inside. Next to it, the **Torre de Salazar** is what remains of the formidable compound built by Juan López de Salazar, a major landowner, in about 1380. The main living area was originally on the second floor – the first was a prison – and the tower was occupied until 1934, when a fire evicted the last residents. One of the Salazar family who lived here, Luis García, was one of the first chroniclers of Vizcaya. He had plenty of time to devote to his writings, as he spent the last few years of his life locked up by his loving sons. For **tourist information** *① T944 958 741, turismo@portugalete.org.*

## ● Sleeping

**Bilbao** *p87, map p90*
Finding accommodation is frequently difficult; it's worth phoning ahead, although some of the *pensiones* won't take reservations. Most budget accommodation is in or near the Casco Viejo, while the classier hotels are spread through the new town.
**LL Gran Domine Bilbao**, Alameda Mazarredo 61, T944 253 300, www.granhoteldomine bilbao.com. This modern 5-star hotel is directly opposite the Guggenheim and has been designed with the same innovation and levity in mind. The original façade of the building consists of 48 mirrors at slightly different angles, while the delightful interior is dominated by a large central atrium. The rooms with Guggenheim views cost a little more, but it's worth it once you're paying prices of this level. There's also a good bar and restaurant. Inspiringly original. Recommended.
**LL Hotel Carlton**, Plaza Moyúa 2, T944 162 200, carlton@aranzazu-hoteles.com. This grand old hotel, set on noisy Plaza Moyúa, is considerably more luxurious inside than out. Its refurbished neoclassical ambience has colonnaded Einstein, Lorca and Hemingway, among other notables.

## ⋮ La Pasionaria

*"It is better to be the widow of a hero than the wife of a coward"*
Dolores Ibárruri

One of the most prominent figures of the Spanish Civil War, Dolores Ibárruri, from the Bilbao suburb of Gallarta, near Portugalete, was known as La Pasionaria (the passion flower) for her inspirational public speaking.

Formerly a servant and a *sardinera* (sardine seller), she suffered grinding poverty, and the loss of two daughters in infancy but rose to prominence in the Communist Party in the 1930s, becoming a deputy in the parliament in 1936 (she was released from prison to take up her post). When the Civil War broke out, she became a powerful symbol of the defence of Madrid and the struggle against fascism as well as empowered womanhood. Straightforward, determined and always dressed in black, she adopted the war cry "No pasarán" (they shall not pass), which was taken up all over Republican Spain. She was instrumental in the recruitment and morale of anti-fascist soldiers, including the International Brigades. When the latter were withdrawn, she famously thanked them: "You can go proudly. You are history. You are legend... We shall not forget you". Ibárruri was never much involved in the plotting and infighting that plagued the Republican cause and was able to claim at the end of the war: "I have neither blood nor gold upon my hands". When Franco was victorious in 1939, she flew to Russia, where she lived in Moscow. The dictator died in 1975 and, after 38 years, Ibárruri was re-elected to her old seat at the first elections in 1977. On her return to Spain the 82-year-old Pasionaria, still in black, proclaimed to a massive crowd "I said they shall not pass, and they haven't". She died in 1989.

LL **Hotel Ercilla**, C Ercilla 37-39, T944 705 700, www.hotelercilla.es. Well located on the city's main shopping street, this large 4-star hotel has a cheerful entrance. It's been newly renovated and is much the better for it. With quality service and a busy, metropolitan feel, it makes an excellent base, and is well priced for the amenities on offer. There are excellent weekend rates, with savings up to 40%. Check the website for current offers. The hotel restaurant, **Bermeo**, is one of Bilbao's best.

L **Hotel Indautxu**, Plaza Bombero Etxariz s/n, T944 211 198, www.hotelindautxu.com. Behind a mirrored façade that bizarrely dwarfs the older building in front, are comfortable executive-style rooms, set on a comparatively quiet square. There's a terrace, and pianists make the occasional scheduled appearance in the bar. More character than many in this category and cheerful to boot.

L **Miróhotel Bilbao**, Alameda Mazarredo 77, T946 611 880, www.mirohotelbilbao.com. Also close to the Guggenheim, with some great views of it, this is a sleek hotel with a Catalan touch; both architect Carmen Abad and interior designer Antonio Miró hail from Barcelona. It's impressively modern, with a pared-back feel not without touches of whimsy. The rooms are excellent: spacious, and with a Nordic feel to the white fittings. As is fashionable these days, rates vary substantially according to when you reserve; you may get better deals from an online dealer or travel agent than the hotel's own website. There are all services, including an enjoyable jacuzzi and a stylish bar. The staff are helpful and friendly.

AL **Hotel Deustu**, C Francisco Maciá 9, T944 760 006, www.nhhoteles.com, Metro Deustu. This colourfully decorated hotel is an enjoyable place to stay on this side of the river. The large rooms, featuring minibar, safe, PlayStation and inviting beds are offset by an attractively arty bar and restaurant downstairs.

A **Petit Palace Arana**, C Bidebarrieta 2, T944 156 411, www.hthoteles.com. With an unbeatable location at the mouth of the warren that is the Casco Viejo, this beautiful building has been very sensitively converted into a smart modern hotel. There's free internet access for guests, and the best of the rooms have a computer terminal and exercise bike. There are innovative family suites with fold-down beds (good value) a pretty upstairs breakfast room, and rooms equipped for the disabled. Book on the internet in advance for the best rates. The closest parking is under Plaza Nueva.

**B Hotel Arriaga**, C Ribera 3, T944 790 001, www.hotelarriaga.com. Very friendly hotel with a garage (rare in the Casco Viejo) and some excellent rooms with floor-to-ceiling windows and views over the theatre. Plush, formal-style decoration and fittings. Good value. Parking underneath for €10.80 per night. Recommended.

**B Hotel Bilbao Jardines**, C Jardines 9, T944 794 210, www.hotelbilbaojardines.com. Right in the heart of the Casco Viejo pintxo zone, this newly-opened hotel is an attractive option. The rooms have a stripped-back, comfortable feel, with light wood floorboards; the best are on the top floor, with sloping ceilings. Management is very friendly, and the price is fair.

**B Hotel Sirimiri**, Plaza de la Encarnación 3, T944 330 759, www.hotelsirimiri.com. Named after the light misty rain that is a feature of the city, this is a small gem of a hotel in a quiet square. The genial owner has equipped it with a gym and sauna, and there's free parking at the back. Rooms come with TV, heating and phone. Recommended.

**C Hostal Begoña**, C Amistad 2, T944 230 134, www.hostalbegona.com. A recent refit has transformed the Begoña into a welcoming modern hotel packed with flair and comfort. From the inviting library/lounge to the large chalet-style rooms and mini-suites at very reasonable prices, this is an excellent option. The hotel also offers free internet access, and can organize a range of outdoor activities. Highly recommended.

**C Iturrienea Ostatua**, C Santa María, T944 161 500, www.iturrieneaostatua.com. This beautiful pensión in the heart of the Casco Viejo pintxo zone is carefully lined in stone, wood, art, and idiosyncratic objects. With delicious breakfasts (€4) and homely rooms, you might want to move in. Recommended.

**C-E Hostal Méndez**, C Santa María 13, T944 160 364, www.pensionmendez.com.

A dignified building with castle-sized doors and an entrance guarded by iron dogs. The 1st floor has *hostal*-grade rooms with new bathrooms, while the 4th floor is *pensión*-style accommodation, simpler, but still very adequate. Many rooms have balconies.

**D-E Hostal Gurea**, C Bidebarrieta 14, T944 163 299. Carefully refurbished and well-scrubbed establishment on one of the Casco Viejo's principal axes. Welcoming and cheerfully vague about bookings. The rooms are equipped with TV and phone, and are available with or without bath (the en suite is €5 more). The owners usually request a 0100 curfew.

**E Albergue Bilbao Aterpetxea**, Ctra Basurto-Kastrexana 70, T944 270 054, http://albergue.bilbao.net. Bus No 58 from Plaza Circular and the bus station. Bilbao's HI hostel is a block-of-flats-sized structure by a motorway on the outskirts of Bilbao. Despite its inconvenient location, it does have good facilities (including bike hire). There's accommodation in dorms, singles or doubles; it's cheaper for under-25s. If there's 2 of you, *pensiones* in the centre are just as cheap. The 0930 check-out is a shock to the system when the rest of the nation runs with midday.

**E Hostal Mardones**, C Jardines 4, T944 153 105. Run by a welcoming and chatty owner and very well situated in *pintxo* heartland. Entered by the side of a newsstand, the *pensión* is fitted in attractive dark wood, and rooms are pleasant, light and airy.

**E Pensión Ladero**, C Lotería 1, T944 150 932, www.pensionladero.com. Right in the thick of it, this small and welcoming option has cork tiles, good shared bathrooms and very well-priced rooms with TV, some of which are reached by a tiny spiral staircase. You'll receive a hearty Basque welcome – just as well, as it's on the 4th floor with no lift. Excellent value. Recommended. No bookings taken.

**E Pensión Manoli**, C Libertad 2, T944 155 636. In the heart of the Casco Viejo with some good-value exterior rooms with balcony and shared bathroom. Bright and well looked after.

### Bilbao's seafront *p95*

Staying here is a good alternative to the city; there are plenty of options.

**AL Gran Hotel Puente Colgante**, C María Díaz de Haro 2, T944 014 800,

www.granhotelpuentecolgante.com.
Euskotren Portugalete; Metro Areeta.
Housed in a reconstructed 19th-century
building with a grand façade, this upmarket
modern hotel is superbly situated right
next to the Puente Vizcaya on the waterfront
promenade. All the rooms face outwards,
and the hotel has all the facilities you
come to expect.

**B Hotel Igeretxe**, Playa de Ereaga s/n,
T944 910 009, F944 608 599, Metro Neguri.
Shaded by palms, this welcoming hotel is
right on Ereaga beach, Getxo's main social
strand. Formerly a *balneario*, the hotel
still offers some spa facilities, as well as
a restaurant overlooking the slightly
grubby sand. Breakfast included.

**D Pensión Usategi**, C Landene 2, T944 913
918, Metro Bidezabal. Well placed on the
headland above pretty Arrigunaga beach,
the rooms are clean and cool, and some
have great views.

**D-E Pensión Areeta**, C Mayor 13 (Las Arenas),
T944 638 136, Metro Areeta. Near the metro
and an iron bar's throw from the Puente
Vizcaya, this is a good place in the heart of
the trendy Las Arenas district of Getxo.
The rooms are smallish but welcoming.

### Camping
**Camping Sopelana**, Ctra Bilbao-Plentzia s/n,
T946 762 120, Metro Sopelana. Very handy
for the metro into Bilbao, this is the most
convenient campsite within range of the
city. Well equipped with facilities, and in easy
range of the shops, it's right by the beach,
too. Bungalows available, reasonable value.

## ❷ Eating

### Bilbao *p87, map p90*
Bilbao's Casco Viejo is undoubtedly the
prime place to head for *pintxos* and evening
drinking, with the best areas being the **Plaza
Nueva** and around the **Siete Calles**. There's
another concentration of bars on **Av
Licenciado Poza** and the smaller **C García
Rivero** off it. The narrow **C Ledesma**, a street
back from Gran Vía, is a popular place to
head for after-work snacks and drinks. There
are some good restaurants in the Casco Viejo
(including a couple geared solely to tourists),
but also plenty of options scattered through
the New Town and Deustu.

**Bermeo**, C Ercilla 37, T944 705 700.
Although it's the restaurant of the **Hotel
Ercilla**, this stands on its own feet as one of
the best restaurants in Bilbao. Specializes in
seafood, prepared either in typical Basque
fashion or more innovative modern styles.

**Guggenheim Restaurant**,
Av Abandoibarra 2, T944 239 333,
www.restaurantegug genheim.com.
A good all-round option in the museum.
The restaurant is administered by one of
San Sebastián's top chefs, and has the quality
and prices to match, but also offers a *menú
del día* for €14 (€18.20 at weekends), which
is first rate. The furniture is Gehry's work.
No bookings are taken for the menu, which
is served (slowly) from 1330 on a first-
come basis. Both the cafés do a fine
line in croissants, coffee and *pintxos*;
the one inside, off Gallery 104 has more
seating and a nice view over the river.

**Guria**, Gran Vía 66, T944 415 780, Metro
San Mamés. One of Bilbao's top restaurants
with plush red walls and a quiet elegant
atmosphere. Its stock-in-trade, like many of
its counterparts, is *bacalao*. After tasting it
here, you may forgive the codfish all of the
bad dishes that have been produced with it
in other kitchens and factories around the
world. There's a *menú de degustacíon* for
€62 and a *menú del día* for €41. Otherwise
you can count on €60 a head minimum,
more if you forsake the fish for the meat,
which is tender and tasty. A cheaper option
is to eat in the bar, where there's a bistro
menu. There's a very respectable selection
of brandies too.

**Victor**, Plaza Nueva 2, T944 151 678.
A quality upstairs restaurant with an elegant
but relaxed atmosphere. This is a top place to
try Bilbao's signature dish, *bacalao al pil-pil*, or
the restaurant's variation on it, and there's an
excellent wine selection. Conforms to the
general Iberian rule of decreasing vegetables
with increasing price. Recommended.

**Victor Montes**, Plaza Nueva 8, T944 155
603. This traditional and excellent restaurant
is known for its huge collection of wines and
whiskies. The elegant upstairs dining room
has the best of Basque cuisine at surprisingly
reasonable prices. Downstairs is a very
popular *pintxo* bar; if you can shoulder your
way to it in the evening, you'll find that not a
square inch is free of posh and delicious bites.

## ♟ Pintxos

From about 1900 in the evening until midnight or so, everyone lives in the street, walking, talking, drinking and eating *pintxos*.

Wherever you go in the Basque country, you'll be confronted and tempted by a massive array of food across the top of bars. Many bars serve up very traditional fare: slices of *tortilla* (potato omelette) or *pulgas de jamón* (small rolls with cured ham). Other bars, enthused by 'new Basque' cuisine, take

things further and dedicate large parts of their day to creating miniature food sculptures using more esoteric ingredients. The key factor is that they're all meant to be eaten. You can ask the bartender or simply help yourself to what you fancy, making sure to remember what you've had for the final reckoning. If you can't tell what something is, ask (*¿de qué es?*). *Pintxos* usually cost about €1.20 to €2.50 depending on the bar.

♟ **Casa Vasca**, Av Lehendakari Aguirre 13-15, T944 483 980. A Deustu institution on the main road – the front bar has a good selection of posh *pintxos* and a couple of comfortable nooks to settle down with a slightly pricey drink. Behind is a restaurant that serves pretty authentic Basque cuisine in generous portions. Another dining room serves a €10 *menú del día*, and there's even a nightclub downstairs, catering for an older crowd.

♟ **Egiluz**, C Perro 4, T944 150 242. Among all the bright modern lights of the Casco Viejo's newer restaurants, this sturdy old family-run place is still the place to go if you fancy a steak or similar. The dining room is upstairs at the back of the bar. They serve a huge *chuletón* – it could comfortably feed 2 – and other excellent grilled and roasted fare.

♟ **Hostaria Marchese del Porto**, C Marqués del Puerto 10, T944 161 680, Metro Moyúa. This elegant Italian restaurant goes slightly over the top with its decor but is deservedly popular with local businessfolk at lunchtimes, when an excellent €10 *menú del día* is served in its *comedor*. Good pasta and gelati too.

♟ **Kasko**, C Santa María 16, T944 160 311. With funky decor inspired by the fish and high-class new Basque food, this spacious bar-restaurant is always busy, and has a very tasty evening *menú* for €18.50 (€26.50 at weekends), which is sometimes accompanied by a pianist.

♟ **La Viña**, C Henao 27, T944 243 602; Metro Moyúa. You could easily miss this tiny bar wedged into a block in the Ensanche. As well as being a hospitable place to have a glass of wine, they serve some very fine food at a very

fair price. Their speciality is seafood, with mussels, crabs, or whatever's fresh to choose from and eat at the handful of small tables.

♟ **Ogetamairu**, C Bailén 33, T944 157 135, www.ogetamairu.com. Although not in the greatest of locations, this minimalist 2-floor restaurant has won itself a big reputation. The clean white dining room hosts an innovative *cocina moderna* that doesn't skimp on quantity. The price (most mains €12-19) is more than reasonable. Alternatively, you may prefer the more intimate downstairs *comedor*.

♟ **Pulpería**, C Nueva 4. This recently-opened restaurant keeps things attractively simple. Although elegant and comfortable, its dishes, from Galicia in northwest Spain, are as they should be, with hearty *lacón con grelos* stew and tasty octopus (*pulpo*). It's good value, and they also have paella (€13.50 per person, order in advance).

♟ **Serantes** and **Serantes II**, C Licenciado Poza 16 and Alameda Urquijo 51, T944 102 066 and 944 102 699, Metro Indautxu. These *marisquerías* (seafood restaurants) are not as pricey as their high reputation would suggest, with fish dishes around the €18 mark. It's all very fresh, and the chefs have the confidence to let the flavours of the seafood hold their own. Go with the daily special – it's usually excellent, or tackle some *cigalas*, the 4WD of the prawn world, equipped with pincers (sometimes called Dublin Bay prawns in English).

♟ **Su@**, C Marqués del Puerto 4, T944 232 292. Metro Moyúa. One of the latest designer restaurants to open in Bilbao, this is ultra-modern but comfortable, with a romantic coloured lighting scheme and a menu of new-style creations that are curiously ordered by temperature that they leave the kitchen at. A gimmick, yes, but the food and atmosphere are pretty good. There's a *menú del día* for €14. Evening bookings essential.

**Taloaska**, Av Madariaga 7, T944 758 264. A more than solid choice in the heart of Deusto, with a bar that stretches as far as the eye can see and is very well endowed with *pintxos*. At the end is the dining room, where there's a good *menú* for €10.50.

**Buda**, C Ayala 1, T944 157 136. Tucked away behind the **Corte Inglés** is this modern Asian fusion restaurant. Choices are mainly centred around Japanese and Thai. There's a *menú* for €8.50 day and night Mon-Thu, which is particularly good value.

**Capuccino**, C Gordóniz 2, T944 436 980. A place for people in the know. This café, run by a friendly Egyptian, and with a map of the old Nile painted on the roof, serves filled pitta rolls, as well as shawarma, musaka, and other snacks. They have an excellent range of teas.

**Garibolo**, C Fernández del Campo 7, T944 273 255, Metro Moyúa. While at first glance Bilbao doesn't seem large enough a Spanish city to sustain a vegetarian restaurant, the colourful Garibolo packs 'em in, particularly for its €10 lunch special. No alcohol.

**Mr Lee**, C Pedro Martínez Artola 12, T944 442 328. Free of the repetitive paraphernalia that adorns other Chinese restaurants in Spain, which tend to become caricatures of themselves, this has an elegant, spacious dining area with Asian artwork of restrained good taste. The menu has a range of decent dishes from different parts ('fusion', if you will) of east and southeast Asia. Good value. The street slopes up from Plaza Zabálburu.

**New Inn**, Alameda Urquijo 9, T944 151 043. The restored art nouveau splendour of the main bar of this popular lunch-spot is reason enough to enter. Workers in Bilbao offices sadly have little time now to grab a 3-course meal, so this place caters for them with a range of excellent sandwiches and similar.

**Río Oja**, C Perro 4, T944 150 871. Another good option on this street, specializing in bubbling Riojan stews and Basque fish dishes, most of which are in big casseroles at the bar. The dishes will come microwave-heated (standard practice in Spain), but it's good value and has friendly service.

**Rotterdam**, C Perro 6, T944 159 772. Small and uncomplicated Casco Viejo restaurant with a *simpático* boss. This is what lunch restaurants have always been like here, with paper tablecloths and a very solid *menú del día* for €8.50

**Saibigain**, C Barrenkale Barrena 16, T944 150 123. This is an intensely traditional and atmospheric place, and one of the best cheap restaurants in the Casco Viejo. It's full of black and white photos of Athletic Bilbao, and has a phalanx of hams hanging over the bar. There's a *menú del día* for €8.30; it's worth waiting to grab a table upstairs. Closed Sun.

## Pintxo bars

**Berton**, C Jardines 11, T944 167 035. The hanging *jamones* and bunches of grapes define this cheerful bar, which has top-notch ham *pintxos* and *raciones* and some quality wines by the glass. Very popular at weekends.

**Café-Bar Bilbao**, Plaza Nueva 6, T944 151 671. A sparky place with top service and a selection of some of the better gourmet *pintxos* (all labelled) to be had around the old town. It's always busy, but the barstaff never seem to miss a trick.

**Lekeitio**, C Diputación 1, T944 239 240. An attentive bar that's a mile long with a fantastic selection of after-work eats. The variety of fishy and seafoody *pintxos* are good, as is the *tortilla*. A palisade of oars and life-buoys sections off a small sit-down eating area.

**Okela**, C García Rivero 8, T944 415 937. A modern bar popular with the office crowd and dominated by a huge signed photo of the footballer Joseba Etxebarría in full stride for Athletic Bilbao. Decent *pintxos*.

**Oriotarra**, C Blas de Otero 30, T944 470 830. A classy *pintxo* bar in Deustu that has won an award for the best bar-top snack in Bilbao. A round of applause for the pig's ear millefeuille.

**Xukela**, C Perro 2, T944 159 772. A very social bar on a very social street. Attractive *pintxos* and some good sit-down food – cheeses and cured meats – and a clientele upending glasses of Rioja at competitive pace until comparatively late.

**Artajo**, C Ledesma 7, T944 248 596, Metro Abando. Uncomplicated and candid bar with homely wooden tables and chairs and good traditional snacks of *tortilla* and *pulgas de jamón*. Famous for its *tigres* (mussels in spicy tomato sauce).

❦ **Bar Irintzi**, C Santa María 8, T944 167 616. *Pintxos* are an art form in this excellent bar, whose remodelled chic styling hasn't changed the quality on offer; there's a superb array of imaginative snacks, all carefully labelled, freshly made and compassionately priced. The recent renovation has removed some atmosphere, but it's still a great choice.

❦ **Gatz**, C Santa María 10, T944 154 861. A convivial bar with some of the Casco's better *pintxos*, which are frequent contenders in the awards for such things. Happily spills on to the street at weekends. Friendly, no-nonsense staff.

❦ **Jaunak**, C Somera 10. One of quite a few earthy, friendly Basque bars on this street, with a huge range of large *bocadillos* at about €3.50 a shot.

❦ **Taberna Taurina**, C Ledesma 5. A tiny old-time tiles 'n' sawdust bar, which is packed top to bottom with bullfighting memorabilia. It's fascinating to browse the old pictures, which convey something of the sport's noble side. The *tortilla* here also commands respect.

## Cafés

**Café Boulevard**, C Arenal 3, T944 153 128. Fans of art deco will love this refurbished defender of the style, which appears unchanged from the early 20th century, when it was Bilbao's beloved 'meeting place'. Not to be missed; a great breakfast spot.

**Café Iruña**, Jardines de Albia s/n, T944 237 021. This noble old establishment on the Jardines de Albia is beginning its 2nd century in style. Well refurbished, the large building is divided into a smarter café space with wood panelling in neo-Moorish style, and a tiled bar with old sherry ads and some good *pintxos* – including lamb kebabs sizzling on the barbie in the corner.

**Café La Granja**, Plaza Circular 3, T944 230 813. A spacious old Bilbao café, opened in 1926. Its high ceilings and long bar are designed to cope with the lively throng that gathers throughout the day. Attractive art nouveau fittings and *pintxos*, although the simple *menú del día* is a little overpriced at €10.40.

**Café Lamiak**, C Pelota 8, T944 161 765. A peaceful and likeable 2-floor forum, the

sort of place a literary genre, pressure group or world-famous funk band might start out. It's a mixed gay/straight crowd, with a relaxed rather than active scene.

**El Kiosko del Arenal**, Muelle del Arenal s/n. Elegant and cool café under the bandstand in the Arenal. Plenty of outdoor tables overlooking the river.

### Bilbao's seafront *p95*

The place for some of Bilbao's best dining.

❦❦❦ **Cubita Kaia**, Muelle de Arriluze 10-11, T944 600 103, Metro Neguri. A highly acclaimed restaurant with views over the water from Getxo's marina. People have been known to kill for the *cigalas* (Dublin bay prawns) turned out by young modern chef Alvaro Martínez. Not to be confused with another restaurant named **Cubita** next to the windmill above Arrigunaga beach.

❦❦❦ **Jolastoki**, Av Leioa 24, T944 912 031; Metro Neguri. Decorated in classy but homely country-mansion style, Jolastoki is a house of good repute throughout Euskadi. Definitely traditional in character, dishes such as *caracoles en salsa vizcaína* (snails) and *liebre* (hare) are the sort of treats that give Basque cuisine its lofty reputation.

❦❦ **Karola Etxea**, C Aretxondo 22, T944 600 868, Metro Algorta. Perfectly situated in a quiet lane above the old port. It's a good place to try some fish; there are usually a few available, such as *txitxarro* (scad) or *besugo* (sea bream). The *kokotxas* (cheeks and throats of hake in sauce) are also delicious.

❦ **El Hule**, C Victor Chavarri 13, T944 722 104. In the narrow, sloping streets of Portugalete's old town (just behind the town hall on the waterfront near the Puente Colgante), this is a cracking spot for lunch. The small but cute upstairs and downstairs dining rooms are cosy and comfortable. The food is traditional, uncomplicated fare (*menú del día* €9.50) served with a smile and plenty of quality.

❦ **Irrintzi**, C Particular de Arlamendi, off Calle Zalama, T944 643 372. This homely bar has an appealing brick and wood décor, an upmarket clientele and about the finest reputation for *pintxos* on the right bank of the *ría*. There's an excellent array, and they are all very tempting. From Areeta metro, head straight ahead and up the hill past the Mandarin Chinese restaurant, and turn right. The bar is un-signed.

# ♪ Bars and clubs

## Bilbao *p87, map p90*

Bilbao's nightlife is fairly quiet during the week, but it makes up for it at weekends. Most bars have to shut at 0400 these days, but there are some *discotecas* that go later. Nearly everywhere in the Casco Viejo shuts by 0130, but you can always dash across the Puente de la Merced to the streets around C Hernani, where there is plenty going on. Be careful in this zone though, as muggings are not unknown. There are lots of bars in the Casco Viejo, including many on the legendary streets of Ronda, Somera and Barenkale.

### Bars

**Bizitza**, C Torre 1. Very chilled predominantly gay bar with a Basque political slant. Relaxed, atmospheric and welcoming, with frequent cultural events. One of the top spots for an after-dinner *copa* in Bilbao – they mix a great drink. Recommended.

**Compañía del Ron**, C Máximo Aguirre 23, T944 213 069. Friends of Ronald will be happy here, with over 100 rums at the disposal of the bar staff, who know how to handle them. Despite the chain-pub feel, this is a good early-evening spot in the heart of the new town.

**El Patio de mi Casa**, C Cosme Echevarrieta 13. A small but quality place, which serves great copas to a discerning crowd in a homely, relaxed atmosphere. Open nightly 2300-0300.

**Errondabide**, C Ronda 20. This is a good place to come to get a feel of what a pro-Independence Basque bar is like. There are political posters everywhere, photos of ETA prisoners (there's a huge campaign to have them repatriated to prisons in the Basque country), a spirited atmosphere, and plenty of smoke and beer.

**Luz Gas**, C Pelota 6, T944 790 823. A beautiful mood bar with an oriental touch. Sophisticated but friendly, and you can challenge all-comers to chess or Connect-4.

**Muga**, C Ronda 10. A long-time favourite, this relaxed café and bar has a rock 'n' roll vibe, with colourful tables, fanzines and CDs for sale, and a down-to-earth clientele.

**Primera Instancia**, Alameda Mazarredo 6, T944 236 545. Buzzing modern bar that's upmarket but far from pretentious. Small restaurant section with a €19.90 *menú de degustacíon* and €9 *menú del día*. Check out the snazzy umbrella wrapper by the door.

**Twiggy**, Alameda de Urquijo 35. Psychedelic colours and a 1960s feel characterize this bar in one of the busiest weekend hubs.

**Zodiako's**, C Euskal Herria s/n (corner of Telletxe), T944 604 059, Metro Algorta. This squiggly bar in the heart of Getxo is one of the best, with a terrace, *pintxos* and service with a smile. There's a *discoteca* underneath.

**Zulo**, Barrenkale 22. A tiny nationalist bar with plenty of plastic fruit and a welcoming set who definitely don't follow the Bill Clinton line on non-inhalation. The name means 'hole' in Euskara.

### Clubs

Many clubs are busiest around 0400-0500.

**Bullitt**, C Dos de Mayo 3. Across the river from the Casco Viejo, this discobar has a variety of music styles. On Sat, it's Black Roots night, with excellent soul and R&B. Other nights offer ska, reggae and 60s rock. After shutting at 0300-0400, at weekends it re-opens at 0600 as an 'afterhours' and the action keeps going all morning.

**Café Indie**, C Doctor Areilza 34. Trendier and sleeker than the name might suggest. Sofas downstairs, and a bar and dancefloor upstairs. At weekends this makes some of the other clubs look empty, with both music and crowd that are suspiciously on the mainstream side of indie. British retro gets some play too.

**Conjunto Vacío**, C Muelle de la Merced 4. Empty by name and packed by nature, at least from about 2 on Fri and Sat nights. The music is fairly light *bakalao*, the crowd mixed and good-looking, the drinks horrendously expensive, but entry is free.

**Distrito 9**, Alameda Rekalde 18. Still probably the best spot in Bilbao for house music. Opens very late and is quite a dressy scene. Drag shows and a €10 cover.

**Heaven**, C Dos de Mayo 4, Bilbao. A men-only gay bar with loud dance music that goes late. There's a lounge area and *cuarto oscuro* (backroom) behind the main bar.

**La Lola**, C Bailén 10. Decorated in industrial style with sheet-metal and graffiti, this is a good Sat night club that varies in character from fairly cheesy dance to pretty heavy garage. Open latish €6 at the door.

**Santana 27**, C Santana 27, Bolueta. Near the Metro station in Bolueta, this vast venue has opened out here to avoid the strict opening hours in central Bilbao. There are so many dance floors that you are bound to find something you like; it often has live bands and special club nights. Usually €6 to get in, including a drink. Open nightly 2300-0600.

## 😎 Entertainment

**Bilbao** *p87, map p90*
For bullfighting and football, see pages 94-95.

### Cinema
**Cines Avenida**, C Lehendakari Aguirre 18, T944 757 796, Metro Deustu. This is one of the better cinemas around, with a tendency to show lower-profile releases and artier films, as well as some Basque pictures.

### Music venues
**Bilbo Rock**, Muelle de la Merced s/n, T944 151 306. Atmospheric venue in a converted church that is now a temple of live rock with bands playing most nights of the week. No license, but canned beer from machines.
**Cotton Club**, C Gregorio de la Revilla 25. Live music venue with a relaxed atmosphere and lined with characterful showbiz trappings. Music ranges from rock to jazz.
**Kafe Antzokia**, C San Vicente 2, T944 244 625, www.kafeantzokia.com. An ex-cinema turned Bilbao icon, this is a live venue for anything from death metal to Euskara poetry, and features two spacious floors with bars which go late and loud at weekends. Sociable, friendly, and a place where you might hear more Euskara than Spanish.
**Palacio Euskalduna**, C Abandoibarra 4, T944 310 310. Top-quality classical performances from the symphonic orchestras of Bilbao and Euskadi, as well as high-profile Spanish and international artists.

### Theatre
**Teatro Arriaga**, Plaza Arriaga 1, T944 792 036. Bilbao's highest-profile theatre is picturesquely set on the river by the Casco Viejo. It's a plush treat of a place in late 19th-century style, but the work it presents can be very innovative. The better seats go for €25 and above, but there are often decent pews available for as little as €5.

## ⊛ Festivals and events

**Bilbao** *p87, map p90*
**Sat after 15 Aug** Aste Nagusia (big week), Bilbao's major fiesta, follows on from those in Vitoria and San Sebastián to make a month of riotous Basque partying. It is a boisterous mixture of everything: concerts, *corridas*, traditional Basque sports and serious drinking.

## ⊙ Shopping

**Bilbao** *p87, map p90*
Bilbao is the best place to shop in Northern Spain. The majority of mainstream Spanish and international clothing stores are in the Ensanche, particularly on and around C Ercilla. The Casco Viejo harbours dozens of quirkier shops. A new commercial centre, **Zubiarte**, just by the Puente de Deustu, has a full complement of fashion chains and a cinema.
**Mercado de la Ribera**, the art deco market by the river where stallholders used to come for the weekly market, has over 400 stalls selling fruit, veg, meat and fish, it's the major centre for fresh produce in Bilbao. Come in the morning if you want to get the true flavour; the afternoons are comparatively quiet.

## ⚓ Activities and tours

**Bilbao** *p87, map p90*
**Barco Pil-Pil, Bilbao**, T944 465 065. Trips Apr-Oct Sat and Sun, Jul and Aug Tue-Sun, €9.30, 1-hr trip and drink. Dinner and dance cruises, 4 hrs, all year Fri and Sat, €49.50, book in advance as the meal is pre-prepared by caterers. Leaves from a jetty not far from the Guggenheim museum.
**Bilbao Paso a Paso**, T944 730 078, www.bilbaopasoapaso.com. Knowledgeable tours of Bilbao and the whole of Euskadi that can be tailored to suit.
**Eroski Bidaiak**, C Licenciado Poza 10, T944 439 012. Travel agent that's part of the Mondragón cooperative.

**Bilbao's seafront** *p95*
**Getxo Abentura**, www.getxo.net. The Getxo tourist office can organize just about any outdoor activity you can think of in the Getxo area, from caving to canoeing, provided there are enough people to make a go of it (usually 4 for group-style outings).

**Maremoto Renting**, Puerto Deportivo de Getxo, T650 439 211. Rental of jet-skis, sailboards, run trips.

**Náutica Getxo**, Puerto Deportivo de Getxo, T609 985 977, www.nauticagetxo.com. On the jetty at the end of Ereaga beach, this company hires out yachts with or without a skipper. Sailing knowledge isn't really required as the boats come with auxiliary power, but if you want to learn to sail, these guys can teach you that too.

## ⊖ Transport

**Bilbao** *p87, map p90*
### Air
Bilbao's airport in **Sondika**, 10 km northeast of the centre, is a beautiful building designed by Santiago Calatrava, seemingly in homage to the whale. A taxi to/from town costs about €15-20. There's an efficient bus service that runs to/from Plaza Moyúa in central Bilbao. It leaves from outside the terminal, takes 20-30 mins and runs every half-hour. One-way €1.15.

Bilbao is served from several European destinations. The cheapest direct flights from the **UK** are with the budget operator **EasyJet**. Bilbao is also served from **London** by Iberia and **British Airways** and directly connected with several other European cities, including several in Germany and Austria with **Air Berlin**, as well as **Zürich**, **Brussels**, **Paris**, **Milan** and **Lisbon**. Note that although **Ryanair** sometimes claim they fly to Bilbao, the flights actually land at Santander, from where a bus service runs to Bilbao (see page 322). Bilbao also has frequent domestic connections with **Madrid**, **Barcelona** and other Spanish cities operated by Iberia and Spanair.

**Airlines offices**  British Airways, Aeropuerto de Bilbao, T944 710 523, www.ba.com; **easyJet**, www.easyjet.com; **Iberia**, C Ercilla 20, Bilbao, T944 245 506, www.iberia.es; **Spanair**, Aeropuerto de Bilbao, T944 869 498, www.spanair.com.

### Bicycle hire
Bilbao currently has a notable lack of cycle hire available. The youth hostel and the **Hotel Nervión** both hire bikes, but normally only to guests, although they might be persuaded.

### Boat
P&O run a ferry service from **Portsmouth** to Bilbao, but in reality it's more of a cruise than a transport connection. The ship, the *Pride of Bilbao*, is the largest ferry operating out of the UK and has several restaurants, a cinema, pool, sauna and casino. While it's certainly not cheap, you wouldn't ever describe it as classy either. It's a 2-night trip and cabin accommodation is mandatory; look at £400-500 return with a car. Boats leave Portsmouth at 2045 every 3 days except during winter, when there are few crossings. The return ferry leaves Bilbao at 1315. Many passengers don't even get off, reasoning they might lose some valuable bar-time. Apart from all the laid-on entertainment, you can often spot dolphins and whales from the deck. The charitable website www.biscay-dolphin.co.uk is worth a look before your trip. Check www.poferries.com for timetable. Book online at www.poferries.com or on T0870 242 4999. The ferry port is at Santurtzi, 13 km from the city centre, accessible by **Euskotren**.

### Bus
The majority of Bilbao's inter-urban buses leave from the Termibus station near the football stadium (Metro San Mamés, tram stops outside). All long-haul destinations are served from here, but several Basque towns are served from the stops next to Abando station on C Hurtado Amezaga.

Bilbao to **San Sebastián**: buses from the Termibus station every 30 mins weekdays, every hr at weekends, operated by PESA (1 hr 20 mins, €8). Also trains from Atxuri station every hr on the hr (2 hrs 40 mins, €5.50). Bilbao to **Vitoria**: buses from the Termibus station about every 30 mins with **Autobuses La Union** (55 mins, €4.80). Other destinations include: **Santander** (almost hourly, 1 hr 30 mins, €5.72), **Pamplona** (7-9 daily, €11.20, 2 hrs), **Logroño** (5 daily, 2 hrs, €10.55), **Burgos** (4 direct daily, 2 hrs, €10.55).

### Car hire
The usual assortment of multinationals dominate this cut-throat trade. The process is fairly painless, and national driving licences are accepted. **Atesa**, C Sabino Arana 9, T944 423 290; Aeropuerto de Bilbao, T944 533 340,

www.atesa.es;. **Avis**, Av Doctor Areilza 34, T944 275 760; Aeropuerto de Bilbao, T944 869 648; www.avis.com; **Hertz**, C Doctor Achucarro 10, T944 153 677; Aeropuerto de Bilbao, T944 530 931; www.hertz.com.

**Metro**
Bilbao's metro runs until about 2400 Sun-Thu, until about 0200 on Fri, and 24 hrs on Sat. A single fare costs €1.15, while a day pass is €3. There's one main line running through the city and out to the beach suburbs, while the recently opened 2nd line will eventually reach the coast on the other side of the estuary.

**Tram**
A single fare costs €1; there are machines at the tram stops. It runs every 10-15 mins or so.

**Train**
Bilbao has 3 train stations. The main one, **Abando**, is the terminal of **RENFE**, the national Spanish railway. It's far from a busy network, and the bus usually beats it over a given distance but it's the principal mainline service.

Abando is also the main terminus for **Euskotren**, a handy short-haul train network, which connects Bilbao and San Sebastián with many of the smaller Basque towns as well as their own outlying suburbs. The other Bilbao base for these trains is **Atxuri**, situated just east of the Casco Viejo, an attractive but run-down station for lines running eastwards as far as San Sebastián. These are particularly useful for reaching the towns of Euskadi's coast. **Gernika** is serviced every hour (18 mins past, 53 mins) and on to **Mundaka** and **Bermeo**. Trains to **San Sebastián** run every hour on the hour (2 hrs 39 mins) via Zarautz, Zumaia, Eibar, Durango.

Narrow-gauge FEVE trains connect Bilbao along the coast to **Santander**, 3 times daily (2½ hrs, €6.50) and beyond. They are slow but scenic and leave from the Estación de Santander just next to Bilbao's main Abando railway station. There's also a daily service from here to **León** (7 hrs 15 mins, €18.45).

**Getxo** *p96*
**Bus**
Buses No 3411 and No 3413 run to/from Plaza Moyúa every 30 mins.

**Metro**
Areeta, Gobela, Neguri, Aiboa, Algorta and Bidezabal. The beaches further on can be accessed from Larrabasterra, Sopelana and Plentzia metros.

**Portugalete** *p97*
**Bus**
Bus No 3152 from the Arenal bus station in Bilbao (Mon-Sat).

**Metro** Areeta (across the bridge).

**Train**
**Euskotren** from Abando (Santurtzi line) every 12 mins weekdays, less frequently at weekends, 20 mins.

## 🅑 Directory

**Bilbao** *p87, map p90*
**Consulates** Eire, T944 912 575; France, T944 249 000; Germany, T944 238 585; South Africa, T944 641 124; UK, T944 157 600; USA, the nearest consular representative is at the embassy in Madrid, T915 872 200. **Internet** Ciber Bilbo, C Pablo Picasso 7, T944 218 176. Internet and *locutorio*; **El Señor de la Red**, Alameda de Rekalde 14, T944 237 425, €2 per hr; **Laser Internet**, C Sendeja 5, T944 453 509, Mon-Fri 1030-0230, Sat and Sun 1100-0230, €0.05 per min, handy and quick, also offers photocopier and fax services; **Web Press**, C Barrancua 11, daily 1000-2200. **Language schools** Instituto Hemingway, C Bailén 5, T944 167 901, www.instituto hemingway.com. **Laundry** Tintorería Lavaclín, Campo de Volantín 15, T944 453 191. Bag wash for €10. **Medical services** Hospital de Basurto, Av Montevideo 18, T944 006 000, T944 755 000, Tram Basurto. **Police** The emergency number for all necessities is 112, while 091 will take you to the local police. **Main police station**, Policia Municipal Bilbao, C Luis Briñas 14, T944 205 000. **Post office** Main post office, Alameda Urquijo 19; **Casco Viejo branch**, C Epalza 4 (opposíte Arenal).

**Getxo** *p96*
**Internet** Getxo Net House, Plaza Villamonte 5 (below Metro Algorta), T944 319 171. €2.70 per hr, daily 1000-2200.

# Vitoria/Gasteiz

→ *Phone code: 945. Colour map 3, B2. Population: 226,490. Altitude: 512 m.*

*Vitoria is the quiet achiever of the Basque trio. A comparatively peaceful town, it comes as a surprise to many visitors to discover that it's actually the capital of the semi-autonomous Basque region. A thoughtful place, it combines an attractive old town with an Ensanche (expansion) designed to provide plenty of green spaces for its hard-working inhabitants. While it lacks the big-city vitality of Bilbao or the languid beauty of San Sebastián it's a satisfying city much-loved by most who visit it. Perhaps because it's the political centre of the region, the young are very vocally Basque, and the city feels energized as a result.* ▸▸ *For Sleeping, Eating and other listings, see pages 112-114.*

## Ins and outs

**Getting there** Vitoria bus station is just east of town on Calle Los Herrán. There are frequent connections with Bilbao and other Basque destinations. Vitoria's **RENFE** station is south of the centre at Calle Eduardo Dato and has better connections with Spain than Bilbao. **Ryanair** serves Vitoria from London Stansted and Dublin.▸▸ *See also Transport, page 114.*

**Getting around** Vitoria is a good two-wheel city with more planned cycle ways and green spots than in busier Bilbao. Vitoria is easily walkable with Calle Dato the focus of the evening Paseo.

**Tourist information** Vitoria's new **tourist office** ⓘ *Plaza General Loma 1, T945 161 598, turismo@vitoria-gasteiz.org, Mon-Sat 1000-1900, Sun 1100-1400*, is near the Plaza de España.

## Background

Vitoria's shield-shaped old town sits on the high ground that perhaps gave the city its name (*beturia* is an Euskara word for hill). After being a Basque settlement first, then a Roman one, Vitoria was abandoned until it was refounded and fortified by the kings of Navarra in the 12th and 13th centuries. An obscure Castilian town for much of its history, Vitoria featured in the Peninsular War, when, on midsummer's day in 1813, Napoleon's forces were routed by the Allied troops and fled in ragged fashion towards home, abandoning their baggage train containing millions of francs, which was gleefully looted. "The battle was to the French", commented a British officer sagely, "like salt on a leech's tail". Vitoria has thrived since being named capital of the semi-autonomous Basque region, and has a genteel, comfortable air, enlivened by an active student population. The city seems divided in two: the old town is the domain of lively Basque youth, and the new town the preserve of middle-aged Spanish strollers.

# Casco Medieval

## Calle Cuchillería and Calle Chiquita

Calle Cuchillería, and its continuation, Calle Chiquita, is the most happening part of the old town, with several impressive old mansions, a couple of museums, dozens of bars, and plenty of pro-Basque political attitude. Indeed, there's an interesting contrast in the atmosphere of the new and old towns; whereas the former feels very Spanish and quite staid, the old streets hum with young Basque energy. Like several in the Casco Medieval, this street is named after the craftspeople who used to have you can see a number of old inscriptions and coats of arms carved on buildings.

Housed in a beautiful fortified medieval house on Cuchillería, the unusual **Museo Fournier** ① *Tue-Fri 1000-1400, 1600-1830, Sat 1000-1400, Sun 1100-1400, free*, is devoted to the playing card, of which it holds over 10,000 packs. The cards are mostly Spanish decks, with swords, cups, coins and staves the suits.

The corner of the old town at the end of Calle Chiquita is one of Vitoria's most picturesque. The **Casa del Portalón**, now a noted restaurant, is a lovely old timbered building from the late 15th century. It used to be an inn and a staging post for messengers. Across from it is the **Torre de los Anda**, which defended one of the entrances in the city wall. Opposite these is the 16th-century house of the Gobeo family that now holds the **archaeology museum** ① *Tue-Fri 1000-1400, 1600-1830, Sat 1000-1400, Sun 1100-1400, free*. The province has been well occupied over history, and the smallish collection covers many periods, from prehistoric through Roman and medieval. There are three floors of objects, of which arguably the most impressive is the so-called *Knight's Stele*, a tombstone carved with a horseman dating from the Roman era.

Opposite here is the current entrance to the older of Vitoria's two cathedrals, the **Catedral de Santa María** ① *tours daily 1100-1400, 1700-2000, €3 per person, pre-book on T945 255 135 or www.catedralvitoria.com*. There's an ongoing restoration project, scheduled to last until 2009. It's currently 'Open for Renovation'; while normal visits have been suspended, you can take a fascinating guided tour of the restoration works. Depending on the progress, you may be able to walk on gangways high above the nave, admiring the vaulting from close up, or see the delicate retrieval of crumbling stonework.

Above the busy square of **Plaza de la Virgen Blanca**, the church of **San Miguel** stands like one of a series of chess pieces guarding the entrance to the Casco Medieval. Two gaping arches mark the portal, which is superbly carved. A niche here holds the city's patron saint, the Virgen Blanca, a coloured late-Gothic figure. On the saint's day, 5 August, a group of townspeople carry the figure of Celedón (a stylized farmer) from the top of the graceful belltower down to the square.

## Los Arquillos

Running off the same square, this slightly strange series of dwellings and covered colonnades was designed in the early 19th century as a means of more effectively linking the high Casco Medieval with the newer town below, and to avoid the risk of the collapse of the southern part of the hill. It leads up to the attractive small **Plaza del Machete**, where incoming city chancellors used to swear an oath of allegiance over a copy of the Fueros (city statutes) and a *machete*, in this case a military cutlass.

Also off Plaza de la Virgen Blanca, the picture-postcard **Plaza de España** (Basques prefer to call it **Plaza Nueva**) was designed by the same man, Olaguíbel, who thought up the Arquillos. It's a beautiful colonnaded square busy with playing children and parents chatting over coffee, housing the town hall and several bars with terraces that are perfect for the morning or afternoon sun.

# New Town

Vitoria's new town isn't going to blow anyone's mind with a cavalcade of Gaudí-esque buildings or wild street parties but it is a very satisfying place: a planned mixture of attractive streets and plenty of parkland. It's got the highest amount of greenery per citizen of any city in Spain and it's no surprise that it's been voted one of the best places to live in Spain. With the innovative Artium in place, the mantle of Basque capital seems to sit ever easier on Vitoria's shoulders.

# Vitoria/Gasteiz

País Vasco Vitoria/Gasteiz

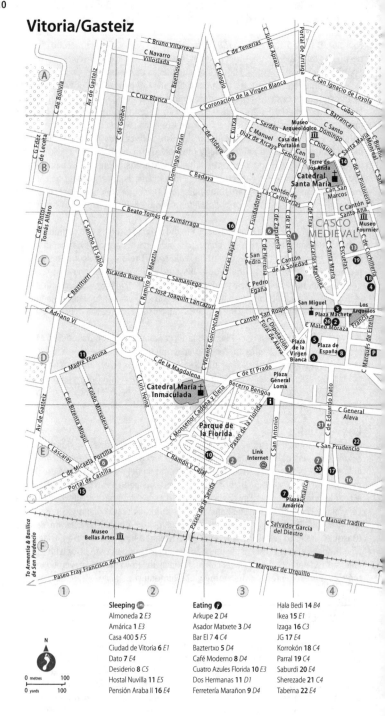

N

0 metres 100
0 yards 100

| Sleeping | Eating | Hala Bedi 14 B4 |
|---|---|---|
| Almoneda 2 E3 | Arkupe 2 D4 | Ikea 15 E1 |
| Amárica 1 E3 | Asador Matxete 3 D4 | Izaga 16 C3 |
| Casa 400 5 F5 | Bar El 7 4 C4 | JG 17 E4 |
| Ciudad de Vitoria 6 E1 | Baztertxo 5 D4 | Korrokón 18 C4 |
| Dato 7 E4 | Café Moderno 8 D4 | Parral 19 C4 |
| Desiderio 8 C5 | Cuatro Azules Florida 10 E3 | Saburdi 20 E4 |
| Hostal Nuvilla 11 E5 | Dos Hermanas 11 D1 | Sherezade 21 C4 |
| Pensión Araba II 16 E4 | Ferretería Marañon 9 D4 | Taberna 22 E4 |

ⓘ *C Francia 24, T945 209 020, www.art ium.org, Tue-Fri 1100-2000, Sat and Sun 1030-2000, €4, Wed 'you decide'.*

The shiny new Artium (opened 2002) is Vitoria's answer to Bilbao's Guggenheim and San Sebastián's Kursaal. It's an exciting project, which features some excellent contemporary artwork, mostly in the form of temporary exhibitions, some of which incorporate some of the older buildings in Vitoria's Casco Medieval. Shiny and white, your attention is grabbed immediately by the building's confident angles and Javier Pérez's *Un pedazo de cielo cristalizado* (A crystallized piece of heaven), a rather large hanging-glass sculpture in the atrium. The galleries are accessed down the stairs. The website has details in English about what's on at any given time; the exhibitions are usually in place for many months. There's a little café which is a good place to hang out.

## Catedral de María Inmaculada

There's no missing the new cathedral, María Inmaculada, constructed in the 20th century in neo-Gothic style; its bulk looms attractively over this part of the town. Built in authentic medieval style, it now houses the **Museo Diocesano de Arte Sacro** ⓘ *Tue-Fri 1000-1400, 1600-1830, Sat 1000-1400, Sun 1100-1400, free.*

## Parque de la Florida

This gorgeous park is an excellent retreat right in the heart of Vitoria. Cool and shady, it has a number of exotic trees and plants and a couple of peaceful cafés. You can watch old men in berets playing *bolas* (boules), and there's an old bandstand with Sunday concerts, guarded by statues of four ancient kings. If you see anyone taking life a little too seriously, they're more than likely politicians – the Basque Parliament stands in a corner of the park.

## Basílica de San Prudencio

ⓘ *Mon-Fri 1000-1400, Sat 1000-1400, 1600-2100, Sun 1000-1200, 1600-2100, guided visit €3.*

It's well worth the half-hour walk or the bus ride to see this church in the village

País Vasco Vitoria/Gasteiz

of Armentia, now subsumed into Vitoria's outskirts. The village is supposedly the birthplace of San Prudencio, the patron saint of Alava Province, and the church was erected in his honour. It was rebuilt in the 18th century, but still has some excellent features from its Romanesque youth, such as a harmonious round apse and the carvings above the doors, one of Christ and the apostles, the other of the Lamb and John the Baptist. At time of writing, it was being renovated, and access to most of the building was by guided tour run by archaeologists who have exposed Romanesque foundations and an adjoining cemetery.

To reach Armentia on foot, continue past the Museo de Bellas Artes on Paseo Fray Francisco de Vitoria, then turn left down Paseo de Cervantes when you reach the modern chapel of **La Sagrada Familia**. The basilica is at the end of this road. It's a pleasant walk; you can also get bus No 9, which runs every half hour from the new cathedral to the basilica.

## ● Sleeping

**Vitoria** *p108, map p110*
**L Hotel Ciudad de Vitoria**, Portal de Castilla 8, T945 141 100, www.hoteles-silken.com. A massive 4-star hotel situated at the edge of Vitoria's centre, where character starts to make way for 'lifestyle'. It's airy and pleasant, with good facilities, including a gym and sauna. Chief attractions, however, are its incredible weekend rates, with doubles from €67, less than half the weekday rate.
**AL Hotel Almoneda**, C Florida 7, T945 154 084, www.hotelalmoneda.com. Attractively situated a few paces from the lovely Parque de la Florida, this hotel has decent spacious rooms with a rustic touch. It's significantly cheaper at weekends. Breakfast included; you can even have it in bed if you ask nicely.
**AL Parador de Argómaniz**, Carretera N1 Km 363, T945 293 200, www.parador.es. This *parador* is some 12 km east of Vitoria in a Renaissance palace. It's a tranquil place with some good views over the surrounding countryside. Napoleon slept here before the disastrous Battle of Vitoria.
**C Hotel América**, C Florida 11, T945 130 506, www.hotelamarica.com Just around the corner from Calle Dato and close to the train station, this friendly hotel is very well placed. The rooms are good value, with TV and good bathroom, warm, and surprisingly quiet, considering it's a busy street.
**C Hotel Desiderio**, C Colegio San Prudencio 2, T945 251 700, F945 251 722. Welcoming hotel with unremarkable but comfy rooms with bathroom just out of the Casco Medieval.
**D Hotel Dato**, C Eduardo Dato 28, T945 147 230, www.hoteldato.com. This *pintxo*-zone cheap hotel is a treasury of art nouveau and

*clásico* statues, mirrors and general plushness, in a comfortable rather than stuffy way. Its rooms are exceptional value too; all are pretty, with excellent facilities, and some have balconies or *miradores* (enclosed balconies). Recommended.
**D-E Pensión Araba II**, C Florida 25, T945 232 588. A good base in central Vitoria. A variety of clean and comfortable rooms with or without bathroom and a genuinely friendly welcome. Parking spaces available (€6).
**F Casa 400**, C Florida 46, T945 233 887. At this price you don't expect many facilities, but this is clean, pretty comfortable, and cheerfully run.
**F Hostal Nuvilla**, C Fueros 29, T945 259 151. Centrally located *pensión* with small rooms with washbasin. It's friendly and it's cheap.

## ● Eating

**Vitoria** *p108, map p110*
**Arkupe**, C Mateo Moraza 13, T945 230 080. A quality restaurant with some imaginative dishes, such as a tasty squid 'n' potato pie, and some inspiring salads. There's a *menú de degustación* for €33.
**Dos Hermanas**, C Madre Vedruna 10, T945 132 934. One of Vitoria's oldest restaurants, and certainly not the place to come for nouvelle cuisine, with generous, hearty and delicious traditional dishes. There's a *menú de degustación* for €39.
**Ikea**, Portal de Castilla 27, T943 144 747. Lovers of homely Swedish furniture will be disappointed to find out that this is in fact one of Vitoria's best restaurants. It is mainly French in style, but there are a few

traditional Basque dishes on the agenda too. The crunchy *pichón* (squab) in a red wine sauce is memorable.

**¶¶ Asador Matxete**, Plaza Machete 4, T945 131 821. A stylish modern restaurant harmoniously inserted into this pretty plaza above Los Arquillos. Specializing in large pieces of meat expertly grilled over coals. There's also a pleasant terrace to enjoy a drink in this peaceful square.

**¶¶ Izaga**, Tomás de Zumárraga 2, T945 138 200. Excellent dining at this fairly formal restaurant in a smart stone building. The focus is on seafood, but there are plenty of other specialities – such as duck's liver on stuffed pig's ear, and some sinful desserts. Mains €13-22.

**¶¶ Restaurante Zabala**, C Mateo Moraza 9, T945 230 099. Although you wouldn't know it from the pleasant but simple decor, this is a well-regarded local restaurant. The dishes on offer, without being spectacular, are solid Basque and Rioja choices, and are priced fairly. The steaks are recommendable, as is the *merluza a la vasca* (hake) or the grilled *sapito* (small monkfish).

**¶¶ Xixilu**, Plaza América 2, T945 230 068. On a small gardened square not far from the train station, this is a great place to eat. The sociable, intimate *comedor* at the back is filled with chunky wooden tables and stools; the food is quite smart, with a tasty *solomillo con foie* and good house salad among a range of tempting dishes. Recommended.

**¶ Parral**, Canton de San Francisco Javier 4. T945 276 833. This relaxed spot on a sloping street above Calle Cuchillería is a vegetarian restaurant by day and a mood bar by night, with regular live music. There's a salad buffet and a *menú del día* offering significant value.

### Pintxo bars

C Eduardo Dato and the streets crossing it are excellent for the early-evening *pintxo* trail.

**¶¶ Baztertxo**, Plaza de España 14, T945 230 436. A fine bar with some great wines by the glass and top-notch *jamón*. Although service can be beneath the dignity of the staff, it's still a good choice, with a terrace on the square.

**¶¶ Saburdi**, C Eduardo Dato 32, T945 147 016. There are some excellent *pintxo* bars in Vitoria, and this is one of the classics, with a great range of delicious bites. It's warmly lit

and welcoming, with several decent wines by the glass. Recommended.

**¶ Bar El 7**, C Cuchillería 7, T945 272 298. An excellent bar at the head of the Casco Medieval's liveliest street. Its big range of *bocadillos* keeps students and all-comers happy. Order a half if you're not starving; they make 'em pretty large. They also do a very acceptable €9.50 *menú del día*.

**¶ Hala Bedi**, C Cuchillería 98, T945 260 411. A late-opening Basque bar with a cheerful atmosphere. It's very lively, and popular with the young and politically conscious. Out of a tiny kitchen come crêpes with a massive variety of sweet and savoury fillings, as well as sandwiches and other simple dishes.

**¶ Korrokón**, C Cuchillería 9. Tasty cheap food can be had here al fresco courtesy of a good range of simple *raciones*. The *mejillones* (mussels) in spicy tomato sauce are particularly good.

**¶ Restaurante JG**, C Eduardo Dato 27, T945 231 132. Another excellent option for *pintxos* on this pedestrian street – the range of *croquetas* comes highly recommended. More substantial eating is also good value in the *comedor*.

**¶ Taberna**, C San Prudencio 21. Simple dynamics: long bar, tables in the sun, big screen showing sport or films, beer, wine and *pintxos*. It spills onto the street in a happy crowd in summer.

### Cafés

**Café Moderno**, Plaza España 4. Sunseekers should head here in the afternoon – the terrace in the picture-postcard arched square is perfectly placed for maximum rays. The trendy bar does good *pintxos*, and the terrace gets very lively in the evenings as the square packs out with socializing Vitorians.

**Cuatro Azules Florida**, Parque de la Florida. One of Vitoria's best spots, with lots of tables among the trees of this peaceful park. Regular games of *bolas* take place nearby.

**Ferretería Marañón**, Plaza de la Virgen Blanca s/n, T945 133 922. In the heart of Vitoria, this former ironmongers is not to be sneered at if you're on the prowl for a morning coffee and croissant. If you grab a spot on its terrace in the early evening you can truly say you are sitting where it's all happening.

**Sherezade**, C Correría 42, T945 255 868.
This is a relaxed café, well frequented by
students, and serving up good coffee and
a range of *infusiones* (herb and fruit teas).

## Bars and clubs

**Vitoria** *p108, map p110*
The old town tends to have boisterous,
no-frills bars with a Basque atmosphere,
while the new town has a more chic scene.
**Bar Río**, C Eduardo Dato 20, T945 230 067.
A decent café with outdoor tables by day, and
one of the last bars to shut at night, when it
caters to a good-natured gay/straight crowd.
Original live music on Thu nights.
**Café Iguana**, Correría 94, T945 122 837. This
recently-opened spot has a great ambience
for an after-dinner *copa* and a friendly mix
of arty people. Plenty of tables and
well-mixed drinks. One of Vitoria's best.
**Cairo Stereo Club**, C Aldabe 9. Great club
with some excellent and innovative DJs and
a mixed crowd. During the week they often
show cult movies or hold theme parties.
**Chip**, C Prudencio María Verástegui 9,
T945 256 561. Just next to the Artium, this
*discoteca* is popular with a 30-something
crowd. It's relaxed, pleasant, and not too
loud or crowded. Open Fri-Sun nights.
**El Bodegón de Gorbea**, C Herrería 26.
A classic. No-frills bar with rock music, cheap
beer, and a bohemian bunch of friendly
Basques chatting and drinking from early until
very late. On the corner of Canton San Roque.
**Gora**, Canton de San Francisco Javier s/n.
A modern, spacious place just off Calle
Cuchillería, with whimsical decor of an
executive pulling off the work clothes.
Green, light, and peaceful.

## Festivals and events

**Vitoria** *p108, map p110*
**25 Jul** Santiago's day is celebrated as
the Día del Blusa, when colour-
coordinated kids patrol the streets.
**4-9 Aug** Fiesta de la Virgen Blanca, the city's
major knees-up, which is recommended.
**Dec  Advent** Vitoria is known for its
spectacular full-sized Nativity scene
(*Belén*), with over 200 figures.

## Shopping

**Vitoria** *p108, map p110*
**Segunda Mano**, C Prudencio María
Verástegui 14, T945 270 007. This is an
amazing shop selling 2nd-hand goods,
which seems to have everything. From
books to grand pianos, skis to tractors.
You name it, it's likely to be there.

## Transport

**Vitoria** *p108, map p110*
**Air**  Vitoria's airport (VIT) is 8 km northwest
of town. There's a connecting bus service
(€3) that meets flights, running from the
bus station. The airport is served by **Ryanair**
from London Stansted and from Dublin,
and by **Iberia** affiliates from Madrid and
Barcelona. A taxi from the centre will
cost about €15.

**Bus**  The bus station is on the eastern
side of town. Buses to **Bilbao** run about
every 30 mins with **Autobuses La Unión**
(55 mins, €4.80). There are 7-8 buses a day
to **San Sebastián** (1 hr 40 mins, €6.55),
to **Madrid** (€20.65), **Burgos** (€6.61),
**Pamplona** (9-14 daily, €6.50, 1 hr 30 mins)
as well as buses to **Logroño**, **Haro**,
**Laguardia**, **Salvatierra** (€1.80).

**Taxi**  A taxi ride from Vitoria train station
to the Basilica at Armentia costs about €5.

**Train**  The train station, south of town,
has regular connections with **Madrid**,
**Zaragoza**, **Logroño**, **Barcelona**, **Burgos**,
and other destinations.

## Directory

**Vitoria** *p108, map p110*
**Internet**  Link Internet, C San
Antonio 31, T945 130 484, €2.10
per hr, Mon-Fri 1000-1400, 1730-2130,
Sat 1030-1400; Nirvana Net Centre,
C Francia 1, T945 154 043, Mon-Sat
1030-1430, 1700-2200, Sun 1700-2200,
€2.10-2.40 per hr. **Telephone**  There's
a *locutorio* at C Portalón 143, opposite
the archaeological museum.

# Alava Province

*The province of Alava is something of a wilderness compared to the densely settled valleys of Vizcaya and Guipúzcoa. It's the place to come for unspoiled nature; there are some spots of great natural beauty and plenty of scope for hiking and other more specialized outdoor activities. The attractive walled town of Salvatierra is worth a visit and a base for exploring the area. The southern part of the province drops away to sunny plains, part of the Rioja wine region Laguardia; the area's main centre is not to be missed.* ➤➤ *For Sleeping, Eating, and other listings, see pages 119-120.*

## Western Alava ◉ ➤➤ *pp119-120.*

➜ *Colour map 3, B1.*
West of Vitoria the green pastures give way to a rugged and dry terrain, home of vultures, eagles and dramatic rock formations. The area is served by bus from Vitoria.

### Salinas de Añana
This hard-bitten half-a-horse village has one of the more unusual sights in the Basque lands. The place owes its existence to the incredibly saline water that wells up from the ground here, which was diverted down a valley and siphoned into any number of *eras* or pans, flat evaporation platforms mounted on wooden stilts. It's something very different and an eerie sight, looking a little like the ruins of an ancient Greek city in miniature. As many as 5500 pans were still being used by the 1960s but nowadays only about 150 are going concerns. The first written reference to the collection of salt in these parts was in AD 822, but it seems pretty likely the Romans had a go too.

During Semana Santa, Salinas comes to life; Judas is put on trial by the villagers. However, it's something of a kangaroo court as he's always convicted and burned.

### Cañón de Delika
To the west beyond Salinas, and actually reached via the province of Burgos, is this spectacular canyon that widens into the valley of Orduña. The Río Nervión has its source near here and when running, it spectacularly spills 300 m into the gorge below: the highest waterfall in Spain. There's a good 90-minute round walk from the car park. Follow the right-hand road first, which brings you to the falls, then follow the cliffs along to the left, where vultures soar above the valley below. When you reach the second mirador, looking down the valley to Orduña, there's another road that descends through beech forest back to the car park. Near the car park is a spring, the **Fuente de Santiago**. Legend has it that St James stopped here to refresh himself and his horse during his alleged time in Spain. To get to the car park, which is about 3 km from the main road, the 2625 (running from Orduña in the north to Espejo in the south and beyond) turn-off is signposted 'Monte Santiago' and is about 8 km south of Orduña. There are buses to Orduña from Vitoria bus station with **La Unión**.

## Eastern Alava ◉◉ ➤➤ *pp119-120.*

➜ *Colour map 3, B2.*
The eastern half of the Alava plain is dotted with interesting villages, churches and prehistoric remains. The town of Salvatierra is the most convenient base for exploration or walking. At the northern fringes of the plain, the mountains rise into Guipúzcoa. Part of the Camino de Santiago passes through the natural tunnel of San Adrián here.

País Vasco Alava Province

The major town in eastern Alava is the not-very-major Salvatierra (Agurain), a well-preserved, walled medieval town with some interesting buildings. Around Salvatierra there's plenty of walking, canyoning and abseiling to be done, while further afield canoeing, windsurfing, paragliding and horse trekking can be arranged. The sleeping and eating possibilities are nothing to write home about, but there are a couple of *pensiones*, both attached to restaurants. The **tourist office**, on the main street half a block up from the square with the **Iglesia de San Juan**, is very helpful. They currently hold keys for the churches in Salvatierra as well as the marvellous church at Gaceo. Unfortunately, though, they don't have permission to lend the keys to visitors so currently the only option is to pay for a guided tour. A one-hour trip to Gaceo and Alaiza costs €7 per person, with a minimum of two: contact Tura (T945 312535; www.tura.org) for details. Tours run every Tuesday and Thursday, but also by arrangement.

## Túnel de San Adrián and around

One of the most interesting walks starts from the hamlet of Zalduondo, 8 km north of Salvatierra. A section of the **Camino de Santiago**, part of it follows the old Roman/medieval highway that effectively linked most of the peninsula with the rest of Europe. It's about 5.5 km from Zalduondo to a small parking area named **Zumarraundi**. From there, the track ascends through beech forest to the Túnel de San Adrián. Shortly after meeting the old stone road, there's a right turn up a slope that's easy to miss; look for the wooden signpost at the top of the rise to your right. The tunnel is a spectacular natural cave cutting a path through the hill. It now houses a small chapel, perhaps built to assuage the fears of medieval pilgrims, many of whom thought that the cave was the entrance to Hell. After the tunnel, the trail continues into Guipúzcoa, reaching the attractive town of Zegama about 90 minutes' walk further on.

*There are numerous adventure tourism options in the area.*

## Eguilaz

The area around Zalduondo and Salvatierra is also notable for its prehistoric remains; in particular a series of dolmens. Near the village of Eguilaz 45 minutes' walk from Salvatierra (just off the N1 to the east) is the dolmen of **Aitzkomendi**, which was rediscovered by a ploughing farmer in 1830. What happened to the plough is unrecorded, but the 11 impressive stones making up the structure all tip the scales at around the 10-ton mark. It's thought that the dolmen was a funerary marker dating from the early Bronze Age. On weekdays, five buses run to Zalduondo from Vitoria/Salvatierra (destination Araia); two run on Saturday and one on Sunday.

## Sorginetxe and around

On the other side of Salvatierra near Arrizala is the equally impressive Sorginetxe, dated to a similar period. The name means 'house of the witch'; in the Middle Ages when the area was still heavily wooded, it could well have been the forest home of somebody of that profession. To the east of here, near the village of Ilarduia, is the **Leze Cave**, a massive crevice in the cliff face. It's 80 m high and a stream flows from its mouth, making access tricky for casual visitors. It's a good place for canyoning (see **Tura**, under Salvatierra, above).

## Gorbeia

North of Vitoria, straddling Vizcaya and Alava, is the massif of Gorbeia, an enticing and inaccessible area of peaks and gorges topped by the peak of the same name, which hits 1482 m. It features in Basque consciousness as a realm of deities and purity. There are several good marked trails around **Murguia**, including an ascent of the peak itself, which, needless to say, shouldn't be attempted in poor weather.

# La Rioja Alavesa ⊜🎵🎏🅾🗩 ►► pp119-120.

→ *Colour map 3, C2.*

Basque Rioja? What's this? The two words don't seem to associate but in fact many of the finest Riojas are from Alava Province. Confusion reigns because the Spanish province of La Rioja is only one of three that the wine region encompasses. Although it's not far from Vitoria, the Rioja Alavesa definitely feels Spanish rather than Basque; the descent from the green hills into the arid plains crosses a cultural and geographical border. As well as the opportunity to visit some excellent vineyards, the hilltop town of Laguardia is one of the most atmospheric places in Euskadi.

## Laguardia/Biasteri

The small, walled hilltop town of Laguardia commands the plain like a sentinel – which it was. It was originally called La Guardia de Navarra (the guard of Navarra). Underneath the medieval streets, like catacombs, are over 300 small *bodegas*, cellars used for the making and storing of wine, as well as a place to hide in troubled times. Most are no longer used – **Bodega El Fabulista** is a fascinating exception.

Even if wine is put aside for a moment, the town itself is captivating. Founded in 1164, its narrow streets are a lovely place to wander. Traffic is almost prohibited due to the *bodegas* 6 m below. The impressive **Iglesia de Santa María de los Reyes** ① *weekend tours at 1730 and 1830, €2, at other times get keys from tourist office*, begun in the 12th century, has an extraordinarily well-preserved painted Gothic façade, while the former Ayuntamiento on the arched Plaza Nueva was inaugurated in the 16th century under Carlos V.

Laguardia's **tourist office** ① *T945 600 845, www.laguardia-alava.com*, is on Plaza San Juan.

## Around Laguardia

The area around Laguardia also has a few non-vinous attractions. A set of small lakes close by is one of Spain's better spots for birdwatching, particularly from September to March when migrating birds are around. There are a series of marked walking and cycling routes in this area, spectacularly backed by the mountains of the Sierra Cantabrica. Getting there: if you're coming from Vitoria by car, it's marginally quicker and much more scenic to take the smaller A2124 rather than the motorway. After ascending to a pass, the high ground dramatically drops away to the Riojan plain; there's a superb lookout on the road, justly known as 'El Balcón' (the balcony).

---

# Wineries

## Bodegas Palacio

① *Ctra de Elciego s/n, T945 621 195, www.cosmepalacio.com, tours Tue-Fri 1300, Sat 1230 and 1330, €3 (redeemable in shop or restaurant); booking essential.*

*All bodegas require a phone call in advance to organize a visit; the more of you there are, the more willing most will be.*

One of the handiest of the wineries, and worth seeing, is **Bodegas Palacio**, located just below Laguardia on the Elciego road, some 10 minutes' walk from town. The winery is modern; the older *bodega* alongside having been charmingly converted into a hotel and restaurant. *Palacio* produces a range of wines, the quality of which has increased in recent years. Their *Glorioso* and *Cosme Palacio* labels are widely sold in the UK.

🍷 *Laguardia was the birthplace of the fable writer Félix de Samaniego.*

País Vasco  Alava Province

The winery was originally founded in 1894 and is fairly typical of the area, producing 90% red wine from the Tempranillo grape, and a small 10% of white from Viura (as well as *crianzas*, *reservas* and *gran reservas*, see box, page 210). Palacio also produce a red wine for drinking young, which is soft, fruity and a nice change from the heavier Rioja styles.

## Bodega El Fabulista

① *Plaza San Juan s/n, Laguardia, T945 621 192. Tours daily at 1130, 1300 and 1730, €5.*
A massive contrast to Palacio, which produces two million bottles a year, is **Bodega El Fabulista**, next to the tourist office in Laguardia. Eusebio, the owner, effectively runs the place alone and produces about 1/50th of that amount. The wine is made using very traditional methods in the intriguing underground cellar from grapes he grows himself. The wines, marketed as *Decidido*, are a good young-drinking red and white. He runs three tours a day, which are excellent and include lots of background information on the Rioja wine region and a generous tasting in a beautiful underground vault.

## Herederos del Marqués de Riscal

① *C Torrea 1, Elciego, T945 180 888, www.marquesderiscal.com, multilingual tours Tue-Sat 1000, 1230, 1600, Sun 1100 and 1300, €6, reserve in advance.*
Founded in 1860, Marqués de Riscal is the oldest and best known of the Rioja *bodegas* and has built a formidable reputation for the quality of its wines. The Marqués himself was a Madrid journalist who, having cooled off in France after getting in some hot political water at home, returned to Spain and started making wine. Enlisting the help of Monsieur Pinot, a French expert, he experimented by planting Cabernet Sauvignon, which is still used in the wines today.

The innovative spirit continues, and Marqués de Riscal enlisted none other than Frank Gehry of Guggenheim museum fame to design their new visitors' complex, a visual treat of a building which opened in 2006. Gehry's design incorporates ribbons of coloured titanium over a building of natural stone. The silver, gold and "dusty rose" sheets are Gehry's response to "the unbroken landscape of vineyards and rich tones". The building incorporates a hotel, a restaurant, and an oenotherapy spa, which combines water treatments with applications of grape and vine extracts.

The winery is modern but remains faithful to the *bodega*'s rigorous tradition of quality. As well as their traditionally elegant *Reserva* and *Gran Reserva*, the more recently inaugurated *Baron de Chirel* is a very classy red indeed, coming from low-yielding old vines and exhibiting a more French character than is typical of the region.

Buses from Vitoria to Logroño via Elciego pass through here and Laguardia, which is 7 km away.

## Other wineries

North of Laguardia, with a waved design echoing the steep mountains behind it, is the new **Ysios Bodega** ① *T945 600 640*, designed by Santiago Calatrava, the brilliant Valencian engineer/architect who seems to have made Euskal Herría his second home. Check with the tourist office for visiting times.

Twenty minutes east of Laguardia is the pretty but parched town of Oyón/Oion. One of the bigger operations here is **Bodegas Faustino Martínez** ① *T945 622 500*, whose range of Faustino wines are a reliable and popular choice both in Spain and the UK. Although not as geared to visitors as might be expected, they run a good tour of their operation in Spanish or English. The tour is all the better for being a bit more in-depth and a little less cursory than some of the other big wineries, but it's thirsty work with no tasting at the end (unless you specifically request a tasting session). Oyon has an excellent restaurant to alleviate this (see Eating, below).

## ● Sleeping

### Salvatierra *p116*

**D Mendiaxpe**, Barrio Salsamendi 22, Asparrena, T945 304 212. Cleverly located in the wooded foothills of the Sierra de Urkilla, this is a superb base for walking in the area. There's use of a kitchen but no meals available except breakfast. The 3 en suite rooms are lovely and light.

**D Merino**, Plaza de San Juan 3, T945 300 052. One of 2 unremarkable *pensiones* in Salvatierra, it offers a *menú del día* in its restaurants.

**E José Mari**, C Mayor 73, T945 300 042. The other unremarkable *pensión*, is above a solid local café with an attached restaurant doing a decent-value daytime and evening *menú* for €8.50. Smiles can sometimes cost extra.

### La Rioja Alavesa *p117*

There are some excellent places to stay in Laguardia.

**LL Hotel Marqués de Riscal**, T945 180 880, C Torrea 1, Elciego, www.starwoodhotels.com This flamboyant structure is visible from afar and is your chance to stay in a Frank Gehry-designed building. The exuberant waves of metal conceal a modern building made from traditional stone. The rooms are, as you'd expect at this price, well designed if not enormous, and have appealingly offbeat shapes and features. You'll get better rates from the website the farther in advance you book. There's also a fine gourmet restaurant here.

**AL Castillo El Collado**, Paseo El Collado 1, Laguardia, T945 621 200, F621 022. Decorated in plush but colourful style, this mansion at the north end of the old town is comfortable and welcoming and has a good, reasonably priced restaurant.

**A Posada Mayor de Migueloa**, C Mayor 20, Laguardia, T945 621 175, www.mayorde migueloa.com. A beautifully decorated Spanish country house, with lovely old wooden furniture and a peaceful atmosphere. Rooms are heated and a/c. The restaurant is of a similarly high standard.

**B Hotel Antigua Bodega de Don Cosme Palacio**, Carretera Elciego s/n, Laguardia, T945 621 195, antiguabodega@cosme palacio .com. A wine-lover's delight. The old **Palacio Bodega** has been converted into a charming hotel and restaurant, adjacent to

the modern winery. The sunny rooms are named after grape varieties, and come with a free ½ bottle. Most rooms feature views over the vines and mountains beyond and have a/c to cope with the fierce summer heat. The rates are reasonable too.

**D Hostal Biazteri**, C Berberana 2, Laguardia, T941 600 026, biazteri@jazzfree.com. Run by the owners of the bar on the corner, this is a very airy and pleasant place to stay, newly fitted and furnished. Rooms are spacious, comfortable and reasonably priced. Breakfast included.

**D-E Larretxori**, Portal de Páganos s/n, Laguardia, T/F945 600 763, larretxori@ euskalnet.net. This comfortable *agroturismo* is just outside the city walls and commands excellent views over the area. The rooms are spruce, clean and good value and the owner is very benevolent.

## ● Eating

### La Rioja Alavesa *p117*

**♦♦♦ Mesón La Cueva**, Concepción 15, Oyón (La Rioja), T945 601 022. If you're visiting wineries over this way, a hearty lunch here is in order. It's a place with a lofty and deserved reputation in the heart of the village, with a new upstairs *comedor* which is light and airy, a significant improvement. The *menú* is €20 but features some excellent Riojan staples, such as *pochas* (young broad beans) and other hearty stews. Recommended.

**♦♦ Castillo El Collado**, Paseo El Collado 1, Laguardia, T945 621 200. There's an excellent, well-priced restaurant in this beautiful fortified hotel at the northern end of Laguardia.

**♦♦ El Bodegón**, Travesía Santa Engracia 3, Laguardia, T945 600 793. Tucked away in the middle of old Laguardia is this cosy restaurant, with a €11 *menú del día* focusing on the hearty staples of the region, such as *pochas* (beans), or *patatas con chorizo*.

**♦♦ Marixa**, C Sancho Abarca s/n, Laguardia, T945 600 165. In the **Hotel Marixa**, the dining room boasts great views over the vine-covered plains below and has a range of local specialities with formally correct Spanish service.

# ♫ Bars and clubs

**La Rioja Alavesa** *p117*
**Café Tertulia**, C Mayor 70, Laguardia.
With couches, padded booths and a pool
table, this is the best place for a few quiet
drinks in Laguardia.

# ○ Shopping

**Laguardia** *p117*
**La Vinoteca**, Pl Mayor 1, T945 621 213.
A worthwhile wine shop in the centre
of town.

# ⊖ Transport

**Salinas de Añana** *p115*
**Bus** There are 5 buses daily from
**Vitoria** bus station.

**Salvatierra** *p116*
**Bus** There are buses hourly from
**Vitoria**'s bus station to Salvatierra,
run by **Burundesa** (€1.80, 40 mins).

**Gorbeia** *p116*
**Bus** There are 4-5 daily buses to
Murguia from **Vitoria**'s bus station

**La Rioja Alavesa** *p117*
**Bus** There are 3-4 daily buses to Laguardia
from **Vitoria** bus station (1 hr 45 mins,
€5.90). These run via **Haro** and proceed
to **Elciego** and **Logroño**. There's one daily
bus from **Bilbao** that stops here (1 hr 45
mins, €9.25), but no return service; you'd
have to go to **Vitoria** or **Logroño**.

# Navarra

## Footprint features

# Introduction

Navarra was for many centuries a small independent kingdom, and an important player in the complex diplomacy of the period. These days as a semi-autonomous province with the same boundaries, it preserves that independent feeling and has plenty of pride in its history. Although fairly small (it's about half the size of Wales or Massachusetts), it's stuffed full of things to see, from the awe-inspiring Pyrenees to dusty, castled plains and sun-drenched wine country.

The Navarra Pyrenees are beautiful, if not quite as spectacular as those further to the east. A series of remote valleys make intriguing places to explore, summer pastureland for generations of cowherds from both sides of the border.

The principal route of the pilgrims to Santiago, the Camino Francés, crosses Navarra from east to west and has left a sizeable endowment of some of the peninsula's finest religious architecture. Entering the province at Roncesvalles, where Charlemagne's rearguard was given a nasty Basque bite, it continues through small attractive towns like Estella and Viana. It's not all hard work; at one lunching stop there's a drinking fountain that spouts red wine.

In the midst of all is Pamplona, a pleasant and sober town which goes berserk for nine days in July for the Fiesta de los Sanfermines, of which the best-known event is the daily *encierro*, or running of the bulls, made famous by Hemingway and more recently by thousands of wine-swilling locals and tourists looking scared on television every year.

The south of Navarra is much more Castilian; sun-baked and dotted with castles, it produces some hearty red wines and some of Spain's best vegetables along the banks of the Río Ebro.

★ **Don't miss...**

1 **Los Sanfermines** Run with the bulls in Pamplona or just watch others run, then enjoy Europe's biggest party, page 128.

2 **Roncal Valley** Walk into the Pyrenees along this beautiful flower-filled valley, page 133.

3 **Roncesvalles** Set out on the long walk to Santiago from this stern monastic complex in a trout-filled valley, page 135.

4 **Zugarramurdi** Sniff out the taint of heresy in this hotbed of witches, page 137.

5 **San Salvador de Leyre** Stop off at one of the north's noblest monasteries, idyllically set among perfumed hills, page 141.

6 **Estella** Follow the pilgrims to this historic town with its fine Romanesque architecture, page 144.

Navarra

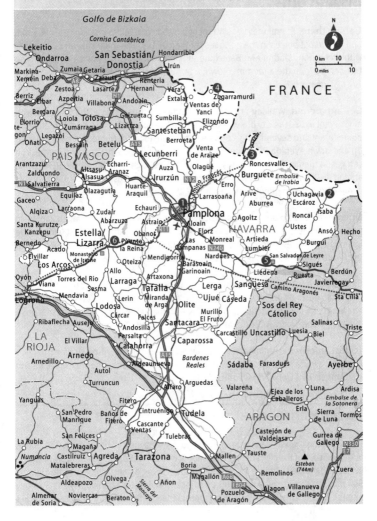

# Pamplona/Iruña

→ *Phone code: 948. Colour map 3, B4. Population: 193,328. Altitude: 444 m.*

*Pamplona, the capital of Navarra, conjures images of wild drunken revelry and stampeding bulls. And rightly so; for that is exactly what happens for nine days every July, Los Sanfermines. Love it or hate it, if you're around you have to check it out. At other times Pamplona is quite a subdued but picturesque city, its high-walled old town very striking when it's approached from below. It's a good place to stop over, with plenty of good accommodation and eating options; you can do pintxos Basque style or sit down to a huge Castilian roast! It's also the hub for all transport in Navarra, so expect to pass through a few times if you're exploring the province by bus.* ▸▸ *For Sleeping, Eating and other listings, see pages 129-133.*

## Ins and outs

**Getting there** Pamplona is easily reached by bus or train from major cities in Spain and from most places in the northeast of the country. There are several daily flights with *Iberia* from Madrid and Barcelona to Pamplona airport, 7 km away. There's no bus service from the airport into town; a taxi will cost about €8. ▸▸ *See Transport, page 133, for further details.*

**Getting around** Walking around Pamplona is the best option; the only time you might want to use the city buses is to reach the Hospitales district where the stadium, planetarium and several hotels and *pensiones* are located. Numerous buses plough up and down Avenida Pío XII connecting the Hospitales district with the centre. You can get on them at Avenida Carlos III, near Plaza del Castillo (€0.82). The **RENFE** train station is inconveniently situated a couple of kilometres north of town, but is connected every 10 minutes by bus.

**Orientation** Pamplona is an easy city to get the hang of: the walled old town perches over the plain above the Río Arga. To the south and west stretch the Ensanches, the newer town, which radiates outwards along avenues beginning near the Ciudadela, a large bastion turned public park.

**Best time to visit** Los Sanfermines are the best time to visit for atmosphere; it's difficult to describe just how big a party it is. Whatever you do, don't visit immediately afterwards (ie mid- to late July); everything's shut and the city seems sunk in a post-alcoholic depression. ▸▸ *See also the boxes on page 128 and 132.*

**Tourist information** Pamplona has an excellent **tourist office** ① *Plaza de San Francisco s/n, T48 420 420, Mon-Sat 1000-1400, 1600-1900, Sun 1000-1400; during Los Sanfermines daily 0800-2000.*

## Background

The Pamplona area was probably settled by Basques, who gave it the name Iruña/Iruñea, but the city's definitive founding was by the Roman general Pompey, who set up a base here around 74 BC while campaigning against the renegade Quintus Sertorius, who had set himself up as a local warlord. No shrinking violet, Pompey named the city after himself (Pompeiopolis). The city flourished due to its important

## The kingdom of Navarra

While the area has been populated for millennia, the historical entity of Navarra emerged in the ninth century after periods of Basque, Roman, Visigothic, Moorish and Frankish control. The Kingdom of Navarra emerged as part of the Reconquista, the Christian battle to drive the Moors southwards and out of the peninsula. Under the astute rulership of King Sancho III in the early 11th century, Navarra was unified with Castilla and Aragón, which meant that Sancho ruled an area extending from the Mediterranean right across to Galicia; not for nothing is he known as 'the Great'. After his death things began to disintegrate, and provinces were lost left, right but not centre until in 1200 it had roughly the boundaries it has today, but including Basse-Navarre, now in France. In 1512, King Fernando of Aragón (who then Regent of Castilla following his wife's death) invaded Navarra and took it easily.

In the 19th century, after centuries of relative peace, things kicked off, first with Napoleon's invasion, then with the rise of the liberal movement and Carlism. These events were always likely to cause schisms in the province, which already had natural divisions between mountains and plains, and families who were Basque, French, or Spanish in alignment. Navarra became the centre of Carlism and suffered the loss of most of its rights as a result of that movement's defeat. During the Civil War, the Carlists, still strong, were on Franco's side; as a result the province was favoured during his rule, in contrast to the other Basque provinces, which had taken the Republican side.

Today, as a semi-autonomous province, the divisions continue; many Basques are striving for the union of Navarra with Euskadi, but the lowland towns are firmly aligned with Spain. Navarra's social and political differences are mirrored in its geography; it is (to use a cliché) 'a land of contrasts'. The northern and eastern parts of the province are dominated by the Pyrenees and its offshoots, and are lands of green valleys and shepherd villages, which are culturally very Basque. The baking southern and central plains seem to reflect the dusty days of the Reconquista and are more Castilian Spanish in outlook and nature.

position at the peninsula's doormat, but was sacked time and again by Germanic tribes. After a period of Visigothic control, it was taken by the Moors in AD 711, although the inhabitants were allowed to remain Christian. There was more territorial exchange and debate before the final emergence of the Kingdom of Pamplona in the ninth century. Sacked and destroyed by the feared caliph of Córdoba Abd-al-Rahman in AD 924, the city only gradually recovered, hampered by squabbling between its municipalities.

Pamplona's rise to real prominence ironically came when Navarra was conquered by Castilla; Fernando built the city walls and made it the province's capital. After a turbulent 19th century, Pamplona expanded rapidly through the 20th century, necessitating the development of successive *Ensanches* (suburbs) south and west of the old centre.

# Sights

## Plaza del Castillo

At the southern entrance to the old town is the pedestrianized Plaza del Castillo, centre of much of the city's social life. Before the Plaza de Toros was built, the bullfights were held in this square. Behind the square to the east is the famous cobbled **Estafeta**, the main runway for the bulls during Los Sanfermines; it's lined with shops and bars. It's amazing how narrow it can look when six bulls are charging down it towards you.

## Cathedral and around

*① T948 224 667, cathedral and museum, Mon-Sat 1000-1330, 1600-1900 (1800 in winter and closed Sat pm), €4.*

The quiet, seemingly deserted part of town east of the Plaza del Castillo is dominated

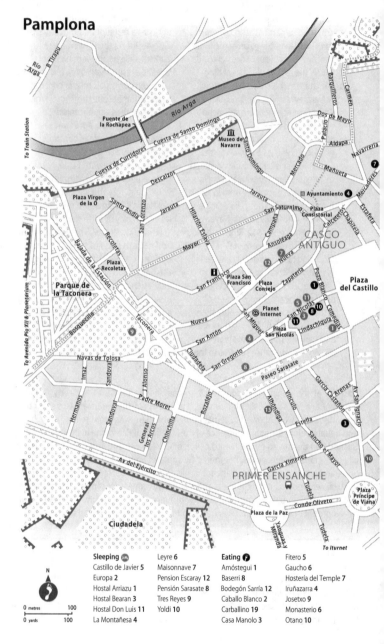

# Pamplona

**Sleeping** 😴

| | |
|---|---|
| Castillo de Javier **5** | Leyre **6** |
| Europa **2** | Maisonnave **7** |
| Hostal Arriazu **1** | Pension Escaray **12** |
| Hostal Bearan **3** | Pensión Sarasate **8** |
| Hostal Don Luis **11** | Tres Reyes **9** |
| La Montañesa **4** | Yoldi **10** |

**Eating** 🍴

| | |
|---|---|
| Amóstegui **1** | Fitero **5** |
| Baserri **8** | Gaucho **6** |
| Bodegón Sarría **12** | Hostería del Temple **7** |
| Caballo Blanco **2** | Iruñazarra **4** |
| Carballino **19** | Josetxo **9** |
| Casa Manolo **3** | Monasterio **6** |
| | Otano **10** |

N

0 metres 100
0 yards 100

by the cathedral. Don't be daunted by the rather austere 18th-century façade, as the interior is a masterpiece of delicate Gothic work. Facing the front, the entrance is up the street to your right. First stop is the gorgeous cloister, a superb space full of delicate harmony with excellent carved reliefs on some of the doorways leading off it. The cathedral itself, which is similarly impressive, houses the tombs of Carlos III ('the noble') of Navarra and his queen. The **Diocesan museum** is located in what used to be the larder, kitchen and dining room, and now holds a reasonably interesting selection of artefacts.

Behind the cathedral, past the shady **Plaza de San José**, is the tranquil corner of **El Caballo Blanco**, named after the inviting bar/restaurant that looks over the ramparts. Walking down the east wall from here you'll reach the **Plaza de Santa María la Real**, another peaceful spot, overlooked by the archbishop's palace.

## Plaza Consistorial and around

The centre of town is occupied by the small Plaza Consistorial, seat of the pretty Baroque **Ayuntamiento**, where the crowd gathers to watch the start of Los Sanfermines. Down the hill from here, near the market, is the impressive **Museo de Navarra** ① *Tue-Sat 0930-1400, 1700-1900, Sun 1100-1400; restricted opening during Los Sanfermines; €2, free on Sat afternoon and Sun*, set in a stately former convent hospital. The museum contains a wide range of material, from prehistoric remains on the ground floor through to modern Navarrese art at the top. There are a few Goyas, as well as much religious art that has been gathered from the many provincial churches and monasteries.

## Primer Ensanche

The Primer Ensanche, the city's earliest expansion, lies immediately to the south of Plaza del Castillo. The Avenida de San Ignacio has a statue depicting the saint, founder of the Jesuit order, wounded while defending the city; the wounds more or less led to his conversion. This avenue ends at the busy **Plaza Príncipe de Viana**; a short way to the west, the bus station stands on the offbeat **Plaza de la Paz**. Beyond the old town, in the Primer Ensanche, stretches the pentagonal wall of the **Ciudadela**, a low military bastion constructed by Felipe II; it houses a chapel and a small arms exhibition. The newer parts of town south of here are blessed with plenty of green space.

*Navarra Pamplona/Iruña*

Sarasate 11        Tropicana 17

**Bars & clubs** 🎵
Ertz 14
La Gruta 15
Okapi 16        Camino de Santiago ·····
Toki Leza 13

# Fiesta de San Fermín

Better known in English as the 'running of the bulls', the nine-day Fiesta de San Fermín lays a serious claim to being the biggest party in Europe. The city goes completely *loca*, and the streets and bars burst with locals and tourists clad traditionally in white with red neckscarves, downing beer and wine with abandon while dancing to the music pumping from a dozen different sources.

It's quite possible to lose a week of your life here and never set eyes on a bull, but it's the *encierros* (bull-runnings) that add the spice. It's difficult to imagine many other country allowing over three tons of bullflesh to plough through a crowd of drunken citizens, but it happens here at 0800 every morning of the fiesta. The streets are barricaded and six bulls are released to run from their *corral* to the Plaza de Toros. If they keep in formation and don't get panicked or distracted they'll only take three minutes to cover the course, but if they find a buttock or two to gore along the way, they can be on the streets for ten minutes or more. Rockets are let off; the first is single and signals the release of the bulls; the next, a double, means that they've all left the corral; and the triple is fired after they've arrived at the bullring and have been safely penned. For good measure, a few cows (with covered horns) are then released into the ring. They always toss a few people, to the amusement of the large crowd gathered in the seats. That evening the bulls are fought in the daily *corrida*.

The festival kicks off each year on 6 July at the Ayuntamiento, with a rocket (*El Chupinazo*) fired at midday and cries of '¡Viva San Fermín!'. The saint himself was a Roman convert to Christianity who became the first bishop of Pamplona. Pushing his luck, he travelled to Gaul to convert the descendants of Asterix and Obelix to the faith. They had his head. The day proceeds with a procession of larger than life papier mâché headed figures (*cabezudos y gigantes*) who parade through town scaring children. 7 July is the biggest day with the first *encierro* and the most revellers, but there are plenty of things going on all week, with live bands, processions, street performers, fireworks and more. Especially noticeable are the *peñas*, large social clubs that travel the length and breadth of Spain to find a party. Loud, boisterous and equipped with their own brass section, their colourful parades are a feature of the week.

When you come to Los Sanfermines, give it a little time. It can be overwhelming at first, and there's plenty to dislike: the stench of stale beer and urine, crowds, inflated prices... but it's enjoyable and addictive. It's also very easy to get away from the hectic atmosphere – walk a few streets into the new town, and you can mix with jovial locals enjoying an equally good-natured, but more civilized, party.

One of the best aspects of the festival is that, despite the tourism, it's still a fiesta with a strong local flavour. How the city keeps functioning is a mystery, as bleary bank tellers struggle to stay awake after being out all night. While things are busiest from 1900, it's great to wander around during the day, seeking out little pockets of good-time in the quiet backstreets. It's a time for family and friends to get together too; you'll see long tables set up in unlikely places for massive al fresco meals.

The festival finally ends at midnight on 14 July, again at the Ayuntamiento, with a big crowd chanting the 'Pobre de mí' (poor me), mourning the end of the fiesta. For practical information, see box, page 132.

Back on the edge of the old town, the **Plaza de Toros** is the first thing you see after winding up the Bajada de Labrit into town from the Puente de la Magdalena, where
the pilgrims cross the river. It's no exaggeration to say that Hemingway's novel *Fiesta*
(*The Sun Also Rises*) has had a massive impact on Pamplona's prosperity over the
years, so it's fitting that there's a bust of him in front of the ring – the street outside is
also named after him.

## ⊜ Sleeping

**Pamplona** *p124, map p126*

There are scores of budget options around
the old town and along Av Pío XII in the
Hospitales district; look for signs saying
'*camas*' above bars and restaurants.
The codes given here do not apply for
San Fermín, when prices are typically
at least trebled. At other times, finding
accommodation is never a problem.
**La Perla**, the hotel where Hemingway
stayed, is currently being converted to 5-star
status and will be shut until mid-2007.
**L Tres Reyes**, C Taconera s/n, T948 226 600,
www.hotel3reyes.com. Pamplona's stellar
hotel is on the edge of the old town and
predictably geared for conferences. This
means that there are excellent facilities,
plenty of staff on call, and weekend rates
that are very good value, up to 50%
cheaper with advance booking.
**AL Hotel Europa**, C Espoz y Mina 11,
T948 221 800, www.hreuropa.com. If there
is a hint of the self-satisfied about this place,
they have good reason, with a small and
superbly located hotel just off the Plaza
del Castillo, and with balconies overlooking
C Estafeta (the main drag of the bull-running).
The restaurant is also one of the better
ones in town.
**AL Maisonnave**, C Nueva 20, T948 222 600,
www.hotelmaisonnave.es. A sleek but
friendly modern hotel with comfortable
furnishings, a decent café and a sauna for
Finnophiles. The a/c rooms are equipped
with every comfort and are pretty good
value for this type of facility, with some
good out-of-season specials.
**B Hotel Leyre**, C Leyre 7, T948 228 500,
www.hotel-leyre.com. Although furnished in
fairly unimaginative 3-star standard style, this
hotel is close to the bullring and offers plenty
of comfort and facilities. It's handy for both

the old and new towns, and offers
very good and notably friendly service.
**B Hotel Yoldi**, Av San Ignacio 11, T948 224
800, www.hotelyoldi.com. Hemingway
stayed here after his friend Juanito Quintana
lost his hotel during the Civil War. It happily
offers modern comforts with surprisingly
reasonable prices. The rooms are a/c and
spacious, if a little unimaginatively furnished.
They have good facilities, including CD player.
**C Hostal Arriazu**, C Comedias 14, T948 210
202, www.hostalarriazu.com. Decorated
with a sure touch, this *hostal* is a delightful
surprise very close to the Plaza del Castillo.
The lovely rooms have polished parquet
floors and firm commodious beds. The
management is very hospitable, and
guests can relax in a beautifully furnished
lounge area. Recommended.
**C Hotel Castillo de Javier**, C San Nicolás 50,
T948 203 040, www.hotelcastillodejavier.com.
This new hotel has a great central location
right on eat street. It's decorated with a light
modern touch; the rooms are smallish but
comfortable, with funky modern art on
the walls. There are several nice touches
throughout, and the rooms have TV and
telephone; for a little more cash you can
have a hydromassage shower in the
bathroom. Downstairs there's a café/bar
and one room is equipped for the disabled.
**D Hostal Bearan**, C San Nicolás 25, T948 223
428. One of several options on this street,
the Bearan has spacious doubles with good
bathrooms. The rooms are fairly unadorned,
and definitely not great value for singles, but
for 2, the location and price are reasonable.
**D Hostal Don Luis**, C San Nicolás 24, T948
210 499. Despite a ragged exterior and
dodgy staircase, this central option is very
comfortable and well-furnished. The double
rooms have colourful pastel walls, attractive

● *For an explanation of the sleeping and eating price codes used in this guide, see inside the*
● *front cover. Other relevant information is found in Essentials pages 39-46.*

129*Navarra* Pamplona/Iruña Listings

fittings and comfy sofa. If there's no-one about, ask in the café of the same name up the street near the Plaza del Castillo.

**E Pensión Sarasate**, Paseo Sarasate 30, T948 223 084, pensionsarasate@wanadoo.es. A small, quiet and friendly *pensión* with well cared-for rooms in the heart of things. This is one of Pamplona's best budget options. The rooms vary; some have balcony; all are decorated in a cheerful and homely style. Recommended.

**E-F Pensión Escaray**, C Nueva 24, T948 227 825. This simple little place is a likeable basic budget option. Run by a solicitous mother-son combination, it has clean and fairly unadorned rooms with shared bathroom. There's a fair difference in quality between the rooms on the 2 different floors.

**F La Montañesa**, C San Gregorio 2, T948 224 380. This old *fonda* has comfortable if basic rooms with shared bathroom above a restaurant on this busy evening street. It's simple and likeable, run by a charming old Navarran lady, but there's little luxury.

### Camping

**Ezcaba**, Ctra N121 Km 7, on the road to Irún, T948 330 315. The closest campsite to Pamplona, with a pool and a few caravans. It's absolutely packed during Los Sanfermines, music festival style.

### 🔅 Eating

**Pamplona** *p124, map p126*

🍴🍴🍴 **Josetxo**, Plaza Principe de Viana 1, T948 222 097. One of Pamplona's most refined restaurants, with wines to match. The *txangurro* (spider crab) stuffed in its own shell is one of a number of outstanding dishes. Closed Sun and Aug.

🍴🍴🍴 **Amóstegui**, C Pozo Blanco 20, T948 224 327. An unglamorous upstairs restaurant that happens to serve some of the nicest mid-priced food in Pamplona. Try some fresh asparagus or artichokes if they're in season, but only go for the fresh foie gras if you fancy something seriously rich.

🍴🍴 **Casa Manolo**, C García Castañon 12, T948 225 102. A dependable 2nd floor restaurant proudly presenting Navarran specialities like *pichón estofado con pochas* (braised pigeon with beans). Good service.

🍴🍴 **Hostería del Temple**, C Curia 3, T948 225 171. A cosy bar and restaurant guarded by a suit of armour and serving some reasonably priced fresh fish and delicious steak; there's also a good-value *menú del día*. Famous for its *moscovita pintxo*, a fried piece of ham, egg and cheese invented by a bloke from Moscow who's a regular here. Closed Sun.

🍴🍴 **Otano**, C San Nicolás 5, T948 227 036. Although you're sometimes left wondering whether style or substance takes precedence here, it's a nice spot, recently re-decorated, with tables overlooking one of Pamplona's livelier weekend streets. It specializes in its roast meats, but if there's *rodaballo* (turbot) about, definitely consider it. The bar downstairs is great, with friendly service and tasty *pintxos*. The *tortilla* is superb.

🍴 **Baserri**, C San Nicolás 32, T948 222 021. This popular chess-board patterned restaurant serves a good value *menú del día* (€10.70) daily except Sun and nightly except Fri and Sat. A more elaborate menu is served at other times. The bar does a good range of *pintxos*.

🍴 **Bodegón Sarría**, C Estafeta 52, T948 227 713. Rows of quality hams hanging from the ceiling; you can try *pintxos* at the bar or sit at the wooden tables and snack on *raciones* which also include tripe and stews.

🍴 **Caballo Blanco**, Rincón del Caballo Blanco s/n. Pamplona's nicest spot, a fantastic location tucked into a quiet corner of the city walls with views over the ramparts. The bar serves some good food in a beautiful stone building, but the beer garden is the place to hang out. Closed Jan/Feb. Superbly peaceful.

🍴 **Carballino**, C Los Teobaldos 2, T948 224 895. A smart modern *pulpería* serving good calamari and octopus with a minimum of fuss and a Galician flair. It's a little away from the hectic centre and can be a good escape during Los Sanfermines.

🍴 **Fitero**, C Estafeta 58, T948 222 006. Award- winning bites on the main drag, which include an excellent spinach and prawn *croqueta*.

🍴 **Gaucho**, C Espoz y Mina. A buzzy little corner bar with good *pintxos* and strong coffee. It's always busy; there's a great variety of beautifully elaborate fare on the bar.

🍴 **Iruñazarra**, C Mercaderes 15, T948 225 167. This spacious and convivial Basque tavern has been going for ages. It's a top spot to eat cheap *raciones* at tables at the back; you can accompany them with cider poured from a big barrel. There's a cheerful mixture of young and old.

**Monasterio**, C Espoz y Mina. Next door to **Gaucho**, this lacks nothing by comparison; it's longer, more brightly lit and more modern in feel but has equally fine snacks, all labelled.

**Sarasate**, C San Nicolás 19, T948 225 727. (Not to be confused with its namesake, until its recent closure one of the heartiest meat restaurants in Navarra.) This cheerful vegetarian restaurant will appeal to all-comers with its cheap and imaginative offerings.

## ♠ Bars and clubs

**Pamplona** *p124, map p126*
The streets in the western part of the old town are full of bars, while C Calderería, C Carmen and around have a vibrant Basque social scene.

**Ertz**, C Tejería 40, T948 222 362. A trendy, mixed crowd fill this place Thu-Sun nights.

**La Gruta**, C Estafeta 36. A well-named cellar bar, which can get mighty stuffy when a crowd's packed in.

**Okapi**, Plaza El Castillo 11, T948 211 572. A bar that serves up quiet *pintxos* and *raciones* by day and kicks off at weekend nights and during Los Sanfermines. Regular live music.

**Toki Leza**, C Calderería 5, T948 229 584. Long and simple, this wood and brick bar is one of the liveliest around. It's Basque in sympathies and atmosphere, and has live music every Sun.

**Tropicana**, Plaza del Castillo s/n. The best option on the main square, with good cold beer and down-to-earth attitudes.

**Zona Límite**, C Intxaurdia s/n, T948 331 554. Hop in a taxi for this club, which doesn't open until 2400. Loud partytime sounds.

## ⊙ Entertainment

**Pamplona** *p124, map p126*
For bullfights, see box, page 128.

### Cinema and theatre
**Cines Carlos III**, C Cortes de Navarra. The handiest cinema for the old town.

**Teatro Gayarre**, Av Carlos III 3, T948 220 139. This noble old theatre doesn't see as much action as in its heyday, but still has regular shows.

### Football
Pamplona's football team, **Osasuna**, are a hardworking and passionately supported *Primera Liga* club; it's one of the nicer places to go and see a game in Spain, but wrap up well. They play at **Reyno de Navarra** (formerly El Sadar) stadium south of the city; you can get there by taking bus 5 from Av Carlos III near Plaza Castilla. Tickets are €30-50 and are on sale office hours at the stadium a couple of days before the match, as well as 2 hrs before kick-off.

## ⊛ Festivals and events

**Pamplona** *p124, map p126*
See **San Fermín** boxes, pages 128 and 132.

## ⊙ Shopping

**Pamplona/Iruña** *p124, map p126*
**Foto Auma**, Plaza del Castillo. During Los Sanfermines, this photography shop has excellent photos of that day's *encierro* available for €4 a shot.

**Librería Abarzuza**, C Santo Domingo 29, T948 213 213, sells decent maps of the city.

## ▲ Activities and tours

**Pamplona** *p124, map p126*
This list covers activities and tours for the entire province.

**Bideak**, Plaza del Castillo 28, T948 221 773, www.bideak@navarraactiva.com. An association of tour operators who will find the company that does what you want done, from architectural tours to canoeing and horse-trekking.

**Ekia**, Camping Osate, Ochagavia, T948 890 184. A friendly set-up organizing mountain activities in Navarra's eastern Pyrenees.

**Roncal Escuela de Esqui**, Ctra General s/n, Izaba, T948 893 266, www.roncaleski.com. A ski school in the Roncal valley running courses in cross-country and downhill skiing for all levels.

## Los Sanfermines: party protocol

**Accommodation** Prices literally triple during the fiesta, and rooms should be booked several months in advance. If you're too late, don't worry; there are rooms available on an impromptu basis – check noticeboards at the bus and train stations, the tourist office and the newspaper. The official campsite is packed, but more secure than the free areas set up by the council to the east of town. If all else fails, sleep out – you'll be in good company and there are plenty of green areas south of the centre or under the walls. The other option is to get a room out of town, party all night and crawl back on the bus in the morning. It's much easier to get rooms for later in the fiesta than for the first few days.

**Bulls** Even if you aren't going to run, come prepared to: staring down the barrel of a drink at 0400 it may suddenly seem like an excellent idea. Wear decent shoes; the cobbled streets are slippery, even before they hose them down. Walk the course beforehand and pick a sensible place to start your run. The tight corner at the bottom of Calle Estafeta is where most carnage occurs, with bulls and people slipping all over the shop. Get there well before the start; women should keep a lowish profile, as the police still aren't too keen for non- males to run. Carry something disposable – chucking a cap or a newspaper can distract a bull if you're in trouble. Don't try to attract a bull's attention; once separated from the herd they are far more dangerous. It's much better to run later in the week; on the first two days there are too many people falling over each other. Try to watch an *encierro* so you've got an idea of what goes on. Above all, respect the bulls as the large, fast, lethal animals they are. People often get seriously injured, occasionally fatally. If you're not from the EU, remember that your travel insurer will probably laugh if you try to claim medical expenses for a horn wound.

**Pitching a spot** Watching the *encierro* can be an anti-climax. It's tough to get a good spot and even if you get one, you may not see much; it's often all over in a blur. The best spots are the private balconies along Calle Estafeta, but you'll have to pay – check for notices on the buildings. Otherwise, grab a seat on the wooden barriers. You're not allowed on the front fence, only on or behind the second one. Get there at least two hours beforehand. If you want to watch the final frolic in the ring, you'll need to queue well in advance.

**Tickets** You can buy bullfight tickets for that day and the next at the Plaza de Toros. These get snapped up, so you may have to buy from scalpers, who drop their prices rapidly once the *corrida* is underway. Avoid the cheaper seats as they often degenerate into a peanut gallery with rowdy food fights.

**Eating and drinking** Prices are predictably high during Los Sanfermines and it can be tough to find space without a reservation. Most people live off *bocadillos*, which are available all over the place, with decreasing prices as you move away from Calle Estafeta. Plenty of shops stay open all night selling beer, *sangría* and wine. The centre is pretty chaotic, with people drinking out of plastic, but walk a few blocks to the new town and you'll find an equally good atmosphere, but with locals, drinking out of proper glasses. There's more scope for tapas and restaurant meals out here, too.

**Parking** There are a couple of free parking areas on the approach roads to town – half-monitored and comparatively secure. Cars cannot enter the old town during the fiesta.

**Safety** San Fermín is Christmas for pickpockets. Don't carry a bag if you can help it, and watch your pockets in the crowds. Although the atmosphere can get volatile with so much being alcohol sunk, there's remarkably little violence. See also box, page 128.

## ⊖ Transport

**Pamplona** p124, map p126
**Bus**
Pamplona is the hub for buses in the area.
**Madrid** (Conda, 6 daily, €22.82, 5 hrs 15
mins) via **Soria** (2 hrs, €10.79). **Zaragoza**
(Conda, 7 daily, €11.62, 2 hrs-2 hrs 30 mins).
**Bilbao** (ALSA/La Burundesa, 7-9 daily,
€11.20, 2 hrs). **Barcelona** (VIBASA, 4 daily,
€24, 6 hrs). **Vitoria** (ALSA/La Burundesa,
9-14 daily, €6.50, 1 hr 30 mins). **San
Sebastián** (Roncalesa, 7-10 daily, €5.61,
2 hrs). **Jaca/Huesca** (Roncalesa, 2 daily,
Jaca €6, 1 hr, Huesca €11.56, 2 hrs)

**Train**
There are 2-3 fast trains daily from **Madrid**
(3 hrs 30 mins, €46.50) and 2-3 from
**Barcelona** via **Zaragoza** (6-8 hrs, €31).

## ⊕ Directory

**Pamplona** p124, map p126
**Emergencies** Phone 112 in any
emergency. **Internet** Kuria Net,
C Curia 15, T948 223 077, 1000-2200,
€3 per hr; Naveganet, Trav de Acella 3,
T948 199 297. Mon-Sat 1030-1330,
1530-2230, €2.50 per hr; Iturnet,
C Iturrana 1, T948 252 820, Mon-Sat
0900-2200, Sun 1000- 2200, €2 per hr.
**Medical services** Hospital de
Navarra, C Irunlarrea s/n, T948 422
100/948 422 212 (emergencies).
**Police** The main police station is at
C Chinchilla. **Post office** Paseo de
Sarasate s/n. **Telephone** There's a
friendly locutorio next to the bullring
at Paseo Hemingway s/n,
1000-2230.

# Western Pyrenees

Navarra's mountainous north is a series of valleys winding up into the Pyrenees towards France. It's fertile and green in summer, when Basque herders still drive their cattle up to the seasonal pasturelands. The landscapes are spectacular, particularly in the east, where the mountains are more imposing. If you're only going to visit one of Navarra's valleys, make it the easternmost, the Valle de Roncal.

Continuing north from Roncal, the slopes of the western Pyrenees rise towards France. One of the two principal branches of the Camino de Santiago descends to Pamplona from the pass near Roncesvalles, a place of rest for millions of pilgrims over the centuries, which still retains some medieval character. Further north, the river Bidasoa runs through some attractive Basque villages before dividing France and Spain at the coast, while one of its tributaries, the Baztan, runs down a peaceful valley that is also worthy of investigation. ▸▸ For Sleeping, Eating and other listings, see pages 137-140.

# Roncal Valley ⊖⊘⊖❋⊖ ▸▸ pp137-140.

Navarra's easternmost Pyrenean valley is also its most enchanting. Here, the mountains are really beginning to flex their muscles – it's a popular base for cross-country (and some downhill) skiing in winter. Summer, though, is when it really comes into its own, when flowers bloom from window boxes in the lovable villages, and the cobblestones aren't icy invitations to a sprained ankle!

## Izaba/Isaba

While it may be the big smoke of the valley, Izaba is not more than a village. Back from the road that winds along its length are unspoiled stony lanes where sheep are still penned on the ground floors of houses and vegetable patches are tended in the heart of town. There's lots of accommodation too, as it's a popular base for walkers, skiers and cross-border weekenders. The village church, **Iglesia de San Cipriano** towers

## ☰ Charlemagne and Roland

Taking the crown of the Franks in 768 at the age of 26, Charlemagne embarked on a lifelong campaign to unite and bring order to western Europe, which resulted in an empire that included France, Switzerland, Belgium, Holland and much of Italy and Germany, as well as the 'Spanish March', a wedge of territory stretching down to the Ebro River. Or so he thought; the locals weren't so sure. Allowing him to pass through their territory to battle the Moors, the local Basques were outraged at Charlemagne's conduct: he destroyed Pamplona's fortifications after taking it; and accepted a bribe from the city of Zaragoza to return to France. As the army ascended the Ibañeta Pass above Roncesvalles on their way home, their rearguard and baggage train was ambushed and slaughtered by locals. Among the dead was Hrudoland, or Roland, governor of the marches of Brittany, a shadowy historical figure immortalized in the later romantic account of the event, *Le Chanson de Roland*.

fortress-like over the settlement, and there's also a local museum. Otherwise, spend a while climbing around the streets, trying to find the perfect photo framing stone houses, geraniums and craggy peaks behind. Izaba has a **tourist office** ① *Mon-Sat 1000-1400, 1630-2000, Sun 1100-1400*.

The valley above Izaba has such lush pastureland in summer that for many centuries French shepherds and cowherds couldn't help themselves and took their flocks over the border to get fat on peninsular grass. After a hard winter, the shepherds in the Roncal Valley were in no mood to be neighbourly, and much strife ensued. Finally, it was agreed that the French would give a gift of three cows to the Navarrese each summer in return for incident-free cud-chewing. The mayor of Izaba, dressed in traditional conquistador-like costume, still collects on it – you can see the two parties solemnly clasp hands on the frontier stone every 13 July at midday, before the Spanish party solemnly select three cows from a frisky herd (sadly, they don't actually keep them any more). If you're going to the ceremony, get there early or be prepared to walk a couple of kilometres, as cars are parked way back down the road on both sides.

## Roncal

Down the valley from Izaba is the village of Roncal itself, famous for its sheep's milk cheese. Its another attractive Pyrenean village with crisp mountain air that must have been a boon to its favourite son, Gayarre, a tenor from opera's golden days in the late 19th century. His tomb in the village cemetery is an ornate riot of kitsch, flamboyantly out of place amid the humbler graves of cheesewrights. In December 1889 his voice gave out during a performance in Madrid. Devastated, he said *"Esto se acabó"* (it's all over), and died three weeks later, aged 45. His mausoleum was so well regarded that it went on tour to exhibitions while his poor bones stayed put.

Roncal's **tourist office** ① *Mon-Sat 1000-1400, 1630-2000, Sun 1100-1400*, is equipped with an internet terminal for public use.

The valley, particularly in its higher reaches, is home to a great variety of wildlife, including rare species such as bear, boar, capercaillie, ptarmigan, chamois and a variety of birds of prey. It offers numerous opportunities for exploring.

West of the Roncal area the Río Salazar, before gouging its way through the Foz de Arbayún (see below), tracks down a low and little-visited valley of beech woods. The main town is Otsagi/Ochagavia, a small place at the point where the Salazar is formed from two tributaries. It seems to have more bridges than it needs – one is a venerable medieval span. On a hill north of town is the Marian **Santuario de Muskildu**.

# 66 99 On a misty evening the stern ecclesiastical complex at Roncesvalles resembles Colditz.

## Roncesvalles/Orreaga and around 🏨🍴🚌 ›› pp137-140.

→ *Phone code: 948. Colour map 3, B4. Altitude: 924 m.*

On a misty evening the stern ecclesiastical complex at Roncesvalles resembles Colditz, but can be deceptive. It is the first stop for pilgrims following the Camino Francés into Navarra from the French town of St Jean Pied-de-Port; it was also the last stop for many of Charlemagne's knights including the famous Roland (see box, page 134).

Roncesvalles/Orreaga is little more than the Colegiata church complex, pilgrim hostel and a couple of *posadas*. It sits just below the Puerto de Ibañeta pass which divides Spain from French Basqueland. Some 3 km closer to Pamplona through an avenue of trees, the village of **Burguete** offers more services than the bare Roncesvalles, and has been made moderately famous by Hemingway, whose characters Jake and Bill put away several gallons of wine there on a trout-fishing expedition before descending to Pamplona in his novel *Fiesta* (*The Sun Also Rises*).

### Sights

A **pilgrim hostel** was originally built in Roncesvalles in 1127. Its fame grew with the growing streams of walkers who were succoured here, aided by the discovery of the Virgin of Roncesvalles, found by a shepherd who was guided to the spot by a deer with Rudolf-style illumination. The statue is said to have been buried to protect it from Moorish raiders; the **Collegiate church** ① *1000-1400, 1530-1730 (1930 in summer, morning only in Jan); €2, or €3.20 including visit to the Iglesia de Santiago and the Silo, which are otherwise kept closed; T948 790 480*, that houses the silver-plated statuette is the highlight of the sanctuary, a simple and uplifting example of French Gothic architecture, with blue stained-glass windows and the Virgin taking pride of place above the altar. On her birthday, 8 September, there's a major *romería* (pilgrimage day) and fiesta here. Off the cloister is the burial chapel of the Navarrese King Sancho VII ('the strong'), whose bones were transferred here in 1912. He lies with his wife under a 2¼-m 14th-century alabaster statue of himself that's said to be life size; in the stained-glass depiction of him battling the Moors at the scene of his greatest triumph, Navas de Tolosa, he cuts an imposing figure. A **warhammer** leaning nearby is predictably said to have been Roland's. The small **museum** ① *daily 1100- 1330, 1600-1800*, attached to the complex is less impressive, but has a few interesting manuscripts, as well as a blue-embossed reliquary known as 'Charlemagne's chess set'.

A few paces away from the church complex are two further buildings, the tiny 14th-century **Iglesia de Santiago** and the 12th-century funerary structure known as the **Silo of Charlemagne** ① *see Collegiate church, above for both*. Legend maintains that the Silo was built on the site where Charlemagne buried Roland and his stricken rearguard. Underneath it is a burial pit holding bones of various origins; some may well have been pilgrims for whom the hard climb over the Pyrenees had proved to be a step too far; the bear and wolf population can't have helped.

Opposite the complex, there's a **visitor centre** ① *1000-1400, 1600-1900, €1*, which is half an excuse for a shop to keep the steady flow of visitors happy. There's also a small exhibition and audiovisual display on Navarra and the Roncesvalles area.

The Roncesvalles **tourist office** ① *1000-1400, 1600-1900, T948 760 301*, is attentive and helpful, although queues can be long.

Navarra Western Pyrenees

**Puerto de Ibañeta**

Not far up the road to France is the pass itself, the Puerto de Ibañeta. Here, there's a modern chapel and a **memorial to Roland**. Some say this is where the grieving Charlemagne buried Roland; at any rate the memorial is slightly strange, seeing as it was the Navarrese who probably did him in. A more recent and appropriate memorial in Roncesvalles commemorates his vanquishers. Continuing from Puerto de Ibañeta, the valley of **Valcarlos/Luzaide** is seen by many scholars as the most likely place for the battle itself. At the border, the town of the same name is pretty enough but is often overwhelmed with French hopefuls paying over-the-odds prices for Spanish ham and wine. There's plenty of accommodation here but no real reason to linger.

## Burguete/Auritz

The austerity of Roncesvalles continues down the hill in the village of Burguete/ Auritz, whose main street is curiously flanked by drains, which give the stone cottages a fortified appearance. A severe church is the town's centrepiece but it's a solid, friendly place to stay with a handful of good-value sleeping and eating options. Hemingway fans will head for the **Hostal Burguete**, which happily seems to have changed little since his day.

---

# Bidasoa Valley 🚍🚲✳️🚌 ▸ *pp137-140.*

Northeast of Pamplona, the road to Irún follows the course of the salmony river Bidasoa, which divides France and Spain at the Bay of Biscay. The road itself is a nightmare of speeding trucks and smelly industry, but the valley houses several likeable villages that are very Basque indeed. Lesaka and Etxalar are charming places; further into the hills Zugarramurdi was a centre of witchcraft in the 17th century, or so the Inquisition thought.

## Bera/Vera de Bidasoa

Closest to the coast is Bera/Vera de Bidasoa, a place where you may hear more Euskara than Spanish, and a hotbed of support for ETA. Below the imposing grey stone church is the Ayuntamiento, with a façade painted with female figures of Fortitude, Temperance, Justice and Prudence, who sometimes seem to dominate this sober town. On the edge of town is the posh farmhouse where the Basque novelist **Pío Baroja** used to spend his summers; it's still a private home (used by his nephew) and very rarely open to the public. The **tourist office** ① *T948 631 222, Mon-Sat 1000-1400, 1600-1900*, is on Calle Errotazar.

## Lesaka

Further inland from Bera, a couple of scenic kilometres off the main road, is Lesaka, prettier and more welcoming than its neighbour. Its architectural highlights are a pair of tower-houses, but there are several impressive homes, many built by *indianos*, colonists returning with fortunes made in the New World. As in Bera, the stone church looms large over the town, but it seems more at ease amid gardens and tranquil pathways. If this was Britain, it is certain that the village would have won some sort of council award for "best geranium window boxes of the northeast" or similar; it's a gloriously colourful place when they're in bloom.

● Francisco Espoz y Mina, one of Spain's heroes of the War of Independence, felt betrayed by
● the Liberals' 1812 constitution that granted no autonomy to the Navarran region. After reading it, he had the document put in a chair and shot by firing squad.

Some 3 km off the main road on the other side of Lesaka is peaceful Etxalar, a stone Basque village with a very attractive pinkish church surrounded by circular Basque gravemarkers, widely thought to be a continuation of pre-Christian tradition. There are several *hostales* and *casas rurales* around here.

## Zugarramurdi

From Etxalar, a deserted road leads up a spectacular valley and around a couple of hills to Zugarramurdi. On entering this spotless whitewashed village you might think it a place of peaceful rural life, the only corruption to be found in shifty-eyed shopkeepers selling overpriced wine and ham to their fellow Basques from across the border. You'd be wrong.

The Inquisition weren't fooled in 1610 when they turned up. Don Juan del Valle Alvarado, sent from the tribunal at Logroño after hearing of an outbreak of witchery in the area, spent several months investigating here and found the village to be a whitened sepulchre, a seething pit of blasphemy and moral turpitude. He accused over 300 villagers (men, women and children) from the surrounding area of witchcraft, and of committing crimes including: whipping up storms to sink ships in the Bay of Biscay; eating the dead and the living; conducting black masses; indulging in various unspeakable acts with Satan in the form of a black goat and more. As in most of the Inquisition's investigations, denunciations by fellow villagers were the dubious source of most of the evidence. Many people turned themselves in; the punishments were far harsher if you didn't. The most heinous of these contemptible criminals were taken to Logroño and left in prison while the evidence was debated. Many died before the verdicts were announced; their effigies were burned or pardoned accordingly. A total of 12 were sentenced to death.

Some five minutes' walk from town is a large **cave complex** ① *1000-2100; €2.40*, said to have been the site for most of the diabolical activity. It certainly would make a fine spot for a black mass, with an impressive natural tunnel overlooked by a couple of viewing galleries. It may well be that various non-Christian rituals were practised here: veneration of traditional Basque deities such as Mari, the mother goddess, was still alive well into the 20th century. It's said that in the year of the witch trials, the local priest came to the caves and daubed them with mustard, declaring that the witches would vanish for as many years as there were mustard grains.

Being so close to France, this whole area was (until the EU era) a nest of smuggling, and many marked walking trails in the area would have been used by moonlight. The unwritten contract between police and smugglers was that, if sprung, the smugglers would drop their booty and make themselves scarce. The law, for their part, would hold their fire and take the goods home with them.

⬤ **Sleeping**

**Roncal Valley** *p133*
There are dozens of places to stay in Izaba and around, many of them *casas rurales*.
**B Hotel Isaba**, Ctra Roncal s/n, Izaba, T948 893 000, hotel_isaba@ctv.es.
A modern and friendly hotel at the edge of town; this is Izaba's most upmarket lodging. It has comfy communal lounges, and happily non-standard rooms. Handily situated right next to the municipal swimming pool, which is open until 2000. Closed mid Oct-early Jan.

**E-F Txabalkua**, C Izargentea 16, Izaba, T948 893 083. A peaceful and pretty *pensión* in the middle of the old town. There's one room with a bathroom; the rest share. It's clean and pleasant, with wooden beams and an authentic mountain touch.
**F Albergue Oxanea**, T948 893 153, Izaba. A hostel that lives a happy life without lockouts, curfews or meddlesome rules. The dorms are crowded but comfortable, and it's right in the heart of the cobbled old town.

F **Refugio de Belagua**, Ctra Izaba-Francia Km 19, T948 394 002. On the way up to the French border, this *refugio* looks like a big tent but is a warm base for skiers and walkers year round. Accommodation in huge dorms, and warming meals.

### Camping
**Camping Asolaze**, Ctra Izaba-Francia Km 6, T948 893 034. This year-round campsite is 6 km from Izaba towards France. Its open all year round and gets very busy, but there's pine forest right up to the back door.

### Roncesvalles/Orreaga and around *p135*
There are plenty of *casas rurales* around Burguete/Auritz should you fail to find a bed.
B **Hostal Loizu**, Av Roncesvalles 7, Burguete/Auritz, T948 760 008, www.hotelloizu.com. The most upmarket of the places to stay in this area, this is a decently modernized old house in Burguete with reasonable rooms with TV and heating, which can be much needed both in summer and winter. The nicest rooms are on the top floor and make use of stripped-back stone to great decorative effect.
C **Hostal Burguete**, C San Nicolás 71, Burguete/Auritz, T948 790 488, F948 760 005. The place where Ernest used to hang out, and the base for Jake and Bill's fishing expedition in *Fiesta* (*The Sun Also Rises*). On the main (only!) street through Burguete; this is a place with plenty of character and decent double rooms.
C-D **La Posada**, Roncesvalles s/n, T948 760 225. It feels like an old travellers' inn and it is one, dating from 1612. The best place to stay in Roncesvalles itself with snug heated en suite rooms for when the weather comes a-calling. There's also a log fire and a more than decent cheap restaurant.
D **Casa Sabina**, Roncesvalles s/n, T948 760 012. While this place's main concern is feeding the pilgrims from the adjacent hostel, it has a few rooms with bathroom and TV that are nicer than the exterior might suggest, although they're not exactly homely.
E **Albergue de Juventud**, Roncesvalles s/n, T948 760 015. An official youth hostel in part of the Colegiata complex. Institutional but friendly and reasonably comfortable. It's early to bed and early to rise, but there's little

going on in Roncesvalles in the way of nightlife anyway. You might wangle a key for late entry.
F **Juandeaburre**, C San Nicolás s/n, Burguete/Auritz, T948 760 078. This simple summer-only *pensión* has unheated rooms with washbasin at a good price. It fills quickly so ring ahead before trudging down from Roncesvalles. Open May-Oct.

### Camping
**Camping Urrobi**, Ctra Pamplona-Valcarlos Km 42, T948 760 200. Just below Burguete, this campsite is reasonably equipped and also has cheap dormitory beds on offer. Open Apr-Oct.

### Bidasoa Valley *p136*
B **Donamaria'ko Benta**, Barrio Ventas 4, Donamaria, T948 450 708, donamariako@jet.es. An excellent place to stay for those with transport, this creeper-swathed inn 3 km from the main road beyond the town of Santesteban/Doneztebe dates from 1815. The welcoming owners rescued it from dereliction and it's now a beautiful place to stay, with rustic floorboarded rooms with no little comfort and style. The adjacent restaurant is excellent.
D **Hostal Ekaitza**, Plaza Berria 13, Lesaka, T948 637 559. A highly central place to stay above a bar in the heart of the village, this offers reasonable double rooms with good bathroom; the best rooms have a balcony. Upstairs is a family suite that sleeps 4. It can get noisy at weekends and during the village festival.
E **Domekenea**, Etxalar s/n, T948 635 031. In Etxalar itself, this typically solid, whitewashed Basque house has a couple of comfy rooms, which are very good value with TV, en suites, and a shared balcony.
G **Matxinbeltzenea**, C Arretxea 22, Lesaka, T948 637 796. This hostel is situated above a noisy and appealing Basque bar in Lesaka. There are loads of bunks, some in 4-berth rooms, some with 8. They cost just €9-10; you can eat cheaply downstairs too.

## ● Eating

### Roncal Valley *p133*
† **Pekoetxe**, Ctra Roncal s/n, Izaba, T948 893 101. An attractive and stylish modern

## ⁞ Patxarán

One of Navarra's most emblematic products is this liqueur, usually taken as a *digestivo* after a meal. Although there are *patxaranes* made from a variety of berries and fruits, the traditional Navarrese one, which now has its own DO (denominación de origen) quality grading, is made from sloe berries macerated in an aniseed liquor. Usually served on ice, the taste can range from the sweet and superbly delicate to the medicinal. The name comes from the Euskara word for sloe, *basaran*. Some folk like to mix it: a *San Fermín* is *patxarán* and *cava* (sparkling wine), while a *vaca rosa* (pink cow) is a blend of the liqueur with milk. Adding a few grains of cinnamon or coffee is another option.

restaurant specializing in grilled meat and fish, but featuring a range of other local options with a touch of flair.
**Ψ Txiki**, C Mendigatxa 17, Izaba, T948 893 118. A lively and atmospheric local bar and restaurant serving a *menú* for €9.70 that's got few frills but plenty of authentic Navarran taste. Closed May & Nov.

**Roncesvalles/Orreaga and around** *p135*
While the **Posada** and **Sabina** in Roncesvalles itself (see above) do fine cheap fare, if you fancy something a little different, head down the road to Burguete.
**ΨΨ Loizu**, Av Roncesvalles 7, Burguete/Auritz. T948 760 008. This hotel restaurant serves up good warming mountain food with a touch of class. There's a *menú* for €18.
**Ψ Burguete**, C San Nicolás 71, Burguete/ Auritz, T948 790 488. If you've read *Fiesta* you'll be eating here, of course. The piano that Bill played to keep warm is *in situ* in the dining room and, while they may have forgotten how to make rum punch, there is a *menú* for €10.11 that is good value and includes trout, as it should. Pictures of the bearded writer adorn the room but it's thankfully far from being a shrine to him.

**Bidasoa Valley** *p136*
**ΨΨ Donamaria'ko Benta**, Barrio Ventas 4, Donamaria, T948 450 708. Excellent modern cuisine with a homely wood-beamed rustic feel beside one of the nicest rural hotels in the area (see above). As you'd guess from the name, there's a definite Basque slant to the menu, but there are even some Japanese dishes.
**Ψ Ansonea**, Plaza de los Fueros 1, Bera, T948 631 155. A well-priced place to try homely Basque specialities like *kokotxas* (stewed hake cheeks; delicious), or red peppers stuffed with crab (*pimientos rellenos de txangurro*). There's a *menú del día* for €7.75.
**Ψ Kasino**, Plaza Zahorra 23, Lesaka, T948 637 287. This charming building houses a dark and homey restaurant with a small terrace. Don't be fooled by the humble surroundings; the *tortilla* here has been voted best in the nation by judges in San Sebastián; not an easy accolade to win by any stretch of the imagination.

## ⋂ Bars and clubs

**Roncal Valley** *p133*
**Ttun Ttun**, Barrikato s/n, Izaga. A great little bar with a terrace in the stone-housed back streets below the main road. The *ttun-ttun* is a zither-like instrument (literally a psaltery), traditional in these parts.

## ⊛ Festivals and events

**Roncal Valley** *p133*
**25-28 Jul** Izaba's main festival
**15 Aug** Roncal festival.

**Bidasoa Valley** *p136*
**7 Jul** Lesaka is famous for its own **San Fermín** festival, starting at the same time as the Pamplona one. The major event is on the morning of 7 Jul, with a dance, the *zubi gainekoa*, performed along both sides of the river to symbolize friendship in the region.
**3 Aug** The start of **Bera's** major fiesta.
**15 Aug** Zugarramurdi celebrates its witchy history.

⊖ **Transport**

**Roncal Valley** *p133*
La Tafallesa, T948 222 886, run one bus from **Pamplona** to Roncal and Izaba, leaving at 1700 Mon-Fri and 1300 Sat. It returns Mon-Sat at 0700 (€7.19). There's one bus from Pamplona to Ochagavía (daily, leaving at 1500 Mon-Thu, 1900 Fri, and 1330 Sat. It leaves Ochagavía Mon-Sat at 0900. This changes in winter; phone T948 303 570.

**Roncesvalles/Orreaga and around** *p135*
Artieda, T948 300 287, run one bus from **Pamplona** to Roncesvalles at 1800 Mon-Fri, 1600 on Sat, no service on Sun (€4.20). On Fri and Sat, this bus continues to **Jaurrieta**. The return bus leaves Roncesvalles at a sociable 0650 Mon-Sat.

**Bidasoa Valley** *p136*
La Baztanesa runs a complex series of buses up and down the Bidasoa and Baztan valleys. There are effectively 3 buses to and from **Pamplona** daily the whole way, although some require a change along the road. For enquiries, T948 226 712 or T948 580 129.

# Camino Aragonés → *Colour map 3, C4.*

*Descending from the mountains, pilgrims on the Camino Aragonés usually make Sangüesa their first stop in Navarra. It's a fine little town with more than its fair share of quirky buildings, and within reach are a few other interesting places – the Monasterio de Leyre and Castillo de Javier are places steeped in religious history, while the Embalse de Yesa reservoir offers a break from the fierce heat. To the west, around the town of Lumbier, are two gorges of great natural beauty.* ►► *For Sleeping, Eating and other listings, see pages 142-143.*

## Sangüesa/Zangoza ⊖🛈⊖ ►► *pp142-143.*

Originally founded by Romans on a nearby hill, Sangüesa served its apprenticeship as a bastion against the Moors before quieter times saw it moved down to the banks of the cloudy green Río Aragón. Most notable among several impressive structures is the Iglesia de Santa María by the bridge. Sweaty pilgrims trudging into town will be happy to know that in Sangüesa the stench from the nearby paper mill makes all bodily odours fade into insignificance. After an hour or so, it's actually not too bad – plenty of locals swear they miss it when they're out of town.

The **tourist office** ① *T948 871 411, Mon-Sat 1000-1400, 1600-1900, Sun 1000-1400 (closed Mon in winter)*, is opposite the church of Santa María is helpful.

### Iglesia de Santa María
① *T620 110 581, tours of this and other churches, summer Mon-Sat 1030-1330, 1600-1830, winter Mon-Sat 1030-1330, €1.20 church only, €3.30 whole town.*
The church's elaborately carved portal takes Romanesque sculpture to heights of delicacy and fluidity seldom seen elsewhere, although some of the themes covered stray a fair way from lofty religion. The inside is less interesting and annoyingly only accessible by guided tour (the office is at the back of the building). This goes for most of the other buildings in town. The church can be visited independently just before mass, which is at 1900 in winter and 2000 in summer.

### Palacio de Vallesantoro
Sangüesa's town hall is based in the outrageous Palacio de Vallesantoro. The doorway is flanked by two bizarre corkscrew (Solomonic) columns, but it's the macabre overhanging eaves that draw even more attention. They make the building

## Iglesia de Santiago

A couple of streets back is the church of Santiago, a late Romanesque building with an impressive fortified tower and several good Gothic sculptures, including one of Saint James himself. He also appears in colour on the building's façade, flanked by two pilgrims who look as though they might have made the journey from the Australian outback.

Off the main street, an elegant arched arcade points the way to the Palacio Príncipe de Viana, formerly a residence of kings of Navarra, while on Calle Alfonso el Batallador, not far from the Ayuntamiento is a working iron forge which uses fairly traditional methods and specializes in forging individualized tokens for pilgrims. Across the river is a statue of St Christopher, patron saint of travellers, which explains the cut-out of a car that's been strangely attached to it.

> ⁑ *The church is only opened at mass times or on the town's guided tour.*

# Around Sangüesa 🚌🚍 ⇢ *pp142-143.*

## Castillo de Javier

Like a lion with its mane plaited, the castle of Javier doesn't seem as formidable as it no doubt once was. Enough of a thorn in the side of Spain for Cardinal Cisneros (also known as Ximénez the Inquisitor) to have commanded its partial destruction, it is better known as the birthplace of the missionary and founding member of the Jesuits, San Francisco Javier. Unlike the birthplace of Francis' former roommate Saint Ignatius, there's not too much ostentatious piety and the castle makes for a good visit. It has been heavily restored; someone foolishly backed a basilica into it in the 19th century, and more work was done in the 1950s, but there's still some feeling of what it might have been like when young Francis roamed its corridors.

## Monasterio de San Salvador de Leyre

ⓘ *T948 884 150, Mon-Fri 1015-1400, 1530-1900, Sat 1015-1400, 1600-1900; €1.65; the monks chant offices at 0730, 0900, 1900 and 2110 in the church.*

Off the N240 northeast of Sangüesa, a road winds 4 km through fragrant hills to the Monasterio de San Salvador de Leyre, a stop on the Camino de Santiago. A monastery was first founded here as early as the eighth century AD, but the beautiful, rugged spot – the name means 'eagerness to overcome' in Euskara – had been a favourite haunt of hermits before that. Nothing but foundations remain from that period – the older parts of today's structure date from the 11th and 12th centuries, when the Navarrese monarchs took a liking to the spot and made it the seat of their kingdom. The centre flourished with religious and secular power and became extremely wealthy before an inevitable decline began. The abbey was abandoned in the 19th century after loss of monastic privileges and was not re-used until 1954, when it was colonized by Benedictines from the Monasterio de Santo Domingo de Silos.

The church itself is of mixed styles but preserves much simplicity and tranquillity inside, above all when it's filled with the Gregorian chanting of the monks during offices. The structure is remarkably off-kilter – lovers of symmetry and proportion will be appallingly ill-at-ease. The portal is a fascinating 12th-century work, filled with Romanesque scenes. While the main groups are of the Last Judgement, Christ and the Evangelists, the sculptors let their fancy run a bit freer elsewhere – you can spot several interesting demons and nightmarish animals, Jonah getting swallowed, and some lifelike prowling lions. Inside, the centrepiece is the Virgin of Leyre, while the adult Christ is relegated to his customary Spanish place in the wings. A large chest on one wall contains the bones of no fewer than 10 Navarrese kings, seven queens and two princes – these were exhumed and boxed in 1915 – their feelings on the matter unrecorded. A small side-chapel has a *retablo* in a pleasingly rustic style.

The crypt, accessed from the ticket office, is a weird space, whose stone altar and ram-horned columns suggest darker ritual purposes. The columns all vary and are tiny – it's strange to have the capitals at waist height. Next to the crypt is a tunnel leading to an image of San Virila – a former abbot. This dozy chap wandered up to a nearby stream and was so enchanted by the song of a bird that he didn't make it back for vespers for another three centuries. If you fancy some time out too, follow his lead and head up to the spring, which is signposted five minutes' walk above the complex. If you like the spot, you might consider staying in the attached *hospedería* (see Sleeping, below).

## Foz/Hoz de Lumbier

ⓘ *Entry is €1.50 when the ticket booth is attended; take swimming gear on a hot day.*
A mile from the small town of Lumbier is the Foz/Hoz de Lumbier, a fashionably *petite* designer gorge. It's a top place, with gurgling stream, overhanging rock walls and a large population of vultures that circle lazily above, in the vain hope that a tourist will drop dead from the heat. Twenty minutes' walk from the car park will get you to the other end of the gorge, where you can see the ruins of the 'Devil's Bridge', destroyed in the Peninsular War but possibly none too safe before that. Return the same way or via a longer circuit around the top of the gorge.

## Embalse de Yesa

The N240 continues on into Aragón, following the shore of the Embalse de Yesa reservoir. This is a pretty way to get to the Roncal Valley (see page 133) if you've got a car.

The Embalse is a beautiful chalky blue colour and good to swim in (watch for submerged trees – check your chosen spot from higher up the bank). On its north shore is the abandoned village of **Escó**, still proudly beautiful on a hilltop. The villagers had to clear out in 1959 when the reservoir was filled (some villages are completely submerged).

---

## ⬤ Sleeping

**Sangüesa** *p140*
C-D **Hostal JP**, Paseo Raimundo Lumbier 3, T948 871 693. A clean, fresh and good option (if slightly hospital-like) just across the river from the Iglesia de Santa María. The rooms are modern and pleasant enough, and have a good bathroom and cable TV.
E **Pensión Las Navas**, C Alfonso el Batallador 7, T948 870 077. Although not the most welcoming of establishments, these rooms are pretty decent value in the heart of town and equipped with bathrooms. There's a restaurant with a cheap *menú* and lift access.

### Camping
**Camping Cantolagua**, Paseo Cantolagua s/n, T948 430 352. A good site by the riverside, with a swimming pool and tennis courts.
There are also bungalows, caravans and rooms available at good cheapish rates.

**Castillo de Javier** *p141*
B **Hotel Xabier**, Plaza de Javier s/n, Javier, T948 884 006, www.hotelxabier.com.
This is the nicer of the 2 hotels in the little touristic zone by the castle of Javier. The old-style rooms have modern comforts, there's some cooling marbled effects, and a reasonable restaurant.

### Monasterio de San Salvador de Leyre *p141*
C **Hospedería de Leyre**, Monasterio de Leyre, T948 884 100, hotel@monasterio deleyre.com. With great views over the plains and the reservoir below, and some very nice walks in the scented hills, this monastery hotel offers much more than monastic comfort, as well as some very good meals. The rooms are simple but welcoming; some are larger than others.

## ❼ Eating

As well as those listed here, all the hotels above have attached restaurants.

**Sangüesa** *p140*
❦ **Mediavilla**, C Alfonso el Batallador 15, T948 870 212. A hospitable *asador* with filling *menús* for €17 and €22. There's a range of very tasty roast meat, but plenty of lighter dishes to accompany it.
❦ **Bar Ciudad de Sangüesa**, C Santiago 4, T948 871 021. There are several bars on this street – this bar does good cheap meals and is popular with locals. The quality is very high for the price, and the style is traditional, with hearty country food.

## Cafés

**El Pilar**, C Mayor 87, Sangüesa. The posh place in town to come for a drink or a coffee.

## ❽ Transport

**Camino Aragonés** *p140*
**Bus**
La Veloz Sangüesina, T948 870 209, runs 3 buses daily to and from **Pamplona** (only 1 on Sun, €3.10). There are also buses from Pamplona to **Liédena** or **Yesa**, from where you can get a taxi to either Javier or the Monasterio de Leyre. For the Foz de Lumbier, take a **Río Irati** bus from Pamplona to the town of Lumbier, and walk from there (1-3 a day, €3.05).

# Western Pilgrim Route

*The two main branches of the Camino de Santiago, the Camino Francés – which has come through Roncesvalles and Pamplona – and the Camino Aragonés – which has tracked through Aragón and Sangüesa – meet at Puente La Reina and continue westwards together. This part of the province is one of Navarra's nicest, with towns such as Estella and Viana joys for the traveller or pilgrim to discover. Off the main route, too, are some perfect little villages, while, to top things off, some of Navarra's best wine is made in the area.* ➵ *For Sleeping, Eating and other listings, see pages 145-146.*

## Puente La Reina/Gares and around ➜ *Colour map 3, C3.*

*"And from here all roads to Santiago become only one."* While this is not completely true, the two principal pilgrim routes converge here just before reaching the medieval bridge that the town grew around, a long and beautiful Romanesque span that emerges from an arched entrance and speaks of many kilometres to come under a beating sun.

The town is small, and a good place to stop for a night if you're inclined. Arriving from the east, on the outskirts, you'll see the strange monument to pilgrims, a wild-eyed and gaunt bronze figure who might provoke more anxiety than comfort in passing peregrines. The pilgrim hostel isn't much further, and stands next to the 12th-century **Iglesia del Crucifijo**.

In the heart of town is another **church** ① *0900-1300, 1700-2030*, dedicated to Santiago himself. The so-called Matamoros ('Moor killer') might not be too impressed to notice that his doorway looks remarkably Muslim in style with its horseshoe notched recessed portal. Opposite is the fine façade of the **Convento de la Trinidad**. The peaceful centre of the town, the **Plaza Julián Mena**, houses the Ayuntamiento and **tourist office** ① *Tue-Sat 1000-1400, 1530-1830 (1700-2000 summer), Sun 1100-1400.*

Near Puente La Reina, the medieval village of **Obanos** is famous for its biennial staging of a mystery play based on a legend of the Camino.

● *For information on the practicalities of walking the Camino de Santiago and the history of the pilgrimage, see pages 52 and 388.*

# Estella/Lizarra 🖂🚻🅿✳🚌🛈 ➠ *pp145-146.*

The major town of western Navarra, Estella is a very likeable place to stay a while. The town likes to dust off the moniker 'the Toledo of the North'; this is a little over-the-top, but its crop of historic buildings are certainly interesting.

Estella's history as a town goes back to 1052 when King Sancho Ramírez, taking ruler and pencil to the burgeoning pilgrim trail, established it as a new stop on the official route. On a hill, close to the Puente de la Cárcel, on the western bank, the older part of town, is the towering grey bulk of the **Iglesia de San Pedro de la Rúa**, with its crusty façade and indented Romanesque portal. The highlight inside is the semi-cloister. It was here that the Castilian kings used to swear to uphold the Navarrese *fueros* after the province was annexed; it was a promise honoured in varying degrees by different monarchs. Apart from the guided tour (see below) the church only opens at about 1900, but you'll have to be prompt, as mass starts at 2000 (1900 in winter).

Opposite is the **Palacio de los Reyes** 🛈 *Tue-Sat 1100-1300, 1700-1900, Sun 1100-1330, free*, another Romanesque edifice, which now houses a museum devoted to the early 20th-century painter Gustavo de Maeztu, who was influenced by the art nouveau movement and lived his later years in Estella.

Across the river, the **Iglesia de San Miguel** is also set above the town on a hillock. Its most endearing feature is the Romanesque portal, richly carved with a scene of Christ in Majesty surrounded by his supporting cast. It's an impressive work. Like San Pedro, the church is only open by guided tour or about an hour before 2000 mass (1900 in winter).

The newer part of town centres around the large **Plaza de los Fueros**, overseen by the **Iglesia de San Juán**, a mishmash of every conceivable style. Nearby is the quiet **Plaza de Santiago**, in whose centre four 'orrible creatures spill water from their mouths into a fountain.

Estella's **tourist office** 🛈 *T948 556 301, summer Mon-Sat 1000-1400, 1600-1900, Sun 1000-1400, winter Mon-Fri 1000-1700, Sat and Sun 1000-1400*, is next to the Palacio de los Reyes; guided tours of the town depart from here.

## Around Estella

A couple of kilometres southwest of Estella, on the way to Ayegui on the Camino, is the **Monasterio de Irache** 🛈 *Tue 1000-1330, Wed-Sun 1000-1330, 1700-1900*, the oldest of the original Navarran pilgrim refuges. It is a bit bare and down at heel these days but scheduled for some restoration work. The light and airy church features an inscrutable Virgin and a bony bit of San Veremundo in a reliquary by the altar.

The monastery is famous for its palatable red table wine, and pilgrims who love the good drop might be tempted to linger on the way here a little: there's a tap at the back of the *bodega* that spouts red wine for the benefit of travellers on the road, a sight to gladden the heart if ever there was one!

There are numerous **wineries** in the Estella area which are happy to show visitors around. The tourist office provides a list of *bodegas* (phone beforehand to arrange a visit). One of the quality labels is **Palacio de la Vega** 🛈 *T948 527 009*, in the small town of Dicastillo, south of Estella. The *bodega*, whose home is a striking 19th-century palace, is a modern producer that has been at the forefront of the successful establishment of French varietals like Cabernet Sauvignon and Merlot in Navarra. A more traditional producer of quality wines is **Bodegas Sarría** 🛈 *based by Puente La Reina, T948 267 562*.

## Viana

One of Navarra's loveliest towns, Viana is the last stop before the Camino descends into the oven of La Rioja. Fortified to defend the kingdom's borders against Castilla, it still preserves small sections of its walls, rising above the surrounding plains. The **Iglesia de Santa María** has a monumental façade and a high Gothic interior, whose sober interior is enlivened by a great number of ornate Baroque *retablos*.

In front of the church is the gravemarker of an unexpected man; Cesare Borgia, a 15th-century Italian noble who could rightly be described as Machiavellian – *The Prince* was largely based on his machinations. Son of a pope, after becoming a cardinal he most probably had his elder brother murdered as part of his scheme, one of a number of opportunistic assassinations he masterminded while conquering significant swathes of Italian territory. It all went pear-shaped for Borgia, though; after having been imprisoned in Spain, Borgia was placed under the protection of the King of Navarra, and he ended up as a minor noble in Viana. After. He was elected constable of the town, but was killed in a siege by Castilian forces in 1507, aged only 30.

The atmospheric ruined Gothic church of **San Pedro** sheltered French troops during the Peninsular War before it collapsed in 1844.

## ● Sleeping

### Puente La Reina/Gares and around *p143*

Puente has a couple of excellent lodging choices. It's close to Pamplona so prices soar during Los Sanfermines.

**L El Peregrino**, C Irunbidea s/n, T948 340 075, www.hotelelperegrino.com. An impressively individual and classy hotel and restaurant on the approach to town. Packed with arty objects and quirky architectural kinks, but with a comfortable stone-and-wood feeling. Lovely pool and surrounding terrace. The restaurant is of a very high standard. Despite the name, one senses eyebrows might rise if a road-weary pilgrim with backpack and staff actually ventured inside.

**B Bidean**, C Mayor 20, T948 341 156, www.hotelbidean.com. A charming hotel in the centre of town with welcoming staff and an old-fashioned homely feel. The beds in the colourful rustic rooms are extremely comfortable.

**F Fonda Lorca**, C Mayor 54, T948 340 127. A cheery place facing the small Plaza Mena, with a balcony, reasonable home-style food, and some cheap rooms.

### Estella *p144*

**C Hotel Yerri**, Av Yerri 35, T948 546 034, F948 555 081. This hotel is Estella's most upmarket option, situated near the bullring. The rooms are modern and have cable TV, good bathroom and telephone, but are fairly blandly decorated. Parking available.

**D Cristina**, C Baja Navarra 1, T948 550 772. A well-positioned *hostal* in Estella's

liveliest part. Nearly all the rooms have a balcony to watch the world go by; those rooms overlooking the Plaza de los Fueros can get a bit noisy. All rooms are en suite.

**E-F Pensión San Andrés**, Plaza Santiago 58, T948 550 448. This is a very good, cheap option on a quiet square in the heart of town. The management is very friendly, and the rooms homely and comfortable. They come with or without bathroom.

### Camping

**Camping Estella**, Ctra Pamplona-Logroño Km 44, T948 551 733. A range of accommodation options are available at this riverbank site. Facilities include a large swimming pool. You'll find it on the road to Pamplona a couple of kilometres from town.

### Viana *p144*

**B Palacio de Pujadas**, C Navarro Villoslada 30, T948 646 464, www.palaciode pujadas.com. This lovely hotel is set in an historic old-town *palacio*. The interior is a lesson in combining modern comfort while staying true to the original building; the rooms are a delight with stately tasteful furniture. There's free internet access for guests.

**E Casa Armendáriz**, C Navarro Villoslada 19, T948 645 078. This, a good choice for lodging, has clean and proper rooms with or without bathroom – the latter are pretty basic – as well as cheerful dining in an old wine cellar.

**⊘ Eating**

### Puente La Reina/Gares and around *p143*

**▦ El Peregrino** (see Sleeping, above). The hotel's restaurant is excellent and classy, giving a chance to sample the fine decor if you're not staying.

**▯ Restaurante Joaquin**, C Mayor 48, T948 341 105. This is a decent lunchtime option with a *menú del día* for €8. The food is typically Navarran, with fine trout and other hearty dishes.

**▯ Valdizarbe**, Paseo de los Fueros s/n, T948 341 009. A bar doing a decent line in cheap *paella*, all good carbohydrates for pilgrims.

### Estella *p144*

Estella's signature dish is *gorrín*, another name for roast suckling pig, a heavy but juicy meal seeded with a potent dose of garlic.

**▦ La Cepa**, Plaza de los Fueros 15, T948 550 032. One of Estella's best, this restaurant makes up for its dull decor with imaginatively prepared Navarrese dishes. There's a *menú* at lunchtime (€11.50) and weekends (€20), otherwise work on €40 a head.

**▯▯ Astarriaga**, Plaza de los Fueros 12, T948 550 802. An *asador* offering a decent *menú del día* for €11.90, and doing the usual good steaks, but also some traditional Navarrese offerings. Good *pintxos* and a terrace on the square.

**▯▯ Katxetas**, Estudio de Gramática 1, T948 550 010. What was once a cheap and cheerful delight has gone upmarket, not unsuccessfully. It's now a Basque cider-house, serving challengingly large portions. The traditional cider-house *menú* is delicious for €19.

**▯ Izarra**, C Calderería 20, T948 550 678. The restaurant above this bar is nothing special, but it does offer a *menú* for €9 day and night. The *bocadillos* and *pintxos* in the bar downstairs are more inspiring.

### ⊙ Bars and clubs

### Estella *p144*

**Pigor**, C La Estrella 6, T948 554 054. A sociable and attractive bar with a range of good *bocadillos*. The music cranks up later on weekend nights.

**Kopa's**, C Carpintería 9. A popular modern bar with a good range of quality imported beers.

### ❀ Festivals and events

### Estella *p144*

**Mid-Jul  Medieval week**, with troupes of *jongleurs* and crumhorn-players roaming the streets, which are enlivened by flaming torches, bales of straw and chickens and rabbits in cages.

**Aug  Estella's fiesta** starts on the first Fri of the month, with *encierros*, *corridas* and more.

### Viana *p144*

**Late Jul  Viana** goes wild for the joint fiesta of **Mary Magdalene** and **St James**; there are 2 *encierros* (bull-runnings) daily.

### ⊙ Transport

### Puente La Reina/Gares and around *p143*

La Estellesa (T948 222 223) runs frequent buses from **Pamplona** to Puente la Reina (20 mins, €1.57, 10 daily); the buses continue to **Logroño**.

### Estella *p144*

La Estellesa (T948 222 223) runs 10 buses a day to and from **Pamplona** (1 hr, €3.04); the journey takes 1 hr. A similar number go to **Logroño**. There are also 6 buses daily to **San Sebastián** and 1 to **Zaragoza**.

### Viana *p144*

La Vianesa (T948 446 227) run a few daily buses to **Logroño** (30 mins, €2.45).

### ⊙ Directory

### Puente La Reina/Gares and around *p143*

**Internet**  Librería Ohiuka, corner C Cerco Viejo and C Las Huertas, 0800-1300, Mon-Sat, 1700-2000.

### Estella *p144*

**Internet**  Ice Net, Plaza Santiago 3, Mon-Fri 1030-1400, 1630-2200; Sat and Sun 1630-2200. **Alfonso**, C De Puy 44, daily 1000-2200 but with only 2 terminals.

# Southern Navarra → *Colour map 3, C4.*

*Not far south of Pamplona, the land flattens and hardens as the Spanish meseta opens up. It's a land where the weather doesn't pull punches; the winters are cold, the summers can be merciless and massive windmills put the relentless westerlies to good use (Navarra is one of Europe's leaders in this form of energy). Corn, wheat, olives and grapes are grown where there's water, while towns and villages stand defiantly under the big sky, seemingly defying nature to do its worst.*

*In easy reach of Pamplona, the delightful towns of Tafalla and Olite, only 7 km apart, are well worth visiting. Although overshadowed from a touristic point of view by its neighbour, Tafalla is the larger and more complete town, whose old quarter boasts an attractively run-down web of medieval streets and little plazas centred around its impressive church. Olite stands in the middle of the baking valley like a bullfighter in the middle of the ring. In its most extravagant phase it was capital of the Navarrese court, but in spite of this there's a Spanish feel to much of the area; perhaps it's just that the sunbaked sandstone seems in such contrast to the softer stone and wood buildings of the Pyrenean villages. Olite's centrepiece is its magnificent castle, which sometimes seems bigger than the town itself. The surrounding area's architecture is magnificent too: even the smallest village seems to have a church tucked away that would draw hundreds of visitors daily in other parts of the world.*

*Further south, Tudela is Navarra's second largest city and centre of the southern region known as La Ribera, for the Ebro, the peninsula's second longest river, meanders lazily through it, giving life to the rows and rows of grapevines that stripe the area. To the west of Tudela are winemaking villages that have given Navarra's reds a very good and growing reputation, to the annoyance of some Rioja producers who, although literally in some cases next door, have to work under more stringent conditions and have limited scope for experimentation.* ▶▶ *For Sleeping, Eating and other listings, see pages 150-152.*

## Tafalla

The biggest town in the area, Tafalla is a busy place, an industrial and commercial centre as well as focus for the surrounding districts. Historically an important stop on the road from Pamplona to Tudela, its architectural charm is as much in the small details – an arch here, a coat of arms there – as its selection of larger monuments.

The major structure in the narrow old town streets is the **Iglesia de Santa María**. Built in the 16th century over older foundations, it's been tweaked a fair bit over the years. The façade is curious in shape but fairly unadorned; it looks as though someone's put up a lean-to along one side. The highlight for most visitors is the *retablo*, an ornate late 16th-century work by the hand of Juan de Ancheta. After working on it for seven years, the strain (perhaps caused by the meddling patrons) killed the maestro, and the work was completed by his colleague and pupil Pedro González de San Pedro. If you find the piece over-ornate, blame the patrons: when the work was finished, they decided it wasn't striking enough, so they got a third artist to touch up some of the paintings and spray paint the rest gold. The bottom row is a brief biography of the Virgin Mary from left to right. The piece is topped by Ancheta's sensitive crucifixion.

> ‡ *Down the hill from the old town, the three-sided Plaza de Navarra is the town's focus these days; the area has several good places to eat and drink.*

There's no tourist office, but the **Casa de Cultura** ① *C Túbal 19, T948 701 654,* provides information.

One of the oldest towns in Navarra, Olite was founded and fortified by the Romans. It wasn't until the 12th century, however, that the town began to rise to prominence within Navarra. The Navarrese monarchs had very itchy feet and were always decamping the court from one capital to the next. Olite became something of a favourite, and a **palace** was built, incorporating what remained of the Roman fortifications. This palace is now a *parador*.

It's the newer **castle** ① *daily Oct-Mar 1000-1400, 1600-1800; Apr-Sep 1000-1400, 1600-1900; Jul and Aug open until 2000; €2.50,* that turns heads though. Carlos III of Navarra, 'the Noble', felt that the ambitions of a kingdom should be reflected in its buildings. Accordingly, he went for broke, building the new palace in the early 15th century. Capitalizing on a period of peace in the Hundred Years' War between England and France (which tended to unavoidably involve Navarra), Carlos was determined that the palace would be a model of elegance, etiquette, and courtly splendour, and put in second-floor 'hanging' gardens, exotic trees, elegant galleries and towers, and a population of African animals including several lions and a giraffe. The castle was unfortunately destroyed in the Peninsular War to prevent it from falling into French hands, but it has been faithfully restored (perhaps overly) to something like its original appearance. It bristles with towers like an extravagant sandcastle, all with flags aflutter, but the highlight is certainly the restored 'queen's garden', a beautiful green space for which Carlos installed a very high-tech irrigation system for the time.

*❖ The remote areas southeast of Olite are difficult to access without a vehicle, and are some of the least populated morsels in Europe.*

As well as several other elegant buildings from Olite's zenith, the town has an intriguing series of **medieval galleries** ① *Oct-Mar Mon-Fri 1000-1400, Sat and Sun 1000-1400, 1600-1800; Apr-Sep daily 1000-1400, 1700-2000; €1.50,* underneath it. Their origins are uncertain, but it seems likely they were created, or at least enlarged by Carlos III, who extravagantly dreamed of linking the towns of Tafalla and Olite with a secret passageway for times of trouble. You can visit the galleries under the main square – they house an exhibition on medieval life.

The **tourist office** ① *Rúa Mayor, T948 741 703, Oct-Easter Tue-Fri 1000-1700, Sat and Sun 1000-1400; Easter-Sep Mon-Sat 1000-1400, 1600-1900; Sun 1000-1400,* is just off the castle square.

## Ujué

Perched above concentric terraces harbouring almond trees, Ujué was founded in the early days of the Navarran monarchy in the ninth century AD. The memorably beautiful walled settlement was ennobled by Carlos I, who built much of the sanctuary complex that perches atop the hill. The **Santuario de Santa María** seems part castle and part church, which it effectively was; the town was seen as an important defensive bastion. The María in question is the 'black virgin', a dusky Romanesque figure with an intense stare who refuses to shiver in the bleak stone church. Carlos II left his heart to the figure, literally; it sits in a box under the altar. How pure a heart it is, is not known: Carlos II was known as 'the Bad' for a number of dodgy political manoeuvres during his reign; he was imprisoned for a while by the French king John, whom history has named 'the Good'.

The most attractive part of the complex is the Paseo de Ronda, a covered walkway around the outside of the church with elegant galleries with beautiful vistas over the surrounding countryside. The road to Ujué starts from the attractive village of **San Martín de Unx**, worth a look in itself for its crypted church and noble old houses.

● *In case you were wondering, the remote village of Ujué, some 17 km east of Tafalla, is the*
● *gorgeous hilltop village on all the Navarrese tourist posters.*

① *Daily 0930-1230, 1530-1800; admission to cloister and garden €1.50.*

The isolated monastery at La Oliva is actually near the village of Carcastillo (18 km east of the main N121 on the NA124) but it feels in the middle of nowhere. The monastery dates from the mid-12th century and is populated by a working community of Cistercians (white monks). Although it was only repopulated in 1927 after a century of abandonment, there's a remarkable feel of living history here. The monks farm and make wine in true Cistercian style, and the smell of the farm yard pervades the monastery air. The beautifully simple portals, long gloomy church, and supremely peaceful cloister make this a very attractive visit.

## Artajona

Some 11 km northwest of Tafalla, its stunningly well-preserved walls are on a huge scale, and speak of a pride and resolve little related to the size of the village. Artajona claims to be the only place in the world whose bells are rung upside down. On *fiestas*, a team of *campañeros* gathers to push the four bells in a steady rhythm until they begin swinging right around. It requires a fair bit of strength and timing: the two heaviest bells each weigh over a ton.

Around Artajona are several **dolmens**, as well as the excavated Iron Age settlement of **Las Eretas** ① *T699 907 650, May-Sep Sat 1100-1400, 1700-1900, Sun 1100-1400; Jul/Aug also Tue-Fri 1100-1400, 1700-1900; phone for the possibility of visiting at other times*, which consists of several houses and burials; some bits have been reproduced, and it's not badly done.

---

# Tudela ⬤🖉✳⬤  ➻ *pp150-152.*

➔ *Colour map 5, A6.*

Even during its chilly winters, Tudela's got a scorched sort of look, while in summer the heat radiating from the footpaths and brown brick buildings can make it feel like a kiln. Apart from this, there's a definite Andalucían or Middle Eastern feel to the place, so it's no surprise to find that this was a place where Christians, Moors and Jews lived in relative harmony together for centuries.

Although there had been a Roman settlement here, it was in fact the Moorish lord Amrus ibn Yusuf who founded modern Tudela in the 9th century. Tudela was a centre of learning and, at times, government during the Middle Ages but its main claim to fame these days is vegetables. Although aridity is the main feature of the area, the silty banks of the Ebro have been a grower's paradise for millennia. If you're eating *alcachofas* (artichokes) or *cogollos* (lettuce hearts) in Spain, one thing's certain: if they aren't from Tudela, they aren't the best.

## Sights

Like many Spanish towns above a certain size, Tudela's outskirts look like no-man's land in a construction war and, like most Spanish towns, the centre is old and remarkably beautiful. The major sight is an example of biting the hand that feeds. When the city was taken by Christians in the early 12th century after centuries of tolerant Muslim rule, the Moors watched in dismay as their mosque was demolished and a **cathedral** ① *Tue-Sat 1000-1330, 1600-1900, Sun 1000-1330, €1.40*, erected on top of it. Despite this unchristian beginning, the cathedral is something of a masterpiece, although seemingly crowded by the surrounding buildings. The Puerta del Juicio is the finest of its entrances, and food for thought for unrepentant sinners passing under it: the Last Judgement is pretty thoroughly and graphically depicted. The high rib-vaulted Gothic interior has several elegant artistic works; the *retablo*, a work of Díaz de Oviedo recounts scenes in the life of Christ and

Mary and is set around a Renaissance sculpture of the Virgin. There's also a small **museum** in the harmonious Romanesque cloister.

The **Plaza de los Fueros**, not far from the cathedral, is a good space with a cute bandstand and several terrace bars. The square used to be used for bullfights, and the surrounding buildings are decorated with scenes of tauromachy, and with the coats of arms of the families of nobles that used to occupy the balconies. Just to the north of the centre is the hill of Santa Bárbara, topped by a statue of Christ on the spot where the old Moorish and Christian castles once stood. From here there's a nice view over the vegetable gardens and the Ebro, crossed by a stately bridge.

Tudela's **tourist office** ① *T948 848 058, Mon-Sat 1000-1400, 1600-1900, Sun 1000-1400*, is next to the cathedral.

## Around Tudela

The town of **Fitero** is home to a beautiful **monastery** ① *Mon 1730-1815, Tue-Sat 1130-1215, 1730-1815, Sun 1200 for guided tours, €2*, whose charming crumbly façade fronts a cavernously attractive church, cloisters and chapterhouse. Dating from 1140, this is the oldest of Spain's Cistercian monasteries. Less attractive, but interesting nonetheless is the memorial to the Falangist dead of the civil war. Next door, the **tourist office** ① *T948 776 600, Mon-Fri 1100-1300, 1700-1830, Sat 1100-1300*, might be persuaded to arrange a visit at other times if you look keen.

On the outskirts of Fitero, **Baños de Fitero** and its adjoining Riojan village **Ventas del Baño** are spa towns in a craggy little valley. Thousands of people still come here to take the waters, which are considered beneficial for many ailments.

North of Tudela, the **Bardenas Reales** is technically semi-desert; a violently rugged expanse of white gypsum flats and scrawny sheep grazing on what little spiky foliage survives. It's a popular location for filmmaking: parts of the recent Bond film *The World is not Enough* were made here. If you've got a car, a few roads are accessible with 2WD; otherwise take a tour from Tudela.

## ● Sleeping

**Tafalla** *p147*
**D Arotza**, Plaza de Navarra 3, T948 700 716. In the heart of things on this busy plaza, this *hostal*, run out of the restaurant **Tubal** next door, is hugely overpriced in Jul and Aug (A) but it's clean and comfortable. The restaurant also has simpler and cheaper rooms above it.

**Olite** *p148*
Olite has no cheap accommodation. For budget places, head for Tafalla or San Martín.
**AL Parador Principe de Viana**, Plaza de los Teobaldos 2, T948 740 000, www.parador.es, olite@parador.es. This recently restored gem of a parador occupies the old palace next to the flamboyant castle of Olite. It feels sober and elegant by comparison. The rooms have modern bathrooms and are centred around a lovely courtyard.

**C Hotel García Ramírez**, R de Medios 1, T948 741 300, www.hotelgarciaramirez.com. Thankfully this place on the main square opposite the castle doesn't live up to its billing as a 'medieval hotel'; in fact it's not short on modern comforts. The best rooms have mock stained-glass windows looking over the square; all are a/c. The hearty *asador* downstairs tends to be heavily booked by tour groups.
**F Albergue de Beire**, Ctra Aragón 1, Beire, T948 740 041, www.beire.com. A 40-min walk from Olite, this hostel is set around the courtyard of a *palacio* and has basic but decent dorms and doubles. During summer, however, the place is normally booked out as a summer camp. Prior reservation essential. There are meals available.

● *For an explanation of the sleeping and eating price codes used in this guide, see inside the*
● *front cover. Other relevant information is found in Essentials pages 39-46.*

### Ujué *p148*

**D Casa Pedro**, Ctra San Martín de Unx-Ujué
Km 1, T/F948 738 257, www.casapedro.net.
A warm, welcoming and individual place
to stay just outside the village of San Martín
de Unx. Comfy and attractive doubles in a
peaceful setting with home-cooked meals
and a great atmosphere. There's an attached
hostel section (**E**) and the place is totally
'green'. Recommended.

### Tudela *p149*

As Navarra's second city, Tudela has
many mid-range business hotels.
**AL Ciudad de Tudela**, C Misericordia s/n,
T948 402 440, ctudela@ac-hoteles.com.
A stately mansion house near the Plaza
de los Fueros, recently converted into
a modern hotel. Good facilities and crisp
modern rooms, although some aren't overly
blessed with natural light. The staff are
helpful, with an enthusiastic attitude.
**D Remigio**, C Gaztambide 4, T948 820 850,
F948 824 123. A cool and shady hotel just
off Plaza de los Fueros, with basic but clean
rooms with bath. Well-priced and popular
local restaurant underneath.
**F Estrella**, C Carnicerías 13, T948 821 039.
A good-value set of rooms above a popular
bar. Basic but acceptable; with reasonable
shared bathrooms and oversoft but
acceptable beds.

### Around Tudela *p150*

**C Balneario Bécquer**, Baños de Fitero,
T948 776 100. The most historic, but less
attractive of the 2 hotels.
**C Virrey Palafox**, Baños de Fitero, T948 776
275. Up the hill, this hotel is more peaceful.
Prices in both are very similar.

## ❼ Eating

### Tafalla *p147*

**❦ Tubal**, Plaza Navarra 6, T948 700 852.
A Tafalla institution and a must on any
*pintxo*- hopping trip in Tafalla; it also does
some tasty smart modern meals.

### Olite *p148*

**❦ Erri Berri**, Rúa del Fondo 1, Olite, T948 741
116. Big chunks of chargrilled meat are very
popular at this *asador*. *Chuletón de buey* is a
big T-bone from a mature ox, packed with

flavour and sold by weight, which usually
approaches 1 kg, a big meal in any language.
**❦ Gambarte**, Rúa del Seco 15, T948 740 139.
A likeable restaurant, which makes a point
of doing traditional Navarrese dishes well.
Try the *cogollos de Tudela*, lettuce rarely
reaches these heights; or the *jarrete de
cordero*, a herb-flavoured lamb stew that
comes with plenty of bones to gnaw.

### Tudela *p149*

**❦ Bargota**, C Virgen de la Cabeza 21,
T948 824 911. A quality place, and one
of the best to try the local vegetables.
One way is to order a *menestra*,which is
delicious here. There's a *menú* for €8.
**❦ Iruña**, C Muro (also called Abilio Calderón)
11, T948 821 000. One of Tudela's most
reliably good restaurants. Smart modern
dining near the plaza with an enticing menu
with distinct Navarrese and Riojan flavour.
Good unobtrusive service.
**❦ Bar Aragón**, Plaza de los Fueros. Bar with
a shady terrace to watch things happening
(or not) in the summer heat. Good beer
and plenty of things to snack on.
**❦ Bar José Luis**, C Muro (also called
Abilio Calderón) 23. A good, cheap place
to eat with outside tables and superb
*ensaladas mixtas*.
**❦ Estrella**, C Carnicerías 13, T948 821 039.
A good and lively bar and restaurant with
a wide selection of *pintxos* and reasonably
priced local dishes.

## ✪ Festivals and events

### Tudela *p149*

**24-30 Jul**  Tudela's big party, the **Fiestas de
Santa Ana**, features *encierros* and general
revelry. A few days before this is the **Bajada
del Ebro**, a competitive and rough-house
regatta on the river.

## ◉ Transport

### Tafalla and Olite *p147*

**Bus**  La Tafallesa (T948 222 886) runs
regular buses from **Pamplona** to Tafalla
(around 10 daily, 45 mins, €2.28), most
of which continue to Olite (€2.86), which
is also served by **Conda** 7 times daily.
A handful of trains link Tafalla and
Pamplona, but the bus is better.

**Ujué** *p148*

**Bus** There's one bus daily from **Tafalla** to Ujué via San Martín.

**Artajona** *p149*

**Bus** Artajona is serviced 2-3 times every Mon-Sat from **Pamplona** by Conda (1hr).

**Tudela** *p149*

**Bus** Conda, T948 221 026, www.condasa.com, runs between **Pamplona** and Tudela 6-7 times daily (1 hr 15 mins-1 hr 30 mins, €5.82-6.34). Some of these services stop in **Olite**, while there are other buses between **Tafalla** and Tudela.

**Around Tudela** *p150*

**Bus** Fitero is serviced by **Conda** buses from **Pamplona** 2-3 times daily (2 hrs 15 mins). In summer, these buses continue to Baños de Fitero. There are also buses from **Tudela** run by **Río Alhama**.

## ⁞ Footprint features

# Introduction

The once-mighty region of Aragón is now one of the peninsula's lesser-known areas. It's the ruggedness of the northern extremes that attracts most visitors; walkers and climbers beckoned by the same remote beauty that once drew legions of monks to establish themselves in lonely corners.

Wandering this sparsely populated region, it's hard to imagine that it was once a major Mediterranean power. Unification with Catalunya was a major part of that and once the two separated, landlocked Aragón was never going to wield the same influence, despite the powerful dynastic union of the Catholic Monarchs. Aragón's strong democratic tradition was a constant stumbling block for later kings desperate for war funds, and to this day the Aragonese enjoy a reputation for stubbornness in the rest of the country. The region saw some of the Civil War's bloodiest stalemates, exacerbated by the extremes of temperature that are a feature of the area.

The north of Aragón is taken up by a large chunk of Spain's most dramatic mountains, the Pyrenees. Whether you're a serious climber, trekker or skier, or you just enjoy fresh air, picturesque villages and proud granite peaks, the area is deeply satisfying and the awe-inspiring mountainscapes live long in the memory.

Further south, Zaragoza is a good lively place with enough museums, bars and Roman ruins to keep anyone happy for a couple of days. This area was the homeland of Goya, one of the world's great painters, and several of his lesser works can be seen in the city, which is gearing up excitedly to stage the 2008 World Expo.

## ★ Don't miss...

1 **Tarazona** Marvel at the *mudéjar* brick of this town, which preserves more feeling of its vanished Muslim and Jewish populations than most, page 165.

2 **Remote villages** Get away from it all in a picturesque village, like Uncastillo, page 167, or Roda de Isábena, page 177.

3 **Canyoning** Head for the area around Alquézar, which has been scoured by nature into one of Europe's best canyoning destinations, page 173.

4 **Jaca** Base yourself in this cheerful, outdoorsy town for some of Spain's best skiing; there are good bars and restaurants too, page 179.

5 **San Juan de la Peña** Revel in the sculptural skills at this atmospheric monastery nestled under an overhanging cliff, page 181.

6 **Pyrenean valleys** Put on a pack and strike out through spectacular mountainscapes such as those around Torla, page 189.

# Zaragoza → Phone code: 976. Colour map 6, B1. Population: 647,373.

*One of Spain's larger cities, Zaragoza is the nicest of places, with an easygoing modern European feel allied to some attractive architecture and good eating options. While it's not a touristed place in other ways, thousands of pilgrims come from all over Spain to visit the Basílica de Nuestra Señora del Pilar, a massive construction that dominates the square of the same name. Formerly an important Roman city, it's now a prosperous centre which stands in stark contrast to the somewhat bleak province that it commands. It sits on the Ebro and was a port in that river's livelier days. Over half of Aragón's population lives in Zaragoza.*

*To great excitement, Zaragoza has been chosen as the venue for the 2008 World Expo, which will run from mid-June to mid-September of that year. The city is hoping for around 7 million visitors to the complex, which is being built on a bend in the Ebro to the northwest of the centre. The theme, somewhat appropriately for this thirsty province, is water; you'll see the Expo's 'ZH2O' logo all over the place.*

▶▶ *For Sleeping, Eating and other listings, see pages 162-164.*

## Ins and outs

**Getting there and around** There's an extensive network of local bus routes; a timetable is available from the Ayuntamiento. Zaragoza's new train station, Las Delicias, is on the **AVE** fast-train network and should be handling all train traffic by the time this guide is in print. It lies just over a kilometre west of the El Portillo train station that was still in use for some services at time of research. Most of the city sits on the south bank of the Río Ebro; the old town being close to the river, and the newer sections spreading east, south and west from there. The majority of the sights are in the fairly compact old town. ▶▶ *See Transport, page 164, for further details.*

**Best time to visit** In high summer the pilgrim crowds in the basilica can be offputting, but they're usually on day trips, so the rest of town is by no means cluttered, although it does get fearsomely hot in August. The week around 12 October is the **Fiesta de La Virgen del Pilar**. ▶▶ *See Festivals and events, page 164.*

**Tourist information** The centre of Zaragoza has various information points. The most useful are the **municipal office** ① *T976 201 200, turismo@zaragoza.es, daily 1000-2000*, in a black glass cube opposite the basilica, and a new **provincial office** ① *T976 212 032, Mon-Fri 1000-1400, 1700-2000, Sat 1100-1400*, on the Plaza de España. There's an exhibition about the Expo in the Torreón Fortea on Plaza San Felipe.

## Background

Zaragoza sits on the Río Ebro, lifeblood of central Aragón, which undoubtedly made it an attractive option for the Romans, who took over the Iberian settlement of Salduie and founded their own town in 14 BC, naming it Caesaraugusta after the emperor. It became something of a focus of Roman culture, and then an important Visigothic city. Taken in AD 714 by the Moors, it resisted Charlemagne's attempts to conquer it and enjoyed a long period of cultural and architectural pre-eminence, known throughout Moorish lands as Al Baida, or the 'White City'. It was reconquered in 1118, and enjoyed a period of religious tolerance but later became a centre of the Inquisition, who didn't have things all their own way: one of their number was famously murdered in the cathedral.

Growing tension between Aragón and Castilla led to rioting in the late 16th century, and the town was annexed by the Castilian armies; effectively that was the end of Aragonese independence. The city's heroic defence against Napoleon's besieging armies in 1808 to 1809 is still a powerful symbol of Spanish independence.

Zaragoza played a full part in the tensions leading up to the Civil War too; the archbishop was murdered in 1923 by the famous anarchists Durruti and Ascaso, while a great general strike in 1933 to 1934 astounded observers, as workers went unpaid for 57 days. Despite these tendencies, the military rising in 1936 took the town by surprise and the Republican forces were never able to regain it, despite a lengthy campaign.

> ❣ There are a number of noble buildings of interest in Zaragoza – many of them are described in the useful pamphlet '100 motivos para visitar Zaragoza', available at the Turismo.

# Sights

## Basílica de Nuestra Señora del Pilar
① *Plaza del Pilar, daily 0545-2030 (2130 in summer), free.*
This enormous basilica, one of the country's foremost pilgrimage sites, is a spectacular building vaguely reminiscent of a mosque with its large coloured dome and slender towers. Saint James (who might have been surprised to learn that he was ever in Spain at all), was preaching in Zaragoza in AD 40 when the Virgin Mary descended from heaven on a jade pillar with words of encouragement for him. The pillar stayed when she disappeared and the basilica was built around it. Such is the Virgin of the Pilar's importance, that Pilar has for many centuries been one of the more popular names for Spanish girls. During the Civil War, the Virgin was named Captain-General of the city, which was under attack by Republican forces. A couple of bombs landed near the basilica but failed to explode; this was of course attributed to the Virgin's presence and intervention rather than the poor quality of the ordnance. The bombs are still proudly displayed in the basilica, hopefully defused.

> ❣ There's a local saying that something long and drawn-out 'goes on longer than the work on El Pilar'.

The church itself is a monumental edifice of a variety of architectural styles. It was built in the 17th and 18th centuries on the site of an earlier church, and not actually completed until 1961. The Santa Capilla chapel at the eastern end of the building houses the pillar itself, entombed in an ornate 18th-century *retablo*. Round the back is a small chink through which the column can be kissed. Nearby, two alcoves have domed ceilings painted by the young Goya.

Visitors throng the building, standing around watching the very public masses and confessions, or lighting candles (both real and LED). The other item of major artistic interest is the main *retablo* by the Aragonese sculptor Damián Forment, an incredibly intricate alabaster work depicting the Assumption of the Virgin. Opposite, the impressive organ has 6250 pipes, which don't seem to be tuned very often.

Behind the basilica is the **Río Ebro**. It's a little disappointing that more hasn't been done with the riverbanks, but it is crossed by a heavily restored 15th-century stone bridge, attractively lioned at each end with modern bronze works.

## Plaza del Pilar
The basilica dominates the Plaza del Pilar, a long rectangular space with a large population of pigeons and tourist shops; there's a roaring trade in cheap religious souvenirs, some of which are in appalling taste. The plaza's western end is given character by the attractive modern **Fuente de la Hispanidad**, while in the east a bronze Goya overlooks sculpted figures derived from his paintings. Next to him is the **Lonja**, a Renaissance building that was originally the influential merchants' guild, but now houses exhibitions in its elegant columned hall.

Northern Aragón Zaragoza

**Museo de Ibercaja Camón Aznar**

ⓘ *C Espoz y Mina 23, T976 397 328, Tue-Fri 0900-1415, 1800-2100, Sat 1000-1400, 1800-2100, Sun 1100-1400.*

Situated in a beautiful Renaissance palace in the heart of Zaragoza, this impressive private collection of Spanish art was donated to the city on the death of the collector, a well-known Zaragozan literary figure. There are several notable paintings by artists such as El Greco and Zurbarán, as well as a large gallery displaying Goya's four major series of prints.

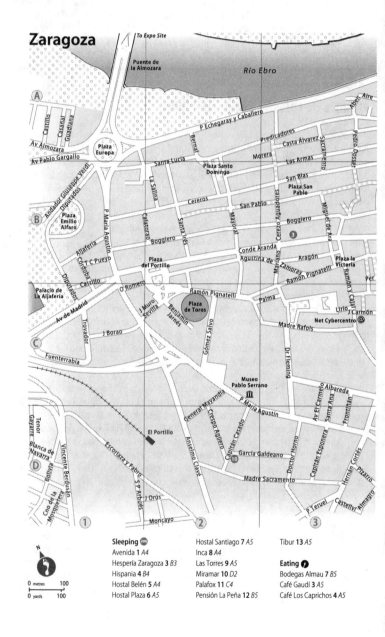

Zaragoza

**Sleeping**
Avenida **1** *A4*
Hesperia Zaragoza **3** *B3*
Hispania **4** *B4*
Hostal Belén **5** *A4*
Hostal Plaza **6** *A5*

Hostal Santiago **7** *A5*
Inca **8** *A4*
Las Torres **9** *A5*
Miramar **10** *D2*
Palafox **11** *C4*
Pensión La Peña **12** *B5*

Tibur **13** *A5*

**Eating**
Bodegas Almau **7** *B5*
Café Gaudí **3** *A5*
Café Los Caprichos **4** *A5*

## Plaza de la Seo and the cathedral

ⓘ *Cathedral: winter Tue-Fri 1000-1400, 1600-1800, Sat 1000-1300, 1600-1800, Sun 1000-1200, 1600-1800; summer Tue-Fri 1000-1400, 1600-1900, Sat 1000-1300, 1600-1900, Sun 1000-1200, 1600-1900; museum open until 1400 Sun, €1.50.*

At its eastern end Plaza del Pilar becomes Plaza de la Seo, dominated by Zaragoza's cathedral of the same name. Built on the site of the city's mosque, it's a blend of styles covering everything from Romanesque to neoclassical. Admire the *mudéjar* tiling and brickwork on its northern side before going inside, where there is an excellent tapestry collection; the amount of work involved in these masterpieces can hardly be imagined.

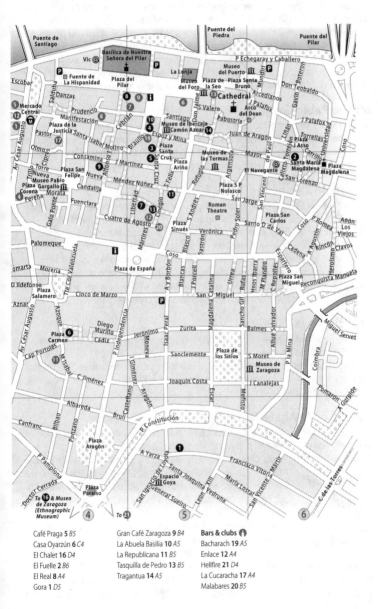

Café Praga **5** *B5*
Casa Oyarzún **6** *C4*
El Chalet **16** *D4*
El Fuelle **2** *B6*
El Real **8** *A4*
Gora **1** *D5*

Gran Café Zaragoza **9** *B4*
La Abuela Basilia **10** *A5*
La Republicana **11** *B5*
Tasquilla de Pedro **13** *B5*
Tragantua **14** *A5*

**Bars & clubs** 🎵
Bacharach **19** *A5*
Enlace **12** *A4*
Hellfire **21** *D4*
La Cucaracha **17** *A4*
Malabares **20** *B5*

Northern Aragón *Zaragoza*

Near Plaza de la Seo, the street is crossed by the pretty Arco del Dean. The dean didn't fancy soiling his robes in the medieval muck when travelling between home and the cathedral, so he had an elegant overhead passage built across the street, with ornate Gothic *mudéjar* windows.

## Roman Caesaraugusta

① *Tue-Sat 1000-1400, 1700-2000, Sun 1000-1400, €1.90 each, €3.80 for all 3.*

As you stroll around the area of Arco del Dean, you're walking over the centre of Roman Caesaraugusta. There are **three underground museums** where the foundations of the Roman forum, riverport and public baths can be investigated. The forum is the most interesting, although all have audiovisual displays in Spanish, English and French.

Other Roman remains to check out are the walls, of which an 80-m stretch is well conserved just west of Plaza del Pilar, and the theatre, which once held 6000.

It's also worth heading down Calle Mayor to inspect the fabulous *mudéjar* tower of the church of **Santa María Magdalena**, a spectacular symphony in decorative brick.

## Museo Pablo Gargallo

① *Plaza San Felipe 3, T976 724 923, Tue-Sat 1000-1400, 1700-2100, Sun 1000-1400, free.*

The Pablo Gargallo museum is set in an attractive 17th-century palacio in the old part of Zaragoza, and fronted by two stocky horses. It contains works by the impressive, if slightly bombastic Aragonese sculptor of the same name.

## Museo de Zaragoza

① *Plaza de los Sitios 6 and Parque Grande s/n; former Tue-Sat 1000-1400, 1700-2000, Sun 1000-1400, latter Tue-Sat 0900-1400, Sun 1000-1400; both free.*

The main provincial museum is divided into two sections, the more interesting of which is on the Plaza de los Sitios, set in an elegant building dating from 1908. This contains art and architecture sections and includes several Goyas, as well as much Aragonese religious art and more modern works. The other section on the edge of the large Parque Grande, a long walk southwest of town, is an ethnographic museum based on Pyrenean life. There's also a pottery collection.

## Espacio Goya

① *C San Ignacio de Loyola 16, Tue-Fri 0830-1430, 1800-2100, Sat 1100-1400, 1800-2100, Sun 1100-1400, free.*

Located in the headquarters of a bank, Espacio Goya is a decorative 16th-century patio from a different building, around which are exhibited Aragonese paintings, including many Goyas.

## Palacio de la Aljafería

① *1 km west of the old town, T976 289 683, daily 1000-1400, 1600-1830 (2000 in summer): closed Thu and Fri pm, except during Jan, Jul and Aug.*

A kilometre west of the old town, the Aljafería was once a sumptuous Muslim palace.

*❉ The most unfortunate incident in the Aljafería's history was its conversion into a barracks, which removed much of its interior character.*

After the city was reconquered, it was lived in by the Aragonese kings, before Fernando and Isabel obtained planning permission to put on a second storey. Felipe II later had the building converted into a military fort, building exterior walls and a moat – he was having problems with the locals at the time. Today the complex holds the Aragonese regional parliament. The most impressive part to visit is the Muslim courtyard, a modern reconstruction with original fragments still visible. It gives a good sense of what it must have been like, with characteristic scalloped arches and delicate carved intricacies. There's a small, ornate prayer room; the niche is the *mihrab*, which points towards Mecca. Upstairs, little

## The Master of Darkness

*Goya, a nightmare full of the Unknown* Baudelaire

The man who reputedly threw a plaster bust at the Duke of Wellington for moving during a portrait sitting was born in the Aragonese village of Fuendetodos in 1746. Francisco José de Goya y Lucientes is widely recognized as being the first artist of the modern age. An artist of great technical skill and imagination Goya was a master of painting and engraving who managed to combine his role at the heart of Spain's art establishment with his own uncompromising artistic vision.

Goya became known outside Spain with the publication in 1864 of his 80 etching series *The Disasters of War*, which depicts in a brutal manner the horrors of the war in Spain after the French invasion of 1808. Not published during his lifetime, this series is almost unique in art history for the dark view of humanity that it portrays. Along with his other series of etchings, *Los Caprichos*, of 1799, a wicked satire on Spanish society, and the 18 etchings of *Los Proverbios* Goya's vision can seem overwhelmingly bleak.

Goya was, however, a man of the Enlightenment and believed that art could instruct and educate. An examination of his enormous number of paintings reveals an artist who worked on many different levels. His designs for the Royal Tapestry factory are rustic and optimistic while his portraits of the family of Carlos IV show him subverting his role as courtly painter by revealing the coldness and ugliness at the heart of the Royal Court.

The darker side of Goya's work was produced during the latter part of his life. The 12 works known as the *Black Paintings*, which he painted on the walls of his house in Madrid, are undoubtedly influenced by his many illnesses which had left him deaf and unable to communicate except through hand signals. His experimentation with new forms and techniques is at its most obvious in these works, typified by the almost abstract *Dog on a Leash*.

Goya's most famous paintings of the clothed and unclothed *Maja* shows his skill in revealing our common humanity stripped of pretensions. His finest works place him in the very highest echelon of European painters and, although his paintings and etchings show at times a pessimistic view of humanity, in much of his work there there is something undeniably life enhancing.

Goya died in Bordeaux in 1828.

remains of the Catholic Monarchs' palace other than some very elaborate ceilings of superb polychrome wood. As it's a parliament building, there's a scanner on the way in, so leave swords and penknives at your *pensión*.

## Museo Pablo Serrano
ⓘ *Paseo María Agustín 20, Tue-Sat 1000-1400, 1700-2000 (1800-2100 summer), Sun 1000-1400.*
A curious bunker-like building near the train station, the Pablo Serrano museum exhibits the work of the sculptor, as well as the painter Juana Francés who married him.

## Monasterio Cartuja de Aula Dei
ⓘ *Open last Sat of each month, but numbers are limited; there's currently an 18-month waiting list; T976 714 934 to get on it.*
On the outskirts of Zaragoza, north along the Z-123, this Carthusian monastery has some wall paintings by Goya, but is almost impossible to get into.

## Sleeping

**Zaragoza** *p156, map p158*
There are over 100 places to stay in Zaragoza, although many of them are clonish business hotels or functional *pensiones*. Prices rocket in mid-Oct for the Virgen del Pilar long weekend.
LL **Hotel Palafox**, Casa Jiménez s/n, T976 237 700, www.palafoxhoteles.com. The most classic of Zaragoza's hotels has undergone a recent redesign, and has been kitted out in very attractive minimalist style. The rooms are large and light, and come with all the trimmings, including video games, a free minibar and round-the-clock room service. There are some rooms available for disabled guests.
L **Hesperia Zaragoza**, Av Conde de Aranda 48, T976 284 500, www.hesperia-zaragoza.com. An efficient modern business hotel. It's much less stuffy than many of its kind and reasonable value. The rooms are spacious and come with satellite TV, excellent bathroom, internet access and a/c. There's also free wireless internet connection throughout the building.
A **Hotel Avenida**, Av César Augusto 55, T976 439 300, www.hotelavenida-zaragoza.com. A clean, fresh spot with mock Roman decor on the street where the old walls used to run. The a/c rooms have parquet floors and are attractive and comfortable. Out of season it's extremely good value (**C**).
B **Hotel Inca**, C Manifestación 33, T976 390 091, www.hotelinca-avil.com. A likeable and stylish small hotel south of the basilica. The wood-floored rooms have simple elegance and the attractive restaurant is suitably classy. Rooms have safe and internet jack.
B **Hotel Tibur**, Plaza de la Seo 2, T976 202 000, www.hoteltibur.com. A smart place in a quiet corner of the Plaza del Pilar area. The rooms have every convenience and are spacious and tastefully furnished. There's also a good restaurant.
B **Hotel Las Torres**, Plaza del Pilar 11, T976 394 250, F976 394 254. Directly opposite the basilica, this pleasant old hotel with friendly owners has large, comfortable rooms, most of which have views and a balcony rail. Parking.
C **Hotel Hispania**, Av César Augusto 103, T976 284 928, www.hotelhispania.com. Well located near the Plaza del Pilar, this handy, pleasant option has modern rooms with all facilities. It's very good value off season and has parking available for €10.
D **Hostal Belén**, C Predicadores 2, T976 280 913, hostalbelen2@yahoo.es. In a brand-new building close to the market, with 5 smallish but nice doubles and friendly management. Rooms have TV, a/c and heating.
D **Hostal Santiago**, C Santiago 3, T976 394 550. A well-placed warren of a hotel near the tourist office and basilica. Management is slightly strange, but it's clean, comfortable, and with a/c. Some rooms are more expensive than others.
D-E **Hostal Plaza**, Plaza del Pilar 14, T976 294 830. A reasonable choice with a top location opposite the basilica. Decent a/c rooms with or without bathroom. Slightly wayward management style, so confirm any bookings!
E **Miramar**, C Capitán Casado 17, T976 281 094. Handy for the station, this is a friendly little *pensión* with clean, quiet rooms with a shower but shared bathroom.
F **Pensión La Peña**, C Cinegio 3, T976 299 089. Simple, cheap doubles with washbasin, in the old part of town.

**Camping**
**Camping Casablanca**, T976 753 870, F976 753 875. The closest campsite to town, large and fully equipped, although only open Apr-Sep. Follow the signs off the N-II west of town, near the Km 317 marker.

## Eating

**Zaragoza** *p156, map p 158*
TTT **El Chalet**, C Santa Teresa 25, T976 569 104. An excellent and not exorbitant restaurant run by chef Angel Conde, an avid historian of Aragonese cuisine. Although his beef dishes are sublime, the careful treatment of vegetables marks the restaurant out from most of its compatriots. In good weather, there's a beautiful garden terrace.
TT **Casa Oyarzún**, Plaza Nuestra Señora del Carmen 1, T976 216 436. Popular with business workers for its good-quality lunchtime *menú* and sunny terrace. The cuisine is Basque in style.
TT **El Real**, C Alfonso I 40. The best of the row of places opposite the basilica, but drinks on the terrace don't come cheap. Roast meats are what they do best, in an attractive stone-faced dining room.

**La Abuela Basilia**, C Santiago 14, T976 390 594. A good downstairs restaurant specializing in suckling pig and milk-fed lamb cooked in their wood-fired oven. The decor is stylish and relaxed.

**Bodegas Almau**, C Estébanes 10, T976 299 834. This enchanting wine bar is well into its 2nd century. It's a temple to Spanish tradition, with old wooden shelves rising to the ceiling laden with bottles of all shapes and sizes. It's a great place to have a glass of local wine.

**El Fuelle**, C Mayor 59, T976 398 033. Zaragoza's most enjoyable tapas spot is large and homely, decorated with farming implements and the neckscarves from dozens of fiestas. The humorous menu continues the rustic theme, with traditional Aragonese *raciones* at knockdown prices.

**Gora**, C Francisco de Vitoria 1, T976 227 983. This trendy modern tapas bar has a stellar reputation for its tortilla, which is succulent in the extreme. At weekends it turns into a trendy disco bar once the tapas are cleared away.

**La Republicana**, C Mendéz Nuñez 38, T976 396 509. A cheap and cheerful little old town tapas bar, cosy and warm. They serve tasty *pinchos* as well as simple, hearty plates of comfort food. The decor, full of bric-a-brac, reminds one of a French bistro, but the cheap breakfasts are pure Spanish: they include a glass of wine. Closed Sun.

**Tasquilla de Pedro**, C Cinegio 3, T976 390 658. There's some good eating to be done here, with a large range of good cold tapas. Ignore the pushy owner who likes to trap tourists with an expensive 'mixed plate' and make your own selections from the bar, which is groaning under the weight of everything.

**Tragantua**, Plaza Santa Marta s/n, T976 299 174. This excellent little tapas bar specializes in seafood. It's always busy with people competing for elbow room to crack open their crustaceans. Good value and very cheerful; there's also a downstairs dining room.

### Cafés

**Café Gaudí**, Plaza Santa Cruz s/n. A good summer option, with outdoor tables in a quiet square. A range of sandwiches and *bocadillos* are on offer.

**Café Los Caprichos**, C Espoz y Mina 25. A good little backstreet bar with a few outdoor tables in summer. The interior is elegant and comfortable, full of character with various Goya prints on the walls and coloured glass. It's a fine spot for a pre- or post- dinner *copa*.

**Café Praga**, Plaza Santa Cruz 13, T976 200 251. A good spot for evening drinks, with a large terrace and good service.

**Gran Café Zaragoza**, C Alfonso I 25. A Zaragoza classic: a beautiful, traditional old Spanish café with a range of small eats. Set on the main pedestrian street, it's a de- rigueur stop for an evening coffee during the *paseo*, or a lunchtime vermouth and *pincho*.

## Bars and clubs

**Zaragoza** *p156, map p158*

**Bar Bacharach**, C Espoz y Mina 10, T976 390 660. A small and very popular bar, carefully decorated in white wood. The walls are decorated with black and white photos of films that Bacharach scored. It's usually full of interesting people; it's also a place where you can eat simple meals and is open late.

**Enlace**, Av César Augusto 45. A large bar with decent house music and a dancefloor. Open very late most nights. Spacious and cheerful.

**Hellfire**, C La Paz 21. A dark and atmospheric darkwave bar, with gothic/industrial sounds and suitable decoration. Open Fri/Sat from 2200. There's a tradition of such clubs in this city, popularly known as Zaragotham.

**La Cucaracha**, C Temple s/n. One of many rowdy bars on this street. This is Zaragoza's prime zone for weekend festivities.

**Malabares**, C Cinegio 2. This popular new bar is mainly worth visiting for its great setting, in an old *palacio* in El Tubo with a beautiful antique ceiling. The interior design is modern and stylish, with a cosy little lounge as well as plenty of tables. There's a range of innovative *pinchos*, but the place really gets going around midnight. Poor service.

## Entertainment

**Zaragoza** *p156, map p158*
### Cinema
**Filmoteca de Zaragoza**, Plaza San Carlos 4, T976 721 853, shows excellent repertory cinema, mostly English-language films with Spanish subtitles. Admission €2.
**Cines Goya**, C San Miguel s/n, T976 225 172, show recent releases, as do **Cines Buñuel**, C Francisco Vitoria 30, T976 232 018.

**Teatro Principal**, C Coso 57, T976 296 090.
**Teatro del Mercado**, Plaza Santo Domingo
s/n, T976 437 662.

## ⊛ Festivals and events

**Zaragoza** *p156, map p158*
**12 Oct**  Fiesta de La Virgen del Pilar.
A week full of parties, concerts and fireworks.

## O Shopping

**Zaragoza** *p156, map p158*
Most shops are around the broad
avenues south of the old town.
**Bacanal**, near the Mercado, is an entertaining
costume shop on C Manifestación.
**Librería General**, Paseo Independencia 22.

### Markets
Try the modernista **Mercado Central**, just
southwest of the Plaza del Pilar. Also worth a
look is the flea market on Sun morning by the
bullring, and the clothes market on Wed and
Sun mornings by the football stadium.

## ▲ Activities and tours

**Zaragoza** *p156, map p158*
A colourful tourist bus runs around a 16-stop
city route. A hop-on hop-off ticket costs €4.
The service is in operation daily from Jul to
mid-Oct, and weekends only from Easter-Jun
and mid-Oct to mid-Dec.The tourist office
also run a variety of tours of the city and
province (www.turismozaragoza.com). Most
of the city's sights have regular guided tours
around them, €1. A **tourist-taxi** service is
also available, with a 1- or 2-hr trip (€18/30)
accompanied by recorded commentary with
various languages available (T976 201 200).

## ⊖ Transport

**Zaragoza** *p156, map p158*
**Air**  The city's airport (ZAZ) is served by
Iberia from **Barcelona** and **Madrid**; by
Ryanair from **London** Stansted and **Milan**
Bergamo; there are also flights to **Frankfurt**.
Airport buses leave from the corner of Gran
Vía and Paseo Pamplona to connect with
flights (20-30 mins, €1.80). About €18
in a taxi. Airport enquiries: T976 712 300.

**Bus**  There are many bus companies serving
a huge variety of destinations. At time of
research, all were still leaving from different
depots, but hopefully, by the time you read
this, all will have been consolidated in the
new bus station, which is to be in the same
complex as the Las Delicias train station.
Bus 51 runs from the centre (passing Puerta
del Carmen) to this station.
    The major long-distance operators are:
**Agreda/ALSA**, who serve **Madrid** (hourly,
3¾ hrs, €12.43), **Barcelona** (more or less
hourly, 3¾ hrs, €11.78), **Valladolid** (5 daily,
6½ hrs, €22.12), **Soria** (3 daily, 2¼ hrs,
€10.97), Bilbao (6-8 daily, 4 hrs, €17). Tezasa
services **Logroño**, **Burgos** and **Teruel**, while
La Oscense, T976 434 510, runs to **Huesca**
(more than hourly, 55 mins, €5.27) and **Jaca**
(5 daily, 2 hrs 10 mins, €10.99). **Tarazona**
is served by **Therpasa** (T976 300 045).
    The **Cinco Villas** are serviced 1-4 times
daily by **Automoviles 5 Villas** (Av de Navarra
81, T976 333 371); **Sos** can also be reached on
the **Sangüesa** bus that leaves at 1900 daily.
    Autobuses Conda go 6 times daily to
**San Sebastián** €16.14), via **Tudela** and
**Pamplona** (€10.65).

**Train**  There are roughly hourly AVE fast
trains from the new Las Delicias station to
Madrid (1hr 30min, €38.60). Ten daily normal
trains run to  **Barcelona** (3-5 hrs, from
€20-40) and two to Madrid (3½ hrs, €18.35).
Other trains run to **Bilbao**, **Pamplona**,
**Burgos**, **Huesca**, **Jaca**, **Calatayud**, **Teruel**,
**Valencia** and more. Bus no 51 runs between
the centre (Puerta del Carmen is one stop)
and Las Delicias station.

## ❶ Directory

**Zaragoza** *p156, map p158*
**Internet**  Conecta-T, Plaza Lanuza s/n;
El Navegante, C Mayor 25, has internet
access at €2 per hr. **Laundry**  There's
a *lavandería* on C Pedro María Ric s/n.
**Medical services**  C Isabel La Católica
s/n. Phone 112 in an emergency. **Police**
C Doctor Palomar 8, T976 396 207. Phone
092 or 112 in an emergency. **Taxis**
Call T976 383 838. **Telephone**  VIC is
a *locutorio* on C Jardel 3, T976 399 055,
by the side of the basilica; there's also
internet access for €1.50 per hr.

# Northwest from Zaragoza

*The most interesting corner of Zaragoza province seems to encapsulate Aragón with its deserted, epic, dry and dusty landscapes and fascinating, forgotten towns and villages redolent of past glories. Intriguing Tarazona takes you back centuries to the era when three faiths lived side by side. With its superb ensemble of mudéjar brick buildings and its precariously perched old town, it has a distinct feel of sandswept North Africa or the Levant. North of here, the enticing Cinco Villas are backwaters today, with beautifully preserved buildings and squares and steep paved streets. Who would believe that remote Sos was the birthplace of one of history's most powerful monarchs, the Catholic King Fernando of Aragón?* ➧ *For Sleeping, Eating and other listings, see pages 167-168.*

## Tarazona and around ●●●●  ➧ *pp167-168.*

➙ *Colour map 5, A5.*

Those who hold stone and wood to be the only noble building materials should pay Tarazona a visit. Brick can be beautiful too, as this town's many *mudéjar* edifices prove. Once home to thriving Muslim and Jewish populations, Tarazona still seems to pine for these expelled people, although a look at the *turiaso* faces suggests that the Catholic purists happily didn't come close to erasing every last drop of non-Christian blood.

The best time to see Tarazona is a summer evening, just as the sun decides it's baked the bricks enough for one day. People emerge from hiding and the buildings glow with a cheery light. Tarazona is an easy day trip from Zaragoza or Soria, but is a nice place to stay too (although the weekday nightlife isn't exactly kicking).

### Background
Tarazona was populated by Celt-Iberians from way back but flowered in the 13th and 14th centuries, when it sheltered a flourishing population of Jews, Muslims and Christians. A frequent target for Castilian expansion, it suffered several sieges. The Aragonese crown generally protected its non-Christian citizens from the pogroms that plagued the land in the late 14th century but, once unified with Castilla, the population was doomed to convert or leave. Later, even the converted Muslims were expelled.

### Sights
Most of Tarazona's *mudéjar* architecture is clustered on a knoll above the struggling Río Queiles. The tower rising imperiously over the town belongs to the Iglesia de Santa María Magdalena, built in a mixture of architectural styles from the Romanesque to the Renaissance. Next to it stands the episcopal palace, formerly a residence of Muslim rulers and Aragonese kings. The ornate Plateresque façade overlooking the river suggests that the local bishops weren't exactly prepared to rough it. There's a tourist office ① *on the main square, T976 640 074, turismo@ tarazona.org, daily 0900-1330, 1630-1900.*

Descending from here, Calle San Juan was the centre of the *morería*, or Moorish quarter. Little remains of the *judería*, the Jewish quarter, which was clustered at the foot of the hill, overhung by houses perched above. The Ayuntamiento is an unusual and attractive building adorned with pictures of the labours of Herakles, perhaps an attempt to flatter Carlos V, the king and emperor at the time it was built. An intriguing sculpture in front depicts *El Cipotegato*, a jester-like character who appears to open the town's annual fiesta on 27 August. He attempts to run from the Ayuntamiento across the town; an easy enough task apart from the minor inconvenience of the entire citizenry trying to stop him by pelting him with tomatoes.

## ⁞ Mudéjar

*Mudéjar* is a style of architecture that evolved in Christian Spain, and particularly Aragón, from around the 12th century. As the Reconquista took town after town from the Muslims, Moorish architects and those who worked with them began to meld their Islamic tradition with the northern influences of Romanesque and Gothic. The result is distinctive and pleasing, typified by the decorative use of brick and coloured tiles, with the tall elegant belltowers a particular highlight. The style became popular nation-wide; in certain areas, *mudéjar* remained a constant feature for over 500 years of building.

Across the river stands the cathedral with an extraordinary *mudéjar* brick tower. Currently closed for major renovation (due to open as this book goes to press), it's another fascinating hotchpotch of styles; the attractive cloister is one of its best features. Nearby, the old Plaza de Toros is an interesting bit of civil history. Annoyed by the lack of a bullring, a group of citizens in the late 18th century decided to build their balconied houses in an octagonal arrangement that both gave them a place to live and the town a venue for tauromachy.

### Monasterio de Veruela
ⓘ *Oct-Mar, Tue-Sun 1000-1300, 1500-1800; Apr-Sep Tue-Sun 1000-1400, 1600-1900.*
Beautifully situated in a valley to the southeast of Tarazona is the Veruela monastery. The Cistercian order, bent on a return to traditional monastic values, found Aragón a suitably harsh terrain for their endeavours. Veruela was the first of many monasteries founded by the White Monks in the 12th century. Its small, gardened entrance conceals the size of the complex, girt by a formidable hexagonal wall. The relatively unadorned church is a blend of Romanesque and early Gothic styles. The cloister is similarly attractive and understated, its capitals crowned with simple fronds and

⁞ *The romantic poet Gustavo Adolfo Bécquer often stayed here with his brother; the monastery inspired many of his works.*

leaves. The monks still work the fields, both inside and outside the walls. During summer there are occasional classical concerts in the grounds. The best way to get there is to take a bus from Zaragoza to Tarazona and get off at the second of the junctions for Vera de Moncayo; the monastery is a 45-minute walk from here. Be sure to prompt the driver to let you off, as they frequently forget. You'll have to signal the return bus clearly, as they tend to thunder past the crossing quite fast.

### Parque Nacional Dehesa de Moncayo
ⓘ *Visitor centre open at weekends in spring and summer 1000-1400, 1500-1900.*
The Dehesa de Moncayo National Park straddles the border of Zaragoza and Soria provinces and is an attractive spot for walks, with scented pine hills and a couple of interesting sanctuaries and villages.

# Cinco Villas 🚍🚻🚌 ↠ *pp167-168.*

Northwest of Zaragoza in a land of harsh hills, cold winds and beating sun are situated these five towns, granted their charter by the Bourbon King Felipe V but important places long before that. If you've got transport you might want to check out all five, but otherwise the bus connections are a bit limiting. Sos del Rey Católico and Uncastillo are the two most rewarding to visit.

# Sos del Rey Católico

Once just called Sos, words were added in memory of its most famous son. Not only did young Fernando become king of Aragón, he also united Spain in partnership with his wife Isabel. She was quite a catch; although she admitted to only having bathed twice in her life, that was still twice more than most people of the time, and what's more, she was heiress to the Castilian throne.

It's a beautiful, atmospheric village; the city wall is partly intact, with houses built into it. It has become a very popular spot for summer outings and weekends but at other times of year you may have it to yourself – pace the lonely streets and plot your own Reconquista. It's the village as a whole rather than individual buildings that impress. In the centre of town *❧ Sos is an architectural gem of medieval streets.* is the **Plaza de la Villa**, presided over by the decorative **Ayuntamiento**, featuring a stern warning from Ecclesiastes. The square used to be used for markets; a hole in one of the columns was for hanging a balance, and next to it is etched an official measure of length of the time, the *bara jaquesa* (Jaca bar). Sos' **tourist office** ① *Tue-Sat 1000-1400, 1700-2100 (2000 in winter)*, run guided walks through the village twice a day.

Ascending from the square you'll reach the church via a haunting underpass. The high-vaulted interior is impressive, a more homely touch is provided by the colourful organ. The highlight is the crypt which preserves some excellent wall-paintings of the life of Christ and the Virgin. At the far end of the village, remains of a castle and walls are backed by the modern but sensitively constructed *parador*. Fernando himself was born in the **Palacio de Sada**, one of the largest of the town's buildings.

# Uncastillo

The most remote of the Cinco Villas, Uncastillo is also its most charming. It's much less visited than Sos and, although not as architecturally perfect, perhaps less austere. Originally fortified by Muslims to counter the Christian Reconquista, it changed hands and became an important bastion for the Navarrese King Sancho the Great, before it passed to the Aragonese monarchy. The town also had a flourishing Jewish quarter.

What's left of the castle, above the town, has been transformed into a small but excellent **museum** ① *T976 679 121, summer 1100-1400, 1700-2000, €2*. The visit commences with a short audiovisual presentation (Spanish or English), which is epic enough for a David Lean feature, and then sends you up the tower where some accessible, light-handed displays give good information about the history of the town and the region. There's a small **tourist office** all week during the summer.

# Ejea de los Caballeros

The 'capital' and largest of the Cinco Villas, Ejea de los Caballeros at first glance lacks the charm of its neighbours, with a dusty feel and traffic thundering through it. However, make your way to the fortress-church of **San Salvador**, which is muscular and elegant and has some vestiges of colour in its portal, which depicts the *Last Supper* and the *Nativity*. The real reason to come here, however, is inside; the main *retablo* is a masterpiece. The Gothic painted panels show clear Flemish influence and have been carefully restored. They depict scenes from the life of Christ, from the *Adoration* to the *Last Judgement*, all in high colour and lively detail.

**Northern Aragón** Northwest from Zaragoza Listings

---

## ● Sleeping

**Tarazona and around** *p165*
C **Hostal Santa Agueda**, C Visconti 26, T976 640 054, www.santaagueda.com. This modern and well-manicured establishment recently opened just off the main plaza. The interior is beautiful, with wooden beams and antique furniture. It's all very stylish, and the management friendly.

D **O Cubillar**, Plaza de Nuestra Señora 12, T976 641 192, F976 199 086. Attractive and cosy rooms, decorated with a nice touch, above a good bar and restaurant.

**D Palacete de los Arcedianos**, Plaza Arcedianos 1/C Marrodón 16, T/F976 642 303, www.palacetearcedianos.com. Good, if sometimes stuffy, rooms in a curious domed building. Bathrooms are shared.

### Sos del Rey Católico *p167*
**AL Parador de Sos del Rey Católico**, C Sainz de Vicuña 1, T948 888 011,  www.parador.es. At the far end of town, this parador is mostly modern but characterful, with a nice veranda terrace and slightly sombre but comfortable rooms and some much nicer mini-suites.
**C Hostal Las Coronas**, Plaza de la Villa s/n, T948 888 408, F948 888 471. In the heart of town, these doubles are slightly overpriced but equipped with TV and bathroom above a good restaurant, with snails a speciality. Some of the rooms look onto the plaza.
**E Fonda Fernandina**, C Alfaro s/n, T948 888 120. A very good and friendly option, with simple but spacious rooms with washbasin. There's also a popular rustic bar/restaurant.

### Uncastillo *p167*
**C Posada La Pastora**, C Roncesvalles 1, T976 679 499, www.lapastora.net.  A fantastic spot, a rural home in the heart of the village. Rooms are tastefully decorated; they're all different, but colourful and beautifully furnished in a way that brings out the stone character of the building. Great breakfast. Recommended.

### Casas rurales
**B Posada la Pastora**, C Roncesvalles 1, T976 679 499, www.lapastora.net This rural hotel is an excellent option. The decor combines light modernity with rustic colours and textures, and the rooms are a delight, particularly the top floor one which has great views and a cosy attic roof (**A**). Breakfast is extra but very good, and the owner is delightful.

There are a couple of other *casas rurales*: a nice one is by the church at Plaza del Ordinario 8, T976 679 012, where a comfy double with shared bath costs about €30. Closed winter.

## ◐ Eating

### Tarazona and around *p165*
**Ⅲ El Galeón**, Av La Paz 1, T976 642 965. It's a fair way from the sea, but this good ship does some excellent seafood – the mussels are especially delicious.

**Ⅲ Mesón O Cubillar**, Plaza de Nuestra Señora 12, T976 641 192. A sound choice with an attractive 1st-floor restaurant, serving modern Aragonese fare and the bar downstairs dishing out inexpensive *raciones* of grilled meats.
**Ⅰ Amadeo I**, Paseo de los Fueros de Aragón s/n. A fine terraced café by the Río Queiles, a spot for early evening drinks and ice creams.
**Ⅰ Bar Visconti**, C Visconti 19. The locals' choice, with a range of *raciones* and tapas, many of them fried morsels of various things.

### Sos del Rey Católico *p167*
Many hotels also have decent restaurants.
**Ⅲ Vinacua**, C Pintor Goya 1, T948 888 071. Eschew the €14 *menú* for à la carte; it's no more expensive. Simple, filling dishes and cheap wine are the order of the day.
**Ⅰ Bar Landa**, C Alfaro s/n, T948 888 158. Good for morning coffee, with a peaceful back terrace and cheap evening meals.
**Ⅰ El Caserio**, C Pintor Goya s/n, T948 888 009. A welcoming bar serving *raciones* of ham and sausage.

### Uncastillo *p167*
**Ⅲ Hostería de Un-Castillo**, next to the tourist office. Splash out on a meal at this *hostería* which has classically hearty Aragonese meats and stews; in the expensive range, but there's a *menú* for €17.75.

## ◐ Transport

### Tarazona and around *p165*
**Bus** Therpasa buses leave from the corner of Av de Navarra and C Arenales. They service **Zaragoza** 7 times daily, and **Soria** 6-7 times daily, falling to 3-4 on Sun. **Cada** leave from Av Estación just off Carrera de Zaragoza for **Tudela** 6 times a day, with no service on Sun. Autobuses Iñigo stop in **Tarazona** on their way from Soria to **Barcelona** once a day. Their station is at the corner of C Teresa Cajal and Ronda de la Rocedo.

### Cinco Villas *p166*
Autobuses Cinco Villas run from Av Navarra in **Zaragoza** to Tauste, Ejea de los Caballeros, and Sádaba (3-4 times daily), some continuing to Uncastillo (1-2 times daily). Sos del Rey Católico can be reached on the **Sangüesa** bus that leaves Zaragoza once daily from the car park under the train station.

# Huesca and around

→ *Phone code: 974. Colour map 6, B3. Population: 48,530.*

*Huesca is in a slightly strange situation – in spite of being the capital of Aragón's Pyrenean province, it has been eclipsed by Jaca as 'gateway to the mountains'. Huesca's town planners need a little kick in the backside too; unlike most Spanish towns, it lacks a pedestrianized zone and a focal point for paseos or cafés. Its old town, albeit interesting, has been allowed to become vaguely seedy, and although the town has plenty of character, it's hard to pin down. That said, it's far from unpleasant, and if you're en route to the Pyrenees, transport connections may well require a stopover.*
▶▶ *For Sleeping, Eating and other listings, see pages 171-173.*

## Ins and outs

**Getting there and around** Huesca is small and easily traversed on foot. The old town is ringed by a road, which changes name several times; south of here is the main area for bars and restaurants, as well as the new combined bus and train station on Calle Zaragoza. There are frequent connections with Zaragoza and regular connections to all major cities in Spain. ▶▶ *See Transport, page 173, for further details.*

**Tourist information** Huesca's active **tourist office** ① *Plaza de Catedral 1, T974 292 170, www.huescaturismo.com, daily 0900-1400, 1600-2000,* is opposite the cathedral. As well as being a good source of information, they run guided tours of the city (1100 and 1700 depending on numbers, two hours, €2). A recent initiative is a vintage bus that has been beautifully restored and runs day trips into the Huescan countryside during summer. It leaves Plaza de Navarra at 0900 daily, returning around 1430. There are dozens of different excursions; it's a great way to reach some hard-to-get-to places. Booking is essential. The trip costs €5. There's also a small **information kiosk** on Plaza de Navarra.

## Background

Huesca's history is an interesting one. An important Roman town, it was known as Urbs Victrix Osca and was used by Sertorius as an education centre for Romanizing the sons of local chieftains. Taken by the Muslims, it was known as Al-Wasqa before Pedro I retook it. It became a significant bastion in the continuing Reconquista, a walled town with 90 sturdy towers that was capital of the young Aragonese kingdom for a few years. Its importance declined, along with Aragón's, after union with Castilla. Republicans besieged it for a long period during the Civil War but unsuccessfully; George Orwell tells how an optimistic general's cry "Tomorrow we'll have coffee in Huesca" became a cynical joke in the loyalist lines.

# Sights

## Cathedral

① *Daily 0800-1300, 1600-1830, free; museum Mon-Sat 1030-1330, 1600-1800 (closed afternoons Nov-Mar, open until 1930 Jul/Aug); €2.*
Huesca's cathedral is a sober Gothic edifice that appears a touch over-restored. It has an attractive portal with characterful apostles, and a quite interesting Diocesan museum, but the highlight is a magnificent alabaster *retablo* sculpted by the Aragonese master Damián Forment. The vivid central pieces depict the crucifixion; the sculpture's naturalistic beauty makes the gold-painted *retablos* in the side chapels look tawdry.

**Museo Provincial**

ⓘ *Tue-Sat 1000-1400, 1700-2000, Sun 1000-1400; free.*

North of the cathedral, the Provincial Museum houses a varied collection, prettily set around the old royal palace and university buildings. The pieces range from prehistoric finds to Goyas and modern Aragonese art. In one of the rooms of the royal palace the famous incident of 'the bell of Huesca' took place. When his two older brothers died heirless, Ramiro II unwillingly left his monk's cell in France and took the throne. The

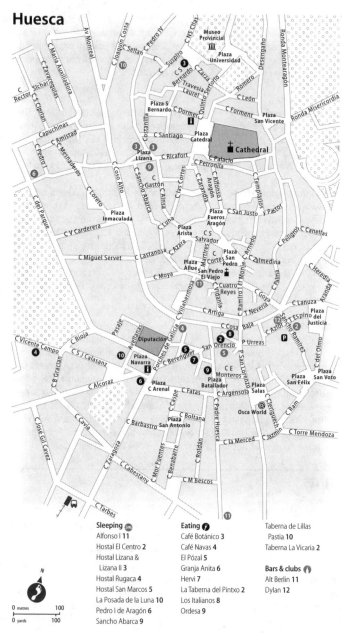

# Huesca

**Sleeping** 🛏
Alfonso I **11**
Hostal El Centro **2**
Hostal Lizana &
   Lizana II **3**
Hostal Rugaca **4**
Hostal San Marcos **5**
La Posada de la Luna **10**
Pedro I de Aragón **6**
Sancho Abarca **9**

**Eating** 🍴
Café Botánico **3**
Café Navas **4**
El Pózal **5**
Granja Anita **6**
Hervi **7**
La Taberna del Pintxo **2**
Los Italianos **8**
Ordesa **9**

Taberna de Lillas
   Pastia **10**
Taberna La Vicaria **2**

**Bars & clubs** 🍸
Alt Berlin **11**
Dylan **12**

0 metres   100
0 yards   100

N

nobles saw him as a pushover, and he was unable to exercise authority. Desperate, he sent a messenger to the abbot of his old monastery, asking for advice. The abbot said nothing, but led the messenger out to the garden, where he chopped the leaves off the tallest plants with a knife. Ramiro got the message, and announced that he was going to forge a bell which would be heard through the kingdom. He summoned the nobles to the palace, and beheaded them as they arrived, making a circle of the heads and hanging one in the centre, thus forming the Bell of Huesca. It was an effective political manoeuvre: Ramiro's difficulties were said to be less from then on.

## Iglesia de San Pedro El Viejo
ⓘ *Mon-Sat 1000-1330; €2; English guided tour available.*
In the south of the old town is the church of San Pedro El Viejo, of old stock indeed, as it stands on the location of a Visigothic church, and was the place of worship of the city's Christians during Muslim rule. The current building was constructed in 1117 and features some superb Romanesque capitals in its small cloister. Featuring scenes of the Reconquista and the story of Christ's life, it's thought that the same sculptor was involved both here and at San Juan de la Peña (see page 181). The plain burial chapel off the cloister houses the earthly remains of Alfonso I and Ramiro II (the monk), whose tomb is faced with a panel from a Roman sarcophagus. Inside the church, the soft Romanesque lines are complemented by a number of excellent wall paintings.

The **Diputación** on Plaza Navarra has an impressive ceiling fresco by Antonio Saura as well as exhibitions of other works. The room is in official use, but is open to the public on weekdays between 1800-2100.

# Loarre 🚍🚌 ↠ *pp171-173.*

First recorded in 1033, shortly after it had been built by Sancho the Great of Navarra, the **Castillo de Loarre** ⓘ *daily 1000-1330, 1600-1900; €2 for guided tour*, became an important centre, a monastery, and also briefly a royal residence, before continuing life as a stout frontier post. The design is functional, with few adornments. The towers in the wall are open on the inside, to prevent attacking enemies using them as a refuge once inside the walls. There are some unusual carvings of monkeys above the entrance, while a small dog marks the ascent from the crypt up a narrow staircase that emerges in front of the altar of the church, an unusually high Romanesque structure. The grim dungeons and remains of the royal hall are other highlights, along with the imposing watchtowers. After the early construction used limestone, the masons decided to switch to sandstone, which is much easier to work. This was bad news for the Muslim prisoners, however, who had to drag the blocks from 20 km away.

> ‡ *The Castillo de Loarre is one of the finest castles in Northern Spain.*

## 🛏 Sleeping

**Huesca** *p169, map p170*
**L La Posada de la Luna**, C Joaquín Costa 10, T974 240 857, www.posadadelaluna.com. An unusual and offbeat small hotel, set in a sensitively and handsomely renovated Aragonese mansion with mystic and astrological decor. The a/c rooms have all the facilities of a business hotel, including wireless internet, flat-screen TV and safe, but it still feels intimate.
**AL Pedro I de Aragon**, C del Parque 34, T974 220 300, www.gargallo-hotels.com. This is a fairly typical modern Spanish hotel, with quiet and cool but vaguely dull rooms

● *The castle of Loarre was recently used to film some of Ridley Scott's crusader film, Kingdom of Heaven.*

and an unremarkable exterior. There are frequent special offers and, best of all, a large outdoor swimming pool.

**A Hotel Sancho Abarca**, Plaza de Lizana 13, T974 220 650, F974 225 169. A good option in the centre of town. The furnishings are fairly stylish and most of the smallish, frilly rooms are exterior.

**C-D Hostal Lizana and Lizana II**, Plaza Lizana 6/8, T974 220 776, www.hostal-lizana.com. These are 2 neighbouring places on a small square, both offering good value. The smallish rooms come with or without bathroom and are clean and comfortable.

**D Hostal El Centro**, C Sancho Ramírez 3, T974 226 823, hcentro@inicia.es. An old-fashioned establishment with decent rooms with bathroom and TV. It's right in the part of town where you want to be, near the cafés and restaurants. However, it can be a touch noisy at weekends if you face the street.

**D Hostal Rugaca**, Porches de Galicia 1, T974 226 449, www.hostalrugaca.com. Right in the heart of things above a popular café, the rooms are simple and small but have a/c, TV and en suite bathrooms. Parking €6.

**D Hostal San Marcos**, C San Orencio 10, T/F974 222 931, www.hotelsanmarcos.es. A friendly spot in the café/bar zone, with clean rooms and attractive new wooden furniture. Breakfast served and parking available at €6.

**E Alfonso I**, C Padre Huesca 67, T/F974 245 454. Small but pleasant rooms with and without bathroom. Hospitable management.

**Loarre** *p171*
**B Hospedería de Loarre**, Plaza Miguel Moya 7, T974 382 706, F974 382 713. A beautiful place to stay and eat, in a big stone building with commodious rooms. The major attraction lies 6 km above, on a rocky outcrop.

## ● Eating

**Huesca** *p169, map p170*
There's not a great deal of action in the old town. Most eating options are in the zone just south, around C Orencio, C San Lorenzo, C Padre Huesca and C Porches de Galicia.
**₩₩₩ Café Navas**, C Vicente Campo 3, T974 212 825. A quality seafood restaurant with a

Basque slant on things. There are drinkless *menús* for €16 and €30, the latter highlighting the best of the fresh shellfish on offer. The decor is classical smart Spanish.

**₩₩₩ Taberna de Lillas Pastia**, Plaza Navarra 4, T974 211 691. A classy, slightly snooty restaurant in the old casino with undeniably good rich fare. A *ménu* costs €24, but expect to pay over €50 a head à la carte. House speciality is *revuelto de trufas*, a delicate combination of truffles and scrambled eggs.

**₩₩ Hervi**, C Santa Paciencia 2, T974 240 333. A popular spot with an outdoor terrace and some excellent fish dishes. Its calamari tapas are particularly highly regarded hereabouts.

**₩₩ La Taberna del Pintxo**, C San Orencio 7, T974 226 063. This place specializes in *pinchos*; just help yourself from the little boxes that line the bar. It's an honesty system whereby you leave the toothpicks on your plate and get charged accordingly. The service is excellent, and you can also enjoy *raciones*, or a €10 *menú del día* at the small wooden tables.

**₩₩ Taberna La Vicaria**, C San Orencio 9, T974 225 195. With stained glass out front, and some distinctly pew-like seats at the tables, this has a churchy theme but is far more about earthly indulgence. A fine range of *pinchos* and tapas are complemented by a selection of meat and seafood *raciones*. The *menú del día* for €8.50 is great; the only problem is that there are few tables so get there early or go hungry!

**₩ El Pózal**, Travesía de Valdés s/n, T974 220 015. A cheery bar serving a good simple *menú del día* for €7.20, often featuring bull stew. There are also *raciones* of home-style Aragonese cooking for very little.

**₩ Ordesa**, C Padre Huesca 20. A decent cheap restaurant with an interesting *menú del día* for €9, often featuring game dishes such as stews of quail or rabbit.

**Cafés**
**Café Botánico**, Plaza Universidad 4, T974 240 401. A popular and attractive spot next to the museum. It's a student favourite and offers a huge range of teas, and usually has some relaxing world music on the stereo.

● *For an explanation of the sleeping and eating price codes used in this guide, see inside the*
● *front cover. Other relevant information is found in Essentials pages 39-46.*

**Granja Anita**, Plaza Navarra 5, T974 215 712. A smart coffee spot opposite the Diputación, with an ornate façade and huge doors. It's popular with Huesca's parliamentarians and as a smart stop on the evening *paseo*.
**Los Italianos**, Cosa Baja 18, T974 224 539. An ice-cream parlour with some tempting pastries and coffee. Try a *pastel ruso*, a traditional Aragonese confection of almonds, meringue, and hazelnut paste.

## ○ Bars and clubs

Huesca *p169, map p170*
The main bar zone is around C Sancho Ramírez and C Padre Huesca.
**Alt Berlin**, Plaza de López Allue 8, T974 230 429. This prettily painted high-ceilinged bar is one of Huesca's best. It offers good beer on an attractive if faded plaza that comes to life during San Lorenzo. There are also some German food options available in the evening.
**Dylan**, C Sancho Ramírez 4, T974 246 040. A homely underground bar open late at weekends. Despite the name, the music is mainly modern pop and rock.

## ⊛ Festivals and events

Huesca *p169, map p170*
**9 Aug** Huesca's big event is San Lorenzo, a week-long festival. It's got all the frills: processions of giants and bigheads, bullfights, cow-dodging in the ring, and copious partying. Like Pamplona, people dress in white, but here the scarves are green rather than red.

## ⊖ Transport

Huesca *p169, map p170*
**Air**
Ten kilometres from town, a local airfield is currently being upgraded into what will become Huesca-Pirineos airport, which will perhaps offer international budget flights as well as connections to Madrid and Barcelona.

**Bus**
Regular buses run from Huesca to **Zaragoza** (more than hourly, 55 mins, €5.27), other major destinations include **Barcelona** (4 a day), **Pamplona** (5 a day), **Lleida** (6 a day). Several buses go to **Jaca** €5.72, 1hour), **Barbastro**, and **Monzón**. 3 a day go to **Ayerbe** (en route to Pamplona). There's one to 2 buses daily to **Loarre**, departing at 0825 (Mon-Sat) and 1330 (Mon-Fri).

**Train**
There are 6-8 trains daily to **Zaragoza** (1 hr, from €4.50), 3 to **Jaca** (2 hrs, €5.75), and a fast train to **Madrid** (2 hrs 40 mins, €50.40).

Loarre *p171*
**Bus** Huesca is 7 km and easily accessible by bus.

## ❶ Directory

Huesca *p169, map p170*
**Internet** Osca World, Plaza Nuestra Señora de Salas 4 (cnr C San Lorenzo), T974 226 110, 1000-2400, €2.40 per hr; Osc@.com, C Calasanz 13, 1600-0100, €2.40 per hr. There are also terminals in the bus/train station.

# East of Huesca

*The southern part of this zone is an agricultural area at the feet of the soaring Pyrenees, little touched by tourism but boasting some good sights, including the excellent Templar castle of Monzón. Aragón's best wine, Somontano, comes from here, around Barbastro, which is also the spiritual home of the Catholic organization Opus Dei. Nearby is the canyoning mecca of Alquézar while, further northeast, towards the Pyrenees, is one of Spain's more enchanting villages, Roda de Isábena.*
▸▸ For Sleeping, Eating and other listings, see pages 177-179.

## Alquézar and the Guara Canyon

The village of Alquézar, tucked away in the Pyrenean foothills, is an attractive place in its own right, but also happens to be the jumping-off point for some of Europe's finest canyoning. There are over 200 canyons in the surrounding Sierra de Guara; some can be strolled without equipment, while others require full climbing, abseiling and water gear. Try and avoid going in the height of summer, as the region gets ridiculously crowded, as well as seriously hot. There's a very French atmosphere here, as enthusiasts from over the border were the first to seriously appreciate the potential of the region.

The village's twisting medieval streets are wholly dominated by a large rock, on which once sat a **Muslim fortress** ① *entrance by guided tour only; Wed-Mon 1100-1300, 1600-1800 (2000 summer), €1.80*, hence the town's name. The foundations and walls are still visible, but following the Christian reconquest of the town in 1067, it was converted into a fortified Colegiata. Although much of it dates from the 16th century, there are some attractive Romanesque elements still present, particularly the double-columned cloister, whose capitals are carved with Old Testament scenes.

There's a **tourist office** ① *C Arrabal, summer daily 1030-1330, 1600-2100, Oct to mid-Jun weekends only.*

The area's most famous canyon is the **Cañón del Vero**, a popular destination for the tour companies. It's not very difficult, but you'll need to get wet in some parts at most times of year. The canyon is spectacular, wide and deep, with immense numbers of vultures; the rare lammergeier occasionally puts in an appearance too. Descending the canyon takes about six hours; during summer there's a shuttle bus to the starting point 20 km from Alquézar (departs daily 15 June to 15 September, 0930 and 1130), otherwise it's about a 4½-hour walk. If you don't fancy doing the whole thing, you can see part of it by walking from Alquézar about an hour to the 'Roman' bridge of Villacantal. ➤➤ *For further information, see Activities and tours, p178.*

# Barbastro and around ⊕❷❷⊕ ➤➤ *pp177-179.*

→ *Colour map 6, B3.*

After enlisting in Barcelona, to fight alongside the Republican Army in the Spanish Civil War, Barbastro was George Orwell's first stop en route to the front. While things have changed since those dark days, you can see what he was getting at when he referred to Barbastro as "a bleak and chipped town"; he had few good words to say about Aragonese towns in general. The place has taken on new life recently as the centre of the **Somontano** wine region, a small core of producers who have risen to prominence with modern winemaking methods allowing high production and consistent quality.

Barbastro was an important Muslim town in its time, but it's the 16th-century **cathedral** ① *1000-1300, 1800-1930; summer 1000-1330, 1630-1930*, that dominates today. Built between 1517 and 1533, it's an elegant structure with a newer, separate bell tower. Archaeological unearthings have revealed parts of a former church and a mosque alongside the building. The church's pride is the 16th-century *retablo*, sculpted from alabaster and polychrome wood by Damián Forment (whose work is also in Huesca cathedral), an Aragonese of considerable Renaissance kudos. He died before he could complete the work, but you wouldn't know – it's a remarkable piece. Barbastro's **tourist office** is in the Museo del Vino complex on Avenida de la Merced on the edge of town.

## Wineries

The Somontano DO (denominación de origen) was approved in principle in 1974 and in practice a decade later. Most of the 10 or so producers are modern concerns, using up-to-date techniques to produce a range of mid-priced wines from 12 permissible red and white grape varieties, some local, some French. The region's cold winters and hot, dry summers are ideal for ripening wine grapes and production has soared in the *bodegas*. The **Museo de Vino** ① *above the tourist office, Mon-Sat 1000-1400, 1630-2000, free*, is an arty but not particularly informative display. There's also a shop downstairs and a good restaurant.

Most of the wineries are on the road to Naval relatively close to Barbastro. The best known both inside and outside Spain is **Viñas del Vero** ① *T974 302 216, www.vinasdelvero.es*, a 30-minute walk from the centre on this road. They're happy to show visitors around by prior appointment on weekdays and Saturday mornings. Some 5 km further on, **Bodegas Enate** ① *T974 302 580, www.enate.es, Mon-Thu 1030, 1130, 1730, Fri 1030, 1130, Sat 1000, 1200*, is in a less attractive building but can be visited without appointment.

## Monzón → *Colour map 6, B3.*

Though seldom visited, Monzón is one of those surprising Spanish towns that has a superb attraction, in this case its relatively unspoiled **castle** ① *Tue-Sat 1000-1300, 1700-2000, Sun 1000-1400, €2, guided visits Sat 1030, 1730, Sun 1030, 1130*, an atmospheric Templar stronghold that feels impregnable, albeit bare. The castle was fought over during the Reconquista, and often changed hands. The mercenary El Cid came here a few times to accept contracts from Muslim governors, while his renowned blade *El Tizón* was later kept here as a relic. Although some reconstruction has been effected, the buildings still preserve the Templar austerity and ambience. There are underground passageways to be explored (take a torch). The **tourist office** is in the bus station, but the admissions booth at the castle also functions as one.

## Torreciudad → *Colour map 6, B3.*

The holy shrine of **Opus Dei** ① *daily 0900-1900 (later in summer)*, is worth a visit if you have your own transport, but don't expect revelation; it's likely to reinforce anyone's pre-existing love or otherwise of the organization (see box page 176). In a spectacular setting on a rocky promontory amid craggy hills, it overlooks the Embalse de El Grado and Franco's dam that created it. The main building, once you're past the security guard (don't look too scruffy, although you'll make it in with shorts and a suitably serious expression), is a curious affair. Virtually windowless, the brick design seems to recall the designs of both Oriental temples and Victorian power stations. Inside, the altarpiece is the main attraction, a very ornate sculptural relief. In the centre is a Romanesque statue of the Virgin – a passage behind leads to a kissable medallion.

Many Catholic theologians see Opus Dei as an organization looking backwards towards ritual piety rather than a more enlightened spirituality; the complex certainly bears this out – visitors are encouraged to seek God in the rosary and stations of the cross in several undeniably attractive locations. The structure was conceived by Saint Josemaría himself, who was born in nearby Barbastro. He died suddenly in 1975, 11 days before the official opening.

## Graus

This small service town doesn't seem much to most who pass through it en route to higher ground. In fact, it's a town with plenty of history, an important bastion of the Reconquista, and long-time marketplace for much of the eastern Pyrenees. While there's not masses to see, what there is, is quality.

The **Plaza Mayor** is an extravagant and beautiful square. Surrounded by beautiful mansions, the **Casa de Barrón** stands out for its red colour and two large paintings on its façade. The female forms are depictions of Art and Science, supposedly created to please the owner's Andalucian wife, perhaps longing for a touch of Mediterranean decadence in dusty Aragón. It's also been suggested, though, that there are several symbols of freemasonry in the paintings, an amusing thought in Opus Dei heartland. Another former resident of the square would not

● The pride of Monzón is the former tennis star Conchita Martínez, the second Spaniard to ● win a Wimbledon title.

## Opus Dei

For this secretive Catholic organization, the stunning recent success enjoyed by the *The Da Vinci Code*, which portrays it in a distinctly unflattering light, was anathema, and spokesmen reacted angrily to what was, after all, a detective novel which made no claim of objectivity. Whatever the mysteries of Opus, we can be fairly certain that self-mutilating albino monk assassins aren't within their *modus operandi*.

It's ironic that after centuries of severe persecution of Freemasons on the grounds that they were a "secretive, power-hungry cult", Spain should have produced Opus Dei, a Catholic sect with marked similarities to the Lodgemen. It was founded in 1928 by Josemaría de Escrivá, a Barbastro lawyer turned priest appalled at the liberalism prevalent in 1920s Spain. He saw Opus (the name means "the work of God" as a way for lay people to devote their life to God; one of his favourite phrases was "the sanctity of every-day life". His book *The Way* is the organization's handbook, with 999 instructions and thoughts for achieving greater spirituality in daily matters. Members are both men and women (although *The Way* has been heavily criticized for its archaic attitude to the latter), and although some follow a semi-monastic life, the majority continue in their worldly professions.

The organization has members all around the world, but Spain has remained its heartland, where membership in boardrooms, staffrooms and parliament remains high but undisclosed. Politically and religiously conservative, Opus was a powerful peacetime ally of Franco's government. This explains part of the considerable hostility towards the sect, as do its capitalistic ventures; the group is very wealthy and owns numerous newspapers, television channels and companies worldwide. Allegations of secrecy about Opus centre around the lack of transparency in its involvement in these enterprises as much as the private nature of personal participation. More serious, perhaps, is its backwards-looking approach to Catholicism, with holiness deemed to derive in a large part from the regular performance of the ritual of the sacraments, and the more recent devotions of the rosary and the stations of the cross, an approach bemoaned by forward-thinking Catholic theologians. The late Pope John Paul II, a devoted admirer of capitalism and conservatism, had a lot of time for Opus, and granted them a privileged status within the Vatican. On 6 October 2002, Escrivá was canonized in Rome as San Josemaría; a controversial event both celebrated and bemoaned in Spain.

have been amused – Tomás de Torquemada, one of the masterminds of the Spanish Inquisition and scourge of the Spanish Jews, who lived here for a period, see box page 237. Not to be outdone, however, the owner of the **Casa de Heredía** did his eaves up with a series of Renaissance female figures. Unable to compete, the **Ayuntamiento** on the square is distinctly restrained by comparison.

# Abizanda ☺⚪ ›› pp177-179.

→ *Colour map 6, A3.*
Heading north from Barbastro towards Aínsa, the village of Abizanda is unmissable, with its **atalaya** (defensive tower, for opening hours see museum, below) looming over the road. Turn the car, it's worth a look. The *atalaya* dates from the 11th century but has been recently rebuilt. Typical of the area, it functioned as a watchtower, one of a chain that could relay signals up and down the valley. A series of levels (sometimes spruced up by art exhibitions) leads to a vertiginous wooden platform with views in all directions through narrow wooden slots. Adjacent is the **Museo de Creencias y Religiosidad Popular** ① *tower and museum Jul to mid-Sep daily 1100-1400, 1700-2100; May and Jun and mid-Sep to mid-Oct Sat and Sun only 1100-1400, 1500-1800, €1.50*, a small but interesting collection of pieces focusing on the local customs that were (and still are, in some villages) designed to keep evil spirits at bay.

## Roda de Isábena → *Colour map 6, A4.*
One of Aragón's gems is tiny Roda, an unlikely cathedral town with a population of 36 in a valley south of the Pyrenees. Apart from the odd tourist shop, the hilltop settlement preserves a superb medieval atmosphere. The Romans established it as a commanding fortification overlooking the valley, but it owes its current appearance to the powerful counts of Ribagorza, sometime troublemakers who made this a major residence.

The **cathedral** ① *admission by guided tour only; €2*, claims to be the smallest in Spain, but it's no chapel. The intricate 12th-century façade (with a later porch) is the portal to several architectural and artistic treasures but is impressive in itself with columns crowned with rearing lions around a massive studded door. The delicate crypt has superb Romanesque wall paintings of which the best is a Pantocrator. There are more in a chapel off the cloister. The earthly remains of San Ramón are housed in an ornately carved tomb, while the 350-year-old organ still belts out a decent note. The cloister is beautiful, swathed with grass and flowers, and centred around a well.

The rest of the town invites wandering around its stone buildings and fortifications; there are several coats-of-arms for heraldists to decipher, and occasional art exhibitions and music recitals.

*Northern Aragón East of Huesca Listings*

## ● Sleeping

**Alquézar and the Guara Canyon** *p173*
There are several places to stay in and around Alquézar, including 2 campsites and a number of *refugios*.
**B Hotel Santa María**, C Arrabal s/n, T974 318 436, www.hotel-santamaria.com. This is the nicest place, with some good views and comfortably attractive rooms with quilts on the beds. The hotel runs the **Avalancha** agency (see page 178).
**E Casa Jabonero**, C Mayor s/n, T974 318 908. One of the nicest of the *casas rurales*. Friendly with attractive rooms and shared bath.
**F Albergue Casa Tintorero**, C San Gregorio 18, T974 318 354. A convivial and well-priced hostel in the town centre.

**Camping**
**Camping Alquézar**, T974 318 300. The closer of the 2 campsites and open all year.

**Barbastro and around** *p174*
A lack of character seems to be endemic in Barbastro's hotels; if you want to stay in the area, Monzón has more peaceful charm, see below.
**C Hotel Clemente**, C Corona de Aragón 5, T974 310 186, hotel clemente@telefonica.net. One of the better options, a touch sterile but spacious, modern and friendly, with a/c and a restaurant.

**Monzón** *p175*

**Ɗ Vianetto**, Av de Lérida 25, T974 401 900, vianetto@monzon.net. The best option in Monzón, with affable management and dull but comfortable doubles with a/c. The restaurant is decent too, with a *menú* for €9.
**Ƒ Pensión El Manchego**, C Antonio Torres Palacio, T974 401 922. A small *pensión* just by the train station and run out of the **Tropical** bar on the corner. The doubles are good for the price, but in summer the singles make the Black Hole of Calcutta seem icy.

**Graus** *p175*

**Ꮯ Hotel Lleida**, C Costa s/n, T974 540 925, www.hotel-lleida.com. In the centre of town, this is the best bet if you want to stay. It's also got a popular bar/restaurant.

**Roda de Isábena** *p177*
There are several places to stay and eat in Roda, which can get busy at summer weekends.
**Ꮯ Hospedería Roda de Isábena**, Plaza la Catedral s/n, T974 544 554, F974 544 500. Virtually touches the cathedral steps, and is garlanded with grapevines. It's a very good, well-priced place to stay, despite a little snootiness. The rooms are comfortable but more atmospheric is the restaurant in the old refectory of the White Monks who founded the cathedral, or the patio overlooking the rocky valley below.

## ❼ Eating

**Alquézar and the Guara Canyon** *p173*
There are many places to eat; you're better off in one of the hotels or *albergues* than in the touristy restaurants around the Plaza Mayor.

**Barbastro and around** *p174*
**▥ El Cenador de San Julián**, Av de la Merced 64. A small and good quality restaurant on the ground floor of the Museo del Vino complex behind the tourist office. The €12 lunch is worthwhile, and there's a €18 evening *menú*, both of which can be enjoyed on the quiet terrace facing the seldom-used bullring.
**▥ Europa**, C Romero 8. A fairly upmarket place specializing in gourmet steaks, rabbit and *longanizo* (an Aragonese sausage along German lines). The bar serves cheaper *platos combinados*.

**♥ La Brasería**, Plaza Mercado s/n. A cheapish upstairs restaurant and downstairs bar serving *raciones* to a porticoed terrace.

**Monzón** *p175*
**▥ La Taberna del Muro**, C Juan de Lanuza s/n. A reasonable restaurant, well-frequented by Monzonese, and with public internet access.
**♥ Acapulco**, Av Lérida 11, T974 400 185. A café/bar on the main drag with a slightly formularized range of food, but a good place to sit out nevertheless. There's both chart and blues music available in different sections for late night atmosphere.

**Graus** *p175*
**▥ Itaka** A good lunch or drink option on the southern edge of Graus, with a very pleasant garden terrace and a variety of eatables and drinkables; there's also an internet terminal.

**Roda de Isábena** *p177*
**▥ Hospedería Roda de Isábena**, see Sleeping, above. A good place for an atmospheric bite to eat.
**▥ Restaurant Catedral**, set in the cathedral building itself, just off the cloister. The cuisine is very Aragonese, with game such as partridge, rabbit and quail featuring large, although the most unusual is certainly *jabalí al chocolate* (wild boar with chocolate). There's a reasonable *menú de la casa* for €10.50.

## ▲ Activities and tours

**Alquézar and the Guara Canyon** *p173*
There are several companies offering guided descents of canyons. Competition keeps prices very similar, but be sure to check exactly what is offered, as well as insurance; your standard travel insurance may well not cover you for this type of activity.
**Avalancha**, C Arrabal s/n, T974 318 299, www.avalancha-guara.com. Solid reputation.
**Guaraqua**, C Pilaseras s/n, T974 318 396, www.guaraqua.com. A reliable company.

## ⊝ Transport

**Barbastro and around** *p174*
**Bus** Barbastro is a major transport junction for the eastern Pyrenean towns. The bus station is near the cathedral in the heart of

things. Many buses connect with ongoing services, so you're unlikely to have to stay unless you want to, although there's enough in the surrounding area to keep you busy for a day or 2.

Buses to and from Barbastro include: **Barcelona** (4 daily, 3½ hrs); **Huesca** (11 daily; 50 mins); **Benasque** (2 a day; 2 hrs); **Lleida** (10 a day); **Monzón** at least hourly (15 mins); **Aínsa** one at 1945 (1 hr), returning at 0700. In summer there's another at 1100, returning at

1515. There are 3 daily buses from Barbastro to **Graus**, and 1 from Barbastro to **Alquézar**.

**Monzón** *p175*
**Bus** There are many daily buses to **Huesca** via **Barbastro**; 4-6 a day to **Lleida**; 4 to **Fraga**, and a couple to **Benabarre**.

**Train Madrid** 3 a day (€31.50); **Barcelona** 7 a day (€15-21; 2½ hrs; **Zaragoza** 11 a day (1 hr).

---

# Western Pyrenean valleys

*Although on a world scale the Pyrenees are no giants, their awesome ruggedness is mightily impressive; they are a formidable natural barrier between the peninsula and the rest of Europe. They gain steadily in height from west to east and are accessed by a series of north-south valleys; just to the south of these, Jaca is the effective capital of the region, a fun-loving outdoorsy place that acts as a supply centre to holiday favourites such as Sallent de Gállego and world-class ski resorts such as Candanchú or Astún. Pilgrims on the Camino Aragonés have their first taste of Spain in this area, which also harbours the stunning carved capitals of San Juan de la Peña, while the quieter vales of Echo and Ansó are home to the distinctive cheso culture.*
▸▸ *For Sleeping, Eating and other listings, see pages 185-189.*

---

## Jaca ⬤🚻🚶🏔🚌🛈 ▸▸ *pp185-189.*

→ *Phone code: 974. Colour map 6, A2. Population: 14,701. Altitude: 820 m.*
A relaxed spot in northern Aragón, Jaca is far from being a large town but it ranks as a metropolis by the standards of the Pyrenees, for which it functions as a service centre and transport hub. The town has enthusiastically bid for three Winter Olympics, most recently for the 2010 event, but with no luck so far. Most visitors to this part of the Pyrenees are in Jaca at some point, and its also the major stop on the Camino Aragonés pilgrim route, so there's always plenty of bustle about the place.

Jaca's **tourist office** ⓘ *Av Regimiento de Galicia 2, T974 360 098, winter Mon-Sat 0900-1330, 1600-1900, summer Mon-Sat 0900-1400, 1630-2000, Sun 1000-1300, 1700-2000,* is on the main road in the centre of town and is very helpful.

### Background
Jaca was the centre of the Aragonese kingdom in the early Middle Ages under Ramiro I and his son Sancho Ramírez, who established the *fueros* (see History, page 445). It was a crucial base in the Reconquista after having been under Moorish control in the 8th century, and a Roman base before that. The city sits on a high plateau above the rivers Aragón and Gállego.

*⁞ The cathedral is usually dark; a coinbox just inside the main door takes half-euro pieces, each of which provides light for five minutes.*

### Sights
Jaca's treasure is its delightful Romanesque **cathedral** ⓘ *1000-1300, 1600-2000,* which sits moored like a primitive ship, surrounded by buildings. Neither majestic nor lofty, it was built in the late 11th and early 12th centuries, although the interior owes more to later periods. The main entrance is a long open portico, which approaches a doorway topped by lions and the Crismon

symbol. The idea was perhaps that people had a few paces to meditate on their sins before entering the house of God.

The south door has a wooden porch and fine, carved capitals depicting Abraham and Isaac, and Balaam with the angel. These were beautifully carved by the 'Master of Jaca'. The interior is slightly less charming; the most ornate of the chapels is that of San Miguel, which contains a fanciful 16th-century *retablo* and a carved portal. Next to this is a 12th-century figurine of a wide-hipped virgin and child, dedicated to Zaragoza's Virgin of the Pillar. The main altar is recessed, with an elaborately painted vaulted ceiling.

Worthy of a quick peek is the Iglesia del Carmen with its interesting façade and scaly columns and a Virgin seemingly flanked by a pair of mandarins.

In the cathedral cloister is the **Diocesan Museum** ① *Tue-Sun 1100-1300, 1600-1830, E2 (closed for renovation when this book went to press, but due to re-open very*

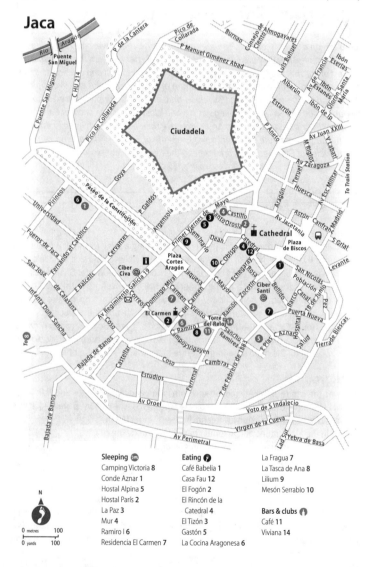

Jaca

| Sleeping | Eating | |
|---|---|---|
| Camping Victoria 8 | Café Babelia 1 | La Fragua 7 |
| Conde Aznar 1 | Casa Fau 12 | La Tasca de Ana 8 |
| Hostal Alpina 5 | El Fogón 2 | Lilium 9 |
| Hostal París 2 | El Rincón de la | Mesón Serrablo 10 |
| La Paz 3 | Catedral 4 | |
| Mur 4 | El Tizón 3 | **Bars & clubs** |
| Ramiro I 6 | Gastón 5 | Café 11 |
| Residencia El Carmen 7 | La Cocina Aragonesa 6 | Viviana 14 |

N

0 metres 100
0 yards 100

*shortly)*, which houses a superb collection of Romanesque and Gothic frescoes, taken from other churches in the area and cleverly reconstructed. The best is an awesome 11th-century set from Bagüés, depicting an abbreviated history of the old and new Testaments, comic-strip style. Another highlight is the apse paintings from Riesto, featuring some marvellously self-satisfied 12th-century apostles. Of the paintings, a prim Saint Michael is standing, as is his habit, on a chicken-footed demon who is having a very bad time of it; a wood-carved Renaissance assembly of figures around the body of Christ is also impressive.

Jaca's **citadel**① *guided visits only 1100-1200, 1600-1700 (1800-2000 summer); wait at the red line for a guide to arrive, €4*, is still in use by the military. A low but impressively large star-shaped structure, it was constructed during Felipe II's reign. The garrison here rose against the monarchy in 1930, before the rest of the Republican movement was ready for action: two young officers who decided to march on Zaragoza were arrested and executed. Their deaths were not in vain, though, as the indignation caused boosted feeling against the monarchy – the Republic was proclaimed shortly afterwards, and the king went into exile. The tour takes about an hour (including a newly inaugurated museum of lead soldiers).

Built over the foundations of the old Royal Palace is the **Torre del Reloj**, an attractive Gothic affair that is now HQ to a Pyrenean taskforce. It sits in Plaza Lacadena, an attractive spot at night, with several bars and a floodlit fountain.

Walking down **Paseo de la Constitución**, the town comes to an abrupt end in a slope down to the **Río Aragón**. A path leads to the river, a bathing spot, which is traversed by a medieval bridge. The **tourist office** is at Avenida Regimento Galicia 19.

## Monasterio de San Juan de la Peña → *Colour map 6, A2.*

① *€3.50 old monastery only, €5 including return bus from the parking area at the new monastery, €5.50 including an audiovisual presentation in the new monastery. Ticket includes entry to the monastery at Santa Cruz de la Serós, 10 km further north. The monastery is difficult to reach without a car, although you can walk the whole way from Jaca on the GR65.3.12 path; otherwise jump off a Pamplona-bound bus at the cruce for Santa Cruz de la Seros; the monastery is just under a 2-hr walk from here.*

This famous monastery allegedly came into being when a noble named Voto was chasing a deer on horseback. The despairing creature took the Roman option and leaped to its death over a cliff. Voto's horse was unable to stop itself from following. Still in the saddle, Voto launched a quick prayer to John the Baptist and, to his amazement, landed safely outside a small cave. Investigating, he found the body of a hermit and a small shrine to the saint. He was so moved by his salvation that he decided to continue the hermitage and settled here with his brother, who was equally impressed with the tale. The monastery became an important centre on the pilgrim route to Santiago in the Middle Ages and today constitutes two separate buildings.

The new monastery is an impressive brick Baroque structure currently being renovated to incorporate a *hospedería* and restaurant. It should be a great place to stay; due to open shortly, it will have 25 rooms, including one with full disabled facilities.

It's the older monastery that draws visitors, spectacularly wedged into the cliff 1 km down the hill. Built around bedrock, the lower part consists of a spooky 11th-century church and dormitory, with fragmentary wall paintings and the tombs of several early abbots. Upstairs is a pantheon, where nobles could (with a hefty donation) be buried; it's decorated with the characteristic *ajedrezado jaqués* chessboard pattern that originated in these parts.

● *"It does exist, love for a building, however difficult it may be to talk about. If I had to talk I*
● *would have to explain why it should be this particular church that, when I can no longer travel, I will want to have been the last building I have seen." Cees Nooteboom, Roads to Santiago.*

## ⦂ The Holy Grail

Relics have always been big in Spain. Fragments of the true cross, feathers from the archangel Gabriel's wings, half-pints of the Virgin's milk, the last breath of San Sebastián in a bottle… But the daddy of them all is the Holy Grail, the cup used to knock back the bevvy at the Last Supper. Several Aragonese monasteries have held this over the years although, irritatingly for Northern Spain, it's now in Valencia. St Peter thoughtfully took the goblet with him after dinner, and brought it to Rome, where it was in the possession of pope after pope until things got dicey and it was handed to a Spanish soldier, who took it home to Huesca in the third century.

When the Moors got too close for comfort, the local bishop took to the hills, and hid the Grail in the monastery of Siresa. After a century or so it was transferred to safer Jaca, where it sat in the cathedral awhile before monks took it to nearby San Juan de la Peña, where it was guarded by Templar knights. The Aragonese King Martino V thought it would look nice on his sideboard, however, and took it to his palace in Zaragoza in 1399. The monks weren't too happy, but he managed to fob them off with a replica (a replica of the replica is still there; the original replica was destroyed in a fire). When the king died, the Grail showed up in Barcelona. When Alfonso V, King of Valencia, acceded to the Aragonese throne, he took it home with him, and it was eventually placed in the cathedral, where you can see it today.

Spoilsport art historians have revealed that it has been embellished in the ninth, 15th and 16th centuries, but its heart is an agate cup dating from Roman times, so you never can tell.

The high church features three apses, one of which holds a replica of the Holy Grail, see box, above, and a martial funerary chapel that holds the remains of the Aragonese kings Pedro I and Ramiro I. It's the open remains of the cloister that inspire most awe; the columns are decorated with superbly carved Romanesque capitals under the conglomerate cliff. Scenes from the life of Christ and the book of Genesis are superbly portrayed; Cain takes on Abel with a particularly fearsome sledgehammer.

# Canfranc Valley ⊟⊞ ⇥ *pp185-189.*

→ *Colour map 6, A2.*

The Canfranc Valley stretches north from Jaca to the French border at Puerto de Somport. Apart from the spectacular mountains at its northernmost extremity, the valley is attractive but not breathtaking. There's not a huge amount of interest; some fine walks to be sure, but the townships seem listless most of the year, perhaps too busy anxiously scanning the skies for the first signs of snow. Pilgrims on the Camino Aragonés branch of the route to Santiago enter Spain along this valley, but the area's main source of tourist revenue is skiing, with two important resorts close to the border.

## Villanúa

The first large settlement in the Canfranc Valley is Villanúa, whose main attraction is a limestone cave, **La Cueva de las Güixas** ① *T974 378 139, the opening schedule is impossibly complex but it's basically summer daily 1000-1330, 1630-2000, rest of the year weekends only, with a morning visit at 1230 and evening one at 1730, €3.90.* Formerly a home for prehistoric man, there are some excellent calcified formations and an underground river. The tour takes about one hour.

## Canfranc and Canfranc-Estación

The village of Canfranc was destroyed by fire in 1944 and plays second fiddle to its neighbour up the valley, Canfranc-Estación, where most of its residents settled after the blaze. Between the two is a small but impressive moated defensive tower built by Felipe II. It now functions as an information centre for the **Somport tunnel** linking France and Spain, which was finally opened in 2003 despite much opposition from environmentalists. Canfranc-Estación's main feature is, sure enough, its railway station, inaugurated in 1928 in a spirit of Franco-Hispanic cooperation. A massive edifice with a platform of prodigious length, it will look familiar to fans of the film *Dr Zhivago*, in which it featured. It's a sad place now, derelict and abandoned; France closed the rail link in the 1970s, although a couple of daily trains still roll in from Jaca. There's a **tourist office** ① *daily 0900-1330, 1630-2000*. On Saturdays at 1030 a guided trip leaves from Jaca station up the valley to here.

## Candanchú and Astún

The ski resort of Candanchú sits amid pretty mountains 1 km short of the border. An ugly place, it's nevertheless equipped with excellent facilities, 40 skiable kilometres at heights from 1500-2500m, a variety of accommodation, and a full range of runs, as well as a cross-country circuit. Check the website www.candanchu.com for further information and for current snwo conditions.

Nearby, Astún is a smaller but equally professional centre, but it lacks cheap accommodation, although it's only a 4 km trudge to Candachú. A day's skiing at either resort costs €29, or €108 for a five-day pass.

# Echo and Ansó valleys ⊜⊝ ▸▸ *pp185-189.*

## Echo and Siresa

Echo (also spelt Hecho) is a small place popular with weekenders. There's a sculpture of a couple in traditional *cheso* costume – these valleys are home to a distinctive micro-culture – with a very distinct dialect and customs – but it's close enough to Basque lands that there's a *frontón* for playing *pelota*. There's a small **ethnographic museum** ① *summer 1030-1330, 1800-2100 (except Mon pm); €1.20.* Behind the **tourist office** on the main road is a **sculpture garden**, a legacy of a former annual festival.

North of Echo, the village of Siresa houses a monastery that was another stop on the long journey of the Holy Grail (see box, page 182). The **Monasterio de Siresa** ① *1100-1300, 1700-2000, €1.50*, a blocky Romanesque construction, dominates the surrounding hillside. There are a few places to stay, including a youth hostel (T974 375 385), which rents bicycles and provides information about walking in the area. Further up, the valley becomes more spectacular; the most popular spot for starting a hike is 11 km north at **Selva de Oza**, where there's a campsite and a bar.

## Ansó

Overlooking a river, Ansó is a characterful town. Belying its chunky exterior, the **church** houses a massive *retablo* and several large gold-framed paintings as well as a small **ethnographic museum** ① €2.

# Tena Valley ⊜⊘✺▲⊝ ▸▸ *pp185-189.*

→ *Colour map 6, A2.*

While not as spectacular as the valleys to the east and west, the Tena Valley is pretty and accessible. It holds two ski resorts, Panticosa and Formigal, and sees most action in winter; during summer it seems a little bit ill at ease without a coating of snow.

## ⦂ Refugios

If you spend time walking in the Pyrenees, you're likely to want to use these comradely places, which are essentially mountain hostels along Scottish 'bothy' lines. The word can mean anything from a one-person lean-to upwards, but the better ones have cosily packed dormitories where wet socks are hung from every available nail, and most of the staffed ones offer meals at good rates; the communal atmosphere is usually excellent. It's always worth booking in summer; no-one is usually turned away (at least in remote areas), but you might find yourself on the floor or outside. The staff are usually knowledgeable about the area; it's a good idea to inform them if you're climbing a peak so they can give advice and alert emergency services in case of trouble. Most also have a book where walkers and climbers write hints, describe routes, and give warnings and advice.

### Sabiñánigo and around

The town at the head of the valley is Sabiñánigo, a fairly dull and uninteresting place useful only for transport connections, see Transport page 188. On the edge of town is a good ethnographic museum, worth a visit if you're stuck here for a few hours. West of here, the semi-abandoned villages of the **Serrablo** region are worth exploring with time and a car; there are numerous small Romanesque gems scattered throughout the near-deserted land.

### Biescas and around

Moving on into the valley, Biescas is a nice quiet little place divided by a pebbly river. There's a road from here leading to **Torla** (see page 189) and the **Ordesa Valley**, with occasional buses plying the route. There's not a lot going on in Biescas, but it's an authentic Pyrenean village and makes a quiet base. The **tourist office** ① *1000-1330, 1700-2030*, is above the main square by the river.

If you've got a car, you may want to drop in at **La Cuniacha** ① *winter 1100-1800, summer 1000-2000 (last entry 2 hrs before closing), €7.21, children 5-12 €4.40, under 5 free*, an open-plan wildlife park/zoo up a side road 5 km north of Biescas. It's a good chance to see some of the Pyrenean animals and plant species, as well as other alpine and cold-climate fauna, although some are a little reclusive.

### Panticosa and around

Some 10 km beyond Biescas, a road branches right to the ski town of Panticosa. It's a pleasant little place, although the odd shop and restaurant break the symmetry of the hotels lining the streets. A cablecar takes skiers up to the chairlift 800 m higher; it also runs in summer, when most visitors are using the town as a base for walks in the area. The hotels are fairly cheap – the skiing is low-key compared to Formigal. You can rent bikes to explore the countryside from **Sport Panticosa**. There's a **tourist office** ① *1000-1300, 1700-2000*.

Further up the narrow valley of the river, 8 km from Caldarés, is an old spa resort, **Balneario de Panticosa**. It's a stately sort of place, given over to leisurely summer lunches and a little light strolling. It's a bit like Hyde Park in the mountains, with a small lake, rowing boats and a tourist train. The location is pretty, and this is the starting point for some more serious hiking up into the mountains; there's a *refugio* (T974 487 571) which can be used as a walking base. Apart from hiking, young children or rheumatism, you won't find many reasons to linger in this pretty place once you've had coffee or a Spanish lunch.

# Sallent de Gállego and around

Back on the main road through the valley, the destination of choice for many middle-class Spaniards is Sallent de Gállego, a stone village on the banks of a stream, still bravely trying to be pretty through the mushrooming clusters of hotels that surround it. There are several easy walks in the area, detailed by the tourist office, but the main attraction outside skiing season is the **Pirineos Sur** world music and culture festival (see Festivals and events, page 186), with high-quality international performers and a market selling more interesting stuff than is the norm at Spanish fiestas. One of the positives to spring from the festival has been the rebirth of the town of **Lanuza**, a couple of kilometres away on the shore of an *embalse*. The Sallent **tourist office** ⓘ *1000-1300, 1700-2000*, is unfailingly friendly; it's set in a square with a curiously attractive sculpture.

## Formigal

The ski resort of Formigal, 4 km above Sallent, enjoys a bleak but spectacular mountain setting, but is by no means attractive; you're better off, as most people do, staying in Sallent. The skiing is good, with dozens of runs, although the wind can bite as it sweeps over the bare hills. Apart from winter sports, there's little reason to stop,

> ♣ For current snow conditions check www.formigal.com.

unless it's for the last drops of Spanish petrol before hitting pricier France. There's a **tourist information centre** ⓘ *daily*. For skiing, see Activities and tours, page 188.

## ● Sleeping

**Jaca** *p179, map p180*

Cheap places are available but not plentiful. For a solo traveller, it can be expensive as many of the hotels don't have single rooms.

**B Hotel Conde Aznar**, Paseo de la Constitución 3, T974 361 050, www.conde aznar.com. A charming hotel with an excellent restaurant that has been completely renovated recently. The modernization hasn't affected the original charm of the place, but has brought facilities up to an excellent level for the price. The doubles vary substantially in size; some are quite small. For a little more money, you can procure one with hydromassage unit, or a 'special' which is part way to being a suite. At peak times, they may only take bookings on a half-board basis; no hardship, as the restaurant is the best in town! Excellent service. Recommended.

**C Hotel La Paz**, C Mayor 41, T974 360 700, www.alojamientosaran.com. A very decent place run by decent folk. The rooms are standard modern Spanish, with TV, tiled floors and bathrooms. Some have balconies.

**C Hotel Mur**, C Santa Orosia 1, T974 360 100, hotelmur@hotmail.com. This is a historic Jaca hotel with a good feeling about it. Bedrooms are airy and have full facilities; the best overlook the citadel, so you can watch the top-secret manoeuvres of the Spanish army.

**C Ramiro I**, C del Carmen 23, T974 361 367, F974 361 361. Middle-of-the-road hotel with courteous management and fairly simple but spacious enough rooms. The restaurant is uninspiring but decent value. Closed Nov.

**E Hostal Alpina**, just down the road from the Hotel La Paz and run by the same people (see above); it has darkish, heated rooms with simple bathroom. Can be noisy if there's a school group in.

**E Hostal París**, Plaza San Pedro 5, T974 361 020, hostalparisjaca@ telefonica.net. A good option near the cathedral with clean doubles with shared bathroom. The doors are locked at night until about 0700, so be sure to make some arrangement if you've got an early bus.

**F Residencia El Carmen**, run by the same people as **Hotel La Paz** (see above); a student residence which can be used out of term time. Adequate rooms cost from €12; it's a good option for the solo traveller. Enquire first in the **Hotel Paz**.

### Campsites

**Camping Victoria**, Ctra Jaca-Pamplona, T974 360 323. A year-round site with less campervan traffic than many, and only 15 mins' walk from town.

Northern Aragón Western Pyrenean valleys Listings

C **Faus-Hütte**, Ctra de Francia s/n, T974 378 136. On the main road, this is a welcoming spot, full of good advice about walks in the area and warm mountain hospitality. It makes a good base for skiing if you've got a car; and the warm, good-value dinners are just the ticket after a day in the snow.

**Canfranc and Canfranc-Estación** *p183*

There are several *albergues* and hotels.

A **Hotel Santa Cristina**, Ctra Candanchú Km 669, T974 373 300, www.santacristina.com. You can't miss this massive hotel, a couple of kilometres beyond Canfranc-Estación. The rooms are spacious and warm and decorated with more subtlety than the exterior would suggest. All facilities for skiers are present, and there's a lively bar and restaurant. The views are great when it's clear.

F **Pepito Grillo**, T974 373 123. This simple mountain hostel has friendly management, dorm beds, and simple en suite doubles. It's a lively hillwalkers' bastion.

**Candanchú and Astún** *p183*

B **Hotel Candanchú**, T974 373 025, www.hotelcandanchu.com. One of the more characterful of the hotels, an old-style Spanish winter hotel with rustic decor, views and a terrace, with a good restaurant. The tariff rises sharply over a few of the crucial ski weekends (A), but this is compensated for by attractive full-board rates; the restaurant is good.

F **Pensión Somport**, T974 373 009. This likeable place is simple and cheap and consequently often full in peak winter periods. They'll also do cheap, filling meals for guests.

**Echo and Siresa** *p183*

D **Casa Blasquico**, Plaza Palacio 1, Echo, T974 375 007, and its restaurant **Gaby**, with charming rooms, good hospitality and great food. There are also cheaper *casas rurales*.

**Ansó** *p183*

C **Posada Magoria**, C Milagros 32, T974 370 049. The nicest of several places to stay in the old town, this is a very homely *casa rural* run by welcoming folk.

**Biescas and around** *p184*

There are 3 good places to stay:

D **Casa Ruba**, C Esperanza 18, T/F974 485 001.

D **La Rambla**, Las Ramblas de San Pedro 7, T/F974 485 177, larambla@publicibercaja.es.

E-F **Habitaciones Las Heras**, C Agustina de Aragón 35, T974 485 027. A friendly place with renovated rooms with or without bath.

**Panticosa and around** *p184*

D **Navarro**, Plaza de la Iglesia s/n, T974 487 181, www.hotelnavarro.com. One of several cheap hotels, it's decked out in typical mountain style with polished wood, cosy rooms, laundry service and ski-rack. There's also a restaurant and pleasant terrace.

**Sallent de Gállego and around** *p185*

There are plenty of places to stay in Sallent.

A **Almud**, C Espadilla 3, T/F974 488 366, www.hotel-almud.com. This stone hotel in the heart of the village is a welcoming and elegant place, full of antique furniture. The nicest room is at the top, with a mirador to sit and admire the view over the lake.

C-D **Hostal Familiar Maximina**, C La Iglesia 3, T974 488 436. A hospitable stone mountain lodge, with good rooms, some perfect for housing families or groups on a ski trip. The price is very reasonable for these parts. Rooms have modern bathroom, TV and phone.

F **Albergue Foratata**, C Francia 17, T974 488 112. The cheapest place in town with bags of dormitory space.

**Formigal** *p185*

The hotels are predictably pricey.

B **Tirol**, T974 490 377, tirol@arrakis.es. The only place you'll find for under €100 a night for a double room. If you're planning to ski here, you are better off either basing yourself further down the valley or booking a package.

## Eating

**Jaca** *p179, map p180*

Jaca has many good options. C Ramiro I is best for tapas, while C Gil Berges is the domain of several late-night bars; C Bellido also has a fair share.

▼▼▼ **El Fogón**, C del Carmen s/n, T974 363 892. An old-fashioned Spanish restaurant with a vaulted chamber. Jaca's proximity to France shows in the careful preparation, but local favourites are the staples, particularly the large tender steaks, succulent venison, and Pyrenean kangaroo!

**La Cocina Aragonesa**, Paseo de la Constitución 3, T974 361 050. One of Jaca's best, a friendly spot serving up Aragonese cuisine with a distinctly French touch. Part of the **Hotel Conde Aznar**. There's a *menú del día* for €13.50, but it's not really representative of the quality on offer. There's a lovely covered and heated terrace; a contrast to the darker, cosier interior.

**Café Babelia**, C Zocotin 11, T974 356 082. Not far from the cathedral, this zappy modern café-bar does some excellent and inventive salads as well as other food. Terrace prices add a hefty kick onto the bill.

**Gastón**, Av Primer Viernes de Mayo 14, T974 361 719. This upstairs establishment offers a €13.15 set menu that features good homestyle cooking. On the main menu, the *lenguado* (sole) in cava is excellent.

**La Fragua**, C Gil Berges 4, T974 360 618. A good hearty *asador*, popular with locals at weekends for its excellent *chuletón de buey* (oxsteaks) and other hearty meat dishes. All portions are enormous.

**Lilium**, Av Primer Viernes de Mayo 8, T974 355 356. On the main street, this spot has a covered terrace and an artistic touch that is manifest in its beautifully presented Pyrenean cuisine. There are a number of menus showcasing local food, as well as one for kids.

**Mesón Serrablo**, C Obispo 3, T974 362 418. An attractive and delicious restaurant in an antique-style stone building. 2 levels, and a good weekend *menú* for €15.50. The value-for-money is high here.

**Casa Fau**, Plaza de la Catedral 3, T974 361 594. This is a great little place, with a homely wooden atmosphere perfect after a day on the slopes; or a sunny terrace for warmer weather. The bar proudly displays an array of tasty *pinchos*, and the service comes with a smile.

**El Rincón de la Catedral**, Plaza de la Catedral 4, T974 355 920. The place to sit and admire the soft Romanesque lines of the cathedral. Large range of meals, salads, and delicious gourmet *montaditos* costing around €1.50.

**El Tizón**, Av Primer Viernes de Mayo 14, T974 362 780. Gregarious and hospitable, this restaurant is a family favourite after a day on the slopes or walking in the hills. There's something for everyone in the ample menu, from pizzas (€5-7) to a huge range of tasty salads, steaks and game. There's also a decent wine list and helpful service.

**La Tasca de Ana**, C Ramiro I 3. An indispensable stop on the Jaca food trail with a very large variety of quality hot and cold tapas, great salads, good wine and more.

### Biescas and around *p184*
Both the **Rambla** and **Casa Ruba** (see Sleeping, above) have good restaurants, well known in these parts, which makes it tricky to get a table at weekend lunchtimes without a reservation.

### Panticosa and around *p184*
**Manél**, Panticosa. A nice place to eat, a stone café/restaurant with a shady terrace; they do a solid *menú del día* for €12.

### Sallent de Gállego and around *p185*
**Martón restaurant**, Plaza Valle de Tena s/n, T974 488 251. A quiet riverside terrace and cosy interior serving cheap dishes, including good roasts cooked in an open brick oven.

**Bar Casino** Ctra Francia 4, T974 488 046. There are many places to eat in Sallent, but if you've never had a beer in a town hall before this is the place.

### Formigal *p185*
**Hotel Villa de Sallent**. The best place in town, it's run by a well-known Spanish chef.

## ⓞ Bars and clubs

**Jaca** *p179, map p180*
**Café**, Plaza de Lacadena s/n. Unremarkable-looking spot, this is actually one of Jaca's best bars, with a great collection of vinyl and a good vibe to boot.
**Viviana**, Plaza de Lacadena s/n. With a mixed selection of Asian prints on the walls, a pool table, and drum 'n bass sounds, this is one of Jaca's best bars.

## ⊛ Festivals and events

### Sallent de Gállego and around *p185*
**Mid-Jul** Pirineos Sur, T974 294 151, www.pirineos-sur.com, a 3-week world music and culture festival with high-quality international performers and a market selling more interesting stuff than is the norm at Spanish fiestas.

## ▲ Activities and tours

**Jaca** *p179, map p180*

Jaca has several tour operators who offer activities throughout the Aragonese Pyrenees.
**Alcorce Pirineos Aventura**, Av Regimiento Galicia 1, T974 356 437, www.alcorceaventura.com. Specialize in mountains, particularly skiing, trekking, climbing and caving.
**Aragón Aventura**, C Mayor 2, T974 485 358, www.aragonaventura.es. Experts in canyoning and skiing, but also offer other activities.
**Deportes Goyo**, Av Juan XXIII 17, T974 360 413. Hire mountain bikes.
**Pirineo Aragonés Aventura**, Av Premier Viernes de Mayo 14, T974 356 788, www.pirineoaventura.com. Primarily a summer operator, running, climbing, canyoning, canoeing trips and more.

**Formigal** *p185*
**Escuela de Esquí de Formigal**, T974 490 135, www.valledetena.com/eef. Has a monopoly on skiing courses in Formigal.

## ❂ Transport

**Jaca** *p179, map p180*
**Bus**
Jaca's bus station is conveniently located on Plaza Biscos in the centre of town. 5-10 daily buses run between Jaca and **Huesca** (1 hr 15 mins, €5.72), some going via **Ayerbe**. These connect in Huesca with buses to **Zaragoza** (2 hrs10 mins, €10.99). There are 2 buses daily to **Pamplona** (1 hr 40 mins, €6.17).

Alosa run buses from Jaca via **Sabiñánigo** up the Valle de Tena as far as **Sallent de Gállego** and **Formigal** (€4.53), detouring to **Panticosa** on the way. They depart from Jaca at 1015 and 1815, arriving at Sabiñánigo 15-30 mins later, and Sallent after 90 mins. The 1015 bus goes all the way to **Formigal** and returns at 1545, arriving in Jaca at 1715. The 1815 bus stops in Sallent and doesn't run on Sun – it leaves for Jaca again at 0700. In Jul and Aug the 1015 bus has a companion that runs all the way up to **Balneario de Panticosa** (€4.16), returning from the spa town at 1730.

There are 5 daily buses from Jaca up the Canfranc Valley, stopping at **Villanua**, **Canfranc Pueblo**, **Canfranc Estación** and continuing to **Candanchú** and **Astún** (45 mins).

For **France**, get a bus or train to Canfranc, and change there for a French rail bus which runs 3-5 times daily to Oloron-Sainte-Mairie, from where you can connect by train to Pau and beyond.

For the **Echó** and **Ansó** Valley, there is 1 bus from Jaca, leaving Mon-Sat at 1850. The return leaves Ansó at 0630.

For **Torla**, **Broto** and **Aínsa**, take 1 of the regular buses to Sabiñánigo (7 daily Mon-Sat, 4 on Sun, 20 mins, €1.26), and change there (see below).

**Car hire**
If you want to hire a car to explore the Pyrenees without relying on the infrequent public transport; head for OscaWeb, Av Oroel 40, T974 360 372, www.oscaw.com; or **Transpemer**, T974 360 781. Both start at around €45 per day for a short hire.

**Train**
The trains are neither as handy nor as useful as the buses and the station is to the east of town. A shuttle bus links to it from outside the bus station. There are 2 trains that head up the **Canfranc Valley** daily as far as the massive station at **Canfranc-Estación**. There are 2 trains that go the other way, from Jaca down to **Huesca** and on to **Zaragoza**.

**Canfranc Valley** *p182*
**Bus**
There are 5 daily buses from Jaca up the **Canfranc Valley**, stopping at **Villanúa**, **Canfranc Pueblo**, **Canfranc Estación**, and continuing to **Candanchú** and **Astún** (45 mins). From Canfranc-Estación, a French rail bus runs 3-5 times daily to **Oloron-Sainte-Mairie**, from where you can connect by train to **Pau** and beyond.

**Train**
2 trains daily head up the **Canfranc Valley** as far as the massive station at **Canfranc-Estación**. 2 trains go the other way, from **Jaca** down to **Huesca** and on to **Zaragoza**.

**Echo and Ansó valleys** *p183*
**Bus**
For the Echó and Ansó Valleys, there is one bus from **Jaca**, leaving Mon-Sat at 1850. The return leaves Ansó at 0630 and Echo at 0702. The schedule is designed for villagers to

spend a day shopping in the 'big smoke' rather than for people wanting to visit the valleys.

**Tena Valley** *p183*
**Bus**
**Alosa** run buses from Jaca via Sabiñánigo up the valley as far as **Sallent de Gállego** and **Formigal**, detouring to **Panticosa** on the way. They depart from **Jaca** at 1015 and 1815, arriving at **Sabiñánigo** 15-30 mins later, and Sallent after 90 mins. The 1015 bus goes all the way to **Formigal** and returns at 1545, arriving in Jaca at 1715. The 1815 bus stops in Sallent and doesn't run on Sun – it leaves for Jaca again at 0700. In Jul and Aug the 1015 bus has a companion that runs all

the way up to Balneario de Panticosa, returning from the spa town at 1730.

From Sabiñánigo buses run to **Torla**, gateway to the Ordesa Valley, at 1100 daily, continuing to **Aínsa**. In Jul/Aug, an additional bus runs at 1830 – both go via **Biescas**. The trip to Torla takes 55 mins.

## ❻ Directory

**Jaca** *p179, map p180*
**Internet** Ciber Santi, C Mayor 42-44 (in arcade), charges €2 per hr, open Mon-Sat 1100-1400, 1700-2300, Sun 1200-1730.
**Post office** C de Correos s/n, on the corner of Av Regimiento Galicia.

# Eastern Pyrenean valleys

*The eastern section of the Aragonese Pyrenees contains some of Spain's most spectacular scenery; towering mountainscapes that loom large over delightful grey stone villages. This is walking and climbing country par excellence, with favourites being the Ordesa National Park, demesne of the mighty lammergeyer, and Maladeta, where the range's highest peaks cluster. There's activity for any ability, from leisurely flower-filled-valley strolls to high-altitude traverses and assisted climbs. A network of hospitable mountain refugios (see box page 184) and hearty alpine cuisine adds to the appeal. Most of the eastern region is deserted in winter, with most services closed until March.* ➤➤ *For Sleeping, Eating and other listings, see pages 193-196.*

## Torla ❶❷▲❸ ➤➤ *pp193-196.*

➔ *Colour map 6, A3.*

Although heavily visited in summer, there's still something magical about Torla, the base most people use to reach the Parque Nacional Ordesa. Torla's sober square grey belltower stands proud in front of the soaring background massif of Mondarruego (2848 m); this massive wall of rock looks like a citadel built by titans. The village is well equipped with places to stay, eat and stock up on supplies and gear for trekking.The beautiful church houses a small ethnographic museum with a small display of traditional working and domestic life – apart from that it's the great outdoors that beckons. There are several banks in town. Torla's summer-only **tourist office** ⓘ *1000-1400, 1700-2000*, is on the Plaza Mayor.

> ❗ *Hit the ground running when you get off the bus to avoid the crowds on the popular trails.*

Further down the valley, **Broto** and **Sarvisé** are pleasant villages with a good range of facilities, but lack the convenience of the Torla shuttle bus that goes to the national park so are only handy if you've got transport. Broto's star attraction is its amazingly muscular and bulky church; there's plenty of accommodation here. Even better is the tiny village of **Oto**, a 10-minute walk from Broto, and featuring some excellent medieval buildings; there's also a good campsite here and a couple of *casas rurales*.

The area isn't one for winter sports; indeed, nearly everything is closed between November and March.

# Parque Nacional Ordesa y Monte Perdido

→ *Colour map 6, A3.*

ⓘ *Access to the park is usually confined to the shuttle bus from Torla in summer, see Transport page 196. There's also a very pleasant 2-hr walk starting from the bridge on the main road in town. Most trails start from La Pradera car park where the bus stops. There's a bar/restaurant here, as well as meteorological information (an important consideration for longer walks even in summer).*

From Torla you can spot the beginning of the Ordesa Valley, taking a sharp right in front of the bulk of Mondarruego. It's the most popular summer destination in the Aragonese Pyrenees, and understandably so, with its dramatic sheer limestone walls, pretty waterfalls, and good selection of walking trails. The valley was formed by a glacier, which chopped through the limestone like feta cheese, albeit over many thousands of years. Beyond the end of the valley looms **Monte Perdido** (Lost Mountain, 3355 m); it's not recorded who managed to lose it, but it must have been a misty day.

The valley and national park is an important haven for flora and fauna – the latter have retreated further into the hills as the stream of visitors became a torrent. You're likely to spot griffon vultures, choughs and wild irises even from the most-used trails, and you may see isard (Pyrenean chamois) and the massive lammergeyer (bearded vulture).

## Hiking in the park

The most popular route is an easy four-hour return up and down the valley, passing the pretty waterfalls of **El Estrecho** and **Gradas de Soaso** before arriving at the aptly named **Cola de Caballo** (horse's tail). It climbs gently most of the way before levelling and widening out above the Gradas.

A much better option, if more strenuous, is to head across the bridge from the car park, following signs for the **Senda de los Cazadores**. As long as the weather is clear you needn't be fazed by the danger sign – the trail has been much improved, although it's not recommended if you don't have a head for heights. After crossing the bridge, you're led straight into a steep ascent 650 m up the valley walls to the small shelter of **Calcilarruego**, where there's a viewing platform. The worst is now over; it's flat and gentle downhill from hereon in. The path spectacularly follows the *faja* (limestone shelf) along the southern edge of the valley, with great views north to the **Brecha de Roldán**, a square-shaped pass on the French border. If you think it looks man-made, you may well be right – Charlemagne's knight Roland is said to have cleared the breach with one blow of his sword *Durandal*. The path continues through beautiful beech and pine forest until you slowly descend to the Cola de Caballo waterfall (3-3½ hours after starting). From here it's a two-hour stroll back down the valley floor. There are several *refugios* around the area, some of which are unmanned.

For attempts on **Monte Perdido** (hard on the thighs but no technical experience required in summer), continue up another hour or two to the **Refugio de Góriz** (see Sleeping, page 193), usually quite full and a touch unwelcoming. From here, you can continue east towards the Pineta Valley and Bielsa, or north towards France.

# Aínsa ●●▲●● » *pp193-196.*

→ *Colour map 6, A3.*

Characterized by its hilltop location and spectacular mountainous backdrop, Aínsa (L'Aínsa) is a remarkably attractive town as well as being an important service centre and transport hub for some of the high Pyrenean villages. Unfortunately, this has its downside in the heart of summer, when the medieval quarter can feel a little like a theme park with hundreds of day-trippers. Come the evening, though, you'll have a freer run, and the sleeping and eating options are good.

The 12th- to 13th-century **old town** stands proud high above the gravelly junction of the Cinca and Ara rivers. From the entrance portal, two narrow streets lead past beautifully preserved houses to the massive cobbled main square, lined with arcades. Every odd year on 14 September there's a play performed here, with most of the town participating – it tells of the defeat of the Moors in AD 724. Legend has it that García Jiménez, attacking the Muslim town with 300 men, was facing defeat. He called on God, and a glowing red cross appeared on a holm oak tree; heartened by this, the Christians won. The top left corner of the Aragonese coat of arms actually refers to this event.

At the other end of the square is what's left of the **castle** ① *summer 1030-1400, 1700-2030*, basically just the still-impressive walls and a reconstructed tower, home to an exhibition of Pyrenean ecology. Back in the narrow streets, there's a better **museum** ① *Plaza San Salvador 5, T974 510 075, summer 1000-1400, 1600-2100, €2.40*, devoted to traditional Pyrenean art. The Romanesque church is Aínsa's other highlight, although the jukebox-style Gregorian chant removes some of the atmosphere. There's a strangely shaped cobbled cloister, frequently hung with the work of local artists. The semi-crypt behind the altar has a small view out of the window, while the tower, when open, offers excellent vistas. The **tourist office** is on the main crossroads below the old town; guided tours of the town run in summer

# Bielsa and around 🏨🍴🚌 ⇸ *pp193-196.*

One of the most peaceful centres in the Aragonese Pyrenees, Bielsa sees most action during the day at weekends, when French Pyreneans nip over the border to secure stashes of cheap whisky and cigarettes. Although the setting isn't as dramatic as Benasque or Torla, it's beautiful here, and the rather unspoiled village atmosphere makes this one of the nicest places to hang out in the area.

> **!** *You may end up staying longer than you meant to – it's easy to miss the only bus out at 0600.*

Bielsa was mostly destroyed in the Civil War; a posse of determined Republicans held the town against the Fascist advance before finally retreating up the valley and across the border. The artillery in the car park, however, is used for a less destructive purpose, to trigger avalanches in controlled conditions. The **Plaza Mayor** houses the **tourist office** and a small ethnographic exhibition; nearby is the simple but attractive 15th-century **church**.

## Valle de Pineta
Beyond Bielsa the main road makes its way into France via a long tunnel. Above the town, a side road winds over a hill and into the Valle de Pineta, a 15-km stretch of road that admits defeat when confronted with the imposing bulk of Monte Perdido. The car park at the road's end is the start or finish for a number of trails, one heading across the Ordesa National Park towards Torla. There's also a parador here, as well as a small chapel with a local Virgin.

Some 2½ km short of the car park, you'll see a sign to **Collado de Añisclo**, a tiring but spectacular ascent of the mountain across the valley. Allow eight hours for a return trip in summer – at other times you'll be after snow gear to reach the top.

## Cañón de Añisclo
South and west of Bielsa, a small, slow and spectacular route links the village of **Escalona** with **Sarvisé** near Torla (there's a quicker way through Aínsa). The road becomes one-way, snaking along a pretty gorge before arriving at a car park, about 12 km from the main road. This is the head of the Cañón de Añisclo, a small-scale

but beautiful gorge with a popular path running down it. Some sections wind easily through oak and beech forest, but other sections are slightly precipitous on one side, although the path isn't steep. Most day trippers walk as far as **La Riparela**, a level grassy plain about three hours from the car park (the return is slightly quicker). It's difficult to get to the canyon without your own transport or a tour from Bielsa or Torla, but it's possible to walk in on the GR15 path, staying at one of the two good *refugios* in tiny **Nerín**, a hamlet with a view. If you're in a car, the return road to Bielsa takes you back a different way, over the top of the hills, while the other option is to continue on to Sarvisé.

## Benasque and around ⊕❷❷❶⛰⊕❶   ➳ *pp193-196.*

→ *Colour map 6, A4.*

One of the major towns of the Aragonese Pyrenees, Benasque is a relaxed resort dedicated to outdoor pursuits. Although some of the modern development is reasonably tasteful, it has buried the old centre, which was outgrown by the massive surge in Pyrenean tourism in the years since Spain's return to democracy. It's a good base – there's plenty of accommodation, though few beds come cheap, several restaurants and bars, and resources for guides, tours, information and equipment.

The intelligent and helpful **tourist office** ① *1000-1400, 1600-1900 (2100 in summer)*, in Benasque is just off the main road. It's more than adequate for most needs, but for more detailed information about the park there's a **visitors' centre** ① *daily in summer from 1000-1400, 1600-2100 and weekends only the rest of the year*, about 1 km from Benasque off the road to Anciles and also a small exhibition.

❢ *There are summer restrictions on vehicles entering the park; you're better off using the bus services provided from Benasque.*

The main attraction in the area is the **Parque Nacional Posets Maladeta**, named after the two highest summits in the Pyrenees, which it encompasses. It's a terrain of valleys gouged by glaciers that extends well into Catalunya. Wild and high, the park includes seven summits over 3000 m. The Maladeta's highest peak, **Aneto**, is the Pyrenees' highest at 3404 m – it's climbable from the **Refugio de Rencluso** (T974 552 106, 45 minutes beyond the bus-stop at La Besurta, see Transport, page 196), but come fully equipped, even in summer: not for nothing is the chain known as the 'Cursed Mountains'. On the other side of the main road, to the east, the dark summit of **Posets** is a similarly difficult climb. There are several marked trails and *refugios* around it – one of the most used is the new **Refugio Angel Oíns in Eriste** (T974 344 044). It's worth checking out some of the area's glaciers, the southernmost in Europe, sadly rapidly diminishing; some estimates give them less than 30 years of life.

There's much scope for shorter walks in the area, around the **Hospital**, **La Besurta** and the **Vallibierna Valley** (also accessible by bus), which is traversed by the GR11 long-distance path. There are several mountain biking routes recommended by the Benasque tourist office.

Some 6 km above Benasque stands the village of **Cerler**, which purports to be the highest place in Aragón to be inhabited year round. It's dominated by a ski resort of average quality but with plenty of runs. There's no shortage of sleeping and eating options, although it lacks the atmosphere of Benasque.

Further up the valley, **Baños de Benasque** is another example of the enduring popularity of spa towns in Spain; there's a hotel here with various regimes targeted at any number of ailments – the beautiful location probably contributes greatly to the healing potential.

# ⊜ Sleeping

## Torla *p189*

**A Hotel Villa Russell**, C Ruata s/n, T974 486 770, www.hotelvillarussell.com. This brand-new hotel is right in the centre of Torla but has stayed true to the attractive stone look of the place. Inside, it's a gem too, with luxurious rustic decoration. The rooms are well equipped, with DVD player, internet access, fridge and microwave; and they are handsome too – some have a terrace but all are of high comfort.

**C Villa de Torla**, Plaza Nueva 1, T974 486 156, www.villadetorla.com. Another excellent place to stay in Torla; although the rooms are nothing to write home about, there's a terrace with great views, a swimming pool, good eating and it's in the heart of town.

**D Casa Frauca**, Ctra de Ordesa s/n, Sarvisé, T974 486 182. A faded but quite charming old inn, with characterful and unusual bedrooms with bathroom and a decent restaurant. Great views. Closed Jan/Feb.

**D Edelweiss**, Ctra Ordesa s/n, T974 486 168, hoteledelweiss@ordesa.com. The best of the cluster of main road hotels, with good en suite rooms, many with pretty wooden balconies and views.

**E-F Casa Laly**, C Fatas s/n, T974 486 168. A welcoming and well-priced *casa rural* in the heart of Torla. The rooms can be a bit noisy with pub-bound revellers passing under the windows, but it's still a very good option, cosy and homely.

**F Refugio L'Atalaya**, C Ruata 1, T974 486 022. Although the manager rubs plenty of people up the wrong way, the rest of the staff and the decoration are welcoming. The bar/restaurant is great, but the 2 dorms don't have a lot of breathing space; if they're filled to capacity you might consider contraception.

**F Refugio Lucien Briet**, C Ruata s/n, T974 486 221, reflucienbriet@eresmas.com. The roomier of the 2 *refugios* in town, with a couple of doubles too. Good restaurant, and board rates offered.

### Camping and refugios

**Camping Río Ara**, T974 486 248. A peaceful campsite in the river valley below Torla. Access by car is 1½ km beyond town, but there's a quicker footpath.

**Refugio de Góriz**, T974 341 201. A crucial *refugio* (see page 190) despite frequent shortages of beds. Book ahead if you don't want to camp out. Meals provided.

**Refugio Valle de Bujaruelo**, T974 486 348. A well-equipped and beautiful site further up the valley, open Apr-Oct.

## Aínsa *p190*

Many of Aínsa's hotels are unattractive options in the new town and budget accommodation is in short supply in summer.

**A Hotel Posada Real**, C de las Escalaretas s/n, T974 500 977, www.posadareal.com. An establishment run out of the Bodegón de Mallacán restaurant, this stately place has an odd mixture of the old and new, with 4-poster beds side by side with modern tiling and art. Still, it's a very comfortable place to stay just off the plaza.

**D Casa del Marqués**, Plaza Mayor s/n, T974 500 977. Another arm of the **Bodegón de Mallacán** restaurant on the plaza, this stone house has rustic and attractive wooden furnishings and a terrace with a view.

**E Casa El Hospital**, C Santa Cruz 3, T/F974 500 750. A good *casa rural* in a stone house next to the church, with charming doubles at a good price.

## Bielsa and around *p191*

**AL Parador de Bielsa**, Valle de Pineta, T974 501 011, www.parador.es. At the end of the Valle de Pineta road, under looming Monte Perdido, this makes an excellent base for walks in the area. Modern but sensitive construction, recently renovated. It's basically just you and the Pyrenees out here; it feels like a last outpost!

**C Valle de Pineta**, C Los Ciervos s/n, T974 501 010, www.monteperdido.com/hotelvalledepineta. Reasonably priced rooms, some overlooking the river valley. There's also a swimming pool. Get your 15 mins' of fame by eating in the pleasant restaurant; diners are telecast onto a screen in the street.

**E Vidaller**, C Calvario 4, T974 501 004. One of the best places to stay in Bielsa, with pleasant top-value rooms with and without bathroom above a small and friendly shop. Simple but very comfortable for this price.

**Northern Aragón** Eastern Pyrenean valleys Listings

**Añisclo Albergue**, Nerín, T974 489 008.
A good place to stop if you're heading for the
Cañón de Añisclo on foot. A top situation,
with great valley views, dorm beds, and
simple but happy meals.

## Benasque and around *p192*

A **Hotel San Marsial**, Av Francia 77, T974 551
616, www.hotelsanmarsial.com. The classiest
option of Benasque, although often booked
out by package tourists. They organize several
activities. Elegant hunting-lodge style decor.
B **Hospital de Benasque Hospedería**, Llanos
de Hospital, T974 552 012, www.llanosdel
hospital.com. With a variety of rooms, this
remote inn offers every comfort. There's a
very welcoming bar and restaurant, but come
prepared to stay a while in winter – every
now and then it gets cut off by snowfalls…
B **Hotel Ciria**, Av Los Tilos s/n, T974 551 612,
www.hotelciria.com. Very nice balconied
rooms on the main street with cheerful
fittings and many facilities. There are also
suites with hydromassage units to soothe
those muscles ailing from hiking or skiing.
C **Casa Mariano**, C Unica s/n, Eresué, T974
553 034, casamariano@imaginapunto
com.com. A top spot for people who want a
base in the great outdoors in a village 10 km
southeast of Benasque. This *casa rural* is very
homely, with 2 large bedrooms and excellent
home-cooked meals. One of the owners is
a mountain guide and will happily help
organize activities and give advice.
C **Hostal Solana**, Plaza Mayor 5, T/F974 551
019, www.hotelsolanabenas.com. Good clean
rooms above an unmemorable but bustling
bar/restaurant. There are 2 separate sections,
a *hostal* and a hotel – both are decent value
and recently refurbished, but make sure they
charge according to the rate sheet.
C **Hotel Avenida**, Av Los Tilos 14, T974 551
126, www.h-avenida.com. A friendly family-
run concern in the heart of Benasque, with
spotless rooms overlooking the main street
and a nice terrace restaurant downstairs.
C-E **Hostal Valero/Hotel Aneto**, Ctra de
Anciles s/n, T974 551 061, F974 551 509.
A large complex across the main road
from the town centre. There's a huge
variety of rooms and prices, as well as
some apartments. The service and staff
are helpful and welcoming.

D **Fonda Vescelia**, C Mayor 5, T974 551 654.
Dormitory accommodation and some
doubles at most un-Fonda-like prices.
Decent bar downstairs, and a shop
that offers massages.

### Refugios and campsites

**Camping Aneto**, Ctra Francia, Km 100,
T974 551 141. Several facilities as well
as some simple bungalows.
**Camping Los Baños**, Ctra Francia s/n,
T974 344 002, F974 551 263. A busier
campsite with more facilities.
**Refugio La Rencluso**, T974 551 490.
Run by the **Hotel Avenida**, this is the
best base for climbing Aneto.

## 🍽 Eating

### Torla *p189*

🍴 **El Rebeco**, Plaza Mayor s/n. Not the
friendliest of places, but there's a good
restaurant upstairs, as well as 2 terraces,
one shady, one sunny. It's named after the
isard/ Pyrenean chamois, which thankfully
doesn't feature on the menu, although
it's a traditional local dish.
🍴 **L'Atalaya**, C Ruata 1, T974 486 022. Funky
bar and restaurant doing a range of quality
dishes in a colourful atmosphere. *Menú
del día* for €9, and a drinkless evening
*menú* for €13. The bar does tapas and
*platos combinados*.
🍴 **A'Borda Samper**, C Travecinal s/n, T974
486 231. One of the nicest places to eat in
Torla – a great range of simple tapas in
a welcoming family atmosphere, and a
good upstairs restaurant.
🍴 **El Taillón** C Ruata s/n, T974 486 304.
A no-nonsense bar featuring a lawn
terrace with superb views of Mondarruego.
The good-value restaurant upstairs does
cheap and filling *menús*.
🍴 **La Brecha**, C Ruata s/n, T974 486 221.
Friendly upstairs restaurant doing a good set
menu for €10.20; a rare exception to the 'don't
eat where they photograph their food' rule!

### Aínsa *p190*

🍴 **Bodegas del Sobrarbe**, Plaza Mayor 2,
T974 500 234. A high-class restaurant with
the best of Pyrenean cuisine, based around
game. Last count featured 11 different
land-based creatures on the menu, but

vegetarians can be consoled by the excellent wild mushrooms. There's a *menú* for €19.26, but it doesn't feature the best on show.
**‼ El Portal**, C Portal Bajo 5, T974 500 138. Just about the first building you pass in the old town, this restaurant has some great views over the rivers below and *menús* for €9.60 and €13.50.

**Bielsa and around** *p191*
**‼ La Terrazeta**, C Baja s/n, T974 501 158. Well set with a dining room overlooking the valley, this is one of Bielsa's better options in summer or winter. There's a *menú* for €9.40 (excluding drinks), but à la carte isn't too pricey either.
**‼ El Chinchecle** is an excellent place in a small courtyard serving home-made liqueurs to the sound of traditional music. Also serves some very nice *cecina de ciervo* (cured venison), and put on 1 or 2 nightly dishes for some excellent simple eating.
**‼ Reyna's Bar**, Av Pineta s/n, T974 501 084. A people-watching spot with outdoor seats, and a good value *menú del día* and snacks.

**Benasque and around** *p192*
**‼ Ixeia**, C Mayor 45, T974 552 875. The smartest restaurant in Benasque with some very classy food. The general tenor is Aragonese, with a variety of meats carefully prepared with local Pyrenean fare: forest fruits and mountain herbs.
**‼ El Pesebre**, C Mayor 45, T974 551 507. A dark stony traditional restaurant with a small terrace, serving traditional Aragonese food, with plenty of lamb and game.
**‼ La Sidrería**, C Los Huertos s/n, T974 551 292. An excellent restaurant run by welcoming Asturians. Cider is the obvious choice but there are several good wines to accompany the delicious food. If there's some home-made cheesecake around, grab a slice – it's a short-priced favourite for the best dessert in Aragón.
**‼ Restaurant La Parrilla**, C Francia s/n, T974 551 134. A spacious and smartish restaurant dealing in well-prepared steaks – eat 'em rare if you want to do as the Aragonese do. There's a *menú del día* for €12.84.
**‼ Hostal Pirineos**, Ctra Benasque s/n, T974 551 307. A couple of kilometres back down the valley on the main road, this terrace is a nice place to sit and enjoy simple but well-done food and wine. There's good rooms available too.

# 🜄 Bars and clubs

**Benasque and around** *p192*
**Petronilla**, C San Marcial 8. A warming resort-style bar that packs a crowd around its pool and football tables.

# ⛰ Activities and tours

**Torla** *p189*
**Aragón Aventura**, C Ruate s/n, T974 486 455, www.aragonaventura.es. One of the 2 major operators in Torla for excursions in the area.
**Casa Blas**, Sarvisé, T974 486 041. All manner of equine activities.
**Center Aventura**, Av Ordesa s/n, T974 486 337. Has a good supply of trekking equipment and maps.
**Compañía Guías de Torla**, C Ruata s/n, T/F974 486 422, www.guiasdetorla.com. The other major operator in Torla for excursions in the area.

**Aínsa** *p190*
**Aguas Blancas**, Av Sobrarbe 4, T974 510 008, www.aguasblancas.com. Run white-water rafting and canoeing expeditions.
**Ignacio Gabás,** in the Bodegón de Mallacán restaurant. Scenic flights over the Pyrenees.

**Benasque and around** *p192*
**Barrabés**, C Francia s/n, T974 551 056. Run a series of alpine, rock climbing, rafting and canyoning activities for all levels. Their massive shop is full of equipment and maps.
**Casa de la Montaña**, Av Los Tilos s/n, T974 552 094. A similar range on offer.
**Centro de Formación de Benasque**, Campalet s/n, T/F974 552 019, fedmeben@sct.ictnet.es. Serious mountaineering, canyoning and skiing courses throughout the year; lasting from 3-5 days, book well in advance. It's part of the **Escuela Española de Alta Montaña**, which has a reputation for excellence.
**Compañía de Guías de Benasque**, Av de Luchón 19, T974 551 336, www.guiasbenasque.com. Organizes all sorts of mountainous activities in the area.
**Centro Ecuestre Casa Palo**, C La Fuente 14, Cerler, T974 551 092. Horse riding trips into the valleys.

Northern Aragón Eastern Pyrenean valleys Listings

**Escuela Español de Esquí**, Centro Cerler, Cerler, T/F974 551 553. Run skiing and snowboarding courses.

**La Garahola**, C San Pedro, Edificio San Pedro, T974 551 360. Run a number of fishing courses and excursions in the Benasque area.

**Radical Snowboard**, Edificio Ribagorza 10, T974 551 425. Snowboard hire and instruction.

## ⊖ Transport

### Torla *p189*
**Bus**

Torla is accessed by bus from **Aínsa** once daily at 1430 (1 hr), the return bus leaves Torla at 1200. 2 buses a day arrive from **Sabiñánigo**, via **Biescas**; they return at 1530 and 1945.

From Jul to Oct (and Easter) a shuttle bus runs from the parking lot at Torla to **La Pradera**, in the valley of Ordesa. Leaving every 15-20 mins from 0600-1900, the last return bus leaves the park at 2200. A return trip costs €2.70; outgoing buses stop at the park's visitors' centre El Parador. This bus is often the only way to reach the park by road, as private vehicle access tends to be cut off. Parking in the car park at the entrance to Torla costs €0.50 per hr or €5.50 per day, but there are other places to park.

### Aínsa *p190*
**Bus**

A bus line runs between Barbastro and Aínsa, leaving **Barbastro** Mon-Sat 1945 (1 hr), and leaving Aínsa at 0700. In Jul and Aug a 2nd bus runs, leaving Barbastro Mon-Sat 1100, and leaving Aínsa at 1510. A bus leaves Aínsa for **Bielsa** at 2045 Mon, Wed, Fri (Mon-Sat in Jul and Aug). The return bus leaves Bielsa at 0600. The service connects with the Barbastro bus.

A daily bus runs from Aínsa to **Sabiñánigo** via **Torla** and **Biescas**, leaving at 1430.

### Bielsa *p191*
**Bus**

Services run from Bielsa to **Aínsa** at 0600 Mon, Wed, Fri (Mon-Sat in Jul and Aug), with a connection to **Barbastro**. The bus into town leaves **Aínsa** at 2045.

### Benasque *p192*
**Bicycle hire**

**El Baúl**, C Francia s/n, hire bikes from €13 a day, as do **Ciclos A Sánchez**, Av del Luchón.

**Bus**

There are buses departing Benasque for **Barbastro** at 0645 and 1500 (2 hrs), which connect directly with buses to **Huesca**, **Lleida** and **Zaragoza**. For **Parque Nacional Maladeta**, a bus runs from Benasque to the trailhead of **La Besurta**, leaving 0430, 0900 and 1300, returning at 1400, 1830 and 2130. The bus also runs to **Vallibierna** and shuttles between La Besurta and the Hospital de Benasque.

## ❶ Directory

### Aínsa *p190*
**Internet** Bar Abrevadero, C Portal Bajo s/n.

### Benasque *p192*
**Internet** Coin-operated terminal in the tourist office, and Bar Surcos also has a computer, available from 1900-2300.
**Laundry** Lavandería Ardilla, Edificio Benás, C Francia s/n, T974 551 504.

# La Rioja

## ⁝ Footprint features

# Introduction

The province of La Rioja is known above all for its red wines, although part of the wine denomination falls in Euskadi. The Río Ebro runs down a shallow valley of enormous fertility, which also produces an important cereal, fruit and vegetable crop. The region was well known by the Romans, who produced and exported much of the good stuff from here; they referred to it as *Rioiia*; the name comes from the Río Oja, a tributary of the Ebro.

La Rioja is Spain's smallest mainland region, given semi-autonomous status for the same political reasons as Cantabria: it was felt that if it was just one more province of Castilla, the people would be more easily swayed by whisperings from separatist movements in Euskadi and Navarra, of which the territory was historically a part. In truth, though, it feels very conservative and Spanish, particularly when the summer sun sends temperatures soaring over 40°C. Pilgrims have a hard time of it walking across this sun's anvil en route to Santiago.

The cuisine is wholly unsuited to the summer sun, being designed more for the chilly winters. Riojan dishes par excellence are hearty stews of beans, or large roasts of goat and lamb, perfect with a bottle of the local.

The southern part of the province is hillier and has an excellent attraction in its multitude of dinosaur footprints hardened and fossilized in the Mesozoic mud. Logroño is a peaceful base for exploring the area's wineries, as is Haro, the effective grape capital.

The wine denomination of La Rioja actually extends into other regions; a good third of it is in El País Vasco; see the Laguardia section (page 117) for more wineries.

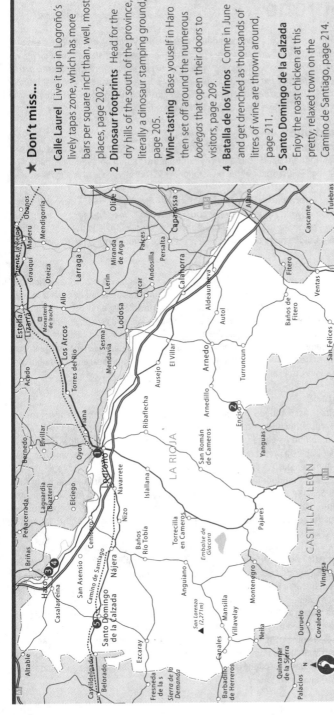

★ Don't miss...

1 **Calle Laurel** Live it up in Logroño's lively tapas zone, which has more bars per square inch than, well, most places, page 202.

2 **Dinosaur footprints** Head for the dry hills of the south of the province, literally a dinosaur stamping ground, page 205.

3 **Wine-tasting** Base youself in Haro then set off around the numerous *bodegas* that open their doors to visitors, page 209.

4 **Batalla de los Vinos** Come in June and get drenched as thousands of litres of wine are thrown around, page 211.

5 **Santo Domingo de la Calzada** Enjoy the roast chicken at this pretty, relaxed town on the Camino de Santiago, page 214.

La Rioja

# Logroño → *Phone code: 941. Colour map 3, C2. Population: 144,935. Altitude: 379m.*

*The capital of La Rioja province is a pleasant small city with plenty of plane trees and opportunities for leisurely outdoor life. It's also an important stop on the Camino de Santiago. If you've got transport it makes an excellent base for exploring the area's bodegas, although the town itself doesn't feel particularly wine-oriented. It happily has several excellent restaurants with Riojan cuisine that's a suitable match for the region's reds. ▶ For Sleeping, Eating and other listings, see pages 202-204.*

## Ins and outs

**Getting there and around** Logroño is a good transport hub, with connections to most of Northern Spain. **Bus** services run from the station on Avenida España. The **train** station is just south of the bus station. ▶ *See Transport, page 204, for further details.*

**Tourist information** The **tourist office** ① *T941 291 260, logrono@larioja turismo.com, winter Mon-Sat 1000-1400, 1600-1900, Sun 1000-1400; summer Mon-Fri 0900-2100, Sat 1000-1400, 1700-2000, Sun 1000-1400,* is in the central Parque Espolón. **Guided tours of town** ① *Mon-Fri 1200, €3,* from behind the tourist office.

## Background

Logroño emerged in history in Visigothic times, and later, along with much of Northern Spain, became part of the Navarrese kingdom until it was annexed by Castilla in 1076 under the name *illo gronio*, meaning 'the ford'. The town prospered as pilgrims flooded through on their way to Santiago, but the city's development was plagued throughout history by fighting; the rich agricultural lands of the region were a valuable prize. The city's name rose when it mounted a legendary defence against a French siege in 1521 and it became an important tribunal of the Inquisition. In more peaceful times, and with Riojan wines drunk all over the world, it can't help but prosper.

## Sights

Logroño's Casco Antiguo sits on the south bank of the Ebro, while the newer town's boulevards stretch west and south to the train station, a 10-minute walk away. Centred around its elegant Renaissance cathedral, not all the old town is actually very old, but it's a pleasant space with arcades and outdoor tables at which to bask in the summer sun.

Logroño's outdoor life is centred around its cathedral, **Santa María de la Real** ① *Mon-Sat 0800-1300, 1830-2045, Sun 0900-1400, 1830-2045, free,* a handsome structure, with a very ornate gilt *retablo* and elaborate vaulting. The impressive Baroque façade still has a faded inscription proclaiming the glory of the Nationalist rising and the *Caudillo*, Franco.

West of the cathedral, along the arcaded Calle Portales, you'll come to **Plaza de San Agustín,** with its impressive post office and the **Museo de la Rioja** ① *Tue-Sat 1000-1400, 1600-1900 (2100 summer), Sun 1130-1400, free.* It's a typical provincial museum, the usual mixed bag of archaeological finds and art; the highlight here is a portrait of Saint Francis by El Greco.

The **Iglesia de Santiago** is a bare and atmospheric Gothic edifice with a sizeable *retablo* of carved polychrome wood. There's an inscription outside to the Falangist leader José Antonio Primo de Rivera, but the front is dominated by a massive statue of Santiago Matamoros trampling some Moorish heads onboard a monster stallion. The **Iglesia de San Bartolomé** is worth a visit for its intricate Gothic portal and *mudéjar*-influenced tower.

# Wineries

The concept of visiting wineries isn't as developed in Spain as in other countries, although this is beginning to change. Most *bodegas* now have set visiting hours, but you'll nearly always have to phone in advance to arrange a tour or tasting. The tourist office have an excellent booklet, *Datos Enoturismo*, with a list of various *bodegas* in the region that welcome visitors. It's in Spanish and English. ▸▸ *See Haro, page 209 and Laguardia page 117, for more wineries in the area.*

One of the closest *bodegas* to Logroño is **Marqués de Murrieta de Ygay** ① *Ctra Zaragoza Km 5, T941 271 370, F941 251 606, Mon-Thu 0900-1400, 1700-1900, Fri 0900-1400 (visits by prior appointment only; mornings only in Jun/Jul, closed Aug), the cost of the tour depends on which wines you choose to taste; tours available in Spanish and English.* An attractive traditional winery, Murrieta has one of the best reputations for quality in the entire Rioja region. Its reds, though complex, are remarkably smooth for a wine with such lengthy ageing potential. To get there, it's about 45 minutes' (unpleasant) walk or €7 in a taxi on the Zaragoza road.

A little closer to town, **Ontañón** ① *Av de Aragón 3, T941 234 200, Tue-Sat 1030-1330, 1600-1830, Sun 1030-1330; ring to book a tour (€4 including tasting),* is

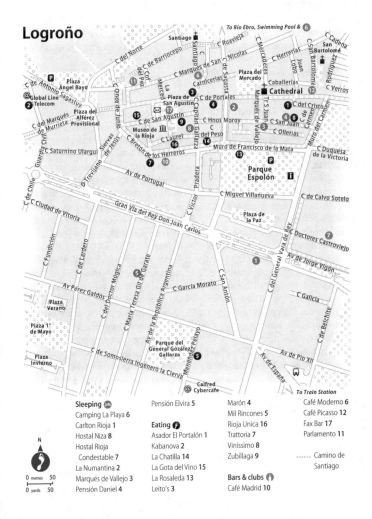

**Logroño**

La Rioja Logroño

| | | | |
|---|---|---|---|
| **Sleeping** | Pensión Elvira **5** | Marón **4** | Café Moderno **6** |
| Camping La Playa **6** | | Mil Rincones **5** | Café Picasso **12** |
| Carlton Rioja **1** | **Eating** | Rioja Unica **16** | Fax Bar **17** |
| Hostal Niza **8** | Asador El Portalón **1** | Trattoria **7** | Parlamento **11** |
| Hostal Rioja | Kabanova **2** | Vinissimo **8** | |
| Condestable **7** | La Chatilla **14** | Zubillaga **9** | |
| La Numantina **2** | La Gota del Vino **15** | | ····· Camino de |
| Marqués de Vallejo **3** | La Rosaleda **13** | **Bars & clubs** | Santiago |
| Pensión Daniel **4** | Leito's **3** | Café Madrid **10** | |

N

0 metres 50
0 yards 50

just a bottling and ageing point; the actual winemaking is done elsewhere. The Bacchanalian sculptures and paintings by a local artist are impressive, but the wine is fairly unremarkable. This *bodega* is handy if you haven't got your own transport; with a car, strike off and head for Haro, Laguardia or other villages in the region.

## ● Sleeping

**Logroño** *p200, map p201*
As many visitors to Logroño are on expenses-paid wine-buying junkets, the hotel accommodation is overpriced.
L **Hotel Carlton Rioja**, Gran Vía 5, T941 242 100, hotelcarlton@pretur.es. One of Logroño's better hotels, this is smart, clean and vaguely minimalist. It's located in the new town a 5-min stroll from the old centre; the rooms are spacious enough without being amazing, and the service is good. Discount for internet bookings.
A **Marqués de Vallejo**, C Marqués de Vallejo 8, T941 248 333, www.hotelmarquesde vallejo.com. This friendly old-town hotel has recently received a major makeover. It's very sleek and stylish, all strategically placed glass, dark wood parquetry and fashionable grey and white minimalism. The brand new beds are mighty comfortable and there's a business lounge with internet access. Underground parking very close by.
C **Hostal Niza**, C Gallarza 13, T941 206 044. This is a reasonable spot right in the centre of the old town. The rooms are wholly uninteresting (apart from a couple with gallery), but are blameless and have comfortable beds and clean spacious bathrooms.
C **Hostal Rioja Condestable**, C Doctores Castroviejo 5, T941 247 288, hosrioja@fer.es. This clean and modern *hostal* has a slightly cramped, lugubrious feel but offers rooms that are significantly good value on a pedestrian street. The owners are welcoming and thoughtful.
D **La Numantina**, C Sagasta 4, T941 251 411. This *hostal* is slightly tacky and faded but it's a place with plenty of comfort in its way. The rooms are all doubles, with en suite bathroom and the location is great, in the heart of the old town.
E **Pensión Daniel**, C San Juan 21, T941 252 948. One of 3 *pensiones* in the same building, right in the heart of things. This is the best of them; it offers comfort at a low price. It's

considerably better than the **Sebastián**, T941 242 800, which has faded, slightly depressing rooms; or the **San Juan**, T619 155 288, with rooms here and further up the street.
E **Pensión Elvira**, C María Teresa Gil de Garate 20, T941 240 150. This *pensión*, situated in the new town, is smart and has good value rooms that are neat as a new pin.

### Campsites
**Camping La Playa**, T941 252 253. By the River Ebro on the opposite bank from town, this is a good place to stay, and relatively handy for town.

## ● Eating

**Logroño** *p200, map p201*
Logroño has a busy tapas scene; the place to head for is C **Laurel**, which proudly claims to have the highest concentration of bars per sq m in Northern Spain (although there are several pretenders to this particular throne). It's a place to just buzz from bar to bar; you'll soon work out what each one specializes in by scanning the other diners' plates or the floor.
♔♔♔ **Marón**, C Portales 49, T941 270 077. A smart modern restaurant with French-inspired cuisine that's more delicate than your average Riojan fare. On weekdays you can enjoy the €25 *menú de degustación* that comes with the works. One of the best wine lists in town is another reason to turn up.
♔♔♔ **Zubillaga**, C San Agustín 3, T941 220 076. A wide mix of Northern Spanish cuisine, with many tasty fish dishes – try the *merluza con setas*, a tasty dish of hake and wild mushrooms. There are also hearty roast meats, as well as more delicate fare like crêpes.
♔♔ **Asador El Portalón**, C Portales 7, T941 241 334. While this *asador* does excellent heavy roast meat, it also has a very nice line in salads to balance out a meal.

**Kabanova**, C Benemérito Cuerpo de la Guardia Civil 9. Despite the Francoist street name, this is a stylish but surprisingly reasonable restaurant with interesting nouveau Riojan cuisine. The menu is short but features such delicacies as pigs' feet stuffed with foie and pear. Closed Sun/Mon.

**La Gota del Vino**, C San Agustín 14, T941 210 146. The tapas bar of a successful restaurant which is upstairs, this is a long, simple, smart and minimalist spot with shell-like chairs and a high metallic bar. There are several wines to choose from at the bar which has excellent and artistic *pinchos*; there are also small rolls and *cazuelitas* (small pots of stew).

**Leito's**, C Portales 30, T941 212 078. Stylish and rich Riojan cuisine, with several surprises on the menu. There's a set lunch/dinner for €12 or €16, both of which are superb value. Atmosphere is classy but warm.

**Rioja Unica**, C Laurel 11. One of the best of the bars on this busy tapas street, this warmly lit stone-fitted spot is a place to enjoy a glass of the local wine along with a delicious *pincho* or 2. At the back are tables where you can enjoy tasty *raciones*; the salads are particularly recommendable.

**Trattoria**, C Bretón de los Herreros 19, T941 202 602. Don't be fazed by the bizarre drive-by-shooting-style glass frontage; this is an excellent Italian restaurant with a split-level interior.

**Vinissimo**, C San Juan 23, T941 258 828. A good choice, with a €9 *menú*. There's a slightly North African flavour here, with dishes like couscous and tajine featuring on the menu, but it's a place to learn about the local wine too. You can book a tutored tasting session in English (€15) as well as purchase a good range of bottles.

**La Chatilla**, C del Peso, T941 206 198. This small, simple, and brightly coloured family restaurant represents good value in the heart of the old town. Tasty home-made paté costs only €4.81 (it's always a good sign seeing prices like this; they are converted directly from the days of the peseta and presumably haven't been victims of the euro price-surge), and there are hearty dishes like *rabo de toro* (bull's tail) and *pochas* (broad beans).

**Mil Rincones**, C Menéndez Pelayo 5, T941 246 965. A character-packed new town eatery, stuffed with curios and with a menu derived from around the world. It looks like a museum but has a much more upbeat atmosphere. The tables have telephones on them to call likely looking diners in other parts of the restaurant. It's also got a popular bar.

**Cafés**

**La Rosaleda**, Parque Espolón s/n. An outdoor café with heaps of tables in the park, open summer only.

## Bars and clubs

**Logroño** *p200, map p201*
There are a number of British-type pubs popular with young Riojans; many of these cluster around C Siervas de Jesús, C Saturnino Ulargui and Av de Portugal.

**Café Madrid**, C Bretón de los Herreros 15. Many of Logroño's young and smartly dressed meet here for an evening coffee or a large mixed drink. On weekend nights, it transforms itself into a disco-bar. It's decorated in American-diner style with padded red booth seating.

**Café Moderno**, Plaza Martínez Zaporta 7, T941 220 042. A very popular local spot lavishly decorated in swish neo-Baroque style with bright lights and black and white photos. It's popular for a pre- or post-cinema drink, but also does tapas and a *menú del día*.

**Café Picasso**, C Portales 4, T941 247 992. A cool café-bar with imported beers fronted by a sleek grey parrot whose daily diet includes fingers. It's cheerful, open-minded, and there's always some local banter being traded across the bar.

**Fax Bar**, Plaza San Agustín s/n. Although the days of curling thermal paper will soon be a distant memory, this is a good dark little bar with a mixed crowd. Its best feature is the summer terrace outside.

**Parlamento**, C Barriocepo s/n, T941 212 836. Lively café-bar with a small stone-faced interior and a terrace. It's opposite the Rioja parliament but often filled with folk much younger than your average politician.

● For an explanation of the sleeping and eating price codes used in this guide, see inside the
● front cover. Other relevant information is found in Essentials pages 39-46.

**Viajero**, C Sagastay s/n, is a smart
cabaret venue just west of the old town.
It's also a good spot for a drink, with a
warm wooden interior. You can't miss it;
there's a huge map of the world painted
on the façade.

## ⊕ Entertainment

**Logroño** *p200, map p201*
**Cines Moderno**, Plaza Martínez Zaporta.
A conveniently central cinema.
**Teatro El Bretón**, C Bretón de los Herreros,
T941 207 231. A theatre but also occasionally
shows *versión original* (subtitled not dubbed)
English-language films.

## ⊛ Festivals and events

**Logroño** *p200, map p201*
**11 Jun** San Bernabé, which is used to
commemorate the town's defence against
the French. Free fish and wine are given
out to the multitudes.
**21 Sep** Harvest Festival. The most
enjoyable time to be in La Rioja is during
harvest time. The festival coincides
with the feast day of San Mateo.

## ○ Shopping

**Logroño** *p200, map p201*
**Vinsa**, C Canalejas s/n (corner C Marqués
de Murrieta). One of the better places to
buy wine in town.

## ▲▲ Activities and tours

**Logroño** *p200, map p201*
**Swimming**
**Las Norias**. If the summer heat is too
much, head across the river to this sports
complex with an outdoor pool. There's
a small admission charge.

**Tour operators**
**Rutas Rioja**, C Hermanos Moroy 18, T941
244 230. Organizes tours of the region
and its wineries.

## ⊝ Transport

**Logroño** *p200, map p201*
**Bus**
The bus station information number is
T941 235 983.

**Local** Within the region, 22 buses a day
(9 on Sun) go to **Nájera**, 2 daily to **San
Millán de Cogolla**, 6 daily to **Calahorra**
(3 on Sun), 7 daily to **Haro** (1 hr, €3.50,
3 on Sun), 3 daily to **Ezcaray**, 6 to **Arnedo**
(3 on Sun), 6 to **Oyón** and 4 to **Laguardia**
(20 mins, €1.05) in **Alava**.

**Long distance** Longer routes include
**Pamplona** (3-5 daily, 1 hr, €6.38), **San
Sebastián** (3-5 daily, 3 hrs, €13), **Vitoria**
(6 daily, 2 hrs, €7.10), **Zaragoza** (6-7 daily),
**Valencia** (2 daily), **Barcelona** (4 daily,
6 hrs, €24), **Bilbao** (5 daily, 2 hrs, €10.55),
**Burgos** (7 daily, 1 hr, €4.50) and **Madrid**
(6 daily, 4 hrs 20 mins, €18.14).

**Train**
Services include **Haro** (3 a day, 40 mins,
€3-10), **Zaragoza** (7 daily, 2 hrs, from
€9.75) and **Bilbao** (3 a day, 3 hrs, €15-20),
but it's not as useful a service as the buses.

## ⊙ Directory

**Logroño** *p200, map p201*
**Internet** Café Picasso (see above) has
2 coin-op terminals for €2.40; **Café
Parlamento** also offers access but doesn't
open until 1530 (closed Sun). **Cálfred II**,
C Menéndez Pelayo 11, T941 247 195,
is a more conventional cybercafé, Mon-
Sat 1100-2200. **Global Line Telecom**,
C Benemérito Cuerpo de Guardia Civil 13,
is a *locutorio* which also has internet access.
**Post office** The main post office is a
pretty affair on Plaza San Agustín, next
to the Museo de la Rioja.

# La Rioja Baja

*The Rioja Baja east of Logroño is a land where wine isn't the be-all and end-all; it's a fertile country (at least near the river), and produces large quantities of high-grade vegetables and cereals. In the southeast, the main attraction is dinosaurs; 100 million years ago prehistoric beasts roamed the land, leaving massive footprints all across the region.*

*Calahorra is the major town of the Rioja Baja, the province's eastern portion. Wine lovers won't find this as good a base as Haro, although there are plenty of producers around. It's a pleasant enough place, but there's little reason to stay unless you're parador-hopping; if you want to check it out, you might be better off making it a day-trip from Logroño.* ⟫ *For Sleeping, Eating and other listings, see pages 206-208.*

## Calahorra

The town is of Roman origin – its fertile riverside situation was what attracted them, and it remains a prosperous agricultural market town. The **old centre** is on a hillock above the river; some of the sloping paths still seem medieval, with chickens running among broken stones and weeds on the side of the hill. The **cathedral** ① *Tue-Sat 1030-1230, 1600-1800 (1700-2000 summer), Sun 1130-1330, 1600-1800 (1700-2000 summer), free*, is by the river, noticeable for its ornate white sculpture on a sandy façade, a side doorway depicting the Assumption and a tiled turreted belltower. Next to it is the similarly hued **Palacio Episcopal**, but the centre of town is the **Plaza del Raso**, down by the square **Iglesia de Santiago**, a church that seems to want to be a town hall. The **tourist office** ① *T941 146 398, calahorra@lariojaturismo.com*, is just off Plaza del Raso, next to the town museum.

There are **Roman ruins**, but they are so fragmentary as to be almost invisible, although it was once an important town, with a circus for chariot-racing. It was the home of the Roman Christian poet Prudentius; the city was one of three in Spain mentioned by the geographer Strabo in the early 1st century AD. Some of the remains can be found in the **Museo Municipal** ① *C Angel Oliván, near Plaza del Raso, Tue-Sat 1200-1400, 1800-2100, Sun 1200-1400*.

## Dinosaur country 🖥️🏍️⬤▲🚌 ⟫ *pp206-208.*

The southern part of La Rioja province feels a bit left out, with few grapevines and less arable soil. There's a major attraction however; the area's former residents, namely stegosaurs, iguanodons and the like, who lived in considerably wetter conditions and left footprints wherever they trod. Some of these tracks have been extraordinarily well preserved. A hundred-odd million years on, it's an unforgettable and slightly eerie sight. Heading into the area south of Calahorra, you hit **Arnedo**, a major Riojan town nestling among rust-red hills. It's a nice enough place, but there's better further on, in the heart of dinosaur country.

**Arnedillo**, 12 km beyond Arnedo, makes a good base. It sits in a gully carved by the Río Cidacos. Compared to many other Spanish villages, it's upside-down – the church is at the very bottom of town, and the main road at the top of the steep streets. Arnedillo has a small **information centre** ① *T941 394 226, arnedillo@lariojaturismo.com*, on the main road opposite the turn-off down to the spa. Half a kilometre from town is a **spa** which offers a large array of treatments and courses, and draws a good number of (mostly elderly) visitors. From here a path follows the banks of the river as far as Calahorra; it's part of a series of former train lines turned walking paths named **Vías Verdes**.

# ▪ Footprint guide

In the early Cretaceous period, about 120 million years ago, what we now see as hot, dry, craggy hills was a flat place with dense vegetation, marshes and lagoons. Herbivorous dinosaurs were drawn here by the abundant plant life, carnivorous ones by the plump prey on offer. While most of the tracks the dinosaurs left in the mud were erased, some hardened in the sun and, over time, filled with a different sediment. This eventually turned to stone, making the footprints clearly distinguishable as the layers eroded again over tens of millions of years.

There are 20-odd marked sites (*yacimientos*) in the region. Just across the river from Enciso is the site of **Virgen del Campo**, a large flat bed of rock with a confusing mixture of trails and fossilized mudslides and ripple patterns. One intriguing set of tracks seems to show an iguanodon being run down and attacked by an allosaurus. The road east from here has a great variety of sites, with fossilized trees, footprints of the massive brachiosaurus, tracks of whole herbivore families, and more. Six kilometres north of Enciso, in the village of **Munilla**, a shockin' dirt road leads a couple more kilometres around the hills to the excellent sites of **Barranco de la Canal** and **Peña Portillo**. The former has a long trail of 33 clear iguanodon footprints, while the latter has a number of well-preserved tracks, including some posited to be those of a stegosaur dragging its tail. Other beds include one, 30 minutes' walk above Arnedillo, and several over the border in Soria province (needless to say, there's no cooperation between the two authorities). The sites are enlivened by decent life-size models of the beasts, with frighteningly pitiless eyes.

**Enciso**, some 10 km further on the road to Soria, is set in the heart of things Cretaceous. Some of the best sites are within a short walk of here, and the village houses the **Centro Paleontológico** ① *Jun to mid-Sep daily 1100-1400, 1700-2000; mid-Sep to May Mon-Sat 1100-1400, 1500-1800, Sun 1100-1400; €2.40.* It's worth stopping here before you go off looking at footprints. There's a decent audiovisual display (in Spanish) and some average exhibits; the overviews of the different sites are the most valuable. On Saturday and Sunday 1200, you can take a two-hour guided visit of some of the footprint sites for an extra €1 (book on T941 396 093).

Beyond Enciso, the road continues into Soria province, and to the city itself. **Yanguas** (actually just over the Sorian border) is a delightfully homogeneous town of stone buildings and cobbled streets on the road between Soria and Arnedo. It's got a very unspoiled feel, and those in need of a quiet stop could do little better. There's a fairly ruinous castle at the eastern end of town that used to house the local lairds; work is in progress to spruce it up a bit. A kilometre north of the town is another reminder from days when these places were thriving; Yanguas actually had a suburb, **Villaviejo**, but it's now in ruins apart from a church, **Iglesia de Santa María**, in rapid decline but still a pretty sight with its curious cupola.

---

## ● Sleeping

**Calahorra** *p205*
**AL Parador Marco Fabio Quintiliano**, Era Alta s/n, T941 130 358, www.parador.es.

Calahorra's modern *parador* sits on the edge of town overlooking the plains below. The Roman remains around can accurately be described as ruins, but the spacious and polished rooms are (of course) a/c, a prerequisite in the baking Riojan summers.

**C Ciudad de Calahorra**, C Maestro Falla 1, T941 147 434. A good, comfortable option in the heart of town. The rooms offer excellent value and lack for nothing except perhaps a dash of levity or character.

**E-F Hostal Teresa**, C Santo Domingo 2, T941 130 332. A clean and tidy place not far from the old town. There are singles and doubles with or without bathroom; they are basic but clean and cheap.

**Dinosaur country** *p205*

**B Hospedería Las Pedrolas**, Plaza Félix Merino 16, Arnedillo, T941 394 401, laspedrolas@ telefonica.net. By far the best in town and indeed one of the nicest places to stay in this part of Spain, this spot is set opposite the church at the bottom of town and is decorated in smart yet welcoming white. The atmosphere is homelike and the rooms, which vary in size, are superbly comfortable. Breakfast included, and home-cooked dinners available. Recommended.

**D El Rimero de la Quintana**, C La Iglesia 4, Yanguas, T975 185 432. There are a couple of *casas rurales*, and this, on the plaza in the heart of the little town, is the most atmospheric. Good meals are also served.

**D La Tahona**, C de Soria 4, Enciso, T941 396 066. A great base; this is a friendly *casa rural* on the main road, with appropriate displays of local fossils, welcoming rustic rooms, and a big terrace by the river. They also rent mountain bikes for €9 a day; the perfect way to get around the footprint sites. The owner can give you all sorts of advice on where to go, and serves a great breakfast. Recommended.

**D-E Hostal Parras**, Av Velasco s/n, Arnedillo, T941 394 034. Right by the massive spa complex, this is a very well-priced retreat. Spacious modern rooms with or without bathroom are available and there's an attractive bar/café as well as a restaurant.

**F Camas Teresa**, Av Cidacos 39, Arnedillo, T941 394 065. One of the cheapest options in the area, this is a no-frills *pensión* with shared bathrooms. It's friendly, clean and good value.

**F Posada de Santa Rita**, Ctra de Soria 7, Enciso, T941 396 071. A clean quiet and cheap little *pensión* with simple rooms.

## ● Eating

**Calahorra** *p205*

¶¶ **Casa Mateo**, Plaza del Raso 15, T941 130 009. A smart restaurant with typical Riojan cuisine, a good spot for lunch on a day-trip if you can handle the jowly men flashing their bulging wallets. Its *menestra de verduras* is justly famous.

¶¶ **Taberna Cuarta Esquina**, C Cuatro Esquinas 16, T941 134 355. Tucked away in the back streets, this is another good bastion of Riojan cuisine with a friendly atmosphere. Closed Tue.

¶ **El Mesón**, C de los Monetes s/n, T941 148 056. Up an arcade off C Ipatro, this *asador* does sizeable roasts and has a *menú del día* for a paltry €6.60.

¶ **Porqus Porqus**, C Cuatro Esquinas 9. A hearty shop to try and buy *jamones*.

**Dinosaur country** *p205*

Eating options in Arnedillo abound, but be aware that late nights aren't the town's forte; many kitchens close shortly after 2200.

¶¶ **Bodega La Petra**, Av del Cidacos 22, T941 394 023. Near the bridge, this atmospheric cave-restaurant is a great place to eat. It does hearty traditional homestyle food, with tasty mushroom croquettes, and good grilled meats in a dark and intimate grotto.

¶¶ **Casa Cañas**, Av Cidacos 23, Arnedillo, T941 394 022. This appealing restaurant spreads over 2 floors and is best for meat and game, which are prepared with Riojan pride.

¶¶ **La Fábrica**, C de Soria 2, Enciso, T941 396 051. There are several restaurants in Enciso, but if you're there at a weekend, try this likeable set-up in an old flour mill.

¶ **Mesón de los Cazadores**, Av del Cidacos 25, Arnedillo, T941 394 138. A cheap and homely spot with hearty no-nonsense fare, which has a good lunch *menú* for €9.

## ● Bars and clubs

**Calahorra** *p205*

**Cinema Lope de Vega**, on the main square, doubles up as a *discoteca* at weekends.

**Oasis**, Paseo del Mercadal 25. This bar is one of a few nightspots on this street.

## ○ Shopping

**Dinosaur country** *p205*
**Factoria**, Av de la Industria s/n, Arnedo, T941 380 005. On the outskirts of Arnedo, this factory outlet has some of Spain's bigger shoe brands for sale at knockdown prices.
**Vinoteca Elias**, Av Cidacos 36, Arnedillo, T941 394 010. A good wine shop, which has a comprehensive range of Riojas.

## ▲ Activities and tours

**Dinosaur country** *p205*
**Spa Balneario Arnedillo**, Av Velasco s/n, T941 394 000, www.balnearioarnedillo.com. If you want to take the waters, this hotel (AL) offers the most comprehensive range of services with various 2- to 6-day programmes as well as one-off sessions. Use of the pool is an outrageous €17 for non-guests.

## ○ Transport

**Calahorra** *p205*
**Bus**
The bus station is convenient and connects the town 6 times daily (3 on Sun) with **Logroño**. Buses also run to **Zaragoza**, **Pamplona**, **Soria** and **Vitoria**.

**Train**
It's a weary uphill trudge from the train station with heavy bags, and there's no *consigna* there. Most eastbound trains from **Logroño** (7 daily, 30 mins, from €3.20) stop here.

**Dinosaur country** *p205*
**Bus**
3 buses a day (1 on Sun) run from **Calahorra** via **Arnedo** to **Arnedillo** and **Enciso**; 1 continues to **Soria** (and vice versa).

# La Rioja Alta

*If you're on the trail of the good drop, you'll want to either head north from Logroño to Alava and base yourself around Laguardia for a day or two, or head northwest towards Haro, which is the wine capital of the Rioja Alta, and a pleasant place to stay. It's definitely the best base for wine tasting in Rioja province, but if you're mobile, explore the pretty villages of the region with the looming mountains in the background.*
▸▸ *For Sleeping, Eating and other listings, see pages 210-212.*

## Wine route

On the road to Haro, first stop is **Fuenmayor**, 16 km out of the capital. A pleasant place with a square and a couple of *pensiones*, it would make a quiet base for visiting wineries if you've got a car. There's also a good campsite (T941 450 330) by the river just out of town.

**Cenicero** is given over completely to wine, with several *bodegas* and the mansions lived in by those who own them. As with all these towns, the backdrop is the mountains of the Sierra de Cantabria to the north, rising sharply from the Riojan plain. Although it sounds mellifluous in English, *Cenicero* actually means 'ashtray'; don't worry, it's really rather nice.

❧ *Most wineries welcome visitors, but phone ahead. See Logroño, page 200, for further information.*

Just south of the main road, **San Asensio** is home to several *bodegas*, and features a smaller version of Haro's *Batalla del Vino* in July, but this free-for-all is strictly rosé only. Further on, **Briones** is dominated by a church spire, as is **San Vicente de la Sonsierra**, main town of a small subsection of the wine region, whose dramatic Romanesque church perches above the town.

**Wineries** in the area include **Marqués de Cáceres** ① *T941 455 064*, based in Cenicero; they don't particularly encourage visitors but will show you around, and they do make decent wine. **Hermanos Peciña** ① *near San Vicente de la Sonsierra,*

1000-1400, are definitely more welcoming and splash out some *vino* for visitors. The tour takes about half an hour and can be arranged in English. **Torremontalbo**, between Cenicero and Briones, is home to **Bodegas Amezola de la Mora** ⓘ *T941 454 532*, who make their very tasty wines in a small castle. In Fuenmayor, **Bodegas AGE** ⓘ *T941 293 500, Mon-Fri 0900-1400, 1500-1800 (last visit 1 hr before)*, operate out of a lovely old 19th-century *bodega*. You don't have to prearrange this visit, but call ahead to arrange a tour in English or French. Their *Azpilicueta crianza* has received many plaudits.

# Haro ⊜𝒇✳❍⊜❶  ⤻ *pp210-212*.

Haro, the major town of the Rioja Alta, is a lively little place. It definitely feels like a wine town, with a clutch of *bodegas* on its outskirts, several decent wine shops, a museum, and a very active tapas and restaurant scene. If it's slightly cliquey, well that comes with the territory too. While its outskirts apparently were designed by a child megalomaniac with a Lego set, the centre is compact and pleasant; most of the *bodegas* are situated on the opposite bank of the river, a 15-minute walk from the centre. For information contact the **tourist office** ⓘ *Plaza Florentino Rodríguez, T941 303 366, haro@lariojaturismo.com, Mon-Sat 1000-1400, 1600-2000 (mornings only Nov-Mar), Sun 1000-1400*.

The **Museo de Vino** ⓘ *C Bretón de los Herreros 4, Mon-Sat 1000-1400; 1600-2000, Sun 1000-1400, €2, free Wed*, is situated in the complex of the **Estación Enológica**, a grapey thinktank. Don't confuse it with a shop on the next block cunningly emblazoned with *Museo de los Vinos*. The real museum is to the point and excellent, with three fairly no-frills floors explaining the winemaking process and regional characteristics in an informative fashion (Spanish, English and French). It's more didactic than interactive, and rather than giving information about individual wineries, it provides details about the region as a whole.

At the top of town is the **Iglesia de Santo Tomás Apostol**, with an impressive portal decorated with scenes of the crucifixion flanked by the Evangelists. Inside it's gloomy and lofty; an ornate organ the most impressive feature. The balconied tower is also attractive. Have a peek at the noble house next door, with its twisted *salomónica* columns and a large coat-of-arms with a very strange base.

## Wineries

One of the best wineries to visit is **Bodegas Muga** ⓘ *T941 310 498, English-language tour Mon-Fri 1100, Spanish tour 1200, €3*. Founded in 1832, the firm relocated here in 1969; it's an attractive and traditional-style *bodega*. There's a firm commitment to time-honoured processes, so everything is fermented and aged in wood; there's no stainless steel in sight. Even the filtration uses actual egg-whites, painstakingly separated, rather than the powdered albumen favoured by most operators. Most interestingly, Muga make their own barrels on site; if the cooperage is working, it's fascinating to see. The wines are of very good quality; an appley white takes its place along a full range of aged reds. The tour is worth the money, and there's a tasting session at the end.

*There are several wineries clustered around the far bank of the river, a 15-minute stroll from town.*

Near to Bodegas Muga is the **Bodegas Bilbaínas** ⓘ *T941 310 147, Apr-Sep Tue-Sat at 1000, 1100, 1200, Sun 1100, ring to book and for winter opening*, another historic *bodega* set in a beautiful building. For a further list of *bodegas*, ask the tourist office for their booklet *Datos Enoturismo* and an updated list of opening hours in the area. Most require a prior phone call, but many are beginning to realize the potential value of tourism and tastings.

# Rioja wine

Spain's most famous wine-producing area is not solely located in the province of the same name, but extends into Basque Alava and even a small part of Navarra. The Ebro Valley has been used for wine production since at least Roman times; there are numerous historical references referring to the wines of the Rioja region.

In 1902 a royal decree gave Rioja wines a defined area of origin, and in 1926 a regulatory body was created. Rioja's DO (denominación de origen) status was upgraded to DOC (denominación de origen calificada) in 1991, with more stringent testing and regulations in place to ensure the high quality of the wine produced. Wine was formerly produced in cellars (bodegas) dug under houses; the grapes would be tipped into a fermentation trough (lagar) and the wine made there; a chimney was essential to let the poisonous gases created escape.

Techniques changed with the addition of French expertise in the 19th century, who introduced destalking and improved fermentation techniques. Nowadays, the odd wine is still made in the old underground bodegas, but the majority of operations are in large modern buildings on the edges of towns.

Although Rioja's reputation worldwide had sunk by the second half of the 20th century, it picked up in the 1990s and is now thriving. Sales are around the 250 million litre mark, about a quarter of which is exported, mostly to the UK, USA, Germany, Scandinavia, and Switzerland.

By far the majority of Riojas are red (85-90%); white and rosé wines are also made. There are four permitted red grape varieties (with a couple of exceptions), these being Tempranillo, which is the main ingredient of most of the quality red Riojas, Garnacha (grenache), Mazuelo, and Graciano. Many reds are blends of two or more

# Sleeping

**Wine route** *p208*
A **Ciudad de Cenicero**, C La Mojadilla s/n, Cenicero, T941 454 888, www.hotel ciudaddecenicero.com. A swish modern hotel in this small town. Rooms are well equipped, with beamed roof, minibar and safe.
E **Mozart**, Plaza de España 8, Cenicero, T941 454 449. A small, clean and likeable *pensión* right on the main square. Good value.

**Haro** *p209*
A **Los Agustinos**, C San Agustín 2, T941 311 308, F941 303 148. A peaceful place set in a beautiful old monastery with a cloister-cum-patio as its focus; this is Haro's best choice. The rooms are remarkably good value for the quality, with plush carpets and beds, and impeccable service.
C **Hostal Higinia**, Plaza Florentino Rodríguez s/n, T941 304 344, F941 303 148. With a little viney terrace outside, this is a cool and

comfortable option in the heart of town run by the same management as Los Agustinos opposite. The rooms are modern, and simply decorated, with a good bathroom and TV. Open Mar-early Dec only.
E-F **Pensión La Peña**, C Arrabal 6, T941 310 022. A rock-solid, well-run option and very attractive rooms with or without bathroom, close to where it all happens in town.
F **Pensión Aragón**, C La Vega 9, T941 310 004. Slightly taciturn but oddly likeable place with decent rooms with shared bathrooms. The mattress springs gave up the ghost years ago but there's a certain charm to the place; perhaps it's the price!

## Camping
**Camping de Haro**, Av de Miranda s/n, T941 312 737. Only a 10-min walk from town across the river, this is a good campsite with some shady spots and decent facilities.

---

of these varietals, which all offer a wine something different. Permitted white varieties are Viura (the main one), Malvasia, and Garnacha Blanca.

The region is divided into three distinct areas, all suited to producing slightly different wines. The Rioja Alavesa is in the southern part of the Basque Country and arguably produces the region's best wines, somewhat lighter and better balanced than some of the others. The Rioja Alta is in the west part of Rioja province and its hotter climate produces fuller-bodied wines, full of strength and character; parts with chalkier soil produce good whites. The Rioja Baja, in the east of Rioja province, is even hotter and drier, and favours Garnacha; wines from here don't have the same longterm ageing potential. Most of the best Rioja reds are produced from a combination of grapes from the three regions.

Oak ageing has traditionally been an important part of the creation of Rioja wine; many would say that Riojas in the past have been overoaked but more care is taken these days and younger styles are more in fashion. The quality of individual Riojas varies widely according to both producer and the amount of time the wines have been aged in oak barrels and in the bottle. Riojas are classified according to the amount of ageing they have undergone. The words *crianza*, *reserva* and *gran reserva* refer to the length of the ageing process (see box, page 45), while the vintage date is also given. Rioja producers store their wines at the *bodega* until deemed ready for drinking, so it's common to see wines dating back a decade or more on shelves and wine lists.

Many of the *bodegas* accept visitors, but be sure to arrange the visit in advance. The best bases for winery visiting are Haro in the Rioja Alta (page 209), and beautiful Laguardia in the Rioja Alavesa (page 117).

## ⊙ Eating

**Haro** *p209*

♥♥♥ **Mesón Atamauri**, Plaza Gato 1, T941 303 220. A top-grade stone restaurant specializing in fish, prepared with a *finesse* that belies the inland location. Richer offerings include some delicious *tornedos* and more traditional Riojan dishes. Excellent *pintxos* in the bar too.

♥♥ **Asador Fharo**, Plaza San Martín 6, T941 311 203. A friendly, family-run place with a decent *menú* for €15, although à la carte won't push you much further. Service is very hospitable. During the week, there's a *menú del día* for €8.

♥♥ **Beethoven I & II**, C Santo Tomás 3 & 10, T941 310 018. A pair of facing establishments, the first a spacious place with comfy wooden furniture serving tapas and *raciones* based around ham and seafood (and an excellent 4-course lunch for €15), the latter a smarter restaurant with a very complete menu of all things fishy and meaty,

as well as an excellent house salad (closed Tue). There's now a third one opposite the Santo Tomás church.

♥♥ **Terete**, C Lucrecia Arana 17, T941 310 023. Founded in 1877, this is a mainstay of the Riojan eating scene. Lamb is the speciality here; any bit of one from half a head to a massive roast. There's a reasonable €9.10 *menú* and a good selection of cheap *raciones* and desserts. The wine list is no disappointment either.

♥ **Mesón Los Berones**, C Santo Tomás 24. A good and popular bar serving inexpensive portions of Riojan food in a warm, friendly atmosphere. Don't bother with the overpriced *menú del día* though.

## ⊛ Festivals and events

**Haro** *p209*

**29 Jun** Batalla de los Vinos (yes that does mean 'Battle of the Wines'). Haro's best-known and messiest festival takes place at the **Riscos de San Bilibio** a couple of km from town. It has its origins in a territorial dispute between Haro and Miranda de Ebro for the area. The mayor climbs the hill, where a medieval castle used to stand, to symbolize Haro's possession of the area, there's a mass in the chapel, a lunch and then all hell breaks loose, with thousands of litres of red wine being sprayed, poured and thrown over anyone and everyone. Not a little disappears down throats too.

**21 Sep** The grape harvest celebration with floats and dancing.

## ◔ Shopping

**Haro** *p209*
**Vinícola Jarrera**, C Santo Tomás 17, T941 303 778, is one of the better places to buy wine. Owned by the Muga family, there's a big range of Riojas, including some very old examples. While most prices here are good compared with the competition, some of the rarer wines are alarmingly overpriced, so shop around a bit before splashing out. Open daily 1000-2200; tapas and tastings available. Case discounts.

## ◔ Transport

**Haro** *p209*
**Bus**
Haro's bus station is situated in the Casa de Cune, former home of the main wine co-operative. There are services to **Logroño** (1 hr, €3.50, 7 daily, 3 on Sun), **Burgos** and **Santander** (1 daily) as well as **Laguardia** (40 mins, €2.30, 3 daily), **Vitoria** (1 hr, €3.60, 4 daily), **Bilbao** (1 hr 15 mins, €7.50, 4 daily), **Santo Domingo de la Calzada** (4 daily, 1 on Sun) and **Nájera** (2 daily).

**Train**
Services are few, and the station is a fair walk from town, but there are trains to **Logroño** (3 a day, 40 mins, €3-10) and **Bilbao**.

## ◔ Directory

**Haro** *p209*
**Internet** Access at 2 neighbouring establishments: **Beep**, C La Vega 40, and **BeMax**, C La Vega 42.

# Pilgrim Route to Santiago

*For those heading to Santiago, the stretch from Logroño is often completed under baking sun, but there are a couple of characterful towns in which to stop. Nájera and Santo Domingo de la Calzada are nice places, and the imposing monasteries of San Millán merit a detour. The area prides itself on being the birthplace of the Spanish language; the earliest known texts in that idiom derive from here.* ▸▸ *For Sleeping, Eating and other listings, see pages 215-216.*

### Nájera → *Colour map 3, C2.*

After passing through the rosé wine centre of Navarrete, the town of Nájera is the first major stop for pilgrims on the road from Logroño to Burgos. It doesn't seem as large as its population of 7000 would suggest; most are housed in the modern sprawl close to the highway, leaving the river and care-worn, but attractive, old town in relative tranquillity. The town's name derives from an Arabic word meaning 'between rocks', referring to its situation, wedged among earthy crags. These are riddled with caves, some of which were used extensively in medieval times and were dug through to make a series of interconnecting passageways. These can be accessed to the south of the town's imposing highlight, the Iglesia de Santa María la Real.

In former times Nájera was an important medieval city and a capital of many Navarran kings; under Sancho the Great in the early 11th century most of Northern

● For information on the practicalities of walking the Camino de Santiago and the history of ● the pilgrimage, see pages 52 and 388.

Spain was ruled from here. In the 14th century, Nájera was the site for two important battles of the Hundred Years War, both won by Pedro the Cruel, while a famous short-term resident was Iñigo de Loyola, waiting on the Duke of Navarra during the period immediately before his wounding at Pamplona and subsequent conversion from dandy to saint.

The impressive **Iglesia de Santa María la Real** ① *Mon-Sat 0930-1300, 1600-1900, Sun 1000-1230, 1600-1830, €2*, is a testament to this period's glories. It was originally founded by Sancho's eldest son, King García, who was out for a bit of falconry. His bird pursued a dove into a cave; following them in, García found them sitting side by side in front of a figure of the Virgin Mary with a vase of fresh lilies at her feet. After his next few battles went the right way, he decided to build a church over the cave; the rest, as they say, is history. Today the figure is in the main *retablo*, still with fresh lilies at her feet, and the cave holds a different Virgin. The present church is a much-altered Gothic construction, which was heavily damaged during the Peninsular War and later, when much looting followed the expulsion of the monks by government order in 1835. Heavy investment in restoration has restored many of its glories. The cloister is entered via an elaborate door crowned by the coat of arms of Carlos V, who donated generously to monastery building projects. Above is an elaborately painted dome. The cloister is pleasant, although many of the artistic details have been destroyed. The church itself is a fairly simple three-naved affair. The *retablo* features the statue of Mary; to either side kneel King García and his queen. Most impressive is the rear of the church, where elaborately carved tombs flank the entrance to the original cave. The tombs hold the mortal remains of several 10th to 12th-century dukes, kings and other worthies, but were made several centuries later. The exception is the sepulchre of Doña Blanca, a beautifully carved Romanesque original with Biblical reliefs and funerary scenes. Above in the gallery the *coro* (choir), although damaged, is a superb piece of woodwork, an incredibly ornate late Gothic fusion of religious, naturalistic, and mythological themes adorning the 67 seats.

Round the corner is the moderately interesting **Museo Arqueológico** ① *Plaza Navarra, Mon-Sat 1000-1400, 1700-2000, Sun 1000-1400, €1.20*, with a range of finds from different periods mostly garnered from volunteer excavations. The area was inhabited by prehistoric man and later by a succession of inhabitants, including Romans, Visigoths and Moors.

The **Iglesia de Santa Cruz** is smaller and simpler than La Real and dates from the 17th century. It seems to be the preferred home for the town's stork population, which have built some unlikely nests in its upper extremities.

The **tourist office** ① *C Constantino Garrán 8*, will provide a map of the town, but they're currently good for little else.

A half-hour walk from Nájera takes you to **Tricio**, famous for its peppers and the **Ermita de Santa María de Arcos** ① *daily 1000-1300, 1600-1930*, which is worth a look. Built over extensive Roman remains, some of it dates to the fifth century AD; it's a curious architectural record and a peaceful little place.

## San Millán de Cogolla
① *Both monasteries open winter daily 1030-1300, 1600-1800; summer 1030- 1330, 1600-1830; admission by guided tour only; €3.50 (Yuso), €3 (Suso).*
Some 18 km into the hills is the village of San Millán de Cogolla, which grew up around its two monasteries. The original is the **Monasterio de Suso**, tucked away in the hills a kilometre or so above town. It was started in the sixth century to house the remains of San Millán himself, a local holy man who lived to be 101 years old. It feels an ancient and spooky place, with low arches and several tombs. Mozarabic influence can be seen in the horseshoe arches and recessed chapels. The saint himself was buried in a recessed chapel off the main church but was dug up by Sancho the Great, who built a solemn carved cenotaph in its place. The bones were

## Chickens in the church

A buff 18-year-old German by the name of Hugonell was heading for Santiago with his parents in the Middle Ages when they stopped here for the night.

The barmaid at the inn liked what she saw but got a terse *nein* from the boy. In revenge she cunningly replaced his enamel camp-mug with a silver goblet from the inn and denounced him as a thief when the family departed. Finding the goblet in his bags, the boy was taken before the judge, who had the innocent teenager hanged outside town. The parents, grief-stricken, continued to Santiago.

On their way back months later, they passed the gallows once again, only to find Hugonell still alive and chirpy; the merciful Santo Domingo had intervened to save his life.

The parents rushed to the judge and told the story, demanding that their son be cut down. The judge laughed sardonically over his dinner and said "Your boy is about as alive as these roast chickens I´m about to eat". At that, the chickens jumped off the plate and began to cluck. The boy was duly cut down.

In memory of this event, a snow-white cockerel and hen have been kept in an ornate Gothic henhouse inside the cathedral ever since. They are donated by local farmers and are changed over monthly.

taken down the hill and had another monastery built around them, **Monasterio de Yuso** (the word means 'low' in a local dialect; *Suso* means 'high'). The current structure is on a massive scale and is a work of the 16th century, far more ornate and less loveable than Suso. Still an active monastery, the highlight is the galleried library, an important archive, some of whose volumes can barely be lifted by one person. San Millán finds himself in an ivory-panelled chest in the museum; this ascetic hermit would also be surprised to see himself depicted over the main entrance door astride a charger with sword in hand and enemies trampled underhoof. There's also a **tourist office** in the grounds of Yuso.

The monastery has styled itself the 'birthplace of Spanish', as the first known scribblings in the Castilian language were jotted as marginal notes by a 10th-century monk in a text found in Yuso's library. A couple of centuries later, the nearby village of **Berceo** produced a monk, Gonzalo, who penned the first known verse to have been written in the language.

### Santo Domingo de la Calzada → *Colour map 3,C2.*

Santo Domingo is a lovely town, worth a stop for anyone passing through the area. It is a town with a curious history behind it, mostly connected with the man for whom it is named. Born in 1019, Domingo dedicated his young life to the pilgrims who were passing through the area. He built a hospice, a bridge and generally improved the quality of the path; it's no wonder he's the patron saint of roadworkers and engineers in these parts. He made himself a simple tomb by the side of the *camino* before dying at the ripe old age of 90, but admirers later had him transferred to the cathedral, which was built in the town that grew up around his pilgrims' rest.

The **cathedral** ① *daily 0930-1330, 1600-1830, €1.80*, with its ornate free-standing tower is the town's centrepiece. Time and the elements haven't quite rubbed off the Fascist slogans on the façade, but inside it's pleasant and light. There's much of interest after you've made it through the officious bureaucracy at the entrance. Santo Domingo himself is in an elaborate mausoleum with a small crypt underneath it. Around it are votive plaques and offerings from various engineering and roadworking firms. An attractive series of 16th-century paintings tell some incidents from the saint's life. One of these concerns his 'miracle of the wheel': a weary pilgrim foolishly had a nap on the road and was run over and killed by an oxcart; Santo Domingo prayed on his behalf and he rose again.

In memory of this event a cartwheel is hung in the cathedral every 11 May. The chooks are the main attraction in their ornate coop, punctuating the pious air with the odd cock-a-doodle-doo (see box, opposite). There's a 16th-century *retablo* with a few nasty fleshy relics of various saints in small cases and a museum around the cloister. Climb onto the roof for some fresh air and a good view over the many narrow streets below. The guided visit includes the cloister and the small museum of religious artefacts.

There are several admirable buildings in the old town, which basically consists of three parallel streets and the northwest section of the old walls is still intact; pilgrims who have passed through Puente la Reina may experience a bit of déjà vu.

The **tourist office** ① *C Mayor 70, T941 341 230, daily 1000-1400, 1700-2000*, is near the cathedral on the main street.

## ● Sleeping

### Nájera *p212*
Places to stay are currently limited.
C **Hotel San Fernando**, Paseo San Julián 1, T941 363 700, www.sanmillan.com. A faded beauty, this is a good option across the river from the old town. It's quite a charming place, and the doubles offer good value, although they aren't exactly modern. There's even a replica British telephone box in the lobby.
D **Hostal Ciudad de Nájera**, C Calleja San Miguel 14, T941 360 660, www.ciudadde najera.com. A brand-new *hostal* decorated with verve in bright colours. The delightful owners have equipped the good-value rooms superbly, with excellent bathrooms, TV and piped music. There's also a cheery guest lounge and downstairs *bodega*. Recommended.
E **Hostal Hispano II**, C La Cepa 2, T941 362 957. Characterless but clean; it's run out of a nearby restaurant.
Cheaper beds yet can be found at the home of **María Emilia del Rey**, Flat 5E, C Espadaña 1, T941 360 808. Just around the corner from the post office, the buzzer (top right) is unmarked, but you'll get a chatty and warm welcome.

### San Millán de Cogolla *p213*
A **Hospedería Monasterio San Millán**, T941 373 277, www.sanmillan.com. An atmospheric place to stay, this is set in a wing of Yuso monastery and offers excellent, spacious rooms, a heavy Spanish décor, and willing service. There are often exceptional special offers, so it's always worth phoning. Opposite is an *asador* which is a decent place to eat, if a little oversized.

### Santo Domingo de la Calzada *p214*
L **Parador de Santo Domingo de la Calzada**, Plaza del Santo 3, T941 340 300, www.parador.es. Right next to the cathedral, this mostly modern *parador* is built around the saint's old pilgrim hospital and is an attractive place with facilities and charm, backed up by a decent restaurant.
B **Hotel El Corregidor**, C Mayor (Zumalacárregui) 14 Av Calahorra 17, T941 342 128, F941 342 115. Bright and breezily decorated modern hotel (although the pink curtains in the rooms are a bit sugar-sweet) in the old town; it's a friendly and comforting spot to stay.
D-E **Pensión Miguel**, C Juan Carlos I 23, T941 343 252. On the main road through town, this *pensión* has rooms that are noisy but not overly so. The en suite ones are significantly nicer than the ones without bathroom, although all are reasonable.
F **Hostal Río**, C Etchegoyen 2, T941 340 277. Faded, simple rooms above a restaurant, run by cheerful management. A good budget option.

## ● Eating

### Nájera *p212*
♥ **Bar Choquito**, C Mayor 23. Good fried fish snacks.
♥ **El Buen Yantar**, C Mártires 19, T941 360 274. This *asador* does a very good *menú* for €8.50, with hearty Riojan bean dishes washed down by tasty grilled meat and decent house wine.

¶**El Trinquete**, C Mayor 8, T941 362 564.
Good *raciones*; you can try fried sheeps' ears,
a waste-not-want-not Riojan speciality.
¶**Las Ocas**, C Descampado 4, T941 362 985. A
*cervecería* specializing in grilled meat.

**Santo Domingo de la Calzada** *p214*
There's good cheap eating in Santo
Domingo; although it might be wise to
off the roast chicken.
¶¶**El Rincón de Emilio**, Plaza Bonifacio
Gil 7, T941 340 527. Tucked away in a tiny
plaza off the main road, this is a charming
chessboard of a place with good Riojan
stews and meats.
¶**Río**, C Etchegoyen 2, T941 340 277. A
cheerful place with a huge range of cheap
and homely dishes, including plenty of fish.

## ◑ Bars and clubs

**Nájera** *p212*
**La Piedra**, C San Miguel 2ª. Rock fans will
want to take their air guitar down to this bar.

## ◉ Festivals and events

**Santo Domingo de la Calzada** *p214*
**12 May**  The town celebrates the anniversary
of the **Santo Domingo's death** in style, with
a series of processions for a couple of weeks
prior to the fiesta.

## ◒ Transport

**Nájera** *p212*
**Bus**
Frequent services run from the spangly new
bus terminal by the **Hotel San Fernando** to
**Logroño** and **Santo Domingo**, and 3 or 4
daily go to **Burgos** and **Zaragoza**. There are
2 daily to **San Millán**, leaving at 0720 and
1320, returning at 1500 and 1945; and 2
to **Haro** and **Ezcaray**.

**Santo Domingo de la Calzada** *p214*
**Bus**
Buses leave from Plaza Hermosilla just south
of the old town. There are regular buses to
**Logroño**, stopping in **Nájera**; to **Burgos**,
and to **Bilbao** via **Haro** and **Vitoria**.

## ◐ Directory

**Nájera** *p212*
**Internet**  Head for **Cybercom**, C Mártires 7,
who charge €1.80 per hr for good access.
**Laundry**  There's a *lavandería* at Ribera
del Najerilla 5.

**Santo Domingo de la Calzada** *p214*
**Internet**  There's free internet access for
pilgrims in the Ayuntamiento, Mon-Fri
0900-1300, 1500-1900. Non-pilgrims
might be able to negotiate something.

Castilla y León

## Footprint features

# Introduction

For many people, Castilla is the image of Spain: a dry, harsh land of pious Inquisition-ravaged cities, ham, wine and bullfighting. Visitors tend to love or hate the dusty *meseta* with its extremes of summer and winter temperatures; it's a bleak, almost desert landscape in parts.

Castilla is named for its huge number of castles, many of them found in the Duero Valley. But it has much more to offer than faded reminders of past glories. The cities of southern Castilla are all interesting: Romanesque Soria glows in the evening light, busy Valladolid preserves an imperial air, Zamora is a model for sensitive urban blending of the old and the new, and Salamanca is a stunningly beautiful ensemble of Renaissance architecture, topped off by Spain's most beautiful main square.

Likewise, the major attraction of northern Castilla is its architecture. The main route to Santiago crosses the heart of the region and there are numerous churches and monasteries in noble Romanesque or Gothic.

The city of Burgos itself is much visited for its elegant cathedral and is a courteous, genteel city. Palencia doesn't attract many tourists, but it deserves more. Quiet and friendly, it's got a definite charm and boasts a province full of treasures.

Despite being amicably joined with Castilla, the province of León is culturally, geographically and socially somewhat distinct. The city of León is vibrant, rich in architectural heritage and draws the crowds to its sublime Gothic cathedral.

This chapter roughly follows two east-west routes: firstly from Soria west along the Duero, then from Burgos west along the Camino de Santiago.

## ★ Don't miss...

**1 Castillo de Gormaz** Step back in time at this massive yet desolate castle looming high over the one-time Reconquista frontline, page 227.

**2 Ribera del Duero** Taste some of Spain's best reds in this wine region near the busy wine capital of Valladolid, page 228.

**3 Plaza Mayor, Salamanca** Pay over the odds for a coffee or vermouth on the most beautiful square in Spain (you won't regret it), page 255.

**4 León** Marvel with the pilgrims at the majestic Gothic cathedral, fine Romanesque frescoes and extravagant Plateresque façade of San Marcos, page 290.

**5 Valle del Silencio** Wind your way through chestnut trees along this remote and barely known valley to the impossibly picturesque stone village of Peñalba de Santiago, page 305.

Castilla y León

# Soria → Phone code: 975. Colour map 5, B4. Population: 37,200.

*One of Spain's smallest provincial capitals, Soria rules a province that's incredibly empty, one of the most sparsely populated in Spain. Although much of it is dry Castilian plains, the River Duero gives it the fullest attention, carving a big horseshoe shape through the province, although it's certainly in no hurry to get to the sea, which it eventually does in Portugal (where it's named the Douro). In the north of the region are some craggy hills and tranquil hilly forests, but few trees remain in the south, for centuries a battleground between Christian and Moor. Dozens of castles are testament to this, as are the gracefully simple Romanesque churches built by the eventual victors. As the Reconquista progressed, however, Christian settlers moved south in search of less thirsty lands, leaving the province a little denuded.*

*Soria is little known in the travel community but is worth a day or two of anyone's time, particularly for its outstanding Romanesque architecture and strong community spirit.* ▸▸ *For Sleeping, Eating and other listings, see pages 224-225.*

## Ins and outs

**Getting there and around**  Soria is well connected by bus to other major cities in Northern Spain. The bus station is a 15-minute walk northwest from the centre of town. A yellow bus runs from Plaza Ramón y Cajal to the train station, a couple of kilometres south. The old town, where most sights of interest are to be found, is easily walkable, tucked between two attractive parks, the hilltop Parque el Castillo and the more formal Alameda de Cervantes. The pedestrianized main street changes name a couple of times but runs the length of the area. ▸▸ *See also Transport, page 225.*

## Soria

**Soria detail**

Sleeping 🛏
Hostal Centro 1
Hostal Viena 2
Hostería Solar de Tejada 3

Parador Antonio
  Machado 4
Pensión Carlos 5
Soria Plaza Mayor 6

Eating 🍴
Casa Augusto &
  El Mesón de Isabel 1
La Patata 5

0 metres 100
0 yards 100

@ Merlin Center
To Train Station

**Tourist information**   Soria's shiny new **tourist office** ⓘ *C Medinaceli 2, T975 212 052, oficinaturismodesoria@jcyl.es, daily 0900-1400, 1700-2000*, is just around the corner from Plaza Ramón y Cajal and is very helpful.

## Background

Although nearby Numancia was an important Celtic settlement, Soria itself didn't really get going until the Middle Ages, when it achieved prosperity as a wool town. But its relative isolation (plus the fact that the sheep ate all the grass) led to its decline, along with that of the rest of Castilla. Once the coast was under central control, there was no percentage left in towns like Soria; the conditions that led to its rise ceased to exist after the Moors had been driven out. The *cabeza* (head) *de Extremadura* – this word formerly referred to the Christian borderlands in the Reconquista – became just another decaying provincial town. Happily, this meant that there wasn't enough money to meddle with its Romanesque architectural heritage too much, a fact that the city is surely grateful for today.

---

# Sights

## Iglesia de Santo Domingo

On the northern edge of the old town, by the main road through Soria, is the Santo Domingo church, built of beautiful pale pink stone, and possessing one of the loveliest Romanesque façades in Spain. The interior is simple; barrel-vaulted and with several interesting capitals that can be a little hard to inspect in the gloom. The portal is the highlight, though, with ornately carved bands depicting a number of Biblical scenes in appealing naïve sculpture. A small guide inside the doorway helps

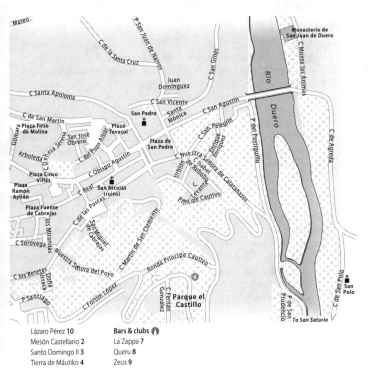

Lázaro Pérez **10**
Mesón Castellano **2**
Santo Domingo II **3**
Tierra de Máutiko **4**

**Bars & clubs** 🎵
La Zappa **7**
Queru **8**
Zeus **9**

**Castilla y León** Soria

## Antonio Machado

*"Por estos campos de la tierra
mía, bordados de olivares
polvorientos, voy caminando solo,
triste, cansado, pensativo y viejo"*
(In the fields of my land, sewn with
dusty olive trees, I walk alone,
sad, weary, pensive, and old).

Along with Federico García
Lorca, Antonio Machado was Spain's
greatest 20th-century poet and part
of the so-called 'Generation of 98'
who struggled to re-evaluate Spain in
the wake of the loss of its last colonial
possessions in 1898. Born in 1875 in
Sevilla, Machado lived in many places
in Spain, including Soria, where he is
a local hero. His poetry is simple
and profound; many examples are
redolent of the landscapes of Castilla,
whose solitude seems to reflect that
which Machado felt in his own soul.
His loneliness was exacerbated
when his young wife Leonor died
after only three years of marriage.

Machado was a staunch defender of
the Republic and became something
of a bard of the war. Forced to flee
with thousands of refugees as the
Republic fell, he died not long after
in a *pensión* in southern France; his
will to live dealt a bitter blow by the
triumph of fascism, and his health
badly damaged by the trying journey.
He was described by Rubén Darío as
"shepherd of a thousand lions, and
also of sheep".

to identify the scenes; including the visitation of the angel to the Magi. The three seem more saucy than wise, all very cosy in bed under a single duvet.

## Monasterio de San Juan de Duero and around

① *Jul-Sep 1000-1400, 1700-2000; Oct-Jun 1000-1400, 1600-1900, closed Mon all day and Sun pm, €0.60.*

Not far from the Iglesia de San Pedro, just on the other side of the river, this is Soria's best sight. Although it started as a humble church, a group of Hospitallers of Saint John of Jerusalem (later known as the Knights of Malta) set up base here on their return from the crusades. The simple church, damaged by fire over the years, preserves some excellent capitals and has decent Spanish display panels on the Romanesque in general. The cloister outside is a strange and striking sight. The knights blended four different types of arch around the square, the simple Romanesque, the Islamic horseshoe and two extroverted criss-cross styles also derived from the east. Throughout the complex, the capitals are an expression of the returning knights' wonderment at the strange world they had seen beyond Christendom: strange beasts and plants, violent battles and weird buildings predominate; there's scarcely a Biblical scene in sight.

On the other side of the main road from San Juan, but on the same side of the river, a lovely riverside walk along the lazy Duero leads past the vine-swathed Templar church of **San Polo** (set in an apple orchard but closed to the public), to the hermitage church of **San Saturio** ① *Tue-Sat 1030-1400, 1630-1830 (1930 in spring and autumn, 2030 in summer), Sun 1030-1400, free.* The saint is a popular local figure who lived in the sixth century. The building is perched on sloping rock above a grotto where he lived as a hermit for 36 years. The chapel is attractively painted floor to ceiling with wall paintings of Saturio's life; there's an impressive bearded icon of him above the altar with very haunted eyes. In another chamber are more paintings of his doings; in one he appears to be boiling sea monsters. He's still the patron of Soria, and numerous offerings and requests are made by locals.

Back in town, above the Plaza Mayor, is another Romanesque treasure in lovely Sorian stone, the **Iglesia de San Juan de Rabanera** ① *Jul-Oct Tue-Sun 1100-1400, 1700-1900; winter closed, but you can sneak a quick look inside before and after Masses (times on the door).* Behind the plaza on the other side is the long and imposing **Palacio de los Condes de Gómara**, whose Plateresque façade features a high gallery with Ionic columns; it's now used by the local government.

A mock-Roman building by the lovely Alameda de Cervantes park houses the **Museo Numantino** ① *Tue-Sat 1000-1400, 1600-1900 (1700-2000 summer), Sun 1000-1400, €1.20.* The very good display, with information in English, is mostly devoted to Roman and Celtiberian finds from Numancia and the province.

# Around Soria ⊟ ➔ *pp224-225.*

Some 6 km north of Soria, just outside the village of **Garray,** a windswept grassy hill is the site of **Numancia**. The inhabitants, doomed to bear the unsatisfactory name of Celtiberians until we can be surer of their origins, weren't too keen to submit to Republican Rome when they came knocking in 153 BC. Despite being outgunned, they amazingly managed to resist for 25 years. Finally, the enforcer Scipio was sent from Rome to sort them out. Not one for mucking around, he decided to encircle the walled town with a massive wall of his own, heavily fortified with camps. The despairing inhabitants lasted another 11 months before succumbing. The Romans built their own town on the site, but many years later the Numancian resistance became a powerful symbol of Spanish heroism and somewhat ironically, was even used by Franco, who surely would have better identified himself with the Romans. Even Soria's have-a-go football team is named after the town.

> ⁝ *Numancia is one of the most important pre-Roman towns of the region, but there's not a great deal to see these days.*

The spread-out site is by no means thrilling today; without your own transport you might be better confining yourself to a visit to the museum in Soria. The ruins include foundations of roads, houses, public baths and a large public building; more approachable are the reconstructed Celtiberian and Roman dwellings. A couple of monuments from 1842 and 1904 commemorate the long-dead heroism of the siege. Numancia is 500 m up a road on the right after passing the centre of the village. There are two buses a day between Soria and Garray. They leave Soria at 1500 and 1745, returning at 0859 and 1415. This effectively means that you'll need to take a taxi in one direction; this costs about €11 each way.

With transport, there are several good parts of the **Sorian hills** to explore north of the capital, towards the province of La Rioja. The N-111 barrels straight north to Logroño, but ascends a picturesque mountain pass on the way, before encountering some seriously craggy hills just over the border in Rioja province. West of the road is a large expanse of forested hills, with several numbered walks. The nicest village in the region is **Molinos de Duero**, a quiet little place with lovely stone houses. Nearby, the village of **Vinuesa** is another potential base, and has a small information centre on the region.

Twenty kilometres north and west of Vinuesa is the **Laguna Negra**, reached by a potholed road. From the car park, it's a couple of kilometres up the hill to the small lake, beautifully opaque under jagged rocky peaks. There's a small information centre here, that can provide details about other walks in the vicinity.

Another good route north of Soria is on the R-115 northeast by bus or car into dinosaur country. **Yanguas**, on the Sorian side of the border, is an extremely peaceful place to stop (see La Rioja, page 205), and the numerous dinosaur footprints are well worth investigating.

East of Soria, the **Dehesa de Moncayo** is another pleasant hillforest on the Aragonese border (see page 166), while the town of **Agreda** is nice enough but has little to offer compared with Tarazona, further on. However, for a couple of decades it played an important part in Spanish history; a nun in the monastery, Sor María de Agreda, became a regular correspondent with the mighty King Felipe II, and gave him much political advice and spiritual comfort over many years.

## ● Sleeping

**Soria** *p220, map p220*

**L Parador Antonio Machado**, Parque del Castillo s/n, T975 240 800, www.parador.es. Soria's *parador* is an attractive modern building peacefully set at the top of a park-covered hill above town. It's named after the famous poet, and selections of his work line the walls. The nicest rooms are suites that overlook the river and don't cost a great deal more, but it's all very comfortable, and is well staffed.

**B Hotel Soria Plaza Mayor**, Plaza Mayor 10, T975 240 864, www.hotelsoriaplaza mayor.com With an excellent location on the tranquil square in the heart of the old town, this new hotel has plenty to offer. There are just 10 rooms, decorated in dark but elegant style, with floorboards and a/c. The ones at the top of the building are not for space freaks, but are very appealing with their sloping roof.

**D Hostal Centro**, Plaza Mariano Granados 2, T975 226 122, F975 229 627. Situated just on the edge of the pedestrian centre, this modern hostal has small but spick 'n' span rooms with good en suite bathrooms.

**D Hostería Solar de Tejada**, C Claustrilla 1, T/F975 230 054, solardetejada@wanadoo.es. This is a great place to stay in the heart of Soria. Original decoration is backed up by warm-hearted service. The rooms, all different, are attractive and brightly coloured, and a solar and lunar theme runs throughout. Recommended.

**E-F Hostal Viena**, C García Solier 1, T975 222 109. A short walk from the centre, this old-fashioned but hospitable *hostal* is set above a café. It's a bargain really for what you get; rooms with or without bathroom are showing their age but comfortable; all have TV and are pretty quiet. You should be able to park free somewhere nearby.

**G Pensión Carlos**, Plaza Olivo 2, T975 211 555. A good option, predictably basic at this price but clean, reasonably quiet and right in the heart of things.

**Around Soria** *p223*

**A-B Real Posada de la Mesta**, Plaza Cañerias s/n, Molinos de Duero, T975 378 531, www.realposada.com. This is a great place to stay in this elegant village; a beautiful, large, old stone mansion with great decoration in heavy rustic style; they serve gourmet meals, and even organize truffle-hunting outings in season.

## ● Eating

**Soria** *p220, map 220*

Much of Soria's eating and drinking is focused around Plaza Ramón Benito Aceña, at one end of C Mayor. Plaza San Clemente has a few foody cafés too.

♥♥♥ **Mesón Castellano**, Plaza Mayor 2, T975 213 045. On the main square, and Castilian it certainly is, with large portions of heavy dishes such as roast goat, balanced by a decent house salad and some good Ribera del Duero reds. They have harsh winters here, and this is the place to combat them.

♥♥ **Casa Augusto/El Mesón de Isabel**, Plaza Mayor 4, T975 213 041. These 2 connected restaurants are among the city's best. In Casa Augusto, you can try traditional Sorian fare such as the tasty *pecho de cordero* or a variety of stews. It's decorated in traditional Castilian style, with excellent service. Adjoining it, **El Mesón de Isabel** has a more relaxed vibe; the stuffed vegetable dishes are good to start off with, and the ambience is pleasant, with a large number of clocks and a romantic feel.

♦♦ **Santo Domingo II**, Plaza del Vergel 1, T975 211 717. An elegant wood-and-curtains type of Spanish restaurant, with mixed Basque and Castilian fare. There are *menús* for 2 or more, which are good value at €16.20 and €22.84, otherwise it'll be about €20-25 a head before drinks. There's a bust of a grumpy Antonio Machado outside.

♦♦ **Tierra de Máutiko**, C Diputación 1, T975 214 948. Opposite the church of San Juan, this is one of Soria's best, with elegant new-style cuisine. An unusual speciality is sweet and sour boar with a mushroom mousse. Closed Sep.

♦ **La Patata**, Plaza San Carlos 1, T975 213 036. This long bar is popular with young and old for its good-value *raciones* and little toasted bar-top snacks. As you'd guess from the name, they take a pride in their *patatas bravas*, served with a spicy home-made sauce. In summer, there's a pleasant outdoor terrace.

♦ **Lázaro Pérez**, C Marqués del Vadillo 52. This traditional place is a favourite on the Soria wine and *tapa* trail. On the main pedestrian street, you can smell the tradition with its crowd of regulars debating bull-fighting or the local football team, Numancia.

## ♠ Bars and clubs

**Soria** *p220, map 220*
The main nightlife starts in C Zapatería and its continuation, C Real. Later it progresses away from the centre to the Rota de Calatañazor zone, where there are several discobars and *discotecas*.
**La Zappa**, C Zapatería 38. A quirky and cool bar open all week; this is the most famous bar in town.
**Queru**, Plaza Ramón y Cajal s/n. A popular bar with Soria's young, this is a fun place right in the heart of town. Banging music and cheap *cubatas* make for a good atmosphere.
**Zeus**, Plaza Ramón Benito Aceña s/n. A smart café/bar on 2 floors, appropriately

decorated with Greek scenes on the walls. It's a good option at any time of the day; morning coffee, pre-lunch *pinchos*, late-night drinks; they cater to all.

## ❀ Festivals and events

**Soria** *p220, map 220*
**Late Jun** Sanjuanes, Soria's main festival. with an array of bullfights, processions, fireworks and wine-drinking.
**2 Oct** San Saturio's feast day is also a big event.

## ⊖ Transport

**Soria** *p220, map 220*
**Bus**
There are 7 daily buses to **Madrid** (€11.82; 3 hrs), and 4 to **Logroño** (1 hr 30 mins, €5.78). 2-3 daily buses go to **Barcelona** (€27-44, 5-6 hrs). There are 6 daily to **Vitoria**, and 4-5 to **Pamplona** (2 hrs, €10.79), some via Tafalla and Olite. 6 buses (3 on Sun) go to **Zaragoza** via Tarazona. Heading west, one heads Mon-Fri to **Berlanga**, 3 daily to **Calatañazor** and **El Burgo de Osma**, and another 3 to **Aranda de Duero** and **Valladolid**.
To the south and north, there are hourly local buses to **Almazán**, and 7 to **Medinaceli**, and 4 to **Arcos de Jalón**. 2 buses daily service the dinosaur country stops of **Yanguas**, **Enciso** and **Arnedillo**.

**Train**
Apart from Almazán, easily accessed by bus anyway, the only rail destination of interest is **Madrid** (2 daily, 3 hrs, €12.25), serviced via **Guadalajara**.

## ❶ Directory

**Soria** *p220, map 220*
**Internet** Merlin Center, C Santa Luisa de Marillac s/n. An internet centre with good connections if there aren't too many online gamers in the house.

Castilla y León Soria Listings

# Along the Duero: West from Soria to Valladolid

*Travelling along the Río Duero you roughly follow the long-time frontline of the Reconquista. There are more castles than you could poke a battering ram at, although many are ruinous. The land is dry and sun-beaten except along the riverbanks, which give their name to one of Spain's best wine regions, the Ribera del Duero. Peñafiel, with its fine mudéjar architecture and vibrant festival, makes the best base for exploring the Duero region. Within easy reach of Berlanga is one of Castilla's more remarkable monuments, the Ermita de San Baudelio. Further west, one of the oldest dioceses in the peninsula, dating from at least AD 598, El Burgo de Osma, once an important Castilian town, makes a worthy stopover, while nearby, the castle of Gormaz stands proud and forlorn on a huge rocky hill.* ▸▸ *For Sleeping, Eating and other listings, see pages 230-232.*

## Calatañazor → *Colour map 5, B3.*

Twenty-five kilometres west of Soria is the village of Calatañazor. This pretty but tiny place, with its cobbled streets, toppling castle and pretty Romanesque chapel, was the unlikely venue for the fall of the great Muslim warlord Al-Manzur (see box, page 444), who was defeated here in a battle in AD 1002, the millennium of which was celebrated with *fiestas* and cultural events. Now home to only 30 inhabitants, the town's name derives from the Arabic 'Qal'at an-Nusur', which means castle of the vultures. It's a picturesque place to stay, although don't expect raging nightlife. A small **tourist office** is at the bottom of the town, opposite the pretty 12th-century chapel, **Ermita de la Soledad**. In the heart of the village is the larger **Nuestra Señora del Castillo**, with a Romanesque portal and small museum. To get to Calatañazor, Burgo de Osma-bound buses from Soria will drop you at the turn-off on the main road, a 10-minute walk away.

## Berlanga de Duero → *Colour map 5, B3.*

Dominated by its impressive castle, Berlanga stands on a slope above the town, which is a likeable jumble of narrow lanes and old buildings set around an attractive plaza. In the centre is the reasonably interesting late-Gothic **Iglesia de Colegiata de Santa María**.

The **castle** ① *Tue-Sat 1100-1400, 1600-1930, Sun 1100-1400, €1*, originated as an Arab fortress, although most of it was built in the 15th and 16th centuries. The walls are preserved in a reasonable state, but little remains of the castle buildings or the elaborate gardens that once surrounded them. It is nevertheless picturesque.

## Ermita de San Baudelio

① *Wed-Sat 1000-1400, 1600-1900, Sun 1000-1400, €0.60.*

Some 8 km south of Berlanga is one of Castilla's more remarkable monuments. On a hillside that until the 19th century was covered in oak forest, the little chapel, Ermita de San Baudelio, was constructed at the beginning of the 11th century. It was close to the border that separated Muslim and Christian lands, and the design is a superb example of Mozarabic architecture. A horseshoe-arched doorway leads into an interior dominated by a central pillar that branches into extravagant ribs that recall a palm grove. There's even a tiny gallery, reached by an unlikely looking stair. Even more inspiring is the painted decoration, added a century-and-a-half later. Incredibly, an American art dealer was permitted to remove most of it in the 1920s (what he took is mostly now in the Metropolitan Museum in New York, although some has been repatriated to the Prado in Madrid). However, there's still enough left to excite: an Islamic hunting scene on the bottom half of the walls sits below a Biblical cycle; both preserve radiant colours and elaborate, sharp imagery.

## El Burgo de Osma → *Colour map 5, B3.*

El Burgo de Osma grew in the Middle Ages, and a large stretch of the wall is still well preserved; a vigilant sentinel on this wall almost changed the course of world history when he lobbed a boulder at a passing shadow one night in 1469. He narrowly missed killing the young prince Fernando, rushing by night to his furtive wedding with Isabel in Valladolid.

The **cathedral** ① *Jul-Oct Tue-Sun 1000-1330, 1630-1930, Nov-Jun 1030-1300, 1630-1800, €2.50,* was started in the 13th century but has been sorely afflicted by later architects who just couldn't leave it alone, and added chapels left, right and centre, as well as an ugly appendix that houses the sacristy. The interior is richly decorated; the *retablo* is a good piece by Juan de Juni, much of whose other work can be seen in Valladolid's sculpture museum. A guided tour will take you to the cloister and museum, the highlight of which is a superb, ornately illustrated manuscript, a copy of the *Codex of Beatus de Liébana* dating from 1086, that has been described as "one of the most beautiful books on earth". A recent replica on the book collectors' market will set you back a cool €5000. The beautiful tomb of San Pedro de Osma, who raised the Romanesque edifice, is also memorable.

The large **Plaza Mayor** has an impressive old building, a former hospital, that now houses both the **tourist office** ① *T975 360 116,* and **Antiqua Osma** ① *summer Tue-Sun 1000-1400, 1800-2000; rest of the year Sat and Sun only 1000-1400, 1700-1900,* a fun little archaeological museum with finds and reconstructed scenes from the Iberian and Roman town of Uxama, whose fragmentary ruins can still be seen to the west of town.

A more earthy note is struck by the **Museo del Cerdo** ① *C Juan Yagüe, 1200-1400, 1630-1900,* or Museum of the Pig, run by a local restaurant. The western part of Soria province is anything but New Age; stag-hunting is a popular pastime, and the eating of vegetables frowned upon. The *matanza*, when the free-range pigs are driven in from the wild and converted into ham and *chorizo*, is a major town event every winter.

## Castillo de Gormaz

① *The castle is little visited, and is permanently open (and free); buses run from El Burgo de Osma to Quintanas de Gormaz, from where it's the best part of a 1-hr walk, including a lengthy climb.*

Some 15 km south of El Burgo de Osma, Gormaz castle, built by the Moors around AD 950 is about the oldest, and certainly one of the largest, castles in western Europe. While not a lot remains inside them, it's well worth a visit just to see its walls, which are nearly 1 km in length and utterly commanding, visible for miles around. The Muslim origin of the citadel can be seen in the Caliph's gate, an ornate horseshoe portal. Although it seems totally impregnable even today, it was taken barely a century after being built, by Alfonso VI. He promptly gave it to El Cid; never let it be said that old Alfonso wasn't good to his friends.

❖ *The castle was one of the 'front teeth' defending Al-Andalus from the Christians.*

## Aranda de Duero → *Colour map 5, B2.*

*"That's red Aranda. I am afraid we had to put the whole town in prison and execute very many people."* (Remark made by the Conde de Vallellano to Dr Junod, Red Cross representative in Spain during the Civil War.)

A cheerful and solid Castilian working town, Aranda was spared the decline of the region by its location on the main road north from Madrid. It's a busy place set on a junction of rivers that still functions as a market town and supply centre for the surrounding area. Aranda's pride is roast lamb, for which it is famous throughout Spain; every eatery in town seems to be an *asador*, and the smell of garlic and cooking meat pervades the air.

The main sights are two attractive churches. **Iglesia de Santa María** has a superb portal still preserving some colour from the original paint job; scenes from the Virgin's life are portrayed, including the *Nativity* and the *Adoration of the Magi*. Nearby, the **Iglesia de San Juan** has a striking, many-layered portal set around Christ and, appropriately enough, a lamb. The **tourist office** ① *Tue- Sat 1000-1400, 1600-1900, Sun 1000-1400*, is on the Plaza Mayor.

## Peñaranda → *Colour map 5, B2.*

East of Aranda is the sweet little town of Peñaranda, all cobbled streets and elegant buildings. There's a 14th-century **castle** on the hill above town, while in the heart, on the **Plaza Mayor**, the hulking **Iglesia de Santa Ana** isn't particularly loveable. Opposite is the more stylish **Palacio de Avellaneda** ① *Oct-Mar 1000-1400, 1500-1800, Apr-Sep 1000-1400, 1600-1930, tours on the hour*. Topped with a bust of Hercules, it was built by the counts of Miranda in the 16th century. The Plateresque façade is suitably grand, and attractively topped by a carved wooden roof. Inside there's an elegant galleried patio, and salons and stairways decorated in rich style. There's a **tourist office** ① *Tue-Sun 1000-1400, 1700-2000*, in the centre.

Further along, near the village of **Peñalba de Castro** are the bare hilltop ruins of **Clunia**, once a significant Roman town. It's far from a world-class attraction, but has the remains of a theatre, bathhouse and several dwellings. There are ordained opening hours when the admission fee is €1, but there are no fences to stop you going for a wander at other times.

# Ribera del Duero ▣❼❶✖▣ ➻ *pp230-232.*

## Peñafiel → *Colour map 5, A1.*

Peñafiel makes the best base for exploring the Ribera del Duero region. The square-jawed **castle** that sits on the hill above Peñafiel was one of the Christian strongholds that flexed its muscles at the Moorish frontline, and the town grew up around it, although the settlement of Pintia nearby had been important in pre-Roman times. It's now an attractive place by the river; there are even some trees, a rare enough site in the Castilian *meseta*.

Nicknamed 'the Ark' because it resembles a ship run aground, the citadel in Peñafiel was important because it occupied a crucial strategic ridge above the Duero. The castle is long and thin, so narrow as to almost resemble a film-set cut-out until you get close and see how thick the curtain walls are, reinforced with a series of bristling towers. It's in very good condition but inside there's disappointingly little medieval ambience, for it now holds the **Museo de Vino** ① *Easter-Sep Tue-Sun 1130-1430, 1630-2030, Oct- Mar Tue-Sun 1130-1400, 1600-1900, €2.50 castle tour, €6 castle tour plus museum, €8 for a tutored tasting session of 4 mostly mediocre wines*, a modern display covering all aspects of wine production in a rather unengaging way. Tastings are available at weekends but are overpriced; you'd be better off buying a bottle from a local *bodega* and drinking it with some ham and cheese by the river. Part of the castle has been left untouched, however, visitable only by guided tour (in English if there's enough demand).

The castle isn't Peñafiel's only point of interest. Down in the town, have a look at the excellent **Plaza del Coso**, a spacious square still used for markets and bullsports. With its beautiful wooden buildings and sand underfoot, it's an unforgettable sight. The town's major fiesta is superb (see page 232). Another highlight is the beautifully ornate brick *mudéjar* exterior of the **Iglesia de San Pablo** ① *daily 1200-1330,*

*1730-1830, €2.* Converted from fortress to monastery in the 14th century, the interior is in contrasting Plateresque style.

The **Aula de Arqueología** ⓘ *winter Sat and Sun 1100-1400, 1630-1930, summer daily 1000-1430, 1700-2030; consult tourist office for midweek winter visits, €2,* on the Plaza del Coso attractively displays finds from the site of Pintia. The site itself can only be visited in summer if an archaeological team is working there. Peñafiel's **tourist office** ⓘ *Plaza del Coso, www.turismopenafiel.com, Tue-Sat 1000-1400, 1700-2000, Sun 1000-1400,* is a good source of information.

## Around Peñafiel

The area east of Peñafiel is worth exploring, even for non-vinous reasons. A good place to start is the small town of **Roa**, whose **tourist office** ⓘ *Mon-Sat 1030-1400, 1630-2030, Sun 1030-1400,* has a wealth of information on the region.

The hill on which the town sits was inhabited in pre-Roman times but lay fallow for centuries until repopulation in the 10th century. Good sections of the medieval walls are preserved, and there's an attractive walk along them, with views across the Valley of the Duero. The church of **Nuestra Señora de la Asunción** is the centrepiece of Roa, and preserves Romanesque and Gothic elements, although the majority is in early Renaissance style. The star vaulting in the interior is especially impressive. Another interesting building in the town is a well-preserved *alhóndiga*, used for storing and trading grain in the Middle Ages.

Roa's most famous inhabitant was Cardinal Cisneros (known in English as Ximenez), powerful archbishop and regent of Spain for a period. He died here in 1517, the day a letter arrived from the new king that dismissed him from his post. The smiling bust of him that looks over the city walls is a charitable interpretation of the authoritarian cleric.

North of Roa, the village of **La Horra** preserves a series of what appear to be conical cairns. Visible all over the region, they are actually air-vents and indicate the presence of an undergound wine *bodega*. All the region's wine was once made in these cellars and the build-up of fumes from the fermentation necessitated the chimneys.

East of here, **La Aguilera** has an unexpectedly large church complex, the **Santuario de San Pedro Regalado** ⓘ *Mon-Sat 0900-1300, 1700-2000; Sun 1700- 2000.* With an ornate interior and impressive flying buttresses, the church is dedicated to a 15th-century saint from Valladolid who spent his life as a monk here, preaching and performing the occasional miracle. He is the patron saint of bullfighters, as he once tamed a fierce bull that had escaped from the square in Valladolid; it's not uncommon for *matadors* to come here to give thanks for a lucky escape.

The attractive town of **Gumiel de Izán** nearby has a church with an impressive Renaissance façade and a large wooden *retablo* detailing the life of Christ, while the village of **Baños de Valderados** ⓘ *Jul-Aug 1030-1400, 1600-2000, T947 534 229 to arrange a visit at other times,* has the remains of a Roman villa, with reasonably preserved if rustic mosaïcs.

## Wineries

Although it's far from being a new wine region, the Ribera del Duero has come to the world's attention in recent years, with its red wines winning rave reviews from experts and public. The wines are based on the Tempranillo grape, although here it's called *Tinta del País*. Many consider the region's top wines superior to anything else produced in the country; the best-known wine, Vega Sicilia's *Unico*, has for many years been the tipple enjoyed by the royal family and is Spain's most expensive label. Dealing with the cold Castilian nights gives the grapes more character, while traditionally a long period of rotation between oak barrels and larger vats has been employed. Ribera soils are also characteristic, and are probably responsible for the wines' very distinctive soft fruity nose.

The excellent Pesquera is produced by **Bodegas Alejandro Fernández** ① *T983 870 037, www.grupopesquera.com*, in the village of Pesquera de Duero west of Peñafiel. Visits need to be arranged by calling a week in advance. In Pedrosa de Duero, near Roa, the tiny **Hermanos Pérez Pascuas** ① *T947 530 100, www.perezpascuas.com*, makes the tasty *Viña Pedrosa*. **Condado de Haza** ① *T947 525 254, www.condadodehaza.com*, another quality producer, is in an attractive building at the end of a long driveway between Roa and La Horra. **Vega Sicilia** is not open to the public.

> *Most wineries can be visited, although they require a call in advance. Visits are rarely possible in Aug or during the vintage in late Sep/early Oct.*

In Peñafiel itself, a handy *bodega* to visit, clearly signposted off the main road, is **Protos** ① *C Protos 24, T983 878 011, www.bodegasprotos.com, daily 1000-1400, 1600-1900*, whose mellow wines are very competitively priced for their quality. Ring in advance to arrange a visit.

East of Sardón de Duero, on the main road west of Peñafiel, is perhaps the most beautiful of the wineries, **Abadía Retuerta** ① *T983 680 317, www.abadia-retuerta.com, Wed and Sat 1000-1300, book by phone or website; you can buy wine here Mon-Sat 1000-1400, 1600-2000*, which stands next to a gorgeous 12th-century Romanesque monastery. The winemaking facilities themselves are modern and the wines aren't actually under the Ribera del Duero denomination, but they are outstanding, some blending Tempranillo and Cabernet Sauvignon to great effect, and there are examples for every budget. Tours of the abbey and *bodega* are possible.

## ● Sleeping

**Calatañazor** *p226*
Tourism is the village's only future and there are 2 good sleeping options.
**A Casa del Cura**, C Real 25, T975 183 631. A *casa rural* with small but nicely decorated rooms, an attractive modern interior and a good restaurant with a large terrace.
**D Hostal Calatañazor**, C Real 10, T975 183 642, www.calatanazor.com. Good rooms and a restaurant decorated in Berber style; there are even regular belly dancers to recall the town's Islamic origins. Superior rooms cost about €10 more.

**Berlanga de Duero** *p226*
**D Hotel Fray Tomás**, C Real 16, T975 343 033. Named after the town's most famous son, a missionary priest, the rooms are pleasant enough, though a little staid and dull. However, the restaurant is good.

**El Burgo de Osma** *p227*
**A Hotel Il Virrey**, C Mayor 4, T975 341 311, www.virreypalafox.com. A plush but courteous hotel in traditional Spanish style. Facilities include gym and sauna, and the rooms are comfortable enough, although some are pokier than the grand decor would suggest; you might prefer to opt for a suite (**L**).

**B Posada del Canónigo**, C San Pedro de Osma 19, T975 360 362, www.posadadelcanonigo.es. An excellent place to stay, just inside the southern gate of the city wall. Decorated with care and style, the rooms are romantic and feature plush beds and floorboards. The *posada* also has an excellent restaurant.
**D Casa Agapito**, C Universidad 1, T975 341 221. A grubby exterior conceals a clean, modern and very decent option on the main road through town. The rooms have good bathrooms and you more or less have the run of the place. You'll likely have to call when you arrive, as the owner lives elsewhere.

**Gormaz** *p227*
**B-C Casa Grande**, T975 340 982. This excellent *casa rural* is in the village of Quintanas below the imposing fortress of Gormaz. It offers great views of the castle and is set in a spick 'n' span yellow mansion. The rooms are delightful, with rustic touches; and there's a lounge with a fireplace. Meals are also available (€14).

**Aranda de Duero** *p227*
See Peñafiel, below, for rural tourism in the villages between Aranda and Peñafiel. Nearly all Aranda's accommodation is set

away from the centre on the main roads. Exceptions include:

C **Hotel Julia**, Plaza de la Virgencilla s/n, T947 501 250, hoteljulia@lycos.es. This central hotel is a comfortable place full of interesting old Spanish objects. The rooms are excellent for this price, and there's friendly management and plenty of comfort.

E **Pensión Sole**, C Puerta Nueva 16, T947 500 607. This *pensión* in the older part of town is a good budget option. It has good clean rooms that are aging but comfortable; they all have TV and you can choose between simple en suite or shared bathroom.

### Peñaranda *p228*

C **Posada Ducal**, Plaza Mayor s/n, T947 552 347. Right on the main square, this beautiful *casa rural* was once the servants' quarters of the nearby palace. The accommodation has probably improved since those days; now it makes an excellent choice, right on the main square, with attractively rustic decoration and a decent restaurant too.

C **Señorio de Velez**, Plaza Duques de Alba 1, T947 552 201, www.hotelvelez.com. This hotel is a decent place to stay in the heart of town. Set in an attractive stone and adobe building, the rooms are clean and acceptable, if a touch overpriced. There's a nice terraced restaurant too.

### Peñafiel *p228*

There is little accommodation in the old centre itself, although nowhere is very far away. If you've got a car, you might like to take advantage of the large numbers of *casas rurales* and *posadas* in the area between Peñafiel and Aranda, particularly around Roa and Gumiel de Hizán. The tourist office will provide a list; prompt them to make sure they give you it for both provinces (ie Valladolid and Burgos) that this area straddles.

B **Ribera del Duero**, Av Escalona 17, T983 881 616, www.hotelriberadelduero.com. A large but attractive hotel cleverly converted from an old flour mill. Some of the rooms have good views of the castle and there's a well-priced restaurant.

D **El Zaguán de Gumiel**, C Real 54, Gumiel de Hizán, T947 544 141, www.elzaguan degumiel.com. One of the best of the rural tourism options in the Ribera del Duero area, this is an attractive stone and adobe building with plenty of character and a restaurant. The rooms are gorgeous: simple in style and wood-beamed, but with TV and a/c as well as a good bathroom. Bikes are available to explore the area.

D **Hostal Campo**, C Encarnación Alonso s/n, T983 873 192. This *hostal* has comfortable and clean brand-new rooms a short stroll from the centre on the other side of the main road. The main problem is a slightly depressing location near the sugar refinery. All rooms have bathroom and modern comforts; it's run out of the down-at-heel **Bar Campo** on the Ctra de Pesquera.

G **Hostal Chicopa**, Plaza de España 2, T983 880 782. This place has 2 important things going for it: price and location. Set right in the centre of the old town above a bar/restaurant, these simple rooms go for a song. The bathrooms are shared; some rooms have a shower; it's pretty basic, but it's not a dive.

## ❼ Eating

### El Burgo de Osma *p227*

₮₮₮ **Virrey Palafox**, C Universidad 7, T975 340 222. This restaurant is run by the same management as the **Hotel Virrey**, and is unashamedly devoted to meat, which is superbly done. On Feb and Mar weekends, the **Fiesta de la Matanza** takes place; pigs are slaughtered and devoured in their entirety.

₮₮ **El Burgo**, C Mayor 71, T975 340 489. Only open at weekends, this restaurant is a temple to meat. The food is great, but some of the steaks are laughably large, so be firm with the pushy owner who is sure he knows what you want.

₮ **Café 2000**, Plaza Mayor s/n. A good cheap place to eat and snack, with a terrace on the main square and a decent €7 *menú*. As everywhere, they also do a good steak.

### Aranda de Duero *p227*

The local speciality is roast lamb, washed down with a bottle of red from the local Ribera del Duero. The lamb's not cheap or particularly subtle, but it's delicious and the portions are huge; you won't have much luck if you prefer soufflé or quiche.

₮₮ **El Lagar**, C Isilla 18, T947 510 683. One of several memorable *asadores* in town, this does succulent milk-fed lamb cooked in a

wood oven and is set in an old wine *bodega*, dozens of which are dug out under the town.
**♯♯ Mesón El Roble**, Plaza Jardines de Don Diego s/n, T947 502 902. The *asador* with the loftiest reputation among *arandinos*; this is part of a chain that has spread Aranda's lamb to cities across Spain. If there's any room left, you can try another local speciality, *empiñonado*, a pine-nut sweet.

### Peñafiel *p228*

**♯♯ Molino de Palacios**, Av de la Constitución 16, T983 880 505. This is a lovely *asador* romantically set in an old watermill on the river. The speciality is predictable, namely roast lamb, but there are also plenty of game and wild mushroom dishes. Recommended.
**♯ Restaurante María Eugenia**, Plaza España 17, T983 873 115. Friendly family-run place decorated with heavy Spanish furniture and decent landscapes. Good seafood and comedy-large steaks.

### Cafés

**Café Judería**, a relaxing place for a coffee or drink, nicely set in the park of the same name by the river.

## ♠ Bars and clubs

### Peñafiel *p228*

**Al Dos**, Derecha al Coso 38. Popular.
**Bar Veray**, Plaza de España. Friendly place with an upstairs that opens at weekends.
**La Charca**, Derecha al Coso 33.
A popular choice.

## ❀ Festivals and events

### Aranda de Duero *p227*

**Sep** Aranda's annual fiesta, in the 2nd week of Sep, is a cheerfully drunken affair.

### Peñafiel *p228*

**14-18 Aug** The town's major fiesta is superb. There are *encierros*, where bulls run through the streets, followed by *capeas* in the plaza, which is basically bull-dodging, sometimes with the aim of slipping rings over the horns. The homeowners sell off balcony seats, but interestingly some families still have hereditary rights to seats during the fiesta, even if the house isn't theirs.

## ⊖ Transport

### Calatañazor *p226*
**Bus**

There are 1-3 buses a day from Soria to **Calatañazor** (25 mins, €1.70). Other Linecar **Valladolid**-bound buses can drop you off just below the village.

### Berlanga de Duero *p226*
**Bus**

There is one bus daily from Soria to **Berlanga** from Mon-Fri (70 mins, €3.65).

### El Burgo de Osma *p227*
**Bus**

The bus station is on the main road; there are 4-6 services to **Soria** (1 hr, €3.25) and 3 to **Aranda de Duero** (45 mins) and on to **Valladolid**.

### Aranda de Duero *p227*
**Bus**

Aranda has good bus connections, being at the junction of major north-south and east-west routes. The bus and train stations are across the Duero from the old part of town.

About 4 buses a day go to **Madrid** (2 hrs, €9.21) and 6-7 to **Burgos** (1 hr 15 mins, €6.45). There are 6 a day to **Valladolid** (1 hr 15 mins), 3 to **El Burgo de Osma** (45 mins) and on to **Soria** (1 hr 30 mins) and **Zaragoza** (3 hrs 45 mins) and 2 to **Roa**.

### Train

Trains go to **Madrid** (1 daily, 2-3 hrs, €19.50), and **Burgos** (1 daily, 1 hr, €13).

### Peñafiel *p228*
**Bus**

There are 6 buses a day from Peñafiel to **Valladolid** (45 mins) and **Aranda de Duero** (30 mins), 3 of which continue to **El Burgo de Osma**, **Soria** and **Zaragoza**.

## ⓓ Directory

### Aranda de Duero *p227*

**Internet** Ciberlibro, Plaza Mayor 19, Mon-Fri 1000-1400, 1730-2030, Sat 1000-1400. **Laundry** Reyna, C Postas 22.

# Valladolid

→ *Phone code: 983. Colour map 4, A5. Population: 321,001. Altitude: 690 m.*

*Valladolid, the capital of the Castilla y León region, is not outstandingly beautiful but it is a pleasant city with a very significant history. It was the principal city of Spain for most of the early 16th century and its streets are redolent with the memories of important people who walked them and events that took place in them. These days it's still an administrative centre, but a fairly relaxed and friendly one; perhaps it looks down the road to sprawling Madrid and breathes a small sigh of relief, as it must have been odds-on favourite to be named capital at one time. As the capital of Castilla y León, however, it still preserves an official function and has a somewhat pijo (a Spanish word that falls somewhere between dandy and yuppie) feel.* ▸▸ *For Sleeping, Eating and other listings, see pages 238-241.*

## Ins and outs

**Getting there** Many visitors to Northern Spain arrive in Valladolid; there's a **Ryanair** connection to the city from London Stansted as well as Brussels Charleroi. Valladolid is a major transport hub, and only two hours from Madrid by road and rail. As the capital of Castilla y León, it has excellent connections within that region, as well as with the rest of Northern Spain. The bus and train stations are close together, about a 20-minute walk south of the centre. They can be reached by local buses Nos 2 and 10 from Plaza de España, or No 19 from Plaza Zorilla. ▸▸ *See also Transport, page 241.*

**Getting around** Situated on the east bank of the Pisuerga, Valladolid's old centre is compact. At the southern end of this part, the large park of Campo Grande is flanked by two long avenues, Paseo de Zorilla, the main artery of the new town, and the mostly pedestrianized Acera de Recoletos. Nearly everything of interest is within an easy walk of the Plaza Mayor.

**Tourist information** The new city **tourist office** ① *T983 219 310, www.asomatea valladolid.com, winter daily 0900-1400, 1700-2000, summer daily 0900-2000,* is in a big glass building by the park on Paseo de Campo Grande; you pass it if you are walking from the train station into town. It has all manner of information on the city and province.

## Background

A site of pre-Roman settlements, Valladolid's profile grew with the Reconquista; it was well placed on the frontline to become an important commercial centre, driven in part by the Castilian wool trade. Although Fernando and Isabel married here in 1469 – a secret ceremony that profoundly changed the course of world history – it was in the 16th century that Valladolid became pre-eminent among Spanish cities. With a population of nearly 40,000, it was a massive place in a hitherto fragmented land, and de-facto capital of Spain; while the court was constantly on the move, the bureaucracy was based here. It was, as it is now, a city of administrators and lawyers: "courtiers died here waiting for their cases to come up" (JH Elliott, *Imperial Spain*).

Valladolid played an important part in most significant Spanish historical events, and was home for periods to people as diverse as Columbus, Cervantes and the inquisitor Torquemada. It was a major centre of the Spanish Inquisition (see box, page 237); *auto de fé's* and burnings were a regular sight in the plaza.

In the year 1550-1551, a significant and famous theological debate took place here between the liberal theologian Bartolomé de las Casas and the historian and philosopher Juan Ginés de Sepúlveda. The former was arguing for an end to indigenous slavery and forced conversions in Spain's American colonies, while the latter deemed the *indígenos* inferior, being incapable of reason and therefore without rights. Las Casas' view prevailed, effectively ending the doctrine of racial purity in the colonies. Las Casas was hardly an enlightened humanist, though; he suggested the labour problem be solved by enslaving Africans instead.

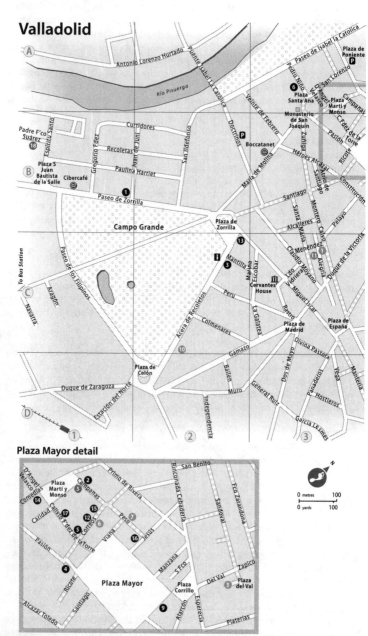

# Valladolid

## Plaza Mayor detail

Felipe II was born in Valladolid, but surprisingly chose Madrid as his capital in 1561. The city lost importance after that, but had a brief reprise. A scheming adviser of Felipe III wanted to keep him away from the powerful influence of his grandmother, and persuaded him to move the capital northwards in 1601. The glory years were back, but only for five years, after which the court moved back to Madrid. Valladolid remained fairly prosperous until the collapse of the wool and grain markets, but enjoyed renewed

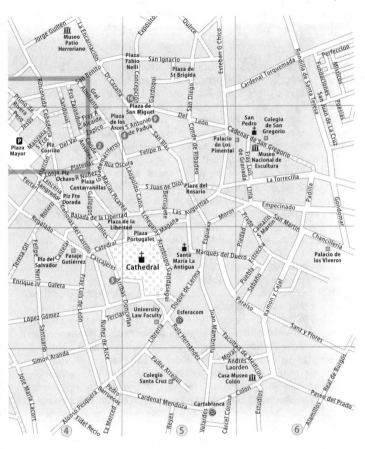

Castilla y León Valladolid

**Sleeping** 💤
Amadeus **1** *C3*
El Nogal **2** *B4*
Hostal Colón **10** *C2*
Hostal del Val **3** *detail*
Hostal Los Arces **4** *B5*
Hostal Zamora **5** *C4*
Hostería La Cueva **6** *detail*
Imperial **7** *detail*
Meliá Olid **9** *B5*
Mozart **11** *C3*

**Eating** 🍴
Bar La Sepia **16** *detail*
Caravanserai **1** *B1*
Don Claudio **2** *detail*
El Figón de Recoletos **3** *C2*
Fátima **4** *detail*
La Balconada **15** *detail*
La Criolla **5** *detail*
La Parrilla de San Lorenzo **6** *A3*
Lion d'Or **9** *detail*
Mil Vinos **14** *detail*

Santi I **12** *detail*
Sol **13** *C2*
Taberna del Herrero **17** *detail*

**Bars & clubs** 🍸
Charlotte **18** *B1*
El Soportal **16** *A5*
La Comedia **5** *detail*
Paco Suárez **18** *B1*

wealth in the early part of the 20th century. The Falange held their first national meeting here in March 1934 and when war broke out Valladolid became an important and brutal Fascist stronghold; it is estimated that over 9000 Republican civilians were shot here behind the lines.

One of Spain's most important post Civil War writers, Miguel Delibes, is a *vallisoletano*. His work deeply reflects the Castilian landscape but is also often bitingly anti-Francoist; much of his journalistic life was spent battling the censors while working for the liberal *El Norte de Castilla*, the regional paper. *The Hedge* is perhaps his best-known translated work; a vicious satire on totalitarian Spain.

## Sights

Valladolid's centrepiece is its large **Plaza Mayor**, attractively surrounded by the red façades of buildings. It was here that *auto de fe*'s and burnings were conducted during the Inquisition's long tenure in the city. Most of Valladolid's buildings of interest are to the north and east of the plaza. The **cathedral**, topped by a statue of Christ standing tall above the city, seems a little crowded-in. The façade is Baroque, the interior fairly bare and disappointing, although the **museum** ① *Tue-Fri 1000-1330, 1630-1900, Sat and Sun 1000-1400; €2.50*, is worthwhile, with some excellent carved tombs among the usual assorted saints and Virgins.

Behind the cathedral stands the Gothic **Iglesia de Santa María la Antigua**, slightly down-at-heel but sporting an attractive tower. Also nearby is the **Pasaje Gutiérrez**, a belle époque shopping arcade with some pleasingly extravagant decoration, if a little careworn these days. The **university law faculty**, also next to the cathedral, is worth a look for its camp Baroque façade guarded by strange monkey-like lions on columns. Across the road, it's faced by a friendly looking Cervantes. Another university building is the lovely **Colegio de Santa Cruz**, a block away, with an ornate Plateresque door; it boasts an attractive central patio with the names of honorary graduates painted on the walls.

North of the cathedral, along Calle Las Angustias, is an interesting collection of buildings. The **Palacio de los Pimentel** was the building that saw the birth, in 1527, of Felipe II, likely to have been a serious little child. His statue faces the palace from across the square, which also holds the **Iglesia de San Pedro**, with a very tall and ornate Gothic façade; the level of intricacy in the stonework is stunning.

Following the pedestrian street at the side of the San Pedro church, you'll soon come to an even more amazing façade. Looking like a psychedelic fantasy in stone, it's an outrageously imaginative piece of work. A pomegranate tree perhaps represents knowledge, while some hairy men represent nature and the value of hermitry. Like much sculpture from centuries ago, it's impossible to really unlock the meaning, but it's certainly a step away from the typical. It belongs to the **Colegio de San Gregorio**, a building commissioned by Fray Alonso de Burgos to house the college he founded, and also to house him after his demise. The building is currently under restoration, but the chapel is still open for visits (with a ticket from the sculpture museum opposite); it features an ornately carved wooded choirstall and a couple of nobles' tombs.

Due to San Gregorio's restoration, the **Museo Nacional de Escultura** ① *Tue-Sat 1000-1400, 1600-1800, Sun 1000-1400, €2.40 (includes admission to the chapel of San Gregorio)*, has moved across the way to the Palacio de Villena. It's a fairly specialized collection, excellent in its field, which is basically Spanish religious sculpture from the 16th-18th centuries. In the first gallery is a portrait of an appropriately brooding Juana I as well as an excellent *retablo* of San Jerónimo, the

● *In 1558, two members of the aristocracy turned up in Valladolid in the royal litter: the king's cat and parrot, sent back to the city by their loving owner Carlos V, who had just died at his monastery retreat of Yuste.*

# Torquemada and the Spanish Inquisition

*"The hammer of heretics, the light of Spain, the saviour of his country"*
Sebastián de Olmedo

Born in 1420, Tomás de Torquemada entered a Dominican monastery in his youth and was appointed as Grand Inquisitor in 1483. He pursued his tasks with considerable energy both reforming the administration of the Inquisition and giving it its uniquely Spanish direction.

Founded by Fernando and Isabel in 1478, the Spanish Inquisition was unusual in that it did not report directly to the Pope but followed a more nationalistic course. Under Torquemada there was a paranoid obsession that the conversions of Muslim and Jewish *conversos* had been insincere; this was to dominate the Inquisition's activities.

Given a remit to extract confessions under torture, the Inquisition was initially content to seize the estates of those Jewish *conversos* it considered to be insincere. This enabled it to quickly build up considerable resources. Later it employed the full range of punishments available including execution by public burning following a theatrical *auto de fé* or trial of faith. It is estimated that during Torquemada's direction there were around 2000 executions, the overwhelming majority of them of Jewish *conversos*.

He was instrumental in ensuring that the Jews were expelled completely from Spain in 1492. It is reputed that when he found Fernando in negotiations with Jewish leaders over a possible payment to the Crown in order to remain, he compared Fernando's actions with those of Judas. The Jews were duly expelled with disastrous long term results for the country.

Torquemada's pursuit of Jewish *conversos* was largely responsible for the development of the cult of *sangre limpia* or pure blood that was to continue to obsess Spain throughout the 16th century. Based on the idea that only those of pure Christian blood could participate fully in the state, it was to cost Spain the services of most of its intellectual class debilitating its development for centuries.

Torquemada stepped down from his role in the Inquisition in 1497. After his directorship it began to diversify into other areas including the maintenance of doctrinal purity and a concern with private morality. It was to retain a formidable grip over Spanish life until its formal abolition at the beginning of the 19th century. Torquemada retired to a monastery where he kept a unicorn's horn close at hand as an antidote to any attempt at poisoning him. He died of natural causes in 1499.

Castilla y León Valladolid

highlight of which is the tiny lion; the painter obviously had only a limited notion of what they were like. An excellent collection of polychrome wooden sculptures by Alonso Berruguete show his mastery at depicting real emotion in that difficult medium, while a curious Zurbarán painting, *La Santa Faz*, displays that superb artist's passion for the subtleties of white cloth. Further highlights include a very creepy *Death* by Gil de Ronza, a range of Mannerist sculpture in alabaster, a gory *Martyrdom of St Bartholomew*, and a Rubens painting of *Democritus and Heraclitus*, who resembles a retired fairground boxer. A couple of interesting pieces round the visit off: an ensemble depicting all the events of a bullfight, and an amazing assembly of Neapolitan dolls, forming a 620-piece Nativity scene. There's a good system of information sheets in English.

Other buildings of note in this part of town are the **Palacio de los Viveros**, where Fernando and Isabel married in 1469, having only set eyes on each other four days before. It now holds an archive and the university library, and isn't hugely interesting. Beyond here is the **Casa Museo Colón** ⓘ *C Colon s/n, Tue-Sat 1000-1400, 1700-1900, Sun 1000-1400, free*, a replica of Columbus' son's house, where the explorer is said to have died, far from the sea and a discontented man. The museum displays a lot of pre-Hispanic American material as well as various displays on his seafaring exploits.

Moving south from the Plaza Mayor down Calle Santiago you pass the **Caja de Burgos** building, topped by a flamboyant eaglerider. The street ends at **Plaza de Zorrilla**, with an energetic fountain. José Zorrilla was a 19th-century poet born in the city, although he spent much of his life in Mexico. On the other side of the plaza stretches the pleasant and busy park of **Campo Grande**. Numerous pro-Republican civilians were shot here during the Civil War, many dying with the words 'Long live the Republic' on their lips.

Cervantes spent three years living in Valladolid, some days of it at his Majesty's leisure on suspicion of being involved in a murder. What was probably his house, a pretty vine-covered building on Calle Miguel Iscar, is nearby; it contains a **museum** ⓘ *Tue-Sat 0930-1500, Sun 1000-1500, €2.40 (currently under renovation)*, part of which recreates the living conditions of the day, and part of which holds a reasonably interesting collection of 19th- and 20th-century Spanish painting and sculpture.

West of the **Plaza Mayor**, a series of attractive streets around Calle Correos hold some excellent eating and drinking options. Beyond, towards the river, is the ugly **Monasterio de San Joaquín** ⓘ *Plaza Santa Ana 4, Mon-Fri 1000-1330, 1700-1900 (2000 in summer), Sat 1000-1430, free*, fronted by a strangely haglike Virgin. In the monastery museum is a collection of religious art, of which the highlight is three Goyas in the church itself.

Finally, the **Museo Patio Herreriano** ⓘ *C Jorge Guillén 6; T983 362 908, www.museopatioherreriano.org, Tue-Fri 1100-2000, Sat 1000-2000, Sun 1000-1500, €4 (€1 on Wed)*, is a contemporary art museum built around a huge Renaissance patio, elegant but rather cold and formal. The permanent collection is housed in various galleries possessed of little levity; there are some good works here (sculptures by the beachcombing Angel Ferrant and the studied ironworker Jorge Oteiza stand out), but the worth of a visit depends largely upon the temporary exhibitions; there have been some excellent ones since the gallery's recent opening.

## ● Sleeping

**Valladolid** *p233, map p234*
Valladolid is full of accommodation; the tourist office can provide a complete listing.
**AL Hotel Imperial**, C Peso 4, T983 330 300, www.himperial.com. Located in a 16th-century *palacio* in the heart of the old town, this has considerable old-Spain charm. The bedrooms are very attractive, the furnishings plush and there's a beautiful if formal bar/lounge with a pianist.
**AL Olid Meliá** , Plaza San Miguel 10, T983 357 200, www.solmelia.com. This well-located hotel is one of the city's most luxurious. The rooms are spacious, light and attractive, and neither they nor the modern bathrooms lack any comfort: minibar, trouser press, satellite TV and safe are all present. The hotel has gym

and parking facilities; there are occasional enticing discounts advertised via the website.
**A Hotel Amadeus**, C Montero Calvo 16-18, T983 219 444, www.hotelamadeus.net. A modern hotel on a central pedestrian street, smartly catering mostly for business travellers. This is good news, because they offer smart weekend rates if you book ahead. The rooms have all the facilities, including cable TV and internet point. The beds are large and comfortable. Parking available.
**A Hotel El Nogal**, C Conde Ansúrez 10, T983 340 333, www.hotelelnogal.com. An intimate modern hotel near the old market. It's a friendly choice and well located. The red-fitted rooms are a touch cramped but are a/c and otherwise comfortable and light.

**B Hotel Mozart**, C Menéndez Pelayo 4, T983 297 777, www.hotelmozart.net. The sister hotel to the **Amadeus**, is set in a noble 19th-century mansion and has a classy feel. The rooms are large and light with windows looking out over the pedestrian streets below. The hotel has its own garage, plenty of charm, and excellent summer rates (**C** in Jul/Aug).

**D Hostal Colón**, Acera de Recoletos 22, T983 304 044. This peaceful and friendly spot is close to the train station on the *paseo* running into the centre. The rooms are comfortable and clean. It's worth paying extra for the en suite.

**D-E Hostal Los Arces**, C San Antonio de Padua 2, T983 353 853, benidiopor@terra.es. This is a fine budget choice, with large (if somewhat noisy) rooms, comfortable beds and a decent atmosphere. Shared bathrooms are good; rooms with en suites available. Doubles are poor value for solo travellers; if there are no singles, go somewhere else.

**E Hostal Del Val**, Plaza del Val 6, T983 375 752. A sound budget option, this *hostal* is very close to the heart of town. The rooms are good for the price; some are equipped with their own bathroom, while there are cheaper but scruffier rooms in another building on the same plaza.

**E Hostería La Cueva**, C Correos 4, T983 330 072. This *pensión* has small, attractive rooms above a restaurant on Valladolid's nicest little street. The better ones have compact en suite bathrooms, but there are rooms with just washbasin available too (**F**).

**E-F Hostal Zamora**, C Arribas 14, T983 303 052. Right by the cathedral, this place has colourful little rooms with bathroom and TV; there are some cheaper ones with shared facilities. They're all heated, and it's pretty good value.

## ❼ Eating

**Valladolid** *p233, map p234*
Valladolid is a gourmet's paradise. The zone of restaurants and tapas bars is in the small streets just west of the Plaza Mayor. Most of the options below function as both; the quality throughout this area is laudably high.

**₮₮₮ El Figón de Recoletos**, Av Recoletos 5. This sleek and fairly posh *asador* is confident in what it does best. While there are always daily specials, there are only a few main dishes on the menu; the quarter roast lamb is enough for 2; the grilled kidneys are unspeakably

delicious if innards are your thing. Not much joy for vegetarians, however.

**₮₮₮ Fátima**, C Pasión 3, T983 342 839. Set in a corner of the Plaza Mayor, this original restaurant is best visited in autumn, as the undisputed speciality is the variety of dishes created using wild mushrooms, although there are several dishes available throughout the year. Portions are on the smallish size, but the creative flair more than makes up for it. There are wines recommended to accompany every dish. Mains are €18-21; if you fancy a splurge, try the truffle menu, with a range of dishes created with that mysterious fungus for €60.

**₮₮ Don Claudio**, C Campanas 4, T983 350 756. A friendly and traditional Spanish restaurant with painted walls and good service. They have a good reputation for their fish dishes – try the grilled sardines if they're about – and is a reliable and likeable, if not spectacular, place.

**₮₮ La Criolla**, C Calixto Fernández de la Torre 2, T983 373 822. A likeable and attractive restaurant, full of intimate nooks and adorned with quotes from *vallisoletano* writers. The fare is based around simple traditional dishes, which have been given an attractive modern boost. There's a terrace in summer and a good tapas bar, which always has an intriguing daily special; you can also order an *espejo* – a mixed tapa selection. Quality food and engaging presentation.

**₮₮ La Parrilla de San Lorenzo**, C Pedro Niño 2, T983 335 088. An atmospheric meaty restaurant in a vault in the depths of a convent building. It specializes in traditional Castilian dishes like roast lamb and is priced fairly. Closed Jul.

**₮₮ Santi I**, C Correos 1, T983 339 355. Superbly situated in the courtyard of a historic inn, named **El Caballo de Troya** after its large painting of the same name, although the Trojan horse looks surprisingly sprightly. The restaurant serves good quality Castilian fare; there's also a *taberna*, which is an atmospheric place for a drink; it serves tapas and *raciones*, but you're better off eating in the restaurant or elsewhere.

**₮ Bar La Sepia**, C Jesús 1, T983 330 769. This Valladolid classic, decorated in wood and brick, is down a side street just off the Plaza Mayor. You can smell the enticing aromas from a block away and when you sample the taste and texture of the *sepia* (cuttlefish) – it comes grilled with a garlic sauce – you'll understand why they're always busy.

**Caravanserai**, Paseo de Zorilla 4, T983 375 822. This relaxed café has window seats to watch the world go by. It's a good place for a snack or some cheap dishes, and is popular with students. There are tasty *pintxos*, sandwiches as well as tofu burgers.

**La Balconada**, C Correos 3, T983 342 114. This small mezzanine restaurant is brightly coloured and very reasonably priced. The brief menu includes *tablas* to share with friends, a good house salad (€5) enlivened by warm prawns, or a tender *solomillo* steak which is great value for €11.50.

**Mil Vinos**, Plaza Martí y Monso s/n, T983 344 336. Looking like a TV studio with its designer furniture and floor-to-ceiling trendy glass, this bar claims to offer 1000 wines (it falls short), many of which are available by the glass. There's excellent service, with staff more than happy to recommend a wine. It's also a restaurant, with a short but decent menu and plenty of cheeses. The wines can also be bought at market prices.

**Taberna del Herrero**, C Calixto Fernández de la Torre 4, T983 342 310. This deservedly popular place sets out its stall to provide wholesome and traditional Castilian fare at popular prices. It succeeds superbly. *Raciones* of such delicious staples as *croquetas*, *lacón*, or a variety of stews are ridiculously cheap and filling (most plates €2-5). Eat at blocky wooden tables or the solid bar. Deservedly popular.

### Cafés

**Lion d'Or**, Plaza Mayor 4, T983 342 057. A lovely old café in the main square, complete with fireman's poles and gilt-framed mirrors. It's very popular with people of a certain age, who have no doubt been coming here every afternoon for several decades; you can see why.

**Sol**, Acera de Recoletos 3, T983 391 058. This elegant café/bar is smartly fitted out in polished wood and dark marble. It's got a fashionable and well-dressed crowd; it's a popular coffee spot or as a place to start off the evening with a relaxing drink. The patterns on the walls look like a 'magic eye' picture; try one of their potent cocktails and then see if you can see anything.

## ☻ Bars and clubs

**Valladolid** *p233, map p234*

There are various zones of bars in Valladolid; some around Plaza Martí y Monso, known as **La Coca**, some smartish ones around Plaza San Miguel, a riot of student nightlife around C Paraíso by the university and Plaza Portugalete near the cathedral, and several *discobares* on and around C Padre Francisco Suárez, between Paseo Zorilla and the river.

**Charlotte**, near **Paco Suárez**, is the last stop, open until midday; everyone heads there once the other places are shut.

**El Soportal**, Plaza San Miguel s/n, T983 371 940. A modern, dark and moody café/bar with a horseshoe bar and plenty of seats. There's hospitable service and a busy, smart crowd at weekends, when it opens very late.

**La Comedia**, Plaza Martí y Monso 4, T983 340 804. This is a reliable choice; a good lively bar with outdoor seating when weather permits. It fills with a fairly smart pre- and post-dinner crowd – there's even a cigar menu – and is lively and buzzy. There's no draught beer, but several good wines and tasty mixed drinks. Open until fairly late and decorated with past stars of the silver screen.

**Paco Suárez**, C Padre Francisco Suárez 2, T983 812 085. This small club has cocktails, a huge range of *chupitos* (shooters) and house music (the best in Valladolid, most reckon) until the sun is well over the yardarm.

## ☻ Entertainment

**Valladolid** *p233, map p234*

**Cines Casablanca**, C Leopoldo Cano 8, T983 398 841. An arthouse cinema that often shows films with subtitles rather than dubbing.

**Cines Roxy**, C Mario de Molina 6, T983 351 672. A small but handy art deco cinema.

**Sala Borja**, C Ruiz Hernández 12, T983 292 400. Frequent theatre performances, less traditional than the **Lope de Vega** or **Calderón**.

**Teatro Calderón**, C Las Angustias s/n, T902 371 137, www.tcalderon.org. The city's main theatre, with mainstream drama and dance.

**Teatro Lope de Vega**, C Mario de Molina 12, T983 213 886. A lovely tiled theatre built in 1861 with regular drama, opera and concerts.

## ⊛ Festivals and events

**Valladolid** *p233, map p234*
**Mar/Apr** Semana Santa (Easter week) is
fairly serious; hooded brotherhoods parade
floats through the streets to the mournful
wailing of cornets and tubas.
**Early Sep** Feast of the Virgen de San Lorenzo,
the streets fill with stalls selling wine and
tapas, there are bullfights, concerts and more.

## ⊖ Shopping

**Valladolid** *p233, map p234*
Valladolid's main shopping area is the
pedestrian zone between Plaza Mayor and
Plaza Zorilla, particularly along C Santiago.
**Oletum**, C de Teresa Gil 12. A wide range of
books with a good English-language section.

## ▲ Activities and tours

**Valladolid** *p233, map p234*
**Football** Real Valladolid is the city's
football team, who dress in slightly tasteless
purple-striped tops. They've spent about half
their life in the *Primera* division, but have
never excelled; 4th place is their highest finish.
At time of writing they were in the *Segunda*.
Their stadium, **Estadio José Zorilla**, Av Mundial
82 s/n, T983 360 342, is to the west of town.

## ⊖ Transport

**Valladolid** *p233, map p234*
**Air** Valladolid's airport (VLL), T983 415 500, is
12 km northwest of town. Regular Linecar
buses run between the bus station and the
airport to connect with flights (20 mins, €2).
ALSA (www.alsa.es) buses running between
Valladolid and León/Madrid will stop here if
you have pre-booked the ticket. A taxi from
Valladolid to the airport costs €16. The airport
is plagued by fog in the winter months and
flights have a history of being cancelled, so it's
best not to rely on making a connection.
    As well as Ryanair flights to **London**
Stansted and **Brussels** Charleroi, there are
international connections to **Paris** and
**Lisbon**, as well as domestic ones to
**Barcelona** and **Málaga**.

**Bus** Intercity buses go from Valladolid to
nearly every major city in Spain. These services

include: **Madrid** hourly (2¼ hrs, €11.14),
**León** 8-9 times daily (2 hrs, €7.69),
**Barcelona** twice daily (10½ hrs, €36-39),
**Segovia** (7-12 daily, 1 hr 50 mins; €6.80)
almost hourly, **Zamora** 7-10 times a day,
**Palencia** hourly, **Bilbao** (3-4 daily, 3½ hrs,
€16.03), **Santander** (2 daily, 4 hrs, €9.94)
and **Zaragoza** (5 hrs) via **Soria** (2¾ hrs)
3 times daily.
    Other destinations include **Aranda**
(5 daily), **Roa** (2 daily), **Medina del Campo**
(8 daily), **Rueda** (7 daily ), **Medina de
Rioseco** hourly (30 mins), **Simancas**
half-hourly, **Tordesillas** hourly. See the
relevant destinations for further details.

**Car hire** There are a few car hire agencies
at Valladolid airport; AVIS, T983 415 530,
www.avis.com; Europcar, T983 560 091,
www.europcar.com; Hertz, T983 415 546,
www.hertz.com.

**Taxi** T983 207 755.

**Train** Services run to **Madrid** (12-15 daily,
2½-3 hrs, €11-22) via Medina del Campo
very regularly, to **Palencia** (35 mins, €3.20)
more than hourly, and less frequently to
most mainline destinations.

## ⊙ Directory

**Valladolid** *p233, map p234*
**Internet** Bocatanet, C Mario de Molina
16, an internet café with unremarkable
connection serving good sandwiches
not far from the tourist office, €2 per hr;
Cartablanca, C de Colón 2, is an option
in the university district; Cibercafé, Paseo
de Zorilla 46, has several coin-op terminals
in a stuffy café, €2.50 per hr; Esferacom,
C Ruiz Hernandez 3, also a *locutorio*, and
fast internet connection. **Laundry**
There's a *lavandería* on C Embajadores
in the *barrio* of Las Delicias, a trek away
on the other side of the railway line in
the south of town. Bus No 6 will take
you there from C Vicente Moliner, near
the Plaza Mayor. **Medical services**
Hospital Universitario, T983 420 000,
emergency 112. **Police** T092 in an
emergency. **Post office** The main post
office is on Plaza de la Rinconada
near the Plaza Mayor.

# West of Valladolid

*Wandering the arid plains and dusty towns of western Castilla these days, it seems difficult to believe that this was once a region of great prestige and power. In the 15th and 16th centuries, towns like Tordesillas and Toro were major players in the political and religious life of the country, while Medina del Campo was a huge city for the time and one of Europe's principal trading towns, a sort of Wall Street of the meseta. Times have changed, and these places are backwaters. Poke about their streets with a rudimentary idea of Spanish history and you may well find them surprisingly rewarding. The excellent dry wines of Rueda or the hearty reds of Toro will banish any remaining dust from the journey across the scorched plains.* ▶▶ *For Sleeping, Eating and other listings, see pages 245-247.*

## Tordesillas and around 🏨🍴✳🚉 ▶▶ *pp245-247.*

→ *Colour map 4, B5.*

Heading west from **Simancas** (a pleasant medieval town 8 km from Valladolid, whose castle was set up as an archive for royal documents by Carlos V and Felipe II; it can be visited by prior appointment, T983 590 003) on the N620 you reach the town of **Tordesillas**. Apart from its imposing *mudéjar* monastery, there's really little to see here, although it is a very pleasant town to wander around. The Plaza Mayor is an attractive arcaded 17th-century affair that would look a lot better if it weren't used as a car park.

In 1494 Tordesillas was the location for the signing of a famous treaty between Spain and Portugal, two major maritime powers at the time. The treaty itself was signed in a building where the reasonably helpful **tourist office** ⓘ *Tue-Sat 1030-1400, 1700-2000, Sun 1000-1400 (closed Tue in winter)*, now stands. A small museum on the history of the treaty is in development at the site.

### Background

The area around Valladolid was the centre of much of Spain's political activity in the 15th and 16th centuries, and Tordesillas was in many ways an important power. Columbus had just got back from the Americas, and there were colonial issues to be sorted out. The 1494 treaty between Spain and Portugal was basically designed to leave Africa for Portugal and the Americas for Spain, but the canny Portuguese suspected or knew of the location of what is now Brazil, so they pushed the dividing line far enough over to give them a foothold in South America. The whole thing had to be re-evaluated within a lifetime anyway, but the very idea of two countries meeting to divide the world in two gives some idea of their control over the Atlantic at the time.

Not too long afterwards, Tordesillas gained an unwilling resident in Juana La Loca (see box, page 243) who was imprisoned here, along with her daughter and the embalmed corpse of her husband. She remained an icon of Castilian sovereignty, and it was due to her presence that Tordesillas became the centre of the *comunero* revolt against the reign of her son Carlos in the early 16th century. The town was viewed with suspicion thereafter and quickly became the backwater that it remains today.

### Real Monasterio de Santa Clara

ⓘ *Access to the convent is by guided tour only; there are some English-speaking guides at weekends. Oct-Mar Tue-Sat 1000-1330, 1600-1745, Sun 1030-1330, 1530-1730; Apr-Sep Tue-Sat 1000-1330, 1600-1830, Sun 1030-1330, 1530-1730; €3.60 (free Wed to EU citizens); Arab baths Tue, Thu-Sat 1000-1200, 1600-1700, (Oct-Mar 1600-1615), Sun 1030-1200, 1530-1600; €2.25.*

## Juana la Loca

There are few more tragic figures in the turbulent history of Spain than Queen Juana, who has gone down in history with the unfortunate but accurate name of 'the Mad'. The daughter of the Catholic monarchs Fernando and Isabel, she was sent off in style from Laredo in a fleet of 120 ships bound for Flanders and marriage to Felipe, heir to the throne. Felipe was known as *El Hermoso* (Philip the Fair) and Juana made the unthinkable mistake of falling in love with her arranged husband. He didn't feel the same way, making it clear he intended to spend his time with mistresses. This sent Juana into fits of *amorous delirium* and hunger strikes; Felipe complained that she refused to leave him alone.

When she was 27, her mother Isabel died and Juana inherited the throne of Castilla. Her husband died shortly after their arrival in Spain, and this pushed the queen over the edge. She took possession of the corpse and had it embalmed, refusing to let

it be buried or approached by women. She roamed the countryside for years with Felipe, whom she occasionally put on a throne. Deemed unfit to rule, she was finally persuaded to enter a mansion in Tordesillas, where she was locked up, with her not-so-fair-nae-more husband with her. Her daughter Catalina was another unfortunate companion – Juana refused to let her be taken from her, and when she was rescued, her mother went on a hunger strike to ensure her return. The wretched Juana lived in rags for 47 years in Tordesillas; she had occasional lucid moments and was a constant focus for those dissatisfied with the new 'foreign' monarchy of the Habsburgs. Many historians (largely Protestant) have implied that her incarceration was a conspiracy, but there can be no doubt that she was mentally unfit to rule the nation. In 1555 she finally passed away at the age of 76. She is buried in Granada alongside the husband that she loved not wisely but too well.

**Castilla y León** West of Valladolid

The Real Monasterio de Santa Clara, where Juana la Loca was incarcerated, is an excellent construction, built in *mudéjar* style, still home to a community of Clarist nuns. It was originally built as a palace by Alfonso XI, and he installed his mistress Doña Leonor here. After the king died of plague, Leonor was murdered on the orders of Pedro (the Cruel), the new king. Following the deaths of Pedro's longtime mistress as well as his son, he ordered his illegitimate daughter to convert the palace into a convent in their memory. The *mudéjar* aspects are the most impressive: a chapel with superb stucco work and attractive scalloped arches, and especially the small patio, an absolute gem with horseshoe and scalloped multifoil arches. Another chapel, the **Capilla Dorada**, also has a fine *mudéjar* interior. The cloister is neoclassical in appearance. The high chapel has a very elegant panelled *mudéjar* ceiling. Some fine alabaster tombs in late Gothic style can be seen in the Saldaña chapel, built by the state treasurer of John II and holding his remains, his wife's, and possibly Beatriz of Portugal, Pedro's daughter, who carried out the conversion of palace to convent.

*♣ Heading north from Tordesillas, off the N-VI motorway that runs to Benavente and beyond, are some excellent, little visited attractions.*

### Urueña → *Colour map 4, A4.*
North of Tordesillas, some 4 km from the N-V1 motorway and not served by buses, Urueña is a small gem of a town. It's the sort of place that ought to be flooded with tourists, but is comparatively unknown. The fantastic walls that surround the village

are the main attraction; their jagged teeth and narrow gateways dominate the plains around; on a clear day you can see a frightening number of kilometres from the sentries' walkway along the top. About a kilometre below the town is the lovely Romanesque **Iglesia de Nuestra Señora de la Anunciada**, unusually built in the Catalan style. The distinguishing feature of this style is 'Lombard arches', a feature that resembles fingers, traced around the apses. The key for the church is in the **tourist office** in town, located in the town hall.

Nine kilometres south of here, the rustic sleepy village of **San Cebrián de Mazote** is named for its fine Mozarabic church. It's well worth a look if you're mobile; track down the keyholder if it's shut; she lives near the small covered market by the lofty walls of the former monastery (T983 780 007).

## Rueda → *Colour map 4, B5.*

Between Tordesillas and Medina del Campo, the straggling town of Rueda is of little interest except for its white wine production. Rueda whites are consistently among Spain's best, and are mostly made from the Verdejo grape, a local variety (not to be confused with Verdelho) which produces wines with a distinctive lemony aroma and crisp finish. Several *bodegas* in the area can be visited, but the white wine process is not nearly as interesting as that of reds, so you're better off picking up a few bottles at the cellar door, and saving your visiting time for the Ribera del Duero east of Valladolid, or for Toro. One of the best wines here is made by **Marqués de Riscal**, located by the motorway just north of the town. About eight buses a day running between Medina and Valladolid stop here.

---

# Medina del Campo ⬤🔘🔘🔘🔘 ›› *pp245-247.*

→ *Colour map 4, B5.*

It's the early 16th century, and you're on your way to one of the biggest cities in Spain to see the queen. Where are you off to? Here, 25 km south of Tordesillas, where massive trade fairs drew the leading merchants from around Europe in their droves. Today, there are few remnants of Medina's past glories. The massive plaza is one of them, and there are some beautiful *palacios* around, but the modern town is ramshackle and poor. The **tourist office** ① *T983 811 357, Tue-Sat 1000-1400, 1630-1900, Sun 1100-1400*, is on the square by the large church.

## Background

Medina was originally an important centre for the export of Castilian wool, but diversified to become, for a while, the pre-eminent commercial city of Spain. Queen Isabel often ran Castilla from here, and she actually died in a house overlooking the square.

In the *comunero* uprising of 1520 to 1521, Medina was burned to the ground after some houses were fired by attacking royalist forces. The town's fairs recovered from this setback, but as financial activity began to surround the court once it was settled in Madrid, Medina lost influence. The commerce was greatly harmed by the royal bankruptcies of the late 16th century, and Medina drifted into obscurity.

## Sights

One of the nicest of the many palaces is the Renaissance **Palacio de los Dueñas**, with a beautiful patio and staircase adorned with the heads of the monarchs of Castilla. ① *Mon-Fri 0900-1445; closed for part of Jul-Aug.*

The **Castillo de la Mota** ① *Mon-Sat 1100-1400, 1600-1800 (1900 summer), Sun 1100-1400, free*, is an impressive *mudéjar* castle across the river from town. Its muscular brick lines are solid in the extreme. While you can walk around inside the walls, there's not much to see inside the building itself, which holds some municipal offices.

The new **Museo de las Ferias** ① *C San Martín 26, T983 837 527, Tue-Sat 1000-*

*1330, 1600-1900, Sun 1100-1400, €2*, is situated in an old church and has an interesting look at the commerce of the great trade fairs and how they influenced the art and politics of the period; there's a large collection of related documents and art.

## Toro 🔲🔲🔲🔲🔲 ⟫ *pp245-247.*

→ *Colour map 4, B4.*

Toro sits high above the River Duero 33 km east of Zamora, from where it can easily be visited on a day trip, if you don't fancy spending the night. Its name might mean 'bull', but its emblem is a stone pig dating from Celtiberian times, which sits at the eastern gate to the city.

The city was repopulated during the Reconquista and changed hands a couple of times. A significant battle occurred near here in 1476 between the Catholic Monarchs (Fernando and Isabel) and Portuguese forces supporting the claim of Isabel's rival, Juana (not the mad one), to the throne of Castilla. The heavy defeat suffered by Alfonso V, the king of Portugal, was a boost to the joint monarchs, and he gave up interfering three years later. The prolific playwright Lope de Vega also made Toro famous by naming one of his plays, *Las Almenas de Toro*, after its battlements.

These days Toro is famous for wine. Its hearty reds don't have the complexity of the Ribera del Duero wines from further up the river, but some of them are pretty good indeed, and full-bodied by Spanish standards.

### Sights

There are several churches in town with *mudéjar* and Romanesque elements, but the highlight is the **Colegiata** ① *Mar-Sep Tue-Sun 1000-1300, 1700-2000, Oct-Feb 1000-1400, 1630-1830, €1 for sacristy and Portada*, near the Plaza Mayor. The interior is graced by a high dome with alabaster windows and a Baroque organ, but the real highlight is the Portada de la Majestad, a 13th-century carved doorway decorated with superbly preserved (and well-restored) painted figures in early Gothic style; the character expressed through such apparently simple paintwork is remarkable. In the sacristy is a celebrated painting, *La Virgen de la Mosca* (the Virgin of the Fly); the insect in question is settled on her skirts.

Overlooking the river is the **Alcázar**, a fort dating from the 12th century built on a Moorish fortification. Juana, pretender to Isabel's Castilian crown, resisted here for a while; she must have enjoyed the views, which stretch for miles across the *meseta*.

### Wineries

Most wineries are happy to show visitors around, but all need to be phoned beforehand. In terms of wine quality, one of the best is **Bodegas Fariña** ① *Camino del Palo, T980 577 673, www.bodegasfarina.com*, who market their wine as *Colegiata* and *Gran Colegiata*. **Covitoro** ① *Ctra Tordesillas, T980 690 347, www.covitoro.com*, the local wine co-operative, also produce some good bottles, with *Gran Cermeño* particularly recommendable as a well-priced, oak-aged red. They're a short walk along the main road east of town. There are plenty of other wineries within easy reach of Toro; the tourist office will supply a list.

‡ *Toro wines received DO (denominación de origen) status in 1987.*

### 🍷 Sleeping

**Tordesillas** *p242*
**L Parador de Tordesillas**, Ctra Salamanca 5, T983 770 051, www.parador.es. Although

this isn't the most characterful of its ilk in Spain, it is still a good lodging option. It is located outside the town in a mansion surrounded by pine trees. The rooms are attractive, and there's a peaceful swimming pool.

**D Hostal San Antolín**, C San Antolín 8, T983 796 771, sanantolin@telefonica.net. Another good choice, just down from the Plaza Mayor. The restaurant underneath is also one of Tordesillas' best, an attractive place with a good traditional *menú* for €12.

**F Pensión Galván**, Ctra Madrid-Coruña Km 182, T983 770 773. One of the closer budget options to the interesting bits of town, this has very simple rooms with heating and TV but shared bathroom.

### Camping

**Camping El Astral**, Camino de Pollos 8, T983 770 953. A decent campsite by the River Duero across the bridge from town (follow signs for the *parador*). There's a swimming pool on the site.

### Urueña *p243*

There are 2 *casas rurales* which make fine places to stay.

**E Villa de Urueña**, C Nueva 6, T983 717 063, 639 738 867. Run out of the restaurant of the same name on the main square, this *casa rural* has 4 simple doubles in a modern house inside the walls.

**E Villalbín**, Travesía La Laguna 1, T616 118 643. A lovely simple *casa rural* just outside the walls. It has adobe walls, a garden and adorable rustic rooms with floorboards and traditional furniture. There are 4 double rooms, 1 equipped for the disabled and a lounge with fireplace. You can also rent the whole house (€140/500 per night/week). Recommended.

### Medina del Campo *p244*

Medina perhaps appeals more as a day trip from Valladolid, but there are many places to stay.

**AL Palacio de las Salinas**, Ctra de Salinas s/n, T983 804 450, www.palaciodelassalinas.es. The most opulent of the town's choices, this is a massive palace 4 km west of town. Set in huge gardens, it's also a spa hotel and has plenty of comfort for a relaxing stay.

**E Hostal Plaza**, Plaza Mayor 34, T983 811 246. Right on the huge main square in town, this *hostal* offers excellent value. It has well-priced, spacious floor-boarded rooms with en suite bathroom.

### Toro *p245*

**B Juan II**, Paseo Espolón 1, T980 690 300, www.hoteljuanii.com. This hotel is on the edge of the old town above the cliff dropping down to the river. The rooms are comfortable; some have great views, and there's some good old-fashioned Spanish hospitality in the air.

**B-C María de Molina**, Plaza San Julián 1, T/F980 691 414, h.molina@helcom.es. A well-priced hotel, modern but attractive, with spacious a/c rooms that lack nothing but hairdryers and minibar. Right in the centre of town.

**F Doña Elvira**, C Antonio Miguelez 47, T980 690 062. Although it's rather unattractively situated by a petrol station on the main road at the edge of the old town, this is the best budget option, with clean en suite rooms at a pittance, and rooms with shared bath for even less (**G**). There's some noise from the road, but it's not too bad.

**G La Castilla**, Plaza de España 19, T980 690 381. This simple *pensión* is basic but comedy-cheap and well placed in the town's centre. Rooms lack every convenience, but the shared bathrooms are clean. Cold in winter though.

## 🍴 Eating

### Tordesillas *p242*

Hostal San Antolín, see Sleeping above, is a good eating option too.

**🍴 El Torreón**, Ctra Burgos-Portugal 11, T983 770 123. This restaurant has a lofty reputation hereabouts and is a favourite weekend lunch choice for the Valladolid bureaucrats. It specializes in meat and is famous for a great steak tartare as well as home-made foie. Service is, however, not their strong point unless you look important.

🔵 *For an explanation of the sleeping and eating price codes used in this guide, see inside the*
⚫ *front cover. Other relevant information is found in Essentials pages 39-46.*

¶ **Palacio del Corregidor**, C San Pedro 14, T983 771 496. Housed in a fine old *palacio*, this friendly restaurant specializes in good *paellas* and fish baked in salt. There are a range of menus on offer. The paella should be ordered earlier in the day; or be prepared to wait.

**Urueña** *p243*
¶ **Pago de Marfeliz**, C Generalísimo 8, T983 717 042. A good option serving generous portions of Castilian food at moderate prices.
¶ **Villa de Urueña**, Plaza Mayor 6, T983 717 063. A hearty option where the locals hang out.

**Medina del Campo** *p244*
E **Mónaco**, Plaza Mayor 26, T983 810 295. The town's most characterful spot, this is a lively bar that has some great *pinchos*, and an upstairs restaurant with some excellent, rich, meaty plates and a good *menú* for €8.

**Toro** *p245*
Toro has a few cheap and cheerful places to eat around the Plaza Mayor.
¶ **Juan II**, Paseo Espolón I, T980 690 300. The best meal in town can be found here. To its infinite credit, it doesn't feel remotely like a hotel restaurant, and is priced very fairly indeed. There's a large dining area, a terrace and a range of excellent Castilian fare.
¶ **Restaurante Castilla**, Plaza de España 19, T980 690 381. This simple and friendly place has decent hearty local cuisine and tapas. You're much better eating outside if the weather's fine, as the cramped *comedor* can get pretty stuffy.

## ⊙ Bars and clubs

**Medina del Campo** *p244*
**La Kapilla**, Ronda de Santa Ana s/n. A good bar set in an old *palacio*.

**Toro** *p245*
**Carpe Diem**, Plaza de España s/n. The town's best drinking option, this thoughtfully stylish spot is a good bar with original church-based decor.

**La Bodeguilla del Pillo**, C Puerto del Mercado 34. A local-style bar, full of character and characters. Nearly every Toro wine is available by the glass.

## ❀ Festivals and events

**Tordesillas** *p242*
**Mid-Sep** Tordesillas' fiesta includes the **Toro de la Vega**, where a bull is released in the open woodlands near the town and the people start running and dodging.

## ⊖ Transport

**Tordesillas** *p242*
**Bus**
Services running between **Valladolid** and **Zamora** stop at the bus station just north and west of the old town. There are 7-10 on weekdays, and 3-4 at weekends. There are several other services to major Spanish cities, as Tordesillas is at an important road junction.

**Medina del Campo** *p244*
**Bus**
While there's a bus terminal next to the train station, most buses to **Madrid** and **Valladolid** leave from outside a bar called Punto Rojo on C Artilleria near the Plaza Mayor. There are about 15 departures for Valladolid daily and 5 for Madrid.

**Train**
Medina is a major rail junction, and there are many trains to **Madrid**, **Valladolid**, **Palencia**, and **Salamanca**, as well as 3 a day to **León**, and 1 to **Lisbon**.

**Toro** *p245*
**Bus**
Services running between **Valladolid** and **Zamora** stop on the main road, a handier option than the train. There are 7-10 a day on weekdays and 3-4 at weekends.

## ⊙ Directory

**Toro** *p245*
**Internet** Cyber Mundo Net, C La Antigua 23.

# Zamora → *Phone code: 980. Colour map 4, B3. Population: 66,123.*

*Like so many other towns along the river Duero, Zamora was a fortress of the Reconquista frontline, although before that it was a Celtic, Carthaginian, then Roman settlement. In the Middle Ages, the city was formidably walled and famous for its resilience during sieges; the saying 'A Zamora, no se ganó en una hora' (Zamora wasn't taken in an hour) dates from these times and is still used widely.*

*Today the city is a relaxed and peaceful provincial capital famous for ceramics and antiques. The centre is attractive with, incredibly, a couple of dozen Romanesque churches, which are at ease with some very harmonious modern urban architecture. The city still preserves large sections of its walls around the old centre, which perches high on the rocky bank of the Duero.* →→ *For Sleeping, Eating and other listings, see pages 252-254.*

## Ins and outs

**Getting there and around** The train station (a beautiful building) and bus station are inconveniently situated a 20-minute walk to the north of town. Rickety local buses run to them from Plaza Sagasta near the Plaza Mayor, or it's a €4-5 cab fare. Nearly all the sights of interest are within the walled old town, of elongated shape but still just about walkable. →→ *See also Transport, page 254.*

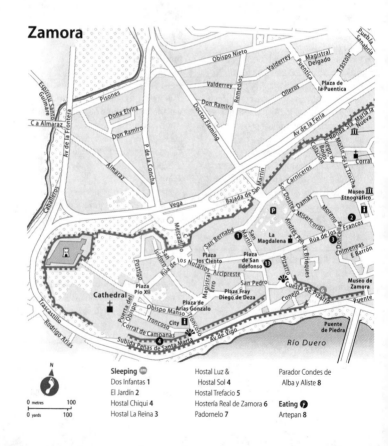

**Zamora**

N

0 metres 100
0 yards 100

**Sleeping**
Dos Infantas 1
El Jardín 2
Hostal Chiqui 4
Hostal La Reina 3

Hostal Luz &
 Hostal Sol 4
Hostal Trefacio 5
Hostería Real de Zamora 6
Padornelo 7

Parador Condes de
 Alba y Aliste 8

**Eating**
Artepan 8

**Tourist information** The city **tourist office** ① *Plaza Arias Gonzalo, T980 533 694, daily 1000-1400, 1600-1900 (1700-2000 Mar-Sep)*, is at the cathedral end of town and is very helpful. There's also a **regional office** ① *C Santa Clara 20, T980 531 845, oficinadeturismodezamora@jcyl.es*. In the heart of the old town, on Plaza Viriato, there is another office, which runs city tours and can give out simple information. The tours (€5 per person) run at weekends from March to June and October to November, and daily from July to September. Most guides will be able to summarize in English as they go along.

## Sights

Where they are preserved, the **city walls** are impressive and worth strolling around. There are a few noble entrances preserved around the perimeter. The western end of the walled town is narrow and culminates at the castle, founded in the 11th century, which looks the goods from the outside but is modern inside and houses a college.

Nearby, Zamora's **cathedral** is an interesting building, especially its dome, which is an unusual feature, with scalloped tiling and miniature pagodas that wouldn't look out of place on a southeast Asian temple. In the squarish interior, you can admire the finely carved stone retrochoir as well as the 16th-century walnut choir itself. The side chapels all have elegant *rejas*, while the stone *retablo* depicts the Ascension. The highlight, however, is the **museum** ① *Tue-Sun 1000-1400, 1630-1830 (Mar-Sep*

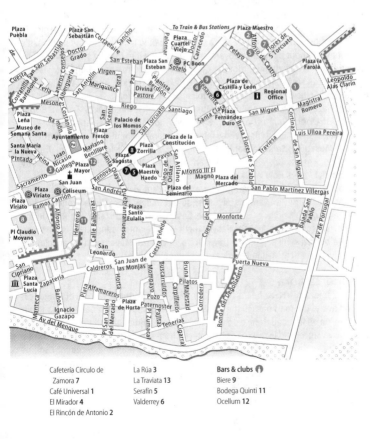

Castilla y León Zamora

| | | |
|---|---|---|
| Cafetería Círculo de Zamora 7 | La Rúa 3 | **Bars & clubs** 🎵 |
| Café Universal 1 | La Traviata 13 | Biere 9 |
| El Mirador 4 | Serafín 5 | Bodega Quinti 11 |
| El Rincón de Antonio 2 | Valderrey 6 | Ocellum 12 |

*1700-2000)*, €3, and its small collection of superb Flemish tapestries. Dating from the 15th and 17th centuries, they are amazing for their detail, colour and size (some of them are around 35 sq m). They depict scenes from antiquity: the conquests of Hannibal, the Trojan War and the coronation of Tarquin.

Zamora has an extraordinary number of Romanesque churches, a pleasing collection, particularly as several of them avoided meddlesome architects of later periods. The **Iglesia de La Magdalena** ① *Tue-Sun 1000-1300, 1700-2000, free*, is one of the nicest, with an ornate portal carved with plant motifs. Inside, it's simple and attractive, with a high single nave, and a 13th-century tomb with an unusually midget-like recumbent figure. Most of the worthwhile churches have the same opening hours.

In the **Plaza Mayor**, the **Iglesia de San Juan**, constructed in the 12th to 13th century, has a thistly façade and a big gloomy interior with unusual arches that run the length of the nave, rather than across it. The alabaster windows are an attractive feature.

The pretty **Iglesia de Santa María la Nueva** is increasingly inaccurately named as its Romanesque lines are going on 900 years old. It has some fine carved capitals outside; inside it's a simple temple with high barrel vaulting, a stone baptismal font, and the faded remains of some frescoes; you can just about make out scenes from the life of Christ and Mary. Next door is a museum detailing the traditions of Zamora's Semana Santa, while, further to the east, look out for the façade of the **Palacio de los Momos**, carved with penitents' chains seemingly at odds with the grandeur of the mansion.

The **Museo de Zamora** ① *Plaza de Santa Lucía 2, T980 516 150, Tue-Sat 1000-1400, 1600-1900 (summer 1700-2000) €1.20*, is housed in two connecting buildings: a 16th-century *palacio*, and a modern construction designed by Emilio Tuñón and Luis Moreno Mansilla, which has won many plaudits since its opening in 1998. The museum was conceived as a chest that would hold the city's valuables; it's imaginative without being flamboyant, and fits quietly into the city's older lines. The collection covers everything from the Celtic to the modern, and is fairly interesting: Roman funeral stelae, gilt crosses from the Visigothic period, and especially a very ornate gold Celtic brooch are all things to catch the attention.

On Plaza Viriato is the elegant Museo Etnográfico **museum** ① *Tue-Sat 1000-1400, 1700-2000, Sun 1000-1400*, €3, which holds an ethnographic display of traditional Castilian life, bolstered by regular temporary exhibitions. A little further on lies the **Museo de Semana Santa** ① *Plaza de Santa María la Nueva s/n, Tue-Sat 1000-1400, 1700-2000*, €3, which has an interesting display illustrating the history of Zamora's famous Holy Week processions.

From parts of the old town, there are magnificent views over the ramparts and down to the Duero River and its picturesque old bridge. From **Plaza Troncoso**, just near the city tourist office, is one of the best, while **Calle Pizarro**, off Rúa de los Francos, is also worthwhile, especially at night. Another interesting street is the steep **Calle Balborraz**, which plunges down from the Plaza Mayor, and is an alluring assembly of character-laden buildings and intriguing shops.

## Around Zamora

West of Zamora, the N122 heads towards the beautiful Portuguese town of **Bragança**, 100 km away. The road passes the massive and attractive reservoir of the Esla River. Some 10 km off the road (from a point 12 km west of Zamora), the church of **San Pedro de la Nave** was moved in the 1930s to protect it from submersion by the rising waters. It's a 17th-century Visigothic structure with lofty doors and some excellent capitals inside, as well as a frieze with various Christian motifs. Unfortunately for the carless, it's in a monumentally depressing little village with no transport options. The keyholder, María Angeles Refoyo, lives in the corner house where the road bends through the middle of the village.

# The fighting bishop of Zamora

In an age which saw the central state increase its power over the individual, Antonio de Acuña, Bishop of Zamora during the *comunero* revolt, stands out as a swaggering medieval individualist whose complete lack of self awareness led to him becoming a central figure of resistance to Carlos V. Born to a wealthy Castilian family who were used to dispensing patronage, Acuña had come to the attention of Fernando and Isabel, who appointed him their ambassador to Rome in 1506.

After Isabel's death, Acuña saw an opportunity to further his own interests and deserted Fernando in preference for Felipe el Hermoso (Philip the Fair). By pledging his absolute loyalty to the Pope he was able to secure his appointment to the bishopric of Zamora despite the opposition of top local bigwig Rodrigo Ronquillo, whose objections were brushed aside when Acuña seized the bishopric by force. His Triumph-of-the-Will-style antics saw him temporarily in charge but at the expense of making a host of powerful enemies.

Although his appointment was eventually confirmed by Fernando, Zamora became a centre of intrigue with Acuña at its centre. When he was eventually expelled from the city at the start of the *comunero* revolt, he raised an army of 2000 men and found himself on the side of the rebels while his implacable enemy Ronquillo was a leading royalist commander. He conducted a series of daring but essentially meaningless campaigns in the *meseta* around Valladolid before deciding in 1521 to march on Toledo where in a great display of showmanship he persuaded the populace to declare him bishop.

It soon became apparent that his individualistic acts of empire building were no substitute for an effective political and military strategy and after the defeat of the *comuneros*, Acuña was forced to flee. But he was captured and held captive in Simancas Castle where Carlos hoped he would be quietly forgotten about.

But in 1526, while attempting to escape, Acuña killed one of his gaolers. Carlos cunningly appointed Ronquillo as custodian of Simancas Castle. Ronquillo wasted no time in settling old scores and sentenced the erstwhile bishop to be tortured and executed. His body was then displayed from the castle walls as warning to others who thought they could challenge royal power.

Although the Pope went through the motions of complaining about this breach of protocol in reality he recognized that Acuña was a son of the Church who had signally failed to bring any credit or advantage to the Papacy. Eventually the whole matter was quietly forgotten about.

Northwest of Zamora, via the unenthralling service centre of Benavente, the A52 heads west into Galicia. It's an attractive route that passes the beautiful **Parque Natural del Lago de Sanabria**. The lake is a haunting glacial feature with plenty of watersports facilities. The nearest town, **Puebla de Sanabria**, is an exceptionally attractive place and makes a good stopover, with plenty of character in the narrow streets around its attractive 12th-century church and blocky castle. Just above the lake, the pretty hamlet of **San Martín de Castañeda** is also worth a look; it too has a fine-looking Romanesque church. From Puebla de Sanabria, a beautiful road winds its way south through a spectacular hilly pass and on to Bragança in Portugal, about a 45-minute drive away.

North of Zamora, on the N630 just before the village of Granja de Moreruela lie the impressive ruins of the **Monasterio de Moreruela** ① *Wed-Sun 1000-1400, 1700-2000 (winter 1530-1830), free.* Built by the Cistercians in the 12th century on a beautiful wooded site, the church and cloisters survive only in outline. Fortunately, the apse and chevet survive intact and convey an impression of the monastery's former glory. It's a romantic spot that you'll almost certainly have to yourself.

## ● Sleeping

**Zamora** *p248, map p248*

**AL Parador Condes de Alba y Aliste**, Plaza de Viriato 5, T980 514 497, www.parador.es. This is a great place to stay in the heart of the old town, in a noble palace built around a beautiful courtyard. The rooms are large and attractively furnished in wood (the new wing is equally comfortable although not quite as atmospheric), while the pool out the back helps with the summer heat.

**AL-A Dos Infantas**, Cortinas de San Miguel 3, T980 509 898, www.hoteldosinfantas.com. This is a modern and stylish option in the centre of town, with surprisingly reasonable rates for their large rooms, which are equipped to business hotel standards. There's parking available as well.

**B Hostería Real de Zamora**, Cuesta de Pizarro 7, T980 534 545, hostzamora@wanadoo.es. Cheaper than the *parador*, but just as atmospheric, this likeable old place is set in a typical *palacio* with attractive patio. The rooms are somewhat simpler, although very good value at this price, except at peak times.

**C Hostal Trefacio**, C Alfonso de Castro 7, T980 509 104. Good mid-range option, with standard modern rooms with decent bathrooms in the heart of the town. The management are warm and friendly. Low end of this price range.

**D Hostal Chiqui**, C Benavente 2, T980 531 480. In the same building as the **Luz** and **Sol**, this is a very acceptable option, with modern rooms with TV, phone and heating.

**E Hostal La Reina**, C Reina 1, T980 533 939. Superbly situated behind the church of San Juan on the Plaza Mayor, this cheery option has rooms with or without bathroom. They are simple enough, but very good at this price and extremely cheap in winter.

**E Hostal Luz** and **D Hostal Sol**, C Benavente 2, T980 533 152, www.hostal-sol.com. 2 *hostales* in the same building, run by the same management. Both are clean and modern, with quiet rooms with bathrooms.

The rooms in the **Luz** have TV and telephone and are very slightly cheaper.

**F El Jardín**, Plaza del Maestro 8, T980 531 827. Some of the cheapest beds in town above a busy tapas bar; simple but clean.

**G Padornelo**, C del Aire 4, T980 532 064. It ain't the Ritz, but it's quiet, clean and seriously cheap.

### Around Zamora *p250*

**AL Parador Puebla de Sanabria**, Ctra Lago 18, Puebla de Sanabria, T980 620 001, www.parador.es. A good modern option, but on the other side of the river from the attractive town centre. Helpful, friendly staff and a decent restaurant.

**D Hostal San Francisco**, Alto de San Francisco 6, Puebla de Sanabria, T980 620 896. With a great location in the old town, this hostel is comfortable, heated and has good views. Offers plenty of value.

## ● Eating

**Zamora** *p248, map p248*

₸₸₸ **El Rincón de Antonio**, Rúa de los Francos 6, T980 535 370. This is an attractive modern restaurant with a stone interior and a big glassed-in terrace. The cuisine is innovative and excellent; the *mollejas* (sweetbreads) come recommended, as does the *rodaballo* (turbot).

₸₸ **El Mirador**, Corral de Campanas 5, T980 535 440. In a quiet street not far from the cathedral, this atmospheric little restaurant is set in an old stone *bodega* that looks out over the Duero. There's quite a contrast between the enclosed stone space and the sweeping views outside; the food is rich and tasty, with such delicacies as *jamón de pato* (duck ham) alongside Castilian favourites, as well as a range of salads and good fish dishes.

₸₸ **La Rúa**, Rúa de los Francos 19, T980 534 024. This likeable and comfortably decorated restaurant is solid for a range of choices, with simple *platos combinados*, a good *menú del día* for €10.85 and some great *zamorano* cuisine. However, it's the rices that give it its good name; the speciality, a paella-like rice with lobster, *arroz con bogavante* (€17.75 per person; best to order it beforehand), comes in a huge deep dish, sizzling with intent to satisfy.

**Serafín**, Plaza Maestro Haedo 10, T980 531 422. Good hearty Zamoran and Castilian fare at reasonable prices, with a pleasant terrace outside. As well as the café, it also has a more upmarket restaurant, serving dishes such as *arroz a la zamorana*, a hearty rice with various porcine morsels.

**Valderrey**, C Benavente 9, T980 532 383. A slightly sombre but satisfactory restaurant with generously proportioned *raciones* of traditional Castilian fare and some very good main courses; their stews with potatoes are recommended.

**Artepan**, C Lope de Vega 2, T980 512 340. A good pastry shop with a top range of *empanadas* and other goodies to take away.

**Café Universal**, Plaza de San Martín. A good choice in summer, one of a couple of adjacent old buildings with massive doors, this has a popular terrace out the front for cheap food, coffees or evening drinks.

**Cafetería Círculo de Zamora**, C Santa Clara 2, T980 530 534. On the first floor of a newly restored art deco building this venerable Zamoran institution serves up good value snacks and meals all day. There's disabled access.

**La Traviata**, Rúa de los Notarios 1. A stylish and attractive café near La Magdalena church.

**Around Zamora** *p250*
**Café Bar Remate**, C Arrabal 3, Puebla de Sanabria, T980 620 920. Though it doesn't look much from the outside, this is a top spot to eat, with lovingly prepared traditional dishes such as *callos* (tripe) or octopus served in a pleasant *comedor*.

# ⊙ Bars and clubs

**Zamora** *p248, map p248*
The bulk of Zamoran nightlife is centred on the boisterous **C de los Herreros**, a narrow curving street off the Plaza Mayor, whose steep length is made of one bar after another; basically you just have to stroll

down and see which one you fancy. There are some quieter bars around the Plaza Mayor too, and a few secluded options seeded throughout the old town.

**Biere**, C Benavente 7. This is a popular and entertaining modern café/bar in an old stone building. It's stylish and cheerfully populated by smart young *zamoranos*.

**Bodega Quinti**, C de los Herreros 23. One of the more atmospheric of bars on this street, this underground bar is in a claustrophobic but smart brick vault. It's better earlier in the night as it gets too packed later on.

**Café La Calle**, C Arcipreste 2. A popular café/bar with brick arches, white walls and a quiet and friendly atmosphere, as well as a small terrace.

**Hacienda Nahuatl**, Pl del Mercado 1, T980 536 436. Opposite the market in an atmospheric stone building, this is a great place for a drink in the early evening when it is full of relaxed stallholders. There is an extensive menu as well, with a mix of Zamoran and international dishes.

**Ocellum**, Plaza Mayor 8, T980 514 848. This high-ceilinged café/bar is popular at several points of the day. Its terrace is a great spot for an afternoon coffee after walking the pedestrian zone of the city; later, it gets busy for after-dinner drinks, then becomes a *discoteca*, with a huge selection in the DJ booth and a downstairs dance floor.

# ⊛ Festivals and events

**Zamora** *p248, map p248*
**Mar/Apr** Zamora's **Semana Santa** (Holy Week) is one of the most famous and traditional in Spain. Book a room well in advance if you fancy a visit. Although there's plenty of revelry in the bars and streets, the main element is the serious religious processions of hooded *cofradías* (brotherhoods) who carry or accompany giant floats; it's effectively a week-long series of funeral processions; they are very atmospheric and traditional, although the mournful music can get a bit much after you've seen a couple of them. One of the most beautiful is the procession on Sat evening, when the much-loved Virgen de la Soledad is carried through the streets, preceded by a sisterhood carrying flickering candles.

**End Jun** Zamora's main fiesta is **San Pedro**, with streetlife, fireworks and bullfights. At the same time, the Plaza de Viriato holds an important ceramics fair; a picturesque sight indeed with thousands of vessels of all shapes and sizes arranged under the trees; they range from traditional plain earthenware to imaginatively painted decorative pieces.

## O Shopping

**Zamora** *p248, map p248*
Zamora is full of interesting shops dealing in antiques and ceramics; there are also characterful shops along the main pedestrian streets selling wine, local cheeses and hams.

## O Transport

**Zamora** *p248, map p248*
Despite Zamora's proximity to the Portuguese border, there are currently no public transport connections with it; you have to go via Salamanca or Madrid.

**Bus**
Some 7 buses a day run north to **León** (2 hrs, €7.90) via Benavente (4 at weekends); 7-10 run to **Valladolid**, some stopping in Toro and Tordesillas (3 at weekends); 6 service **Madrid**; a massive 13 cruise south to **Salamanca** (40 mins-1 hr, 6 on Sun), 5 go to **Oviedo** (3 hrs 30 mins, €14.01), among other Northern Spanish destinations.

**Train**
Trains are few; 3 a day run to **Madrid** (3-4 hrs, €24); more go to **Medina del Campo** (55 mins, €4.50-€13.50), but you're better off with the buses.

## O Directory

**Zamora** *p248, map p248*
**Internet** Plaza Viriato, Plaza Viriato s/n, is a cybercafé opposite the *parador*; PC Boon, Plaza del Cuartel Viejo s/n, has access during business hours; **Recreativos Coliseum**, C Ramos Carrión, is a gaming arcade with internet terminals; CyberZamor@, C Juan II 10, €2 per hr. **Laundry** A friendly no-name laundry on the corner of C de Balborraz and C San Andrés just off the Plaza Mayor (look for the *Tintorería* sign) will do a service wash and dry for about €6. **Police** Police station is in the Plaza Mayor in the old town hall.

# Salamanca

→ *Phone Code: 923. Colour map 4, B3. Population:160,331. Altitude: 780 m.*
*Salamanca has a strong claim to being Spain's most attractive city. A university town since the early 13th century, it reached its apogee in the 15th and 16th centuries, the Golden Age of Imperial Spain. The old town is a remarkable assembly of superb buildings; a day's solid sightseeing can teach you more about Spanish architecture than you thought you ever wanted to know – Plateresque and Churrigueresque were more or less born here. By night, too, it's a good spot; today's university students just don't seem to tuck up in bed with a candle, hot milk and a theological tract like they used to, and bar life is busy seven days a week, bolstered by the large numbers of tourists and foreign students learning Spanish. If you can handle the heat and the crowds, there are few better places in Spain to spend a summer evening than the superb Plaza Mayor; sit at an outdoor table and watch storks circle architectural perfection in the setting sun.* ➤➤ For Sleeping, Eating and other listings, see pages 260-263.

## Ins and outs
**Getting there** Salamanca is about 200 km west of Madrid, but don't you dare consider the words 'day trip'. The bus station is west of town along Avenida Filiberto Villalobos. There are plenty of buses from Madrid, Valladolid and other Castilian cities. If you're in a car, the straight *meseta* roads make easy driving; it's well under one hour south of Zamora, for example. There are also several train connections.
➤➤ See also Transport, page 263.

**Getting around** You won't have much cause to stray from the old town, which is very walkable indeed. The bus and train stations are a 15-minute walk from the centre.

**Best time to visit** If you visit in summer you are guaranteed heat, tourists and outdoor tables. In many ways this is the nicest time to come, but the students aren't about (although there are always plenty of American language students) and the nightlife is correspondingly quieter. Like the rest of Castilla, Salamanca gets cold in winter, but never shuts down and accommodation is cheap.

**Tourist information** There are two handy tourist offices, one in the **Plaza Mayor** ① *T923 218 342, Mon-Fri 0900-1400, 1600-1830, Sat 0900-1830, Sun 0900-1400, summer Mon-Sat 0900-2000, Sun 0900-1400*, and one at **Rúa Antigua 70** ① *Casa de las Conchas, T923 268 571, oficinade turismodesalamanca@jcyl.es, daily 0900-1400, 1700-2000, Jul- mid Sep Sun-Thu 0900-2000, Fri and Sat 0900-2100*. The former has more information on the city, the second is better for information on the rest of Castilla y León. A few summer-only kiosks are scattered about, notably at the transport terminals. Regular **walking tours** of the city run from the tourist office on the Plaza Mayor; they leave daily throughout the year at 1100 (€6, Spanish only). In summer there may be English-language tours available. Otherwise, the tourist office can provide a list of English-speaking official guides.

> ‡ *Opening hours for Salamanca's monuments change frequently; it's best to get a sheet listing them from the tourist office, who should have their fingers on the pulse of the chaos.*

# Background

Salamanca's history is tied to that of its university (see box, page 259), but the town itself was founded in pre-Roman times. An Iberian settlement, it was taken by Hannibal (pre-elephants) in 218 BC. The Romans later took it over but, as with most cities in these parts, it was abandoned and only resettled during the Reconquista. The university was founded in AD 1218 and rapidly grew to become one of Europe's principal centres of learning. Flourishing particularly under the Catholic Monarchs, the city became an emblem of Imperial Spain; the think-tank behind the monarchy that ruled half the world.

Salamanca's decline in the 18th and 19th centuries mirrored that of its university and indeed the rest of Castilla. The city suffered grievously in the Napoleonic wars; the French general Marmont destroyed most of the university's buildings before his defeat by Wellington just south of the city in 1812. In the 20th century, during the Civil War, Major Doval, a well-known butcher, cracked down fiercely on Republican sympathizers after the coup. The city was the conspirators' command centre for a while, and Franco was declared *caudillo* in a cork grove just outside the town.

In 2002 Salamanca revelled in its status as joint European Cultural Capital, and the city has benefitted from the success and structural improvements.

# Sights

## Plaza Mayor

Among strong competition, Salamanca's main square stands out as the most harmonious plaza in Spain. Built in the 18th century by Alberto Churriguera, it has nothing of the occasional gaudiness of the style to which he and his brother unwittingly lent their names. Paying over the odds for a coffee or a vermouth at one of its outdoor tables is still a superb option; there can be fewer nicer places to sit, especially on a warm summer's evening with storks circling their nests above. Around the perimeter are medallions bearing the heads of various illustrious Spaniards; the more recent additions include Franco (often defaced by paint) and King Juan Carlos ('JC'), and there are plenty of blank ones for new notables.

ⓘ *The university is open Mon-Fri 0930-1300, 1600-1900, Sat 0930-1300, 1600-1830, Sun 1000-1300, €4/€2 students; entrance includes the university museum.*

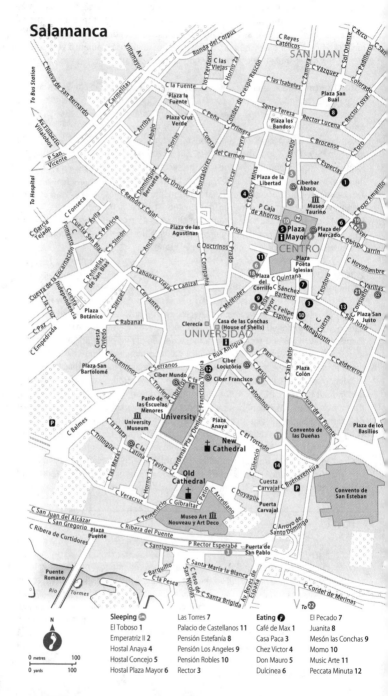

Salamanca

| Sleeping 🛏 | | Eating 🍴 | |
|---|---|---|---|
| El Toboso 1 | Las Torres 7 | Café de Max 1 | El Pecado 7 |
| Emperatriz II 2 | Palacio de Castellanos 11 | Casa Paca 3 | Juanita 8 |
| Hostal Anaya 4 | Pensión Estefanía 8 | Chez Victor 4 | Mesón las Conchas 9 |
| Hostal Concejo 5 | Pensión Los Angeles 9 | Don Mauro 5 | Momo 10 |
| Hostal Plaza Mayor 6 | Pensión Robles 10 | Dulcinea 6 | Music Arte 11 |
| | Rector 3 | | Peccata Minuta 12 |

Rúa Mayor links the plaza with the cathedral and the old buildings of the university. It's lined with restaurants that take over the street with tables for pleasant overeating and drinking in the summer sun. On the right about halfway down is the distinctive **Casa de las Conchas** (House of Shells), named for the 400-odd carved scallop shells of its façades. Now a library (with occasional exhibitions), its nicest feature is the courtyard, graced by an elegantly intricate balcony and decorated with well-carved lions and shields. Opposite the Casa de las Conchas is the **Clerecía**, a Jesuit college founded in the early 17th century by Felipe III – a plaque commemorates the event. An imposing Baroque cloister can be visited to the right of the church entrance.

Leave the Clerecía on your right and take the second left to reach the **Patio de las Escuelas**, a small square surrounded by beautiful university buildings. In the centre stands Fray Luis de León (see box, page 259). He faces the edifice where he once lectured, the main **university** building. Its incredible façade is an amazing example of what master masons could achieve with soft Salamanca sandstone. The key for generations of students and visitors has been to spot the frog; if you manage to do it unguided, you are eligible for a range of benefits: good exam results, luck in love and more. If you don't need any of these and want some help, see the note on the following page. It's rather underwhelming if you've just spent a couple of hours searching it out.

The interior of the building, which is dominated by a mighty cypress, is interesting, but not nearly as impressive, and feels positively stark after the exuberant exterior. There are several impressively worked ceilings inside. The old halls radiate around the courtyard; the largest, the Paraninfo, is hung with Flemish tapestries. One of the halls is preserved as it was in the days when Fray Luis lectured here, with narrow wooden benches, while upstairs, the impressive library is a beautiful space, with ornate wooden shelves lined with thousands of ancient texts; these days you can only peer from the entrance, however. Fray Luis' remains are in the chapel.

The **university museum** is housed around a patio on the other side of the square, the Escuelas Menores. The patio is attractively grassed behind its Plateresque portal. The arches, looking a little like

Castilla y León Salamanca

devils' horns, are typical of Salamanca, an exuberant innovation of the 15th century. There's a reasonable collection of paintings and sculptures, the best by foreign artists resident in Salamanca in its glory years, but the highlight is the remaining part of the fresco ceiling painted by Fernando Gallego. It illustrates the signs of the Zodiac and various constellations; a *mudéjar* ceiling in one of the rooms for temporary exhibits is also well worth a peek.

## Cathedrals

Unusually for Spain, Salamanca's **Catedral Nueva** (new cathedral) ⓘ *Mon-Sat 0900-1300, 1600-1800 (2000 summer), Sun 0900-1300, free; cathedral tower daily 1000-1730, €2.50*, is built alongside, rather than on top of, its Romanesque predecessor. It's a massive affair that dominates the city's skyline from most angles. While the later tower is unimpressively ostentatious, the western façade is superb; a masterpiece of late Gothic stonework, with the transition into Plateresque very visible. It is the sheer number of statues and motifs that amazes, more than the power of any particular scene. The central figure is of the Crucifixion, flanked by Saints Peter and Paul. Around the corner to the left, the façade facing the Plaza de Anaya is also excellent. The door is named Puerta de las Palmas for the relief carving of Jesus entering Jerusalem on Palm Sunday, but take a look at the archivolts on the left-hand side; an astronaut and an imp with a large ice-cream are entertaining recent additions.

Inside, the new cathedral impresses more by its lofty lines than its subtlety. It's a mixture of styles, mostly in transitional Gothic with star vaulting and colourful, high Renaissance lantern. The *coro* is almost completely enclosed; the stalls were carved in walnut by the Churriguera brothers. At the back, in a *capilla* of the squared apse, the bronze figure of the *Cristo de las Batallas* is said to have been carried into war by the Cid. In another chapel is the grisly dried hand of Julián Rodríguez Sánchez, a Salamancan priest murdered in the Civil War, and beatified in 2001. The cathedral tower has been recently restored and offers an exhibition of medieval documents and a terrace with a fine city view.

The **Cathedral Vieja** ⓘ *Mon-Sat 1000-1230, 1600-1730 (1930 in summer), Sun 1000-1230, €3.50*, is accessed from inside the new one. It's a much smaller, more intimate space. It dates mostly from the 12th century; while the design is Romanesque, the pointed arches anticipate the later Gothic styles. On the wall by the entrance are wall paintings from the early 17th century; they depict miracles attributed to the *Cristo de las Batallas* figurine. The *retablo* is superb, a colourful ensemble of 53 panels mostly depicting the life of Christ. Above, a good *Last Judgement* sees the damned getting herded into the maw of a hake-like monster. In the transepts are some excellent coloured tombs, one with its own vaulted ribs.

Around the cloister are several interesting chambers. The Capilla de Santa Bárbara is where, until 1843, the rector of the university was sworn in. It was also where the students used to take their final exams; if they failed, it was straight across the cloister and out via the opposite door, and thence no doubt to the nearest boozer.

## Convents

The **Convento de San Esteban** ⓘ *Mon and Tue 1600-1830 (2000 in spring and summer), Wed-Sat 0900-1300, 1600-1830 (2000 in spring and summer), Sun 0900-1300, €1.50*, not far from the cathedrals, is slightly cheerless but worth visiting. Its ornate Plateresque façade depicts the stoning of Esteban himself (St Stephen); the door itself is also attractive. Entry to the church is via the high cloister, which has quadruple arches. The top deck, floored with boards, is the nicest bit; it would cry out for a café-bar if it weren't in a monastery. There's a small museum with various

⬤ *The frog is on the right pilaster; at the top of the second tier you'll see three skulls; the frog*
⬤ *perches on the left-hand one.*

# Salamanca University and Fray Luis de León

Founded in 1218, Salamanca is the second-oldest university in Spain (after Palencia). The patronage of kings allowed it to grow rapidly; in 1255 it was named by the Pope as pre-eminent in Europe, alongside Paris, Oxford and Bologna. It was the brains behind the Golden Age of Imperial Spain; its *Colegios Mayores*, or four Great Colleges, supplied a constant stream of Spain's most distinguished thinkers, and exerted plenty of undue political influence to get their own graduates appointed to high positions. The university had in excess of 10,000 students in its pomp and was forward thinking, with a strong scientific tradition and a female professor as early as the late 15th century.

Spain's closed-door policy to Protestant thinkers was always going to have a bad effect, and Salamanca declined in the 18th century; Newton and Descartes were considered unimportant, the chair of mathematics was vacant for decades, and theologians debated what language was spoken by the angels. The Peninsular War had a terrible effect too; French troops demolished most of the university's colleges. But the university is thriving again: although not among Spain's elite, it has a good reputation for several disciplines, and the student atmosphere is bolstered by large numbers of foreigners who come to the beautiful city to learn Spanish.

Among many notable teachers that have taught at Salamanca, two stand out; Miguel de Unamuno (see box, page 96), and Fray Luis de León. Born to Jewish *conversos* (converts), at 14 the latter came to Salamanca to study law; he soon moved into theology, becoming a monk of the Augustinian order. In 1560 he was appointed to the chair of theology. Well versed in Hebrew, Fray Luis continued to use Hebrew texts as the basis of his Biblical teaching; he was responsible for many translations of the testaments and scriptures from that language into Spanish. Enemies and anti-Semites saw these actions as being in defiance of the Council of Trent, and on March 27, 1572 Fray Luis was arrested mid-lecture by the Inquisition and imprisoned in Valladolid, where he was charged with disrespect and imprudence. After a five-year trial he was sentenced to torture by the rack; the punishment was, however, revoked. Returning to Salamanca, he famously began his first lecture to a crowded room with *Dicebamus hesterna die* (As we were saying yesterday…). He maintained his firm stance, and got into fresh trouble with the Inquisition five years later. He was made provincial of the Augustinians and died in 1591.

Apart from his theological writings, he was an excellent poet, one of the finest in Spain's history. His verses bring out the deep feelings of a man better known as having been severe and sardonic, understandably, given the religious hypocrisy that he struggled against.

Filipino saints, a silver reliquary in the shape of a *sombrero*, and a couple of amazing early Bibles. One of them, dating from the late 13th century or so, is so perfect it's almost impossible to believe that it was handwritten.

The church is dominated by its *retablo*, a work of José Churriguera. A massive 30 m by 14 m, it's exuberantly over the top, but more elegant than some of the style's later examples.

Opposite, the **Convento de las Dueñas** ⓘ *daily 1200-1245 (1030-1300 summer), 1630-1730, €1.50*, also houses Dominicans, this time in the shape of nuns who do a popular line in almond cakes. The irregular-shaped cloister is open for visits and is beautiful, with views of the cathedral in the background. Dating from the first half of the 16th century, its lower floor is fairly simple compared with the top level, decorated with busts and shields, as well as ornate capitals of doomed souls and beasts.

## Museo Art Nouveau y Art Deco

ⓘ *C Gibraltar 14, T923 121 425, www.museocasalis.org, Apr to mid-Oct Tue-Fri 1100-1400, 1700-2100, Sat and Sun 1100-2100, mid-Oct to Mar Tue-Fri 1100-1400, 1600-1900, Sat and Sun 1100-2000, €3.*

If you fancy a break from sandstone and Plateresque, head for the Museo Art Nouveau y Art Deco. It's superbly housed in the **Casa Lis**, an art nouveau *palacio* built for a wealthy Salamancan industrialist; there's a particularly good view of the building from the riverbank. The collection of pieces is very good; you're sure to find something you love and something you can't stand. Representative of the traditions of many countries, there are porcelains, sculpture, glassware, ceramics, Fabergé jewelling and dolls. The stained-glass ceiling is particularly impressive too.

Nearby, check out the pretty **Puente Romano**, a bridge over the Tormes with Roman origins.

## ● Sleeping

**Salamanca** *p254, map p256*
Salamanca's traditional old **Gran Hotel** has closed, and is unlikely to re-open as a hotel. Luckily, the city is replete with other choices; there are well over 100 places to lay your head.
**L NH Palacio de Castellanos**, C San Pablo 58, T923 261 818, www.nh-hotels.com. This imposing hotel occupies what was once a late 15th-century palace, although much of what remains dates from the 19th century. The rooms have all the conveniences of a business hotel but considerably more charm than most, with wrought-iron balconies, a pillow menu, video games and more.
**AL Hotel Rector**, Paseo Rector Esperabé 10, T923 218 482, www.hotelrector.com. An excellent option near the river, this small and exclusive hotel is in a beautiful sandstone *palacio*. Its very plush inside, with leather sofas, art-nouveau glass and elegant wooden furniture; the rooms are decorated with a lighter touch, with olive-wood bedheads and large windows admitting plenty of natural light. Service is excellent. Book ahead. Parking available.
**AL-B Hotel Las Torres**, C Concejo 4, T923 212 100, www.hthoteles.com. Some rooms in this sensitively refurbished

18th-century building have balconies overlooking the Plaza Mayor. It's one of a new generation of hotels, offering smart facilities such as internet access, hydromassage showers and, in the best rooms, PC with flat-screen monitor and exercise bike. There's free internet and business facilities for guests and specially adapted rooms for families and for the disabled. The rates are on a sliding scale and vary considerably; it's best to book over the internet to see what's on offer.
**B Hostal Concejo**, Plaza de la Libertad 1, T923 214 737, www.hconcejo.com. Another well-placed option, this friendly *hostal* has faultless modern rooms around the corner from the Plaza Mayor. It's in the pedestrian zone and has been recently renovated.
**C Hostal Plaza Mayor**, Plaza Corrillo 19, T923 262 020, hostalplazamayor@ hotmail.com. Though not quite on the square that it's named after, it's only a few paces away. You pay a little for the location, but the rooms are compact, modern and comfortable, although slightly in need of a bit of tender loving care.
**C Hotel El Toboso**, C Clavel 7, T923 271 462, F923 271 464. Value-packed choice in the heart of things, with very pleasing decor in

an attractive stone building. The prices are very good; the double rooms are spacious and light and the apartments (sleeping 3 or 5) are especially attractive for a family stay and priced very reasonably.

**C Hotel Emperatriz II**, Rúa Mayor 18, T923 219 156. Though the rooms can get stuffy in summer, this hotel couldn't be better placed, on the main pedestrian street through the old centre. There's not a lot of luxury, but the hotel does have its own garage, a useful asset in this part of town, although some manoeuvering around café tables may be required.

**D Hostal Anaya**, C Jesús 18, T923 271 773. A very central option, with attractive and spacious modern rooms with sparklingly clean en suite and friendly management. They can provide breakfast too, and have good-value rooms for 3 or 4.

**E Pensión Los Angeles**, Plaza Mayor 10, T923 218 166. The nicest rooms in this decent spot overlook the Plaza Mayor, but there are also cheap no-frills options (**F**) often booked out by foreign students. The better rooms come with a small but adequate en suite bathroom.

**F Pensión Estefanía**, C Jesús 3, T923 217 372. A very cheap and handy option in the centre of Salamanca. Though the welcome is hardly effusive, the rooms are good value, at least in summer. In winter, you might like to consider elsewhere, as there's no heating. Bathrooms are shared but clean.

**F Pensión Robles**, Plaza Mayor 20, T923 213 197. The best reason to stay at this basic but clean place is that some of its rooms overlook the beautiful plaza, but the price is good too. It's regularly booked out.

## ❷ Eating

**Salamanca** *p254, map p256*
Salamanca abounds in cheap places to eat. Some of the places around the Plaza Mayor and Rúa Mayor are a bit tourist-trappy, but it's hard to beat their terraces for alfresco dining.

**♔♔♔ Chez Victor**, C Espoz y Mina 26, T923 213 123. Surprisingly reasonably priced for its lofty reputation, this spot deals in rich creations from traditional Spanish

ingredients with a definite Gallic influence. Closed Sun evenings and Mon.

**♔♔♔ El Pecado**, Plaza Poeta Iglesias 12, T923 266 558. One of the city's best restaurants, this upstairs restaurant brings back a touch of colour and fun into modern design. Zebra-stripes, bookshelves and rich red walls live up to the name (Sin), but there's substance here in abundance. The menu is startlingly original and innovative; try the turbot with onion ice cream. The *menú del día* is the price-conscious way to appreciate its charms at €20.

**♔♔♔ Victor Gutiérrez**, C San Pablo 82, T923 262 975. A smart urban modern restaurant with nouvelle Spanish cuisine as well as heartier, traditional fare.

**♔♔ Casa Paca**, Plaza del Peso 10, T923 218 993. Big portions of hearty Castilian dishes are this attentive restaurant's stock in trade. A full feed of roast goat or pig costs €14-16, and there's a great wine list. Out front is a historic tapas bar, with an awe-inspiring array of scrumptious *pinchos*, theatre seats and wine-based decor.

**♔♔ Don Mauro**, Plaza Mayor 19, T923 281 487. A quality modern restaurant with a small but attractive selection of meats and salads, this is also a popular spot for a smart evening coffee or drink among older *salmantinos*. There's an excellent duck and corn salad (*canónigo*) for €12, and exquisite *lubina al sal* (whole sea bass baked in salt for 2).

**♔♔ Mesón Las Conchas**, Rúa Mayor 16, T923 212 167. A top choice for a main-street bite, with excellent *raciones* and tasty *pinchos* to accompany a drink, as well as fuller choices. You can eat in the cheery upstairs dining room or out on the street. There's a wide choice, from salads and roasts to a delicately flavoured duck with honey glaze. It's all good value, especially considering its location.

**♔♔ Momo**, C San Pablo , T923 280 798. A stylish modern restaurant and bar with some excellent classy *pinchos* and a range of innovative modern Castilian cuisine downstairs. The *menú del día* is good for €12; otherwise mains are €8-15. There's plenty of vegetarian choice. It's also a good spot for breakfast, opening at 0800.

**♔♔ Sakana**, C San Justo 9, T923 218 619. Rare for Northern Spain, this is a Japanese restaurant, pretty good too, although often booked out by tourist groups. The carpaccio-like beef *tataki* is very tasty (€13.50), while the *menú de degustación* for 2 is a snip at €33. The decor is modern but typically thoughtful, with bamboo screens and hessian-clad walls.

**Dulcinea**, C Pozo Amarillo 5, T923 217 843. Although it doesn't look up to much from the outside, this is a very reliable and likeable little place far from the tourist trail but only a short step from the Plaza Mayor. The fare is traditional for the region; a simple range of stews and meat dishes. Best value is at lunchtime, when there's a €9 *menú del día*; the *pollo al ajillo* (chicken pieces sizzled in garlic) is excellent if it's on.

**Peccata Minuta**, C Franciso Vitoria 3, T923 123 447. A very pleasant café/restaurant with a range of good tapas and *raciones* – the prawns are particularly good – as well as friendly service and a generous line in rum 'n' Cokes.

### Cafés

**Café de Max**, C Toro 22. A nice spot for breakfast in a little courtyard off C Toro. It's cheerful but relatively quiet, and popular with students. There's a selection of imported beers and simple tapas too.

**Juanita**, Plaza de San Bual 21. Situated on an engagingly dog-legged plaza, this café features warm, decadently ornate Baroque decor in an intimate basement setting. These contrive to make it one of Salamanca's most loveable and atmospheric spots.

**Music Arte**, Plaza Corrillo 20. An excellent place for breakfast, a friendly and stylish café near Plaza Mayor.

## ⊕ Bars and clubs

**Salamanca** *p254, map p256*
When the students are in town, Salamanca's nightlife can kick off any night of the week. *Lugares* is a free monthly paper with listings of events and what's going on in bars and clubs; you can pick it up in cafés. There's a zone of student bars around C Librerías and

C La Latina, but the main night owl area is on Gran Vía and around; Plaza de Bretón and C Varillas have a high concentration of spots.

**De Laval Genovés**, C San Justo 27. One of Salamanca's best gay choices, with a spacious interior and cool decor that has earned it the nickname 'El Submarino'. It's in the heart of the Salamanca bar zone.

**El Barco**, Puente Principe de Asturias s/n. It's hard to beat dancing on a boat at 0900. Moored in the river near the Puente Principe de Asturias bridge, this goes late from Thu-Sat and has a pretty happy atmosp here indeed. There are sometimes live bands at weekends.

**El Savor**, C San Justo 28, T923 268 576. This large and stylish bar packs out with people keen on dancing to salsa and other Latin American rhythms. It's a fun, uninhibited sort of place; if you want to get your feet moving right, there are free dancing classes at 2300 on Thu and Fri.

**Gaia**, Plaza Comillo 18. A cellar bar just off the Plaza Mayor with frequent live music and a devoted if slightly serious student crowd.

**Potemkin**, C Consuelo 2, T923 219 620. Another late opener in the Salamanca zone with heavyish rock music played loud. It's big, spacious and has a great atmosphere, particularly when there's a live band playing. Popular with people from all walks.

**Tío Vivo**, C Clavel 3, www.cafebartio vivo.com. This intriguing bar is packed with curios; there's everything from machine guns and army uniforms to carousel horses, giving it a slightly macabre and dreamlike quality. It's a great place with a good atmosphere; there are live shows and live music several days a week and excllent G&Ts.

## ⊕ Entertainment

**Salamanca** *p254, map p256*
**Multicines Salamanca**, C Vázquez Coronado, T923 266 468. A convenient central cinema.
**Teatro Liceo**, Plaza de Liceo s/n, T923 272 290. A modernized theatre near the Plaza Mayor, with occasional flamenco and other performances.

## ❀ Festivals and events

**Salamanca** *p254, map p256*
**7 Sep** Salamanca's major **fiesta** is a 2- week binge of drinks, bullfights and fireworks.

There always seems to be some type of fiesta at other times; student faculties combine to make sure there's rarely a dull moment.

## ○ Shopping

**Salamanca** *p254, map p256*
**Bookshops**
**Librería Cervantes**, Plaza de Santa Eulalia s/n, is one of many bookshops in this university city.

**Food**
A good thing to buy in Salamanca is ham. The main shopping streets are north of the Plaza Mayor, along C Toro and C Zamora.

A convenient, if slightly overpriced, ham shop is **La Despensa**, Rúa Mayor 23, which has a good selection of all things piggy.

The market just below the Plaza Mayor is a good spot for food shopping.

## ❂ Transport

**Salamanca** *p254, map p256*
**Air**
Salamanca's airport is 15 km east of town on the Avila road. Its only flight at the time of writing is a domestic connection to **Barcelona** (but with the growth of the budget sector, it's a possible destination); if you're coming from Madrid you'll have to take the bus. A taxi to or from the airport to the centre costs €15.

**Bus**
The bus station is west of town along Av Filiberto Villalobos, T923 236 717. Within the province, there are buses roughly hourly to **Alba de Tormes**, **Béjar** and **Ciudad Rodrigo**, among other destinations.

Further flung destinations include **Avila** (4-6 weekdays, 2 at weekends), **Madrid** hourly, **Oviedo/Gijón** (4-5 daily, 4 hrs 30 mins-5 hrs, €17.44), **León** (4 daily), **Santiago** (2 daily, 6 hrs, €21.29), **Bilbao** (3 daily, 6 hrs, €22.44), **Sevilla** (5 daily, 8 hrs,

€26.80), **Zaragoza/ Barcelona** (2 daily), **Zamora** (more than hourly), **Valladolid** (6 daily), and **Cáceres** (10 daily, €12.08, 3 hrs 30 mins). There's also a daily bus to **Porto** in Portugal (5 hrs 30 mins, €24) with a connection to Lisboa (9 hrs, €33).

**Taxi**
For local taxis, call T923 250 000.

**Train**
The train station, T902 240 202, is northeast of town along Av de la Estación. There's a (very) early morning train to **Lisbon** (6 hrs) and **Porto**, 4 daily to **Burgos** (2 hrs 30 mins-4 hrs, from €18.50), 7 to **Avila** (1 hr, €7.40), and 9 to **Valladolid** (1 hr 30 mins, from €5.75). There are 6 daily trains to **Madrid** (2 hrs 30 mins, €14.55).

## ❶ Directory

**Salamanca** *p254, map p256*
**Internet** There seems to be an internet café on every corner in Salamanca. **Ciber Locutório Jesús**, C Jesús 10, T923 281 571, has good rates for international calls and decent internet access at €1.20 per hr; **Ciberbar Abaco**, C Zamora 7, has access at €1.20 per hr; **Ciber Los Angeles**, Plaza Mayor 11, is handy, but slow; **Ciber Francisco**, C Francisco Vitoria 5, is not the fastest, but is handily close to the cathedral; **Ciber Anuario**, C La Latina 8, is open 0900-0100, from €1 per hr;. **Ciber Mundo**, C Librerías 20, Olver, C Varillas 24, €1 per hr. **Language schools** Apart from the university itself, which has a highly regarded Spanish-language programme, there are several smaller schools: **Letra Hispánica**, C Librerías 28, www.letrahispanica.com, has a reasonable reputation. **Laundry** Coin Laundry, C Azafranal 26, is a self-service laundromat in an arcade. **Medical services** Hospital Clínico, Paseo de San Vicente 58, T923 291 100. **Police** Call T092 or T923 194 433. The handiest police station is on the Plaza Mayor. **Post office** The main post office is on Gran Vía 25 near Plaza de la Constitución.

# Burgos → *Phone code: 947. Colour map 5, A2. Population: 172,421. Altitude: 860 m.*

*"They have very good houses and live very comfortably, and they are the most courteous people I have come across in Spain." Andres Navagero, 1526*

The Venetian traveller's comment on 16th-century Burgos could equally apply today to the city where courtesy and courtliness still rule the roost. Formerly an important and prosperous trading town, Burgos achieved infamy as the seat of Franco's Civil War junta and is still a sober and reactionary town, the heartland of Castilian conservatism.

Burgos' collection of superb Gothic buildings and sculpture, as well as its position on the Camino de Santiago, make it a popular destination, but the city copes well with the summer influx. Just don't come for gentle spring sunshine; Burgos is known throughout Spain as a chilly city, epitome of the saying 'nueve meses de invierno, tres meses de infierno' *(nine months of winter, three months of hell)*. The chills can be banished with the traditionally hearty local cuisine. → *For Sleeping, Eating and other listings, see pages 270-272.*

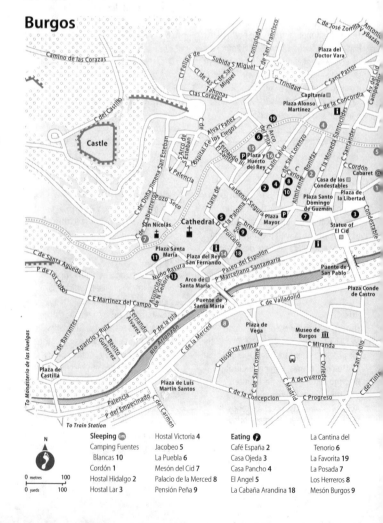

# Burgos

| | | | |
|---|---|---|---|
| **Sleeping** | Hostal Victoria **4** | **Eating** | La Cantina del |
| Camping Fuentes | Jacobeo **5** | Café España **2** | Tenorio **6** |
| Blancas **10** | La Puebla **6** | Casa Ojeda **3** | La Favorita **19** |
| Cordón **1** | Mesón del Cid **7** | Casa Pancho **4** | La Posada **7** |
| Hostal Hidalgo **2** | Palacio de la Merced **8** | El Angel **5** | Los Herreros **8** |
| Hostal Lar **3** | Pensión Peña **9** | La Cabaña Arandina **18** | Mesón Burgos **9** |

**Getting there** Burgos is roughly in the centre of Northern Spain and easily accessed from most parts of the country by bus or train. There are regular services from Madrid and the Basque country as well as Santander and all Castilian towns. ▸▸*See also Transport, page 272.*

**Getting around** As usual, the old centre is fairly compact, but you may want to use the local bus service to access a couple of the outlying monasteries and the campsite.

**Best time to visit** Burgos has a fairly unpleasant climate with short hot summers and long cold winters (it often snows) punctuated by the biting wind that 'won't blow out a candle but will kill a man'. The most moderate weather will be found in May, June and September.

**Tourist information** The handiest office is across from the cathedral on **Plaza del Rey San Fernando** ① *daily 1000-2000*; there's one on **Paseo Espolón** ① *Mon-Sat 1000-1400, 1700-2000, Sun 1000-1400*, and also one on **Plaza Alonso Martínez** ① *daily 0900- 1400, 1700-2000*. There are **city tours** and a rather tacky **tourist train** ① *daily in summer and at weekends Oct-Jun, €2.50*, which rolls around the sights, leaving from outside the cathedral square tourist office.

**BurgosCard** is a potential money-saver; bought at the cathedral or tourist offices, it allows free entry to all of the monuments, a guided visit to Atapuerca and free travel on both the tourist train and the **Burgos Vision** bus, which does a circular hop-on hop-off route around the city. It costs €10 for one day or €16 for two days.

## Background
Burgos is comfortably the oldest city in Europe, if you count the nearby cave-dwellers from Atapuerca, who were around 500,000 years ago. That aside, the city's effective foundation was in the late ninth century, when it was resettled during the Reconquista. Further honours soon followed; it was named capital of Castilla y León as early as the 11th century.

The city's position at the northern centre of the Castilian plain, near the coastal mountain passes, made it a crucial point for the export of goods. Burgos flourished, becoming a wealthy city of merchants and beasts of burden; in the 16th century its mule population often exceeded the human one, as bigger and bigger convoys of wool made their way over the mountains and by ship to Flanders.

Mesón La
    Amarilla **10**
Mesón La Cueva **11**
Mesón San
    Lesmes **12**
Rincón de España **13**

**Bars & clubs** 🎵
Fox Tavern **14**
La Negra
    Candela **15**
Mondrian **16**
Ram Jam Club **17**

···· Camino de Santiago

*Castilla y León* Burgos

The Consulado de Burgos, a powerful guildlike body, was created to administer trade, and succeeded in establishing a virtual monopoly; Burgos became one of three great 16th-century trading cities, along with Sevilla and Medina del Campo. The strife in Flanders hit the city hard, though, and other towns broke into the market. Burgos' population declined by 75 per cent in the first half of the 17th century, and the city lapsed into the role of genteel provincial capital, apart from a brief and bloody interlude. During the Civil War the Nationalist *junta* was established here; the city had shown its credentials with a series of atrocities committed on Republicans after the rising.

# Sights

## Cathedral
ⓘ *The cathedral and museum are open summer Mon-Sat 0930-1915, Sun 0930-1500, 1530-1915, winter daily 1000-1315, 1600-1845, €3, €1 for pilgrims. Some of the chapels are only accessible on guided tours; the guides are independent and prices vary. Before entering the cathedral, you must buy a ticket in the reception office on the square below.*

Burgos' famed cathedral is a remarkable Gothic edifice whose high hollow spires rise over the city. Its beauty is an austere and solemn one, and the technical excellence of its stonework can only be admired. It also houses a collection of significant artwork.

The current structure was begun in 1221 over an earlier church by Fernando III and his Germanic wife, Beatrice of Swabia, with the bishop Maurice overseeing things. Beatrice brought him with her from Swabia, and the Northern influence didn't stop there; Gil and Diego de Siloé, the top sculptors who are responsible for many masterpieces inside and throughout the province, originated from those parts, while the towers were designed by master builder Hans of Cologne, a city whose cathedral bears some resemblance to this.

Entering through the western door, under the spires (only completed in the 19th century), one of the strangest sights is in the chapel to the right. It's reserved for private prayer, but the figure you see through the glass is the **Christ of Burgos**. Made from buffalo hide and sporting a head of real hair, the crucified Jesus wears a green skirt and looks a little the worse for wear. The limbs are movable, no doubt to impress the 14th-century faithful with a few tricks; apparently the Christ was once so lifelike that folk thought the fingernails had to be clipped weekly. Opposite, high on the wall, the strange figure of Papamoscas strikes the hours, the closest thing to levity in this serious building.

Like those of many Spanish cathedrals, the **Choir** is closed off, which spoils any long perspective views. Once inside, admire the Renaissance main *retablo* depicting scenes from the life of the Virgin. Underfoot at the crossing are the bones of El Cid and his wife Doña Jimena, underwhelmingly marked by a simple slab. The remains were only transferred here in 1927 after being reclaimed from the French, who had taken them from the monastery of San Pedro de Cardeña. They lie under the large octagonal tower, an elaborate 16th-century add-on. The choir itself is incredibly elegant and intricate – you could spend hours examining the carved wooden images; Bishop Maurice's tomb is in the centre of it.

✱ *The cathedral is the main reason many people visit Burgos.*

There's a wealth of side chapels, many unfortunately shielded by grilles, although if an attendant is around they are happy to open them up. The chapels date from different architectural periods; some of the Renaissance ones feature stunningly fine stonework around the doorways. The **Capilla de Santa Teresa** sports a riotous Churrigueresque ceiling, while the soaring late Gothic *retablo* in the **Capilla de Santa Ana** and the painted Romanesque tombs in the **Capilla de San Nicolás** are also striking.

The grandest, however, is at the very far end of the apse, the **Capilla de los Condestables**. The Velasco family, hereditary Constables of Castilla, were immensely influential in their time, and one of the most powerful, Don Pedro Fernández, is entombed here with his wife. Few kings have lain in a more elaborate setting, with a high vaulted roof, fabulous stonework and three *retablos*, the most ornate of which, the central one, depicts the purification of Mary. The alabaster figures on the sepulchre itself are by another German, Simon of Cologne, and his son. The room is oddly asymmetrical and is a memorable shrine to earthly power and heraldry. Just outside, around the ambulatory, a series of sensitive alabaster panels depicts Biblical scenes.

The **museum**, set around the top of the two-tiered tomb-lined cloister, is reasonably interesting. After passing through the Baroque sacristy, the first stop is the chapterhouse, where, high on the wall, hangs a coffer that belonged to the Cid; possibly the one that was involved in a grubby little deed of his, where he sneakily repaid some Jews with a coffer of sand, rather than the gold that he owed them. In the adjacent chamber is a pretty red *mudéjar* ceiling. A 10th-century Visigothic Bible is the highlight of the next room, as well as the Cid's marriage contract, the so-called *Letter of Arras*. Finally, the museum has an excellent collection of well-restored 15th-century Flemish paintings. They are full of life and action – the mob mentality of the Crucifixion is well portrayed. There are several reliquaries holding various bits of saints (including Thomas Becket) and nothing less than a spine from the crown of thorns. A *retablo* depicts Santiago in Moor-slaying mode.

## Iglesia de San Nicolás

ⓘ *Jun-Sep Mon-Sat 1100-1300, 1700-1900, €1; free Mon; currently only open before and after evening Mass in winter.*

This small church above the cathedral has a superb *retablo*, a virtuoso sculptural work, probably by Simon and Francis of Cologne. It's a bit like looking at a portrait of a city, or a theatre audience, so many figures seem to be depicted in different sections. The main scene at the top is Mary surrounded by a 360-degree choir of angels. The stonework is superb throughout; have a look for the ship's rigging, a handy piece of chiselling to say the least. There's also a good painting of the *Last Judgement* in the church, an early 16th-century Flemish work, only recently rediscovered. The demons are the most colourful aspect; one is trying to tip the scales despite being stood on by Saint Michael.

## Around the old town

The old town is entered across one of two main bridges over the pretty Río Arlanzón, linked by a leafy *paseo*. The eastern of the two, the **Puente de San Pablo**, is guarded by an imposing mounted statue of El Cid, looming Batman-like above the traffic, heavy beard flying. The inscription risibly dubs him "a miracle from among the great miracles of the creator". The other, **Puente de Santa María**, approaches the arch of the same name, an impressive if pompous gateway with a statue of a very snooty Carlos V. East of here is the **Plaza Mayor**, which is normally fairly lifeless. The **Casa Consistorial** has marks and dates from two of Burgos' biggest floods; it's hard to believe that the friendly little river could ever make it that high.

❧ *Above the town, a park covers the hilltop and conceals the remains of a castle, which was blown up by the French in the Napoleonic Wars.*

Other interesting buildings in the old centre include the **Casa de los Condestables**, with a massive corded façade. Felipe I died here prematurely; it was also here that the Catholic Monarchs received Columbus after he returned from his second voyage. The ornate neo-Gothic **Capitanía** was the headquarters for the Nationalist *junta* in the Civil War. Still used by the army, the façade bears pompous plaques to the memory of Franco and Mola; the fact that they are still there speaks much about conservative Burgos, where 'the very stones were Nationalist'.

## ⁝ El Cid

Although portrayed as something of a national hero in the 12th-century epic *El Cantar de Mío Cid* (Song of the Cid ), the recorded deeds of Rodrigo Díaz de Vivar actually suggest a degree of ambiguity in the fight for places in the pantheon of Spanish heroes. Born in a village just outside Burgos in AD 1043, El Cid (the Boss) was in fact a mercenary who fought with the Moors if the price was right.

His ability to protect his own interests was recognized even by those who sought to idolize him. The Song of the Cid recounts that on being expelled from Burgos the great man wrapped up his beard to protect it from being pulled by irate citizens angry at his nefarious dealings.

Operating along the border between Christian and Muslim Spain, the Cid was a man of undoubted military guile who was able to combine a zeal for the Reconquista with an equal desire to further his own fortune. The moment when he swindled two innocent Jewish merchants by delivering a chest filled with sand instead of gold is celebrated with gusto in Burgos cathedral where his mortal remains now lie.

Banished by Alfonso VI for double dealing, his military skills proved indispensable and he was re-hired in the fight against the Almoravids. The capture of Valencia in 1094 marked the height of his powers and was an undoubted blow to the Moors. If having his own city wasn't reward enough, the Cid was given the formidable Gormaz castle as a sort of fortified weekend retreat.

By the standards of his own time where the boundaries, both physical and cultural, between Christian and Moorish Spain were flexible, the Cid's actions make perfect sense. It is only later ages, preferring their heroes without ambiguity, that had to gloss over the actual facts. By the time of his death in 1099 the Cid was well on his way to national hero status.

The Cid's horse, Babieca, immortalized in the Charlton Heston film, has her own marked grave in the monastery of San Pedro de Cardeña. The Cid himself was buried here for 600 years until Napoleon's forces , perhaps fearing a re-appearance by the man himself, removed the body to France. He was reburied in Burgos in the 1930s.

Attractively set around the patioed **Casa Miranda** sections of the **Museo de Burgos** ⓘ *Tue-Sat 1000-1400, 1600-1900 (1700-2000 summer), Sun 1000-1400; €1.20*, have prehistoric finds from Atapuerca (see page 270), Roman finds from Clunia, religious painting and sculpture, and some more modern works by Burgalese artists.

## Monasterio de las Huelgas
ⓘ *Tue-Sat 1000-1300, 1545-1730, Sun 1030-1400, €5; buses Nos 5, 7 and 39 run there from Av Valladolid across the river from the old town.*

A 20-minute walk through an upmarket suburb of Burgos, the Monasterio de las Huelgas still harbours some 40 cloistered nuns, heiresses to a long tradition of power. In its day, the convent wielded enormous influence. The monastery was founded by Eleanor of England, daughter of Henry II and Eleanor of Aquitaine, who came to Burgos to marry Alfonso VIII in 1170. The Hammer of the Scots, Edward I, came here to get hitched as well; he married Eleanor, Princess of Castilla, in the monastery in 1254. Las Huelgas originally meant 'the reposes', as the complex was a favourite retreat for the Castilian monarchs. Here they could regain strength, ponder matters of state – and perhaps have a bit on the side; several abbesses of Las Huelgas bore illegitimate children behind the closed doors.

To keep the nuns separate from the public, the church was partitioned in the 16th century, and the naves separated by walls. The public were just left with a small aisle, where the visit starts. In here are a couple of curios: a moving pulpit that enabled the priest to address both the congregation and the separated nuns; and a strange statue of Santiago, sword in hand. Part of the coronation ceremony of the kings of Castilla used to involve them being knighted; as they judged no-one else in the land fit to perform the task, a statue of the saint with moveable arms used to perform the deed; this is probably one of those. There's also a *retablo* by the tireless Diego de Siloé in here.

The real attractions are on the nuns' side of the barricade. The church contains many ornate tombs of princes and other Castilian royals. These were robbed of much of their contents by Napoleon's soldiers. All were opened in 1942 and, to great surprise, an array of superb royal garments remained well preserved 700 years on, as well as some jewellery from the one tomb the French had overlooked. In the central nave are the tombs of Eleanor and Alfonso, who died in the same year. The arms of England and Castilla adorn the exquisite tombs. They lie beneath an ornate Plateresque *retablo* which is topped by a 13th-century crucifixion scene and contains various relics.

Around a large cloister are more treasures; a *mudéjar* door with intricate wooden carving, a Moorish standard captured from the famous battle at Navas de Tolosa in 1212, and a postcard-pretty smaller cloister with amazing carved plasterwork, no doubt Moorish-influenced. For many, the highlight is the display of the clothing found in the tombs: strange, ornate, silken garments embroidered with gold thread. The colours have faded over the centuries, but they remain in top condition, a seldom-seen link with the past that seems to bring the dusty royal names alive.

## Cartuja de Miraflores
① *Currently under restoration, but will still usually be open for visits depending on the nature of the work at the time; check with the tourist office. To get there, catch bus No 26 or 27 from Plaza de España and get off at the Fuente del Prior stop; the monastery is a 5-min walk up a marked side road. Otherwise, it's a 50-min walk through pleasant parkland from the centre of town.*

This former hunting lodge is another important Burgos monastery, also still functioning, populated by silent Carthusians. Juan II de Castilla, father of Isabel (the Catholic Monarch), started the conversion and his daughter finished it. Like so much in Burgos, it was the work of a German, Hans of Cologne. Inside, the late-Gothic design is elegant, with elaborate vaulting, and stained glass from Flanders depicting the life of Christ. The wooden choir stalls are carved with incredible delicacy, but attention is soon drawn by the superb alabaster work of the *retablo* and the tombs that lie before it. These are all designed by Gil de Siloé, the Gothic master and they are the triumphant expression of genius. The central tomb is star-shaped, and was commissioned by Isabel for her parents; at the side of the chamber rests her brother Alonso, heir to the Castilian throne until his death at the age of 14. The *retablo* centres on the crucifixion, with many saints in attendance. The sculptural treatment is beautiful, expressing emotion and sentiment through stone. Equally striking is the sheer level of detail in the works; a casual visitor could spend weeks trying to decode the symbols and layers of meaning.

## Monasterio de San Pedro de Cardeña
① *Tue-Sat 1000-1300, 1600-1830, Sun 1200-1400, 1600-1800; wait in the church for a monk to appear; admission by donation; accommodation is available at the monastery.*

Close to the city, at a distance of some 10 km, the Monasterio de San Pedro de Cardeña is worth a visit, especially for those with an interest in the Cid. The first point of interest is to one side, in front of the monastery, where a gravestone marks the supposed burial site of the Cid's legendary mare, Babieca. The monastery has a community of 24 Cistercians; a monk will show you around the church, most of which dates from the 15th century. In a side chapel is an ornate tomb raised (much later) over the spot where the man and his wife were buried until Napoleon's troops nicked the bones in the 19th century; they were reclaimed and buried in Burgos cathedral. The *mudéjar* cloister dates from the 10th century and is the most impressive feature of the building, along with a late Gothic doorway in the *sala capitular*.

## Atapuerca

ⓘ *Ibeas is 13 km east of Burgos on the N120; the site is 3 km north of here. T947 421 462, www.paleorama.es; in Jul and Aug tours leave 4-6 times daily, some from the site itself, others from the hall on the main road in Ibeas. At other times you can arrange visits at weekends by prior appointment.*

Some 13 km east of Burgos, an unremarkable series of rocky hills were the site of some incredibly significant palaeontological finds. The remains of *homo heidelbergensis* were discovered here; dating has placed the bones from 500,000 to 200,000 years old. It's a crucial link in the study of hominid evolution; Neanderthals seemed to evolve directly from these Heidelbergers, but there's not a huge amount to see. There's a small hall displaying some of the finds from the nearby village of **Ibeas**, and some walkways around the excavation sites, which are accessed by guided tour.

## ● Sleeping

**Burgos** *p264, map p264*
**LL Palacio de la Merced**, C La Merced 13, T947 479 900, www.nh-hoteles.com. Attractively set in a 16th-century *palacio*, this hotel successfully blends minimalist, modern design into the old building, whose most charming feature is its cloister in Isabelline Gothic style. The rooms are comfortable and attractively decked out in wood. Recommended.

**L Hotel Mesón del Cid**, Plaza Santa María 8, T947 208 715, www.mesondelcid.es. Superbly located opposite the cathedral, this hotel and restaurant is an excellent place to stay, with spacious, quiet and modern rooms and helpful staff. There are larger rooms available for families.

**AL Hotel Cordón**, C La Puebla 6, T947 265 000, www.hotelcordon.com. This is a reasonable option in the centre, geared up for business travellers. There's nothing particularly stunning about the rooms, but there are very reasonable weekend rates if you book ahead.

**A Hotel La Puebla**, C La Puebla 20, T947 200 011, www.hotellapuebla.com. An intimate new hotel in the centre of Burgos with classy modern design, good facilities, and comfortable furnishings. Parking available for €7.

**B-C Jacobeo**, C San Juan 24, T947 260 102, hoteljacobeo@totalburgos.com. This smallish central hotel is well managed and features good en suite rooms with comfortable new

beds in a pretty old building. It's much better value outside of the summer months.

**D Hostal Lar**, C Cardenal Benlloch 1, T947 209 655, F947 209 655. This quiet and decent place have well-priced en suite rooms with TV and telephone. The management is friendly; the only problem is that the bathrooms are tiny.

**E Hostal Victoria**, C San Juan 3, T947 201 542. A good choice with friendly management, this *hostal* is central and relatively quiet, and the rooms with shared bath are comfortable and fairly spacious.

**F Hostal Hidalgo**, C Almirante Bonifaz 14, T947 203 481. A nice quiet *pensión* on a pedestrian street. It's clean, neat and friendly; the rooms are heated and the shared bathrooms are good.

**F Pensión Peña**, C Puebla 18, T947 206 323. An excellent cheapie, well located and maintained on a pedestrian street. The rooms are heated and have good shared bathrooms. It's often full, however, so don't hold your breath.

### Camping
**Camping Fuentes Blancas**, Ctra Burgos-Cartuja s/n, T947 486 016, F947 486 016. A well situated campsite in woody riverside parkland about 4 km from the centre. Take bus No 26 or 27 from Plaza de España (not terribly frequent); the **Burgos Vision** bus (see page 265) also stops here.

## ❶ Eating

**Burgos** *p264, map p264*
Burgos is famous for its *morcilla*, a tasty black pudding similar to a British one in texture, unlike the more liquid ones in other parts of the country

🍴🍴🍴 **Casa Ojeda**, C Vitoria 5, T947 209 052. One of Burgos' better-known restaurants, backing on to Plaza de la Libertad. Traditional cuisine a bit on the heavy side, but good. Oven-roasted meats are the pride of the house.

🍴🍴🍴 **El Angel**, C Paloma 24, T947 208 608. A smart restaurant near the cathedral with a range of succulent dishes like wild turbot as well as Castilian specialities.

🍴🍴🍴 **La Posada**, Plaza Santo Domingo de Guzmán 18, T947 204 578. This central spot is a likeable restaurant with comforting home cooking. There's a *menú* for €11 at lunchtime, which is good value for this quality. The roast lamb is also memorable.

🍴🍴🍴 **Mesón Burgos**, C Sombrerería 8, T947 206 150. One of Burgos' better tapas bars downstairs is complemented by a friendly upstairs restaurant with good, if unexceptional fare. The service is good and the decor traditional and comfortable.

🍴🍴🍴 **Mesón La Cueva**, Plaza de Santa María 7, T947 205 946. A small dark Castilian restaurant with good service and a traditional feel. The *menestra de verduras* is tasty and generous, and the roast meats are predictably tasty.

🍴🍴🍴 **Rincón de España**, C Nuño Rasura 11, T947 205 955. One of the better of the terraced restaurants around the cathedral, this is no stranger to tourism but does good fish and roast meats; à la carte is much better than the set menus.

🍴 **Casa Pancho**, C San Lorenzo 13, T947 203 405. Another good option on this street, Casa Pancho is large, warm and light. An array of excellent *pinchos* adorn the bar, and the service is cheerful. The tapas are more hit and miss; prawns or mushrooms are a good bet.

🍴 **La Cabaña Arandina**, C Sombrerería 12, T947 261 932. Since its recent opening, this spot near the cathedral has quickly become a Burgos favourite. It's cheery and light and there's plenty of competition to sit at the wooden tables and enjoy *raciones* of cheeses, *revueltos* or *morcilla*; or stand at the bar and sample the delicious tapas.

🍴 **La Cantina del Tenorio**, C Arco del Pilar 10, T947 269 781. This delicatessan and bar is a buzzy and cosy retreat from the Burgos wind. A range of delicious fishy bites and small rolls is strangely complemented by baked potatoes, given a Spanish touch with lashings of paprika. Characterful and friendly.

🍴 **La Favorita**, C Avellanos 8, T947 205 949. This large barn-like spot is modern but feels traditional with its hanging hams, rows of wine bottles and wooden fittings. There's plenty of space to enjoy tasty *pinchos* – try the chopped ham with mayonnaise for a rich treat – or *raciones* of traditional products.

🍴 **Los Herreros**, C San Lorenzo 20, T947 202 448. This old favourite is an excellent tapas bar with a big range of hot and cold platelets for very little; its popularity with Burgos folk speaks volumes.

🍴 **Mesón La Amarilla**, C San Lorenzo 26, T947 205 936. A good sunken bar serving some decent *tapas*, some seeming to use a whole jar of mayonnaise. There's a good cheap restaurant upstairs too.

🍴 **Mesón San Lesmes**, C Puebla 37, T947 205 956. This likeable little corner place offers cheerful cheap eats in a gregarious downmarket bar. Simple *raciones* of things like *callos* (tripe), calamari and mixed salad cost €3-7 and are filling and satisfying. Or you could weigh down the checked tablecloth with a monster *chuletón* steak.

### Cafés

🍴 **Café España**, C Laín Calvo 12, T947 205 337. There's a sepia tinge to this venerable old-style café in the heart of Burgos. Warm in winter and with a terrace in summer, it's friendly and specializes in liqueur coffees.

## ❶ Bars and clubs

**Burgos** *p264, map p264*
During the week, nightlife is poor, but it picks up at weekends, when on C Huerta del Rey the bars spill out onto the street.

**Fox Tavern**, Paseo del Espolón 4, T947 273 311. Impossible to miss, this is a decent pub which doesn't push the Irish theme too far. Comfy seats including a terrace looking up at the cathedral; the food is OK but overpriced.

**La Negra Candela**, C Huerta del Rey 18,
T947 202 844. One of the best options
in this busy weekend drinking zone,
warm and attractively dark.

**Mondrian**, C Huerta del Rey 25,
opposite **La Negra Candela**, is another
popular Fri night spot.

**Ram Jam Club**, C San Juan 29, T607 7
84 339. A popular basement bar with
a good vinyl collection, mostly playing
British music from the 1970s and 1980s.
It's always filled with interesting people.
The decor changes regularly but currently
features classic comic strips. There's live
music fairly often here too.

## Entertainment

**Burgos** *p264, map p264*
**Teatro Principal**, Paseo del Espolón s/n,
T947 288 873, is Burgos' main theatre,
on the riverbank.

## Festivals and events

**Burgos** *p264, map p264*
**Jan 30** Fiesta de San Lesmes,
Burgos' patron saint.

**Mar/Apr** Semana Santa (Easter week)
processions are important in Burgos,
with a fairly serious religious character.
**End Jun** Fiesta de San Pedro, Burgos'
main festival of the year.

## Shopping

**Burgos** *p264, map p264*
Burgos is a fairly upmarket place to
shop, focused on the old town streets.

### Books
**Luz y Vida**, C Laín Calvo 38. A decent
bookseller's spread over 2 facing shops.
**Sedano**, Paseo del Espolón 6, T947 202 220.
A small shop with a good range of maps
and travel guides.

### Food
**La Vieja Castilla**, C Paloma 21,
T947 207 367. A tiny but excellent shop
to buy ham, Burgos *morcilla* (black
pudding) and other Castilian produce,
with friendly management.

## Activities and tours

**Burgos** *p264, map p264*
**Viajes Burgos**, C Miranda 1, T947 256
445. Organizes day and half-day trips to
interesting towns and sights in the country
around Burgos, including the Cartuja
de Miraflores, San Pedro de Cardeña,
Covarrubias, and Santo Domingo de Silos,
leaving from the cathedral square.

## Transport

**Burgos** *p264, map p264*
Burgos is a transport hub, with plenty
of trains and buses leaving to all parts
of the country.

### Bus
The bus station is handily close to town,
on C Miranda just across the Puente de
Santa María. All buses run less often on Sun.

Within the province buses run to **Aranda
de Duero** 6-7 a day (1 hr 15 mins, €6.45),
**Miranda** 3 a day, **Santo Domingo de Silos**
1 a day (none on Sun), **Roa** 1 a day Mon-Fri
(1 hr 30 mins, €6.15), **Sasamón** 1 a day (none
on Sun), **Castrojeriz** 2 a day, **Oña** 3 a day.

Further afield, there are services to
**Madrid** hourly (2 hrs 45 mins, €14.04),
**Bilbao** 4 direct a day (2 hrs, €10.55), **León**
1 a day, **Santander** 3-5 a day (2 hrs 45 mins,
€9.71), **Logroño** 7 a day (2 hrs), **Valladolid**
5 a day (2 hrs, €7.40), **Zaragoza** 4 a day
(4 hrs, via Logroño), **Barcelona** 4 a day
(7-8 hrs, €30.24).

### Trains
The trains stop a 5-min walk west
of the bus station.

## Directory

**Burgos** *p264, map p264*
**Internet** Ciber Ocio, Parque del Manzano,
open 1100-1400, 1700- 2300; **Colón 11 net**,
C Colón s/n, Mon-Sat 1100-1400, 1700-2000;
Cabaret, C La Puebla s/n, quite a cool bar
with internet access Mon-Thu 1600-0200,
Fri and Sat 1600-0400, Sun 1700-0200. **Post
office** The main post office is just across
the river from the old town on Plaza
Conde de Castro.

# Burgos Province

*While the barren stretches to the east and west of the city of Burgos are relatively dull and relentless, there are some very worthwhile trips to be made to the north and south, where the country is greener and hillier. To the south, the cloister of the monastery of Santo Domingo de Silos is worth a journey in its own right, but there's more to see. To the north are quiet hidden valleys and one of Northern Spain's most lovable Romanesque churches, the Iglesia de San Pedro de la Tejera.* ▸▸ *For Sleeping, Eating and other listings, see pages 277-279.*

## South of Burgos 🏨🍴🚌 ▸▸ *pp277-279.*

### Covarrubias → *Colour map 5, A2.*
This attractive village gets a few tour coaches but hasn't remotely been spoiled. Its attractive wooden buildings and cobbled squares make a picturesque setting by the side of a babbling brook. Its impressive 10th-century **tower** stands over the big town wall on the riverbank; it's a Mozarabic work that's said to be haunted by the ghost of a noble lady who was walled up alive there. Behind it is the **Colegiata** ⓘ *Wed-Mon 1030-1400, 1600-1900; €2 guided tour*, a Gothic affair containing a number of tombs of fat-lipped men and thin-lipped ladies, including that of Fernán González, a count of these lands who united disparate Christian communities into an efficient force to drive the Moors southwards, thereby setting the foundations of Castilla. Opposite the church is a statue of the Norwegian princess Kristina, who married the former archbishop of Sevilla here in 1257; her tomb is in the 16th-century cloister. The village has several places to stay and makes a relaxing stop (see Sleeping, page 277).

### Santo Domingo de Silos → *Colour map 5, A2.*
ⓘ *Tue-Sat 1000-1300, 1630-1800, Sun and Mon 1630-1800, €2.40, also includes admission to a small museum of musical instruments in the village.*
The monastery of Santo Domingo de Silos' **cloister**, the equal of any in the peninsula, should not be missed. It was started in the 11th century and the finished result is superb: two levels of double-columned harmony decorated with a fine series of sculptured capitals. It's not known who the artist was, but the expertise is unquestionable. Most of the capitals have vegetable and animal motifs, while at each corner are reliefs with Biblical scenes. Curiously, the central column of the western gallery breaks the pattern, with a flamboyant twist around itself, a humorous touch. The ceiling around the cloister is also memorable; a colourful *mudéjar* work. A cenotaph of Santo Domingo, who was born just south of here, stands on three lions in the northern gallery.

Another interesting aspect is the old **pharmacy**, in a couple of rooms off the cloister. It's full of phials and bottles in which the monks used to prepare all manner of remedies; even more fascinating are some of the amazing old books of pharmacy and science that fill the shelves. Other rooms off the cloister hold temporary exhibitions. Next door, visitors are welcome to attend offices in the **monastery church** ⓘ *Mon-Fri 0600, 0730, 0900, 1345, 1900, 2140; Sat 0600, 0730, 0900, 1300, 1345, 1900, 2140; Sun 0600, 0800, 1030, 1200, 1345, 1900, 2140*, where the monks use Gregorian chant. The church itself is bare and uninteresting but an office is well worth attending, especially in the evening; wrap up well.

● *In the 1990s the monks of Santo Domingo de Silos went platinum with their CD of Gregorian chant.*

Three kilometres away is a small natural chasm, the **Desfiladero de La Yecla**. Follow the road towards Caleruega; a snaky path leads down into the gorge just before a long tunnel. The path follows the tortuous twists of rock with vultures circling above; it's only a five- or 10-minute walk, but it's atmospheric, although the path is in need of some repair.

## Lerma → *Colour map 5, A2.*

Although Lerma was once a reasonably important local town, what we see today is a product of the early 17th century, when the local duke effectively ruled Spain as the favourite of Felipe III. He wasn't above a bit of pork-barrelling, and used his power to inflict a massive building programme on his hometown. Six **monasteries** were built for different orders between 1605 and 1617, but the **Palacio Ducal** tops it all; a massive structure out of all proportion to the size of the town. It bears a passing resemblance to Colditz castle in some ways; there's certainly a martial aspect to both it and the parade-ground-style square that fronts it. Inside, however, it's a more sympathetic space, and has recently been converted into a *parador*. Nearby, the **tourist office** ① *C Audiencia, Tue-Sun 1000-1400, 1600-1900 (2000 in summer)*, itself located in a former monastery, will point out the other monasteries (three of which are still functioning) on the town map for you. **San Blas** is the most interesting, with a fine 17th-century *retablo* in the church.

# North of Burgos ⊜⊜ ‣ *pp277-279.*

The land to the north rises into the Cordillera Cantábrica, where the beautiful valleys are excellent, little-visited places to explore. Avoid coming in winter, when temperatures can drop well below zero.

## El Gran Cañón del Ebro → *Colour map 2, C5.*

From Sotopalacios, the N623 continues, through increasingly mountainous terrain, finally descending to the coast and Santander on the other side of the range. The Ebro, near its source here, has carved a picturesque canyon into the rock; it's a lovely cool valley full of trees and vultures. A marked trail, **El Gran Cañón del Ebro**, can be walked, starting from the spa village of **Valdelateja**; the whole trail is a six-hour round trip.

## Valdivielso Valley → *Colour map 2, C5/6.*

Accessible via a windy road through the village of **Pesquera**, the Valdivielso Valley is a quiet little gem. Green (or white in winter), pretty and reasonably isolated, the valley is perfect for walking, climbing or even canoeing, but it also has several buildings of interest. As an important north-south conduit it was fortified with a series of towers; one of the better examples is at the valley's northern end, in the village of **Valdenoceda**.

Above the pretty village one of the finest Romanesque churches you could hope to see. The **Iglesia de San Pedro de la Tejera** ① *T947 303 200 or T636 264 447 to arrange a visit, €1.50*, is a beautiful little structure overlooking the valley. It's in superb condition, built in the 11th and 12th centuries. The façade is fantastic, exquisitely carved with various allegorical scenes, including a lion eating a man. Around the outside are a series of animal heads in relief. The sunken interior features more carvings of animals, musicians and acrobats as well as an impressively painted *mudéjar* gallery, installed in the 15th century. The simple apse is harmonious; it's the beautiful Romanesque proportions as much as the carvings that make this building such a delight. Oña, see below, makes the best option for getting up here by public transport as it is connected three times daily with Burgos by bus (via Briviesca).

**Oña,** a tiny town at the southern end of the Valdivielso Valley, is worth a visit for its monuments. The massive **Monasterio de San Salvador** ① *admission by guided* *visit only, Tue-Fri 1030, 1130, 1245, 1600, 1700, 1815, Sat and Sun 1030, 1130, 1230, 1315, 1600, 1700, 1815, €2*, is an attractive fortified former monastery that seems bigger than the rest of the town put together. It's now a psychiatric hospital but its quite remarkable church can still be visited.

The royals of the Middle Ages always favoured burial in a monastery; they shrewdly figured that the ongoing monkish prayers for their souls (after a sizeable cash injection of course) lessened the chance of being blackballed at the Pearly Gates. A number of notable figures are buried here in an attractive pantheon; foremost among them is the Navarran king Sancho the Great, who managed to unite almost the whole of Northern Spain under his rule in the 11th century. The main pantheon is in Gothic style, with *mudéjar* influences, and sits at the back of the church. There are lesser notables buried in the harmonious cloister, a work of Simon of Cologne.

There's a small **tourist office** ① *Easter-Oct Tue-Fri 1030-1330, 1600-1900, Sat and Sun 1030-1400, 1600-1900; Nov-Easter Tue-Fri 1000-1400, 1600-1800, Sat and Sun 1000-1400, 1530-1800*, in the square outside the church.

*Botas*, the goatskin winebags once an essential possession of every farmer and shepherd who couldn't return to their village at lunchtime, are still used to drink from at fiestas and bullfights. Drinking from them is something of an art; it's easy to spray yourself with a jet of cheap red that was meant for the mouth. There's a traditional little *botería*, one of the few left of a formerly widespread craft, on the main road through town. Have a look even if you don't want to buy one; the process hasn't changed much over the years, although the premium models now have a rubber interior to improve the storage of the wine.

## Medina de Pomar → *Colour map 2, B6.*

Northeast of Valdivielso, the town of Medina de Pomar was the stamping ground of the Velascos, a powerful Castilian family. Their legacy includes a sturdy castle and the 14th-century **Monastery of Santa Clara**, which they basically founded to be buried in; it features an attractive *retablo* by Diego de Siloe and a small museum. It's a more popular holiday base than the Valdivielso and as a result there are more facilities for tourism.

---

# East of Burgos 🏨🍴 » *pp277-279.*

The N120 crosses wooded hills on its way to Logroño, while the N1 makes its way to Miranda de Ebro and the Basque hills. This is one of the most unpleasant roads in Spain, a conga-line of trucks enlivened by the suicidal overtaking manoeuvres of impatient drivers. If travelling by car, it's worth paying the motorway toll to avoid it.

Some 4 km north of the N120, peaceful **San Juan de Ortega** is the last stop before Burgos for many pilgrims on the way to Santiago. In the green foothills, it's nothing more than a church and *albergue*, and has been a fixture of the Camino ever since Juan, inspired by the good works of Santo Domingo de la Calzada down the road, decided to do the same and dedicate his life to easing the pilgrims' journey. He started the church in the 12th century; the Romanesque apse survives, although the rest is in later style. It's a likeable if unremarkable place. San Juan is buried here in an ornate Gothic tomb. Pilgrims stay at the hospital that he founded.

Further along towards La Rioja, **Villafranca Montes de Oca** is an unremarkable pilgrim stop with a small *ermita* in a green valley. North again from here, just off the N1, is an unlikely picnic spot. The hamlet of **Alcocero de Mola**, 2 km from the main road on the BU703, bears the name of the general who masterminded the Nationalist rising. He was killed before the end of the Civil War in a plane crash, probably to Franco's relief. Three kilometres up a neglected side road from Alcocero is a massive concrete monument to him, on the wooded hilltop where the plane hit, with good views across the plains. All of 20 m high and completely forgotten, it's in characteristically pompous

Fascist style; an intriguing reminder of a not too distant past. The concrete's in decline now, and weeds carpet the monumental staircase; take a torch if you want to climb the stairs inside.

Further east, **Briviesca** is a sizeable service town, which seems to have beaten the decline that afflicts so many towns of Castilla. The tree-lined plaza is pleasant and shady; on it stands the nicest of the three big churches, with a damaged Renaissance façade. The **tourist office** is on the square too.

Beyond here, the main road passes through a dramatic craggy pass at **Pancorbo**, which would be a nice hiking base were it not for the trucks thundering through. This is geographically where Castilla ends; the *meseta* more or less gives way here to the Basque foothills.

Castilla officially ends at **Miranda de Ebro**, a hardbitten town which, while attractive in parts, is mostly dusty and vaguely depressing; and is full of big boulevards where nothing much happens. The main reason to come here is to change bus or train; by all means take a stroll down the pretty river, but don't miss your connection.

---

# Southwest from Burgos: the Pilgrim Route
■⚡🚌 ▸ *pp277-279.*

## Castrojeriz → *Colour map 2, C4.*
West of Burgos, the principal branch of the Camino de Santiago tracks southwest to the town of Castrojeriz, a somewhat bleak place unlikely to cheer the heart after a long trudge across treeless Castilian terrain. It was formerly a Celtic settlement, and the *castro* hilltop structure has been preserved. The **church of San Juan** is the village's

> ❢ *Among the fairly bleak towns on this stretch, this stands out like a beacon.*

main attraction; it's a clean, if over-restored Gothic building influenced by the Burgos German tradition and features a nice double-columned cloister. As well as the bare ruin of a castle on the hill, there are a couple of impressive buildings in the town, most notably the **Casa de Gutiérrez Barona**, a large knightly residence. This predates Castrojeriz' only moment in the spotlight. During the *comunero* revolt (see History, page 448) this town was deemed unlikely enough to rebel that the Council of Castilla took up residence here, and the place briefly buzzed with noblemen who were doubtless happy enough to leave again.

## Sasamón → *Colour map 2, C4.*
A more interesting, if longer route would take the pilgrim through Sasamón, just north of the main Burgos-León road. The **Iglesia de Santa María la Real** ① *daily 1100-1400, 1600-1900 (ask in the bar opposite if shut), €1.25 includes a helpful explanation by the knowledgeable and justly proud caretaker*, is its very lovely church in light honey-coloured stone. It was originally a massive five-naved space, but was partitioned after a fire destroyed half of it in the 19th century. The exterior highlight is an excellent 13th-century Gothic portal featuring Christ and the Apostles, while the museum has

> ❢ *The town is famous for its almond biscuits but there's little to see here.*

some well-displayed Roman finds as well as a couple of top-notch pieces; a couple of Flemish tapestries featuring the life of Alexander the Great, and a Diego de Siloe polychrome of San Miguel, the pretty-boy bully. It's fairly plain, a reflection of the Inquisition passing into irrelevance. In the church itself, two works of the German school stand out; the ornate pulpit, from around 1500, and a large baptismal font. A 16th-century Plateresque *retablo* of Santiago is one of many that adorn the building, so monumental for such a small town.

📍 *For information on the practicalities of walking the Camino de Santiago and the history of the pilgrimage, see pages 52 and 388.*

A statue of **Octavian** stands in a square nearby. The Celtiberian town of Segisama was used as a base in 26 BC for his campaigns against the Cantabrians and Asturians. The inscription reads *Ipse venit Segisamam, castro posuit* (then he came to Segisama and set up camp).

There's a **tourist office** in the Plaza Mayor, but the church warden knows all there is to know about the area.

Don't leave town without checking out the **Ermita de San Isidro**, dominated by a massive 6-m carved crucifix that once would have stood at a crossroads to comfort weary souls. Under Christ is the Tree of Knowledge, Adam, Eve, Cain and Abel. It dates from the 16th century and is a lovely work. Atop it is a nesting pelican; it was formerly believed that a pelican short of fish to feed the kids would wound itself in the breast to let them feed on its own blood. This became a metaphor for Christ's sacrifice, and pelicans are a common motif in Castilian religious sculpture.

---

## Sleeping

**Covarrubias** *p273*
B-C **Hotel Arlanza**, Plaza Mayor 11, T947 406 441. This is a good option on the main square set attractively in a stately old house. The rooms are beautiful, particularly those on the top floor with sloping attic roof. There's an atmospheric restaurant too which has riotous medieval dinners on Sat nights in spring and autumn.
C **Los Castros**, C Los Castros 10, T947 406 368. This is a very cosy *casa rural* with a comfy lounge and 5 excellent homely doubles. The decoration is in enchanting rustic style; and breakfast is included.
F **Pensión Galin**, Plaza Doña Urraca 4, T947 406 552. This *pensión* above a bar isn't exactly brand new but has plenty of charm. The rooms come both with and without bathroom; the best look over the square.

**Camping**
**Covarrubias**, on the road to Hortiguela, T947 406 417. Close to town with some bungalows also available.

**Santo Domingo de Silos** *p273*
B **Tres Coronas de Silos**, Plaza Mayor 6, T947 390 047, F947 390 065. Attractive and comfortable, set in a solid stone mansion just across from the monastery. The rooms are rustic and charming.
C-D **Hotel Santo Domingo de Silos**, C Santo Domingo 16, T947 390 053, www.hotelsantodomingodesilos.com. Set in 2 adjacent buildings on the main road, this offers excellent quality for the price. There's a variety of rooms available, but all have plenty of space, and comfortable

furnishings. The newer ones have excellent bathrooms. The hotel restaurant does an excellent *cochinillo* (sucking pig). Recommended.
D **Arco de San Juan**, Pradera de San Juan 1, T/F947 390 074. This is a hotel and restaurant peacefully set by a stream just past the monastery. The rooms are quiet and clean, and there are some nice terraces to relax on.

**Lerma** *p274*
L **Parador de Lerma**, Plaza Mayor 1, T947 177 110, www.parador.es. Set in the massive Ducal Palace, this recently inaugurated *parador* has a sumptuous interior and makes a fine place to stay. Built around a high-arched covered patio, it oozes class, and the cool tiled-floor rooms have excellent facilities and bathrooms; many have great views.
D **El Zaguán**, C Barquillo 6, T947 172 165, F947 172 083. This makes another very comfortable base in Lerma. It's a 17th-century *casa rural* with attractive stone walls and interesting furniture. The rooms are great, and equipped to hotel standard; a couple have lovely wooden sloping ceilings.

**El Gran Cañón del Ebro** *p274*
A-B **Posada del Balneario**, Camino del Balneario s/n, Valdelateja T947 150 220. A big attractive place by the river with a high level of comfort and service, swimming pool and jacuzzi included. Readers have recommended sleeping here but eating elsewhere.

C **Casa de Lolo y Vicent**, C Callejón 18, T947 150 267. Cheaper but no less welcoming is this *casa rural* in the village of Escalada further up the road. It's set in a sensitively restored 15th-century house, and offers a good welcome and pretty views.

### Valdivielso Valley *p274*

E **Casa Tipi**, Ctra Quecedo s/n, near Valdenoceda in the hamlet of Puente Arenas, T947 303 130. A small *casa rural* with just 2 doubles that share a bathroom and a lounge. The owners will happily make meals or arrange watersports or horse riding.
F **Hostal Once Brutos**, C del Pan 6, Oña, T947 300 010. A simple but clean place just off the square that also provides simple meals. Some rooms have a lot more natural light than others.

### Medina de Pomar *p275*

A **Hotel Ciudad de Medina**, Plaza Somovilla s/n, T947 190 822, F947 191 556. Good a/c rooms with minibar and modern bathrooms set in a lovely old arcaded building on the square.

### East of Burgos *p275*

E **Hostal El Parque**, C Francisco Cantera 1, Miranda de Ebro, T947 331 383. A good place with clean rooms opposite a pleasant park named after the Sorian poet Antonio Machado. Cheaper rooms with shared bathroom are available.
E-F **Fortu**, C Marqués de Torresoto 11, Briviesca, T947 590 719. Simple but clean rooms with shared bathrooms. The restaurant downstairs does cheap but good food.

### Castrojeriz *p276*

Apart from 2 pilgrim *albergues*, the best place to stay is:
D **La Posada**, C Landelino Tardajos 5, T947 378 610, F947 378 611. A *casa rural* with some charm, set in an historic old mansion built around a pleasing interior patio. There's also a very good restaurant.

### Sasamón *p276*

E **Casa Gloria**, C Arco 1, T947 370 059. The village's only accommodation option, this is right opposite the church. It's cordial, clean and well presented; the simple rooms have spick and span white-sheeted beds and small bathrooms. They're heated, the owner will lend you a bike, and you can eat downstairs.

## 🍴 Eating

### Lerma *p274*

🍴 **Casa Brigante**, C Luis Cervera Vera 1, T947 170 594. A good *asador* on the giant Plaza Ducal. Their speciality is roast milk-fed lamb, *lechazo asado*.

### Castrojeriz *p276*

🍴 **La Taberna**, C General Mola 43, T947 377 610. One of a handful of cheap restaurants catering to locals and pilgrims. It's decent and also has internet access and simple rooms.

## 🚌 Transport

### Covarrubias *p273*

**Bus** There are 3 buses a day to Covarrubias from **Burgos** (none on Sun).

### Santo Domingo de Silos *p273*

**Bus** There is a daily bus Mon-Thu and Sat from **Burgos** in the afternoon (2 hrs), returning in the morning.

### Lerma *p274*

**Bus** There are several daily buses and the odd train that make their way to Lerma from **Burgos** and to a lesser extent **Madrid**.

### Valdivielso Valley *p274*

**Bus** There are daily buses from **Burgos** to Oña via Briviesca.

**Car** Take the C629 north from **Sotopalacios**, a strange road that crosses a sort of Alpine plateau. A series of large stone waymarkers irregularly dot the route marking the road that Carlos V used on entering Spain to claim the throne.

🎈 *For an explanation of the sleeping and eating price codes used in this guide, see inside* ⚫ *the front cover. Other relevant information is found in Essentials pages 39-46.*

**East of Burgos** *p275*

**Bus and train** Briviesca is visited by 7 daily buses from **Burgos** and there are also a few trains.

Miranda de Ebro is well connected to major cities in Northern Spain, particularly **Bilbao**, **Vitoria**, **Burgos**, **Logroño** and **Madrid**. It's a major transport hub between the Basque regions and the rest of the nation.

**Castrojeriz** *p276*

**Bus** Buses run from from **Burgos** to Castrojeriz twice a day (none on Sun).

**Sasamón** *p276*

**Bus** There are 2 buses a day to Sasamón from **Burgos** (none on Sun).

---

# Palencia → *Phone code: 979. Colour map 4, A6. Population: 81,439. Altitude: 740 m.*

*Although its population surpasses a healthy 80,000, never a sentence seems to be written about Palencia without the word 'little'. And it's understandable; on some approaches to the provincial capital, it seems that you're in the centre of town before even noticing there was a town. It is, as Hemingway once said, a nice place – quiet and friendly, bypassed by pilgrims, tourists and public awareness of its presence. This is partly an accident of geography – the town is situated in the middle of a triangle of more important places, Valladolid, Burgos and León – but also one of history.*

*Palencia sits on the Carrión, so murky and green it surely merits mangroves and crocodiles. The old town stretches along its eastern bank in elongated fashion. It is studded with churches, headed up by the superb cathedral.* ▸▸ *For Sleeping, Eating and other listings, see pages 284-286.*

## Ins and outs

**Getting there and around** The train and bus stations are just beyond the northern end of Calle Mayor, a pedestrian street stretching the length of the old town. Palencia's main sights are all within easy walking distance of each other, concentrated in the old town. ▸▸ *See also Transport, page 286.*

**Tourist information** The city's **tourist office** ① *C Mayor 105, T979 740 068, oficina deturismodepalencia@jcyl.es, winter daily 0900-1400, 1700-2000, summer Mon-Fri 0900-2000, Sat and Sun 0900-2100,* is at the southern end of Calle Mayor and has a big range of information on the city, the province and the rest of Castilla y León.

## Background

Like many towns in Castilla, Palencia has a proud past. Inhabited in prehistoric times, the local villages resisted the Romans for nearly a century before Pompey swept them aside in 72 BC and set up camp here. Pliny the Elder cited Palencia as one of the important Roman settlements of the 1st century AD. It wasn't until the 12th century that the city reached its zenith, however; *fueros* (legal privileges) were granted by Alfonso VIII, and Spain's first university was established here. In 1378 the city became legendary for resisting a siege by the Duke of Lancaster, fighting for Pedro I. The defences were mounted by the Palentine women, as the men were off fighting at another battleground. But things turned sour in the *comunero* revolt, a Castilian revolution against the 'foreign' regime of Carlos V, which became an anti-aristocratic movement in general. The *comuneros* were heavily defeated in 1521 and Palencia suffered thereafter, as Castilian towns were stripped of some of their privileges and influence.

# Sights

Palencia's scenic highlight is its superb **cathedral** ① *T979 701 347, Mon-Sat 0845-1330, 1600-1830 (1930 mid May-Sep), Sun 1115-1300; regular guided visits; €3; crypt only €1*, known as *La Bella Desconocida*, (the unknown beauty). Built in the 14th century on Visigothic and Romanesque foundations, it's a massive structure, although it hardly dominates the town, tucked away somewhat on a quiet square. The magnificent main portal depicts the Virgin flanked by apostles. Inside, the massive *retablo* paints the story of Christ's life; it's a work of the Flemish master Jan of Flanders, who also painted an attractive triptych on one side of the choir. The city's patron, the Virgen de la Calle, sits on a silver coffer in the ambulatory, while there's an amusing sculpture of lions eating a martyr at the back end of the *coro*. There's a

# Palencia

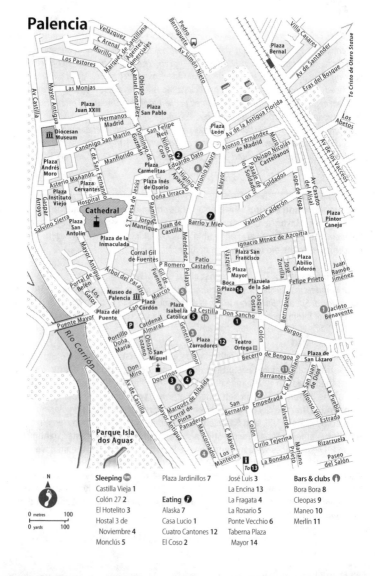

| Sleeping 🛏 | Plaza Jardinillos 7 | José Luis 3 | Bars & clubs 🍸 |
|---|---|---|---|
| Castilla Vieja 1 | | La Encina 13 | Bora Bora 8 |
| Colón 27 2 | Eating 🍴 | La Fragata 4 | Cleopas 9 |
| El Hotelito 3 | Alaska 7 | La Rosario 5 | Maneo 10 |
| Hostal 3 de | Casa Lucio 1 | Ponte Vecchio 6 | Merlín 11 |
| Noviembre 4 | Cuatro Cantones 12 | Taberna Plaza | |
| Monclús 5 | El Coso 2 | Mayor 14 | |

N

0 metres 100
0 yards 100

painting by El Greco just off the cloister, but this and the Visigothic/ Romanesque crypt are only accessible on the guided tours. Similarly annoying is the lighting system; to see all the impressive works of art around the building will cost you a small fortune in euro coins.

A couple of blocks away is the **Diocesan museum** ① *open by tour only Mon-Sat 1030 and 1130, €3*, set around a cloister, and with a decent collection of paintings and *retablos* from around the province.

Further south, the Romanesque **Iglesia de San Miguel** is a knobbly affair with an alarmingly hollow tower. It's fairly unadorned inside, with elegant vaulting. There's a small gilt *retablo* of the saint, and some fragmentary wall paintings.

Nearby, the **Museo de Palencia** ① *T979 752 328, Tue-Sat 1000-1400, 1600-1900 (Jul-Sep 1700-2000), Sun 1000-1400, €1.20, free at weekends*, is housed in an attractive building on Plaza del Cordón, named for the sculpted cord that is tied around the doorway. It's a good display with plenty of artefacts from the province's Roman and pre-Roman past. The museum is situated in what was once Palencia's Jewish quarter.

> ❢ *Ernest Hemingway summed up Palencia as a "nice Castilian town with good beer".*

Palencia's **Plaza Mayor** sits secluded just to the east of the long Calle Mayor. It's a lovely space with trees, *soportales*, and a monument to the Renaissance sculptor Alonso Berruguete.

Just out of town, the looming Lego-like **Cristo de Otero** claims to be the second tallest statue of Jesus in the world (after Rio). There are good views from the 850-m elevation. The sculptor's last wish was to be buried at the statue's feet; his body is in the small chapel.

---

# Around Palencia ⬤❂⬤❂⬤ ⇥ *pp284-286.*

## Basílica de San Juan de Baños
① *T979 770 338, winter Tue-Sun 1030-1330, 1600-1800; summer 1000-1330, 1630-2000, €1 (Wed free); ring to confirm in winter.*
South of Palencia and around 2 km east of Venta de Baños, a mainline train hub with frequent connections to Palencia, is a church that's well worth visiting, the Basílica de San Juan de Baños. At least some of the pretty little building is awesomely old; an inscription above the altar states that it was founded by the Visigothic King Recesvinth in AD 661. To be sure, it's been altered substantially over the years, but it still preserves much of its original character, principally in the central aisle. Its architectural value is high, as clear links are evident with late Roman building traditions, but apart from all that, it's an enchanting simple structure, a relic from a time when Christianity was (comparatively) young. Opposite is a decent *asador*, **Mesón El Lagar**.

## Ampudia → *Colour map 4, A5.*
For a good off-the-beaten track Castilian experience, head west from Palencia five leagues to the town of Ampudia, unexpectedly dominated by an imposing **castle** ① *guided visits mid-May to Sep; Sat 1030-1430, 1830, 1930, Sun 1200, 1300; rest of year Sat only 1130, 1230, 1330; €3.50; if there are a few of you, or you are especially keen, T629 768 247 to arrange a visit at other times.* It's in top nick, bristling with castellation, but visits are limited, as it's still lived in. There's an ornate collection of objets d'art on show as well.

The **Colegiata de San Miguel Arcángel** is a floor-boarded Gothic and Renaissance affair, light and breezy and with a spiky tower that looks ready to blast off to join the archangel himself. Its known as the *Novia de los Campos* (Bride of the Plains; this area of the province is known as *Los Campos*). The main altarpiece is a Renaissance work; more interesting perhaps is the Gothic side chapel of San Ildefonso, containing the tombs of the men who paid for the building, and also a pretty Plateresque *retablo*.

Next to the Colegiata is the **Museo del Arte Sacro** ① *May-Sep Tue-Sun 1030-1400, 1630-2000, Oct-Apr 1030-1400, 1600-1800, closed early Jan-early Mar,* €2.50, quite a good museum of religious art. The town itself is typical and pleasant, with just enough passing visitors to warrant a few eating and staying options.

## Medina de Rioseco → *Colour map 4, A5.*

A little further west, and once quite an important wool and wheat merchants' town in the province of Valladolid, Medina de Rioseco still retains a little from those times, like an old soldier with a carefully mothballed uniform tucked away in a bedsit wardrobe. It's well served by buses, so hop off and take a look, especially on a Wednesday morning, when there's an entertaining livestock market. It lies on the main road between Valladolid and León, so makes a good stop if going between those cities too.

The most endearing aspect of the town is the pedestrian street Calle Lázaro Alonso, colonnaded in warped old wood. Following this from the main road, you'll come to one of Medina's three churches, the **Iglesia de Santa Cruz**. More than a bit mausoleum-like from the outside, it houses the **Museo de Semana Santa** ① *Tue-Sun 1100-1400, 1600-1900 (1700-2000 in summer),* devoted to Holy Week celebrations in different towns and villages of Castilla y León.

More beautiful is the church of **Santa María**, built from attractive white-ish limestone in the 15th and 16th centuries. Gothic in style, it's topped by a flamboyant Baroque spire. Inside it's fairly ornate, with showy star vaulting and a big gilt *retablo*. Flashest of all is the intricately decorated funerary chapel of the Benavente family. The pretty little coloured organ provides a homelier touch. There's a small museum inside; the attendant has the keys to the **Iglesia de Santiago** ① *Tue-Sun 1100-1400, 1600-1900 (1700-2000 in summer),* a squareish structure further down the hill.

The new **tourist office** ① *T983 720 319, www.medinaderioseco.com,* can be found by the Canal de Castilla in a converted flour mill.

---

# Camino de Santiago ⊖❼♠⊜ » *pp284-286.*

## Frómista → *Colour map 2, C4.*

In northern Palencia, Frómista, as well as lying on the Camino de Santiago, seems to be a compulsory stop on the Romanesque circuit; for a tiny town it gets its share of tour buses. The reason is the **Iglesia de San Martín** ① *winter 1000-1400, 1530-1830, summer 1000-1400, 1630-2000,* €1, €1.50 with San Pedro, a remarkable 11th-century Romanesque church, one of the purest and earliest, derived almost wholly from the French model that permeated the peninsula via the pilgrim route. From the outside it's beautiful, an elegant gem standing slightly self-satisfied in the sunlight. The church happily managed to survive the Gothic and Baroque eras without being meddled with, but a late 19th-century restoration brought mixed benefits. While the building owes its good condition to this, it also has lost some of the weathered charm that makes the Romanesque dear to modern hearts. That said, the purity of its lines make it well worth a visit. Inside, it's the capitals of the pillars that attract the attention. While some were sculpted during the restoration (they are marked with an R, with creditable honesty), the others are excellent examples of Romanesque sculpture. There are no Biblical scenes – many of the motifs are vegetal, and some are curious juxtapositions of people and animals, particularly lions and birds. The church is crowned by an octagonal tower as well as two distinctive turrets.

Nearby, **San Pedro** is an attractive Gothic building with a small museum. There's a small **tourist information centre** on the main crossroads in town.

🎈 *For information on the practicalities of walking the Camino de Santiago and the history of*
⬤ *the pilgrimage, see pages 52 and 388.*

## Astudillo → *Colour map 4, A6.*

Just off the Camino, southeast of Frómista, the town of Astudillo is a beautiful little place. All that remains of its medieval walls is the **Puerta de San Martín**, a striking gateway. The central square is an attractive tree-lined affair, and there are several noble *palacios* and mansions. On the small hill above town is a castle; the hill itself is honeycombed with old wine *bodegas*.

## Villalcázar de Sirga → *Colour map 2, C4.*

The Camino continues through an awesomely empty landscape before arriving at the village of Villalcázar de Sirga, which is built around a memorable church, **Santa María la Blanca** ① *Easter-Oct daily 1030-1400, 1630-1930, Nov-Easter Sat and Sun 1200-1400, 1630-1830, €1.* It's a majestic sight, a massive Gothic affair quite out of proportion to everything else around it. The exterior highlights include a finely carved rose window and a portal topped by a frieze depicting the Pantocrator with evangelists and apostles, and, below, Mary in the Annunciation and the Adoration. Inside, particularly noteworthy are the impressive painted tombs of the Infante don Felipe, prince and brother of King Alfonso X, and his wife. Both date from the late 13th century.

## Carrión de los Condes → *Colour map 2, C4.*

Carrión de los Condes provides some relief after the hard slog across the Castilian plain. The Carrión is the river on which the town lies. A couple of shabby churches can be found north of the main road, but the nicest part of town is around the plaza to the south of it. The **Iglesia de Santiago** is the town's showpiece, with an excellent late 12th-century façade, an unusual affair with zigzag columns and an actor doing a backflip among the figures on the archivolt. The Christ in Majesty has been described as the most impressive in Spain. There's also a small **museum** inside. Another church, **Santa María**, is a clean-lined affair with a large porch and some chessboard patterning. It's relatively unadorned inside apart from a massive gilt *retablo*. A statue of St Michael is camp even by his lofty standards; the archangel looks as if he's just stepped off the set of *Starlight Express*. On Thursday mornings, a market stretches between the two churches. There's a nice park by the river too. Just west of town, the monastery of **San Zoilo** has been converted into a beautiful hotel (see Sleeping, page 284).

## La Olmeda and Quintanilla → *Colour map 2, C4/C3.*

① *Both villas and the museum are open Tue-Sun Apr to mid-Oct 1000-1330, 1630-2000; mid-Oct to Mar 1030-1330, 1600-1800; the Quintanilla villa is closed from Nov-Easter. Entry to each villa €3; La Olmeda includes entry to the Saldaña museum.*

Near Carrión are two of the little-known highlights of Palencia Province, the Roman villas of La Olmeda and Quintanilla. The former, north of Carrión, near the town of Saldaña and just outside Pedrosa de la Vega, is slightly more impressive than the latter. Dating from the late Roman period, the villa is set around a large central courtyard. The numerous small rooms around it are decorated with geometrical and vegetal mosaic flooring, but in a larger room is a superb mosaic with Achilles and Ulysses as well as a hunting scene, with all manner of beasts in a flurry of complex activity.

Quintanilla, just off the N120 west of Carrión, has a similarly large villa, also featuring some excellent mosaics as well as a hypocaust underfloor heating system for the cold Castilian winters. In **Saldaña** itself, an attractive if hard-bitten *meseta* town, some of the finds from the two villas have been assembled in a **museum** set in an old church; it's well worth visiting, as there are some excellent pieces, particularly those found at a funerary complex by the Olmeda villa. Buses run to Saldaña from Palencia, Burgos and León.

## ⬤ Sleeping

**Palencia** *p279, map p280*
Accommodation is very reasonably priced.
**A-B Castilla Vieja**, Av Casado del Alisal 26,
T979 749 044, www.hotelessuco.com.
While this hotel on the edge of the old town
isn't exactly interesting, it's modern, well
equipped and fairly priced. The rooms are
spacious, with polished wooden floorboards
and decent bathrooms. The mini-suites,
which have extra space and a lounge area,
are only €15 more than the standard
double. Parking available.
**C Hotel Colón 27**, C Colón 27, T979 740 700,
www.colon27.com. Despite the rather
unimaginative name, the hotel is pleasant
with spacious rooms and a welcoming
attitude in the heart of town. Good value for
the price (which is at the bottom end of this
category), although there's some morning
racket from the school opposite.
**C Hotel Monclús**, C Menéndez Pelayo 3,
T979 744 300, F979 744 490. This brick,
slightly stuffy hotel is in the middle of town.
The rooms are comfortable but kitted out
in sombre brown. Nevertheless, it's quiet
and central and parking is available.
**C Hotel Plaza Jardinillos**, C Dato 2, T979
750 022, F979 750 190. A hotel with a bit of
character, with interesting prints on the walls
and helpful staff. Recently renovated, it has
comfortable rooms with bathroom and
offers breakfast and parking (nearby).
**D Hostal 3 de Noviembre**, C Mancornador
18, T979 703 042. With surely the smallest
lobby of any Spanish hotel, this is a good
Palentine choice. Doubles are all exterior
and comfortable, although the singles are
predictably cramped (though cheap).
Parking available. Reception open 1900-
2330 only, so phone ahead at other times.
**E-F El Hotelito**, C General Amor 5, T979 746
913, hotelito@yahoo.com. Small but decent
rooms, which offer fine value above a bar
at the southern end of the old town. It's
a friendly place with parking available.
Rooms come with or without bathroom;
the price difference is minimal.

**Ampudia** *p281*
**L Casa del Abad de Ampudia**, Plaza Gromaz
12, T979 768 008, www.casadelabad.com.
An excellent accommodation and eating

option is this beautiful and originally
renovated 16th-century abbot's house
in the main square. A riot of colour and
subtle beauty, every room is different and
comfortable. There's even a gym and sauna.
The meals are delicious – the restaurant has
recently been awarded a Michelin star – and
the wines are superb. Recommended.
**D Atienza**, C Duque de Alba 3, T979 768
076. Another welcoming choice, this is a
*casa rural* in an old workers' cottage with
a restored wine *bodega*. The rooms are
charming, meals are served and there's
a peaceful garden.

**Medina de Rioseco** *p282*
**F La Muralla**, Plaza Santo Domingo 4,
T983 700 577. Just at the bottom of
C Lázaro Alonso, this is clean, airy and
remarkably good value.
**G Fonda Santo Domingo**, Plaza Santo
Domingo 3, T983 700 030. Although basic,
it's clean and adequate at prices that will
bring a glow to the heart of the budget
traveller (€6 per person).

**Frómista** *p282*
**D Hostal San Telmo**, C Martin Veña 8,
T979 811 028. This is a great place to stay;
a large, light and tranquil *casa rural* with
a large garden/ courtyard and charming
but cheap rooms.
**F Pensión Marisa**, Plaza Obispo
Almaraz 2, T979 810 023. This is a
simple and welcoming choice on the
main square, with spotless but basic
rooms with shared bathroom.

**Villalcázar de Sirga** *p283*
**D-E Hostal Las Cántigas**, C Condes de
Toreno 1, T979 880 015, www.turwl.com/
infantadonaleonor. This excellent modern
*hostal* is right by the church of Santa María
la Blanca in this tiny and tranquil village. It
makes a great rural base and is well priced.
Rooms have bathroom, heating and there's
a bar and restaurant.

**Carrión de los Condes** *p283*
**B Real Monasterio San Zoilo**, T979 880 050,
www.sanzoilo.com. The best of several
options. A characterful setting in an old

monastery with a peaceful garden which has more grass than the rest of the province put together. There's also a good restaurant with a €15 lunch which offers plenty of choice.
**F Hospedería Albe**, C Collantes 21, T979 880 913, F979 880 874. Hospitable, pleasant and cool, with charming rustic decoration.

---

## 🍴 Eating

### Palencia *p279, map p280*
Palencia's not exactly a gourmet paradise and restaurants are a little thin on the ground.
**🍴🍴🍴 La Encina**, C Casañe 2, T979 710 936. This Castilian *asador* is considered the city's best and most reliable restaurant. It is famous for its roast meats, but also for its *tortilla*, which has twice been voted the best in the nation.
**🍴🍴 Casa Lucio**, C Don Sancho 2, T979 748 190. A bright, traditional and warmly lit basement bar and restaurant dealing in standard Castilian fare with a spring in its step (or was that the garlic?). Good value.
**🍴🍴 La Fragata**, C Pedro Fernández de Pulgar 8, T979 750 129. There are 2 options on offer here; well-prepared fish and seafood in the restaurant, or cheap, simple and effective *raciones* and *platos combinados* in the bar on the corner.
**🍴🍴 La Rosario**, C La Cestilla 3, T979 740 936. A staid and typical Spanish restaurant, which still relies on the good old typewriter to produce the menu. The *pimientos rellenos*, the house speciality, live up to their billing; there are also some good wines on offer. Mains are in the €15-20 range.
**🍴🍴 Ponte Vecchio**, C Doctrinos 1, T979 745 215. Atmospheric and spacious Italian restaurant located opposite the church of San Miguel in a lovely stone building. The food is upmarket and excellent. Closed Mon.
**🍴🍴 Taberna Plaza Mayor**, Plaza Mayor 1, T979 740 410. This is a warm wooden tavern right on the main square, with tiled bar and walls. You can hang out in the bar and enjoy *raciones* of calamari and the like, or head upstairs to the restaurant, which looks down into the bar through a hole in the floor. There's a terrace outside in summer.
**🍴 El Coso**, C Eduardo Dato 8, T979 746 758. A characterful and yellow-tiled café which does a range of cheap meal options. It's very convivial and fills up in the evenings with people browsing *pinchos* and *raciones*.

**🍴 José Luis**, C Pedro Fernández de Pulgar 11, T979 741 510. A varied range of cheap and hearty *menús* are on offer at this decent, no-frills restaurant. The lunchtime *menú* costs €8, while the daily specials include a tasty paella on Thu.

### Cafés
**Alaska**, C Mayor 24. A tiny café/bar bedecked with massive paintings, a popular terrace, and a toilet accessed by a tight spiral staircase. They also do good tapas.
**Cuatro Cantones**, C Mayor 43, T979 700 463. A loveable, old-style Spanish café, all tiles and ornate light fittings, a top place for a coffee or a *coñac*.

### Medina de Rioseco *p282*
**🍴🍴 Mesón la Rúa**, C San Juan 25, T983 700 519. This restaurant is a pleasant surprise. After entering from the street, you enter a sumptuous dark interior with a staircase that could have come from a Renaissance *palacio*. The menu is bristling with Castilian specialities, such as *pichón* (squab) and hearty stews (mains €6-12). The *menú del día* is great value at €9; the sullen service is the only drawback.
**🍴 Los Pasos**, C Lázaro Alonso 44. A homely place serving big portions.

### Cafés
**Mente**, Av Juan Carlos II 4. A popular terraced café/bar on the main road.

### Frómista *p282*
**🍴🍴 Hotel San Martín**, Plaza Obispo Almaraz 7, T979 810 000, also on the square, although service can border on the hostile.
**🍴 Pensión Marisa**, Plaza Obispo Almaraz 2, T979 810 023. See Sleeping, above. Serves meals in a homely atmosphere.

### Carrión de los Condes *p283*
**🍴🍴 Bodegón El Resbalón**, C Fernán Gómez 17, T979 880 799. This dark and inviting spot is in an attractively refurbished traditional building. Stone and wood give a typical *bodega* feel, and the typical local cuisine matches it. There are few tables, so you might have to wait at lunchtime, but the €8 *menú* is worth it.

## ♠ Bars and clubs

**Palencia** *p279, map p280*

**Bar Maneo**, C La Cestilla 5. A trendy modern bar with chrome furniture and red walls that packs in a busy night crowd. By day it's also a restaurant, serving a bright contemporary *menú del día* for €12.

**Bora Bora**, C Maura 9, T979 746 388. 'It's a Samoan pub'. Well, OK, French Polynesian then, but the cocktails are as frilly as anything you'd find. Cheerful and relaxed atmosphere.

**Cleopas**, C Pedro Fernández de Pulgar 9. A cheery bar popular for evening drinks with the Palentine young.

**Merlin**, C Conde de Vallelano 4, T979 742 947. One of many bars around this block, where the weekend evenings kick on late with young Palencians driving the *marcha*.

**Frómista** *p282*

**Bar Garigolo**, around the corner from Hotel San Martín, has an internet terminal.

## ✺ Festivals and events

**Palencia** *p279*

**1st week of Sep** Palencia has lots of fiestas, but the main one is San Antolín. While hardly over the top by Spanish standards, there are plenty of markets, street stalls, bullfights, fireworks and concerts.

**Ampudia** *p281*

**1st weekend of Sep** Ampudia's fiesta includes bullfights.

## ⊙ Transport

**Palencia** *p279, map p280*

**Bus** For bus information, phone T979 743 222. There are hourly buses to **Valladolid**,

4 a day to **Burgos** (1 hr 15 mins) and **Madrid** (5 daily, 3 hrs 15 mins, €26.32). Within the province, there are 4 a day to **Aguilar de Campoo** via Frómista and Osorno, hourly buses to **Dueñas** via Venta del Baños, 2 daily to **Ampudia**, 2 to **Cervera**, 2 to **Astudillo** and 3 to **Saldaña**.

**Train** Palencia is on the main line, and is very well served by rail. For information, phone **RENFE** on T902 240 202. There are heaps of trains to **Frómista** (4 daily, 25 mins, €2.25), **Aguilar de Campoo** (6 daily, 1 hr, from €4.95), **Madrid** (3 hrs 30 mins, up to 12 daily, €16.20), **Valladolid** (at least hourly, 30 mins, from €2.80), **León** (12 daily, 1 hr 10 mins, from €7.20), and other destinations in Northern Spain.

**Ampudia** *p281*

**Bus** There are 2 buses daily to and from Palencia to **Ampudia**, and 1 to **Valladolid**.

**Medina de Rioseco** *p282*

**Bus** ALSA buses stop here on their way to and from **Valladolid**. There are about 20 services a day to that city, as well as 8 to **León**, 7 to **Madrid** and one to **Sahagún** via Mayorbo.

**Frómista** *p282*

**Bus ands train** There are regular buses and trains to Frómista from **Palencia**.

**Astudillo** *p283*

**Bus** There are 2 daily buses to and from **Palencia**.

**Carrión de los Condes** *p283*

**Bus** There are regular buses from Carrión de los Condes to **Palencia**.

# North towards Santander

*The northern part of Palencia province is an incredible haven of Romanesque architecture; every little village seems to have a round-arched gem tucked away. Fans of the style could spend many happy days exploring the area, based at Aguilar de Campoo. The Department of Tourism have a number of useful booklets and pamphlets on the subject, which they rightly regard as the province's chief attraction.* ➤ *For Sleeping, Eating and other listings, see pages 288-289.*

# Canal de Castilla

North of Frómista, the road heads north towards Santander. Alongside it stretches part of the Canal de Castilla. A major work, it was started in 1749 with the aim of transporting goods from the interior to the coast more easily. In those times of war and political turmoil it took over a century to complete. One branch begins at Valladolid, one at Medina de Rioseco, and they meet and continue north to Alar del Rey, from where the mountains made a continuation impossible and goods once again were put to

*Take insect repellent if planning a stroll or a hike.*

the road. It was a significant engineering feat for its time but sadly saw only 20-odd years of effective use before it was rendered redundant by the railway. Long stretches of it have a canalside path to walk, and there are a couple of information centres along the way.

## Monasterio de San Andrés de Arroyo → *Colour map 2, C4.*

① *30-min tours daily at 1000, 1100, 1200, 1300, 1600, 1700, 1800 and 1845, €1.50.* Make every effort to get to San Andrés de Arroyo, south from Aguilar de Campoo, and 8 km west of Alar del Rey. A working monastery populated by Cistercian nuns, it boasts a superb late 12th-century cloister, which you will be shown around by a friendly inhabitant. The cloister is double-columned and features some exceptionally intricate work, especially on the corner capitals. How the masons managed to chisel out the leaves and tendrils is anybody's guess. The far side of the cloister is more recent but features equally ornate work. The Sala Capitular is a Gothic affair with an ornate tomb supported by lions, in which rest the mortal remains of Doña Mencia Lara, a powerful local countess in her day. Traces of paint remain, a useful reminder that the bare Gothic style that we admire was often probably rather garishly coloured. The centrepiece of the cloister is a Moorish fountain originally from Granada.

Closer to the main road (2 km east) is the crumbly red Romanesque monastery **Iglesia de Santa María de Mave**. The keys are housed in the *hospedería* that's built into the monastery.

## Aguilar de Campoo ●🍴🏠🚌❶ → *pp288-289.*

→ *Colour map 2, C4.*

The lovely town of Aguilar sits where the Castilian plain gives way to the northern mountains of the Cordillera Cantábrica. Chilly, even snowy, in winter, its pleasant summer temperatures make it a place of blessed relief from the *meseta* heat. It makes an excellent base for exploring the area's Romanesque heritage. The **tourist office** ① *Plaza de España, T979 123 641, Tue-Fri 1000-1400, 1700-1845, Sat and Sun 1000-1345, 1700-1845, 1-hr guided walks leave Tue-Sun 1100, Tue-Sat 1700, €3,* is helpful.

The town sits on the Río Pisuerga and is centred on the long **Plaza de España**, which is where most things go on. At one end of the plaza is the **Colegiata de San Miguel** ① *T979 122 231, summer only 1030-1330, 1700-2000; guided tours Mon-Sat 1100, 1200, 1700, Sun 1300; €1.50,* which conceals a Gothic interior behind its attractive Romanesque façade. Inside, there's a big dusty *retablo*, a scary sleeping Christ with real hair and a small museum.

A number of **gateways** remain from the old walls; that on Calle Barrio y Mier has a Hebrew inscription, a legacy of the once substantial Jewish population, while the one behind the church is topped by griffins.

Across the river, the **Monasterio de Santa Clara** is home to a community of nuns that follow the Assisi saint. Its **Gothic church** ① *daily 1200-0100, 1800-1900,* can be visited. Appropriately in this town, baking is one of the principal activities here; the delicious pastries can be bought inside.

Castilla y León North towards Santander

## ⁞ Box o' biscuits

Aguilar is named after its 'eagle's nest', a slightly exaggerated description of the modest hill capped by a castle that overlooks the town. In latter days, however, the town has been known for biscuit-making; the rich smells wafting through the streets make a visitor permanently peckish. While iconic Fontaneda biscuits, first made by a local family in 1881, are no longer produced here, there are still three biscuit factories here, producing a wide range of crunchy delights.

The **Museo Ursi** ① *C Tobalina s/n, Tue-Sat 1300 and 1900, Sun am only*, is the workshop of the sculptor Ursicino Martínez, whose work, mostly from wood, is a blend of the sober, the abstract and the light-hearted.

Worth looking at is the Romanesque **Ermita de Santa Cecilia**, a chapel with a leaning tower on the hillside below the castle. You'll have to get the key from the priest's house (the tourist office will direct you). The interior is simple; the highlight is a superb capital showing the Innocents being put to the sword by chainmailed soldiers. Above, up a path, little remains of the castle but its walls; the view is good, but the town looks better from lower angles.

### Monasterio de Santa María la Real

On the road to Cervera, 1 km west is the Monasterio de Santa María la Real. The cloister is attractive enough, although bound to be disappointing after San Andrés de Arroyo, which is similar. The columns are doubled, but many of the capitals are missing (some are in Madrid). The Sala Capitular features clusters of multiple columns, their capitals impressively carved from a single block of stone. The **Museo Románico** ① *Jul and Aug daily 1030-1400, 1600-2000 (guided visits 1100, 1230, 1630, 1800), Sep-Jun Tue-Fri 1600-1900; Sat and Sun 1030-1400, 1630-1930, cloister free, museum €1.80*, housed in the monastery, is a little disappointing. Perhaps useful for planning a Romanesque itinerary as it contains many models of churches in the province, there is no information on the history or features of the style.

### Cervera de Pisuerga

Some 25 km west of Aguilar is the quiet town of Cervera de Pisuerga, set in the foothills of the Cordillera Cantábrica. It's not a bad base for outdoor activities; walkers will have a good time of it, at least as long as it's not quail season. The town's highlight is the Gothic **Iglesia de Santa María del Castillo** ① *May-Jun Sat and Sun 1030-1330, 1700-2000, Jul-Sep daily 1030-1330, 1700-2000, €1*, imperiously enthroned above the town. It's not of huge interest inside, but worth checking out is the side chapel of Santa Ana, with polychrome reliefs adorning the walls above the *retablo*. There's also a small **Museo Etnográfico** ① *summer Tue-Sat 1100-1400, 1700-2000, winter Sat and Sun 1100-1400, 1700-2000; €2*, of moderate interest. The **tourist office** ① *Parque El Plantío s/n, T979 870 695, summer only Mon-Sat 1000-1400, 1700-2000, Sun 1000-1400*, on the edge of town, has lots of information on driving and walking routes.

## ⬤ Sleeping

**Monasterio de San Andrés de Arroyo** *p287*
C **Posada Hostería El Convento**, T979 123 611, F979 125 492. A peaceful place to stay, apart from the odd goods-train rattling by.

**Aguilar de Campoo** *p287*
C **Hotel Valentín**, Av Ronda 23, T979 122 125, F979 122 442, www.hotelvalentin.com. This slightly larger-than-life complex can't be missed as you approach. On the main

road on the edge of town, it has a disco, restaurant, shops and a hotel that actually manages to be quite calm and pleasant, with large light rooms.

**F Albergue Nido de las Aguilas**, C Antonio Rojo 2, T979 128 036, www.albergue aguilas.com. The official hostel is a friendly place, which organizes several outdoor activities. Doors close between 2400 and 0730.

**F Hostal Siglo XX**, Plaza España 9, T979 126 040, F979 122 900. A good choice, with cosy rooms with TV and shared bath above a restaurant. Try and grab one of the front rooms, which have access to enclosed balconies overlooking the square.

### Camping

**Monte Royal**, Av Virgen del Llano s/n, T979 123 083. Near the lake to the west of town, this is a campsite with all the trappings.

### Cervera de Pisuerga *p288*

**A Parador Fuentes Carrionas**, Ctra de Resoba s/n, T979 870 075, www.parador.es. 2 km above the town is this large pinkish *parador*, which enjoys a privileged natural setting. There are great views from all the balconied rooms (which cost a little more), particularly those in the front, which overlook a lake. It's a lovely peaceful spot, where cows graze quietly in the grounds.

**D La Galería**, Plaza Mayor 16, T979 870 234. Right in the heart of this pretty village, this is a fine option with nice rooms on the charming square,

**E Casa Goyetes**, C El Valle 4, T979 870 568. Right opposite the church, this attractive wood-beamed *casa rural* is a relaxing and comfortable base. It's excellent value, and the homely rustic interior is a delight.

## 🍴 Eating

### Aguilar de Campoo *p287*

🍴 **El Barón**, C El Pozo 14, T979 123 151, F979 125 430. An excellent restaurant attractively set in an old stone building, and atmospherically decorated. There's a good *menú* for €15, and a lunch option for €9. Recommended.

🍴 **Siglo XX**, Plaza España 9, T979 126 040. Inside the *hostal*, there's a restaurant of good quality, while in the bar (and outside, weather permitting), a range of *raciones* and snacks are available.

### Cafés

**Café El Pueblo**, Paseo la Cascajera s/n. A friendly café on a small plaza by the river.

### Cervera de Pisuerga *p288*

🍴 **Gasolina**, near the plaza, T979 122 900. Worryingly named, this one serves cheap and simple but hearty food in an old stone building; there's some lovely chunky wooden furniture outside.

## 🍸 Bars and clubs

### Aguilar de Campoo *p287*

**Al Socano**, C Puente s/n. A bar with a good riverside beer garden.

### Cervera de Pisuerga *p288*

**Al Aire**, C Licenciado Fraile de la Hoz, is a pretty little courtyard bar.

## 🚎 Transport

### Aguilar de Campoo *p287*

**Bus**

The bus station is in the heart of town next to the **Hotel Valentín**. There are regular services to **Palencia**, **Santander**, **León** and **Burgos**, as well as **Cervera**.

**Train**

RENFE station is to the east of town and has frequent trains to **Palencia**, **Santander**, and **Madrid**.

### Cervera de Pisuerga *p288*

**Bus**

Cervera is linked by bus to **Aguilar** and **Palencia** a couple of times daily.

## ☎ Directory

### Aguilar de Campoo *p287*

**Internet** Playnet, C Comercio 8, has internet access amidst bursts of gunfire from online gamers. Open 1200-1400, 1700-2230, €2/hr. **Laundry** Salmar, Av Ronda 16, Mon-Fri 0930-1400, 1630-2000, Sat 1030-1400.

# León → *Phone code: 987. Colour map 2, C2. Population: 130,916 Altitude: 820 m.*

*León is one of the loveliest of Northern Spain's cities, with a proud architectural legacy, an elegant new town and an excellent tapas bar scene. Once capital of Christian Spain, it preserves an outstanding reminder of its glory days in its Gothic cathedral, one of the nation's finest buildings. After crossing the dusty meseta from Burgos, pilgrims arriving here should put their feet up for a couple of days and enjoy what León has to offer.* → *For Sleeping, Eating and other listings, see pages 296-300.*

## Ins and outs

**Getting there and around** León's bus and **RENFE** train stations are close to each other just across the river from the new town, a 10-minute walk from the old town. The bus station is the best bet, as **ALSA** and other buses have a comprehensive network both within the province and with other northern Spanish cities. → *See also Transport, page 299.*

**Best time to visit** Like Burgos, León's high altitude results in freezing winters and roasting summers; spring and autumn are good times to visit, as there's little rain.

**Tourist information** León's cheerful **tourist office** ① *T987 237 082, oficinade turismodeleon@jcyl.es, Mon-Fri 0900-1400, 1700-1900 (2000 in summer), Sat and Sun 1000-1400, 1700-2000*, is opposite the cathedral on Plaza de la Regla.

## Background

León was founded as a Roman fortress in AD 68 to protect the road that transported the gold from the mines in El Bierzo to the west. It became the base of the *Legio Septima*, the seventh legion of Imperial Rome; this is where the name originates (although León means 'lion' in Spanish). The city was Christianized in the third century and is one of the oldest bishoprics in western Europe. After being reconquered in the mid-eighth century, León became the official residence of the Asturian royal line in the early 10th century; the royals were thereafter known as kings of León. The city was recaptured and sacked several times by the Moors until it was retaken for the final time by Alfonso V in 1002. León then enjoyed a period of power and glory as the centre of Reconquista pride and prestige; the city flourished on protection paid from the fragmented *taifa* states.

In 1188 there was a meeting of nobles and ecclesiasts that set the pattern for what was later to become the system of *cortes*, regional quasi-parliaments that kept Spanish kings on a tight leash. As the Reconquista moved further south, however, León found itself increasingly put in the shade by the young whippersnapper Castilla, which had seceded from it in the 10th century.

In 1230 the crowns were united, and León is still bound to Castilla to this day, a fact bemoaned by many – spraycans are often taken to the castles on the coat of arms of the region, leaving only the Leonese lion. When the Flemish Habsburg Carlos V took the throne of Spain, León feared further isolation and became one of the prime movers in the *comunero* rebellion. One of the most extreme of the *comuneros* was a Leonese named Gonzalo de Guzmán, who declared a "war of fire, sack and blood" on the aristocracy. The rebellion was heavily put down, and León languished for centuries.

The region's coal provided some prosperity in the 19th century, but it has really only been relatively recently that the city has lifted itself from stagnating regional market-town to what it is today; a modern and dynamic Spanish city.

# 66 99 León cathedral has more glass than stone, more light than glass, and more faith than light (Pope John XXIII)

## Sights

León's **old town** is to the east of the River Bernesga and surrounded by the boulevards of the newer city. Walk up the pedestrianized Calle Ancha and prepare to be stunned by the appearance of the white Gothic cathedral, a jewel in Spain's architectural crown.

### Cathedral

ⓘ *Mon-Sat 0830-1330, 1600-1900; Sun 0830-1430, 1700-1900 (summer closing 2000); free. Guided tours leave Tue-Sat at 1200 and 1600 from the tourist office, €4.50.*
Effectively begun in the early 13th century, León's cathedral is constructed over the old Roman baths; this, combined with the poor quality of the stone used and the huge quantity of stained glass, has made the building fairly unstable. A late 19th-century restoration replaced many of the more decayed stones, an impressive engineering feat that required removing and replacing whole sections of the building.

Approaching the cathedral up Calle Ancha, its spectacular bulk is suddenly revealed. The main western façade is flanked by two bright towers, mostly original Gothic but capped with later crowns, the northern (left hand) one by one of the Churriguera brothers. Walking around the outside, there's some superb buttressing as well as numerous quirky gargoyles and pinnacles. Back at the main door, investigate the triple-arched façade, expressively carved. The central portal features a jovial Christ above a graphic Hell, with demons cheerfully stuffing sinners into cooking pots. To the right are scenes from the life of the Virgin; a brief biography of her son is on the left side.

As you enter through the wooden doors, look up at the back corner behind you. The leathery object hanging above the door is supposed to be the carcass of the *topo maligno* (evil mole) who was blamed for tunnelling under the building works and destroying the masons' labours. In reality, the Roman baths underneath were the cause of all the tunnels; while the mole was apparently captured and killed, the hanging carcass is that of a large tortoise.

The beautifully untouched Gothic interior of the cathedral is illuminated by a riot of stained glass, a patchwork of colour that completely changes the building's character depending on the time of day and amount of sun outside. The sheer amount of glass is impressive; some 1700 sq m. The oldest glass is to be found in the apse and in the large rose window above the main entrance; some of it dates to the 13th century, while other panels span later centuries. There's a general theme to it all; the natural world is depicted at low levels, along with the sciences and arts; normal folk, including nobles, are in the middle, while saints, prophets, kings and angels occupy the top positions. Every so often at night, instead of floodlighting the building, it is illuminated from the inside, a spectacular sight.

Another of the cathedral's appealing attributes is that, although there's a Renaissance *trascoro* illustrating the Adoration and Nativity, there's a transparent panel allowing a perspective of the whole church, a rarity in Spanish cathedrals. The *coro* itself is beautifully and humourously carved of walnut, although you'll have to join one of the frequent guided tours to inspect it at close quarters. The *retablo* is an excellent painted work by Nicolás Francés, although not complete. Scenes from the lives of the Virgin and the city's patron, San Froilán, are depicted.

‡ *León's cathedral is one of the most lovable of Spain's grand buildings.*

*Castilla y León* León

Much venerated is the 13th-century statue of the Virgen Blanca, in one of the apsidal chapels; there's also a replica of the elegant sculpture in the portal. Inside the north door of the cathedral is another Virgin, also with child; she's known as the Virgin of the Die, after an unlucky gambler lobbed his six-sider at the statue, causing the Christ-child's nose to bleed.

Also worth a peek are two excellent 13th-century tombs in the transepts. Holding the remains of two bishops involved in the cathedral's construction, they are carved with scenes from the prelates' lives; although heavily damaged, the representations are superb.

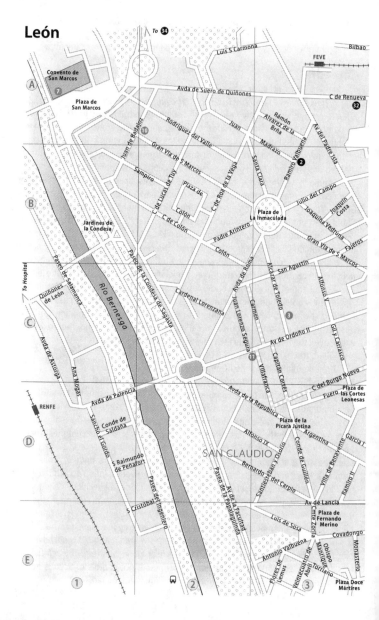

León

The **cathedral museum** ⓘ *Oct-May Mon-Fri 0930-1330, 1600-1900, Sat 0930-1330, Jun Mon-Sat 0930-1330, 1600-1900, Jul-Sep Mon-Fri 0930-1400, 1600-1930, Sat 0930-1400, 1600-1900, €3.50, €1 cloister only, last museum visit 1 hr before closing*, is housed in the cloisters and sacristy. Most of the cloister is Renaissance in style, with several tombs of wealthy nobles and frescoes; note too the star vaulting. The museum, part of which is accessed up a beautiful Plateresque stair, is a good collection, with many notable pieces. Outstanding items include a Mozarabic bible dating from the 10th century, fragments of stained glasswork, and a superb crucifixion by Juan de Juni, portraying a twisted, anguished Christ.

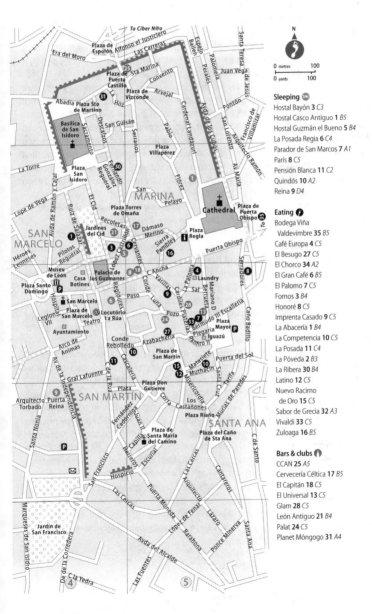

**Sleeping** 🛏
Hostal Bayón **3** *C3*
Hostal Casco Antiguo **1** *B5*
Hostal Guzmán el Bueno **5** *B4*
La Posada Regia **6** *C4*
Parador de San Marcos **7** *A1*
París **8** *C5*
Pensión Blanca **11** *C2*
Quindós **10** *A2*
Reina **9** *D4*

**Eating** 🍴
Bodega Viña Valdevimbre **35** *B5*
Café Europa **4** *C5*
El Besugo **27** *C5*
El Chorco **34** *A2*
El Gran Café **6** *B5*
El Palomo **7** *C5*
Fornos **3** *B4*
Honoré **8** *C5*
Imprenta Casado **9** *C5*
La Abacería **1** *B4*
La Competencia **10** *C5*
La Posada **11** *C4*
La Póveda **2** *B3*
La Ribera **30** *B4*
Latino **12** *C5*
Nuevo Racimo de Oro **15** *C5*
Sabor de Grecia **32** *A3*
Vivaldi **33** *C5*
Zuloaga **16** *B5*

**Bars & clubs** 🍸
CCAN **25** *A5*
Cervecería Céltica **17** *B5*
El Capitán **18** *C5*
El Universal **13** *C5*
Glam **28** *C5*
León Antiguo **21** *B4*
Palat **24** *C5*
Planet Móngogo **31** *A4*

**Castilla y León** *León*

① *Sep-Jun Mon-Sat 1000-1330, 1600-1830, Sun 1000-1330, Jul-Aug Mon-Sat 0900-2000, Sun 0900-1400, €3, free Thu pm.*

As well as the Gothic cathedral, León also has a cracker of a Romanesque ensemble in the Basílica de San Isidoro. Consecrated in the 11th century over an earlier church, it was renamed in 1063 when Fernando I managed to get that learned saint's remains repatriated from Sevilla (see box, page 442).

The complex is built into the medieval city walls, much of which is preserved. The façade is beautiful, particularly in the morning or evening light; it's pure Romanesque in essence, although the balustrade and pedimental shield were added, harmoniously, during the Renaissance, and there are Gothic additions in other parts of the building. Facing the building, the right-hand doorway is named the **Puerta del Perdón** (door of forgiveness); pilgrims could gain absolution by passing through here if they were too infirm to continue their journey to Santiago. The door is topped by a good relief of the Descent from the Cross and Ascension.

To the left is the **Puerta del Cordero** (door of the lamb) with an even more impressive tympanum depicting Abraham's sacrifice. Atop this door is the Renaissance pediment, decorated with a large shield surmounted by San Isidoro in Reconquista mode (like Santiago, this bookish scholar made surprise horseback appearances to fight Moors several centuries after his death). The interior of the church is dark and attractive, with later Gothic elements in accord with the Romanesque; large multifoil arches add a Moorish element. The *retablo* dates from the 16th century and surrounds a monstrance in which the Host is permanently on display (the basilica is one of only two churches in Northern Spain to have been granted this right). Below is a casket containing the remains of Isidore himself – or whoever it was whose bones were found in Sevilla long after the saint's burial place had been forgotten.

The real treasure of San Isidoro lies through another exterior door which gives access to the **museum**. On entering, the first chamber you are given access to is the Panteón Real, an astonishing crypt that is the resting place of 11 kings of León and their families. The arches, the ceiling and some of the tombs are covered with Romanesque wallpainting in a superb state of preservation (it's barely needed any restoration). There are scenes from the New Testament as well as agricultural life; if you're at all jaded with religious art and architecture, this sublime space will fix it. The short columns are crowned with well-carved capitals, mostly vegetal, but some with Biblical scenes or motifs derived from Visigothic traditions.

The next stop on the visit is the first of the two cloisters, above which rises the emblematic **Torre del Gallo**, (tower of the cock), topped by a curious 11th-century gold-plated weathercock that wouldn't look out of place at White Hart Lane.

The treasury and library is the other highlight of the visit to the museum. Although the complex was sacked and badly damaged by French troops in the Napoleonic Wars, most of the priceless collection of artefacts and books survived. More remains of San Isidoro reside in an 11th-century reliquary beautifully decorated in Mozarabic style; another reliquary is equally finely carved from ivory. The ornate chalice of Doña Urraca is made from two Roman cups and studded with gems. The library contains some beautiful works, of which the highlight is a 10th-century Mozarabic bible.

At the back of San Isidoro is a guesthouse used mostly for retreats. An intriguing option is to have lunch in its restaurant; you get to see parts of the building normally not open to the public. You need to reserve by phoning T987 875 088, and, while you don't get a choice of what you eat, it's always generously proportioned and tasty, costing €12 including drinks.

● León was the birthplace of one of the most significant Jewish cabalistic writers, Moses de
● León, known as the author of the mystical Zohar.

## Convento de San Marcos

León's other great monument is the San Marcos convent by the river, which doubles as a sumptuous *parador*. Not a bad place to stay, you might think; so, no doubt, did generations of pilgrims who laid their road-dusted heads down here when it was administered as a monastery and hostel by the Knights of Santiago.

The massive façade is the highlight. It postdates the pilgrim era and is 100 m long, pure Plateresque overlaid by a Baroque pediment, and sensitively dignified by a well-designed modern plaza. The church itself is attractive if rather unremarkable; more inspiring is the adjoining cloister with its figure-adorned arches. You can also access it from the *parador*. There are daily tours of the hotel, but it's easy enough to take a stroll around the ground floor areas (ask first); the bar and lounge are attractive and open to the public.

Next to the *parador* on the riverbank a crowd gather at weekends and on some weekday evenings to watch the curious game of *bolos*, in which old men toss  a wooden hemisphere at skittles aiming, not to knock them over, but to roll it in an arc between them.

## Old town

On the edge of León's old town, the **Museo de León** ① *Plaza Santo Domingo 8, T987 236 405, Tue-Sat 1000-1400, 1600-1900 (1700-2000 summer), Sun 1000- 1400, €1.20*, opened its doors in early 2007 to some acclaim. It's a very impressive modern display that comprehensively covers the city's significant Roman, royal, and Jewish past. Among the pieces on display is the famous Cristo de Carraza, an exquisite 11th century ivory crucifix.

Other sights in the old town include the nearby **Casa Botines**, a *palacio* built by Gaudí in subdued (for him) fairytale style. It now functions as an exhibition centre, but the top floors are a bank. You have to catch them in a very good mood at the front desk if you want to go upstairs and have a look; if they let you in, it's amusing to watch executives trying to look corporate whilst working in a pointy turret. The building's façade features St George sticking it to a dragon; a bronze sculpture of Gaudí observes his creation narrowly from a park bench outside. Next door is the elegant **Palacio de los Guzmanes**, a 16th-century Renaissance palace with a fine façade and beautiful patio. Across the square, the old Ayuntamiento is from the same period; next to it is the fine tower of **San Marcelo**.

Wandering around León's old quarter will reveal many time-worn architectural treasures and hidden nooks. The area north of Calle Ancha contains several, but the area south is the most interesting. This is the **Húmedo**, the 'wet' *barrio*, named after its massive collection of tapas bars, the most popular of which are around Plaza de San Martín, which hums with life most evenings and explodes at weekends. Near here is the beautiful **Plaza Mayor**, an extremely elegant porticoed 18th-century design which holds a fascinating and extremely traditional Wednesday and Saturday morning fruit and veg market. Delve a little further into the area and you'll come to the **Plaza de Santa María del Camino**, popularly known as Plaza del Grano (grain square) for its one-time wheat exchange. It's a lovely time-worn space with rough cobbles, wooden arcades and a pretty Romanesque church.

## Valdevimbre

An excellent lunch or dinnertime excursion is to head some 20 km south of León to **Valdevimbre**, a historic winemaking village with spacious *bodegas* dug into the hills. Several of these have been converted into atmospheric restaurants with fine, well-priced food (see Eating, page 298). To get to Valdevimbre, turn off the N630 18 km south of León. Public transport isn't great, but you can hop off a Zamora/ Benavente bound bus at the turn-off, from where it's a half-hour walk. A taxi either way costs €18-26.

# ● Sleeping

**León** *p290, map p292*

**LL Parador de San Marcos**, Plaza San Marcos 7, T987 237 300, www.parador.es. One of Spain's most attractive hotels, housed in the former monastery and pilgrim hostel of San Marcos. The furnishings are elegant but not over the top, and the building itself is a treasure. The rooms are comfortable and attractive, even if they don't quite live up to the rest of the building.

**A La Posada Regia**, C Regidores 9, T987 218 820, www.regialeon.com. This is a superb, characterful place to stay in León's old quarter. Just off busy pedestrian C Ancha, this 14th-century building has hugely enticing rooms with floorboards, pastel shades and many thoughtful touches; get one away from the street though, as there's a motorcycle shop next door. The restaurant is excellent, and there's underground parking very close by.

**B Hotel Paris**, C Ancha 18, T987 238 600, www.hotelparisleon.com. This is something of a León staple; a bright modern hotel on the main pedestrian street near the cathedral. The rooms are well-equipped and very comfortable for the price – with minibar, good bathroom, and pillow menu. There's also a good café, and atmospheric downstairs restaurant and tapas bar.

**B Hotel Quindós**, Gran Vía de San Marcos 38, T987 236 200, www.hotelquindos.com. This is a very pleasant modern hotel near San Marcos, with inventively chic decor, modern art on the walls, rooms all decorated differently from each other and with plenty of colour, as well as an excellent restaurant. Good value.

**D Hostal Casco Antiguo**, C Cardenal Landázuri 11, T987 074 000. This new spot is attractively modern and enjoys a fabulous location in the heart of old León, very close to the cathedral but on a quiet street. The rooms aren't huge but have good bathrooms; an added plus are the ruins of a Roman camp in the basement.

**D Hostal Guzmán el Bueno**, C López Castrillón 6, T987 236 412. This is a good choice in the old town, with attractive woody rooms in a spruce old building in the *barrio* of the Cid. They're a little dark because it's on

a narrow street, but they are well-equipped, and the management is friendly.

**E Hotel Reina**, C Puerta de la Reina 2, T987 205 200. This hotel was a faded beauty until enterprising new management took it over; now it is charmingly Spanish retro and offers excellent value. Rooms are bright and cheery, and come with or without old-fashioned bathroom (only 2 rooms use each shared one). There's a lift and roof terrace, and always a genuine welcome. Recommended.

**E Pensión Blanca**, C Villafranca 2, T987 251 991/678 660 244. This is an exceptional budget option; the rooms are light and colourful, tastefully decorated with brand new furnishings. Rooms have private or shared bathroom; guests have use of a kitchen and there's free internet access if the friendly owner isn't busy on the computer. Breakfast is included in the price, and you can have you're your laundry done. Highly recommended.

**E Hostal Bayón**, C Alcázar de Toledo 6, T987 231 446. This is a fine and homely choice, with comfy rooms with en suite or shared bath (**F**) in a friendly *pensión*. It's got character and it's quiet and leafy with house plants.

# ● Eating

**León** *p290, map p292*

Eating in León is a pleasure. Nearly all the tapas bars give a free snack with every drink; it's standard practice to order a *corto* (short beer) to take full advantage – these cost €0.80 or so. The most concentrated tapas zone is around Plaza San Martín in the Barrio Húmedo; for a quieter scene, head across C Ancha into the Barrio Romántico. There's also a popular knot of modern tapas bars near the river on Av de los Reyes Leoneses (Las Eras).

**♥♥♥ Restaurante Vivaldi**, C Platerías 4, T987 260 760. Widely regarded as the province's finest restaurant, this classy and welcoming spot serves up memorable gourmet food, many of the recipes using the traditional ingredients of the region. Mains are €15-25, and there are several *menú de degustación* options. The wine list is long and impressive.

**El Palomo**, C Escalerilla 8, T987 254 225. A good little restaurant in the Húmedo area, with well-priced, high quality fare and a friendly attitude. The cuisine is typically Leonese, with plenty of dishes to share as well as steaks and fine fish dishes.

**Imprenta Casado**, C Varillas 3, T987 218 235. Formerly a printers, this Barrio Húmedo restaurant continues the theme on its walls and charmingly presented menu. The upstairs dining room is intimate and looks out over the pedestrian street below. All the food is good, but the steaks, the house pâtés, and the croquettes are especially tasty.

**La Póveda**, C Ramiro Valbuena 9, T987 227 155. The curious fact that the boss here is almost universally loathed yet manages to constantly fill his restaurant says much about the quality of the cooking. Dishes are mostly *raciones*, and are absolutely delicious – the *sesos* (brains) have incredible flavour and texture, and the octopus is as good as you'll get outside Galicia.

**Restaurante Zuloaga**, C Sierra Pambley 3, T987 237 814. This very original modern restaurant is set in a large space with a pretty courtyard in a 19th-century mansion, with surprisingly large tables. The dishes are prepared with some French influence and plenty of originality, and the service is warm. The *menú del día* isn't really worth bothering with. Recommended.

**Sabor de Grecia**, C Renueva 11, T987 224 628. A welcoming family-run restaurant not far from San Isidoro, this is much visited for its short but very delicious menu of Greek cuisine. Dishes such as meatballs or broad beans ooze with flavour, and can be accompanied by a number of Greek wines. Best to book ahead. Recommended.

**Bodega Viña Valdevimbre**, C San Guillermo 44, T987 255 413. A very traditional sort of place, with cheap wine from the nearby village of Valdevimbre served out of big barrels. There are simple tapas of ham, chorizo and the like. Very characterful.

**El Besugo**, C Azabachería 10, T987 256 995. This is an old-style León tapas bar; a big spacious place that doesn't deal in frills but rather simple free *morcilla* and *jamón*. There are tables to devour reliable and good-value *raciones* of the same sort of fare, and an upstairs restaurant. It's one of the classics of León.

**El Chorco**, Av Reyes Leoneses 14, T987 279 090. One of the best of a string of popular tapas bars in a new zone not far from San Marcos. The free snacks here are generous, and the service prompt. It gets very lively around 2030, when the local office workers down tools for the day.

**Fornos**, C El Cid 8, T680 857 544. This longstanding León favourite has recently reopened in rebuilt premises. Light and modern, it specializes in traditional Leonese fare, accompanied by a range of wines. Grab a table and try the calamari, the *mollejas*, or any of the other delicious *raciones*. Good tapas at the bar too.

**La Abacería**, C Ruiz de Salazar 14, T987 234 273. This delicatessan, which specializes in classy produce from around the region doubles as a wine bar, with cheery hosts and a good range. The tapas are very tasty ham, chorizo and *lomo*, and there's usually a photo exhibition. Excellent.

**La Competencia**, C Conde Rebolledo 17/C Mulhacín 8, T987 212 312. A León classic, this deservedly popular place serves very good cheap pizzas in 2 locations in the heart of the Barrio Húmedo. They serve until late at weekends; the 2-level bar at C Mulhacín is also much visited as a tapas bar.

**La Posada**, C la Rúa 33, T987 258 266. Opposite the casino, this is a lovely cosy family-run place serving a range of simple, tasty, and well-priced *raciones* in a checked-tableclothed *comedor*; it all comes with a welcoming smile from the humour-filled boss.

**La Ribera**, C Fernando González Regueral 8, T987 270 408. The locals crowded into this place will show you that it's one of León's best tapas bars. Once you squeeze your way to the bar, you'll find out why; as well as the home-made fried potatoes, you can enjoy some of the tastiest innards around: tripe, kidneys and *asadurilla* to remember. If that's not your thing, try the delicious mussels.

**Latino**, Plaza de San Martín 10, T987 262 109. This is a great tapas bar and is always busy and cheerful. The free snacks are tasty and generous; there's also a restaurant which has high-quality fare; the spinach and bacon salad stands out, as do the steaks. There's a terrace on the square in summer.

**Nuevo Racimo de Oro**, Plaza San Martín 8, T987 214 767. One of the best bars on this busy square, this is a beautiful spot with old brick and timber walls and a range of *raciones* to be devoured on foot. There are also 2 atmospheric *comedores* above and below the bar, where pricier, but rich and tasty dishes are served.

**¶Restaurante Honoré**, C Serradores 4, T987 210 864. A welcoming place to eat with French-influenced gourmet choices at very low prices. Everything on the menu is good; the *solomillo al foie* is the tenderest of steaks, and comes smothered in rich sauce, while the duck dishes are also excellent. Be prepared to wait a long time for service and food, but it's worth every minute; if this restaurant charged double the price, it'd be famous throughout the region. Highly recommended.

### Cafés

**Café Europa**, Plaza la Regla 9, T987 256 117. With a great location looking up at the cathedral, this café has a relaxed atmosphere, and a good range of coffees and teas.

**El Gran Café**, C Cervantes 9, T987 272 301. This classic café is a popular and atmospheric spot for an afternoon coffee, with a beautiful upstairs *sala* used for cabaret and meals. Regular live music.

### Valdevimbre *p295*

**¶La Cueva del Cura**, T987 304 037. Slightly more upmarket than Cueva San Simón with similarly excellent food; but don't try the *potro* if you are a horse lover.

**¶La Cueva San Simón**, T987 304 096. A spacious warren of a place with the main dining area in the chimneyed fermentation chamber; try the *solomillo a la brasa*, morsels of tenderest steak that you rapidly cook on a sizzling grate that's brought to the table.

## ⊙ Bars and clubs

### León *p290, map p292*
León's nightlife is busy; the **Barrio Húmedo** is the best place for concentrated action – wander around these streets and you'll find any number of bars that will suit you, but by law they shut at 0400; for later dancing and drinking, head for the zone around **C Burgo** Nuevo in the new town, where there are several options.

**CCAN**, Plaza Puerta Castillo 10, T987 230 609. Virtually unmarked on the street, and reached via a colourful staircase, this 2nd-floor members' club is a haven for everything offbeat and outside the León mainstream. Its dark, cosy attic bar sees the lot; from chess tournaments and environmental debates to frenzied flamenco and heavy rock. At other times the varied crowd (non-members very welcome) just relaxes and chats. Due to move to a new location while the premises are being renovated - ask. Open nightly from 2000 until late. Closed Jul/Aug.

**Cervecería Céltica**, C Cervantes 10, T987 230 774. This large and bright bar has an excellent range of Belgian beers, and several draught options, all expertly poured. Always buzzy and cheerful.

**El Capitán**, C Ancha 8, T987 262 772. A reliable and atmospheric nightspot, with candlelit tables and a romantic range of curios and furniture. The drinks aren't cheap, but it's one of the nicest places to sit with friends for a quiet chat. Open nightly until after 0200; there's more of a mixed crowd than many places.

**El Universal**, Pl Mayor s/n. On a corner of the Plaza Mayor, this is one of León's best bars, standing out from the crowd for its mix of all types of people, good music, well-made drinks, and busy, cheerful bar staff. In summer there's a terrace out on the square – a great place to be.

**Glam**, C Platerías 10. The trendiest late-night spot with León's young, this spacious and extravagantly decorated *discoteca* is absolutely mobbed at weekends around 0200. The music is far from glam rock, usually centring around the latest pop and dance hits and enlivened by live acts and go-go dancers. Bands sometimes play here too.

**León Antiguo**, Plaza Ordoño IV s/n, T987 226 956. A good bar with a friendly upmarket vibe and a nice outdoor terrace in the quieter part of the old town. Always busy and cheerful.

**Palat**, C Pozo s/n. One of the city's better pink choices, with a gay-mixed crowd, cool decor and decent music.

**Planet Móngogo**, Plaza Puerta Castillo 5. People come from all over Northern Spain to visit this unique bar, which is flexing its zebra stripes and leopard spots in better form than ever. Rock 'n' roll and trash horror are the themes, and it's a memorable spot for drinks – including the worryingly fluorescent Zombie Zumo – and food, with the kitchen turning out high-quality Mexican plates at low prices. Highly recommended. Open Tue-Sun from 1800.

## ⊛ Festivals and events

**León** *p290, map p292*
**Mar/Apr** León's **Semana Santa** (Easter Week) is a very traditional, serious affair, with many mournful processions conducted by striking hooded *cofradías* (religious brotherhoods and sisterhoods). Carrying the heavy *pasos* (floats bearing sculptures of Jesus and Mary) is thirsty work; relief comes in the form of *limonada*, a *sangría*-like punch; a throwback to Christian Spain's dark past is that going out to drink a few is traditionally known as *matar judíos* ('kill Jews').
**Late Jun** The feasts of **San Juan** (24th) and **San Pablo** (28th) are León's major fiestas of the year. There's a good range of activities over 10 days, including bullfights, concerts and high alcohol consumption.
**Early Oct** Fiesta de **San Froilán**, the city's patron, is the first weekend of Oct. There's a Moorish/medieval market, processions and dances; there's also a good Celtic music festival.

## ○ Shopping

**León** *p290, map p292*
The main shopping street is **Av Ordoño II** in the new town; more quirky shops can be found in the old town.

### Books
**Galatea**, C Sierra Pambley 1, T987 272 652, near the cathedral, has an surprising and high-quality selection of English-language fiction and non-fiction.
**Iguazú**, C Plegarias 7, T987 208 066. A good place to go for maps and travel literature.

### Food
**Don Queso**, C Azabachería, is a good cheese shop. Nearby is a delightful shop that sells all the necessary to make your own sausages and *chorizo*.

## ▲ Activities and tours

**León** *p290, map p292*
**Mundileón**, T987 212 266, www.mundi leon.com. This agency is a good option for people on public transport. They arrange a variety of tours around this fascinating province, in English or Spanish, and will pick up from any hotel in the city.

## ⊖ Transport

**León** *p290, map p292*
**Bus**
**Local** Within the province, **Astorga** (30-45 mins, €2.90) is served hourly, **Sahagún** 2-3 times daily (1 hr, €4.09), **Riaño** 3 times (1 hr 45 mins, €6.60), one to **Posada de Valdeón**, **Ponferrada** hourly (1-2 hrs, €7.15), and **Villafranca del Bierzo** 3 times (2 hrs 30 mins, €8.30).
**Long distance** There are 10 to 12 departures for **Madrid** (4 hrs, €18.86), 8 to **Valladolid** (€7.70, 2 hrs, stops at Valladolid airport on request), a similar number north to **Oviedo** (1 hr 30 mins, €7.31) and **Gijón**, 5-7 to **Zamora** (2 hrs, €7.90) via Benavente, 2 to **Salamanca** (3 hrs, €10.15), 3 to **Barcelona** (10 hrs, €39.19), 1 to **Palencia**, 3 to **Burgos** (2hrs, €12.09) and 3 into **Galicia**.

**Train**
From the RENFE station, trains run to **Madrid** 8 times a day (4 hrs 30 mins, from €19.65), north to **Oviedo** (2 hrs, from €6.80) and **Gijón** 7 times, east to **Barcelona** 3 times daily (10-11 hrs, from €40) via **Palencia**, **Burgos**, **Logroño**, **Vitoria**, **Pamplona** and **Zaragoza**, and 2 daily westwards to **A Coruña** and **Santiago**.
A dozen trains run east to **Sahagún**, and several daily go west to **Astorga** and **Ponferrada**.
The FEVE station is on Av Padre Isla, northwest of the centre. The line runs to **Bilbao**; it's a scenic but slow journey via every village (1 daily, 7 hrs 15 mins, €18.45). The luxury train service, **Transcantábrico**, follows this route and onwards to Santiago, see Sport and special interest travel, page 49.

## ⊙ Directory

**Internet** Locutório La Rúa, C La Rúa 8, T987 230 106, provides internet access and reasonably priced phone calls; **Ciber N@o**, Av Nocedo 16, €1.70 per hr. **Laundry** La Paloma, C Paloma 6, near the cathedral.

**Medical services** Hospital Virgen Blanca, C Altos de Nava, T987 237 400. Call 112 in an emergency. **Police** Paseo del Parque s/n, T987 255 500. Call 092 in an emergency. **Post office** The main post office is on Plaza de San Francisco and open continuously from 0800-2000 Mon-Fri and 1000-1400 Sat.

# León Province

*Although joined in semi-autonomous harmony with Castilla, the province of León is fairly distinct, and offers a different experience to the vast Castilian plain. In fact, it's got a bit of everything; a look at the map confirms that it's part* meseta, *part mountain, and part fertile valleyland.*

*León was an important early kingdom of the Christian Reconquest, but soon lost ground and importance as the battlegrounds moved further south and power became focused around Valladolid and then Madrid. Mining has been a constant part of the area's history; the Romans extracted gold in major operations in the west of the province, while coal, cobalt and copper are all still extracted, although with limited future.*

*The west of the province is a region of hills and valleys known as El Bierzo. It's a busy rural zone of grapevines,vegetables, mines and more; further exploration reveals superb natural enclaves and vibrant local fiestas.*

*The pilgrim route crosses León province, stopping in the towns of Sahagún, Astorga, Ponferrada and Villafranca del Bierzo as well as the capital; good places all to regain lost strength for the climb into Galicia and the last haul of the journey.* ▸▸ *For Sleeping, Eating and other listings, see pages 307-310.*

## Camino de Santiago 🍴🚲🚶✳️🛏 ▸▸ *pp307-310.*

### Sahagún → *Colour map 2, C3.*

Sahagún is one of those rare towns whose population is only a quarter of that it housed in the Middle Ages. These days it's a likeable enough place; wandering its dusty streets it's hard to imagine that Sahagún was ever anything more than what it is today – an insignificant agricultural town of the thirsty *meseta*.

Sahagún's main attraction is its collection of *mudéjar* buildings. These differ from Aragonese *mudéjar* and are to some extent Romanesque buildings made of brick.

The area around Sahagún was settled by Romans and the town is named for an early Christian basilica dedicated to a local saint, Facundo (the Latin name was Sanctum Facundum). The town began to thrive once Santiago-fever got going, and it gained real power and prestige when King Alfonso VI invited a community of Cluny monks to establish the Roman rite in the area. They built their monastery, San Benito, on the site of the old Visigothic church; once Alfonso had granted it massive privileges and lands, it became one of the most powerful religious centres of Spain's north.

Sahagún's most famous son was a 16th-century Franciscan missionary to the Americas, Friar Bernardino, a remarkable figure. His respect for Aztec culture made him a controversial figure at the time; he mastered the *náhuatl* language and wrote texts in it. He is commemorated in his hometown by a small bust near the Plaza Mayor.

🎈 *For information on the practicalities of walking the Camino de Santiago and the history of the pilgrimage, see pages 52 and 388.*

**Iglesia de San Lorenzo** is the most emblematic of Sahagún's *mudéjar* buildings; a church dating from the early 13th century and characterized by a pretty belltower punctured with three rows of arches. The interior is less impressive, remodelled in later periods. It's worth climbing the tower if restoration work permits.

The **Iglesia de San Tirso** dates from the 12th century and is similar, with a smaller but pretty tower. The interior has suffered through neglect, but it's worth popping in to see the floats from Sahagún's well-known **Semana Santa** celebrations, as well as a well-carved 13th-century tomb, later reused. At the time of writing, San Tirso was closed for restoration. Visits run daily to another church on the hill, **Santuario de la Virgen Peregrina** ① *ask at the tourist office or the pilgrim albergue for tours; free, but donations are badly needed for restorative work*, formerly a Franciscan monastery. The interior is again sadly in need of restoration, but the point of the visit is to see a little chapel at the back of the church, where fragments of superb Mozarabic stucco work were found when the plaster that covered them began to flake off in the mid-20th century. The chapel was commissioned by a local noble in the 15th century to house his own bones.

By the church is what's left of the **Monasterio de San Benito**; a clocktower and a Gothic chapel. The portal also survived and has been placed across the road behind the building; it's an ornate Baroque work from the 17th century with impressive lions. Nearby, in the still-functioning **Monasterio de Santa Cruz** ① *1000-1300, 1615-1830, €1.20*, is a small museum of religious art which also has architectural and sculptural fragments from the burned monastery.

## Around Sahagún

If your legs aren't weary from peregrination, or if you've got a car, there's a good excursion from Sahagún. It's an hour's walk south to the **Convento de San Pedro de las Dueñas**, which preserves some excellent Romanesque capitals and attractive *mudéjar* brickwork. The keyholder is a curious old man named Pablo; if he doesn't appear, seek him out in the house below the castle by the main road.

Head east from the convent for around half an hour to **Grajal de Campos**, with an excellent castle of Moorish origin but beefed up in the 15th and 16th centuries. It's a very imposing structure indeed. There's not a great deal to see inside, but it's fun to climb the crumbling stairs and walls. While you're in town, have a look at the nearby *palacio*, which has seen better days but preserves an attractively down-at-heel patio. From here, it's about an hour back to Sahagún.

### Mansilla de la Mulas → *Colour map 2, C2.*

Beyond Sahagún, the pilgrim trail continues to Mansilla de la Mulas. There are few mules around these days, and what remains of its once proud heritage are the ruins of its fortifications. Some 8 km north, however, is the lovely Mozarabic **Iglesia de San Miguel de Escalada** ① *Oct-Mar Wed-Sat 1030-1315, 1630-1800, Sun 1030-1315; Apr-Sep Wed-Sat 1030-1345, 1630-2000, Sun 1030-1345*, dating from the 10th century, it was built by a group of Christian refugees from Córdoba. There's a pretty horseshoe-arched porch; the interior is attractively bare of ornament; the arches are set on columns reused from an earlier structure, and are beautifully subtle. A triple arch divides the altar area from the rest of the church. It's a lovely place, well worth the detour.

## Valencia de Don Juan

West of Sahagún, and south of León, the chief attraction in this small town is its weird twisted ruin of a castle, with strange-shaped battlements rising above green grass. It was built in the 15th century; the pretty bullring is also worth a look; it sees taurine action in late September. The villages nearby are warrened with curious tomblike *bodegas* burrowed into the hills; they produce slightly effervescent red and rosé wine. South of here is Toral de los Guzmanes with a massive adobe palace. The road continues south of here into Zamora province.

The road west from León starts out through urban sprawl to the village of **Virgen del Camino**, where a modern church houses a respected Virgin. Beyond here, the village of **Hospital de Orbigo** is a reasonably attractive little place, and the best option for pilgrims to stop over between León and Astorga; the *albergue* is a friendly spot with a pleasant patio. Nearby, a bridge was the scene of a curious event in 1434. A local noble, iron chain around his neck and doubtless suffering some form of insecurity, decided to take up residence on the bridge for the fortnight leading up to the feast day of Santiago. Passing pilgrims were forced to either declare his chosen lady the most beautiful in Christendom or have a joust with the knight or one of his heavies. The event became known as the *Paso Honroso*; how fair the fights were is not known, but the knights unhorsed over 700 weary pilgrims, killing one and wounding several more. Ah, for the days of chivalry.

## Astorga → *Colour map 2, C1.*

While Astorga is a small town with an interesting history, nothing much goes on here now. In fact, the Leonese are fond of saying that "in Astorga there are only priests, soldiers and whores" – but it's a very pleasant, relaxed place with some attractive buildings and a peaceful small-town atmosphere.

Astorga and its surrounding villages are particularly famous for being the home of the Maragatos (see box, page 303), a distinct ethnic group that for centuries were considered the bravest and most trustworthy of muleteers and guides.

As a major Roman centre for administering the goldmining region further to the west, Astorga was known as Asturica Augusta, having been founded by Augustus during his campaigns against the never-say-die tribes of the northwest of the peninsula. Astorga was one of the earliest of Christian communities in Spain; the archbishop of Carthage, San Cipriano, wrote a letter to the presbyter and faithful of the town as early as AD 254. After the disintegration of the Empire, the area was settled by the Sueves who made the journey from Swabia, now in southwest Germany. They made Astorga their capital and fought constantly with the Visigothic rulers until Astorga finally fell for good in the sixth century.

*In August there's a Roman festival, togas and all.*

Astorga's most important sight is its **cathedral** ⓘ *0930-1200, 1630-1800, summer 0900-1200, 1700-1830*, on which construction began in the 15th century. The best view of the cathedral is to be had from below it, outside the city walls. Most of it is in late Gothic style, but the façade and towers are later Baroque constructions and seem overlarge and ornate for the comparatively small town. The sculptural reliefs depict events from Christ's life, and are flanked by numerous cherubs and flights of Churrigueresque fancy. Inside, the marble *retablo* is impressive, while the highlight of the **Museo Diocesano** ⓘ *1100- 1400, 1530-1830, summer 1000-1400, 1600-2000, €2.50 (€4 including Palacio Episcopal)* are the paintings of the temptations and trials of St Anthony, who is bothered during his hermitage by some memorable demons.

Next to the cathedral, the **Palacio Episcopal** ⓘ *Tue-Sat 1100-1400, 1600-1800, Sun 1100-1400; summer Tue-Sat 1000-1400, 1600-2000, Sun 1000-1400, €2.50 (€4 including Museo Diocesano)*, is something of a contrast. In 1887 a Catalan bishop was appointed to Astorga. Not prepared to settle for a modest prefab bungalow on the edge of town, he decided that his residence was to be built by his mate Gaudí. The townsfolk were horrified, but the result is a fairytale-style castle with pointy turrets. Little of the interior was designed by the man, as he was kept away by the hostility of the locals, but there are a couple of nice touches, notably in the bishop's throne room and chapel. Much of the (chilly) interior is taken up by the **Museo de los Caminos**, a collection of art and artefacts relating to the pilgrimage to Santiago. The garden is guarded by some scary angels. The **tourist office** ⓘ *Tue-Sat 1000-1400, 1600-1900, Sun 1000-1400*, is opposite the Palacio Episcopal.

## The Maragatos

The matter of origin of the Maragatos has provoked much scholarly and unscholarly debate. They have been variously touted as descendants of Moorish prisoners, Sueves, Visigoths and Phoenicians, but no one is really sure. Until fairly recently they kept pretty much to themselves; it is still common to see them in their characteristic national dress. The men wear a red waistcoat, bowler-style hat and a black tunic, while the women have a shawl and a headscarf.

The Maragatos are famous for their *cocido*; usually served in reverse to the standard Spanish custom; the meal starts with the stewed meats; usually a bit of everything, chicken, lamb, sausage and chunks of pork from various parts of the pig. The chickpea and cabbage part of the stew follows on a separate plate, and is washed down by the broth after. There are many restaurants in Astorga serving it up, but some of the best are in the small villages of the *maragatería*, the surrounding district.

Astorga's **Plaza Mayor** is attractive, and notable for the figures of a Maragato man and woman that strike the hour on the town hall clock. Some of the city's Roman heritage can be seen at the **Museo Romano** ① *Tue-Sat 1000-1330, 1600-1800 (1600-2000 summer), Sun 1100-1400, €2.50 (€3 including Museo de Chocolate)*, constructed over some of the old forum by the Ayuntamiento. Finds from many of the archaeological excavations around the town are on display. There are many **Roman remains** of some interest around the town; the tourist office will provide a map of the *Ruta Romana*; guided tours run in summer.

Another museum is the **Museo de Chocolate** ① *Tue-Sat 1030-1400, 1630-1900 (2000 summer), Sun 1030-1400, €1 (€3 with Museo Romano)*, where you can learn how chocolate was, and is, made and how it can be purchased.

### Around Astorga

Some 5 km from Astorga, **Castrillo de los Polvazares** is somewhat touristy, but it's still one of the most attractive of the **Maragato villages**. Built of muddy red stone, it's been attractively restored, and you still expect the rattle of mulecarts down its cobbled streets. There are many other less-developed Maragato villages around that are worth checking out if you've got transport. There are around 40 or 50 of them in all; some of the nicest are **Murias de Rechivaldo, Luyego** and **Santiago Millas**. All have at least one hearty restaurant dishing up the famed *cocido*.

### El Bierzo

The lands immediately west of Astorga mainly consist of low scrubby hills. There's little of interest until the Bierzo region in the west of the province. The Bierzo is criss-crossed by middling mountain ranges and pretty valleys. The Romans mined gold and other metals here, and some coal mines are still creaking on towards their inevitable closure. It's now mainly famous for red wine and vegetables; its peppers have DO (denominación de origen) status and are famous throughout Spain. There are many hidden corners of the region to investigate; it's one of Northern Spain's least known and most interesting corners that could merit a sizeable guidebook on its own.

### Ponferrada → *Colour map 1, C6.*

Although afflicted by rampant urban sprawl, industrial Ponferrada has a small, attractive old centre above the river Sil. It's a fast-growing and vibrant young city and capital of the Bierzo region. The main feature of the centre is a superb **Templar castle**

Castilla y León León Province

① *Oct-Apr Tue-Sat 1030-1400, 1600-1800, Sun 1030-1400, May-Sep Tue-Sat 1030-1400, 1700-2100, Sun 1100-1400, €2.50*, low but formidable, with a series of defensive walls and a steep underground passage descending to the river.

Some lovely buildings are preserved in the old town; check out the small lanes around the Plaza de Ayuntamiento, an attractive space in itself; nearby a pretty clocktower arches across the street. The **Basílica de la Virgen de Encina** sits in another square and is an attractive building. The **Museo de Bierzo**, set in an old *palacio* in the centre, is a good display, with items of interest from the region's Celtic cultures as well as the Templar period. There's a nice patio and cobbled courtyard. There's also a small **railway museum** ① *Tue-Sat 1100-1400, 1600-1900 (1700-2030 summer), Sun 1100-1400, €2.50*, on the edge of the new town, with several lovable old locomotives. The **tourist office** is by the castle walls.

## Molinaseca

Some 5 km southeast of Ponferrada, on the Camino de Santiago, this excellent stone village sits by a babbling river, scene of a frenetic water-fight during the village fiestas. It's full of *bodegas* which have been converted into bars, where the typical order is a cheap local wine and a tapa of chorizo. It's particularly popular on Sundays with folk from Ponferrada. There's a pilgrim hostel here, and plenty of accommodation and eating options. For pilgrims it may make a more relaxing stay than Ponferrada itself.

## Villafranca del Bierzo

West of Ponferrada, the Camino de Santiago heads west to Galicia and the road leads into dark wooded uplands. The next stop for most Santiago-bound walkers is Villafranca del Bierzo. An attractive town, it's a nice spot to gather strength and spirit before the long ascent into Galicia. In medieval times, many pilgrims were by this stage not physically capable of continuing into the harsher terrain and weather conditions. That being the case, if they reached the church here, they were granted the same absolutions and indulgences as if they had completed the whole journey to Santiago. The **Iglesia de Santiago** is where they had to go, at least from when it was built in the late 12th century. Although Romanesque, it's unusual in form, with a cavernous, barn-like interior with a calming feel. There's a crucifixion above the simple altar, with Christ looking very old and careworn; the side chapel is a more recent affair with an 18th-century *retablo*. The side door, the Puerta del Perdón, is what the pilgrims had to touch to receive all the benefits of their journey. It has some nice capitals around it, including one of the three wise men cosily bunked up in a single bed.

Nearby, the foursquare **castle** has big crumbly walls as well as a restored section. It's still lived in and therefore cannot be visited. There's a late **Gothic Colegiata** with some local architectural influences; near here make a point of walking down Calle del Agua, a superbly atmospheric street lined with old buildings. Villafranca's **tourist office** ① *daily 1000-1400, 1600-2000*, is very helpful.

## Valle del Silencio

One of the most charming spots in Northern Spain is this hidden valley south of Ponferrada. The treeless plains of Castilla seem light years away as you wind through grape vines into the narrow valley carved by the River Oza. Chestnuts and oaks, as well as abundant animal and bird life accompany the cheerful stream through villages that are utterly tranquil and rural. A circular walk around the valley, waymarked PR L-E 14, is an excellent way to spend a day; it takes about six hours.

This village of **Villafrancos** is one of the prettiest in the valley, with a delightfully picturesque stone bridge, and villagers going about their business as if the passing of centuries is a curious but inconsequential matter. There's a small bar here, but no accommodation. Further along the valley floor is a campsite and *refugio*, **El Molino de San Juan**, with a restaurant.

Perched below the hamlet of **San Pedro de Monte**, signposted down a side road, is a monastery, mostly in ruins but of a venerable age. You can visit its Baroque church, which has a Romanesque tower. The road ends at Peñalba de Santiago, and you feel it's done well to get this far. Peñalba, a village of slate where three mountain ranges meet, has eked out an existence on chestnuts for centuries. Although in good modern repair (restored a few years ago to beautiful effect), it's a grey beauty, with wooden balconies and an ends-of-the-earth feel. Enjoy a glass of home-made wine and a tapa of *cecina* at Cantina opposite the church, a bar steeped in tradition and the focus of village life.

The centrepiece of the village is a 10th-century **Mozarabic church** which belies its solid exterior with elegant horseshoe arches inside, as well as many fragments of wall painting. The restoration here is ongoing, but it's sometimes open for a look around.

It's about a four- to five-hour stroll from Ponferrada to Peñalba, through beautiful surroundings; much of the distance is a marked trail that follows the river.
▸▸ *See Transport, page 310, for details.*

## Las Médulas and around

The Romans found gold all over Bierzo, but here at Las Médulas they had to perform engineering wonders to get at it. Mining open-cast, they diverted river waters in elaborate ways and employed thousands of labourers in what was a massive ongoing operation. Las Médulas are the eerie and surreal remains of their toil, a large stretch of terrain sculpted into strange formations and criss-crossed by paths and tunnels, some of which are amazingly extensive. The best viewpoint in the area is near the village of **Orellán** not far away; from here there's an amazing vista over the tortured earth. Pliny described one of the mining techniques as *ruina montium* (the destruction of a mountain); vast quantities of water were suddenly channelled through a prepared network of wells and sluices, literally blowing the whole hillside out and down the hill to the panning areas below. A few hills survived the process; these stand forlorn, sharp little peaks red among the heathery valleys.

Near the *mirador* is a network of galleries to explore; ponder Pliny's account of the labour as you walk through them: "The light of day is never seen for months at a time. The galleries are prone to collapse without warning, leaving workers buried alive. Any rocks that blocked their passage were attacked with fire and vinegar, but the smoke and fumes often choked people in the caves. So they were broken into smaller pieces with blows from iron mallets and carried out on shoulders day and night, handing them along a human chain in that infernal darkness."

The incomprehensible thing is that these mines were not even particularly lucrative; recent estimates put the annual production of gold at around 25 kg; extraordinarily low from such a vast operation.

The area is some 20 km southwest of Ponferrada; you're best to drop in at the small visitor centre at the village of Las Médulas itself to get an idea of the layout of the place.

---

# North of León 🖿🍴 ▸▸ *pp307-310.*

The mountainous northern reaches of León province are little known except by locals but merit plenty of exploration. It's a favourite destination of cavers and rockclimbers from the city. A series of spectacular mountain passes join the province with neighbouring Asturias; these are often snowbound in winter. A car is the best way to nose around the area, although the **FEVE** trains and the odd bus makes its way out from León to many outlying villages in the zone.

**Las Hoces and the Cuevas de Valporquero** → *Colour map 2, B2.*

A good day out from León could see you head north to the region of Las Hoces, two narrow gorges carved from the grey stone. Take the LE-311 which follows the course of the Torio River and continue past Matallana de Torio up the first of the gorges, **Las Hoces de Vegacervera**. The villages in this area continue much as they have done for years, pasturing sheep in the summer and grimly hanging on through the cold winters. Look out for *madreñas*, a wooden clog worn over the shoes when tramping around the muddy fields, and the famous Leonese *mastín*, or mastiff, an enormous shaggy beast.

Off the road through the gorge are the stunning limestone caves of **Valporquero** ① *Jun-Sep daily 1000-1400, 1600-1900, Oct-mid-Dec and Apr-May Fri-Sun 1000-1700, €4.20*, much of which remains to be discovered. Some of the chambers are amazingly large, and (in spring and autumn) there is an underground river plunging into the depths, as well as the fascinating limestone sculpture.

> ‼ *Take warm clothing, non-slip footwear and some sort of waterproof, as it can get pretty wet if the rain's been falling.*

Beyond the Valporquero cave turn-off, take a right-turn up the LE-313 through the other gorge, the **Valdeteja**. Before you reach the turn is the hamlet of **Getino**, which has an excellent place to eat, the **Venta de Getino** (see Eating, page 309). Continuing through the gorge, take another right just after Valdeteja itself on the LE-321. About 6 km down this road, look out for a small paved area on the right. A path leads to a spectacular waterfall pounding through a hole in the rocky hill. Once you've described the horseshoe shape through both gorges, the road ends at the village of **La Vecilla**, 4 km from the waterfall and serviced several times daily by **FEVE** trains from León. There are several accommodation options in this region (see Sleeping, page 308).

# Northeast to the Picos ⬛🍴🏨📧 ➤ *pp307-310.*

The northeastern section of León province is isolated and fairly poor, climbing steadily towards the Picos de Europa. Formerly a significant coalmining region, little of that goes on here now; farming and sausage-making are the mainstays of the small towns in the area.

## Boñar and around → *Colour map 2, B2.*

**Vegaquemada**, a small village on the way to Boñar, has nothing of interest except a strange church in an Italianate style, with an ornate layered belltower and a porch with filigreed ironwork. ➤ *For the Leonese Picos, see page 341.*

Boñar is served by buses from León, but also has a train connection to Santander on the private **FEVE** network. From Boñar, the quickest route to the peaks is east via Sabero, a coalmining town amid low mountains that look to be melting.

Boñar itself is liveliest in winter as there's a **ski resort** nearby. It's a somewhat bleak place like much of this region, but there are a couple of decent places to stay.

## Riaño

Forgive Riaño its slightly ugly, gawky appearance overlooking an often empty lake; the construction of the controversial dam and reservoir forced the town to reluctantly relocate to the top of the hill in the 1980s.

Although it's the southern gateway to the Picos, not an awful lot goes on here except hunting and people passing through. If you're wanting to explore this side of the range, **Posada de Valdeón** makes a smaller but more inviting and convenient base (see page 341).

There's a tourist kiosk at the entrance to the town, a couple of banks, a service station, and a handful of places to stay.

### Sahagún *p300*

If you're not walking the *camino*, Sahagún is best seen as a day trip from León, but there are decent places to stay.

**C Hostal El Ruedo**, Plaza Mayor 1, T987 780 075. This is another good choice, on the main plaza with clean modern rooms, recently renovated and equipped to hotel standard, above an *asador*. There are only 4 rooms so you might want to book ahead.

**C La Codorniz**, C Arco , T987 780 276, F987 780 106. Right opposite the tourist office, this is Sahagún's most comfortable lodgings. The rooms are unremarkable in decoration but large, light and comfortable and the restaurant is decent, decked out in *mudéjar* brick.

**E-F Hostal Pacho**, Av Constitución 86, T987 780 775. This is a cheaper option, with a variety of rooms both with and without bathroom above a cheap restaurant on the main road through the middle of town.

### Valencia de Don Juan *p301*

**C El Palacio**, C Palacio 3, T987 750 474. One of the best places to stay in town, this is set in a beautiful old mansion and has friendly Asturian management and a good bar (where you can try Asturian cider) and restaurant.

### Astorga *p302*

**B Hotel Gaudí**, C Eduardo de Castro 6, T987 615 654, F987 615 040. Opposite the Palacio Episcopal, this is one of Astorga's best, a beautiful and stylish place with a good restaurant and café. There are some good-value suites available as well.

**C Hostal La Peseta**, Plaza San Bartolomé 3, T987 617 275, F987 615 300. Good rooms above what is widely considered one of Astorga's best restaurants. The rooms are excellent for this price, and the staff incredibly welcoming.

**F Pensión García**, Bajada Postigo 3, T987 616 046. One of the cheaper choices in town, this is clean and decent, if fairly unremarkable.

### Around Astorga *p303*

**C Cuca la Vaina**, C Jardín s/n, Castrillo de los Polvazares, T987 691 078. If you're exploring the area, this is a top base in the village of Castrillo de los Polvazares, with a lively bar and

excellent restaurant. The rooms are rustic and beautiful, with elaborately carved headboards, and much-needed heating in winter.

**C Guts Muths**, Santiago Millas, El Bajo s/n, T987 691 123. A superbly peaceful and welcoming place run by a Dutch expat; the rooms are decorated by art students and are out-of-the-ordinary, to say the least.

**D-E El Molino de Arriero**, Av Villalibre 5, Luyego, T987 601 720, www.molinodel arriero.com. This is another characterful and welcoming *casa rural* managed by a Russian and serving good cheap meals.

### Ponferrada *p303*

Few of Ponferrada's accommodations are in the old town; most are in the new zone across the river.

**A Hotel Temple**, Av Portugal 2, T987 410 058, F987 423 525. The town's top hotel is set in a large stone building with pseudo- Templar furnishings; it doesn't lack comfort, although still has a of touch of 'big hotel' impersonality.

**B Hotel Bierzo Plaza**, Pl del Ayuntamiento 4, T987 409 001, www.hotelbierzoplaza.com This appealing modern hotel has an excellent location in the old town, on the town hall square. The rooms are decorated with a light touch, and are pretty good value for the price.

**B Hotel El Castillo**, Av del Castillo 115, T987 456 227, elcastillo@picos.com. Just across from the castle, these slightly noisy rooms are modern with good bathrooms but worth it for the location.

**E-F Santa Cruz**, C Marcelo Macías 4, T987 428 351. There are numerous basic *pensiones* in the new town, but this is a cut above with good-value rooms with or without bath.

### Peñalba de Santiago *p305*

There are 2 accommodation options, both *casas rurales* available only to rent as a whole.

**Casa Elba**, Arriba de la Fuente 2, T988 322 037. Very cosy, with 3 twin rooms, kitchen, balcony, heating and lounge with log-fire. If there are a few of you, it's a bargain at €100 a day or €570 for a week.

**Turpesa**, Plaza de la Iglesia s/n, T987 425 566. Not quite as cosy as **Casa Elba**, but still a good deal for €75 a day (minimum stay 3 days) or €490 a week. It sleeps 3-4. Both need to be booked in advance.

### Villafranca del Bierzo *p304*
There are several good places to stay in Villafranca.

**AL Parador Villafranca del Bierzo**, Av Calvo Sotelo-Constitución s/n, T987 540 175, www.parador.es. This cheerful cottage affair, draped in creepers has all the comfort and style associated with the *parador* chain.

**C Hostal San Francisco**, Plaza Mayor/Generalísimo 6, T987 540 465, F987 540 544. This is a solid option on the attractive main plaza. As it's right in the centre, you pay a little for location, but it's an enjoyable place to stay.

**D Hospedería San Nicolás**, Travesía de San Nicolás 4, T987 540 483. This is located in a 17th-century Jesuit college and pilgrims' rest and has excellent rooms and a very good restaurant.

**F Hostal Comercio**, Puente Nuevo 2, T987 540 008. This is a great budget spot, an intensely characterful building attractively set in an old stone building. It offers fairly basic comfort at bargain rates.

### Las Hoces and the Cuevas de Valporquero *p306*
**E Hostal El Pescador**, Felmín s/n, T987 576 623. Just beyond the Valporquero cave turn-off, this hostal has good views over the mountains.

### Boñar and around *p306*
**D El Negrillón**, Plaza El Negrillón s/n, Boñar, T987 735 164. The nicest place to stay in Boñar, a cosy wood-lined *casa rural* on the square by the church.

### Riaño *p306*
**C Hotel Presa**, Av de Valcayo 12, T987 740 637, F987 740 737. The best option, with views across the lake and mountains, a good restaurant, and cosy if frilly rooms.

## 🍴 Eating

### Sahagún *p300*
🍴 **Restaurante Luis**, Plaza Mayor 4, T987 781 085. Sahagún is famous for its *puerros* (leeks), and the best place to try them is here; it's a great restaurant with a log fire, courtyard and a large fresco depicting market day. There's a *menú* for €10.80 at lunchtimes but it's much more interesting to go à la carte.

### Astorga *p302*
🍴 **Hostal La Peseta**, Plaza San Bartolomé 3, T987 617 275. See Sleeping, above. The best *cocido* in town.

🍴 **Parrillada Serrano**, C Portería 2, T987 617 866. This is spacious and cosily stylish; there's a big range of dishes (including an excellent fish soup), and a *menú del día* for €8.40.

🍴 **Pizzería Venezia**, C Matías Rodríguez 2, T987 618 463. Popular with all types of Astorgan, this is an inexpensive option with poor service and excellent pizza.

### Cafés
**Café Kavafis**, C Enfermeras 3, T987 615 363. This cosy little place has internet access and books to browse. The peaceful atmosphere changes at weekends, when it transforms itself into a small discobar, with good DJs.

**Taberna Los Hornos**, Plaza del Ayuntamiento s/n. Right on the main square, this is an atmospheric spot and a good place for snacking and drinking.

### Around Astorga *p303*
🍴 **Cuca la Vaina** C Jardín s/n, Castrillo de los Polvazares, T987 691 078. See Sleeping, above. The restaurant naturally serves a good *cocido*; there's also a *menú* for €14.

🍴 **La Maruja**, C Real 24, Castrillo de los Polvazares, T987 691 065. The best *cocido* in town at a beautiful little house with a warm welcome and filling meal. Reservations are essential. Closed Sep.

Castilla y León León Province Listings

## Ponferrada *p303*

There are many good tapas bars in Ponferrada, some in the old centre, and some around Plaza Fernando Miranda.

**Ψ Las Cuadras**, Trasero de la Cava 2, T987 419 373. A good dark Spanish restaurant with gutsy fishes and meats and a good set lunch for €10.

**Ψ La Bodeguilla**, Plaza Fernando Miranda. One of the best bars for its delicious ham *pinchos*.

**Ψ La Fonda**, Plaza del Ayuntamiento 10, T987 425 794, with a nice covered terrace and excellent *alubias* (stewed beans) and generous meat dishes.

### Villafranca del Bierzo *p304*

**Ψ Viña Femita**, Av Calvo Sotelo-Constitución 2, T987 542 409. This restaurant is worth a look just for its massive chimney, proudly emblazoned with the word 'alcohol'. The reason is that it's a former distillery. The restaurant serves up solid mountain fare and has several menus and a terrace in summer.

**Ψ Mesón Don Nacho**, C Truqueles s/n, T987 540 076, has good hearty portions of tapas and stews.

### Las Hoces and the Cuevas de Valporquero *p306*

**Ψ Venta de Getino**, Getino, T987 576 424. The food is excellent and plentiful, and the family-run atmosphere very welcoming. There's a *menú del día* for €7 (10 at weekends), but don't expect to be able to finish it all.

### Boñar and around *p306*

**Ψ Hostal Inés**, Av Constitución 64, Boñar, T987 735 086. Decent food.

---

## ⊙ Bars and clubs

### Ponferrada *p303*

Ponferrada has famously boisterous nightlife; in the streets behind the **Temple** hotel there are any number of *discobares* with all types of music.

**Morticia**, Av la Plata 19, is one of the best-known, with gruesomely detailed horror decor and a rock 'n' roll crowd.

Later on, the action moves out to the large bars in the purpose-built complex known as **La Gran Manzana**.

A rather unique venue in the heart of the old town is **Sala Tararí**, C del Reloj 17, www.salatarari.com, with an inclusive feel, friendly folk, exhibitions, concerts, and a rocking Thu night jam session.

### Boñar and around *p306*

**Cervecería Sierra**, Ctra Cisuerna 11. One of the better spots for a drink.

---

## ⊛ Festivals and events

### Ponferrada *p303*

**Mar/Apr** Freakland, a well-attended rock festival, takes place here over Easter weekend.

---

## ⊙ Transport

### Sahagún *p300*
**Bus**
A few buses stop in Sahagún but they are significantly slower than the train.

**Train**
There are a dozen or so feasible daily trains linking **León** and Sahagún, a journey of 30 mins (from €3.40). Some of the trains continue to **Grajal**, 5 mins away, before heading to **Palencia**.

### Mansilla de las Mulas *p301*
**Bus**
There are buses at least hourly from **León** to Mansilla (€2, 20 mins). 2 buses continue Mon-Fri, and 1 Sat to **San Miguel de la Escalada** (40 mins, €2.20)

### Valencia de Don Juan *p301*
**Bus**
Buses run to Valencia from **León** 6-8 times a day.(€3.05, 30 mins). A similar number head on to **Valladolid**.

### Astorga *p302*
**Bus**
There are 15 daily buses from **León** to Astorga. There are a few trains too, but the station is inconveniently situated 20 mins' walk from the centre.

**Ponferrada** *p303*
### Bus
Ponferrada's bus station is across the river from the old town; it's a bit of a trudge, but there are frequent city buses crossing the river. Many buses go to **León**, several a day go on west to **Villafranca**, and several continue into **Galicia**, mostly to **Lugo** and **Santiago**.

### Trains
Trains run east to **León** via **Astorga** 6 times a day, and some go west to **A Coruña**, **Ourense** and **Vigo**. The train station is also across the river from the old town.

### Villafranca del Bierzo *p304*
### Bus
Villafranca is served by ALSA buses from **León** and **Ponferrada**. Many buses continue into **Galicia**.

### Peñalba de Santiago *p305*
### Bus
There are 2 buses monthly from **Ponferrada** up the valley to Peñalba, which run on the 1st and 3rd Wed of the month. They run twice on both days, leaving Ponferrada at 0800 and 1330. They are principally to allow carless villagers to do the monthly shopping.

A better option is to **hitch**; there are few cars, but a high lift percentage.

### Riaño *p306*
### Bus
There are 3 buses daily (only 1 on Sun) from **León** to Riaño. The 1830 bus continues to **Posada de Valdeón** in the heart of the Leonese Picos. On Fri and Sat there's an additional bus running between León and **Santander** that passes through Riaño.

Cantabria and the Picos de Europa

## Footprint features

# Introduction

Genteel Cantabria is an island of reaction between the more radical Asturians and Basques. Historically part of Castilla, it prospered for many years as that kingdom's main sea access, and is still known as a well-heeled sort of place: "people are prone to go to puerile lengths in their vanity about heraldry", claimed writer Gregorio Marañón in the early 20th century.

Way back beyond then, from 18,000 BC onwards, a thriving Stone Age population lived in the area. They've left many remains of their culture, most notably the superb cave paintings at Altamira. These are now closed to the public, but you can see a replica of their very sophisticated art; for a more authentic atmosphere, head to one of the smaller caves in the region.

Apart from the Picos de Europa, Cantabria's principal attraction is its coast. Santander itself has some superb beaches and excellent restaurants. Santillana del Mar is misnamed (it's not on the sea…) but is within easy reach of the sand; it's a touristed but captivating and memorable town of stone mansions and cobbled streets, while Comillas has some startling modernista architecture, including a flamboyant Gaudí building.

For such a small area, the Picos de Europa have a high reputation among visitors, who eulogize this part of the vast Cordillera Cantábrica that's blessed with spectacular scenery, superb walking, abundant wildlife and most crucially, comparatively easy access. They encompass the corners of three provinces: Asturias, Cantabria and León and have a fairly mild climate due to their proximity to the sea.

There's a slightly different feel in each part of the Picos, and if you have time it's a good idea to visit all three provinces.

★ **Don't miss...**

1 **Cuevas del Castillo** Contemplate the staggering age of the prehistoric paintings in these caves, page 317.

2 **Santander's bodegas** Head for the converted wine warehouses in Santander's old town; they're great places to eat and drink, page 320.

3 **Cangas de Onís** Explore the Picos from this Asturian town then sample the local cider at one of several excellent *sidrerías*, page 332.

4 **Potes** Base yourself off season in this pretty riverside town (it gets crowded in summer) and try the hearty local *cocido*, page 337.

5 **Fuente Dé** Battle against vertigo while ascending this breathtaking rock theatre in a cablecar, page 338.

6 **Puerto San Glorio** Take in the views from this mountain pass; it's a highlight of the Picos, page 339.

# Santander and around

→ *Phone code: 942. Colour map 2, B5. Population:183,955.*

*Still an important Spanish port, Santander has for years encouraged visitors to turn their attentions away from its industrial side and towards its series of superb beaches. These gird the barrio of Sardinero, which became a genteel and exclusive resort for the summering upper classes from the mid-19th century on. An earthier lifestyle can be found around the old centre, which has an excellent collection of restaurants and bars, where old wine warehouses have been converted into some of the region's best tapas venues. Santander's ferry link to Plymouth makes it many visitors' first point of entry into Spain; it's a relaxing and pleasant, if a little unexciting, introduction to the country.*

*Inland Cantabria is still very rural; mulecarts and cow traffic jams are still a common sight once off the main roads. The N611 and N623 forge south to Palencia and Burgos respectively through attractive countryside. The main towns in the area, Torrelavega and Reinosa, are both depressing and dull industrial centres, but there are enough small attractions to make a trip in the area interesting.*

*The eastern Cantabrian coast is a fairly uncomplicated place, with decent beaches and a sprinkling of resorts and fishing towns that attract many summer visitors from Madrid and the Basque lands. The nicest place by far is Castro Urdiales, while the large beach town of Laredo offers a great stretch of sand, pretty centre, watersports and good sunny season nightlife. It's not the most interesting stretch of the Spanish coast if sand and sea aren't your thing, and the area between Santander and Laredo is blighted by ugly development.* ➤➤ *For Sleeping, Eating and other listings, see pages 319-323.*

## Ins and outs

**Getting there** Santander is connected by bus and train with the rest of Northern Spain, and by plane domestically with Madrid and Barcelona, and internationally with London Stansted, Liverpool, Rome Ciampino and Frankfurt Hahn on **Ryanair**. Its only international **ferry** service runs from the centre of town to Plymouth, operated by **Brittany Ferries**. In the past, this has sometimes switched to Poole or Portsmouth in the winter months. ➤➤ *See also Transport, page 322.*

**Getting around** Santander is long and thin, with its beaches a good couple of kilometres from its old centre. Fortunately, buses are very frequent, with nearly all lines ploughing the waterside. Taxis are fairly prevalent too; a fare from Sardinero to the centre won't cost much more than €4-5.

**Best time to visit** August is the best time to visit Santander, with the International Festival in full swing and superb weather guaranteed. The downside is the number of sunseekers, and the difficulty of finding accommodation, which increases in price. The sea is pretty chilly, so if you're not too worried about staying out of the water, April and May should offer decent warm weather and not too much rain; apart from Easter week, the accommodation is a bargain outside the summer months.

**Tourist information and tours** The main **Cantabrian tourist office** ① *daily 0930-1330, 1600-1900, T942 310 708, ofitur@cantabria.org*, is in the Mercado del Este building in the centre of town. There is a **municipal office** ① *T942 203 000*, near the ferry terminal in the Jardines de Pereda park, as well as a **summer-only office** at the beach in Sardinero. A **tourist bus** plies a circular route around the town and its beaches, with information and a 'hop-on hop-off' system. Tickets and schedules are available at the tourist office in the Jardines de Pereda. From a jetty on the Paseo de Pereda you can take a **boat tour** of the bay. These leave four times daily, take an hour and cost €6.20.

As the Reconquista progressed and the Moors were driven southwards, the north coast became increasingly important as an export point for Castilian produce. The northern ports joined together in 1296 to form the **Hermandad de las Marismas**, a trading union that included Santander along with La Coruña, San Sebastián and nearby Laredo. Although Laredo was a more important port for much of Spain's Imperial period, Britain's Charles I picked Santander to sail home from after his incredible jaunt through France to Madrid in 1623 (see box, page 446).

Santander's major growth period as a port came in the 19th century; this was also the time that it achieved fashionable status as a resort, which it has retained. Despite the aristocratic feel of parts of the town, Santander was firmly in the Republican camp during the Civil War but finally fell in August 1937. Much of the town centre was destroyed in a fire in 1941, which originated in the Archbishop's palace (did he burn the toast or was he smoking in bed?). The Franco years didn't treat Santander too badly, though, and it's one of very few cities not to have changed its Fascist street names since the return to democracy; a statue of the *caudillo* himself still sits on a horse outside the town hall, facing the industrial suburbs defiantly, with conservative Santander at his back.

# Sights

In the centre, the **cathedral** ① *1000-1300, 1600-1930*, is reasonably interesting. Largely destroyed by the 1941 fire, its church is dull although the cloister offers a chance to relax for a moment from the city streets. The **crypt** ① *0800-1300, 1700-2000*, around the back, is used for masses, and is an intriguing little space, with curious stubby columns and ill-lit Roman ruins under glass. A reliquary holds the silver-plated heads of San Emeterio and San Celedonio, the city patrons.

Nearby, the **Ayuntamiento** is fronted by a statue of Franco; it says much about Santander that he hasn't dismounted and slipped away into history as he has in most other Spanish towns (although you wouldn't bet on him remaining in situ too much longer). Behind the building is the excellent **Mercado de la Esperanza** with lashings of fruit, fish, meat and deli products; the place to buy your hams and olive oils if you're heading back home on the ferry.

Not far from here is the **Museo de Bellas Artes** ① *C Rubio 5, T942 239 485, Mon-Fri 1000-1300, 1700-2000, Sat 1000-1300; opens 30 mins later in summer, free*, a fairly mediocre collection. The highlight is many of Goya's *Horrors of War* prints, a dark and haunted series; there's also a portrait of Fernando VII, which isn't one of his better works. A small Miró is also notable, as are several sculptures by the late Basque, Jorge Oteiza, among them an expressive *Adam and Eve*.

> ‡ *Santander doesn't possess a wealth of historical buildings or noteworthy museums; the principal attraction is its excellent town beaches east of the centre.*

Other museums in town include the **Museo Marítimo** ① *Tue-Sat 1000-1300, 1600-1800 (Jul/Aug 1100-1400, 1700-1900), Sun 1100-1400, €6*, which celebrates the city's fishing heritage as well as exhibiting some live fish and molluscs in tanks; and the **Museo de Prehistoria y Arqueología** ① *C Casimiro Sainz 4, T942 207 105, Tue-Sat 0900-1300, 1600-1900 (opens at 1000 in summer), Sun 1100-1400, free*, a collection of well-presented pieces from the province's past, many of which are creations of Neanderthal and modern man, and were found in several caves around the region.

The **waterfront** is the nicest part of this area; it's a walk that fills with people during the *paseo*; there's also a bike lane. The **Puerto Chico** is the leisure marina; after passing this you come to the huge festival centre; quite attractive floodlit, but ugly by day.

## The beaches

Past the festival centre, Avenida de la Reina Victoria heads for the sands past some very flashy houses (some chalets go for over €4 million, an incredible sum in Spain).

The **Península de la Magdalena** protects the bay of Santander from the Atlantic and is topped by a flashy *palacio*. This was a gift from the city to the king but it now houses the renowned summer university that draws people from around the globe. Jan Morris described the building as 'like a child's idea of a palace, surrounded on three sides by the sea and on the fourth by loyal subjects'. A small **zoo** nearby holds marine animals.

On the bay side of the peninsula are a couple of pretty beaches, **Playa de la Magdalena** and **Playa de los Bikinis**; just around on the sea side is the artificial **Playa del Camello**, named for the humped rock that sticks out of the water opposite it.

**Sardinero** is the centre of the sand suburbs; an attractively unmodern collection of belle époque buildings that back two superb beaches, perceptively named **La Primera** and **La Segunda**. The Primera is the beach to be seen at; it's backed by the elegantly restored casino and several pricey hotels. The Segunda is less crowded and usually gets better waves, either at the far end or around the spur that divides the two. Both are kept creditably clean and have enough sand that you're never hurdling bodies to reach the water.

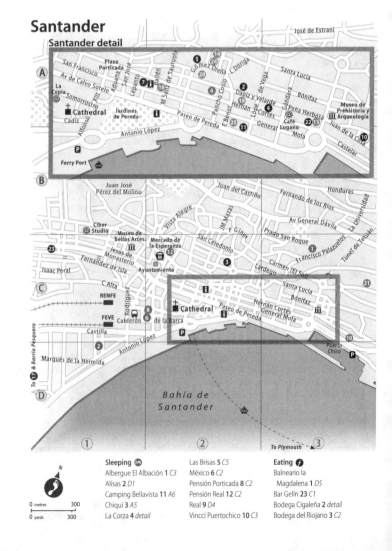

# Santander

**Santander detail**

0 metres 300
0 yards 300

**Sleeping**
Albergue El Albación **1** C3
Alisas **2** D1
Camping Bellavista **11** A6
Chiqui **3** A5
La Corza **4** detail

Las Brisas **5** C5
México **6** C2
Pensión Porticada **8** C2
Pensión Real **12** C2
Real **9** D4
Vincci Puertochico **10** C3

**Eating**
Balneario la
  Magdalena **1** D5
Bar Gelín **23** C1
Bodega Cigaleña **2** detail
Bodega del Riojano **3** C2

# South of Santander 🚉🚌 ▸▸ *pp319-323.*

**Puente Viesgo**, 30 km south of Santander, is a peaceful spa village long used as a weekend retreat from Santander but of great interest because of the caves up on the hill above, 1½ km from town and one of the highlights of the province.

## Cuevas del Castillo
ⓘ *T942 598 425, May-Sep daily 1000-1400, 1600-2030; Oct-Apr Wed-Sun 0930-1655; entry is by guided tour in Spanish, but the guides speak very clearly and slowly and make every effort to be understood. €2; tours run roughly every hour and last 45 mins; daily visitors have a maximum limit; it's worth booking in summer and also in winter, to avoid the lengthy wait for a group to form.*

The Cuevas del Castillo were home to thousands of generations of Neanderthal man and Cro-Magnon man (*homo sapiens sapiens*); with the earliest occupation being

Bodegas Bringas **4** *detail*
Bodegas Manzón **22** *detail*
Café Suizo **11** *detail*
La Casa del Indiano **7** *detail*
La Conveniente **5** *detail*
La Gaviota **17** *D1*

La Posada del Mar **10** *detail*
Rhin **12** *C5*

**Bars & clubs** 🎵
Blues **24** *detail*
del Puerto **13** *detail*

Fortunny **14** *detail*
La Floridita **16** *detail*
Pachá **25** *detail*
Rocambole **18** *detail*
Ventilador **20** *detail*
Zona Límite **21** *C3*

dated at some 130,000 years ago. Both left extensive remains of tools and weapons (Teilhard de Chardin and Albert of Monaco both got their hands dirty in the excavations here), but Cro-Magnon man did some decorating in a series of paintings that extend deep into the cave complex; these were discovered in 1903. The earliest efforts date from around 30,000 years ago and some are of several outlines of hands, created with red ochre. Interestingly, most of the prints found are of the left hand, suggesting that most folk were right-handed even back then. More sophisticated works are from later but still predate the more advanced work at Altamira. There are outlines of bison here too, as well as deer, and a long series of discs that has mystified theorists.

Although the quality of the art is nothing to touch Altamira, it's a much more satisfying experience to see the originals here than the replicas. It's atmospheric too, for the caves are fantastic; the one open for visits is a sort of Gothic cathedral in lime.

The tourist board of Cantabria produce an excellent booklet (*Patrimonio Paleolítico*; in Spanish but with clear details and well illustrated) detailing a number of other caves in the area with Palaeolithic art.

---

# Eastern Cantabria ⬤⬤⬤⬤⬤⬤ ⤻ *pp319-323.*

## Laredo

Part of the *Hermandad de las Marismas* (brotherhood of seatowns), Laredo was once an important port and the place whence Juana La Loca set sail in a fleet of 120 ships to her arranged marriage in Flanders; an alliance that led to her complete mental breakdown. Her son Carlos V used the port too, to return to Spain weary and old, on his way to retirement and a peaceful death at the monastery of Yuste. In earlier times, Laredo was a big Roman seaport, named Portus Luliobrigensium, scene of a major naval engagement. There's a cheerfully efficient **tourist office** ① *T942 611 096, daily 0900-1400, 1700-1900*, in the Alameda Miramar park.

Laredo still nurses a handful of small fishing smacks in its harbour, but the town's sole focus these days is tourism, powered by its sunny climate and superb beach, **La Salvé**, 5 km of golden sand arcing round the bay. It's a big town, and there are kilometres of ugly resort housing along the beach; if you're prepared for that, it's a likeable place, particularly if you spend some time in its compact old town. It's worth visiting the 13th-century **Iglesia de San Francisco**, as well as sniffing out a tunnel carved in the 1860s that makes its way through the headland to a small harbour. Otherwise, relax on the sand and prepare for the lively summer nightlife.

## Castro Urdiales and around

Eastern Cantabria's nicest town, Castro Urdiales is a good-humoured seaside place with just the right mixture of resort and original character to make it attractive. The coastline here has the Basque rockiness and Castro is still an important fishing port (famous for anchovies) with a big harbour. The **tourist office** ① *Av de la Constitución, year round 0900-1400, 1700-1900*, is on the waterfront.

The **waterfront** is attractive and long; at its end is a decent beach, **Playa Brazomar**. At the other end of the harbour a couple of imposing buildings stand high over the town. The **castle**, now a lighthouse, preserves its Templar walls; a picturesque medieval bridge links it with the massive **church**. This is a surprising building of great architectural and artistic merit. The reliefs on the outside present strange but damaged allegorical scenes of animals kissing and other exotica, while the interior is beautifully Gothic, all arches and blue stained glass; the holy water is kept in a giant clam shell. Further around the headland is a beautiful sheltered **rockpool**, occasionally used as a venue for concerts.

Castro Urdiales is big on *traineras*, large rowing boats that are raced in regattas on the sea in fierce competition with other towns. These are testosterone-fuelled events that draw big crowds.

**Oriñón,** an excellent stretch of sand dramatically set between rocky mountains, only slightly spoiled by the ugly development.

## ● Sleeping

**Santander** *p314, map p316*
As befits its resort status, Santander has dozens of places to stay. Many of these are in lofty price brackets, especially in the beachside *barrio* of Sardinero. There are several cheap *pensiones* around the bus and train stations, most fairly respectable if a bit noisy. Prices in Jul-Aug are outrageously high. Rates drop significantly once the summer rush is over.

**LL Hotel Real**, Paseo de Pérez Galdós 28, T942 272 550, www.hotelreal.es. Santander's top hotel was commissioned by the king when the royal family started summering here in the early 20th century. It's a luxurious and magnificent palace with a French feel to the decor; it has superb views over the bay and prices to match (a double in summer can cost up to €280). It's a byword for style and sophistication in these parts and has seen its fair share of celebrity guests.

**L Hotel Chiqui**, Av García Lago 9, T902 282 700, www.hotelchiqui.com. This large hotel is very well placed at the quiet end of the Sardinero beaches. While service and staff aren't as professional as the **Real**, the front rooms have all the conveniences and superb views out to sea. Excellent off-season and weekend specials are on offer on the website.

**L Hotel Vincci Puertochico**, C Castelar 25, T942 225 200, puertochico@vinccihoteles. com. A good hotel right on the marina. The rooms are comfortable and modern, but the best, which overlook the water, cost up to €32 more. ADSL line, pillow menu and other conveniences are on offer.

**AL Hotel Las Brisas**, Travesía de los Castros 14, T942 275 011, www.hotellasbrisas.net. A block back from the main Sardinero beach, this quirky hotel is in the thick of it and has homely, characterful decor and welcoming owners. All the rooms are enticingly different and decorated with a heavy Spanish charm.

**B-C Hotel Alisas**, C Nicolás Salmerón 3, T942 222 750, www.celuisma.com. A comfortable, clean hotel, which is overpriced in Aug but reasonable at other times. Rooms are largish and come with television, direct dialling, and clean, modern bathroom.

**D-E La Corza**, C Hernán Cortés 25, T942 212 950. A very good choice right on the central Plaza del Pombo and a block from the water. The rooms are clean and spacious, decorated with a colourful charm, and the management is friendly. Book ahead. Recommended.

**E Pensión Porticada**, C Méndez Núñez 6, T942 227 817. Convenient for the ferry, and very near the bus station, this is a good and friendly budget option. Nearly all the rooms have a *mirador* (glassed-in balcony), and while the bathrooms are shared, they are clean and adequate. There are also 2 en suite rooms and a drinks service. Recommended.

**E Pensión Real**, Plaza de la Esperanza 1, T942 225 787, pensionreal@hotmail.com. Good-value rooms in a warm and well-maintained family home. Warm in this instance refers to the ambient temperature rather than the smug owner, but it's a very good deal at this price and located a block behind the town hall.

**F Albergue El Albación**, C Francisco Palazuelos 21, T942 217 753, F942 211 452. A decent independent hostel, close to the centre. The staff are exceedingly upbeat and friendly and the facilities reasonable, although the dorms are a little cramped. No curfew.

### Camping
**Camping Bellavista**, T942 391 530, is a year-round campsite well located by the Mataleñas beach just north of Sardinero. Bus 9 goes to the campsite via the coastal boulevards from the Ayuntamiento.

### South of Santander *p317*
**AL Gran Hotel Balneario**, C Manuel Pérez Mazo s/n, Puente Viesgo, T942 598 061, www.balneariodepuenteviesgo.com. The waters of the town are reportedly effective for skin disorders and rheumatism; this massive spa hotel complex is the place to take them. These types of places are very popular in Spain, and there are all manner of treatments available, as well as fine food, well-appointed rooms and pleasant grounds.

**E Pensión El Carmen**, Puente Viesgo s/n, T942 598 141. This is a much homelier place to stay, set by the small stream. The rooms are well appointed for this price, and there's a friendly welcome. Open Jul-Sep only.

### Laredo *p318*

Most places to stay are unattractive but functional beach hotels and apartments to rent, although few are right on the sands.

**A Miramar**, Alto de Laredo s/n, T942 610 367, proinasa@arrakis.es. It would be staggering if there weren't a hotel called **Miramar** here; luckily this one has excellent views over the bay and is very well priced off-season.

**D-E Pensión Esmeralda**, Fuente Fresnedo 6, T942 605 219. Set in the old, hilly part of town this has attractive, clean doubles with bath.

**E Pensión Salomón**, C Menéndez Pelayo 11, T942 605 081, is an excellent option despite an unremarkable exterior.

**F Albergue Casa de la Trinidad**, C San Francisco 24, T942 606 141. 1 of 2 hostels in the old town run by nuns, this sparklingly clean place is to be found up the side of the church of the same name; head through a metal gate. Facilities are excellent, with a good kitchen and comfy dorms, and the nuns – who are cloistered; if you need anything you speak to them through a hatch. When speaking to nuns, the convention is to address them 'Ave María Purísima', to which the stock reply is 'Sin pecado concebida' (Hail Mary most pure/Conceived without sin).

### Castro Urdiales and around *p318*

**C Pensión La Sota**, C Correría 1, Castro Urdiales, T942 871 188, F942 871 284. This good-looking and sparklingly clean place is a street back from the water. The rooms come with TV and bathroom and are slightly overpriced in summer but good value at other times. Owners looking to sell, so new management might be in place.

**D Lantarón**, Playa de Arenillas s/n, Islares, T942 871 212. A relaxed hotel right by the sands.

**D-E Pensión La Mar**, C La Mar 1, Castro Urdiales, T942 870 524, F942 862 828. A simpler choice than **La Sota**, this central *pensión* is a good bet with rooms with or without bath that come with TV and heating.

### Camping

There's a campsite at **Oriñón** and a summer-only *fonda*; **Islares** is only a 20-min walk and has more to offer.

## ❷ Eating

**Santander** *p314, map p316*

Santander's status as elegant holiday resort and active fishing port assures it of a good selection of excellent places to eat. Top seafood restaurants compete for attention with characterful ex-wine cellars and no-frills joints doling the best of fresh fish. Sardinero has excellent eating options, but for concentration, head for the zone around **Plaza Cañadio** in the old town. **C Peña Herbosa** also has a selection of cheap tapas bars.

**♥♥♥ La Posada del Mar**, C Juan de la Cosa 3, T942 215 656. A fairly formal old restaurant with a formidable wine list. Although the seafood is good (try a whole salt-baked fish – memorable), this restaurant is perhaps better known for its meat and game dishes. The *menú del día* is good value at €18. Closed Sun and all Sep.

**♥♥♥ Rhin**, Plaza Italia 2, T942 273 034. An obvious choice overlooking the Sardinero beaches, this pleasant light restaurant has excellent if conservative dishes, with seafood the highlight. It's worth it for the view alone, looking right over the beach through massive windows. The bar and café are also popular places, particularly on a Sun, when *rabas* (calamari) are the order of the day.

**♥♥ Balneario la Magdalena**, C La Horada da s/n, T942 032 107. Excellently located café and restaurant on the peaceful and calm Magdalena beach. The dining room inevitably has fantastic views and the seafood is of the highest order without breaking the bank. There's a huge range of fish and other dishes; the red mullet (*salmonete*) with a sea-urchin sauce is particularly good.

**♥♥ Bodega Cigaleña**, C Daoiz y Velarde 19. This warm snug narrow bar is lined with wooden cabinets. It looks like the workshop of a mad alchemist convinced that the Philosopher's Stone was to be found at the bottom of a bottle of Rioja or *anis*. An excellent place for tapas, but you can also sit down for a meal; the menu focuses on game and other hearty fare.

**♥♥ Bodega del Riojano**, C Río de la Pila 5, T942 216 750. This loveable *bodega* has what is, for Spain, an almost reverentially hushed atmosphere as people seem awed by the ageing wine bottles that line the place from floor to ceiling. This old wine merchants' is famous for its decoratively painted barrels. The *tortilla con bonito* (tuna omelette) is the best around, while there's a range of cheeses, cured meats and stews. *Raciones* cost €6-12. Recommended.

**Bodegas Bringas**, C Hernán Cortés 47, T942 362 070. An excellent tapas bar, one of several set in old wine merchants' warehouses. The atmosphere is great and the food good and well priced. It's a convivial spot with a tasty array of *pinchos* adorning its long bar. Closed Tue.

**Bar Gelín**, C Vargas 29, T942 232 637. This bar has a stellar reputation for its *rabas* (pieces of fried calamari) and is the centrepiece of a popular tapas zone with a number of bars specializing in seafood snacks and home-made vermouth. The bar is usually known as the **Rey de Rabas**.

**Bodegas Manzón**, C Hernán Cortés 57, T942 215 752. This cavernous bar is big enough to park several buses in and is a Santander institution, having been in business more than a century. The huge vats of wine have the menu of cheap and cheerful *raciones* chalked up on the side; the smaller barrels still bear the names of the sherries and other wines that were once shipped from the port here. Chunky wooden tables and down-to-earth staff and customers add to the atmosphere. *Raciones* €3-10. Open daily.

**La Conveniente**, C Gómez Oreña 9. Another atmospheric *bodega* by Plaza Cañadío with a spacious, beamed interior, several shiploads of wine and a good variety of cheap food. It's a memorable place with its art nouveau panels about the only adornment to the chipped marble and aged wood, all with a patina of decades of chatter and good cheer. Open Mon-Sat from 1900.

**La Gaviota**, C Marqués de la Ensenada 35. One of a series of downmarket but deservedly popular seafood restaurants in the Barrio Pesquero, an earthy zone by the fishing harbour. Excellent grilled sardines are on offer here for a pittance. Take bus 4 or 14 from anywhere on the Santander waterfront to get here; better this than the slightly seedy walk.

## Cafés

**Café Suizo**, Paseo de Pereda 28, T942 215 864. This large and light 2-level café's white wooden balustrades give it the feeling of a filmset. It's well known as one of the best breakfast spots in town, with a range of sandwiches, pastries and little rolls, as well as a large terrace out on the waterfront road.

**La Casa del Indiano**, Mercado del Este s/n. The recently renovated 19th-century market now houses a variety of specialist shops, as well as this cheerful café/bar.

### Laredo *p318*

For tapas, restaurants and bars, head up the steps next to the town hall to the cobbled old-town street **C Rúa Mayor**, a long, narrow affair with plentiful choice.

**San Román de Escalante**, Escalante s/n, T942 677 728. Around the headland from Laredo, in the village of Escalante 3 km short of the anchovy-fishing town of Santoña, this restaurant is set superbly in an old mansion house by a Romanesque church. The cuisine is of the highest order; the memorable seafood, such as monkfish on crab paste, has won it many plaudits. There are also rooms (**AL**) available.

**La Abadía**, C Rúa Mayor 18, T942 612 028. Attractively set in a house partly dating from the 15th century, this restaurant has a fairly traditional sort of Spanish menu drawing from different parts of the country. The paella is excellent, as is the roast lamb, but don't decide until you've found out what the stew of the day is (*guiso del día*).

### Castro Urdiales and around *p318*

Basques often come here for day trips and weekends, so the food standards are high!

**El Segoviano**, Plaza del Ayuntamiento s/n, T942 861 859. Opposite the **Marinero**, this low-beamed restaurant serves up heavier fare, with roast meats the order of the day.

**Mesón Marinero**, Plaza del Ayuntamiento s/n, T942 860 005. This is an excellent restaurant with a wooden terrace, under the arcade in the main plaza. The seafood, of which there is a huge variety, is superb and is allowed to stand on its own merits rather than being over-smothered in other flavours. The *marmitakos* (spicy Basque fish stews) are especially tasty.

# ♪ Bars and clubs

**Santander** *p314, map p316*
**Bar del Puerto**, C Peña Herbosa 22, T942 212
939. A sleek bar, popular with the upwardly
mobile after work. It's a tapas bar and
restaurant too, but after hours the lights
dim and it becomes a cool and stylish bar.
**Blues**, C Gómez Oreña 15, T942 314 305.
A packed and popular bar with a good
mix of people. The music, as you may have
guessed, rests on a base of blues and soul.
**Fortunny**, C Moctezuma s/n. A weird little
bar, with a red girder exterior and chrome
'n' stone interior. The flashing lights and
pumping *bacalao* music make it a reliable
weekend destination for a 20s-30s crowd.
**La Floridita**, C Bailén s/n. A cheerful and
very lively bar, with a youngish crowd and
unpretentious scene. Good mixed drinks.
**Pachá**, C General Mola 45, T942 310 067.
Big 2-level *discoteca* that packs out late
at weekends with Spanish top-40 hits.
**Rocambole**, C Hernán Cortés 24. A late-
running bar with frequent live jazz and
blues and a lively dancefloor. There are
often 'open jam' nights where anyone
with an instrument can join in.
**Ventilador**, Plaza Cañadio s/n. A popular
bar with outdoor tables on this lively
night-time square. The atmosphere is
a bit more relaxing in the quieter
early evening.
**Zona Límite**, C Tetuán 32. A lively gay
spot, particularly during summer.

**Laredo** *p318*
**Cafe IV**, C Rúa Mayor 12. More a bar
than a café, this cheerful nightspot is
decorated with pseudo-Egyptian murals
and has a few tables out on the street
that are eagerly sought after. As well
as a selection of wines, they have a
couple of Belgian beers – Brugs
and Grimbergen – on tap.
**Playamar** on the beachfront, T942 610
150. A popular summer-only *discoteca*.

**Castro Urdiales and around** *p318*
There's plenty of weekend nightlife in Castro.
**Safari**, C Ardigales 26, T942 863 489. Good
for mellow music and a happy crowd.
**Twist**, C Rúa 16, T942 863 489. Offers
some serious dancefloor action.

# ◉ Entertainment

**Santander** *p314, map p316*
**Bahía Cinema**, Av Marqués de la
Hermida s/n. A big-release cinema.
**Filmoteca de Cantabria**, C Bonifaz 6, T942
319 310. Arthouse films and movie festivals.
**Gran Casino**, Plaza Italia s/n. 2000-0400
(0500 in summer). Dress code and proof of
age regulations apply. €3 cover charge.
**Palacio de Festivales**, C Castelar s/n. A
spacious venue for concerts and exhibitions.

# ◉ Festivals and events

**Santander** *p314, map p316*
**28 Jul** The province's main **rowing regatta**.
**Aug International Festival**, Santander's
major event of the year, featuring some
top-drawer musical and theatrical
performances. The liveliest street action
comes at its end, which coincides with
the fiesta of the city's patron saints.

# ◉ Shopping

**Santander** *p314, map p316*
Santander's main shopping streets are near
the town hall, cathedral and to the west.
**Librería Estudio**, Paseo Calvo Sotelo 19.
A good bookshop with a largish selection.

# ▲ Activities and tours

**Santander** *p314, map p316*
**Football**
Racing Santander yo-yo between the *Primera*
and *Segunda* divisions in Spanish football.
At time of writing, they were in the top flight,
and entertain the likes of **Real Madrid** in their
stadium in Sardinero. Tickets can be bought
at the stadium on Fri and Sat for a Sun fixture,
as well as from 2 hrs before the game.

# ◉ Transport

**Santander** *p314, map p316*
**Air**
Air services arrive at the Parayas airport,
5 km southwest of the centre. **ALSA** runs
buses to the airport every ½ hr or so (€1.50,
15 mins), and also connect the airport
directly with other cities, such as Laredo and
Bilbao – check their website www.alsa.es for

timetables. A taxi costs about €15 from the centre. Ryanair currently serve this airport from **London Stansted**, **Rome Ciampino**, **Liverpool**, and **Frankfurt Hahn**. Iberia run domestic flights from here to **Barcelona** and **Madrid** as well as other Spanish cities. The airport's phone number is T942 251 004.

**Airlines** Iberia, Plaza Pombo s/n, www.iberia.es.

### Bus
There's a handy online timetable at www.santandereabus.com, or you can phone the bus station on T942 211 995. Many buses ply routes from Santander to other Spanish cities. Up to 6 buses a day go to **Burgos** (3 hrs, €9.71) and on to **Madrid** (5½ hrs, €23.74), while buses east to **Bilbao** (90 mins, €5.72) are almost hourly. Several a day follow the coast westwards as far as **Gijón** and **Oviedo** (10 daily, 2½-3 hrs, €10.39) , while there are also buses serving **Zaragoza**, **Valladolid**, **A Coruña** and others.

Within Cantabria, there are 5 daily buses (2 on Sun) running to **Santillana del Mar** (40 mins, €2.30) and **Comillas** (55 mins) and 10-15 daily buses to **San Vicente de la Barquera** (1 hr if direct, €4). **Laredo** is served roughly hourly (€3.30), as is **Castro Urdiales** (1 hr, €4), while for the **Picos de Europa**, there are 1-3 buses daily to **Potes**, some of which have a connection to **Fuente Dé**.

### Car
**Car hire** Hertz, Puerto Ferrys, T942 362 821; Atesa, C Marcelino Sanz de Santuola, T942 222 926.

### Ferry
Brittany Ferries run a service between Santander and **Plymouth**. These leave the UK on Sun and Wed mornings, taking a shade under 24 hrs. Return ferries leave Santander on Mon and Thu. Book online at www.brittany ferries.co.uk, or by phone on T08705 561 600 (UK) or T942 360 611 (Spain). Prices are variable but can usually be found for about £70-90 (€115-150) each way in a reclining seat. A car adds about £140 (€225) each way, and cabins start from about £80 (€130) for a twin. The service runs year-round.

### Taxi
If none on the street calle, T942 333 333.

Santander is both on the national RENFE network and the private coastal FEVE service. The stations are next to each other (as is the bus station). Call the RENFE station on T942 280 202; the FEVE station on T942 364 718.

RENFE runs 3-5 trains daily to **Madrid** (6 hrs, €34.50) and 7 or so to **Valladolid** and **Palencia** on the same line. There are *cercanía* trains to **Torrelavega** and **Reinosa** every ½ hr.

FEVE trains run east to **Bilbao** 3 times daily (2½ hrs, €6.50) and west along the coast as far as **Oviedo**, **Gijón** and **Ferrol** in Galicia twice daily (to Oviedo/Gijón, it's 4 hrs and costs €11.85). It's a fairly slow but scenic service, and invaluable for accessing smaller coastal towns.

### South of Santander *p317*
### Bus
Puente Viesgo is accessible by bus from **Santander** (operated by various companies; about €1.85, ½ hr) up to 6 times daily.

### Laredo *p318*
### Bus
Frequent buses connected Laredo and **Santander** (½-hourly, €3.30, 45 mins).

### Castro Urdiales and around *p318*
### Bus
Castro Urdiales is connected very regularly by bus with both **Santander** (more than hourly, €4.85, 60-90 mins) and **Bilbao**, which is only ½ hr away.

## ● Directory

**Santander** *p314, map p316*
**Internet** Café Lugano, C Hernán Cortés 55, T942 224 280, Sun-Thu 0730-2200, Fri/Sat 0830-0100; Ciber Studio, C Magallanes 48; La Copia, C Lealtad 13, T942 227 680 (by cathedral). **Laundry** Lavandería del Palacio, C Juan de la Cosa 15, T942 076 390, 6-kg service wash for €10.22. **Post office** The main post office is on C Alfonso XIII, at the corner with Av de Calvo Sotelo. **Telephone** There's a *locutorio* near the station at C Madrid 2, and one at C Burgos 9.

**Castro Urdiales and around** *p318*
**Internet** Check email at Cibercafé Link, C De Jardines 4, Castro Urdiales.

# West Coast of Cantabria

*Cantabria's western coast has plenty to detain the visitor. As well as some good beaches, there are some very attractive towns; these are headed up by Santillana del Mar, a superb ensemble of stonework which also boasts the newly opened museum at nearby Altamira, the site of some of the finest prehistoric art ever discovered. Comillas will appeal to fans of Modernista architecture and, beyond, the coast continues towards Asturias, backed spectacularly by the bulky Picos de Europa mountains.*
‣ *For Sleeping, Eating and other listings, see pages 327-329.*

## Santillana del Mar and around ⬤🚻🏃👤🚌🎈 ‣ *pp327-329.*

➔ *Colour map 2, B5.*

Although it may sound like a seaside town, it isn't; it's 4 km inland. A cynical old saying claims that it's the town of three lies: '*Santillana no es santa, no es llana, y no hay mar*' (Santillana's not holy or flat, and there's no sea). Nevertheless, Santillana is delightful, despite the high number of strolling visitors captivated by the architecture of the place that Sartre immortalized (albeit in *Nausea*) as "the most beautiful village in Spain". While it's still a dairy region – cows are still brought back into the village in the evening – every building within the old town is now devoted to tourism in some form. It's definitely worth staying overnight, as the bulk of the visitors are on daytrips, and the emptier the town, the more atmospheric it is. Try and come out of season, and avoid weekends if possible; the opening of the Altamira museum has increased the daily flow of visitors.

### Background

Founded by monks, the town became important in the Middle Ages due to the power of its monastery, which had a finger in every pie going. What the town is today is a result of the nobility wresting control of the feudal rent system from the abbot in the 15th century. Once the peasants were filling secular coffers, the landowners grew wealthy, donated money in exchange for titles and started trying to outdo each other in ostentatious *palacio* construction. Though undoubtedly antidemocratic and tasteless at the time, these buildings are now exceedingly beautiful!

### Sights

The **Colegiata** ⓘ *daily 1000-1330, 1600-1830 (closes 1930 in summer), €2.50 (includes entrance to the Diocesan Museum at the other end of town)*, sits at the end of the town and has a jumbled, homely façade in orangey stone. The current Romanesque building replaced a former Benedictine monastery in the 12th century. An arcaded gallery runs high above the portal, and a round belltower to the right outrages hardcore symmetry fans. Wander around the side to gain access to the church and cloister. To the latter can be applied all the adjectives normally used to describe its kind; its shady Romanesque arches also feature many different motifs on the capitals, ranging from mythological creatures to geometric figures and Biblical scenes.

The church is spacious with impressive stone vaulting; there is some of the *ajedrezado jaqués* chessboard patterning originally used in the town of Jaca and disseminated through Northern Spain by wandering masons and pilgrims. The building is dedicated to Santa Juliana, a third-century saint for whom the town is named. She was put to death by her husband for not consummating their marriage on their wedding night (or any other night); her bones were originally brought here by the community of monks that founded the monastery and town. One of her achievements in life was the taming of a demon, whom she used to drag around on a rope (to the despair of their marriage counsellor); scenes from her life can be seen on her tomb in the centre of the church, and the *retablo*, a 16th-century work. There's a figure of Juliana in the centre, standing above a chest that holds various parts of her earthly remains.

The other major sight in town is the collection of grandiose *palacios* emblazoned with (in some cases hugely oversized) coats-of-arms. They are concentrated down the main street, **Calle Cantón**, and around the main square. The square has two Gothic towers, one of which is an exhibition hall. In front of the church, the former **abbot's house** was later occupied by the Archduchess of Austria; further down this street note the former marquis' house (now a hotel). The **Casa de los Villa** near the main road has a façade emblazoned with a pierced eagle and the motto *un buen morir es honra de la vida* (a good death honours the life); a precursor to the Falangist Civil War cry ¡*Viva la muerte!*

As Santillana is a popular place to spend holidays, there's always plenty on for young and old, with frequent temporary exhibitions, craft displays and festivals. Permanent attractions include a decent **Zoo** ① *daily 0930-dusk, €8, kids €4*, on the edge of town, which has a snow leopard among its constricted but cared-for captives. There is a **Torture Museum** ① *daily 1000-2000, 2200 in summer, €3.60*, near the church with all sorts of horrible fantasies in iron used during the Inquisition and other dark periods in human history. The **Diocesan Museum** ① *Tue-Sun 1000-1330, 1600-1830 (closes 1930 summer, also open Mon); joint ticket with the Colegiata, €2.50*, on the main road, which is a good example of its kind, has a large collection that includes some Latin American pieces brought back to Santillana by *indianos*.

The **tourist office** ① *daily 0900-1330, 1600-1900*, at the edge of the old town near the main road, is busy and occasionally understandably brusque. They supply a decent map/guide to the town in a variety of languages.

## Altamira Caves

① *T942 818 005, www.mcu.es/nmuseos/altamira, Jun-Sep Tue-Sat 0930-1930, Sun 0930-1700, Oct-May Tue-Sun 0930-1700, last admission to the Neocueva 1 hr before closing; €2.40, free Sat after 1430 and Sun all day. To apply to visit the original cave, write to the museum at Museo de Altamira, 39330 Santillana del Mar, or F942 840 157, but you now have to have a serious scientific reason to gain admission.*

In 1879, in the countryside 2 km from Santillana, a man and his daughter were exploring some caves only discovered a few years before when they looked up and saw a cavalcade of animals superbly painted in ochre and charcoal. The man, Marcelino Sanz de Sautuola, was interested in prehistoric art, but the quality of these works far exceeded any known at the time. Excitedly publishing his findings, he wasn't believed until several years after his death, when the discovery of similar paintings in southern France made the sceptics reverse their position. The paintings are amazing; fluid bison, deer and horses, some 14,000 years old. Understandably, they became a major tourist attraction, but the moist breath of the visitors began to damage the art and admission had to be heavily restricted; the waiting list is about three years at present and may be entirely terminated in the future.

Enter the **Neocueva**, opened in 2001 with much pomp and ceremony. It's a replica of part of the original cave and paintings and is part of a museum that puts the art in context. The exhibition begins with an excellent overview of prehistoric hominids so you can get your Neanderthals sorted from your Cro-Magnons before moving on to more specific displays about the Altamira epoch and ways of life at the time.

The Neocueva itself is accessed in groups with a guide; there can be quite a wait if the museum is busy. It's an impressive reconstruction, and the explanations are good. You can admire the replica paintings, particularly as they were probably painted from a prone position but, although impressive, they lack some of the

# 66 99...they looked up and saw a cavalcade of animals superbly painted in ochre and charcoal.

emotion that comes from actually feeling the incomprehensible gulf of 14,000 years. All told, it's a very good museum and an impressive substitute for the original cave, which the government were absolutely right to protect from destruction.

## Comillas → *Colour map 2, B5.*

Comillas is a fashionable Cantabrian beach resort and has been popular with the well-to-do for over a century. As well as its beach and pleasant old centre, the town is worth a visit for its architecture, out of the ordinary for a seaside summer town. Rather than drab lines of holiday cottages, it boasts some striking Modernista buildings ostentatiously perched on the hilltops around the town. They are a legacy of Catalan architects who were commissioned by competitive local aristocrats to create suitably extravagant residences for them. The **tourist office** ① *Mon-Fri 1130-1430, 1600-1800 (2000 summer), Sat 1130-1400, 1630-1930,* in the town hall building on the main road through Comillas is efficient and helpful.

The town's most unusual architectural flourishes are found in **Gaudí's El Capricho**. Rightly named (the caprice), it's an astonishingly imaginative flight of fancy embossed with bright green and yellow tiles and adorned with Mediterranean sunflowers. The best feature is a whimsical tower, an ornate Muslim fantasy with a balcony. Apart from a tourist shop with Gaudí paraphernalia, the interior is filled by an upmarket restaurant.

Next door is the **Palacio de Sobrellano** ① *Oct-Jun Wed-Sun 1030-1400, 1600-1930, Jul and Aug daily 1000-2100, Sep daily 1030-1400, 1600-1930, €2 palace, €2 chapel (guided tour),* commissioned by the Marqués de Comillas, a heavy pseudo-Gothic structure full of quirky furniture. A small plot in the parish graveyard wasn't the marquis' vision of resting in peace, so he had an ornate chapel put up next to the family summer home to hold flashy tombs that would have done justice to a Renaissance monarch!

On the eminence opposite, the **Universidad Pontificia** was built as a theological college in similarly avant-garde style. It's a majestic and grandiose structure in reddish stone that dominates the town. Whether the priests-in-training were imbued with Christian humility in such a building is open to question, but in any event the college moved to Madrid in 1964. The building is now subject to various plans for its future and is not open for visits.

*♣ The town is a fair walk from the beach, but still functions as an important fishing port.*

The town itself has several attractive squares and mansions that seem positively modest by comparison. Keep your eyes up as you wander around to appreciate some of the fine carved balustrades. The cobbled Plaza de la Constitución is at the heart of the area and is winningly beautiful, with fabulous balconies and rustic rubble masonry. There are two good beaches 10-minutes walk from the centre. West of Comillas is another strand, **Playa Oyambre**, with a campsite and cheap but tasty restaurant.

## San Vicente de la Barquera → *Colour map 2, B4.*

Although blessed with a stunning mountain backdrop when you can see it for the mist, San Vicente is a fairly low-key although pleasant resort. While the town's seafood restaurants and natural setting at the mouth of two rivers appeal, the attractive old-town streets have been surrounded by some fairly thoughtless modern development. The architectural highlight is the transitional Gothic **Iglesia de Nuestra**

**Señora de los Angeles,** which has a wooden floor like a ship's deck and attractive Gothic vaulting. The church was built in the 13th century, when Romanesque was going pointy, and it's an interesting example of this phase. There are good views from here over the river estuary and the long bridge crossing it.

On the same ridge, the **castle** ⓘ *Tue-Sun 1100-1400, 1700-2000, €1.20,* is in reasonable shape but isn't overly compelling. The big **tourist office** ⓘ *Av Generalísimo 20, T942 710 797, Tue-Fri 1000-1300, 1600-1900, Sat and Sun 1000-1330, 1630-1830,* is on the main street; the Fascist street names live on for some reason.

---

## ● Sleeping

**Santillana del Mar** *p324*
Santillana has a good range of accommodation for all budgets. There are many hotels on the main road, or worse, in an ugly expansion on the other side of it that tried to retain that old-town look but failed; however, there are enough in the old centre itself to make sure you end up there, though you should definitely book ahead in summer. Many private homes put signs out advertising *camas* or *habitaciones* at peak time; some of these are very good options.
**LL La Casa del Marqués,** C Cantón 26, T942 818 888, www.casadelmarques.com. Santillana's priciest hotel is excellently set in a large *palacio* that belonged to the local marquis, who had to display his superior status with 3 coats of arms. The interior decoration is simpler, with attractive wooden furniture but numerous facilities. Service lets down the overall effect, but it's still a memorable place to stay.
**L Parador Gil Blas,** Plaza Ramón Pelayo 11, T942 028 028, www.parador.es. In a modernized *palacio* on the beautifully bare Plaza Mayor, this *parador* is named after a famous fictional character from Santillana created by the French novelist Lesage in the 18th century. There's a good restaurant, and the rooms have every comfort.
**A Altamira,** C Cantón 1, T942 818 025, www.hotelaltamira.com. This is cheaper than the *parador* but also charterfully set in another sumptuous *palacio*, with appropriate decor. There's also a good patio restaurant, an excellent spot to eat or have a drink.
**A-B Posada La Casa del Organista,** C Los Hornos 4, T942 840 352, www.casadel organista.com. Set in a smaller but still

impressive 18th-century home; this is a welcoming place with lovely wooden furnishings and rustic bedrooms. The quality of the welcome, the stone walls and the sharp off-season prices (**C**) make this a great place. Recommended.
**B-C Posada Ansorena,** C Cantón 10, T942 818 228, F942 818 280. This delightful stone mansion is right on the main cobbled street and makes a great place to stay. Inside it's all rustic dark wooden furniture and creaking floorboards; rooms are large and varied, many with a balcony overlooking the garden. There's also a guest lounge with board games. Breakfast included; very good value, especially outside Aug.
**E Casa Octavio,** Plaza de las Arenas s/n, T942 818 199. A peaceful and very attractive spot to find a bed in an alley off the Plaza de las Arenas by the side of the church. There's a variety of rooms on offer, but all are rustic and charming.

### Camping
**Camping Santillana,** T942 818 250. 5-mins' walk down the main road west out of town, this is a good campsite, although packed during summer. There are bungalows available too.

**Comillas** *p326*
There are many places to stay, with the usual summer price hike.
**A Casal del Castro,** C San Jerónimo s/n, T942 720 036, hccastro@infonegocio.com. The best option in town, an attractively renovated mansion with a garden and thoughtfully homely rooms. Well priced for this coast.

● *For an explanation of the sleeping and eating price codes used in this guide, see inside the front cover. Other relevant information is found in Essentials pages 39-46.*

**B Esmeralda**, C Antonio López 7, T942 720 097, F942 722 258. This good friendly choice is right in the centre, set in a great old stone building. The rooms are large and sensitively modernized and the management offer sharp off-season prices (**D**). Restaurant downstairs.

**D Pensión Pasiegos de la Vega**, Paseo del Muelle s/n, T942 722 102. An upmarket *pensión* with good facilities, this is comfy if not stylish and overlooks the beach 5-10 mins' walk from the centre of town.

**F Pensión Fuente Real**, C Fuente Real 19, T942 720 155. This curious little *pensión* is right behind **El Capricho** and its shabby but clean rooms are cheap and pretty good value for the area.

**San Vicente de la Barquera** *p326*
You'll have no problems finding a room on spec; there are many places.

**D Pensión Liébana**, C Ronda 2, T942 710 211 This *pensión* is right in the centre of things and has decent rooms with bathroom and TV, that become exceedingly cheap (**F**) once summer's over.

## ❷ Eating

### Santillana del Mar *p324*

**❅❅❅ Altamira**, C Cantón 1, T942 818 025. The best of the hotel restaurants and fairly reasonably priced. The seafood here is excellent; at lunchtime you can eat on the patio. If you fancy something heartier, try the *lechón* (sucking pig) served with chestnut mash. Mains are €12-19.

**❅❅❅ Gran Duque**, C Escultor Jesús Otero Orena. A good restaurant, with views over the meadows outside town and much attractive seafood on the list, and a good set menu for €15. Closed Feb.

**❅ El Castillo**, Plaza Mayor 6, T942 818 377. Although in the heart of the town, this bar/restaurant is refreshingly unpretentious and does some good dishes at reasonable prices. The *menú de cocido* is particularly hearty; broth followed by a big serve of chickpeas and salt pork.

### Comillas *p326*
The pleasures of eating fish 'n' chips by the sea are lost on holidaying Spaniards – there are several excellent restaurants.

**❅❅❅ El Capricho de Gaudí**, Sobrellano s/n, T942 720 365. If you're a fan of Gaudí's building, you'll probably want to eat here. Happily, there's no gimmickry or reliance on the building here; the food is top class. It's new Spanish cuisine with a heavy emphasis on seafood; there are some excellent fishes, such as *rodaballo salvaje con ajetes* (wild turbot with fresh garlic shoots), or *rape con setas* (monkfish stew with wild mushrooms).

**❅❅❅ Gurea**, C Ignacio Fernández de Castro 11, T942 722 446. A Basque restaurant that lives up to all the good things that implies. Mains such as *bacalao a la vizcaína* (a cod dish) or *kokotxas* (hake cheeks in spicy sauce; excellent) cost €10-15 and are served in a cosy atmosphere. Closed Sun pm and Mon.

**❅ Filipinas**, C de los Arzobispos s/n. Where the locals eat; this is a lively bar on the intersection in the middle of town. There are simple *raciones* of seafood and meat, as well as hearty stews in tin pots. During the week the *menú del día* is €8, which rises (along with the choice) to €12 at weekends, when you'll wait for a table.

### San Vicente de la Barquera *p326*

**❅❅❅ Boga-Boga**, Av Generalísimo, T942 710 135. The food at Boga-Boga lives up to its excellent name, which is a traditional Basque sea-shanty. There's a great variety of seafood and some good wines to knock back with it. There are also decent rooms upstairs.

**❅❅❅ Augusto**, C Mercado 1, T942 712 040. This excellent seafood restaurant sees plenty of visitors at its terraced tables and in its shiplike interior. There are plenty of good- value mixed platters to choose from; you can have a good meal here at a number of different price levels depending on what crustaceans take your fancy.

## ❸ Bars and clubs

### Comillas *p326*
**Don Porfirio**, C Victoriano Pérez de la Riva s/n. A riotous outdoor bar, open in summer only, with loud music, cold beer and picnic-style wooden seats in a grassy plot of land in the old town.

**Pamara**, C Comillas s/n, is a good summer *discoteca* with an upmarket set.

## ⊝ Transport

**Santillana del Mar** *p324*
**Bus**
There are 5 daily buses (2 on Sun) running
to and from **Santander** (30 mins, €2.30).

**Comillas** *p326*
**Bus**
There are 5 daily buses, 2 on Sun, running
to and from **Santander** via **Santillana del
Mar**. They continue westwards to **San
Vicente de Barquera**.

**San Vicente de la Barquera** *p326*
**Bus**
10-15 daily buses run to **Santander**
(1 hr if direct, €4), some going via
**Comillas** and **Santillana**. There are
also 10 westbound buses to **Oviedo**
and **Gijón**.

## ❶ Directory

**Comillas** *p326*
**Internet** Kiosco Ataf, C Cervantes 2,
is a shop with an internet terminal.

# Los Picos de Europa

*The Picos de Europa are a small area of the vast Cordillera Cantábrica blessed with
spectacular scenery, superb walking, abundant wildlife and, most crucially,
comparatively easy access (but take your hat off to the engineers who built the roads...).
They encompass the corners of three provinces: Asturias, Cantabria and León, and have
a mild climate due to their proximity to the sea. It is this fact that probably gives them
their curious name (the Peaks of Europe); they often would have been the first sight of
land that weary Spanish sailors got on their return from the Americas.*

*The Picos are comprised of three main massifs of limestone cut and tortured over
the millennia by glaciation, resulting in the distinctive rock formations given the
adjective 'karstic'. The central part of the range is a national park, expanded from the
original Parque Nacional de la Montaña de Covadonga, the first such beast in Spain,
denominated in 1918.*

## Ins and outs

**Getting there** The Picos de Europa are easily accessed from Santander or Oviedo,
and slightly less so from León. The two principal towns for Picos tourism are Cangas
de Onís (Asturias) and Potes (Cantabria); both make excellent bases, especially if
you lack private transport. Potes is serviced regularly by bus from Santander and the
Cantabrian coast, while there are frequent buses from Oviedo and Gijón to Cangas.
▸ See Transport, page 337.

**Getting around** Travelling around the Picos de Europa is simple with your own
transport and time-consuming without. The Picos is basically a rectangular area
with a main road running around its perimeter and several smaller roads dead-
ending into the heart of the mountains from it. Buses run on the main roads and to
popular destinations like Covadonga and Fuente Dé. Fewer buses run on Sundays
on routes indicated within each travelling text section; if the buses just don't get
you where you need to go, taxis are a reasonable alternative, if there are two or more
of you. There are also jeep services that act as shared taxis. Hitching is easy in the
Picos too. The ideal solution for some is to walk; it's only three hours through the
Cares gorge, and you've crossed the Picos from north to south; the journey wouldn't
take much less by car.

**Tourist information** The Picos de Europa National Park offices run free guided tours around the Picos region during summer, an excellent service. The schedule changes each year and is organized from the three regional information centres; phone for details: **Cangas de Onís, Asturias,** T985 848 614; **Posada de Valdeón, León,** T987 740 549; **Camaleño/Potes, Cantabria,** T942 730 555. There's also a head office in **Oviedo,** at Calle Arquitecto Reguera 13, T985 241 412, F985 273 945. All the major towns have year-round tourist offices, and in addition many villages have summer-only kiosks. The best tourist information office for the Picos is in Cangas de Onís.
▸▸ *See sections Cangas de Onís, page 332, and Potes, page 337.*

**Best time to visit** The best time to visit the Picos is either side of high summer; September/October and May/June are ideal, in July and August prices are well up and the crowds can hamper enjoyment of the natural beauties of the area. The Picos

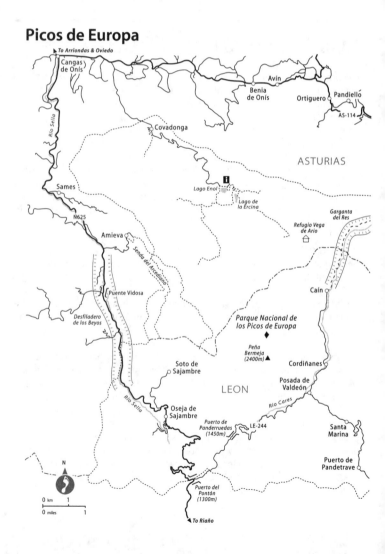

# Picos de Europa

have a fairly damp and temperate maritime climate so you're never assured of clear days, but neither does it get extremely cold, at least on the north side of the range. Mists descend regularly; so take a compass and check the forecast.

**Flora and fauna** The Picos are home to a wide variety of fauna and flora, due partly to the hugely varying climactic zones within its terrasculpted interior. Among the birds, vultures are common; rarer are eagles and capercaillies. Less glamorous species include choughs and wallcreepers. Chamois are a reasonably common sight, as are wild boar; there are also mountain cats, wolves and bears about, but they are much scarcer. A frequent and pretty sight on roads are herds of soft-eyed cows, an attractive variety from these parts. Insect and reptile life is also abundant; clouds of butterflies are about in spring and summer. The flora varies widely from the temperate to the Alpine; in spring the mountain fields are full of wildflowers.

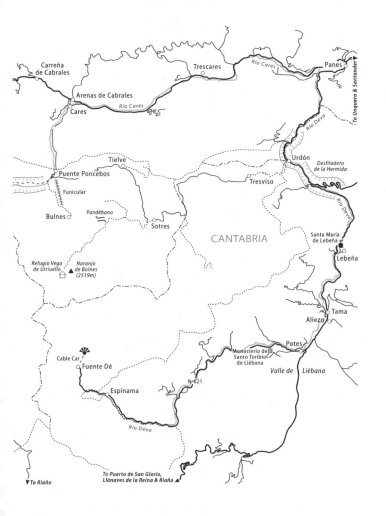

# Asturian Picos

*Asturias claims the largest slab of the Picos massif and has the most advanced environmental and tourism infrastructure of the region. The area's main town, Cangas de Onís, is an excellent place to begin a trip to the Picos, while nearby Covadonga is revered as the birthplace of Christian Spain. The area is also famous for producing the strong blue cheese known as Cabrales after the villages in which it is produced. Similar in style to Roquefort, it lends its flavour to many a gourmet dish, but is also enjoyed by the locals as a smotherer of chips. Some of the most dramatic rocky scenery of the region is accessed south of here; there are some fantastic hikes in the area around Puente Poncebos, including the three-hour gorge walk to Caín, a route that crosses the Picos from north to south.* ▸▸ *For Sleeping, Eating and other listings, see pages 335-337.*

## Cangas de Onís ▸▸ *pp335-337.*

This service town is a typically cheerful Asturian centre, with plenty of places to stay, and some top *sidrerías* in which to drink and eat. Its highlight is a superb medieval bridge across the Río Sella with an alarmingly steep cobbled arch. It's at its best when eerily floodlit at night; locals inaccurately name it the **Puente Romano** (Roman bridge). Also of interest is the **Ermita de Santa Cruz**, just across the other river (the Güeña), a tiny 15th-century chapel, which has fifth-century origins and was built over a dolmen; the key can be collected from the tourist office.

After his victory at Covadonga (see below), Pelayo set up base here and Cangas proudly claims to be the first capital of Christian Spain as a result. A statue of a very rugged Pelayo stands defiantly outside the church, a 20th-century construction with *indiano* and Italian influences visible in its three-storey belltower. There are many *indiano* buildings in town; a good number of eastern Asturians left to seek their fortunes in the New World.

Cangas' **tourist office** ① *T985 848 005, daily 1000-1400, 1600-1900*, is the best equipped in the Picos region. It sits on the main square and has plenty of information about the whole Picos area. Grab all the information you can here, as the smaller offices in other towns have less regular opening and sometimes run out of maps, etc.

### Around Cangas
South of Cangas the road to Riaño soon plunges into the Desfiladero de los Beyos. It's a popular spot for walking and salmon fishing and vultures are a common sight.

North of Cangas, the town of **Arriondas** is a popular base for canoeing the Río Sella, but lacks the appeal of Cangas, which also operates canoeing trips. The descent is brisk but not too challenging; a fun introduction to the sport. A typical half-day involves transport to the launch point, descent, lunch and return to the town, be it Cangas or Arriondas.

## Covadonga ▸▸ *pp335-337.*

→ *Colour map 2, B3.*
Some 4 km east of Cangas, a side road leads a further 6 km up a wooded valley to Covadonga, a name written large in Spanish history, more for what it represented after the fact than for what it was. Thronged with Spanish pilgrims and visitors, its main touristic interest lies in its pretty setting and in the observation of just how deep the Reconquista is embedded as the country's primary source of national pride.

## Background

The facts are few and lost in time and propaganda. What is conjectured is that Pelayo, an Asturian leader, defeated a Moorish expedition here some time around AD 718. Some accounts from the Middle Ages claim that 124,000 Moors were killed here by 30 men. This is an obvious exaggeration, it would seem more likely that the force was of a small expeditionary nature and the defeat a minor one. For the Moors, the defeat was certainly of little military significance; it was another 14 years before their serious reverse occurred at Poitiers, a good distance into France. But Spanish history has seen Covadonga as the beginning of the Reconquista, the reconquest of the peninsula by Christian soldiers, a process that wasn't complete until 1492, nearly 800 years later. In truth, the battle may have had some effect, at least in establishing Pelayo as pre-eminent among Asturian warlords and sowing the seeds for the foundation of a Christian kingdom in the mountains, a kingdom that did play a significant role in unravelling Muslim dominance in Iberia. But it's hard to sit at Covadonga, watching the coaches roll in, and not wonder what it's all about.

## Sights

The focus of Covadonga is the **cave** where the Christian reconquest of the peninsular allegedly began, a pretty little grotto in a rockface with a waterfall and small chapel. Pelayo is buried here at the scene of his triumph, in a plain but powerfully simple sarcophagus in a niche in the cave wall. A pink **basilica** was erected in the late 19th century; it houses the Virgin of Covadonga and is surprisingly unadorned inside; the focus is on a replica of the Asturian victory cross forged by Pelayo to commemorate the victory. There's also a **museum** ① *Wed-Mon 1030-1400, 1600-1930; €2*, on site, which primarily displays a collection of expensive gifts lavished on the Virgin over the years.

Beyond Covadonga, a 12-km road leads further into the mountains, offering a couple of spectacular panoramas to the north. At the top are two lakes, **Enol** and **Ercina**, neither particularly appealing in themselves, but in superb surroundings bristling with peaks that are often snow capped. From Ercina, a 10-minute walk beyond Enol, there are some good walks: one heads south up the face of the Reblagas to an isolated *refugio*, Vega de Ario (six hours return); others head westwards and south to various viewpoints and *refugios*. A small information centre at the lake is open in summer and has reasonable maps of the area; otherwise grab them in Cangas.

---

# Arenas de Cabrales and around ⬛🌀🚌 » *pp335-337.*

→ *Colour map 2, B4.*

The road east from Cangas to Arenas de Cabrales is very attractive, and there are numerous hamlets both on and off the road, which offer potentially relaxing rural stays.

The **Arenas de Cabrales Valley** and the surrounding hillsides are famous throughout Spain for the strong blue cheese made here, *cabrales*. If you've been underwhelmed by Spanish cheeses so far, you're in for a treat. Not for nothing is the stuff known as the 'Spanish Roquefort'; it shares many similarities in taste and production methods with the classic French blue cheese. It's made from cows' milk, often with a percentage of sheep or goat milk added, and is matured in damp caves, where the bacteria that give it its sharp taste and distinctive colour develop.

Arenas is a busy place, as it's here that many people cut south into the heart of the Picos around Poncebos and Sotres. It makes a good base for the region, with banks, restaurants, shops and plenty of hotels. There's a small tourist kiosk by the bridge.

In **Cares**, a five-minute walk south of Arenas, the **Cueva del Cares** ① *Apr-Oct daily 1000-1400, 1600-2000, Nov-Mar weekends only; €2.50*, is a small factory and cave where Cabrales cheese is made in the traditional manner. A guided tour takes visitors through the process and finishes up with a tasting of the blue-blooded stuff.

# Into the mountains ⬛ ➤ *pp335-337.*

## Hiking the Cares Gorge trail

An hour's walk south of Arenas, the road reaches **Puente Poncebos**, a small collection of buildings set among high, bleak mountains. There's a shared-jeep service running to here and Sotres from Arenas. The main reason people come here is to walk the Cares Gorge, one of the Picos' most popular trails. It's about three hours from here to **Caín**, at the other end of the gorge; there's accommodation there, or you can continue another three hours to **Posada de Valdeón** (see page 341), if you don't meet up with a jeep that connects those two towns. This is the best direction to walk in, it gets more spectacular as you go, and Posada de Valdeón is a welcoming place to finish up.

The trail is there thanks to a hydroelectric scheme, and it follows the course of a small, fast-flowing canal that would itch for a fairground-style dinghy ride if it didn't plunge underground every few metres. It's not the best walk if you don't like heights or enclosed spaces; there are several claustrophobic tunnels (a torch helps) and the path runs alongside steep drops to the river much of the time. It's incredibly popular, so don't do it at weekends or in high summer unless you fancy a conga-line experience. From Poncebos, the trail climbs moderately for the first hour or so, leaving the river far below. If you hear jangling far above, it probably comes from belled goats, who seem to reach completely impossible locations high on the precipitous rocks.

The walk gets prettier and more dramatic as you approach the tail of the **Valdeón Valley**; the massive slabs of rock get bigger and more imposing, but provide shelter for a large range of tree and plant life. You'll probably see vultures circling lazily overhead and you may spot wallcreepers thumbing their beaks at gravity as they hop up perpendicular stone faces. After two hours or so, you'll reach a large green bridge; the path gently descends from here to Caín, crossing the river a couple more times. There are swimming holes here to refresh you, although the water is never less than icy. ➤ *See the Leonese Picos section, page 341, for Caín and beyond.*

## Hiking from Poncebos to Bulnes

Another walk from Poncebos is the steep hour-and-a-bit's climb to Bulnes, a remote village in the midst of lofty mountains. Until 2001, this was the only way to get to the place, and villagers lugged their provisions up this trail as part of everyday life. There's now a **funicular railway** ① *every ½ hr or so, a massive €13.52 one way/€15 return,* in place at Poncebos, a controversial scheme that outraged environmentalists but pleased the villagers (although it certainly wasn't built for their benefit).

The walk leaves from near the car park for the Cares Gorge walk, and crosses the river before zigzagging steeply up the hill. The first half is the hardest, but the trail continues to climb before reaching Bulnes, which is two separate hamlets, a higher and a lower. Most facilities are in the lower one, **La Villa**: there are two *albergues* that also do meals (**Bulnes**, T985 845 934, and **Peña Main**, T985 845 939), although the funicular will no doubt necessitate more options. The village's setting is superb, surrounded by threatening grey peaks, but with enough pastureland to sustain a grazing economy.

## Hiking from Poncebos to Sotres

From Poncebos, a spectacular road winds through the brooding mountains to the remote village of Sotres (this route is also serviced by shared jeeps in season), another walking base. Sotres is slightly on the grim side, especially in bleak weather, but there are a couple of good lodging and eating options.

## Hiking from Sotres to Vego de Urriello

One of the best walks from Sotres is the 4½ hours to the *refugio* of **Vega de Urriello** (T985 925 200; year-round), in a grassy meadow near the signature peak of **Naranjo** de Bulnes, which is basically a massive rock jutting out from the massif; it's not a climb for the inexperienced. The walk to the *refugio* crosses the pass at **Pandébano,** from where there are excellent views.

## East to Panes

Panes itself isn't worth a stop; it is characterized by a modern bridge in rusted iron and a shocking 19th-century church topped by a pastel-blue Jesus. South of here, the N621 winds into Cantabria towards Potes along the spectacular **Desfiladero de la Hermida.**

---

## ● Sleeping

### Cangas de Onís *p332*

There are many places to stay – even in summer there should space. The tourist office has a full list. Most are great value off-season.

**L** **Parador de Cangas de Onís**, Villanueva s/n, T985 849 402, www.parador.es, cangas@ parador.es. Set in an old Benedictine monastery 3 km north of Cangas, this new *parador* offers excellent comfort and some good views. Most of the rooms are in a modern annexe; those in the original building are less comfortable but more atmospheric.

**AL** **Ciudad de Cangas de Onís**, Av Castilla 36, T985 849 444, www.hotelcangasde onis.com. 5 mins' walk from the centre on the road to Riaño, this is a fairly stylish modern hotel with all the trimmings. €10 extra gets a spa-bath in the room; a good option for weary hiking legs.

**A** **El Rexacu**, Bobia de Arriba s/n, T985 844 303, www.elrexacu.com A reader alerted us to this excellent rural hotel in a village 18km east of Cangas. It's a welcoming, nothing-too-much-trouble sort of place, and has fabulous views. There's a sociable lounge with books, games, and films, and the restaurant serves up excellent food, including home-grown vegies and even ostrich meat from the farm.

**B** **Hotel Puente Romano**, C Puente Romano s/n, T985 849 339, puenteromano@ hispa portal.zzn.com. An authentically heavily decorated 19th-century mansion across the Sella, with courteous management and comfortable heated rooms.

**C** **Los Robles**, C San Pelayo 8, T985 947 052, F985 997 165. A nice sunny option a street back from the main road.

**C-D** **Hotel Los Lagos**, Jardines de Ayunta-miento 3, T985 849 277, loslagos@fade.es. Good hotel with a warm, professional attitude and modern, attractive and quiet rooms on the main square. Closed Nov-Mar.

**D** **Hotel La Plaza**, C La Plaza 7, T985 848 308, F985 848 308. Simple and cheery rooms with bathroom. The best options have a balcony and look out towards the mountains.

**E** **Pensión Reconquista**, Av Covadonga 6, T985 848 275. Modern, 6th-floor rooms with balconies overlooking the town, and that rarest of beasts, a good shower. Run out of the bar on the corner. An excellent option.

### Around Cangas *p332*

**B-C** **Hotel Puente Vidosa**, Puente Vidosa s/n, T985 944 735, www.puentevidosa.com. Slap-bang in the middle of the gorge; a romantic and lonely spot.

### Covadonga *p332*

**A** **Gran Hotel Pelayo**, Covadonga s/n, T985 846 061, www.granhotelpelayo.com. Right in the middle of the complex at Covadonga, the **Pelayo** is devoid of warmth but is reasonably well equipped, with a good restaurant. The price halves off-season.

**B** **Peñalba**, La Riera, T985 846 100. Half way between the sanctuary and the main road. Overpriced in summer but a good option at other times, set in a nice roadside village by the lively Covadonga stream.

**C** **El Texu**, La Riera. A cosy rural hotel in the village of La Riera.

### Camping

**Covadonga**, T985 940 097. A bland campsite at Soto by the main road.

### Arenas de Cabrales and around *p333*

**A** **Picos de Europa**, Ctra General s/n, T985 846 491, www.hotelpicosdeeuropa.com. A little faded but still Arenas' grandest hotel, with a swimming pool, rooms with great views and a granary feature by the bar in the garden.

B **Villa de Cabrales**, Ctra General s/n, T985 846 719, villacabrales@hotmail.com. In a big stone building, this is a more modern affair, with smart rooms with balconies (although there's some traffic noise). The off-season rates here are appealing.

C **Hotel Torrecerredo**, Barrio Los Llambriosos s/n, T985 846 640, www.hoteltorre cerredo.com. About 0.5 km west of the centre of Arenas, this hotel is a breath of fresh air. With plenty of space, welcoming, humorous owners, and numerous activities able to be organized, it makes a great base. Add to that great breakfasts and evening meals, and you have an excellent package.

F **Fonda Fermín Cotera**, T985 846 566. This has simple, clean rooms with shared bathrooms in traditional Spanish *pensión* style.

**Camping**

**Camping Naranjo de Bulnes**, Ctra Cangas-Panes Km 32.6, T985 846 578. A 10-min walk east along the main road, open Mar-Oct.

**Hiking from Poncebos to Bulnes** *p334*

B **El Mirador de Cabrales**, Poncebos, T985 846 673, www.hotelmirador.com. The top accommodation option in Poncebos. Although overpriced in summer, it does have a great location and good restaurant.

C **Hostal Poncebos**, Poncebos, T985 846 447. Dwarfed by mountains and with reasonable rooms and a restaurant by the chilly Río Cares.

E **Garganta del Cares**, Poncebos, T985 846 463. This is a comfortable *hostal* above a bar with en suite rooms that are heated and good value except in the height of summer (**C**).

**Hiking from Poncebos to Sotres** *p334*

D-E **Casa Cipriano**, Sotres, T985 945 024. A convivial mountain *hostal*, which runs many guided excursions in the area. The rooms are good, and there's a bar and restaurant.

D **La Perdiz**, Sotres, T985 945 011, hotel.laperdiz@terra.es. Opposite **Casa Cipriano**, has good rooms with bath.

F **Peña Castil**, Sotres, T985 945 049. An *albergue* with a restaurant.

**◑ Eating**

**Cangas de Onís** *p332*
The *sidrerías* in Cangas are a superb eating and drinking option.

♥♥ **El Abuelo**, Av Covadonga 21, T985 848 733. A cheerful, warming restaurant specializing in hearty stews and *fabadas*.

♥♥ **El Molino de la Pedrera**, C Bernabé Pendas 1, T985 849 109. A smart cider bar with some great fishy stews on offer, as well as roast chestnuts in season. One of Cangas' best.

♥♥ **Mesón El Puente Romano**, Av Covadonga s/n. The chief virtue of this place is its terrace looking at the medieval bridge. Simple but reasonable Asturian fare, including *fabada*.

♥♥ **Sidrería Los Arcos**, Av Covadonga 17, T985 849 277. A popular cider bar on the main street, serving some good Asturian food.

♥ **El Corcho**, C Angel Tárano 5, T985 849 477. Great seedy *sidrería* with fantastic food; try the grilled *gambones* (king prawns).

**Arenas de Cabrales and around** *p333*

♥♥ **La Panera**, C General s/n, T985 846 505. Set away from the main-road bustle on a terrace above the town. It's a good spot for a quiet drink, but the food is attractive too. There's a set menu, which is reasonable for €11, and plenty of dishes making full use of *cabrales* cheese; try it with wild mushrooms.

♥ **San Telmo**, Ctra General s/n, T985 846 505, gets plenty of tourists on its roadside terrace, but the food is great; try the ultimate expression of *cabrales*, chips 'n' cheese.

**◑ Bars and clubs**

**Cangas de Onís** *p332*
**César Llosa**, C Constantino González 2. A friendly bar, good for late drinks or breakfast.

**◉ Festivals and events**

**Cangas de Onís** *p332*
**25 Jul** The **Fiesta de Santiago** is celebrated with gusto at Cangas de Onís. On the same day, the **Fiesta del Pastor** is a big party with shepherds and visitors mixing on the shores of Lake Enol near Covadonga.
**Aug** Regattas down the Río Sella from Arriondas. This **Descenso de la Sella** features everyone from canoeists to professional partiers. The fiesta starts in Arriondas and ends in Ribadesella amid boisterous scenes; it's one of the region's most memorable events.
**8 Sep** The Picos' biggest day is **Asturias Day**, the feast of the Virgen de Covadonga, celebrated with processions and partying.

## Shopping

**Cangas de Onís** *p332*

**La Barata**, Av Covadonga 13, T985 848 027. An attractive shop dealing in Asturian handicrafts, deli produce and souvenirs.

## Activities and tours

**Cangas de Onís** *p332*

**Cangas Aventura**, Av Covadonga 17, T985 849 261. Canoeing trips on the river and quad excursions into the mountains.

**Escuela Asturiana de Piragüismo**, Av de Castilla s/n, T985 841 282. By the Puente Romano in Cangas, they organize canoeing trips on the Río Sella as well as horse riding and canyoning.

**K2 Aventura**, Las Rozas s/n, T985 849 358, www.k2aventura.com. A canoeing outfit based on the river between Arriondas and Cangas. There's a bar on hand for *après-kayak* ciders.

**La Ruta Quads**, Ctra Cangas-Cabrales Km 10, T629 127 323. A quad-tour company based between Cangas and Arenas de Cabrales.

## Transport

**Cangas de Onís** *p332*

**Bus** Cangas de Onís is serviced very regularly by ALSA buses from **Oviedo** and **Gijón** (almost hourly; 1 hr 20 mins).

**Covadonga** *p332*

**Bus** From **Oviedo** and **Cangas**, 4 buses a day ascend to Covadonga. In summer a couple a day continue to the lakes (as does a cavalcade of families in cars); about 4 a day continue along the AS114 to **Arenas de Cabrales** and **Panes**.

**Arenas de Cabrales and around** *p333*

**Bus** There are 4 ALSA buses a day from **Cangas de Onís** and **Oviedo** to **Panes** via Arenas de Cabrales. From Arenas, ALSA run buses to the Bulnes funicular at **Poncebos**. Shared-jeep taxis also do this trip in summer, and continue to **Sotres**.

## Directory

**Cangas de Onís** *p332*

**Laundry** Higiensec, Av de Castilla 24, T985 947 471. For those dirty hiking clothes. Just off the road to Riaño. Service wash €13.22.

# Cantabrian Picos

→ *Colour map 2, B4.*

*This is the most heavily visited section of the Picos due to its easy road access and good tourist facilities. The region's main centre is the town of Potes, a very attractive place that at times struggles to accommodate the numbers passing through it. The heart of the area is the Liébana Valley, a green swathe watered by mountain streams and the Río Deva. It's noted for its cheeses, its chestnuts and its* orujo, *a fiery grape spirit that comes in original form as well as more mellow-flavoured varieties. A hefty shot in a cup of black coffee is another popular way of taking it. West of Potes, the road winds up to the spectacular natural theatre of Fuente Dé, starting point for plenty of memorable walks.* *»For Sleeping, Eating and other listings, see pages 339-340.*

## Potes and around

» *pp339-340.*

Potes is a gorgeous little town on the side of a hill by the Río Deva, with cobbled streets and a few noble stone buildings; those that survived the Civil War damage. The most striking of these is a large tower, looking like a medieval fort, but in fact built as a mansion by the Marqués de Santillana in the 16th century; it's now the town hall. Another tower nearby holds changing exhibitions, while there's a small **cartography museum** next door. It makes the best base in this part of the Picos, although in summer there's an unbroken line of cars winding through its centre.

There are several banks and supermarkets in town, as well as a petrol station. And there's a **tourist office** ① *daily 1000-1400, 1600-2000*, on the tower side of the river. There's also a **national park information office** ① *T942 730 555, daily 0900-1430, 1630-1830*, a couple of kilometres out of town on the Fuente Dé road. If you're going to do some walking in the area, make sure you pick up a proper map from one of these places. Even on the brightest of days, mists can descend rapidly, and in any event some trails are ambiguously marked.

A 45-minute walk from Potes, off the Fuente Dé road, is a monastery of great importance, **Monasterio de Santo Toribio de Liébana**. Although in a magnificent setting, the building itself isn't of massive interest, but makes up for it with two claims to fame.

❧ *Potes is a centre for tour agencies that operate activities in the mountains, see page 340.*

The first is that it was here that the Abbot Beatus de Liébana wrote his apocalyptic commentaries on the book of Saint John; one of the superb illustrated copies of this work is kept here, far from the public gaze (see box page 339). Prints of some of the pages of this beautiful work are displayed around the cloister (you may recognize some from the film *In the Name of the Rose*), and there are some good laminates on sale for €1.50 in the shop. The other item of interest here is kept locked away in a side chapel off the main church. It is nothing less than the largest fragment of the True Cross in existence, a hefty chunk of cypress wood that measures 63 x 40 cm and has one of the nail-holes. It's embedded in an ornate silver Gothic crucifix.

# West of Potes to Fuente Dé 🖹 ➤ *pp339-340.*

→ *Colour map 2, B3.*

The N621 follows the Río Deva upstream to the west of Potes, passing through several pretty hamlets. It's a well-travelled route, but just off the main road there are some pretty tranquil *casas rurales* where you can stay.

The road stops at Fuente Dé, and it's not hard to see why; there's a massive semicircle of rock ahead; a spectacular natural wall that rises 800 m almost sheer. Named Fuente Dé for this is where the Deva springs from the ground, there's little here apart from two hotels, a campsite and a cablecar station. The **cablecar** ① *daily 1000-1800, €6 one-way/€10 return*, takes 3½ minutes to trundle to the top of the rocky theatre; it's a bad one for claustrophobes, as you're jammed with 25 or so others into the tiny capsule. Expect a long wait in summer.

## Hiking around Fuente Dé → *See map, page 330*

There are some superb walks in this area, some leaving from the top cablecar station; don't worry if you don't fancy the trip up, as there's a steep path that'll get you there eventually. At the top station, there's an unremarkable tourist complex and the start of a jagged, rocky plateau, an Alpine landscape in contrast to the lush meadows below. In clear weather the views from here are magnificent, with the *parador* hardly more than a dot below. Following the track from here, you'll soon leave the crowds behind and start a gentle ascent to the top of a rise. Descending to the right from here, you'll come to the **Refugio de Aliva**, (see Sleeping, below), a year-round hotel and *albergue*. From here, a spectacular 1½-hour descent winds around the valley and down to its floor at Espinama, from where you can follow the river back up to Fuente Dé. The whole circuit takes about four hours and is one of the most beautiful walks in the Picos. Other walks start from the campsite and provide equally spectacular valley and mountain views.

## North towards Panes

North of Potes, the N621 heads into Asturias towards Panes through the very narrow gorge of La Hermida. At **Lebeña**, half a kilometre off the road through the gorge, and 8 km from Potes, is a worthwhile church, **Iglesia de Santa María de Lebeña** ① *Tue-Sat*

## Beatus and a medieval bestseller

In the middle of the eighth century when the future of Christianity in Europe was in the balance, a monk writing in the remote mountains of Cantabria produced a work which was to be the equivalent of a European bestseller for the next 400 years. Writing from the monastery of Liébana, Beatus wrote a commentary on Saint John's Apocalypse that struck a note with readers who, as well as fearing further invasions from the Moors, also believed that the approaching millennium would bring the coming of the Antichrist. Only 22 of these manuscripts still survive, nearly

all of them in academic libraries. Produced in various monasteries in Northern Spain, the text of each is the same, but the illustrations differ. The quality of the illustrations make these manuscripts masterpieces of medieval art. The one in Burgo de Osma has been described as "the most beautiful book in the world".

Umberto Eco used the Beatus manuscripts as the basis for his novel *In the Name of the Rose*. However if you fancy reading the original for yourself be warned: Eco describes the Beatus text as "tortuous , even to those well acquainted with medieval Latin".

*1000-1330, 1600-1900, Sun 1100-1400*, €2, set against a superb backdrop of massive rock. Founded in the 10th century, its interior is Mozarabic, with horseshoe arches on a rectangular ground plan. It's a beautifully simple space; most interesting is the altarstone, carved with a series of circles deemed to represent nature, the heavens and the redemptive power of Christ; symbols that go back to the Visigoths and beyond.

## South to León

South from Potes, the road winds through the green **Liébana Valley** for a while, then begins to ascend to the **Puerto San Glorio** and **León** province. This stretch of road offers perhaps the best views in the entire Picos; the contrast between the lush green valley and the harsh grey mountains is superb.

## ⬛ Sleeping

**Potes and around** *p337*
**C Posada La Antigua**, C Cántabra 9, T942 730 037, eltarugu@mixmail.com. A characterful mountain inn, with beautiful wood-beamed rooms with balustraded balconies.
**D Casa Cayo**, C Cántabra 6, T942 730 150, www.casacayo.com. A very good option above Potes' best bar and restaurant. The rooms are large, comfortable and tastefully furnished; some overlook the river.
**E-F Hostal Coriscao**, C La Serna s/n, T942 730 458. A simple but friendly and cheap option by the car park on the west side of the river. Rooms are basic, with shared bathroom, and can be chilly in winter.
**F El Fogón de Cus**, C Capitán Palacios 2, T942 730 060. Cheap, clean, modernized rooms above a restaurant; something of a bargain.

**Camping**
**Camping La Viorna**, T942 732 021. On the road to the Santo Toribio monastery, this is a good campsite in a nice setting with a swimming pool.

**West of Potes to Fuente Dé** *p338*
**A Parador de Fuente Dé**, Fuente Dé, T942 736 651, www.parador.es. The top place to stay. A modern but fairly sensitive building, this is one of the cheaper *paradores* but loses nothing on location, particularly when the day-trippers have gone home. The rooms are spacious and attractive, most with views of some sort, and the restaurant focuses on Picos cuisine. Open Mar-Oct.
**C Rebeco**, Fuente Dé, T942 736 601, F942 736 600. Cheaper and not lacking in comforts either, and also has a bar/restaurant.

**Camping El Redondo**, T942 736 699.
5 mins' walk beyond Rebeco. A campsite
which also has bunkbed accommodation.

**Hiking around Fuente Dé** *p338*
C-F **Refugio de Aliva**, T942 730 999 (see
page 338). A hotel and *albergue* (with double
rooms or dorms), open mid-Jun to Oct. It has a
popular restaurant (popular because there's a
jeep running from the top of the cablecar
station) that does a *menú del día* for €12.

## ● Eating

**Potes and around** *p337*
♯♯♯ **El Fogón de Cus**, C Capitán Palacios 2,
T942 730 060. Excellent modern mountain
cuisine, with good wine and a set lunch for €9.
If you're after a hearty splurge, try the 2-person
*menú degustación*, a 5-courser for €45.
♯♯ **Casa Cayo**, C Cántabra 6, T942 730 150.
Potes' best option, very lively and cheerful
with huge portions. The *cocidos* (chickpea
stews) are good, as are the the *revueltos*
(scrambled eggs mixed with just about
everything). Some tables overlook the river.
♯♯ **El Bodegón**, C San Roque 14, T942 730
247. Set in a stone building off an old-timers'
bar, this restaurant lacks a bit of warmth, but
is a good place to tuck into a hearty *cocido
lebaniego* (the local chickpea stew garnished
with sausage and pork). *Revuelto de erizos*
(scrambled egg with sea-urchins) is also
delicious, but an acquired taste.
♯ **Casa Nisio**, C San Roque 24, T942 730
626. Slightly tacky *après-ski* decor, but this
is a spacious and friendly bar with some
decent bartop food and *raciones*.
♯ **Los Camachos**, C El Llano, T942 732 148.
Cheap, decent food in a lively Cantabrian bar
that has won prizes for its home-made *orujo*.
♯ **Tasca Cántabra**, C Cántabra s/n, T942 730
714. A pleasing no-frills option with an upstairs
*comedor*. In winter, try the *alubias con jabalí*
(beans with wild boar), a real belly warmer.

## ● Bars and clubs

**Potes and around** *p337*
**Bar Chente**, Bajos la Plaza s/n, T942 730
732. A good summer terrace on the hidden
square below the road. The restaurant also
does good cheap meals.

**Cucu**, Bajos la Plaza s/n. A warren of a
*discoteca* with several bars under the square
by the river; you wouldn't even guess it was
there during the day. Good atmosphere
at weekends and in summer.

## ❂ Festivals and events

**Potes and around** *p337*
**2 Jul** Romería (pilgrimage procession)
and festival in the Liébana Valley.
**1st week in Nov** Orujo festival in Potes;
can be messy.

## ▲ Activities and tours

**Potes and around** *p337*
**Europicos**, C San Roque 6, T942 730 724,
www.europicos.com. One of several tour
operators based in popular Potes, this group
organizes everything from quad tours or
4WD trips to paragliding. They also hire
mountain bikes from €20 for a ½-day.
**La Liébana**, C Independencia 4, T942 731
021. Organize a range of activities including
horse trekking and paragliding.
**La Rodrigona**, Cillorigo de Liébana s/n,
Tama, T615 970 442, F942 730 506.
A specialist horse-trekking operator
based in a village north of Potes.
**Picostur**, C Obispo 2, T942 738 091,
www.picostur.com. Another firm offering
the lot. Most guides speak decent English.
**Potes Tur**, C San Roque 19, T/F942 732 164,
potestur@ceoecant.es. Specialize in quad
trips into the mountains, also other options.

## ● Transport

**Potes and around** *p337*
**Bus**
A bus service from **Santander** to Potes runs
3 times daily, stopping along the western
Cantabrian coast, turning inland at **Unquera**,
and stopping at **Panes**. This connects with
2 of 3 daily buses from Potes to the cablecar
at **Fuente Dé**.

## ● Directory

**Potes and around** *p337*
**Internet** Ciber-Plaza, on the main street,
and **Cyber-Liébana**, in an arcade, are 2
neighbouring options in the centre of town.

# Leonese Picos

*Although this part of the Picos range isn't as endowed with tourist facilities as the Asturian or Cantabrian sections, it contains much of the area's most dramatic scenery, with breathtaking mountainscapes suddenly revealed as you round a bend in the path or road. While Riaño (see León page 290), is the area's biggest town, it's a bit far from the action and not especially charming; a better bet is Posada de Valdeón, spectacularly set in a lush valley surrounded by rocky peaks.* ▸▸ *For Sleeping, Eating and other listings, see page 342.*

## South to the Naranco Valley

The N621 running south from Potes meets León province at the spectacular **Puerto de San Glorio** pass, site for a controversial ski station. Descending rapidly through dark rocks and grassy pasture, the first settlement is **Llánaves de la Reina**.

## Valdeón Valley ⊜⊘⊛⊜ ▸▸ *p342.*

### Santa Marina → *Colour map 2, B3.*
Some 6 km further south is the turn-off for the Valdeón Valley. The road climbs to the **Puerto de Pandetrave** at 1562 m, which suddenly reveals a superb view of the valley, dwarfed by the imposing stone masses of the Picos. The first village in the valley itself is Santa Marina, a very rural settlement of simple stone houses. It's a friendly village with a good campsite.

### Posada de Valdeón
Around 4 km up the lovely grassy valley is the area's main settlement, Posada de Valdeón. This is the southern terminus for the popular walk along the Cares Gorge (see page 334), and is well equipped for a small place, with a supermarket and bank, but no cash machine. The setting is spectacular, with the intimidating mass of **Peña Bermeja** behind it contrasting with the lush pasturelands around.

The Picos de Europa National Park has an **information office** ① *T987 740 549, Mon-Fri 0900-1700, Wed 1400-1700 only*, in Posada from where it runs free guided trips during the summer months (phone for details). There are several places to stay.

### Caín
North from Posada de Valdeón, a steep and narrow road makes its way to the village of Caín, a walk of just over 1½ hours. Jeeps run a shared-taxi service between the two towns. Not far from Posada, a fantastic view opens up as the valley seems to be swallowed up by lofty mountains; it's an awe-inspiring sight in good weather. The **Mirador de Pombo** is one vantage point to appreciate the vista; it's marked by a slender chamois and a confusing diagram of the peaks around. Before you reach here, the hamlet of **Cordiñanes** has a good rustic *pensión*.

Caín itself would be about as isolated as a rural village gets were it not for the number of walkers passing through the **Garganta de Cares**. As it is, there are a couple of restaurants, shops and a few lodging options.

### West to Asturias
From Posada de Valdeón, the LE244 runs west over the Panderruedas Pass to meet the main N625 near the windy Puerto de Pontón Pass. Continuing northwards, the road enters the maw of the **Desfiladero de los Beyos**, a narrow gorge framed by massive rockfaces; a haunt of vultures and anglers that winds its way into Asturias.

# ● Sleeping

## Santa Marina *p341*

**D Casa Friero**, C Amapolas 1, T987 742 658.
A very good, if slightly pricey, *casa rural* in
the village; kitchen facilities are available for
guests' use. Sleeps 6 and is only available
as an entire rental; €90 per day or €400
for a week.

**F Ardilla Real**, Plaza de la Esquina. Serves
meals and has dormitory accommodation.

### Camping

**Camping El Cares**, 1 km out of town,
T987 742 676. A campsite where you
can rent horses to explore the valley.

## Posada de Valdeón *p341*

**C Posada El Asturiano**, Ctra Cordiñanes s/n,
T987 740 514. A favourite with many Picos
regulars, this has warm and comfortable
rooms just off the square.

**D Hostal Campo**, Ctra Cordiñanes s/n, T987
740 502. In the centre of the town, this has
big, warm and comfy rooms with modern
bathrooms and views at a reasonable price.

**F Pensión Begoña**, C Amador Campo
Pérez s/n, T987 740 516. Run by the same
management as the **Hostal Campo**, this
is a friendly option, cheap, fairly basic and
likeable; rooms have clean shared bathroom
and a down-to-earth walkers' vibe.

### Camping

**El Valdeón**, T987 742 605. The closest
campsite is a couple of kilometres out
on the road to Soto.

## Caín *p341*

**C Posada del Montañero**, Caín, T987
742 711. The nicest option, open Apr-Sep,
a comfortable but overpriced inn with a
good simple restaurant.

**E Rojo**, C Santiago 8, Cordiñanes, T987
740 523. A good rustic *pensión*, clean and
comfortable with an unbeatable location if
you're not scared of big, powerful mountains.

**G Casa Cuevas**, Caín, T987 742 720. Basic,
with small simple rooms; a sleeping bag will
be handy at chillier times of year.

# ● Eating

## Posada de Valdeón *p341*

**Ψ Posada El Asturiano** (see Sleeping
above), has a good restaurant.

**Ψ La Begoña**, see Pensión Begoña in
Sleeping, above. This is the place for the most
characterful meal in town. The **Begoña** does a
cheap set menu in traditional and delicious
no-frills mountain style. You might get trout,
which abound in the streams around here, or
stew made from a freshly hunted wild boar,
but its bound to be hearty and good.

# ● Festivals and events

## Posada de Valdeón *p341*

**Sep 8** The Picos' biggest day is **Asturias
Day**, the feast of the **Virgen de Covadonga**,
celebrated with processions and partying,
and the fiesta of the **Virgen de Corona** in
the Valdeón Valley.

# ● Transport

## Posada de Valdeón *p341*
### Bus

The southern part of the Picos is a bit
problematic when it comes to transport.
There's 1 daily **Santander-León** bus (and
vice versa), which stops at **Panes**, **Potes**,
**Llánaves de la Reina** and **Riaño**. Occasional
buses link Riaño with Posada de Valdeón.

There are 2 buses a day hit Riaño from
**León** and there's 1 bus daily from León to
Posada de Valdeón.

### Taxi

There's a shared taxi service from Posada
de Valdeón to **Caín**, at the head of the
Cares Gorge walk.

# Introduction

Earthy Asturias has a different feel to much of Northern Spain. It's a land of mining, fishing and good cheer, exemplified by its superb cider culture – a legacy of the Celts. There are few more interesting places to have a drink than an Asturian *sidrería*, with sawdust-covered floor and streams of booze poured from alarming heights. Round off the meal with some of the province's great seafood and you'll be in gastro heaven.

Asturias has had the foresight to look after its natural heritage. While the province is heavily industrialized, there are vast swathes of untouched old-growth forest inland that still harbour bears and wolves. A well-documented network of trails gives access to these places, maintained by an enthusiastic army of ecologists.

The cities of the region are no less appealing. Oviedo, an elegant and beautiful capital, claims some of the best of the ancient pre-Romanesque architecture left by the Asturian monarchs; Gijón is a lively place with an excellent beach; while Avilés shields a beautiful old town inside its ring of industry.

Although the sea temperatures aren't exactly Caribbean and rain is never unlikely, it's not hard to see why the Asturian coast is so popular in summer: the mix of sandy beaches and pretty fishing ports is hard to beat. Hit the east coast for a more developed summer scene, or the west for some more low-key places.

Asturias is a tough, proud land that suffered greatly in the 20th century, when its radical miners were put down brutally by the army in 1934 and again in the Civil War. It is is still one of the more left-wing and egalitarian regions in Northern Spain and, along with Euskadi, its friendliest. Wherever you head in the province you're guaranteed a gruff, genuine welcome and the sound of a cider cork popping.

**Asturias**

## ★ Don't miss...

1 **Oviedo** Satisfy your architectural appetite with the achingly beautiful pre-Romanesque churches, a highlight of the province, page 346.

2 **National parks** Delve into Asturias' superb forested parks, such as Somiedo and Muniellos; they still harbour wolves and bears, pages 351 and 369.

3 **Gijón** Splash the cider around at some of the province's best *sidrerías* in this vibrant beachside city, page 359.

4 **Avilés** Take this pretty town by storm in fancy dress during the lively *Carnaval* celebrations, page 361.

5 **West coast** Explore this enchanting stretch of coast; it's a mixture of fine fishing towns and great beaches; Tapia de Casariego has both, page 367.

6 **Taramundi** Step back in time when you visit the local ethnographic projects at this remote and charming hill village, page 367.

# Oviedo and around

➜ *Phone code: 985. Colour map 2, B2. Population: 212, 174.*

*Oviedo, the capital of Asturias, seems to have come a long way since Clarín wrote in 1884, "he looked down on...the old squashed and blackened dwellings; the vain citizens thought them palaces but they were burrows, caves, piles of earth, the work of moles". Luckily, the description is from a novel written in a characteristically hyper-critical style. Nowadays, after an extensive programme of pedestrianization and restoration, the new town is a prosperous hive of shops and cafés, while old Oviedo is an extremely attractive web of plazas and old palaces built of honey-coloured stone. Three of the best and most accessible examples of the distinctive and beautiful Asturian pre-Romanesque style, are to be found in and around Oviedo; other highlights include the cathedral, the Museo de Bellas Artes, and the never-say-die nightlife. In the local dialect, Bable, Oviedo is written and pronounced Uvieu.*

*There's plenty to explore outside the city too. Many of the valleys south of Oviedo are pockmarked with coalmines, which are gradually being closed down. Towns to the west, such as Pravia, ancient Asturian capital, and Salas, hometown of an arch-inquisitor, can be easily visited as day trips from Oviedo or Gijón, although they also make good bases in themselves; there are several rewarding walks in the area. This is salmon country – in season, the rivers teem with them, and also with phalanxes of local and international fly-fishers making survival a dim prospect. Perhaps none make it back to warn the others.*

*One of the typical sights in this area are the hórreos, wood and stone huts raised on legs for the storage of grain. Most of these are at least a century old, and many are much older. You'll often see strings of peppers or corncobs hung out to dry from the eaves. There's also a Galician version of the huts, which are smaller and made of stone.* ▸▸ *For Sleeping, Eating and other listings, see pages 353-358.*

## Ins and outs

**Getting there** Flights arrive at the Aeropuerto de Ranón, on the coast near Avilés, and is reached by regular buses from Oviedo. Most of the intercity buses are run by **ALSA** (T902 422 242, www.alsa.es), an efficient service that connects Asturias with much of Spain. These connections are typically faster than the train. **RENFE** trains connect with the major cities in Northern Spain, as well as Madrid and Barcelona, while the slower **FEVE** network connects Oviedo with the coast eastwards and westwards to Galicia. ▸▸ *See Transport, page 357, for further details.*

**Getting around** Buses are useful for reaching outlying areas – there are 12 or so routes, clearly labelled at bus stops. Taxis are easy to find, but bear in mind that, due to Oviedo's commitment to pedestrianization, many locations aren't easily accessible by car. Hemmed in by hills, Oviedo is a fairly compact city, and easy to walk around. From the bus and train stations it's a 15-minute walk to the heart of the old town down Calle Uría; most of the accommodation is closer to the centre.

**Best time to visit** Oviedo has a comparatively mild climate; neither winter nor summer usually hits uncomfortable extremes, although it is notoriously rainy in autumn and winter. Oviedo's major fiesta is in September (see page 357), but the *sidrerías* (cider bars) and other haunts are busy year-round.

**Tourist information**  The **tourist office** ⓘ *C Cimadevilla 4, T985 213 385, ofiturio@ princast.es, Oct-May daily 1000-1900, Jun-Sep daily 1000-2000*, is located near the Ayuntamiento. There are plans afoot (but they've been standing there a while) to move it down the road to Plaza de la Constitución. There's a smaller **municipal office** ⓘ *Campo de San Francisco park, T985 227 586, Mon-Fri 1030-1400, 1630-1930, Sat and Sun 1000-1400*. There's also a tourist information desk in the bus station. The website www.infoasturias.com is a valuable resource run by the tourist board.

## Background

Oviedo was born in the early years of the stubborn Asturian monarchy, when a monastery was founded on the hill of 'Ovetao' in the mid-eighth century. Successive kings added other buildings until Alfonso II saw the city's potential, rebuilt and expanded it, and moved his court here in 808. He saw it as a new Toledo (the former Christian capital having long since fallen to the Moors). It was this period that saw the consolidation of the pre-Romanesque style, as Alfonso commissioned an impressive series of buildings. A glorious century in the spotlight followed, but Oviedo soon returned to relative obscurity when the court was moved south to León. Oviedo continued to grow through the Middle Ages, however, partly as a result of pilgrim traffic to Santiago. The university was founded in about 1600, which helped to raise the city's profile. Real prosperity arrived with the Industrial Revolution and, crucially, the discovery of coal in the green valleys near the Asturian capital. Asturias became a stronghold of unionism and socialism, and Oviedo suffered massive damage in the 1934 revolt, and again in the Civil War. Franco had a long memory, and it's only fairly recently that Oviedo has emerged from his shadow. A progressive town council has transformed the city, embarking on a massive program of pedestrianization (there are over 80 pedestrian streets), restoration, and commissioning of public sculpture. Now, painted and scrubbed, Oviedo is taking new pride in living up to its coat of arms as the "very noble, very loyal, meritorious, unconquered, heroic, and good city of Oviedo".

# Sights

## Cathedral

ⓘ *Mon-Fri 1000-1300, 1600-2000, Sat 1000-1300, 1600-1800 (no lunchtime closing in summer); admission to Cámara Santa, museum, and cloister €3, Cámara Santa only €1.25 (guided visit).*

The cathedral, a warm-coloured and harmonious construction, dominates the **Plaza de Alfonso el Casto** with its delicate and exuberant spire. While most of the building is a 14th- and 15th-century design, it contains a series of important relics of the Asturian kings in its Cámara Santa. This chamber, originally part of Alfonso II's palace, contains the Cruz de los Angeles and the Cruz de la Victoria; the two emblematic, bejewelled crucifixes were gifts to the church by Kings Alfonso II and III respectively. The former is now the symbol of Oviedo, while the latter features on the Asturian coat of arms. Also behind glass in the Cámara Santa is a silver ark containing relics perhaps brought

❗ *Across the square from the cathedral is a statue of Clarín's La Regenta.*

from the Holy Land to Spain in the seventh century. One of the relics, supposedly the shroud of Christ, is behind a panel in the back wall; it is brought out and venerated three times a year. The ark itself contains a bumper crop including a piece of the true cross, some bread from the Last Supper, part of Christ's clothing, some of his nappies, and milk of the Virgin Mary. The cathedral also has an attractive cloister and a museum with a good collection of objects, although these are left to the visitor's interpretation.

**Asturias** Oviedo & around

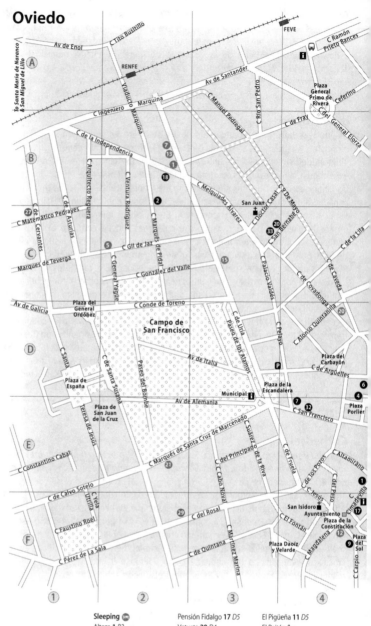

FEVE

C Ramón Prieto Bances

Av de Enol

C Tito Bustillo

RENFE

Av de Santander

Plaza General Primo de Rivera

C Ingeniero Marquina

Viaducto Marquina

C de la Independencia

Marquina

C Manuel Pedregal

C Río San Pedro

C de Frat

Cefer

General Elorza

Ciel

C de la Lila

C Arquitecto Reguera

C Ventura Rodríguez

C de Asturias

C Matemático Pedrayes

C de Levantes

Marques de Teverga

C General Yagüe

C Gil de Jaz

C Marqués de Pidal

C González del Valle

C Melquiades Álvarez

San Juan

C Doctor Casal

C de Pío de Mayo

C de San Bernabé

C Palacio Valdés

C de Caveda

C de Covadonga

C Alonso Quintanilla

Av de Galicia

Plaza del General Ordóñez

C Conde de Toreno

**Campo de San Francisco**

C de Uría

Paseo de los Álamos

C Pelayo

Plaza del Carbayón

C de Arguelles

Plaza de la Escandalera

Av de Italia

Municipal

Plaza Porlier

C de Santa Susana

Paseo del Bombé

Santa

Plaza de España

Plaza de San Juan de la Cruz

Teresa de Jesús

Av de Alemania

C san Francisco

C Marqués de Santa Cruz de Marcenado

C del Principado

C Cabo Noval

Suárez de la Riva

C de Frúela

Altamirano

C Constantino Cabal

C de Calvo Sotelo

C y la Utilla

Faustino Roél

C del Rosal

C Martínez Marina

C de los Pozos

C del Peso

C de Jesús

San Isidoro

Ayuntamiento

Plaza de la Constitución

C El Fontán

Plaza Daoíz y Velarde

Magdalena

C Carpio

Plaza del Sol

C de Quintana

C Pérez de la Sala

N

0 metres 200
0 yards 200

**Sleeping** 🛏
Alteza **1** B2
De la Reconquista **5** C2
El Magistral **6** D5
Favila **7** B2
Gran Hotel España **8** D5
Hostal Arcos **12** F4
Hostal Belmonte **13** B2
Hostal Romero **15** C3
Libretto **21** E2
Ovetense **16** E5

Pensión Fidalgo **17** D5
Vetusta **20** D4

**Eating** 🍴
Bocamar **2** B2
Café Dólar **4** D4
Casa Conrado **6** D5
Casa Fermín **7** E4
Casa Montoto **33** C3
El Café de Juliotón **9** F4
El Cogollu **10** F5

El Pigüeña **11** D5
El Raitán &
  El Chigre **12** F5
Faro Vidio **1** E4
La Corrada
  del Obispo **14** F5
La MásBARata **17** F4
La Paloma **18** B2
La Pumarada **3** D5
Las Campanas de
  San Bernabé **20** C3

## Museo Arqueológico

ⓘ *C San Vicente, Tue-Sat 1000-1330, 1600-1800, Sun 1100-1300, free. Currently under renovation; due to re-open in mid 2007;*

Behind the cathedral is the museum of archaeology, which is built around a beautiful monastery cloister. The sparsely labelled finds somehow lack context, but it's a pleasant stroll around the old building.

## Museo de las Bellas Artes de Asturias

ⓘ *Sep-Jun Tue-Fri 1030-1400, 1630-2030, Sat 1130-1400, 1700-2000, Sun 1130-1430; Jul and Aug Tue-Sat 1100-1430, 1700-2100, Sun 1100-1430; free.*

The fine arts museum is housed in a 17th-century palace and a grand 18th-century townhouse that are joined back-to-back. There are two entrances, one on Calle Santa Ana, and one on Calle Rua. The museum has an excellent collection of 20th-century Asturian art and a good selection of Spanish masters. In the vestibule at the Santa Ana entrance hangs José Uría y Uría's tragic *Después de una huelga* (After a Strike). Painted in 1895, it evocatively demonstrates that the events of 1934 and 1936 were a long time in the making.

## Old town

The old town is made for wandering. The walk-through **Ayuntamiento** is on **Plaza de la Constitución**, as is the honey-coloured **Iglesia de San Isidoro**, still daubed with ancient graffiti, as graduating students traditionally painted their names there. Other pretty plazas include **Trascorrales**, and **Porlier**; the latter is home to the mysterious sculpture *El regreso de William B Arrensberg (The Return of William B Arrensberg)*, one of many street sculptures that invigorate Oviedo. From here, walk down Calle San Francisco (the Assisi saint passed through Oviedo on his way to Santiago) to the large park of the same name. *Maternidad*, a sculpture by the Colombian artist Botero, is an unmissable landmark here on the **Plaza de la Escandalera**; it's irreverently nicknamed *La Muyerona (The Big Woman)* by locals.

Asturias Oviedo & around

Rialto **32** *E4*
Tierra Astur **34** *D5*

**Bars & clubs** 🎵
Asturianu **24** *F5*
Ca Beleño **25** *E6*
El Cuelebre **26** *F5*
La Perrera **33** *F5*
· La Real **27** *C1*
Paddock **29** *F2*
TKC **31** *F5*

**North of the old town**

Heading north, **Calle Gascona**'s sharpish slope serves to drain away all the cider spilled in its numerous and gregarious *sidrerías*. The pre-Romanesque **Iglesia de San Julián de los Prados** ① *T607 353 999, Oct-Apr Tue-Sat 0930-1130, May-Sep also 1600-1800; Mon 1000-12300 unguided; guided visits take half-an-hour, last entry 30 mins before closing time €1.20, Mon free*, was built by Alfonso II in the first half of the ninth century. Northeast of the old centre, beyond the fountained **Plaza de la Cruz Roja**, it now struggles for serenity beside the Gijón motorway. Designed with the characteristic triple nave, the highlight of the church is its superbly preserved frescoes, which show interesting similarities with first-century AD Roman wall-paintings from Pompeii.

## New town

The elegant facades of the new town, many of them coloured, are an attractive feature. Off busy Calle Uría on Calle Gil de Jaz stands the **Hotel de la Reconquista**, see also page 353. It's worth a look for its beautiful courtyard and galleries.

## Los Monumentos

① *Both monuments Apr-Sep Tue-Sat 0930-1330, 1530-1930, Sun and Mon 0930-1330; Oct-Mar Tue-Sat 1000-1300, 1500-1700, Sun and Mon 1000-1300. Admission by tour only; €3, free Mon; last tour ½ hr before closing. Tour covers both buildings, so if no one seems to be around, wait; or check the other building. The guardian's phone number is T676 032 087.*

The pre-Romanesque structures of Santa María de Naranco and San Miguel de Lillo, collectively known as Los Monumentos, overlook the city on Naranco hill to the northwest. There's a good view over Oviedo, which, it has to be said, isn't super-attractive from up here, but is backed by beautiful mountains.

**Santa María de Naranco**, built as a palace by Ramiro I (1842-1850), is arguably the finest example of this architecture. The columns in the upper hall could almost be carved from bone or ivory, such is the skill of the stonework. Balconies at either end add to the lightness of the design; one contains an altar with an inscription of the king. A range of sculptural motifs, many of them depicting alarming animals, decorate the hall, and have been attributed to Visigothic and Byzantine influences. Underneath the hall is another chamber variously identified as a crypt, bathhouse, and servants' quarters.

The **Iglesia de San Miguel de Lillo**, a stone's throw further up the road, is a church also constructed during the reign of Ramiro I. What remains is a conglomeration of the original building – much of which collapsed in the 13th century – and later additions. The original building was undoubtedly an amazing structure for the time in which it was built. What remains is impressive, with a series of intricately carved lattices, and some remaining fresco decoration. Carved panels appear to show gladiatorial or circus scenes. To get there it's about a 30-minute brisk walk up Avenida de los Monumentos from above and behind the railway station. Bus No 3 plies the route hourly from Calle Uría, or it's a €5-7 cab ride from central Oviedo. From the bus, get off at the car park – Santa María is a five-minute walk up the hill; San Miguel a short way beyond.

---

# South from Oviedo 🖼️🚶🚌 ⇢ *pp353-358*.

Due south of Oviedo, just off the motorway to León, the town of **Mieres** can be accessed very easily on the **FEVE** *cercanías* from Oviedo (line F8). It's a likeably honest place, a working town which gives a taste of Asturian mining heritage. It has excellent nightlife, even more so during **Carnaval**. Not far to the east, in the village of El Entrego, the **Museo de la Minería y de la Industria** ① *Oct-Jun Tue-Sat 1000-1400, 1600-1900,*

## Asturian pre-Romanesque

From the late eighth century, the rulers of the young Asturian kingdom began to construct religious and civil buildings in an original style that drew on Roman, Visigothic and Eastern elements.

Some of the buildings which remain are strikingly beautiful. There are some 20 standing churches and halls that preserve some or many of their original features. The style was characterized by barrel-vaulted, usually triple naves and a rectangular or cross-shaped ground plan. The roof is supported by columns, often elaborately carved with motifs derived from Moorish and Byzantine models. The transepts are wide, and the altar area often raised. A triple apse is a common feature, sometimes divided from the rest of the building by a triple arch; the windows, too, are characteristic, divided by a miniature column. The exterior is typically buttressed; the supports line up with the interior columns.

The style progressed quickly and reached its peak in the mid-ninth century under Ramiro I. From this period are the supreme examples outside Oviedo, Santa María de Naranco and San Miguel de Lillo. Other excellent example of the Asturian pre-Romanesque style (a term coined by Jovellanos, see box page 449), are San Salvador de Valdedios not far from Villaviciosa; San Julián de los Prados in Oviedo, and Santa Cristina de Lena, south of Oviedo, on the way to León.

*Sun 1000-1400; Jul-Sep Tue-Sat 1000-2000, Sun 1000-1400*, €4, is a proud display of the region's coalmining history. There is a good collection of working replicas of old mining devices, but the highlight is a guided descent into an excellent replica mine, bringing to life the conditions underground. El Entrego is accessed from Oviedo on a different *cercanía* line (hourly to El Entrego station on **RENFE** C2, and **FEVE** F6-F5 five times daily; get off at San Vicente if the train stops there).

### Iglesia de Santa Cristina de Lena
① *Apr-Oct Tue-Sun 1100-1300, 1630-1830, Nov-Mar Tue-Sun 1100-1300, 1600-1800; €1.20. Contact the keyholder on T985 490 525 if there's no one about.*
South of El Entrego, overlooking the motorway near the border with León province, it's worth making the effort to visit another excellent pre-Romanesque church, Iglesia de Santa Cristina de Lena. Dating from the mid-ninth century, it's a pretty thing on the outside, but its hauntingly beautiful interior is better. A delicately carved raised triple arch is topped by symbols of early Christianity, not without some Islamic influence. The altarstone inscriptions have clear Visigothic/Germanic parallels, and there are several stones reused from a Visigothic edifice. To get there, take the *cercanía* line C1 to La Cobertoria, from where it's a short walk; you thus avoid the depressing town of Pola de Lena.

### Parque Natural de Somiedo → *Colour map 2, B2.*
Southwest of Oviedo, the national park (and UNESCO biosphere reserve) of Somiedo is a superbly high, wild area of Asturian forest, home to bears and wolves, as well as some exceedingly traditional Asturian villages. There are many superb walks in the park, one of the best starting from the hamlet of **Valle de Lago**, from where there's a walk to (you guessed it), Lago del Valle, a 12-km round trip up a high grassy valley with abundant birdlife. If you're scared of dogs, take a bribe or two; they're really big softies. The trail is waymarked as PR 15.1. You can stay in Lago del Valle, or in the bigger village of **Pola de Somiedo**, a 1½-hour walk back on the main road.

Asturias Oviedo & around

# West from Oviedo 🚌🚻🍴🚍 ⇢ *pp353-358.*

## Salas → *Colour map 2, A1.*

West of the fishing centre of Cornellana, along a valley of eucalyptus and wild deer, is the town of Salas. Although it features prominently on most maps of Asturias, it is in fact a small, picturesque, and tranquil place. Salas' most famous son was Hernando de Valdés, whose formidable presence still looms large in the town over 500 years after his birth. An extremely able theologian and orator, he rapidly ascended the church hierarchy until, in 1547, he became Inquisitor-General for the whole of Spain. His rule was, like the man himself, strict, austere and inflexible. Quick to crack down on any books, tracts or people with so much as a sniff of liberalism or reformation about them, he can be seen as a symbol of the "Spain that turned its back on Europe".

*‡ Down the hill a little stands the Colegiata de Santa María la Mayor, where the body of the inquisitor now rests in an alabaster mausoleum.*

Valdés came from a notable local family, whose small castle and tower still dominate the town. Inside is the **tourist office** and a small **museum** ① *tourist office and museum, T985 830 988, mid-Sep to mid-Jun Mon-Thu 0930- 1430, 1600-1900, Fri 0930-1430; mid-Jun to mid-Sep Tue-Sun 1030-1430, 1630- 1930, Mon 1030-1430; admission €1.20.* The museum, which is in the tower, has a display of pre-Romanesque inscriptions and ornamentation. The rest of the castle is mostly a hotel set around the pleasing courtyard.

## Pravia and Santianes → *Colour map 2, A1.*

Little-known **Pravia** is another small gem in the crown of Asturias. Founded in Roman times, it was briefly the home of the Asturian court in the eighth century before being forsaken for Oviedo in AD 808. Now a small agricultural town, its small centre is a relaxing collage of perfect façades, which are at their best in the soft evening light. The town feels oddly South American, perhaps as a result of the large numbers of *indianos* who returned home having made their fortunes in the new colonies. Many *indiano* houses dot Pravia and the surrounding area (as well as much of Asturias) – they are typically tall and grandiose, and often have gardens planted with palms and cactus. In the heart of town there's a **tourist office** ① *Parque Sabino Moutas s/n, T985 822 355, Tue-Sat 1000-1300, 1600-1900, Sun 1100-1330.*

The centre of Pravia is presided over by the bulky **Colegiata de Pravia** and the connected **Palacio de los Moutas**, good examples of Spanish Baroque architecture. The oldest building in the town proper is the **Casa del Busto**, a large and dignified *casona* now tastefully converted into a hotel. Built in the 16th century, it was a favourite refuge of Jovellanos, the 18th-century Spanish Enlightenment figure par excellence, whose sister-in-law lived here.

In the nearby village of **Santianes**, the **Iglesia de Santianes de Pravia** ① *call or visit the town hall, T985 823 510, for the key*, the oldest of the series of existing pre-Romanesque buildings of this size, is 3 km from town. It preserves little of its original character, having been substantially altered over the years, but is an attractive building nonetheless. It stands on the site of an earlier Visigothic church. Santianes is one stop from Pravia on the **FEVE** line and is also accessible by bus, but if you're after a nice walk on a dry day, go down Calle de la Industria from the centre of Pravia, cross the river and two roundabouts, and continue up the hill. Santianes is signposted to the right about 1½ km up this road.

● *Spain's biggest-selling soap brand, Heno de Pravia, is named after the aromas of hay* ● *in the district.*

**Oviedo** *p346, map p348*

There's a cluster of cheap accommodation near the train station on and around the main new-town street C Uría.

**LL Hotel de la Reconquista**, C Gil de Jaz 16, T985 241 100, www.hoteldelareconquista.com. Oviedo's top hotel, fantastically built around, and faithful to, the 18th-century Hospital of the Principality. Set around galleries, courtyards and chapels brimming with period objets d'art, the Prince of Asturias, heir to the Spanish throne, stays here when he's in town. Visitors are welcome on the ground floor – it's well worth a look. Check the website for special offers.

**L Gran Hotel España**, C Jovellanos 2, T985 220 596, www.granhotelespana.com. This noble giant is typical of a certain type of smart Spanish hotel slightly yearning for the glory days of the 1920s. Untypically, this has been sensitively renovated, and the courteous staff complement the plush interiors. The rooms are equipped to business-hotel standard, and the location right on the edge of the old town is also a plus. Parking and wireless internet available.

**AL Hotel Libretto**, C Marqués de Santa Cruz 12, T985 202 004, www.librettohotel.com. A bright new star on the Oviedo hotel scene, this strikingly innovative hotel faces the San Francisco park. Facilities are impressive, with DVD/CD players, posh TV, rentable laptops, wireless internet access, and even an umbrella for the regular drizzle, but it's the striking and sleek design that lives long in the memory. A minimalist mix of the classic and the avant-garde, it somehow works brilliantly. There are often excellent weekend or promotional deals.

**AL-A Hotel El Magistral**, C Jovellanos 3, T985 215 116, www.elmagistral.com. The steel-and-bottle glass decor gives an intriguingly space-age feel to this original establishment. The rooms are softer, well-lit and with lacquered floorboards and pastel colours accompanied by the expected facilities. Parking available.

**A Hotel Vetusta**, C Covadonga 2, T985 222 229, www.hotelvetusta.com. Small and welcoming central hotel with modern design that exudes warmth and personality. All rooms are exterior, half come complete with a mini sauna/massage unit. There's a sunny café-bar downstairs. Parking available. Recommended.

**C Hostal Romero**, C Uría 36, T985 227 591, hostalromero@telecable.es. Well located in the new town in shopping centre, this well-renovated *pensión* has big and inviting rooms, all with bathroom and TV. The owners are welcoming and enthusiastic. Recommended.

**C Hotel Favila**, C Uría 37, T985 253 877. Very handily placed for trains and buses and situated on Oviedo's main shopping street, this has comfy rooms with cable TV and smart bathroom, as well as cheery staff. The restaurant downstairs does a cheap, tasty and filling lunchtime *menú*.

**C-D Hostal Belmonte**, C Uría 31, T985 241 020, calogon@telefonicanet.es. An inviting and hospitable option in a lovely green and cream building, this is probably the best of the range of accommodation on this street. It's been attractively renovated, with a wooden floor and a variety of rooms, all with TV and bathroom. Student discount available.

**D Hostal Arcos**, C Magdalena 3, T985 214 773. A very friendly place in the heart of the old town, just off the Plaza de la Constitución. Most rooms share bathrooms, which are clean and modern; there's 24-hr access; basically it's a top central-city budget option. Recommended.

**D Hotel Alteza**, C Uría 25, T985 240 404. This is a decent, cheap hotel in a flamboyant building on Oviedo's main shopping street not too far from the station. The rooms are compact but snug, and there's a comfy guest lounge. All rooms have TV and bathroom; they are warm in winter and a little hot in summer. Breakfast included.

**D Hotel Ovetense**, C San Juan 6, T985 220 840, www.hotelovetense.com. In a prime central location just near Plaza Porlier, this hotel has cosy rooms, which, although small, are top value. It can be a little stuffy in summer, but it's quiet and friendly nonetheless. There's a restaurant and pay parking available nearby.

**D Pensión Fidalgo**, C Jovellanos 5, T985 213 287. This homely, welcoming, and colourful set-up is well placed between the old and new towns and just a hop, skip and jump away from the cider houses of C Gascona. The rooms facing the street are a little noisy but the friendly old couple running it make up for it. Recommended.

### Somiedo *p351*
**E Mierel**, T985 763 993. A good comfy spot to sleep and refuel on hearty Asturian food.

### Salas *p352*
**B Castillo de Valdés-Salas**, Plaza de la Campa s/n, T985 830 173, www.castillo valdesalas.com. This is an excellent rural hotel situated within the small castle, a beautiful setting indeed with its charming rustic central patio. The rooms are very true to the building but have much more than castle comfort. Recently renovated, they feature bright homely fabrics on comfortable beds, pastel-shaded walls and polished floorboards.
**D Hotel Soto**, C Arzobispo Valdés 9, T985 830 037. This cheap hotel is set in a pleasant old building right next to the Colegiata, which the best rooms overlook. While far from luxurious, the rooms are heated and have bathroom and television, and the price is very reasonable.

### Self-catering
The hills to the northeast of Salas have a number of good options for self-catering.
**Ca Pilarona**, Mallecina, T629 127 561, www.capilarona.com. One of the best options, Ca Pilarona is in the tiny village of Mallecina, 11 km from Salas. It is a series of 4 restored houses, modernized with excellent facilities. All have either 1 or 2 bedrooms, and cost from €40-90 per night, depending on length of stay.

### Pravia and Santianes *p352*
**A Casa del Busto**, Plaza Rey Don Silo 1, Pravia, T985 822 771, www.hotelbusto.com. One of the best places to stay in the area, this elegant hotel is set in a 16th-century *casona*. From the hallway to the rooms it's charming; the use of period-style furniture perfectly sets off an already striking building. The rooms all have individual character, with plenty of wooden furniture and hessian giving a taste of the colonial era. There's also a good restaurant, with tables in the open atrium. Recommended.

**D Pensión 14**, C Jovellanos 8, Pravia, T985 821 148. This is a small and welcoming *pensión* with 2 home-from-home rooms, lavishly appointed with stove, sink, utensils, TV, pine wood and skylights. It's on a small street in the centre of town; don't confuse it with the hotel of the same name at the bottom of Pravia. Recommended.

## ❼ Eating

### Oviedo *p346, map p348*
Head to the 'Boulevard of Cider', **C Gascona**, for a wide choice of places to try the life-blood of Asturias; most also do tasty seafood.
**♔♔♔ Casa Conrado**, C Argüelles 1, T985 223 919. A fairly traditional Spanish *mesón*, all dark wood and cigar smoke, this is a local byword for quality and elegance. The cuisine has Asturian favourites accompanied by fine meat and fish dishes; main courses are €15-25 and there's a top wine list. Closed Sun and Aug.
**♔♔♔ Casa Fermín**, C San Francisco 8, T985 216 452. This central spot specializes in high quality Asturian dishes, with *merluza a la sidra* (hake cooked in cider) a speciality. A hefty multi-course *menú* showcasing a range of Asturian cuisine is €40 not including wine; otherwise mains are €15-22. Closed Sun.
**♔♔♔ La Corrada del Obispo**, C Canóniga 18, T985 220 048. This stylish restaurant on a lovely square near the cathedral is beautifully decorated, with plenty of natural light as well as chandeliers, polished wood floors and all the trimmings. The thoughtfully prepared food matches the surroundings and feels slightly underpriced. Delicious mains include such temptations as monkfish and sea-bass in asparagus sauce. There's a €41 *menú de degustación* showcasing the best on offer. Closed Sun night.
**♔♔ Bocamar**, C Marqués de Pidal 20, T985 271 611. In the heart of the shopping district, this is a warmly lit, reasonably upmarket fish and seafood restaurant that offers a good €15 *menú* at lunchtime.
**♔♔ El Cogollu**, Plaza de Trascorrales 19, T985 223 983. This is a little gem of a restaurant in the southeastern corner of Plaza de Trascorrales. Its peaceful stone and ochre interior is decorated with traditional

ceramics; there's imaginative Asturian cuisine and a 4-course *menú*, which is superb value at €18.60. Recommended.

**El Pigüeña**, C Gascona 2, T985 210 341. For those with a largish appetite, this is an excellent choice for cider and seafood. While the à la carte fish dishes are around €16-20, *raciones* are generous here as well and a fair bit cheaper.

**Faro Vidio**, C Cimadevilla 19, T985 228 587. This extremely popular restaurant specializes in well-priced Asturian home cooking. The hearty stews and casseroles are simple and filling, while the extensive seafood dishes are prepared and presented in an uncomplicated and authentic manner.

**La MásBARata**, C Cimadevilla 2, T985 213 606. A sparky modern but casual tapas bar specializing in rice dishes. It's popular with smart young Asturians who choose from a huge range of *raciones* for €6-11; other mains are €9-16; delicious accompaniments to a *caña* at the bar.

**Tierra Astur**, C Gascona 1, T985 203 411. Spacious and very popular, this ciderhouse is one of the best-value places to eat in Oviedo. The solid wooden tables groan under the weight of some of the *raciones* that come out of the kitchen; many would feed 2, such as a selection of Asturian cheeses, all labelled with a cute little flag. The bar itself is convivial and has the smooth and lenient Trabanco cider.

**El Raitán** and **El Chigre**, Plaza de Trascorrales 6, T985 214 218. A long-term favourite for Asturian cuisine, this 2-in-1 establishment offers a smart traditional restaurant alongside a typical Asturian cider-bar. In the former, you can take advantage of various set menus (€15-28) including one for kids; in the latter, a hearty range of tapas and stews (such as broad beans or wild boar) cost just €4-7. It's all pretty good value and there's a good terrace outside in summer.

**Casa Montoto**, C San Bernabé 9. This is a simple, no-frills establishment of a sort sadly dying out in Spain. The only adornment is photos of roller-hockey teams, but the crowds flock in for a cheap wine and a *bollo preñao*, a favourite Asturian snack consisting of chorizo sausage baked in a bread roll. They don't come better than they do here.

**La Paloma**, C Independencia 3, T985 235 397. An Oviedo classic, this double-sided bar swells with people for morning coffee or a pre-lunch vermouth and *tapa*, and it makes a good evening rendezvous-point. They have their own vermouth *solera* which has been going over a century, there are daily specials such as paella and smart seafood snacks; try some *bígaros* (winkles).

**La Pumarada**, C Gascona 8, T985 200 279. A busy sidrería with impressively fast and efficient service. The excellent value *menú del día* offers a variety of Asturian and other specialities with wine for €8.50. The enormous portions may intimidate those on diets, but more robust diners will be able to savour cooking of a very high standard.

**Las Campanas de San Bernabé**, C San Bernabé 7, T985 224 931. An attractive faded façade in the shopping district conceals a popular restaurant with beautifully painted beams and a good line in bistro-style Asturiana, seafood dishes and rices. It's deservedly busy; the warming stews are particularly good at €6-9, washed down with a jar of wine.

### Cafés and bars

A traditional Oviedo pastry is the *carbayón*, an eclair-like almond creation. It's named after the oak tree, the traditional centre and meeting place of Asturian villages. A large *carbayón* was controversially chopped down in Oviedo in 1879 to make more room on C Uría; a plaque marks the spot where it stood.

**Café Dólar**, Plaza de Porlier 2. A very typical, rather than noteworthy, café with a relaxed ambience and a good location. It's decorated with a modern but classical touch that seems somehow very characteristic of contemporary Oviedo.

**El Café de Juliotón**, Plaza del Sol 4. Pleasant place for a coffee, snack or cheap lunch, nicely situated on a plaza near the town hall.

**Rialto**, C San Francisco 12, T985 212 164. With over 80 years in business, the Rialto must be doing something right. Its pastries are widely considered the best in Asturias and are absolutely delicious; browse them at the counter at the front, then eat them at your leisure at the cosy tables in the rear.

In the town of Mieres, **Plaza San Juan** is an elegant little square easily recognizable by the statue of a cider-pourer in full flow. Its placement here is no accident, as several of the town's many excellent *sidrerías* are nearby.

**El Rinconín**, Plaza San Juan 5, Mieres. One of the best of the *sidrerías*, and notably welcoming.

**Salas** *p352*

Salas isn't bursting with places to eat.

**Castillo**, Plaza de la Campa s/n, T985 830 175. Undoubtedly the best option in town, this is the **Castillo de Valdés-Salas** hotel restaurant. It offers a cheap and tasty lunch *menú* for €8 and cooks up some of the local trout catch in season. If you're not a guest and want dinner, phone ahead to reserve a spot. Closed Tue nights.

**Bar La Campa**, Plaza de la Campa s/n. A pleasing option for simple tapas and *raciones*, with a range of wines to accompany them. Its best feature is a breezy terrace over looking the castle.

**Pravia and Santianes** *p352*

**Balbona**, C Pico de Merás 2, Pravia, T985 821 162. Don't be fooled by the somewhat garish neon sign; this is actually a restaurant with a weighty reputation for quality Asturian fare. There's always a wide selection of fresh fish caught just down the road, while the beef is also recommendable. Despite the traditional atmosphere, there's plenty of modern flair in the preparation, as well as a bar where you can relax with tapas or a bottle of cider.

**La Hilandera**, C San Antonio 8, Pravia, T985 822 051. This good-looking *sidrería* is immediately recognizable by its green façade. There are various cheeses and meats to enjoy with the cider, as well as heartier *raciones* like tripe. Upstairs is a very cute stone-walled dining room, with a wider selection. *Raciones* are €5-8.

## Bars and clubs

**Oviedo** *p346, map p348*

Many of the bars only open at the weekend. Much of Oviedo's nightlife is centred in the rectangle bounded by Calles Mon, Postigo Alto, San José and Canóniga. Other areas are C Rosal, for a grungier scene and, of course, the area around C Gascona and C Jovellanos.

**Asturianu**, C Carta Puebla 8, T985 206 227. While there's nothing particularly Asturian about this bar, it's super-friendly, is a monument to good beers from around the world, and is lively till very late. Live music some nights and a weekly pub quiz.

**Ca Beleño**, C Martínez Vigil 4. This is a legendary Oviedo bar focusing on the Asturian folk scene with its Celtic roots fully intact. Frequent live music.

**El Cuelebre**, C Mon 9. The best of a selection of similar bars on this street, pleasing a youngish crowd at weekends with chart Spanish hits and international pop. It gets packed and boisterous!

**La Perrera**, C Postigo Alto 5. An excellent bar decorated with plenty of character, and dedicated to rock 'n' roll from the 1960s on. The name literally means 'the doghouse', so you get the idea.

**La Real**, C Cervantes 19, www.lareal.org. The top spot in Oviedo, and perhaps Northern Spain, for house music, with big-name DJs from Madrid, France, and the UK frequently appearing. It's open Sat nights only from 0100 until 0800. €6-16 entry (depending on the DJs) includes a drink. Check the website for upcoming nights.

**Paddock**, C Rosal 70. On a street with several late-drinking options, this place is for those with an ear tuned to heavy metal. It's suitably dark and loud.

**TKC**, C Canóniga 12. An indefatigably cheery spot, much favoured for its *chupitos*, a range of inventive and tasty shooters, with varying degrees of mortality. The music is loud Spanish pop.

## Entertainment

**Oviedo** *p346, map p348*
**Cinema**

The **Cajastur** bank on Plaza de la Escandalera has a programme of art house films.

**Cinés Brooklyn**, C General Zubillaga 10, T985 965 856.

**Theatre**

**Teatro Campoamor**, Plaza del Carbayón, T985 207 590. A well-regarded mainstream theatre prgoramme, and weekly Sun morning performances of Asturian folk music.

# ✺ Festivals and events

**Oviedo** *p346, map p348*
**Feb/Mar** Carnaval in Oviedo is gaining
a reputation; the main day here is the Sat
after **Shrove Tue**, ie 43 days before **Easter
Sun**,when you can see the traditional end of
Carnaval ceremony: the burial of the Sardine.
**Sep** Oviedo's major festival is the fiesta of
**San Mateo**, the city's patron. The 3rd week
of Sep is given over to street parades,
dances, bullfights, an opera season
and similar celebration.

# O Shopping

**Oviedo** *p346, map p348*
Oviedo is a good place to shop, with a wide
range of chain and boutique outlets. **C Uría** is
the place to find smart fashion, as are the
pedestrianized streets east of it.

## Books
**La Palma Libros**, C Rúa 6, T985 214 782.
Good bookshop for information on Asturias;
also has a good English language section.
**Librería Cervantes**, C Doctor Casal and
C Campoamor. Bookshop with an excellent
range of English-language books, as well
as Asturian and Spanish literature.

## Department stores
**El Corte Inglés**, C Uría 9. Another Corte
Inglés superstore with anything anybody
could want.

## Food
**Mercado El Fontán**, behind the Plaza Mayor.
This covered central market is a good place
to stock up on Asturian produce. The curious
might be interested in the horse butcher.

# ☏ Transport

**Oviedo** *p346, map p348*
## Air
There are several flights daily from **Madrid**
and **Barcelona** operated by Iberia and
Spanair. For international flights, which
include **Easyjet** services to London and
Berlin, see Getting there, page 28. A bus
service operates to the airport from Oviedo,
and **Gijón**; (11 daily, scheduled to connect
with outgoing flights, 45 mins, €5.25). Buses

run ½-hourly from **Avilés**, which is only ⟨357⟩
15 mins away. A taxi from Oviedo or
Gijón costs around €40.
   **Airlines** Iberia, Plaza de Juan XXIII 9,
T985 118 783.

## Bicycle hire
**Salvador Bermúdez**, C/ Postigo Alto, opposite
C/Fueros, rents and repairs bicycles.

## Bus
Local city buses are blue and run on 12
clearly marked routes around the city. The
basic fare is €0.75. Bus No 3 runs hourly
from C Uría up to Santa María de Naranco
and San Miguel de Lillo. The new intercity
bus terminal is near the train station (T985
969 696). There are many buses to **Gijón**,
30 mins, and many companies run services
across Asturias. The major intercity operator
is **ALSA** (www.alsa.es), T902 422 242, who
connect **Oviedo** with A Coruña (4 daily,
4-6 hrs, €22.46 single), **Santiago** (6 daily,
7 hrs, €26.54), **León** (9 daily, 1½ hrs, €7.29),
**Valladolid** (4 daily, 4 hrs, €15.49), **Madrid**
(14 daily, 5½ hrs, €27.10), **Santander**
(10 daily, 2½ hrs, €10.39), and **Bilbao**
(9 daily, 5 hrs, €17). Some of these services
are premium class, being slightly quicker
and more expensive. There's also a service
to **London** (26 hrs, change in **Paris**).

## Taxi
Call T985 220 919 if you can't flag one
on the street.

## Train
There is a bewildering number of short-
distance *cercanía* train routes around the
central valleys of Asturias. These are run
by both **FEVE** and **RENFE** out of the train
station. Details of individual lines can be
found in the relevant destination section.
For long-distance services, **RENFE** links
Oviedo with **León** (7 per day, 2 hrs, from
€14 single), **Madrid** (3 per day, 6 hrs, €36),
**Barcelona** (2 per day, 12 hrs, €42), and
points in between. Note that the bus is
generally quicker on these routes. FEVE's
coastal network links Oviedo (slowly) with
**Santander** (2 through trains per day, 4 hrs,
€11.85), **Bilbao** (1 per day, 6½ hrs, €18.35),
and westwards as far as **Ferrol** in Galicia
(2 per day, 6½ hrs, €17.35).

**Train** FEVE trains run to Mieres from **Oviedo** (Line F8, frequent, 20 mins), and most southbound RENFE trains also stop here.

**Bus** There are regular buses from **Oviedo** and **Gijón** (at least hourly, 35 mins, €3.15).

**Somiedo** *p351*
**Bus** ALSA runs 4 buses on weekdays and one on weekends (leaves at 1000) to **Pola de Somiedo** (2 hrs 15 mins, €6.35).

**Salas** *p352*
**Bus** ALSA runs hourly buses from **Oviedo** to Salas (1 hr 15 mins, €3.55) via Cornellana.

**Pravia and Santianes** *p352*
**Train** Pravia is served hourly by FEVE trains from **Oviedo** (Line F7) and **Gijón** (F4), 1 hr.

**Bus** ALSA also runs buses here from Oviedo and Gijón (2 a day, 1 hr).

## ● Directory

**Oviedo** *p346, map p348*
**Internet** Café Oriental, C Jovellanos 12, T985 202 897. Cybercafé at €1.80 per hr; CyberExpress, upstairs in the train station, Mon-Fri 1000-1400, 1600-1900, Sat 1000-2100, €0.04 per min; Laser Internet Center, C San Francisco 9, T985 200 066, www.las.es. Internet centre open 24 hrs, €0.05 per min.
**Language schools** Alea, C Fray Ceferino 10, T985 216 349, www.mundoalea.com. A highly professional company that organizes Spanish courses in Oviedo. Good reputation.
**Laundry** Riosol, C Capitán Almeida 31, T985 222 090. **Libraries** The provincial library is on C Quintana near Plaza del Fontán, T985 211 397. **Medical services** There's a large medical centre that deals with emergencies at C Naranjo de Bulnes behind the train station, T985 286 000. **Post office** The main post office is on C Alonso Quintanilla. **Telephone** There is a *locutorio* (telephone centre) at C Caveda and C Alonso Quintanilla, and another at C Foncalada 6.

# Gijón and Avilés

→ *Phone code: 985. Colour map 2, A2. Population: 273, 931 (Gijón), 83,855 (Avilés).*
*Following what seems to be the established law for such things, there is no love lost between Gijón and Oviedo. People in Gijón, the larger of the two, feel that it should be capital of Asturias instead of Oviedo, which some consider soft and effete. Those in Oviedo aren't too bothered, but occasionally enjoy riling Gijón by referring to it, tongue in cheek, as 'our port'.*

*Gijón is a fun city set around two beaches and a harbour. The larger and nicer of the beaches, Playa de San Lorenzo, is an Asturian Copacabana, fronting 2 km of city blocks with a stretch of very clean sand, which almost wholly disappears at high tide – and in summer, under rows of bronzing bodies. There's a fair-sized surf community here, and a thriving summer gay scene. The small old quarter, at the base of the Cimadevilla promontory, is heady with the yeasty cider smell from dozens of small bars. The council has also done a good job of highlighting the city's heritage with small museums and information plaques. In the local dialect, Bable, Gijón is written and pronounced Xixón.*

*A little further west is Avilés, whose reputation is slowly changing from grim to vivid. For a long time, the only travellers to pass through this large industrial centre were business travellers under company orders. Now, having tackled its pollution problems, the city is capitalizing on its major asset, a remarkably beautiful historic centre. On the back of its carnival, widely regarded as the best in Northern Spain, Avilés makes a concerted effort to welcome tourists. While there aren't many bona fide sights to visit, the beauty of the centre, the quality of the cafés and restaurants, and the openness of the people make it an excellent destination.* ▸▸ *For Sleeping, Eating and other listings, see pages 361-365.*

# Gijón 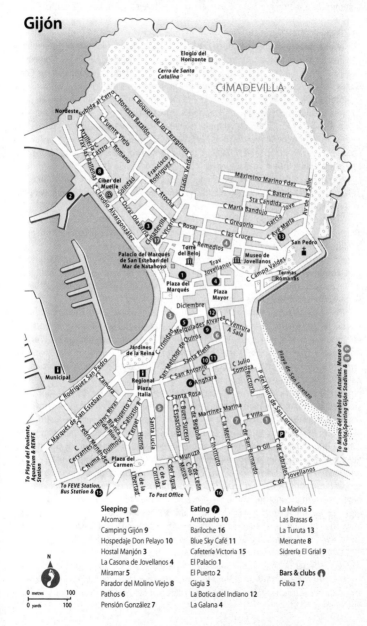 » pp361-365.

## Ins and outs

**Getting there** Gijón's bus station is on Calle Magnus Blikstad, between Llanes and Ribadesella, with regular long-distance connections to other cities in Northern Spain and local regional services. Just about all buses inbound from and outbound to other provinces stop in both Oviedo and Gijón. Train services depart from the nearby **FEVE**

## Gijón

**Sleeping** 🛏
Alcomar **1**
Camping Gijón **9**
Hospedaje Don Pelayo **10**
Hostal Manjón **3**
La Casona de Jovellanos **4**
Miramar **5**
Parador del Molino Viéjo **8**
Pathos **6**
Pensión González **7**

**Eating** 🍴
Anticuario **10**
Bariloche **16**
Blue Sky Café **11**
Cafetería Victoria **15**
El Palacio **1**
El Puerto **2**
Gigia **3**
La Botica del Indiano **12**
La Galana **4**

La Marina **5**
Las Brasas **6**
La Turuta **13**
Mercante **8**
Sidrería El Grial **9**

**Bars & clubs** 🍸
Folixa **17**

Asturias Gijón & Avilés

station on Plaza del Humedal. Most **RENFE** trains stop here, although the main RENFE station (Gijón Jovellanos) is on Avenida de Juan Carlos I, about 20 minutes' walk from the old centre.▸▸ *See Transport, page 364, for further details.*

**Tourist information** The helpful **municipal tourist office** ① *Dársena Fomento pier, T985 341 771, daily 0900-2000*, is just around the harbour from the old town. The staff are multilingual and well informed. There's a **regional office** ① *Jardines de la Reina park by the harbour, Mon-Fri 0900-1400, 1630-1830.* There's also a network of summer information kiosks, including one at each end of San Lorenzo beach.

## Sights

The **Ayuntamiento** of Gijón has been busily populating the city with small museums of varying degrees of interest. There are also numerous small art exhibitions leading brief lives in unlikely places. At the tip of the Cimadevilla headland is a small hill, the **Cerro Santa Catalina**, at the tip of which stands Eduardo Chillida's *Elogio del Horizonte* sculpture, which has become the symbol of the town. Further around the headland to the west stands the equally photographed *Nordeste*, a work by Vaquero Turcios.

A few blocks back through the old town's web, the birthplace of Jovellanos has been turned into the **Museo de Jovellanos** ① *Plaza Jovellanos, T985 346 313, Tue-Sat 1000-1300, 1700-2000 (mid-Jun to Aug 1100-1400, 1700-2100), Sun 1100-1400, free.* More interesting than the handful of Jovellanos memorabilia are the modern works of Navascués and the massive wooden depiction of the old Gijón fish market by Sebastián Miranda, a work he patiently restarted from scratch after the first was lost during the Civil War.

The nearby **Torre del Reloj** ① *Recoletas 5, T985 181 329, Tue-Sat 1000-1400, 1700-2000 (mid-Jun to Aug 1100-1400, 1700-2100), Sun 1100-1400; free*, houses an exhibition of Gijón's history in a modern clock tower.

Although now a bank, the succinctly named, sandstone **Palacio del Marqués de San Esteban del Mar de Natahoyo** is one of Gijón's most beautiful buildings, particularly in the evening sun. Behind it, the **Plaza Mayor** leads a double life as stately municipal square and lively hub of cider drinking.

The **Playa de San Lorenzo** stretches to the east of here, watched over by the **Iglesia de San Pedro** and a statue of Augustus Caesar, who stands near the entrance to the city's moderately interesting remains of the Roman public baths, **Termas Romanas** ① *Tue-Sat 1000-1300, 1700-2000 (Jul and Aug 1100-1330, 1700-2100), Sun 1100-1400, €2.30, free Sun, T985 345 147.* The beach's long boulevard is the natural choice for the evening *paseo*.

At the other end of the beach, the sluggish **Río Piles** is flanked by pleasant parks studded with palms. On the east side, about a 10-minute walk back from the beach, is the **Museo del Pueblo de Asturias,** an open-air ethnographic park with reconstructions of various examples of traditional Asturian buildings and life. It's a very worthwhile exhibit but, if you are heading for southwest Asturias, the museum at Grandas de Salime is even more engaging. Also in the complex is the **Museo de la Gaita** ① *Paseo del Doctor Fleming s/n, T985 182 963, Tue-Sat 1000-1300, 1700-2000 (Jul and Aug 1100-1330, 1700-2100), Sun 1100-1400, 1700-1900; €2.30, free on Sun*, devoted to bagpipes from around the world. Bagpipes have a long history in Asturias – the local type has a more austere tone than the Scottish kind. Information (audio) is Spanish only. The museum has a *sidrería*/restaurant with a pleasant terrace. On the other side of the river, by the **Sporting Gijón** stadium, is the busy Sunday *rastro* (flea market).

Gijón's other beach, **Playa de Poniente**, is a short walk west of the centre. It's also nicely sanded, but has more industrialized views. At its western end is the recently opened **Gijón Aquarium** ① *Oct-Mar Mon-Fri 1000-1900, Sat and Sun 1000-2100, Apr-May Mon-Fri 1000-2000, Sat and Sun 1000-2200, Jun-Sep daily 1000-2200, €10, €5 for children.*

➡ *Colour map 2, A2.*

The heart of Avilés is **Plaza de España**, from which a number of pedestrian streets radiate. One side of it is occupied by the **Ayuntamiento**, an attractive arched building that is a symbol of the post-medieval expansion of the town. Opposite is the elegant bulk of the **Palacio del Marqués de Ferrera**, recently converted to a luxury hotel.

Avilés' **tourist office** ① *C Ruiz Gómez 21, T985 544 325, turismo@ayto-aviles.es, Mon-Fri 0900-1400, 1630-1830, Sat and Sun 1000-1500,* is a block down from Plaza de España. It's very helpful and English is spoken.

From the Plaza de España (many locals refer to it as the Plaza Mayor), Calle San Francisco runs up to the **Plaza Domingo A Acebal**, where it becomes the colonnaded Calle Galiana. This whole area is lined with bars and cafés, several of which have tables outdoors. It's a popular and recommended evening meeting spot. Calle San Francisco is dominated by the 13th-century **Iglesia de San Nicolás de Bari** with a pretty Romanesque cloister, now partly occupied by a school. In front is the quirky **Fuente de los Caños** (fountain of the spouts), which pours water into a basin from six lugubrious bearded faces.

Further up Calle Galiana, the **Parque de Ferrera** was part of the impressive back garden of the counts of Ferrera before being given over to public use. It's now a rambling network of paths filled with strolling *avilesinos*.

On the other side of Plaza de España, Calle Ferrería leads into the oldest part of town; this part of the city was originally walled. At the bottom of the street are the early Gothic **Capilla de los Alas**, and the earlier **Iglesia de los Padres Franciscanos**, started in the late 12th century. The latter's sandy Romanesque façade is appealing; inside is the tomb of a notable *avilesino*, Pedro Menéndez, who founded the city of San Agustín in Florida, which claims to be the oldest city in the USA (Saint Augustine). West of here, in the **Plaza Camposagrado**, is a statue of another famous local, the shaggy Juan Carreño de Miranda, a notable 17th-century Spanish painter. A few blocks further west again, past the waterfront park of **El Muelle**, is Avilés' prettiest square, the **Plaza del Carbayo**. This is in the *barrio* of **Sabugo**, where the majority of Avilés fisherfolk used to live. It was almost a separate town, and the plaza was its centre, where whaling and fishing expeditions were planned. Walking back towards town along Calle Bances Candamo gives further flavour of this tiny district.

The nearby town of **Salinas** (4 km northwest of Avilés) is a somewhat bland place whose raison d'être is its long, sandy beach, thronged in summer but quiet at other times. At its western end is one of Asturias' best restaurants (see page 363), and a the view from the headland is good; there's also a vaguely surreal collection of anchors. Salinas can be reached by city buses Nos 1 and 11 from Avilés bus station.

## ⊜ Sleeping

**Gijón** *p359, map p359*

Gijón bristles with hotels, but many are dull cells for business travellers. Happily, there are several options with more charm.
**L Parador del Molino Viejo**, Av Torcuato Fernández Miranda s/n, T985 370 511, www.parador.es. This *parador*, in a suburban setting in a duck-filled park at the eastern end of Gijón, is mostly modern but its restaurant is set within the walls of an old

mill. Rooms are spacious, stylish and well lit. It's next door to the **Sporting Gijón** stadium.
**AL-A Hotel Alcomar**, C Cabrales 24, T985 357 011, www.hotelalcomar.com. Although slightly starchy, this hotel has an excellent location at the old-town end of the San Lorenzo beach. The rooms with a view are predictably lovely and light, and come with minibar, safe and the standard conveniences of a hotel of this level.

**A Hotel Pathos**, C Santa Elena 6, T985 176 400, www.celuisma.com. This is a refreshingly offbeat modern crashpad close to the Plaza Mayor. Pop art decorates the walls and each of the small but stylish rooms is dedicated to a 20th-century icon: Jagger, Thatcher, Gandhi? Your choice. Bathrooms are modern and swish, while there's wireless internet, minibar, and a safe in the rooms. Great value off-season. Recommended.

**B La Casona de Jovellanos**, Plazuela de Jovellanos 1, T985 341 264, hotel-lacasona@jazzfree.com. A smallish hotel in the heart of old Gijón with simple, elegant rooms in a historic building with characterful wooden *objets*, including an alarming dragonboat prow on the stairs.

**B Hotel Miramar**, C Santa Lucia 9, T985 351 008. Although right in the heart of Gijón's shopping and bar-hopping area, this small boutique-like hotel is remarkably quiet. The friendly management keep the rooms just-so.

**C Hospedaje Don Pelayo**, C San Bernardo 22, T985 344 450. A newcomer to the Gijón accommodation scene, this upmarket *hostal* is in a noble old townhouse very close to the beach. The rooms are comfortable and bright, with gleaming modern bathrooms, heating, hairdryers and cable TV.

**D Hostal Manjón**, Plaza del Marqués 1, T985 352 378. Very well-located hostel. Rooms with a view are much nicer but at weekends you're better joining the late cider-drinkers in the square rather than letting them keep you awake. Recommended.

**E Pensión González**, C San Bernardo 30, T985 355 863. Basic but wholesome option with high ceilings, wooden floorboards, and a significant population of porcelain dogs. Particularly cheap off-season.

### Camping

**Camping Deva**, 4 km east of town just off the highway, T985 133 848, www.campingdeva-gijon.com. Well equipped and with a swimming pool, something of a resort .

**Camping Gijón**, T985 365 755. Well situated at the tip of the headland to the east of the Playa de Lorenzo.

**Avilés and around** *p361*

**LL-AL Palacio de Ferrera**, Plaza de España 9, T985 129 080, www.nh-hotels.com. This newly opened hotel has been sensitively converted from a 17th-century palace right on the main square in the heart of Avilés. The rooms aren't cheap, but they have all the facilities of a business hotel, including internet connection and pillow menu. There's a gym, sauna, and underground parking. Rates vary extensively depending on availability and the time of year.

**B Hotel Don Pedro**, C La Fruta 22, T985 512 288, donpedro@asturvia.cajastur.es. Just down the hill from Plaza España, this small hotel is run out of a busy café. The staff are welcoming, the stone-faced rooms are charmingly grotto-like and have an Arabian feel. Currently being expanded so ring ahead to confirm that it's open. Recommended.

**B-C Hotel de la Villa**, Plaza Domíngo A Acebal 4, T/F985 129 704. This likeable hotel is well situated in the historic centre, looking over a pleasant plaza and the church of San Nicolás de Bari. Rooms are appealing, with dark wood floors and prints of Kandinsky and Klee, and the staff are friendly.

**D Pensión La Fruta**, C La Fruta 21, T985 512 288. This well-equipped *pensión* is run out of the friendly **Hotel Don Pedro**, and is directly opposite it. Every room comes with its own bathroom (either en suite or next to the room), and TV. Recommended.

## ● Eating

**Gijón** *p359, map p359*

Gijón offers some excellent eating around the Plaza Mayor and the marina. The black spiny *ericios* (sea-urchins) are a local favourite, as are *zamburiñas*, (a tasty small scallop).

**₩ El Palacio**, Plaza de Marqués 3, T985 341 368. In an elegant restored building between the port and the Plaza Mayor, this has a popular cider joint and terrace downstairs. Above is quite an elegant restaurant, decorated in differing shades of red. Some tables have fine views over the bobbing yachts in the harbour. The *magret de pato* (duck magret) is delicious, as is the seafood and salads. Closed Mon.

**El Puerto**, Paseo de Claudio Alvargonzález s/n, T985 349 096. An upmarket restaurant on the jetty, whose reputation for seafood makes it a popular destination for people stepping off their yachts. Fairly dark despite the large windows, but the food is superb. Local grouper (*mero*) comes in a green pepper sauce, while the expensive *quisquillas* are a tiny shrimp highly regarded in Spain. Mains €13-21.

**La Galana**, Plaza Mayor 10, T985 172 429. This distinguished looking *sidrería* on the main square is a prime spot to eat and drink. The huge barrels, painted ceiling and heavy wooden beams give plenty of atmosphere. You can snack on *tapas* (€3-5 for a decent plate), or head up the back for some more serious seafood and stews. The lunchtime *menú* is great value at €10 for 4 courses.

**La Marina**, C Trinidad 9, T985 346 246. This colourful cider place is gregarious, buzzy and warmly lit. There's maritime decor and a fine range of free *pinchos* laid out on wooden boards. Sit down for tasty *oricios*, or *almejas a la marinera*, a clam stew served in a tin pot.

**Mercante**, Cuesta del Cholo 2, T985 350 244. A very good harbourside option with an excellent €9 lunch *menú* in the upstairs restaurant. In fine weather, a popular choice is to grab a cold drink from the bar and sit on the stone wall outside. Recommended.

**Sidrería El Grial**, C Melquiades Alvarez 5, T985 344 497. A good little basement *sidrería* tucked into the backstreets near the Plaza Mayor, which prepares some excellent plates of shellfish, including *zamburiñas* in a spicy sauce (€12.50). Other mains cost €6-15, and there's a cheap *menú del día* (€7.50).

**Cafetería Victoria**, C Magnus Blikstad 5, T985 357 020. Half-an-hour until the bus and not sure whether you can fit in a 4-course lunch and coffee? Let this place show you how; its €8.10 *menú* is good and served by speedy staff high on stress (or is that the other way around?).

**Gigia**, C Oscar Olivarriá 8, T985 344 509. The crates of cider stacked in the corner give a good clue to this bar's raison d'être. It's earthier and not as glamorous as some of the other ciderhouses, which gives it a certain authentic appeal, as does its reliably good food; sit at the cute wooden tables and enjoy anchovies with ham, grilled baby sardines (*parrochas*), or goat chops.

**Las Brasas**, C Instituto 10, T985 356 331. No-frills *parrilla* restaurant with a range of *platos combinados* and *menús*. The smells of the grilling meat will lure you in; things such as *chorizo criollo* (an Argentinian sausage) are particularly tempting. The half *parrilla* (€16; €20 with salad) can comfortably feed 2 people and features a range of meats. Eat upstairs if you fancy a quieter meal.

**Cafés**

**Anticuario**, C San Antonio 9, T985 344 441. A fairly upmarket café during the day, this place changes once the sun goes down, as a white-collar (and mixed) crowd move from the *café con leche* to the gin and tonics. Particularly lively at weekends; closes late.

**Bariloche**, Plaza del Instituto 1, T985 350 169. One of the city's classic cafés, with a characteristic duplex style much in vogue in the 1970s in Spain. There are tasty rolls and good coffee; a breakfast not to be sniffed at.

**Blue Sky Café**, C San Antonio, next door to **Anticuario**. Dark, sleek, styled and also gay-friendly. A DJ and lively crowd turns it into a disco-bar at weekends.

**La Botica del Indiano**, Plaza Mayor. This large and convivial bar-café is on the main square and kitted out with all manner of decoration from Old Habana. It's a popular spot to meet, whether for morning coffee or pre-dinner *copa*.

**La Turuta**, C Avé María 21. With posters of Che Guevara and Bob Marley on the walls, this relaxed Cimadevilla bar in the back streets has what is euphemistically called a liberal atmosphere. Quiet, friendly and studenty.

**Avilés and around** *p361*

Avilés is an excellent place for eating out; especially **C Galiana** and the old streets north of Plaza de España.

**Casa Tataguyo**, Plaza del Carbayedo 6 (unsigned at the back), T985 564 815. Amazing split-personality restaurant that has been an legend for years. The back bar dishes out cheap workers' lunches at shared tables in a satisfyingly no-frills atmosphere. The other part is an expensive and attractive 2-level restaurant dealing in very classy Asturian fare.

**Real Balneario**, Av Juan Sitges 3, Salinas, T985 518 613. One of Asturias' top restaurants, beautifully set on the beach at

Salinas. Predictably specializing in seafood, the €17 lunch *menú* is definitely the most economical way to enjoy the haute cuisine.

**Casa Lin**, Av de los Telares 3, T985 564 827. This is a historic *sidrería* near the station serving up excellent seafood and a well-poured apple juice. Its kidneys stewed in sherry (*riñones al jerez*) also have a stratospheric reputation.

**Casa Moisés**, C La Muralla 4, T985 526 000. This new restaurant opened by the former boss of the Casa Lin has quickly gained a big following. It's a spacious ciderhouse with an excellent selection of seafood.

**La Posada**, C Ruiz Gómez 12, T985 512 062. This new restaurant is across the road from the tourist office and is warmly decorated in a modern but traditional style on 2 levels. There are plenty of warming Asturian stew-type dishes on offer, and they prepare fine *bacalao* (cod). There's a lunch *menú* for €10.

**La Serrana**, C La Fruta 9, T985 565 840. A spacious seafood restaurant under the Luzana hotel with a good-value lunch *menú* for €9.62. There's a good wine list too, and the place has bags more character than the hotel.

**La Coruxa**, Plaza del Carbayo 16, T985 565 381. Another restaurant on the square, with an elegant upstairs *comedor* and a bar downstairs. Unpretentious and good-quality food.

### Cafés

**Cafetería El Delfín**, Plaza Domingo A Acebal 7. A busy and enticing café that does a range of rolls and snacks best consumed from its shady outdoor tables on the attractive square.

**Café Don Pedro** (see Sleeping). Set in the hotel of the same name, this café is decorated in similar stony style. The coffee is very good.

**Cafetón**, C Del Sol 4. Cosy bar/café with board games and a happy bohemian crowd.

## ⊙ Bars and clubs

### Gijón *p359, map p359*

There are many cheerful drinking bars along C **Rivero** off the Plaza de España. The small streets around C **Santa Lucía** are a mass of bars, many operating only at weekends. For every bar calling last orders in the early hours, another is probably just throwing open its doors, although the council is having things close earlier (around 0500) than before.

**Folixa**, C Oscar Olavarría 6. A small intimate locale dedicated to rock music, and open very late (0530 at weekends). The low tables have leopard-printed stools, and the walls are covered with posters of legendary Spanish gigs.

### Avilés and around *p361*

The main area for weekend nights is the barrio of Sabugo, where pubs like **Camelot** and **El Angel Azul** are always busy. See also Cafés, above.

## ⊙ Entertainment

### Gijón *p359, map p359*
### Cinemas

**Cines Centro**, behind Playa San Lorenzo in a shopping centre off C San Agustín, T985 353 757. The most convenient cinema to the centre of town.

## ⊛ Festivals and events

### Avilés and around *p361*

**Feb/Mar** Carnaval, known as *Antroxu*, in Avilés is big and getting bigger every year. The town happily submits to a week of parties and events centred around the Plaza de España. On the Sat, C Galiana sees a riotous procession of boats on a river of foam, while the Tue hosts a more traditional, but equally boisterous, procession. The whole town is in fancy dress, including the bars, which undergo a change of identity. **Ash Wed** sees the traditional **Burial of the Sardine**. Accommodation is tight, but FEVE run trains all night from Gijón and Oviedo on the main nights.

## ⊙ Transport

### Gijón *p359, map p359*

See Oviedo pages 346 and p357 for information on the Asturias airport, reached by regular bus from Gijón (11 daily, 45 mins, €5.25).

### Bus

Local services run very regularly to **Oviedo** (30 mins) and **Avilés** (30-40 mins). The major intercity operator is **ALSA** www.alsa.es, T902 422 242, who connect Gijón with **A Coruña** (4 daily, 5-6 hrs, €22.46 single), **Santiago**

(6 daily, 7-8 hrs, €26.54), **León** (9 daily, 2 hrs, €7.29), **Valladolid** (4 daily, 4½ hrs, €15.49), **Madrid** (14 daily, 6 hrs, €27.10), **Santander** (10 daily, 3 hrs, €10.39), and **Bilbao** (9 daily, 5½ hrs, €17). Some of these services are premium class, being slightly quicker and more expensive.

**Train**
There are FEVE coastal connections to **Santander** (2 through trains daily, 4 hrs, €11.85), **Bilbao** (1 daily, 6½ hrs, €18.35), and westwards as far as **Ferrol** in Galicia (2 daily, 6½ hrs, €17.35). More regular services run to **Llanes**, **Cudillero** and **Avilés**.

RENFE links Gijón with **León** (7 daily, 2½ hrs, from €15), **Madrid** (3 daily, 6½ hrs, from €37), **Barcelona** (2 daily, 12½ hrs, €42-46) and points in between. Note that the bus is generally quicker on these routes.

**Avilés and around** p361
**Bus and train** The RENFE, FEVE, and bus stations are all together on Av de los Telares on the waterfront to the west of the old town,

and about 15 mins' walk. Both RENFE and FEVE connect the town frequently with both **Oviedo** and **Gijón** (35 to 40 mins), as does the bus company ALSA. There are frequent buses bound for the western Asturias.

## ❶ Directory

**Gijón** p359, map p359
**Internet** Ciber del Muelle, on the harbour, C Claudio Alvargonzález 4, T985 190 252. A decent cybercafé, Sun-Fri 1100-2200, Sat 1100-0300; €1.50-1.95 per hr. **Post office** The main post office is on Plaza 6 de Agosto, south of the centre, not far from the bus station. **Telephone** There are *locutorios* in the FEVE station, and on the boulevard above Playa de San Lorenzo, at the western end.

**Avilés and around** p361
**Internet** Café Bongo, C Rivero 25, near Plaza de España, has internet access. **Post office** The main post office is on Plaza Alfonso VI, just north of Plaza de España.

# Western Asturias

*The west coast of Asturias is a rugged green landscape, speckled with fishing villages and gouged by deep ravines. George Borrow describes the arduousness of crossing these in the 1830s in* The Bible in Spain, *but nowadays they are spanned by massive road and rail viaducts. It makes a great place for a enjoyably low-key Asturian stay. The fishing towns of Cudillero, Luarca and Tapia bristle with character, and there are many excellent beaches, some with good surf.*

*Southwestern Asturias is something of a wilderness, whose steep green valleys still contain villages that are not accessible by road. It's a hillwalker's paradise: there are several good bases with a range of marked trails, such as Santa Eulalia de Oscos, or Taramundi, famous for its knives and centre of a fascinating ethnographic project. The village of Grandas de Salime is another rewarding place to stay and is home to an excellent ethnographic museum. It's also worth applying to visit the Parque Nacional Muniellos, in the far southwest corner of Asturias – the old growth European forest is home to several endangered species, including a small community of bears.*
▸▸ *For Sleeping, Eating and other listings, see pages 369-373.*

## Along the west coast ⬤🕐🕙▲🅱 ▸▸ pp369-373.

### Ins and outs → *Colour map 2, A1.*
The FEVE line from Gijón and Oviedo to Galicia follows this coast faithfully, although the stations tend to be at a short distance from the town centres, and there are only three trains a day in either direction. ALSA buses are much more frequent.
▸▸ *See also Transport, page 372, for further details.*

Asturias Western Asturias

The houses of this small fishing town are steeply arrayed around the harbour like the audience in a small theatre. Its picturesque setting and fishing harbour small enough not to have any unsightly associated industry have made this prime outing territory during summer holidays. Entirely dormant during winter, in season Cudillero makes a good destination, having enough restaurants and bars to keep things interesting, but still a long way from being a resort. It's a lovely place.

The town, called 'Cuideiru' in Bable, effectively has just one street, which winds its way down the hill to the harbour. There's not a lot to see; the setting of the town itself is the main attraction. Most of the action takes place around the waterfront, where the smell of grilling fish is all pervading at lunchtime.

There are some wildly shaped cliffs in this area, and while the summer sea might seem almost Mediterranean, in winter the waves give the sea wall a pounding. The village of **El Pito**, just off the main road east of town, has its own **FEVE** station and a few places to stay. It's an attractive walk down into the town but a steep return trip.

## Luarca → *Colour map 2, A1.*

The charm of Luarca, one of this coast's best destinations, is that although summer visitors are drawn by its attractive harbour and plentiful facilities, it gives the refreshing impression that fishing remains its primary concern. While it has grown a little since Borrow exclaimed that it "stands in a deep hollow...it is impossible to descry the town until you stand just above it", it's still a compact place, centred around the Río Negro, which often seems in danger of relegation to 'stream' status. Luarca was formerly a big whaling port; the whale still has a proud place on the coat of arms.

Once again, the **harbour** is the biggest attraction, filled with colourful boats of all sizes. A variety of restaurants line it; beyond them you can walk around to the sea wall and watch it take a fearful pounding if the sea is in the mood. At the other end of the harbour is the **beach**, a rather apologetic affair with dirty grey sand and lined with changing huts. A much better beach is **Playa de Taurán**, a few kilometres west.

Just by the water opposite the church is the *lonja*, where the freshly caught fish is sold in the middle of the day. It's decorated with tiled murals depicting the town's fishing history, one of which shows the curious custom of deciding whether to put to sea or not in bad weather: a model of a house and of a boat were put at opposite ends of a table and the fishermen lined up according to their preference. If the majority chose to stay home, nobody would go to sea that day.

As with much of the coastline, the **tourist office** ① *by the river on Paseo del Pilarin, T985 640 083, Easter-Sep Mon-Fri 1230-1400, 1630-2100,* is only open in summer. The library on the hill behind it usually has free maps to hand out.

## Navia and around

At the mouth of the river of the same name, Navia is a more commercial port than the others on this coast, with a significant boatbuilding and plastics industry. It can be noisy, with trucks and buses shuddering through town to and from Galicia. Unlike most of the others, Navia's charm is to be found away from its harbour, in the narrow paved streets above. The **tourist office** is in the old town at the top of Calle Las Armas.

The valley of the Río Navia, winding inland to **Grandas de Salime** and beyond, is one of Asturias' natural highlights, dotted with Celtic *castros*, small hillforts, most of which are between 2000 to 2500 years old. While some of the remoter ones are well worth exploring with transport, the most accessible is 4 km from Navia, at **Coaña** ① *T985 978 401, Oct-Mar Tue-Sun 1100-1500, Apr-Sep Tue-Sun 1100-1400, 1600-1900, closed Mon; €1.50*. It's an impressive, well-conserved structure commanding a spur in the valley. There's a café and a small visitor centre. Infrequent buses run there from Navia; if you want to walk, cross the bridge over the river and take the first road on the left. The fort is a short way past the village of Coaña.

## ⁝ El Cambaral

El Cambaral was the most famous of the Moorish pirates who terrorized the Cantabrian and Asturian coasts. The scourge of local shipping, he was finally tricked by a local knight, who put to sea in an apparently harmless ship bristling with hidden soldiers. El Cambaral was wounded and captured. The knight took him home, as the trial had to wait until he had healed, but foolishly let his young daughter tend to the pirate's wounds. The two predictably fell in love and decided to elope. Reaching the port, where a boat was waiting, and thinking themselves safe, they stopped for a kiss, but the enraged knight had been warned. He arrived at the quay and chopped off both the kissers' heads with one blow.

Luarca remembers the ill-fated couple in the name of its bridge, El Beso (The Kiss), and the fishermen's quarter, El Pirata Cambaral.

## Tapia de Casariego and around

Tapia, one of the most relaxed places on this coast, deserves a look. While there is a small harbour, the town's beautiful beach west of the centre is deservedly the main attraction. There's a small surf community here, established by the semi-mythical Gooley brothers – two Aussies who fetched up in a campervan one day in the 1970s – and it certainly feels more like a beach town than a fishing port. The town itself is charming, with a quiet elegance radiating from its whitewashed stone buildings and peaceful plazas watched over by the dominant Christ on the church tower. Opposite the church, there's a small tourist information kiosk open in summer. Apart from Tapia, the best surf beaches are **Peñarronda** to the west, where there are two campsites, and **Frejulfe**, further east. Waves also get ridden under the bridge that crosses into Galicia.

## Castropol and the Galician border

Asturias ends at the Ría de Ribadeo, a broad estuary at the mouth of the Río Eo, notable for the cultivation of shellfish. The N634 highway blazes straight on over a massive bridge into Galicia. While the main town in this area, Ribadeo, is across the water, Asturias still has a little more to offer in the village of Castropol.

With a great setting on the estuary, the onion-like village is a peaceful and seldom-visited gem. Formerly an important ferry crossing, it has been completely bypassed by the massive bridge, and now does little but cater to passing traffic on the Lugo road. If you've got a spare hour or two, it won't be wasted exploring the narrow streets of this lovely place. The central plaza contains a memorial to the Spanish-American war of 1898. The naval defeats of this war, and subsequent decline in shipping due to the loss of all Spain's remaining colonies, was a big factor in the decline of towns on this coastline. To reach Castropol, take the Lugo turn-off from the coast road a few kilometres before Galicia.

# Southwest Asturias 🏨🍴🚌 ›› *pp369-373.*

## Ins and outs

Travelling is time consuming even with your own car. The local bus system, although slow and infrequent, has fairly good coverage. See Transport, page 372, for details.

## Taramundi and around

More easily accessed from the coast, the road to Taramundi beetles up green valleys where mules and donkeys still draw carts, and herds of cows take priority over

# Cider House Rules

Wine may be Bacchus' choice of drink in the rest of Spain but in Asturias it is cider that is to be found when refreshment is needed. Drunk all over the province in thousands of *sidrerías*, *sidra* has developed a complex ritual of its own that at times seems as mysterious as the Japanese tea ceremony. Ordered by the bottle and not by the glass, Asturian cider is a medium-strength drink containing around 6% alcohol.

The most obvious aspect to the ritual is the method of pouring (the verb *escanciar*). It is a case of once seen never forgotten as the waiter holds aloft the crystal-like bottle of cider and pours it from arms length into a glass without looking. This is done not just for show but to create bubbles in the cider which are an essential part of the drinking process. The smaller the bubbles the higher the quality of the cider.

The drinker then has a small period of grace known as the *espalmar* during which the bubbles remain in the glass and the small quantity of poured cider must be drunk. Normally a maximum of 10 seconds. So a leisurely sip is not the norm for Asturian drinkers who usually down the glass or *culín* in one. Normal practice is then to wait for the eagle-eyed master of ceremonies to refill the glass. However, those feeling a little impatient or emboldened after a bottle or two are welcome to try themselves (if it's not too smart a place!). Just be ready to smell of fermented apples for the rest of the evening.

The different types of cider are a result of the various blends of apples used. There are around 20 varieties used in Asturias, each one falling into a different category of sweetness. Usually the cider will be made of 80% dry and semi-dry varieties. The apples are harvested between mid-September and mid-October and important local festivals are based around the harvest. The best known is in Villaviciosa. Another notable cider festival is held in Nava on 11 and 12 July each year.

Not surprisingly, given its importance in Asturian culture, cider is widely used in local cooking. Most *sidrerías* will produce their own dishes with cider added as a flavouring. It is important to realize though that more than three bottles may seriously impair the diner's judgment. Local people are reported to have a number of traditional hangover cures all of which will be denied the intemperate visitor. You have been warned.

vehicles. The village itself is an earthy place, which draws its fair share of summer tourists, many of whom are attracted by its numerous knife workshops. The Taramundi blades are renowned throughout Spain; the range available runs from professional-standard kitchen knives to carved tourist souvenirs. Most of the workshops welcome visitors – there are plenty to choose from. Taramundi is only a couple of kilometres from Galicia, and the locals speak a bewildering mixture of *Bable* and *Gallego* that they cheerfully admit is incomprehensible to outsiders. There's a **tourist office** ① *Tue-Sun 1000-1400, 1630-1930*, on the main road at the bottom of town.

In the valley around Taramundi are a number of ethnographic projects, where traditional Asturian crafts and industries have been re-established. The best of these is possibly **Teixois** ① *T985 979 684, daily 1100-1800, €1.50*, in an idyllic wooded valley with a working mill and forge powered by the stream. If there aren't many people about, it feels uncannily as if you've just stepped back in time. There's a small restaurant, which cheerfully serves up simple but abundant food, much of it produced by the local projects. Teixois is about one hour's walk from Taramundi – head straight down the hill and follow the signs. The road passes near several of the other projects en route.

This sleepy little municipal centre is notable for an excellent museum, the **Museo Etnográfico** ① *Sep-Jun Tue-Sat 1130-1400, 1600-1830, Sun 1130-1430, Jul-Aug Tue-Sun 1130-1400, 1600-1930, €1.50*, an ambitious and enthusiastic project that seeks to recreate in one place a range of traditional Asturian crafts, industries and daily life. Working mills, grape presses, and pedal-operated lathes are fascinatingly and lovingly put to work by the informative staff. Here you can see the making of the characteristic *madreñas*, wooden clogs worn over shoes when working outdoors, still very much in use. It's an important project and indicative of the deep pride Asturians hold for their heritage.

## Reserva Natural Integral de Muniellos → *Colour map 1,B6*

① *Access is strictly limited to 20 visitors a day; reservations are taken on T985 105 545.*
This large protected area of mountain oak forest is situated west of the AS-15 some 30 km south of Cangas. Much of it is unspoiled old-growth forest and it is home to many protected species including badgers, capercaillie, deer, bears, short-toed eagles, otters and serpents. The enthusiastic visitor centre is 7 km from the main road and is the starting point for a seven-hour walking trail through the forest. One inhabited village remains in the far north of the park. Since 2002, it has been reduced to seven inhabitants, a sad example of the depopulation of the Asturian mountains.

## ● Sleeping

**Cudillero and around** *p366*
**A-B La Casona de la Paca**, El Pito, T985 591 303, www.casonadelapaca.com. This red 3-storey house is a typical *casa de indiano* with a walled garden. Fairly formal in style, it's a relaxing and secluded hideaway. As well as the comfortable rooms, there are also good-value apartments for daily or weekly hire. Turning left out of the El Pito station, it's 5 mins' walk on the right. Closed Jan.
**B La Casona del Pío**, C Riofrío 3, Cudillero, T985 591 512, www.arrakis.es/casonadepio. This beautiful stone hotel and restaurant is just off the harbour. It's run by warm and friendly people, and has welcoming rooms with hydromassage mini-tubs. Closed Jan. Recommended.
**D Pensión Alver**, C García de la Concha 8, Cudillero, T985 591 528. On the main street through the village, this friendly *pensión* in a bright blue building has good-standard rooms that are as clean as a whistle. Open Easter-Sep.
**D Pensión El Camarote**, C García de la Concha 4, Cudillero, T985 591 202. In the top half of the main street, this upmarket *pensión* has well-equipped rooms and is considerable value. It's often full in summer, so book ahead. Open Apr-Sep.

**Camping**
There are 2 summer-only sites, both inconvenient for town but good for the beach.

**Camping Cudillero**, T985 590 663. Inaccurately named, but the nicer of the 2. Also with cabins.
**L'Amuravela**, to the east of Cudillero, beyond El Pito, T985 590 995. With a swimming pool and cabins.

**Luarca** *p366*
Several of the hotels shut for the greater or lesser portion of Jan and Feb.
**B Hotel Gayoso**, Plaza Alfonso X, T985 640 050. Founded in 1860 but refurbished since, this offers some sharp off-season prices. The rooms aren't memorably decorated, but are comfortable enough, with standard facilities.
**B Torre de Villademoros**, T985 645 264, www.torrevillademoros.com. Between Cudillero and Luarca, this is a beautiful old Asturian farmhouse with an extremely stylish modern interior situated on a cliff above the sea with a large medieval tower in its backyard. There's a FEVE station in Cadavedo, about 3 km from the hotel, but it would be quicker to jump off an ALSA bus at the Villademoros stop on the main road. From there, cross the railway bridge and turn left when you reach a small *parrillada*. The hotel is signposted from there.
**C Hotel Baltico**, Paseo del Muelle 1, T985 640 991. Stolid but adequate hotel well situated on the harbour. The rooms have plenty of light and are quiet.

**C La Colmena**, C Uría 2, T985 640 278, www.lacolmena.com. This attractively modern option has smallish but newly refurbished rooms with attractive wooden floors and furnishings and plenty of light.

**D Hotel Rico**, Plaza Alfonso X, 6, T985 470 585. An excellent budget option, this has value-packed and spacious rooms above a café. There's cable television, heating and good en suite bathrooms. Heated debates from downstairs can echo through the building, but it's a winner at this price. Recommended.

**E Pensión Moderna**, C Crucero 2, T985 640 057. A simple, old-style *pensión* with 3 spotless doubles and polished floors.

### Camping

**Playa del Tauran**, T985 641 272. The best campsite in this part of Asturias, on a clifftop west of Luarca with access to a small cove beach. Excellent atmosphere and facilities. Bar, shop and cabins can be found among the eucalypts. It is some 3 km from the main road, near the hamlet of San Martín. Quicker access by foot from the far end of Luarca beach. Open Easter-Sep. Recommended.

### Navia and around *p366*

**B-C Hotel Palacio Arias**, Av Emigrantes 11, Navia, T985 473 675, palacioarias@fade.es. One of the most lavish and eccentric *I ndiano* constructions in western Asturias, surrounded by the trademark walled garden and furnished in period style. The hotel's modern annexe offers cheaper but less characterful accommodation. Neither section is immune from the noise of the road, which is still widely known as Av José Antonio.

**D Hotel Arco Navia**, C San Francisco 2, Navia, T/F985 473 495, www.hotel elarco.com. Attractive slate building by an arch on a historic medieval street. St Francis is said to have stayed in what is now the hotel's rental apartments.

**E Pensión San Franciso**, C San Francisco s/n, Navia, T985 631 351. On a tiny plaza, this whitewashed *pensión* is clean and simple.

### Tapia de Casariego and around *p367*

Accommodation in Tapia is unremarkable but perfectly adequate.

**C La Xungueira**, T985 628 213. By the beach, on the main road just west of the centre, is the best option in Tapia. The pastel-shaded rooms are unoriginal but blameless. Significant off-season discounts. Closed Jan and Feb.

**D Hotel Puente de los Santos**, Av Primo de Rivera 31, T985 628 155, F985 628 437. On the main road, where the buses stop. You've seen this type of set-up in beach towns in any given country, but it's friendly and comfy.

### Camping

**Camping Playa de Tapia**, T985 472 721. On the other side of the beach from town, this summer-only campsite has reasonable facilities. Road access a couple of kilometres west of town but on foot it's much quicker across the beach.

### Castropol and the Galician border *p367*

**B Palacete de Peñalba**, C El Cotarelo s/n, Figueras, T985 636 125, F985 636 247. On the hill above Figueras, this flamboyant apricot-coloured edifice dominates the fishing village. Set in a huge garden, it was built in the early 20th century by a modernista disciple of Gaudí. It's now a lavish place with an expensive French-influenced restaurant.

**C Peña Mar**, Ctra General s/n, T985 635 481. The nicer of the 2 uninspiring motel-style set-ups on the main road.

**D Casa Vicente** Ctra General s/n, opposite Peña Mar, T985 635 051. The cheaper of the 2.

### Taramundi and around *p367*

**L La Rectoral**, Cuesta de la Rectoral s/n, Taramundi, T985 646 760, www.la rectoral.com. This historic hotel is housed in the 18th-century building that used to be the home of the parish priest, with superb views over a fairytale valley. The rooms are extremely comfortable – the best have balconies over-looking the valley, as does the dining room.

**C Casa Petronila**, C Mayor s/n, Taramundi, T985 646 874, www.casapetronila.com Attractive rooms in an old stone building on the main street.

**C-D Hotel Taramundi**, C Mayor s/n, Taramundi, T985 646 727, www.hotel taramundi.com. This friendly hotel has bedrooms plum-full of Asturian comfort. It's a small and intimate place and real care has been paid to the decoration. Recommended.

**E Pensión La Esquina**, C Mayor s/n, T985 646 736. The cheapest beds in town in a simple *pensión* above a café. Small and comfy (unless you're tall, as the beds have footboards).

### Casas de aldea
The area around Taramundi is brimming with *casas de aldea*. 2 to consider are **Freixe**, T985 621 215, near the village of Barcia, and **Aniceto**, T985 646 853, a small nucleus of houses in Bres. Pricier, but with character and setting is **Las Veigas**, T987 540 593, where, as part of the ethnographic project, a deserted village has been restored to life; the 2 buildings of the priest's house can be rented.

### Reserva Natural Integral de Muniellos *p369*
The nearest accommodation to the park is on the main road.
**D Hotel La Pista**, T985 911 004. A short distance south of the turn-off, in the village of Vega de Rengos, dominated by a massive coal plant. It is welcoming, however, with colourful rooms, a restaurant and a cosy sitting room.
**E Pensión La Pescal**, T985 918 903. In the tiny village of the same name north of the turn-off, this is more a hotel than a *pensión*, with a garden, elegantly quirky bedrooms with the original furniture of the old house and comforting home-cooked meals.

## ⊘ Eating

### Cudillero and around *p366*
There are plenty of seafood 'n' cider places of varying quality, many featuring meet-your-meal style aquarium tanks.
**La Casona del Pío**, see Sleeping, above. An excellent seafood restaurant in the slate dining room with layered wooden ceiling. The philosophy is to produce '*cocina de siempre*' with high-quality ingredients; they succeed. Lunch *menú* for €19.
**Restaurante Isabel**, C La Ribera 1, T985 590 211. Bang on the harbour with lifebuoy-and-anchor style nautical decor and appropriately high-class seafood.
**Bar Julio**, on the harbour. A good café. Sitting on the outside terrace you can watch on the whole town stretching up above you.

**El Ancla**, C Riofrío 2, T985 590 023. Seafood restaurant specializing in *paella* and a mixed seafood *parillada*, but also does a range of *raciones* and tapas. The calamari are particularly tasty, generous portions.

### Luarca *p366*
**Villa Blanca**, Av de Galicia 25, T985 641 035. The gourmet option in town, with a choice of dining rooms. The seafood is of excellent quality, as you would expect from this proud fishing town, paintings of which decorate the walls.
**Café Riesgo**, C Uría 6. Pleasant 1st-floor café with lots of windows for contemplation.
**El Barómetro**, Paseo de la Muelle 4, T985 470 662. The old wooden object in question stands on the wall outside this excellent seafood restaurant. The decor is warmly maritime, and the host is solicitous. Try a whole oven-baked *sargo* (white sea bream, €14.50) or the *oricios* (sea urchins), which have an unusual but acquirable taste. High quality dining at a very reasonable price. Recommended.
**Mesón de la Mar**, Paseo de la Muelle 35, T985 640 994. Massive old stone building on the harbour with plenty of character and a big range of *menús*. There are also tasty *raciones* to be eaten at homely wooden tables in the bar, which features a circular table and trough for pouring your own cider. They also do an excellent seafood rice for 2 (€24).
**Restaurante Sport**, C Rivero 8, T985 641 078. This smart harbourside joint specializes in shellfish, including river oysters from the nearby Eo. It is characterized by excellent service and lovely large wine glasses. There's a great wine list and also a bar, where they'll try and tempt you to dine by serving a delicious free tapa.
**Cambaral**, C Rivero 14, named after the swashbuckling pirate, see page 367, this is another good tapas and drinks option. There's a conservatory space for a quiet coffee, while the bar is always lively with locals. The tapas are simple but delicious, like mussels or *lacón*.

### Navia and around *p366*
**El Sotanillo**, C Mariano Luiña 24, T985 630 884. Restaurant with a range of seafood with a good *menú del día*. Café upstairs does a range of snacks for smaller appetites.

**Asturias** Western Asturias Listings

**La Barcarola**, C Las Armas 15, T985 474
528. Fairly upmarket restaurant in a heavy
3-storey stone building in the old part of
town. Attractive interior with dark wood and
soft, coloured lights. Good reputation in
these parts, particularly for seafood rice.

**Tapia de Casariego and around** *p367*
The majority of restaurants and bars are
huddled around the harbour. Fresh fish is
understandably their stock-in-trade.
**El Bote**, C Marqués de Casariego 30, T985
628 282. This thoughtful seafood restaurant
has a very homely feel and excellent fresh
fish. Try the *percebes* (goose barnacles)
if they are on offer.
**La Cubierta**, C/Travesia del Dr Enrique
Iglesias Alvarez, T985 471 016. A good
*sidrería* with a simple and effective layout.
A long bar crowded with locals is faced by
wooden tables on one side which need to
be sturdy in order to support the massive
*raciones* on offer at knockdown prices.

**Castropol and the Galician
border** *p367*
**El Risón**, El Puerto s/n, T985 635 065.
The best option in town for a meal or a drink,
this is a friendly and peaceful place on the
water with outdoor tables looking over the
oyster and clam beds of the *ría*, and over
to Ribadeo in Galicia. Closed Feb.

**Taramundi and around** *p367*
All 3 Taramundi hotels have
good restaurants.
**Hotel Taramundi**, C Mayor s/n,
Taramundi, T985 646 727. In the centre of
town, this one is attractively stone-faced.
The meat dishes stand out; the *churrasco*
(ribs) and *solomillo* steak are particularly juicy.
**Pantaramundi**, C Mayor s/n, T985 646 821.
Their bread is prized throughout Asturias.
A friendly café, good for snacks.
**Sidrería Folleiro**, further down the
hill. Another decent place.

**Reserva Natural Integral de
Muniellos** *p369*
**The Restaurante Pousada**, T985 911 431,
is a popular country restaurant just off the
main road opposite the turn-off to the park;
it's a good spot for a filling late lunch after
the park trail.

# ☉ Bars and clubs

**Cudillero and around** *p366*
**Txomi** and **La Luna** are the summer nightspot options. They're happy places, but but
not exactly at the cutting edge of the
international music scene.

**Luarca** *p366*
**Los Corsarios del Mar Chico**, C Rivero 28.
The liveliest of Luarca's bars, this long dark
nightspot on the pedestrian main street gets
lively at weekends, when it's open very late.

**Navia and around** *p366*
**El Bar de Siñe**, C Las Armas 17, Navia.
A good bar on one of Navia's nicest streets.
**Te Beo**, Av del Muelle. One of Navia's best
bars, with a good range of beers.

**Tapia de Casariego and around** *p367*
**El Faro**, by the harbour. A friendly bar
decorated with photos and paintings of
lighthouses. A good place to discuss the
surfing options hereabouts.

# ▲ Activities and tours

**Luarca** *p366*
**Jatay**, based 3 km west of Luarca, T985 640
433/600 665 763. Organizes tours on horses
and quad-buggies in the area; on more of a
holiday-fun than serious trekking footing. .
**Valdés Aventura**, T689 148 295. Offers
more serious adventures on mountain
bikes or horseback.

**Castropol and the Galician
border** *p367*
**Ondabrava**, based in Castropol, T985 626
002. Organizes an excellent range of
activities throughout southwest Asturias.

# ☉ Transport

**Along the west coast** *p365*
**Bus** ALSA buses run westwards more or
less hourly along the coast from **Gijón**
and **Oviedo** (changing at Avilés).

**Cudillero and around** *p366*
**Bus and train** The railway station is
at the top of the town, while most **ALSA**
services only stop on the main road about

½ hr's walk away. A few go into town, these mostly go to/from **Avilés**.

**Luarca** *p366*
**Bus and train** The bus station is next to El Arbol supermarket on Paseo de Gómez on the river, while the **FEVE** station is a little further upstream, on the accurately named Av de la Estación, 10 mins' walk from the centre of town. There are regular bus services from **Oviedo**, **Gijón** and **Avilés**.

**Navia and around** *p366*
**Bus and train** The FEVE station is on Av Manuel Suárez, Navia. There are 3 services a day to and from **Oviedo** (2 of which continue to Galicia). The **ALSA** station is on the main road, Av de los Emigrantes.

Autos Piñeiro service the **Navia** valley to **Grandas de Salime**.

**Tapia de Casariego and around** *p367*
**Bus and train** ALSA buses stop on Av Primo de Rivera in the centre of town. The FEVE station is an inconvenient 20-min walk.

**Taramundi and around** *p367*
**Bus** Taramundi can be reached by bus from **Vegadeo**, on the N640 that links Lugo with the Asturian coast.

**Grandas de Salime** *p369*
**Bus** 4 buses a day run from **Oviedo** to Grandas de Salime, stopping at every house on the way. It takes 4 hrs 30 mins and costs €11.10.

# East coast of Asturias

*The coast east of Gijón is popular with Spanish summer tourists but it's always possible to get away from the crowds; the sheer number of small villages and accommodation options sees to that. There are dinosaur footprints scattered around; pick up the tourist office brochure if you're interested in tracking them down. You'll find some good examples, although not to the standard of those in the Rioja.*

➤ *For Sleeping, Eating and other listings, see pages 374-376.*

## Villaviciosa and around ➔ *Colour map 2, A2.*
Set back from the sea on a marshy inlet, Villaviciosa is a busy market town with an attractive historic centre. It's famous for *avellanas* (hazelnuts), but more importantly, it's the foremost producer of cider in Asturias, and is worth a visit even if you don't fancy a night on the apple juice.

The centre boasts several elegant *indiano* buildings, as well as a church, the **Iglesia de Santa María de la Oliva** ① *Tue-Sun 1100-1300, 1700-1900*, a Romanesque building with very attractive zigzagged portals.

In a square nearby is a statue of Carlos V (Carlos I of Spain). In 1517, intending to make his first entry to Spain a grand one, Carlos' fleet was ravaged by storms and finally managed to limp into harbour at Tazones just north of here, thus making Villaviciosa his first sizeable stop. He stayed at a nearby *palacio*, **Casa de Hevia** ① *C José Caveda y Nava*, which is marked with a plaque.

A good chunk of the town's population work in the **cider factories**, some of which are open for tours, such as **El Gaitero**, a 10-minute walk from the centre. The tourist office will give details of visiting hours for this and others.

Southwest of Villaviciosa at a distance of about 10 km is the ninth-century pre-Romanesque **Iglesia de San Salvador de Valdedios** ① *T985 892 324, Oct-Mar Tue-Sun 1115-1300, Sat and Sun 1115-1300, 1600-1730, Apr-Sep Tue-Sun 1100-1300, 1630-1830, €1*, one of the province's finest. Believed to have been the spiritual centre of the Asturian kingdom and part of a palace complex for Alfonso III, it is attractively proportioned with its typical three naves and carved windows. Plenty of paintwork remains, as well as charming leafy capitals and dedicatory inscriptions. Bat-phobes should avoid the place entirely; several of the little creatures call the dark church home.

**Asturias** East Coast of Asturias

**Lastres and around** → *Colour map 2, A3.*

Lastres is a quiet fishing port with attractive views over the sea and rocky coast. Its steep streets see plenty of summer action, but little at other times, when the town gets on with harvesting *almejas* (clams) and fishing. There's nothing really to see; it's a working town with some accommodation and makes a good, relaxing waterside stay, even when the nights are chillier and the sea mist rolls over the green hills. Some 3 km away by road (but a shorter walk) is **Playa La Griega**, an excellent beach shaped strangely by a small river. There are sets of dinosaur prints on the southeast side, and a decent campsite, **Costa Verde**, T985 856 373 (June to September).

## Ribadesella → *Colour map 2, B3.*

Ribadesella is a town of two halves, separated by a long bridge. On the western side is the beach, a long, narrow strip of sand with plenty of accommodation and holiday homes. Across the bridge is the fishing port, a more characterful area with plenty of good eating and drinking options, particularly in the summer season. The **tourist office** ① *Tue-Sun 1000-1400, 1600-2000,* is near the bridge on the harbourside.

Just outside the town is a good place for a break from the beach, the **Cuevas Tito Bustillo** ① *Apr-Aug Wed-Sun 1000-1630, visits (1 hr) every 25 mins, maximum 24 per tour so get there early, €2.10,* not recommended for children under 11, a limestone cave complex with some prehistoric art from the Magdalenian culture that created Altamira, only discovered in 1968. Groups of up to 25 people are admitted every 25 minutes, but there's a daily limit, so get there earlier rather than later in summer. There's a small information hall.

The Sella river that flows into the sea here is a popular venue for canoeing. See page 376, for details of tour operators.

## Llanes → *Colour map 2, B4.*

Llanes is the most important town on this stretch of coast and a delightful place to stay. Although it sees plenty of tourists, it has retained a very pleasant character around its fishing port and walled, pedestrianized medieval centre. There are plenty of good beaches within reasonably easy reach. It was an important whaling town, and still hauls in a good quantity of fish every day; the best spot to see them is in the *lonja* where they are sold off every day at around midday. The **tourist office** ① *Mon-Fri 1000-1400, 1600-1830, Sat 1030-1330, extended hours in summer,* is located in an old tower within the walled town.

There's a tiny beach close to the town walls, **Playa del Sablón**, that soon fills up in summer. For more breathing room, head 20 minutes' walk east to **Playa de Toró**. (Note the accent, as for some reason locals never fail to be amused by people calling it 'beach of the bull', *toro*.)

At the end of the harbour wall, Basque artist Agustín Ibarrola had the novel idea of cheering things up by painting the concrete blocks in exuberant colours. The *Cubes of Memory* are striking and best viewed from near the lighthouse on the eastern side of the harbour.

## Towards Cantabria

The last stretch of Asturias has many beaches and pretty pastures, with looming mountains in the background. Just across in Cantabria, **Devatur** (see Activities and tours, page 376) run all kinds of canoeing, rafting and horseriding activities.

---

## 🔵 Sleeping

**Villaviciosa and around** *p373*
There are 2 good places to stay, opposite each other in the heart of town.

**B Casa España**, Plaza Carlos I 3, Villaviciosa, T985 892 030, www.hcasaespana.com. This friendly and attractively renovated *indiano-*

style house has good bedrooms, modern bathrooms, and cheap off-season rates.
**C Carlos I**, Plaza Carlos I 4, Villaviciosa, T985 890 121, F985 890 051. An old *palacio* decorated in period style with modern comfort.
**F Pensión Sol**, C Sol 27, Villaviciosa, T985 891 130. A bit tatty but friendly and low priced.

### Lastres and around *p374*
Both hotels are much cheaper off-season.
**B Hotel Eutimio**, C San Antonio s/n, Lastres, T985 850 012. Near the tourist office, this is a well-maintained and modernized old *casona* with friendly staff and good seafood restaurant.
**C-D Miramar**, Bajada al Puerto s/n, Lastres, T985 850 120. This hotel wins no prizes for the name, but has decent, clean and slightly boring rooms, some with excellent views.

### Ribadesella *p374*
There are many places to stay. Along the beach is a series of upmarket hotels, while the few cheaper options are in the town.
**A Casa de Paloma Castillo**, C Ricardo Cangas 9, T985 860 863, This is one of the nicer of the beachfront hotels, and conveniently close to the town end of it.
**A Villa Rosario**, C Dionisio Ruiz Sánchez 6, T985 860 090, www.hotelvillarosario.com. A very blue and ornate mansion on the beach that could have come out of the Addams Family; one of the best things about the interior is that you can't see the exterior, but the rooms are good, with excellent facilities, some top views and a good restaurant.
**D-E Hotel Covadonga**, C Manuel Caso de la Villa 9, T985 857 461. A good-value and cheerful place with rooms with or without bath above a convivial bar.
**E-F Albergue Roberto Frassinelli**, C Ricardo Cangas 1, T985 861 380. An official YHA hostel on the beachfront in a ramshackle old building. Reception is only open 1700-2100.

### Camping
**Camping Los Sauces**, T985 861 312, near the beach. The nicer of 2 campsites. It's open from the last week of Jun to mid-Sep.
**Ribadesella**, T985 858 293, in the small village of Sebreño, 1 km inland. This campsite has more facilities than Los Sauces (including a pool), and is open Apr-Sep.

The town makes a pretty good base, with plenty of accommodation and eating choices.
**A La Posada del Rey**, C Mayor 11, T985 401 332, www.laposadadelrey.iespana.es. A very attractive tiny hotel near the port, decorated with *cariño* and style by an enterprising and energetic old lady. The tiny but cute bar is another highlight; off-season rooms are significantly cheaper. Recommended.
**A-C Hotel Mira-Olas**, Paseo de San Antón 14, T985 400 828, www.hotelmiraolas.com. This quiet hotel is on the eastern side of the harbour and overlooks the colourful cubes. It's been recently refurbished and makes a very pleasant base. The front-facing rooms are large and light. Closed Feb.
**C Pensión La Guía**, C Parres Sobrino 1, T985 402 577. A very nice central *pensión* in an old stone building in the heart of town. The rooms are decorated with a sure touch and have modern bathrooms and reading lamps; some have a glassed gallery. There's some noise from the road, but it's worth putting up with. Recommended.
**C Sablón's**, El Sablón s/n, T985 400 787. A well-located hotel/restaurant, with views out to sea – perfect for dashing down after breakfast and staking a claim on the tiny beach.

### Camping
**Camping Las Bárcenas**, T985 402 887. One of many campsites, this one not far from Toró beach. Open Jun-Sep.

## 🍴 Eating

### Villaviciosa and around *p373*
Good eating options can be found all along C Generalísimo by the town hall.
🍴 **El Congreso de Benjamín**, C Generalísimo 25, T985 891 180. Perhaps the town's best option, this specializes in seafood (and there's plenty of cider to wash it down with), and has a *menú* for €9.65. Seafood mains are €12-18.

### Lastres and around *p374*
🍴 **Hotel Eutimio** See Sleeping, above. Good seafood restaurant (closed Mon).
🍴 **El Cafetín**, C Pedroyes s/n, T985 850 085, just above the tourist office. A decent bite, although hardly inspired, and the wooden seats are a penance, but some of the stews and seafood are pretty good and cheap.

Apart from the hotel restaurants, most of the characterful eateries are in the old town, as are the bars.

**¶¶ El Rompeolas**, C Manuel Fernández de Juncos 11, T985 860 287. A massive bar and restaurant with a good range of seafood and snacks.

**¶¶ Sidrería Carroceu**, C del Marqués de Argüelles 25, T985 861 419. A good harbourside venue for classy seafood and cider, a typical Asturian combination.

**¶ Bar Del Puerto**, Paseo del Puerto s/n. This simple place hasn't got a frill in sight, but their grilled sardines are a treat for €6; there's also a range of other fish on offer.

**Llanes** *p374*

Most of the action is on C Mayor, where there are many *sidrerías* and restaurants.

**¶¶ Caroni**, C Mayor 8, T985 400 852. This trendy modern place is a cosy and cheerful wine bar. You can taste wines from many different regions of Spain by the glass, or sit down and graze on a plate of octopus or ham. There are various offers scrawled on the mirrors on the wall, and there's usually something tempting as a free snack on the bar.

**¶¶ El Campanu**, La Calzada s/n, T985 401 021. Set on the riverside a block back from the port, this is a good seafood destination. There's an earthy downstairs cider-bar, but above is a warmly lit restaurant serving excellent fresh fish. They do a good seafood paella too.

**¶¶ Mesón El Galeón**, C Mayor 20. A very good seafood restaurant in the old town near the port. What's on offer encouragingly depends on the catch. Try the *oricios* (sea urchins) or the selection of grilled meats. There's a gregarious bar downstairs.

**¶ Bar Casa del Mar**, C del Muelle s/n. Underneath the ugly fishermen's club, this cheap place serves excellent fish to locals. *Menú del día* on offer for €7.

## ❶ Bars and clubs

**Lastres and around** *p374*

**Azor**, C San Antonio 18. A great place to hang out with a drink. Floor-to-ceiling windows, great view, cheesy 1980s beach decor and a monster dog.

## ▲▲ Activities and tours

**Llanes** *p374*
**Golf**
There's a well-placed golf course east of town.

**Tour operators**
**Güe**, C El Castillo s/n, T985 402 430. Runs a variety of excursions in the surrounding area, including canoeing on the Río Sella.

**Watersports**
**Escuela Asturiana de Surf**, T670 686 801, www.escuela.surfastur.com. Can arrange surfing lessons at a variety of locations on the Asturian coast.

**Towards Cantabria** *p374*
**Devatur**, Edificio Estación s/n, Unquera, T942 717 033. All kinds of canoeing, rafting and horse-riding activities.

## ❷ Transport

**Villaviciosa and around** *p373*
**Bus** Several buses a day to **Oviedo** and **Gijón**, and some heading east to **Lastres.**

**Lastres and around** *p374*
**Bus** ALSA buses from **Oviedo** and **Gijón** come several times a day and stop outside the summer-only tourist office.

**Ribadesella** *p374*
**Bus** Ribadesella and Llanes are linked by bus to **Gijón** and **Oviedo**, and east to Santander.

**Llanes** *p374*
**Bus and train** For buses, see under Ribadesella, above. The **FEVE** station is to the east of town and is another means of reaching **Oviedo**, **Gijón** and other coastal destinations.

## ❸ Directory

**Villaviciosa and around** *p373*
**Internet** There's internet access for €3 per hr at the **Hotel La Ría** on C Marqués de Villaviciosa 5, T985 891 555.

**Llanes** *p374*
**Internet** Cyberspacio, Av de la Paz 5. Slow internet connection.

# Galicia

## ⁝ Footprint features

# Introduction

Remote Galicia's Celtic history can still be keenly felt in this northwestern region of Spain, about the size of Belgium. It's dotted with hill villages and dolmens, and the *gaita*, or bagpipe, is a strong element of Galicia's musical heritage. Another point it shares with other Celtic nations is its rainfall, which is high; in the northwest, for example, it rains 150 days of the year.

The course of Galicia's history was changed forever when the tomb of the apostle St James was allegedly discovered. Pilgrims flocked from across Europe, as they have recently started to do again, and the noble granite city of Santiago de Compostela that grew up around the tomb is a fitting welcome for them.

Apart from religion, fishing is Galicia's main business; the ports of Vigo and around furnish much of Spain with its fish, and shellfish are intensively farmed in the sheltered *rías* (inlets).

The variety of Galicia's rural and urban landscapes make it a fascinating part of the country; the unifying factor is the seafood, which is uniformly superb, particularly the 'national' dish, *pulpo* (octopus), which is deliciously served both in no-frills *pulperías* and gourmet restaurants.

Galicians have a reputation for being superstitious and introspective, not hard to understand when you've seen the Atlantic storms in full force. A Celtic melancholy known as *morriña* is also a feature, expressed in the poems of Galicia's favourite writer, Rosalía de Castro. To visitors, though, *galegos* are generous and friendly; the region's cities are as open and convivial as anywhere in Northern Spain.

# ★ Don't miss...

1 **Lugo**  March along the fantastic walls, then get down to business at the great tapas bars, page 382.
2 **Santiago**  Stagger into the cathedral square at the end of your five week pilgrimage or just turn up for a memorable visit, page 386.
3 **A Coruña**  Make a detour to this, one of the nicest cities in Northern Spain, with everything a traveller could ask for, page 405.
4 **Costa da Morte**  Whisper tales of smugglers and shipwrecks in the secretive villages of this beautiful rocky coast, page 410.
5 **Cabo Finisterre**  Gaze out at the limitless Atlantic from this romantic spot at the end of the earth, page 412.
6 **Pretty plazas**  Probe the fine square of little-visited Pontevedra, page 423, and Ourense, page 433.
7 **Vigo**  Dine on octopus and *albariño* wine in gritty, fascinating Vigo, after a day at the beautifully unspoiled Illas Cíes, page 425.

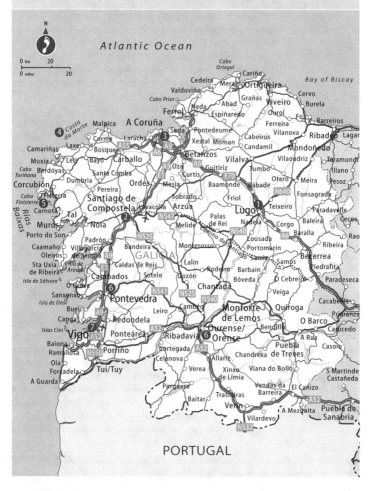

Galicia

# Pilgrim Route to Santiago

*The climb from western León province into Galicia is one of the most gruelling parts of the pilgrim route, particularly if the local weather is on form. The first stop, O Cebreiro is a pretty village that offers a well-deserved welcome; from here it's all downhill to Santiago through rolling green hills and a number of interesting Galician towns. Off the route to the north is the enjoyable city of Lugo, girt by a seriously impressive wall, originally built by the Romans in typically no-holds-barred fashion.* ▸▸ *For Sleeping, Eating and other listings, see pages 384-386.*

## Piedrafita and O Cebreiro

The most spectacular approach into Galicia is via the pass of Piedrafita, a wind- and rainswept mountain location which can be hostile in the extreme. Sir John Moore and his ragtag British forces were pursued up here by the French army, and many died of cold. Not much further, they found themselves without explosive to mine a bridge, and were forced to ditch all their gold over the edge so that they could travel faster and avoid being set upon from behind.

On the main road, Piedrafita has banks, other services and lodging options, but it's best to move on down a side road to the pilgrims' rest stop of O Cebreiro. In many

❧ *The area is famous for its mountain cheeses.*

ways, this tiny village of attractive stone buildings is where the modern Camino de Santiago was reborn. The church and former pilgrim hostel were rebuilt in the 1960s and the energetic parish priest, Elías Valiña, found suitable people to run hostels in other waystations and began to popularize the notion of the pilgrim way once again.

Although O Cebreiro can be indescribably bleak as the winds, rains and snows roll in and the power fails, it's atmospheric and friendly and has all the services a weary pilgrim could desire. Here you'll see four reconstructed *pallozas*, a circular dwelling of stone walls and straw roofs originating in Celtic pre-Roman Galicia: two house an ethnographic exhibition; the other two provide accommodation for pilgrims. The church has a reliquary donated by Fernando and Isabel to accompany the chalice known as the 'Grail of Galicia', after the host and communion wine became real flesh and blood one day as a skeptical priest went through the motions at mass. In high summer, pilgrims can outnumber locals (there are 31) by 30 or 40 times, and the army comes in to set up an outdoor canteen.

## Samos

Pilgrims shortly have a choice of routes (they soon meet up again). The more interesting, but slightly longer, goes via the village of Samos. Significantly wetter than the Greek island where Pythagoras was born, this Samos is wholly dominated by the large monastery of **San Julián** ⓘ *Mon-Sat 1000-1230, 1630-1830; Sun 1130, 1230 only, €2; admission by interesting tour only, leaving on the ½ hr.* The Benedictines first came here in the sixth century, and a tiny slate chapel by the river dates back to the ninth and tenth; it's shaded by a large cypress tree. The main monastery is a huge structure entered via its elegant western façade. If you think it looks a bit too square, you're right; towers were planned but the coffers ran dry before they could be erected.

Much of the interior has been rebuilt: in 1951 a monk took a candle too close to a fermenting barrel in the distillery and burned most of the complex down. Although a Romanesque doorway is still in place where it used to give access to the old church, most of the architecture is Baroque, but a far more elegant and restrained Baroque

● *For information on the practicalities of walking the Camino de Santiago and the history of*
● *the pilgrimage, see pages 52 and 388.*

than is usual in these parts. There are two cloisters; a pretty fountain depicting water nymphs from Greek mythology is the highlight of the smaller one, its pagan overtones appear not to trouble the monks, whose cells and eating quarters are here. Sixteen Benedictines still live here and run a small farm on the edge of the village.

The larger cloister abuts the raised church and is centred around a statue of Feijóo, the notable and enlightened writer who was a monk here early in his career. He donated much money derived from his writings to enable the dome of the church to be completed. The upper level sleeps guests (males can apply in writing to join the community for a contemplative break) and was decorated in the 1960s with a series of murals to replace those paintings lost in the fire. They're pretty bad – the artist painted cinema posters for a living – but give the monks credit for courage; it would have been all too easy to whack in a series of insipid replicas.

> ♣ Ask at the monastery for a guide to visit the little chapel by the river it it's not already open.

The church itself is large, elegant, and fairly bare. An Asturian cross above the altar is a reference to the kings that generously donated money to the early monastery; statues of them flank the nave. The dome, as with the one in the sacristy, has a touch of the Italian about it.

## Sarria

Pilgrims continue from here to Sarria, preferably with a stout stick or a joint of meat; the dogs in these hills have forgotten the 'man's best friend' bit. Sarria is a bit dull; a busy service and transport centre for the region with a traffic problem. The few charms there are lie in the old town, on the side of the hill. There's a simple Romanesque church with a charming cloister and above it, a privately owned castle that needs a couple of ravens as a finishing touch to its creeper-swathed tower. Sarria is famous for antiques, and there are many such shops in the town – beware reproductions!

## Portomarín

At first glance you wouldn't know it, but this village is only about 40 years old. The original lies underwater, submerged when the river Miño was dammed. Hearteningly, the villagers were helped to move the historic buildings to the new site, and Portomarín escaped becoming the sad and soulless concrete shambles that many such relocated villages in Spain are. The main street is attractive, with an arcade and whitewashed buildings, and the Romanesque parish church is well worth a look for its rose window and beautifully carved tall portals.

Further along the Camino, it's worth taking a short detour to see the church at **Vilar de Donas**, see Around Lugo, page 384.

## Melide, Sobrado and Lavacolla

Once the Camino hits the main road, it's a fairly characterless final stretch to Santiago, with fairly lifeless towns and villages straggling along the highway. The best of them is **Melide**, the geographical centre of Galicia, which has a very attractive plaza and a moderately interesting church with Romanesque origins.

If you've got transport, it's worth heading north to the small town of **Sobrado**, where one of Galicia's largest monasteries is gradually being saved from dereliction by the small community of monks that live there. The **church** ① *guided tour Mon-Sat 1030-1300, 1615-1815, Sun 1215-1300, 1615-1815, €0.60*, is impressive if not lovable, with a strange sober façade of squares and geometrical patterning. The interior is softer, with ornate cupolas; there are also three down-at-heel cloisters and the massive kitchen.

The last fraction of the pilgrim trail follows the busy main road due west to Santiago and has little of interest. At **Lavacolla** pilgrims used to bathe in the river so as to be clean when arriving at the apostle's tomb (the name may derive from the

**Galicia** Pilgrim Route to Santiago

Latin for 'wash arse'). Ascending the hill of Monte del Gozo, now cluttered with tasteless *hostales* and roadside brothels, the first pilgrim to spot the cathedral would be dubbed the 'king' of the group. A large metal pilgrim figure marks the beginnings of the long outskirts of Santiago itself. If you're a pilgrim arriving in a very busy period, it may be an idea to overnight just before reaching Santiago, thus arriving first the next morning to grab a cheap bed before the rest do.

---

# Lugo 🚌🚹🏠⊕🔲🚍🄲 ➤ pp384-386.

→ *Phone code: 982. Colour map 1, B4. Population: 92,271. Altitude: 470 m.*

The Romans weren't ones for half measures, so when they decided their main Galician town needed walls, they didn't hang around. Still in top condition today, the wall impressively circles the old town and is the most obvious feature of what is a small and remarkably pleasant inland provincial capital. Attractive architecture within the perimeter adds to the appeal, and there are several good bars and restaurants.

Lugo was founded in 15 BC as Lucus Augusti, named after Augustus, the emperor of the time. It rapidly became an important outpost; the Roman province that contained Galicia had its capital in distant Tarragona (near Barcelona), so the city had an important local administrative role. The main streets in the town still follow the Roman axes. Today, Lugo is a busy little place, a centre for the surrounding farming districts and capital of Galicia's largest province.

The main **tourist office** ① *www.lugoturismo.com, Mon-Fri 0930-1400, 1630-1830*, is set in an arcade off the Praza Maior. There's also a handy and friendly new **tourist kiosk** ① *Mon-Fri 1100-1400, 1630-2000, Sat and Sun 1030-1400, 1600-2000*, in the small park outside the bus station.

## Sights

Lugo's **walls** were erected in the third century AD and built to last. Made of slabs of schist, they are still almost complete and run over 2 km right around the centre of town at a height of some 10 m. Their width is impressive too; you could race chariots along the top, where the walkway is some 4-5 m wide.

The wall has been shored up over the years, and most of the 82 towers that punctuate its length are of medieval construction. If you feel a bit exposed on the top, that's because the upper portions of the towers were removed during the Napoleonic wars because it was thought they wouldn't withstand cannon fire and would topple into the town's centre.

Walking around the walls is the best way to appreciate their construction, and walking along the top them is the best way to see the town. There are six points of access and 10 gates, of which the most authentically Roman is **Porta do Carme** (also called Porta Minha).

The 19th-century traveller George Borrow must have been having a bad day when he described Lugo's **cathedral** ① *1100-1300, 1600-1800*, as "a small, mean building"; although it's not the finest cathedral in Northern Spain, it's a large and interesting place. It was first built over earlier remains in the 12th century, but its big twin-towered Baroque façade, somewhat reminiscent of Santiago, is what dominates today. Inside, some Romanesque features remain, such as the distinctive *ajedrezado jaqués* chessboard patterning associated with the Camino de Santiago.

The town was granted the right to have the consecrated host permanently on view; an honour seldom granted by the Catholic church, and still a source of some pride; Galicia's coat-of-arms depicts the host and the chalice for this reason. The host is displayed above the altar in an ornate silver and gold monstrance, surrounded by marble cherubs and flanked by angels. Above is a shower of silver around the eye-in-triangle symbol of the all-seeing God. In the apse is the famous and much-venerated statue of *La Virgen de los Ojos Grandes* (Virgin with the Big Eyes), a beautiful and sober Romanesque wood carving set in a Baroque chapel. The **cathedral museum** and treasury is set around the small cloisters.

Nearby, the **Praza Maior** is large, attractive, and guarded by fierce stone lions. At its top end is the town hall, an 18th-century building in Galician Baroque, a style that (whisper it) owes something to Portuguese architectural traditions.

The **Museo Provincial** ① *Mon-Sat 1030-1400, 1630-2030 (2000 Sat), Sun 1100-1400, Jul and Aug Mon-Fri 1100-1400, 1700-2000, Sat 1000-1400, free*, includes the **Iglesia de San Pedro**, with a curious 15th-century door, beautiful Gothic tracery on the windows, and a strange tower. There's an eclectic display, ranging from Roman pottery and coins to sundials, Celtic jewellery, Galician painting and ethnographic displays.

Lugo's **Roman baths** were built shortly after the city was founded, taking advantage of the natural hot spring by the river. What's left of them is within the spa hotel complex by the **Miño**. A walkway over the warm waters lets you see the ancient changing rooms, with alcoves in the wall to stash your toga; another room nearby is of uncertain function. The bridge across the river nearby is also of Roman origin.

One of Lugo's pleasures apart from strolling the walls is exploring the small streets within their sturdy circle. **Rúa Nova** is the centre for tapas bars and restaurants, while the shopping streets are in the eastern end of the old town.

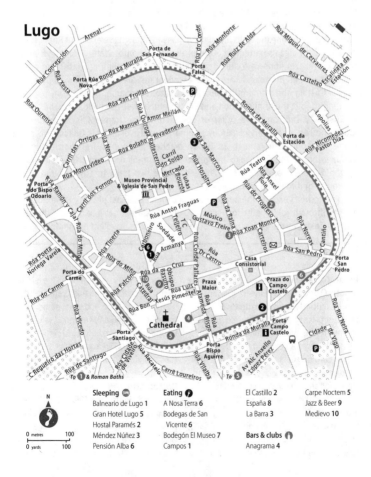

**Lugo**

N

0 metres 100
0 yards 100

| Sleeping 🛏 | Eating 🍴 | El Castillo **2** | Carpe Noctem **5** |
|---|---|---|---|
| Balneario de Lugo **1** | A Nosa Terra **6** | España **8** | Jazz & Beer **9** |
| Gran Hotel Lugo **5** | Bodegas de San | La Barra **3** | Medievo **10** |
| Hostal Paramés **2** | Vicente **6** | | |
| Méndez Núñez **3** | Bodegón El Museo **7** | **Bars & clubs** 🍸 | |
| Pensión Alba **6** | Campos **1** | Anagrama **4** | |

The area **southwest of Lugo** is out of the ordinary; a sort of microcosm of Galician rural life that seems to have changed little over the decades. A web of tiny roads connects a series of hamlets where tractors are still outnumbered by mulecarts and villagers still bear loads on their heads.

Within this area are two excellent churches. The first, in the tiny settlement of **Santa Eulalia de Bóveda** ① *guided tour only, Tue-Sat 1100-1400, 1530-1700 (1630-2030 summer), Sun 1100-1400*, is something of an enigma. Originally a Celtic and Roman temple, the mystery centres around an atrium and a small chamber with columns surrounding a basin. Very well-preserved paintings of birds and trees decorate the walls. Perhaps used for baptism, there can be no doubt that it dates to early Christian times, perhaps while rural religion was still heavily intertwined with pagan rites. Santa Eulalia can't be reached by public transport; get an Ourense or Santiago-bound bus to drop you off at the turn-off and hitch (it's a good 1½-hour walk). If you have your own transport, take the Ourense road (N540), turn right after 4 km, left about 1 km further on, then right about 6 km down that road. It's all signposted.

More accessible is the church at **Vilar de Donas** ① *1100-1300, 1600-1800; admission by donation (the knowledgeable and kindly warden lives nearby and may come and open it outside these hours if you hang around)*, it's also only a shortish detour off the Camino de Santiago. It's worth the trouble; it's one of Galicia's most interesting buildings. Built in the 12th century, it was modified at the behest of the Knights of Santiago to serve as a place of burial for the prestigious members of that order. The tombs line the walls after you've passed through the excellent Romanesque doorway with zigzag patterning. One of the finest tombs dates from 1378 and is mounted on two lions who are squashing a boar, representing wrath, and a wolf, symbolizing evil. In the apse are some excellent frescoes commissioned by Juan II, king of Castilla and father of Isabella, the Catholic monarch. Dating from 1434, the paintings depict the Annunciation and Pantocrator as well as shields with the devices of Castilla y León and the order of Santiago. In the transept is a *baldacchino* (baldachin) an ornate carved canopy commonly used over altars in Galicia; this one is made of stone. The church is easily reached by public transport; take any Santiago-bound bus from Lugo and get off at the turn-off on the main road; it's 500 m up a side road from here. If you're getting the bus back to Lugo, signal it very vigorously or it may sail on by.

Few tourists explore the peaceful green countryside east of Lugo; the road winds its way through rolling hills to western Asturias. In a hamlet just outside the small town of **Castroverde**, 20 km or so east of Lugo, is some excellent accomodation.

## ● Sleeping

**Piedrafita and O Cebreiro** *p380*
D **Hotel O Cebreiro**, O Cebreiro, T982 367 125. Next door to the church, this is an excellent place to stay, with spacious wood-beamed rooms and a restaurant serving an incredibly generous evening *menú* for €9.
E **Casa Carolo**, O Cebreiro, T982 367 168. A good option serving meals. The double rooms are heated and offer good value for money.

**Sarria** *p381*
B **Alfonso IX**, Rúa do Peregrino 29, T982 530 005, www.nh-hoteles.com. The town's most luxurious option, this chain hotel is modern

and pleasant; the rooms have all the facilities (some are disabled-equipped), and it also boasts a gym, sauna, and swimming pool as well as a restaurant. Very good value.
E **Londres**, Av Calvo Sotelo 153, T982 532 456, F982 533 006. A comfortable place to stay, clean rooms with bath and no frills.

**Portomarín** *p381*
E **Mesón de Rodríguez**, T982 545 054. This bastion of peregrine comforts on the main street, is a good place for a bed and/or a meal; clean and good value, the food is generously proportioned and compassionately priced.

**Lugo** *p382, map p383*

**L Gran Hotel Lugo**, Av Ramón Ferreiro 21, T982 224 152, www.gh-hoteles.com. Lugo's top option, this massive hulk of a hotel is modern with a considerably better interior than exterior. The rooms are blessed with many facilities. Internet and a swimming pool.

**C Balneario de Lugo**, Barrio del Puente s/n, T982 221 228, www.lugonet.com/balneario. Although the atmosphere is staid, and it's a wee walk downhill from the walled town, this spa hotel is very well priced, right by the Miño river, and on the site of the old Roman baths. The rooms are well equipped, with a garden to stroll in.

**C Hotel Méndez Núñez**, C Reina 1, T982 230 711, F982 229 738. This grand old hotel is right in the centre. It has plenty of period charm with large rooms but slightly stuffy decor. Reasonably good value.

**D Pensión Alba**, Praza Campo Castelo 31, T982 226 056. This sparkling modern *pensión* is tucked up against the city walls near the town hall. The rooms are excellent, with firm new mattresses and wooden floorboards; it makes a very good central spot to stay.

**F Hostal Paramés**, Rúa Progreso 28, T982 224 816, hparames@wanadoo.es Within the walls, this *hostal* is a snip at the price, with faded but faultless rooms with TV and bathroom for very little cash. It's good value for singles too. Recommended.

### Around Lugo *p384*

**A Pazo de Vilabade**, near Castroverde, T982 313 000, www.elpazo.com. One of Galicia's nicest places to stay, an old mansion with a classy but homely atmosphere and a spirited *dueña* who makes a mean afternoon tea. Closed Christmas-mid Mar.

## ⊘ Eating

### Sarria *p381*

**¶ A Carreta**, Av Calvo Sotelo 142, T982 830 549. One of many for eating and drinking on the main street, including the heart-warming simplicity which does tasty stew-type dishes and cheap Galician favourites.

### Lugo *p382, map p383*

Lugo's tapas trail centres on two streets; Rúa Nova and Rúa da Cruz. Most of these bars give a small free tapa with each drink.

**¶¶¶ La Barra**, C San Marcos 27, T982 252 920. A sleek, stylish seafood restaurant widely considered Lugo's best. It's decorated in executive style; dishes such as *rodaballo* (turbot) or *kokotxas* (hake cheeks in sauce) hover around the €20 mark.

**¶¶¶ Restaurante España**, Rúa Teatro 10, T982 242 717. This modern restaurant serves gourmet Galician food. The menu is short and full of quality, with dishes like beef carpaccio or monkfish medallions on ratatouille well presented and delicious. Out the front is a popular bar for coffee or *pinchos*, with parchment lamps, and tables stretching as far as the eye can see.

**¶¶ A Nosa Terra**, Rúa Nova 8, T982 229 235. A great place to eat, this is a spot to devour tasty raciones in an atmospheric old wine cellar, beautifully spruce in stone and wood. Out the front is a busy and excellent tapas bar; the *pinchos* are very tasty, there's a quaffable house Rioja, and the walls decorated with wood carvings of Galician poets and quotations from them.

**¶¶ Bodegas do San Vicente**, Rúa Nova 6, T982 253 318. This low, small and atmospheric spot has bags of character, which is why you'll usually wait for a table. The boss is always chopping away at something at the front counter, be it hams, cheeses, or *chorizos*, which are served in the traditional manner on greaseproof paper. At the front are some barrels where people socialize with a glass of wine.

**¶¶ Campos**, Rúa Nova 4, T982 229 743. A top range of seafood is available at this place, which does a *menú* for €14.50, but also has got a very high reputation for its meats; the game, when in season, is a must. Hospitable and popular, and shortly to be enlarged.

**¶ Bodegón El Museo**, Rúa Nova 21, T982 253 351. Opposite the museum, this traditional bar is run by a hospitable Galician couple and is gloriously untrendy, with wooden beams and local folk enjoying the cheap wine. Out the back are tables where there are incredibly cheap *raciones* served; the house specialty is *pulpo* (octopus), which is absolutely delicious and only €7.

**¶ El Castillo**, Praza do Campo Castelo 14. This attractive café and bar is an appealing spot for a coffee near the walls. It also does cheap and tasty food, ranging from good *bocadillos* to a set lunch for €8.

## ♠ Bars and clubs

**Lugo** *p382, map p383*
Lugo's lively and late bar scene is centred
in the small streets around the cathedral
and around Rúa de Cruz.
**Anagrama**, Praza Alférez Provisional 5.
A lively bar by the side of the cathedral
with some very cool interior pseudo-
classical design. Open nightly until late.
**Carpe Noctem**, Rúa Dois Clérigos 17.
Atmospheric bar in the cathedral zone, one of
the better bars in Lugo. Sleek modern chrome
decoration, a good range of people and a
variety of music. Open Thu-Sat from 2300.
**Jazz and Beer**, Rúa Obispo Basulto 2, T982
250 951. This intimate and comfortable bar
is a Lugo favourite for an after-dinner *copa*.
With mellow music, friendly service, and
well-mixed drinks, it's a very likeable spot.
**Medievo**, Rúa Catedral 14, T982 242 021.
One of Lugo's most-frequented late-night
bars, this is a place of 2 halves. Downstairs,
the medieval decoration of armour, shields,
and the like belies a friendly bar dishing out
popcorn and jelly beans with drinks and
coffee. Upstairs is where the music is;
it tends to fill up after 0200 at weekends.

## ● Entertainment

**Lugo** *p382, map p383*
**Cineplex Yelmo**, Praza Viana do
Castelo 3, T982 217 986.

## ● Shopping

**Lugo** *p382, map p383*
**Books** There are 2 good bookshops on
Rúa Bispo Aguirre: **Aguirre**, at No 8,
T982 220 336, with a good selection of
maps; and **La Voz de la Verdad**, at No 17.

## ● Transport

**Lugo** *p382, map p383*
**Bus**
Lugo's bus station is conveniently located
just outside the walls near the Praza Maior;
there are services to the other Galician
cities and all over Northern Spain.
   Within Galicia, there are buses to
**A Coruña** (roughly hourly, 1 hr-1 hr
30 mins, €7.40), 4 to **Ferrol**, 8 to **Ourense**
(2 hrs, €6.80), 10 to **Santiago** (2 hrs
15 mins, €9.71), 5-6 to **Viveiro** and the
north coast, 6 to **Ribadeo**, and 1 to **Vilalba**.
   There are 8-10 services eastwards to
**Ponferrada** (€7, 1 hr 30 mins), some going
via Sarria. There's 1 bus a day to **Salamanca**
(5 hrs 30 mins, €17.86) via Zamora, one
night bus to **Barcelona** (10 hrs, €52.52)
via Zaragoza, 6-8 to **Madrid** (5 hrs 30 mins,
from €29.53), and 4 to **Gijón** and **Oviedo**
(5-6 hrs, €16.83) via the Asturian coast.

**Train**
The train station isn't too far away from
the eastern side of the old town.
   There's an overnight train to **Madrid**
(9 hrs, €47.50), 3 a day to **A Coruña** (2 hrs,
€5.75), 4-5 to the rail junction of **Monforte**
(1 hr, €3.40), and 2 to **Barcelona** (14-15 hrs,
from €46). You can buy tickets at a handy
**RENFE** office in a little arcade off the Praza
Maior, next to the tourist office.

## ● Directory

**Lugo** *p382, map p383*
**Internet** CiberMania, at Camiño Real 143,
1100-1400, 1600-0100, €1.20 per hr.
**Post office** Lugo's main post office is
in the old town on Rúa San Pedro
near the Praza Maior

# Santiago de Compostela

→ *Phone code: 981. Colour map 1, B2. Population: 92,919.*
"The true capital of Spain" Cees Nooteboom, Roads to Santiago
*Archaeologists in the ninth century weren't known for their academic rigour, so when a
tomb was discovered here at that time it was rather staggeringly concluded to be that of
the apostle Santiago, or Saint James. Christianity was in bullish mode, and the spot
grew into the major pilgrimage destination in Europe as people walked thousands of
miles to pay their respects, reduce their time in purgatory, or atone for their crimes.*

*The city has transcended its dubious beginnings to become one of the most magical cities in Spain, its cathedral the undisputed highlight of a superb architectural ensemble of mossy granite buildings and narrow pedestrian lanes. Simply walking the streets is a pleasure (even in the rain), particularly Rúa Vilar, Rúa Nova and the streets around the university.*

*The late 20th century saw a massive revival of the pilgrimage tradition and Santiago is today a flourishing, happy place, seat of the Galician parliament and a lively student centre. Don't come for a suntan, though; HV Morton accurately if unkindly described the city as a "medieval aquarium", but the regular rain can add to the character of the place, at least for the first three days or so.* ➤➤ *For Sleeping, Eating and other listings, see pages 394-397.*

## Ins and outs

**Getting there** The traditional and now increasingly popular way to get to Santiago is a five-week walk from the French Pyrenees, but there are ways to cheat. If flying, for example, **Ryanair** runs a daily service from London Stansted to Santiago's airport (SCQ), situated 11 km east of town in Lavacolla. Ryanair also serve the city from Liverpool, East Midlands, Rome, and Frankfurt Hahn. There are also daily flights from London run by **BA/Iberia**, as well as frequent internal connections, and flights to other European destinations including Brussels and Amsterdam. Buses run from the airport to the corner of Rúa de República de El Salvador and Rúa do Xeneral Pardiñas, a couple of blocks southwest of Praza de Galicia. Another bus runs from Praza de Galicia to coincide with Ryanair flights. Santiago is well served by interurban buses. The bus station is a 20-minute walk northeast of the centre. Bus No 5 and C5 run there from Praza de Galicia via Rúa da Virxe da Cerca. If arriving by bus, head up the hill directly opposite the bus station café and turn left at the big intersection. The train station is south of the centre, about a 15-minute walk down Rúa de Hórreo (off Praza Galicia). There are trains to the rest of Galicia and Spain. ➤➤ *See also Transport, page 397.*

**Getting around** The interesting bits of town are mostly very close together. The main places you'll need public transport to access are the airport and the bus station.

**Best time to visit** During summer Santiago is thronged with tourists and pilgrims; if you don't mind that, this can be the best time to be there. It rains slightly less, the old town is buzzing, and there's the fiesta of Santiago on 25 July. If you're prepared to get wet, spring and autumn are good times to visit; there are fewer people, accommodation prices are down, and the university is in session, guaranteeing rampant nightlife until dawn.

**Tourist information** Santiago has several tourist information offices. The three most useful are the **municipal office** ① *Rúa do Vilar 63, T981 555 129, Mon-Fri 1000-1400, 1600-1900, Sat 1100-1400, 1700-1900, Sun 1100-1400*; the **Galician regional office** ① *Rúa do Vilar 43, T981 584 081, a few doors up, and a **kiosk** ① Praza de Galicia, T981 584 400, Mon-Sat 1000-1400, 1600-1900*. A two-hour guided walk (in Spanish) leaves daily from the Banco de España on the Praza das Platerías. It costs €8 (free for under 12s) and leaves at 1200. There's an additional tour at 1800 from Apr to mid-Oct. There's also an information office at the airport. Galicia's tourist board, **Turgalicia**, has upped its act in recent years, and publishes useful booklets and brochures. Their website, www.turgalicia.es, is also worth a browse.

The **pilgrim office** ① *Rúa do Vilar 1, Easter-Oct 0900-2100, Nov-Easter 1000-1900*, is around the corner from the cathedral. This is where you can get your pilgrim passports examined and pick up the Compostela certificate. The process has been streamlined somewhat, but there are still long queues in summer.

● *For information on the practicalities of walking the Camino de Santiago and the history of the pilgrimage, see pages 52 and 388.*

## Saint James and the Camino de Santiago

The patron saint of Spain is one of the most revered of figures in the country, probably coming a close second behind Mary, and a good way ahead of Christ. St James, or Santiago, was the son of Zebedee, brother of the apostle John, and a fisherman who gave up his nets to follow Christ. In AD 44 he was martyred at swordpoint by King Herod Agrippa. Several centuries later, a small west European kingdom flexing its Christian muscles, was in need of a holy warrior.

We move to Galicia, and a spot near the end of the world, Finisterre. In the early ninth century, 800 years after James was martyred and thousands of miles away, a shepherd is guided by an angel and stars to a tomb in the woods at a place now called Compostela. The local bishop, evidently not a man to reserve judgement, deemed it to be Saint James himself. The news spread fast, and gave the Christians new faith for their fight against the Moors. Even handier than faith on a muddy battlefield is a back-from-the-dead apostle on a white charger, and Santiago obliged. He brutally slew hundreds of hapless Muslims in battle, winning himself the nickname Matamoros, or slayer of Moors.

All very well, but how and why was his body in Spain in the first place? He had, after all, been killed in Caesarea. But tradition, however historically debatable, has it that he preached in Spain at some point, and the Virgin Mary is said to have appeared to him in Zaragoza (at the time called Caesarea too; a possible source of the confusion). James went back to the Holy Land with a few keen Spanish converts. After his death the followers rescued his body and set forth for home with it. Not experts in boat buying, they selected a stone yacht, but with the saint on board, they managed to navigate it to the Pillars of Hercules and around to Galicia. Along the way, the saint performed a miracle, saving a gentleman whose panicked horse had dashed headlong into the sea with him in the saddle. Man and horse rose from the seabed safe and sound; some traditions hold that they were covered in scallop shells; this became the apostle's symbol. His followers landed near Padrón and requested oxen from the local pagan queen so that they could transport the body inland. In mockery, she gave them a pair of ferocious bulls, but the apostle intervened and transformed them into docile beasts, thus converting the

### Background

Relics have been a big deal in Christendom since the early Middle Ages, and especially in Spain. Christ physically ascended into heaven, and the Virgin was bodily assumed there too. With the big two out of the question, the apostles were the next best thing. However, whether you believe that the bones of Saint James are, or were ever, under the altar of the cathedral (see box, above) is beside the point; the city has transcended its origins completely, as the number of atheist pilgrims trudging towards it attests.

After the discovery of the tomb in the early 9th century, Santiago's PR people did a good job. Pilgrims soon began flooding in, and the city had achieved such prosperity by 968 that it was sacked by none other than the Vikings, who were never averse to a long voyage for a bit of plunder. Some 29 years later Santiago had another bad day, when Al-Manzur (see box, page 444) came from the south and sacked it again. Legend says that an old monk was praying by the tomb of Saint James while chaos reigned around. The Moorish warlord himself burst in and was so impressed by the old man's courage that he swore on his honour to safeguard the tomb and the monk from all harm.

Although the city was razed to the ground, Santiago continued to flourish as Saint James became a sort of patron-cum-field marshal of the Reconquista. Pilgrims

amazed queen. After the long journey, Santiago's loyal companions buried him and he was conveniently forgotten until the shepherd's discovery centuries later.

**The pilgrims** News that an apostle's tomb was in Christian Galicia travelled fast. A church was built and granted a perpetual *voto*, a tax payable by every inhabitant of Spain; this was levied until the 19th century. Pilgrims began to make the journey to Galicia to venerate the saint's remains. Most of the early pilgrims were from France, and the main route across Northern Spain came to be known as the *Camino Francés* (French way). Waystations for pilgrims were set up, and French settlers and monks became a significant presence in the towns and villages along the route, and continued to be so; many of the churches and cathedrals are based on models from France. In the 12th century a French monk, Aimery Picaud, wrote the Codex Calixtinus, part of which was an entertaining guidebook for pilgrims making the journey to Santiago; the dangers mentioned include robbers, con-artists and wolves.

The pilgrimage became phenomenally popular, helped along by the Pope's declaration that all pilgrims to Santiago would have their time in Purgatory halved; if they went on a Holy Year (when the feast of St James, 25 July, falls on a Sunday) they would get a full remission (plenary indulgence). They came from all over Europe; some by boat (Chaucer's Wife of Bath made the journey), some walking for more than a year. At its peak, some half a million pilgrims arrived annually in Santiago, which rapidly became a flourishing city.

The pilgrimage declined in the 19th century, although there was a brief revival when the bones of Santiago, missing for a couple of centuries, were rediscovered (it was proved because a fragment of Santiago's skull from Pistoia in Italy fit exactly into a handy notch in the Compostela skull) and by the mid-20th century only a handful of people were following the route, whose pilgrim hostels had long since disappeared.

In the late 20th century there was a surprising revival in the pilgrimage, whose popularity has continued to grow. In the most recent Holy Year (2004; the next is 2010) over 170,000 people made the journey at least in part, and many hundreds of thousands more visited Santiago.

came from across Europe and the cathedral was constructed to receive them in appropriate style; they used to bed down for the night in its interior. Constant architectural modifications followed from Santiago's swelling coffers, which also paid for the 40-something churches in the small city. This restructuring reached its peak in the 17th and early 18th centuries, from which period most of the granite-built centre that exists today dates. A rapid decline followed as pilgrimage waned and A Coruña thrived at Santiago's expense. The French occupied Santiago during the Napoleonic Wars, and carried off a large amount of plunder.

The late 20th century brought a rapid revival as the age of tourism descended on Spain with bells on. Santiago is high on many visitors' lists and, unexpectedly, the Camino itself is now phenomenally popular again, with pilgrims of all creeds making the journey in whole or part on foot or bicycle saddle. Although A Coruña remains the provincial capital, Santiago is the seat of the Xunta (semi-autonomous Galician government established in 1982), which has provided a further boost to the town's economy. The recent Holy Year in 2004 saw a flood of visitors to the city; with more than a million in town on the feast day of Santiago, this ancient pilgrimage city is definitely back in the big time.

# Santiago de Compostela

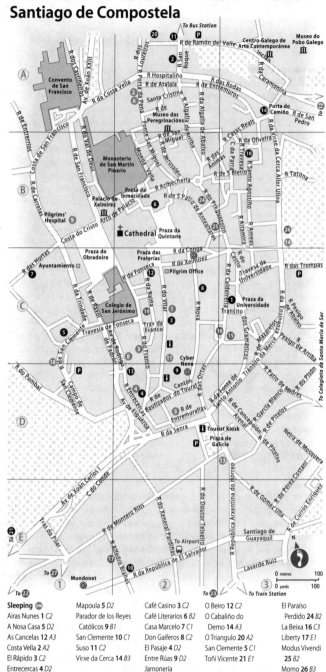

**Sleeping** 
Airas Nunes **1** *C2*
A Nosa Casa **5** *D2*
As Cancelas **12** *A3*
Costa Vella **2** *A2*
El Rápido **3** *C2*
Entrecercas **4** *D2*
Hesperia
  Compostela **13** *D3*
Hospedaje Mera **6** *A2*
Hostal 25 de Julio **8** *C2*

Mapoula **5** *D2*
Parador de los Reyes
  Católicos **9** *B1*
San Clemente **10** *C1*
Suso **11** *C2*
Virxe da Cerca **14** *B3*

**Eating** 
Asesino **1** *C3*
Belgo **18** *B3*
Cachimba **2** *A2*

Café Casino **3** *C2*
Café Literarios **6** *B2*
Casa Marcelo **7** *C1*
Don Gaiferos **8** *C2*
El Pasaje **4** *D2*
Entre Rúas **9** *D2*
Jamonería
  Ferro **10** *E2*
La Bodeguilla de
  San Roque **11** *A2*
Marte **13** *D2*

O Beiro **12** *C2*
O Cabaliño do
  Demo **14** *A3*
O Triangulo **20** *A2*
San Clemente **5** *C1*
Toñi Vicente **21** *E1*

**Bars & clubs** 
Alamique **22** *E1*
A Novena Porta **15** *C3*
Cervecería Jolgarria **23** *E3*

El Paraíso
  Perdido **24** *B2*
La Beixa **16** *C3*
Liberty **17** *E1*
Modus Vivendi
  **25** *B2*
Momo **26** *B3*
N-VI **27** *E1*
Séptimo Cielo
  **19** *C2*

# Cathedral and around

*① Cathedral 1000-2030, except during Mass; entry at these times is via the Praza das Praterías only. There's a Mass for pilgrims daily at 1200, and evening Mass at 1930; both last for about 45 mins. Admission is free, apart from the museum (see below).*

Santiago's past, present and future is wrapped up in its cathedral and its emblematic grey towers. Pilgrims trudge for weeks to reach it, many tourists visit Galicia specifically to see it, and locals go to mass and confession in it as part of their day-to-day lives.

While the original Romanesque interior is superbly preserved, what first greets most visitors is the western façade and its twin towers. Granite is the perfect stone to express a more sober face of Spanish Baroque; its stern colour renders the style epic rather than whimsical, and it's hard enough to chisel that masons concentrated on broader, nobler lines rather than intricacy. The façade rises high above the square, the moss-stained stone towers (which incorporate the original Romanesque ones) seem to say 'Heaven this way'. The façade was added in the 18th century and is reached by a complex double staircase that predates it.

The plaza that it dominates, named **Obradoiro**, is the main gateway to the cathedral, but it's worth strolling around the building before you enter. Walking clockwise, you pass the façade of the Romanesque **Palacio de Xelmírez**, which adjoins it and forms part of the cathedral museum. Turning the corner, you emerge in the **Praza da Inmaculada**, where the north façade is a slightly underwhelming 18th-century Baroque construction that replaced the earlier Romanesque portal, which, from fragments of stone and textual descriptions, was superb. It faces the **Monasterio de San Martín Pinario**, with a huge façade that's wasted next to this magnificent cathedral; this part of it is now a student residence. The plaza used to be known as the Azabachería; this is where craftsmen made and sold rosaries made of jet (*azabache*) to the arriving pilgrims.

Continuing around, the **Praza da Quintana** is a curious space, with an upper and lower half; these are known as the halves of the living (the top) and the dead (below); the area used to be a cemetery. A plaque here is dedicated to the Literary Batallion, a corps of student volunteers who fought in the French in the Napoleonic wars. The portal on this side is known as the Puerta Santa, or holy door. It is only opened on the feast day of Santiago (25 July) in a Holy Year (ie a year when this date falls on a Sunday). The façade is 17th century, but contains figures salvaged from the Romanesque stone choir. The 18th-century clocktower soars over the square.

The last square on the circuit is **Praza das Praterías**, with an entrance to the cathedral through an original portal, the oldest that remains, with scenes from the life of Christ.

Come back to the western façade and ascend the complex staircase. Once through the Baroque doorway, you're confronted with the original Romanesque façade, the **Pórtico de la Gloria**. Built 1168-1188 by a man named Master Mateo, it is one of the finest pieces of sculpture in Spain, and a fitting welcome for weary pilgrims. Three doorless arches are intricately carved with Biblical scenes; a superb last Judgement on the right, and variously interpreted Old Testament scenes on the left. In the centre Santiago himself sits under Christ and the Evangelists, who are surrounded by elders of the Apocalypse playing medieval musical instruments.

Upon entering the church, pilgrims queue to touch the pillar by the feet of Santiago; over the centuries five clear finger marks have been worn in the stone. On the other side of the pillar, carved with the Tree of Jesse, many then bump heads with the figure of Master Mateo, hoping that some of his genius will rub off. Many mistakenly butt the head under Santiago's feet; this is in fact Samson; Master Mateo faces into the church.

The interior itself is still attractively Romanesque in the main. High barrel vaulting and the lack of a *coro* in the centre of the nave give an excellent perspective down the church, although it's a pity the original stone *coro* by Master Mateo was destroyed in the early 17th century to make way for a wooden one that is no longer there either (the stone one has been re-assembled in the cathedral museum, the wooden one in the Monasterio de San Martín Pinario).

The massive altar is over-ornate and features some rather out-of-place cherubs on the *baldacchino* (baldachin), which is topped by an image of Santiago in Moor-killing mode; the whole thing belongs on a circus caravan. Above in the cupola is the eye-in-triangle symbol of the all-seeing God. Behind the altar is the image of Santiago himself. Pilgrims ascend behind the statue and give it an *abrazo* (embrace); this, a kiss to the back of his head, and a confession below, was the symbolic end to the pilgrimage.

On special occasions (which seem to be becoming more and more frequent), a large silver censer (*botafumeiro*) is hung from the ceiling at the crossing and slowly swung by eight men until it covers the whole length of the transept and reaches frightening velocities, diffusing incense and sparks all the while. It's a fantastic and unnerving thing to see, and it's only flown off twice (once in a mass celebrated for Catherine of Aragón to wish her luck on her journey to wed Henry VIII in England; it was considered a bad omen, as it proved to be).

## Cathedral museum

① *Mon-Sat 1000-1330, 1600-1830, Jun-Sep 1000-1400, 1600-1930, Sun 1100-1400, €5.*
Back in the Praza do Obradoiro, investigate the Romanesque **crypt** at the base of the main staircase. One of the three sections of the cathedral museum, it was built by Master Mateo to support the weight of his Romanesque façade above; it's an interesting space dominated by a sturdy loadbearing pillar. There are reproductions of some of the musical instruments that appear on the façade above, as well as some processional crosses and, more interestingly, the 14th-century battle-horn of Alfonso XI, made from an elephant's tusk.

The main section of the museum is accessed from the cathedral or the Praza do Obradoiro. Entering from the square, the first rooms contain fragments of Romanesque sculpture, including one of the *Punishment of the Damned*, with two naked sinners having their sensitive bits eaten by beasts. The highlight of this section is the re-construction of the stone **coro** by Master Mateo, which must have looked superb in the cathedral until it was destroyed in 1603 to make way for a wooden one. Some granite slabs elegantly painted in *mudéjar* style are also noteworthy. Upstairs, there's a range of religious sculpture in both polychrome wood and granite, including a sensitive San Sebastián in gold shorts and a fine *Last Judgement*, with an hirsute San Miguel presiding over the psychostasis (weighing of souls). There's also a wooden relief of the bells of the original church being carried back from Córdoba, where they had been taken after Al-Manzur sacked the city. They were triumphantly reclaimed during the Reconquista, although, underwhelmingly, they were allegedly found in a pantry, being used to hold olive oil. A 10th-century Moorish dirham coin is another item of interest.

The **cloister** is absolutely massive in scale, and has a slightly neglected feel. The star vaulting is ornate Gothic and the arches heavily elegant. There are several tombs and fragments around, as well as some large, 18th-century bells. A small **library** contains one of the ex-*botafumeiros* (see above), and there are some mediocre tapestries; but don't despair, there are some better ones upstairs, especially three depicting the life of Achilles by Rubens. Others are factory-made ones depicting rural life, some based on Goya cartoons.

Between the cloister and the cathedral is the **treasury**, a rather vulgar display of wealth donated by various bigwigs; the collection includes a goblet that belonged to Marshal Pétain. Next to this is the **Panteón**, which contains tombs of various kings of León and other nobles. There's also an immense *retablo* holding the cathedral's impressive collection of relics; these include the head of the other apostle James, the Lesser (Alpheus), encased in a gilt bust, and a spine from the crown of thorns.

The other section of the museum, on the other side of the cathedral façade, is the **Palacio de Xelmírez**, interesting for being a Romanesque civil building (it was built as an archbishop's residence), although it was heavily modified in the 16th century. Features of it include an attractive patio and large kitchen and two beautiful halls.

The other buildings on the Praza do Obradoiro are also interesting. To the left as you face the cathedral is the massive **Pilgrims' Hospital**, built by Fernando and Isabel, the Catholic Monarchs. Now a *parador*, pilgrims still have the right to three days' worth of free meals here on presentation of their *compostela* (see box, page 52). The meals are served in a canteen around the back, but the food's still pretty nice. The hotel has four pretty courtyards named after the evangelists and several elegant halls. Access is limited if you aren't a guest, but the bits you are allowed to wander around are worthwhile.

Opposite the cathedral, the **Ayuntamiento**, is housed in an attractive neoclassical building, while the fourth side, opposite the *parador*, is partly taken up by the **Colegio de San Jerónimo**, a 15th-century structure now part of the university, with a nice little patio and a portal that looks distinctly Romanesque; perhaps the architects didn't want to clash with the Pórtico de la Gloria of the cathedral. Next to it, the **Colegio de Santiago Alfeo** is a Renaissance construction used by the local government.

## Monasterio de San Martín Pinario and around

North of the cathedral, the **San Martín Pinario monastery** ① *daily 1000-1400, 1600-1800, €2* is half restricted to students, but you can enter the church and museum from the back. The door is high and rather overbearing; it's reached via an attractive downward staircase. The interior is lofty and bare, with a massive dome. In contrast to the sober architectural lines is the huge altarpiece, described by the 19th-century traveller Richard Ford: "In the *retablo*, of vilest Churrigueresque, Santiago and San Martín ride together in a fricasee of gilt gingerbread."

Similarly decorative *retablos* decorate the side chapels. Of more interest is the *coro* behind the altar; see if you can find the hidden door that the monks used to enter through. The museum has some old printing presses, an interesting old pharmacy and the wooden choir from the cathedral. There's also a multimedia exhibition on Galicia.

Near to the monastery is the **Convento de San Francisco**, founded by Saint Francis when he made the pilgrimage here in the early 13th century, and the newish **Museo das Peregrinacións** ① *Tue-Fri 1000-2000, Sat 1030-1330, 1700-2000, Sun 1030-1330, €2.40*, a three-floor display about the pilgrimage to Santiago, images and iconography of the saint, the Pórtico de la Gloria, and the medieval life of the town. It's reasonably interesting, more so if you're a pilgrim, but ducks a few crucial Saint James issues.

## Around Porta do Camino

At the eastern end of town, opposite the Porta do Camino where pilgrims enter the city, are two more museums. The **Museo do Pobo Galego** ① *Tue-Sat 1000-1400, 1600-2000, Sun 1100-1400, free*, was originally founded by Saint Dominic as a monastery. Inside is a monumental cloister and many ethnographic exhibits relating to Galician life. It's worth a look just for the architecture, including a stunning spiral staircase. There's also a chapel where the poet Rosalía de Castro is buried. Next to the museum, the **Centro Galego de Arte Contemporánea** ① *Tue-Sun 1100-2000, free*, is a modern building whose attractive white spaces provide a break from the timeworn granite. Exhibitions are of a high international standard. There's also a bookshop and café.

## Colegiata de Santa María de Sar

The Colegiata de Santa María de Sar is a Romanesque church a 15-minute walk south of the centre. Built in the 12th century, on insecure ground, it is remarkable chiefly for the alarming lean its interior columns; after the Lisbon earthquake of 1755, massive buttresses had to be added. There's a small **museum** ① *Mon-Sat 1000-1300, 1600-1900, €0.60*, with a tiny bit of Saint Peter in a reliquary, and a cloister, of which one side survives with carvings attributed to Master Mateo. To get there from the Rúa Fonte de San Antonio off Praza de Galicia, take the second right down Rúa Patio de Madres and follow it down the hill; the church is on your right after the railway bridge.

**Santiago de Compostela** *p386, map p390*
There are literally dozens of places to stay in
Santiago, with plenty in the budget range to
cater for the pilgrim traffic. Many restaurants
in the centre have a few cheap rooms too.
Rooms can be hard to find in summer, but
it's just a matter of persistence.

**LL Parador de los Reyes Católicos**, Praza do
Obradoiro 1, T981 582 200, www.parador.es,
santiago@parador.es. Although beyond the
budgets of many 21st-century peregrines,
the pilgrims' hostel built by the Catholic
monarchs is a luxurious place to lie up and by
far the city's most atmospheric place to stay.
Built around 4 beautiful courtyards, it's still
worth splashing out at €195 a double. It's on
the cathedral square, and the rooms lack
nothing of the class of the building.

**L Hesperia Compostela**, Rúa Hórreo 1, T981
585 700, www.hesperia-compostela.com.
This large and dignified hotel occupies a
noble old building just off the Praza de
Galicia. It's decorated in classically weighty
Spanish period style. The rooms are
comfortable but not overly memorable;
some seem to have been more recently
renovated than others.

**AL Virxe da Cerca**, Rúa Virxe da Cerca 27,
T981 569 350, www.pousadasde
compostela.com. This lovely old stone
building on the road circling Santiago's old
town has been converted into this stylish and
characterful hotel. While the rooms are as
well equipped as in any big hotel, there's a
more enchanting feel here, particularly
around the delightful central patio.

**B Costa Vella**, Porta da Peña 17, T981 569
530, www.costavella.com. This smart,
comfortable hotel is one of the best in this
price range. It's got a romantic feel, not least
for its fantastic garden studded with apple
and lemon trees and offering fantastic views.
Some of the rooms overlook it (they are
slightly more expensive); the interior decor is
stylish and beautiful, and the welcome from
the owners is genuine. Recommended.

**B Hotel Airas Nunes**, Rúa do Vilar 17, T981
569 350, www.pousadasdecompostela.com.
Right in the thick of things, this modern and
stylish hotel has excellent facilities and plenty
of attractive charm in a 17th-century
building. Rooms are on the small side but

comfortable and the location is hard to
better. Top end of this price category.

**B Hotel San Clemente**, Rúa San Clemente
28, T981 569 260, www.pousadasde
compostela.com. An excellent option
located in the old town below and close to
the cathedral. The charm of the old house
still shines through, but the rooms are
equipped to modern standards with good
if small bathrooms and internet sockets.

**C Hostal 25 de Julio**, Av Rodrigo de Padrón 4,
T981 582 295, www.25dejulio.com. This
intimate little luxury *pensión* is a very
charming choice. It's run by *simpático*
management with an aesthetic eye. The
rooms abound in good taste and are soft on
mind and body. There's disabled access and
an alluring little café too. Recommended.

**C Hotel Entrecercas**, Rúa Entrecercas 11,
T981 571 151, F981 571 112. A charming
little hotel that's central but tucked away
from the busier parts. It's got charm as well
as courteous and helpful management.
Breakfast included. Underground
parking close by. Recommmended.

**E A Nosa Casa**, Rúa Entremurallas 9, T981
585 926, www.anosacasa.com. One of 2
worthwhile lodging options on this narrow
little street in the old town near Praza de
Galicia. They're not related, but they both
offer a warm welcome and very good
rooms, a budget traveller's dream.
It's hard to pick between them for
value and comfort. Recommended.

**E Mapoula**, Rúa Entremurallas 10, T981 580
124, F981 584 089. The second of the 2
worthwhile lodging options on this street
(see **A Nosa Casa**, above). The **Mapoula** is
very slightly pricier and has somewhat
newer bathrooms. Recommended.

**E Suso**, Rúa Vilar 65, T981 586 611.
This central pilgrims' favourite is handy
for everything in town. Its en suite
rooms are very good value year-round
(it's worth getting here early to avoid
disappointment) and there's a friendly
vibe from management and the happy
walkers at journey's end (unlike the pilgrims
of yesteryear, they don't have to turn around
and walk back home again too!).

**F El Rápido**, Rúa Franco 22, T981 584 983.
Foolishly cheap rooms above a restaurant in

seafood central. The en suite bathrooms are basic; also rooms with shared bath available. The beds are fine for this price and location.
**F Hospedaje Mera**, Porta da Pena 15, T981 583 867. This quiet and cheap option is on a pedestrian street in the centre of town. Facilities are basic – no towels – but some rooms have balconies and views, and it's in a great location.

## Camping
**As Cancelas**, T981 580 266. A good campsite, frequently served by city bus No 9. There's a shop and a pool. Open year-round.
**Ciudad de Vacaciones**, Monte do Gozo, Ctra Aeropuerto s/n, T981 558 942. A massive summer-only campsite on the hill 2 km east of town with regular public transport and all facilities including a pool.

## ● Eating

**Santiago de Compostela** *p386, map p390*
Seafood is the thing to eat in Santiago, as indeed in much of Galicia. One of the main streets, **Rúa Franco**, is something of a tourist trap (although locals eat here too); prices are high and quality variable. Scallops (*vieiras*) are an obvious choice, served in a bacon and onion sauce, but they're expensive at about €6 per scallop. *Percebes* are also popular, as are *cigalas* (a word to the wise: *cigalas* are expensive and menus often somewhat misleadingly list the price per 100g; 6 chubby *cigalas* can weigh well over 500g). The *Tarta de Santiago* is an almond cake often engraved with a sword; patisseries along Rúa Franco give out free morsels to taste.
**TTT Casa Marcelo**, Rúa das Hortas 3, T981 558 850. This little gourmet's paradise is on one of Santiago's most picturesque streets just below the Praza do Obradoiro. You won't spend hours browsing the menu, for it's *table d'hôte* only. The feast on offer changes daily, but consists of 5-6 courses full of delicate flavours for €38.52. Open Wed-Sat. Recommended.
**TTT Don Gaiferos**, Rúa Nova 23, T981 583 894. A dark and moody but modern place that offers plenty of choice of the finest Galician produce. Excellent daily seafood specials, but you might also be tempted by the meat on offer; the *tournedos* are delicious, and the steak tartare just as it should be. Mains are €15-22; eschew the pricey set menu.

**TTT El Pasaje**, Rúa Franco 54, T981 557 081. A class above the other fish restaurants on this street, this is at the open end near the Alameda and has room for 3 or 4 outdoor tables. The seafood is sublime, though expensive. The fish cooked *a la parrilla* is memorable, and there's a fine range of wine to accompany it. The *zamburiñas* (mini-scallops) make a fine appetizer. Be aware of the price/weight equation. Recommended.
**TTT Toñi Vicente**, Av Rosalía de Castro 24, T981 594 100. Galician nouvelle cuisine is the order of the day at this top restaurant. The dishes are elaborately decorative and subtle, with a range of exotic seafood-based salads, delicious lampreys available in season, and superbly delicate fish creations. Rated by foodies as Galicia's finest restaurant. Closed Sun.
**TT Asesino**, Praza Universidad 16, T981 581 568. Almost unmarked, this restaurant opposite the university opens when it chooses, and offers excellent homestyle food accompanied by appropriately familiar bric-a-brac decor. Recommended.
**TT Marte**, Av Rodrigo de Padrón 11, T981 584 905. Cops usually know where to eat well at sensible prices, so it's a good sign that this no-nonsense family-run place is much patronized by the police station opposite. The *menú del día* is superb value for €15 (there's an even cheaper one for €9) and doesn't hold back on the seafood; there's turbot, monkfish and plenty more. There's a terrace outside too. Top value. Recommended.
**TT O Beiro**, Rúa da Raíña 3, T981 581 370. This upmarket *vinoteca* is the place to work your way through an impromptu tasting session. The attractive decor – flagstones, low wood-beamed ceiling – lives up to its fantastic selection of *gallego* wines and other local produce. There's a restaurant upstairs too.
**TT San Clemente**, Rúa San Clemente 6, T981 565 426. This is a great place to eat when the sun is shining. The colourful awnings conceal tables where the service and seafood are exemplary and pretty good value. The *cigalas* are excellent indeed.
**T Belgo**, Rúa Travesa 22, T981 578 235. The owners of this likeable spot is run by folk that have their own mussel farm – and that is all they serve, they are delicious. It's also a good spot for a drink. Last Thu of every month is a promotion night, with free dishes of their black and orange offerings.

**Entre Rúas**, Ruela de Entreruas 2. An enchanting terrace in a minute hidden square, this is the place to conduct an illicit affair, at least when the sun's shining. It's a great spot for a drink; there's also a very acceptable *menú del día* for €8.

**Jamonería Ferro**, Rúa República de El Salvador 20, T981 592 399. A deli that's also a popular bar, with free nibbles and some good *raciones*, especially of the hammy kind.

**La Bodeguilla de San Roque**, Rúa San Roque 13, T981 564 379. A good bar, popular with students for its cheap and filling *raciones*. These are best eaten in the pretty upstairs *comedor* which also serves up a value-packed *menú del día*.

**O Cabaliño do Demo**, Porta do Camiño s/n, T981 588 146. A welcoming veggie option with a wide variety of dishes (including some vegan options) and a relaxing vibe.

**O Triangulo**, Praciña das Penas 2, T981 577 181. Another sound veggie choice.

#### Cafés

There's nowhere better in town for a relaxing outdoor drink than the garden of the **Hotel Costa Vella** (see Sleeping above). Just watch out for apples falling into your drink.

**Cachimba**, Rúa San Roque 7, T981 566 505. This spot, marked by a pipe, is a popular meeting point for students and a good place to relax on a rainy day. The window is useful place to look for flat-share notices.

**Café Casino**, Rúa do Vilar 35, T981 577 503. This historic café is awash with 19th-century plushness. It's a massive space, beautiful, elegant and popular with young and old for evening coffee. Once you sink into those chairs you may be there for some time.

**Café Literarios**, Praza Quintana 1, T981 565 630. A great spot on this attractive and unusual square, named after the redoubtable student batallion of this granite city. Its still got an arty feel inside, while the terrace gazes over the architectural glories of the city.

newspaper *Compostelán* or *7 Días Santiago* for bar, club events and venues listings.

**Alamique**, Rúa Nova de Abaixo 17. A good bar for pre-dance drinking and chat, always reasonably busy and cheery.

**A Novena Porta**, Rúa Cardenal Payá 3. The 9th door is a modern and bright bar popular for evening drinks with white-collar Santiago folk.

**Cervecería Jolgarria**, Rúa da República Arxentina 41, T981 596 210. A cross between a fastfood restaurant and a student bar, this massive joint is a basic and popular place to start an evening's drinking in this lively zone.

**El Paraíso Perdido**, Rúa San Paio de Antealtares 3. This basement bar has an intriguing 'hell gate' entrance. Inside it's decorated with mosaïcs, and there's a chilled-out, buzzy, hippy-trippy atmosphere.

**La Beixa**, Rúa de Tras Salomé 3. A popular student haunt playing 70s music in a cosy and friendly environment.

**Liberty**, Rúa Alfredo Brañas 4, T981 599 181. Santiago's students don't get going until the wee hours, and neither does this large discoteca, which is busy even on weeknights and doesn't let up until well after dawn.

**Modus Vivendi**, Praza Feijóo 1, T981 576 109. Once a stable of sorts, you can still use the old horse trough as a table and see the old stone ramp down which they were once led. The dodgy-looking stone arches lend a medieval ambience.

**Momo**, Rúa da Virxe da Cerca. This massive bar on the edge of the old town comes equipped with its own street and zebra crossing! In summer the terrace opens – it's a fantastic spot to be, with great views.

**N-VI**, C Santiago del Estero s/n. It's rare that you get to drink in an underground car park, so take the opportunity. At the old-town end of Rúa Nova de Abaixo off Praza Roxa.

**Séptimo Cielo**, Rúa da Raíña 20. This late-opening bar near the cathedral plays Spanish chart hits to a cheery crowd. There's a good atmosphere and cheapish drinks.

## ⊙ Bars and clubs

**Santiago de Compostela** *p386, map p390*
The student nightlife kicks off around **Rúa Nova de Abaixos** near Praza Roxa; try some of the small bars in the arcades. They may look dead, but they'll spark up some time after midnight, even on weekdays. Get the free

## ⊙ Entertainment

**Santiago de Compostela** *p386, map p390*
**Auditorio de Galicia**, T981 552 290. North of town. Classical concerts and opera.

**Teatro Principal**, Rúa Nova 21, T981 586 521. A council-run venue for theatre and occasional cinema festivals.

**Sala Yago**, Rúa do Vilar 51, T981 589 288. Good value shows for €5; also a cinema.

Others include: **Cinesa Area Central**, Rúa Fontiñas, T902 333 231; **Cine Compostela**, Rúa Ramón Piñeiro 3, T981 560 342 and **Teatro Galán**, T981 585 166, www.teatrogalan.com.

## ✱ Festivals and events

**Santiago de Compostela** *p386, map p390*
**25 Jul** Santiago's main fiesta is the day of the Saint James himself. When this day falls on a Sun, it's known as a **Holy Year** (the next one is 2010). Apart from partying, there's a solemn mass attended by thousands, and a spectacular pyrotechnic display the night before.

## ○ Shopping

**Santiago de Compostela** *p386, map p390*
**Books** Librería Universitas, Rúa Fernando III el Santo 3, T981 592 438; **Librería San Pablo**, Rúa do Vilar 39.

**Food and drink** The Mercado de Abastos is a lively food market in the old town on Praza de Abastos. O Beiro, Rúa da Raiña 3, is a good place to buy (as well as drink) Galician wines.

**Gems** Santiago is a good place to buy *azabache* (jet), but beware of vendors near the cathedral who make a living preying on tourists.

## ⊖ Transport

**Santiago de Compostela** *p386, map p390*
Buy a copy of the newspaper *El Correo Gallego* for a complete list of transport times.

### Air
There's a daily **Ryanair** flight to London Stansted, as well as services to Liverpool, East Midlands, Frankfurt Hahn, and Roma. There are regular flights on mainstream airlines to **London**, **Brussels**, and **Amsterdam**, as well as internal ones to **Madrid** and **Barcelona** and, less frequently, **Bilbao** and **Sevilla**; there are also several flights to the **Canary Islands**. Buses connect the airport with the city centre and bus station, stopping at the corner of Av Xeneral Pardiñas and Rúa da República de El Salvador; they run approximately hourly. A separate Ryanair bus runs from Plaza Galicia to coincide with their flights.

### Bus
**Local** Within Galicia, buses run hourly to **A Coruña** (€4.15; via motorway 45 mins, via road 1 hr 20 mins), 3 a day travel to **Fisterra** and **Camariñas**. 8 buses go to **Lugo**, hourly ones to **Pontevedra** (45 mins, €4.85) and **Vigo**, and 7 to **Ourense**. Buses run hourly to **Ribeira**, and 6 times a day to **Vilagarcía**, **Cambados** and **O Grove**.

**Long distance** Services connect with **Bilbao** (3 daily, 11 hrs, €45.04), **Ponferrada** (5 daily, 3½-4 hrs, €16.72), **Madrid** (5-6 daily, 8-9 hrs, €36.42), **Oviedo** (6 a day, 5 hrs 30 mins, €26.54) and **Gijón**, **Burgos** (2 daily, 9 hrs, €32.29) and **Salamanca** (2 daily, 6 hrs 15 mins, €21.34) via **Zamora**, among other destinations.

### Car hire
Autos Brea, C Gómez Ulla 10, T981 562 670, is a reasonably central agency. There are several multinationals at the airport.

### Train
Trains run regularly to **A Coruña** (1 hr 10 mins, from €3.40), **Vigo** (1 hr 40 mins, from €5.20), and **Ourense** (6-8 a day, 1 hr 40 mins, from €6.30) ; there's also a sleeper and a day train to **Madrid** (8-9 hrs, €40.30).

## ❶ Directory

**Santiago de Compostela** *p386, map p390*
**Internet** Cyber Nova 50, Rúa Nova 50, €1.50 per hr. Mundonet, Rúa República de El Salvador 30, and Av de Coimbra 2, €1.50 per hr. Internet, Rúa do Xelmírez 19, from €1 per hr. **Laundry** Lavandeira, Av Rosalía de Castro 116, T981 942 110. A self-service laundromat with plenty of machines. **Medical services** The Hospital Xeral is fairly central on Rúa das Galeras, T981 950 000. **Police and emergencies** Dial 112 for an emergency; 092 contacts the municipal police. The handiest **police station** is on Av Rodrigo de Padrón around the corner from the post office. **Post office** The main post office is on Travesa de Fonseca a block from the cathedral. **Telephone** There's a *locutorio* on C Bautizados 15, but only use it for very quick calls, as they charge about 5 times the going rate. There are several better ones in the streets around Praza Roxa.

# Rías Altas → *Colour map 1, A2/3.*

*The north coast of Galicia, not as overdeveloped as the west coast, features some interesting fishing towns and a few cracking beaches. The inlets of the Rías Altas are deep, making perfect natural harbours and sheltered (if chilly) swimming spots. Of the two major ports on the north coast, Ferrol is an earthy industrial centre that makes few concessions to tourism, while A Coruña is a jewel set on a promontory with a harbour on one side, a great beach on the other and a lively seafood tapas scene in between. For violent cliffscapes, Garita de Herbeira is hard to beat.* ➠ *For Sleeping, Eating and other Listings, see pages 402-404.*

## Ribadeo 🖳🍴🛏 ➠ *pp402-404.*

→ *Colour map 1, A5.*
ⓘ *There's a tourist office in the centre where you can gather information on Galicia if just arriving from Asturias.*

Ribadeo faces its Asturian counterpart Castropol across the broad expanse of the inlet at the mouth of the river Eo; thus the town's name. It's a functional but pleasant place, with a waterside promenade by the harbour at the bottom of the steep streets leading down from the old centre. The views across to Asturias a mile away across the water are picturesque, and the modern bridge over the *ría* impressive despite the thundering traffic. Past the bridge there's a small fort, the **Forte de San Damián**, built to protect the town from seaward invasion. The old centre is pleasant too, with a good square with plenty of palm trees. There are many *indiano* houses, attractive structures built by Galicians returned from the Americas.

### West of Ribadeo
Along this first stretch of Galician coast are some of the region's best **beaches**, all within a 20-minute walk of the main road. **As Catedrais** (the cathedrals) is a pretty little stretch named for its spectacularly eroded cliffs and rocks lying in the water. It all but disappears at high tide. Nearby **Reinante** is a superb length of whitish sand, as is **Arealonga**, while a little further, **Praia de Lóngara** and adjacent Fontela are the best options for surfing.

## Foz and around 🖳🍴 ➠ *pp402-404.*

→ *Colour map 1, A5.*
The best feature of Foz is its attractive working fishing port, where the fishermen's families come down to wave at the boats heading out to sea in the late afternoon. The rest of the town is friendly but not particularly interesting. A good excursion is the walk or drive to **San Martín de Mondoñedo**, a hamlet whose **church** ⓘ *usually 1100-1300, 1600-1900 (the keyholder lives nearby)*, was once a cathedral; the bishop must have been the least stressed of primates. It's about 8 km from town along a pleasant road heavy with the scent of eucalypts. Although the church's origins are ninth century, most of what is visible is later Romanesque. It's on soft ground and is heavily buttressed; the apse has Lombard arching, a feature of the Romanesque of Catalunya. There's an attractive *cruceiro* outside, and the portal features the Lamb. Inside are some excellent Romanesque wallpaintings, good carved capitals and the tomb of Gonzalo, yet another Galician saint.

# 66 99 ...Spaniards, strive to imitate the inimitable Galicians (Duke of Wellington)

## West of Foz

Moving westwards, the coast becomes a little more rugged, but there are still some decent beaches. As well, a multitude of rivers flow down to the sea from the Galician high country and are good spots for trout fishing. The straggling village of **Xove** is less impressive than its name, which derives from the Latin *Iovii*, meaning 'of Jupiter'.

Few places appeal as a stopover until you reach the **Ría de Viveiro**. Near the town of Celeiro is the excellent patrolled beach of **Area**, a duney stretch that looks across to an islet.

# Viveiro and around 🕮🍴▲🚌 ▸ *pp402-404.*

→ *Colour map 1, A4.*

Viveiro is a curious place, which makes the best stop on this stretch of coast. Right at the tail of the *ría*, its small boats get marooned on mudflats at low tide. Viveiro is reasonably lively in summer, when there's a small but steady flow of holidaymakers, but it's strangely lifeless for the rest of the year. Viveiro is particularly known for its Easter festival, a serious event with a candlelit procession enacting the stations of the cross. The town is within easy range of many fine beaches, including Area (see above).

The old town is interesting, and still preserves fragments of its walls as well as a couple of gates, one a very tight squeeze at the top of the town. Built in the 12th century, the Romanesque **Iglesia de Santa María del Campo** is in the centre of the old town. Inside is a pretty processional cross dating from the 16th century, as well as a sculptural assembly that used to adorn one of the gates of the town wall. Nearby is a replica of the grotto at Lourdes; locals seem to trust it; there's many an offering of plastic body parts, soliciting intervention for physical ailments.

The coastline continues in rugged vein after Viveiro; as the road ascends the western headland there are some excellent views over the *ría* and out to sea. The small fishing village of **O Barqueiro** is a peaceful spot to stay, although the roadside sprawl above isn't so attractive. There's a bank in town, and a choice of places to stay on the small harbour.

From here, it's an hour's walk through eucalypt forest to **Punto da Bares**, the northernmost point in Spain. A winding road leads up to a viewpoint (signposted *Semáforo*), while at the cape itself is a lighthouse and whipping winds. There are some shops in the village, a good restaurant and a superb sandy beach a mile long and sheltered by a reef that was probably built by the Phoenicians.

# Ortigueira and around 🕮 ▸ *pp402-404.*

→ *Colour map 1, A4.*

The town of Ortigueira is a fairly workaday fishing port, transformed in mid-July for a massive festival of Celtic music and culture (www.festivaldeortigueira.com). Otherwise, there's no real reason to stop here; a quick look at its gardened port will suffice. A short distance west of Ortigueira, the main road cuts inland, but it's worth exploring the headland, a wild and rugged landscape battered by some of Galicia's worst weather. Apart from the dull sprawl of **Carriño**, it's a bleak and lonely place populated mainly by wild horses. North of Carriño, the pretty **Cabo Ortegal** has a

# The sphinx without a mystery

*"A less straightforward man I never met"* John Whitaker, American journalist

Francisco Franco y Bahamonde looms over 20th-century Spanish history like the concrete monoliths he was so fond of building and, like them, his shadow is long. Born in 1892 in the Galician naval port of Ferrol, this son of a naval administrator wanted to join the navy but was forced to choose the army due to lack of places at the academy. Sent to the war in Morocco at the age of 20, he excelled, showing remarkable military ability and bravery. As commander of the new Foreign Legion, he was largely responsible for the victory achieved there in 1925; this success saw him made Spain's youngest ever general at the age of 33.

The authoritarian Franco was just the man the government needed to put down the rebellion of the Asturian miners in 1934; this he achieved brutally. Sent to a command in the Canaries, out of harm's way as the government thought, he agreed to join the conspiracy against the Republic late. He took command of the army in Morocco, which was transported across to the Spanish mainland with German assistance, an intervention crucial in the context of the war.

Franco's advance was successful and rapid – he soon manoeuvred his way into the Nationalist leadership, reluctantly being given supreme power by his fellow generals. He assumed the title of *Caudillo*, or 'head' and installed himself in Burgos.

Throughout the war, he was known for his ruthlessness, never more so than when the German Condor Legion razed Gernika from the air on market day, killing 1650 civilians (see box, page 81). After the Nationalist victory, the *Generalísimo* showed no signs of giving up power, although in 1949

he declared himself as a regent pending the choice of a king. He ensured that there was to be no leniency for those who had supported the former Republic and a cruel purge followed. Franco wasn't exactly a relaxed and charismatic prankster; after meeting him at Hendaye in 1940 to discuss possible Spanish involvement in the Second World War, Adolf Hitler said he "would rather have three or four teeth out" than meet him again.

After the war Franco's dictatorship was shunned by the western democracies until Cold War politics made the USA adopt him as an ally, betraying the governments-in-exile they had continued to recognize. A massive aid package in exchange for military bases gave Franco the cash required to begin modernizing a country that had been crippled by the Civil War, but for much of his rule parts of Spain remained virtually Third World. Franco was recognized by other countries, and Spain was accepted into the United Nations, but remained politically and culturally stagnant. Separatism was not countenanced; Franco banned Euskara and even Gallego, the tongue of his native Galicia. He never forgot an enemy; the regions that had struggled to uphold democracy were left to rot while he conferred favours on the Nationalist heartlands of Castilla and Navarra. The ageing dictator appointed Juan Carlos, grandson of the former king, as his designated successor in 1969.

Franco died in 1975; "Españoles – the Spanish people were solemnly informed – Franco ha muerto". The man described as "a sphinx with no mystery" was no more: those who mourned the passing of this plump, shy, suspicious, authoritarian general were comparatively few, but Francoism is still alive within the Spanish political right, and memorial services on the anniversaries of his death are still held.

lighthouse and good views; it's a nice walk along the green clifftops. Further west, the **Garita de Herbeira** makes a very worthwhile little visit; it's an atmospheric and desolate arch of high granite cliffs 600 m high, and pounded by waves and weather.

Back on the coast, the **Santuario de San Andrés de Teixido** is in a sturdy stone hamlet. It's a simple chapel that was established by the Knights of Malta, who brought a relic of Saint Andrew here back from the Holy Land. The saint is much venerated along this understandably superstitious coast, and there's always a good pile of *ex voto* offerings that range from representations of what intervention is being sought for, such as models of fishing boats or plastic body parts to simple gifts of pens and cigarettes. There's a well-attended *romería* (pilgrimage procession) to the sanctuary on 8 September; some of the pilgrims make the journey in coffins to give thanks for narrow escapes, mostly at sea.

# Cedeira and around ● ›› *pp402-404.*

→ *Colour map 1, A3.*
South of the sanctuary of San Andrés de Teixido, and back on the main road is Cedeira, a pleasant town on yet another picturesque *ría*. There are some excellent **beaches** around, although the town beach isn't the best of them; try **A Magdalena**, a shallow-watered strip of sand a couple of kilometres further along the coast. The two halves of Cedeira are linked by a bridge; the old town is across it from the main road, and is a warren of steep and narrow streets.

## Cedeira coastline
West of Cedeira is some of the nicest coastline in these parts, heavily wooded and studded with excellent beaches, particularly **Villarube** and **Do Rodo**, one of Galicia's best surf beaches. **Da Frouxeira** is another excellent strip of sand, 2½ km long, and backed by a lagoon that is an important haven for waterfowl. There's a good (if slightly pricey) campsite at **Valdoviño**, on the main road near Da Frouxeira beach. There's a simpler campsite near the Praia do Río, which also has good surf (see Sleeping, below). Buses are the only way to access the coast on public transport, as the **FEVE** line has cut inland by this point.

# Ferrol ●◐◐◑● ›› *pp402-404.*

→ *Colour map 1, A3.*
While Ferrol's glory days as a naval harbour ended abruptly (along with most of Spain's fleet) during the Peninsular War, it's still an important port, and the navy is very much in evidence. Although poor and with high unemployment, Ferrol has not been shorn of its dignity; the streets around the harbour are lined with once-noble terraced houses, and locals are proud of their city and its hardworking heritage. Perhaps Ferrol's greatest claim to fame, however, is seldom mentioned these days: in the winter of 1892 an uptight little boy was born to a naval family in a house near the harbour. Francisco Franco y Bahamonde went on to rule Spain with a concrete fist for the best part of four decades (see box, page 400).

❧ *Although some 155,000 souls live in Ferrol and its sprawling suburbs, it's not a place of huge interest.*

Hurry through Ferrol's outskirts and modern expansions, some of the most depressing urban landscapes in modern Spain. In some of the poorer, high-density areas, the council inexcusably hasn't even bothered to give the streets proper names; just letters. Nevertheless, the city centre conserves a certain charm.

Although the **waterfront** is mostly taken up by naval buildings and dockyards, it's well worth strolling along: from the **Paseo de la Marina** at the western tip of the old

Galicia Rías Altas

town, you can get a good idea of just how large Ferrol's excellent natural harbour (the Ría do Ferrol) is. Near here is one of the twin forts defending the port. Most of Ferrol's character is in the five or six parallel streets back from here. The elegant balconied buildings tell of days of prosperity, as do the several indiano buildings. The white-washed neoclassical church and post office show some of these influences; nearby is the busy modern market. Franco was born on Rúa María, four streets back from the shore at No 136 (although the street was called Frutos Saavedra when he was a nipper). There's a **regional tourist office** ① *T981 311 179, Mon-Sat 1000-1400, 1600-1900 (1700-2000 summer), Sun 1000-1400,* on Praza Camilo José Cela, while the new **city tourist office** is inconveniently located east of the train and bus stations on Estrada de Castela, on a concrete island at a freeway junction.

# Pontedeume and the Caaveiro Valley 🚌🚍 » *pp402-404.*

→ *Colour map 1, A3.*
South of Ferrol, the rivermouth town of Pontedeume is a prettier and more relaxed place to hang out despite the almost constant line of traffic through town. Its main features are its long bridge across the Eume and an impressive 14th-century tower. Both were originally built by the Andrade family, local lairds, *bon viveurs* and boar hunters (see Betanzos, page 409). A weathered stone boar faces across the bridge. The tower holds the **tourist office**, which can advise on things to see in the area, of which there are several.

"The valley of Caaveiro", wrote Richard Ford in the mid-19th century, "is one of the most secluded in Spain". Not much has changed. The valley is a refuge of much wildlife; there are many otters (mostly further up, above the hydroelectric station), boar, ermine and birds. Fishing has been suspended on the river to allow the salmon and trout levels to restabilize.

Some 10 km up the valley is an atmospheric ruined monastery, **Monasterio de San Xoán de Caaveiro**. It was founded by the boy-bishop San Rosendo in the 10th century. The remaining Romanesque walls look over the river; it's a lovely setting. Nearby, a rapid watercourse feeds the Eume with yet more water. Don't be put off by the unlikely figure who may meet you at the information panel; he has chosen to live up here self-sufficiently and is an excellent source of knowledge about the area and its nature. From here, you may want to strike off for a walk: the **GR50 long-distance path** crosses the bridge at the monastery. The whole walk is recommended; it stretches from Betanzos to Cabo Ortegal at the top of Galicia, and can be done comfortably in four days, or strenuously in two.

# ◉ Sleeping

### Ribadeo *p398*
**AL Parador de Ribadeo**, Rúa Amador Fernández 7, T982 128 825, www.parador.es. The town's best place to stay, this *parador* is modern and not the most characterful of its kind but has views across the *ría* and a reasonable seafood restaurant.
**C Hotel Mediante**, Praza de Espanha 8, T982 130 453, www.hotelmediante.com. This hotel is on the main square and has good en suite rooms, which are slightly overpriced in Jul and Aug but top value at other times (**E**).

### Camping
There are several campsites to the west of town, including **Ribadeo**, T982 131 167, which boasts a swimming pool and has bungalows (open Jun-Sep only).

### West of Ribadeo *p398*
**C Casa Guillermo**, Vista Alegre 3, Santiago de Reinante, Barreiros. T982 134 150, www.casaguillermo.net. A good place to stay if you've got kids; it's near to the beach and has a large garden and comfortable rooms.

## Camping

**Nosa Casa**, by Reinante beach, T982 134 065. One of several campsites in this stretch, Nova Casa is open year-round and also has simple rooms.

### Foz and around *p398*

**C Hotel Leytón**, Av da Mariña 6, T982 140 800, F982 141 712. This is a good option despite the slightly garish decor. The rooms are well equipped, with internet point and heating; it's good value except in the first fortnight of August (**A**).

### Viveiro and around *p399*

**A Hotel Ego**, East of Viveiro, T982 560 987, www.hotelego.com. This hotel has an excellent situation above Area beach. It's a relaxed and well-equipped hotel for stress-free summer holidays. The terrace and most rooms boast excellent views over the strand and *ría*, and there's a good restaurant. **AL** in August.

**C Hotel Orfeo**, Av García Navia Castrillón 2, Viveiro, T982 562 101, F982 560 453. This is an excellent choice on the water in Viveiro itself, with comfortable, modern rooms, many of which come with a balcony and a view at no extra cost. It's more expensive in Aug (**B**).

**D Hostal O Forno**, O Barqueiro, T981 414 124. This is a great little place to stay, lovingly renovated and cared for; it looks over the water and also has a good seafood restaurant.

**D-F La Marina**, O Barqueiro, T981 414 098. Simpler than **Hostal O Forno** but still dapper and very cheap off season.

**F Fonda Nuevo Mundo**, Rúa Teodoro de Quirós 14, Viveiro, T982 560 025. At the upper end of town, this is a good friendly budget option if you don't mind the odd pealing of churchbells.

### Camping

**Camping Viveiro**, T982 560 004. Across the estuary from the heart of town and on a popular patrolled beach with greyish sand. Open Jun-Sep.

### Ortigueira and around *p399*

**C Río da Cruz**, in the middle of the headland, some 9 km inland from Garita de Herbeira, T981 428 057, www.riodacruz.com. A lovely old stone farmhouse with cosy pinewood rooms, one of which is an appealing duplex

that costs a little more (**B**). They serve nice meals, which can be eaten on an outdoor terrace.

### Cedeira and around *p401*

**E Chelsea**, Praza Sagrado Corazón 10, T981 482 340. The most appealing option in town, this is an acceptable place on a nice square very near the beach, across the bridge from the main part of town. Open May-Oct only.

### Cedeira coastline *p401*
### Camping

**Fontesín**, T981485028, near the Praia do Río, which is simpler than the one at Valdoviño, but also has good surf; it's open Jun-Sep only.

**Valdoviño**, on the main road near Da Frouxeira beach, T981 487 076. A good (if slightly pricey) campsite, open from Easter-Sep, it has bungalows and many facilities.

### Ferrol *p401*

Ferrol has a *parador*, an unlikely choice that probably had something to do with it being the dictator's hometown. The other options are filled with naval officers and sailors.

**L Parador de Ferrol**, Rúa Almirante Fernández Martín s/n, T981 356 720, www.parador.es. Situated in a good spot, at the end of the old town near the water, this *parador* has comfortable rooms, many with views, although these cost a handful more.

**F Hostal Da Madalena**, Rúa Magdalena 98, T981 355 615, madalenahostal@wanadoo.es Clean and cheap and far better than some of the seedier options around Ferrol.

### Pontedeume and the Caaveiro Valley *p402*

There are several lodging options in Ponte-deume and several *casas rurales* in the area.

**B Hotel Eumesa**, Av de A Coruña s/n, T981 430 925, F981 431 025. This well-equipped and friendly hotel has a garish neon front, but good rooms, many overlooking the rivermouth.

**E Allegue**, Rúa Chafaris 1, T/F981 430 035. A good little place with clean and comfortable rooms with simple bathrooms; it's on a square dominated by an old convent with an attractive patio. There are a couple of other options on this plaza.

# 🍴 Eating

## Ribadeo *p398*

🍴 **Solana**, C Antonio Otero 41, T982 128 635. This is a reliably good seafood restaurant; try the oysters if they're on, as Ribadeo is known for them; you can see their growing platforms out in the *ría*.

## Foz and around *p398*

🍴 **Restaurante O Lar**, Rúa Paco Maañon s/n, Foz. This place is a good, traditional and solid harbourside eatery with reliable and cheap seafood.

## Viveiro and around *p399*

🍴 **O Asador**, Rúa Meliton Cortiñas 15, T982 560 688. This is the best restaurant in Viveiro, a friendly upstairs spot looking over the narrow lane below. The fish, octopus and service are superb. Recommended.

🍴 **O Muro**, C Margarita Pardo de Cela 28, T982 560 823. This is a popular local *pulpería* with cheap bar snacks and an upstairs restaurant.

## Ferrol *p401*

🍴 **Casa Rivera**, Rúa Galiano 57, T981 350 759. This well-priced restaurant has excellent seafood and land-based dishes, with cheering stews and tasty octopus.

# 🍷 Bars and clubs

## Ferrol *p401*

As you'd expect from a naval town, Ferrol has a lively bar scene, mostly centred in the old town.

**Vétula**, Rúa Cantón de Molíns 6, T981 354 712. A friendly place for a drink or a coffee, this bar, facing the park, is one of the more pleasant spots.

# ▲ Activities and tours

## Viveiro and around *p399*

If you fancy a bit of boating, you can rent canoes on the Praia de Covas beach just across the *ría* from town.

**Roq Sport**, T646 514 60. Arranges land-based activities including guided hikes, mountain biking and archery.

# ⊖ Transport

## Ribadeo *p398*

**Bus** Ribadeo is well supplied with buses, with 8 daily to **Lugo**, 7 along the coast to **Oviedo**, 4 to **Santiago**, and several running to **A Coruña** along the coast. 2 buses head inland to **Vilalba** and **Mondoñedo**.

**Train** The coastal FEVE train line stops here on its way between **Ferrol** and **Oviedo**. It's a good way to access some of the smaller coastal towns.

## Viveiro and around *p399*

**Bus** Buses run from here both ways along the coast and inland to **Lugo** and **Santiago**. The bus station is by the water 200 m north of the old town. There's a small but helpful tourist kiosk opposite it.

**Train** The FEVE line stops at O Barqueiro near the main road, as do buses on the coastal road.

## Ferrol *p401*

The FEVE station, RENFE station and bus station are close together near Praza de España a short way north of the old centre.

**Bus** There are very frequent services to **A Coruña**. **Santiago**, **Pontevedra**, **Vigo**, **Betanzos** and the north coast are also regularly serviced by bus.

**Ferry** A launch service zips across the *ría* to Mugardos from Paseo de la Marina. You get a good view of the port, and Mugardos is a pretty little fishing town; you might want to stay for lunch and try the famed local recipe for octopus.

**Train** 4 FEVE trains a day head eastwards towards **Oviedo**; 2 only make it to **Ribadeo**. RENFE trains connect Ferrol with **A Coruña** (3 daily, 1 hr 10 mins, €3.40).

## Pontedeume and the Caaveiro Valley *p402*

**Bus and train** Train services between **Ferrol** and **A Coruña** call in at Pontedeume, as do buses on the same route.

# A Coruña and Costa da Morte

→ *Phone code: 981. Colour map 1, A3. Population: 243,349.*

*Don't even think about seeing Santiago and slipping out of Galicia without coming to A Coruña. A superb city where, at least when it's not raining, everyone seems to stay outdoors enjoying the privileged natural setting. Coruña has a bit of everything; a harbour, a good beach, top seafood, great nightlife, Romanesque architecture, entertaining museums, quiet corners and a football team that came from nowhere and took Europe by storm. It's one of the most enjoyable cities in the north of Spain but still an important working port and commercial centre.*

*The rugged coast west of A Coruña is named the 'coast of death', and has an interesting and dark history of marine disasters, wreckers and 'five and twenty ponies trotting through the dark' smuggling. There are some excellent beaches and some fairly authentic towns, who get on with their fishing and farming as the majority of tourists zip straight down to Finisterre.* ▸▸ *For Sleeping, Eating and other listings, see pages 412-416.*

## A Coruña 🏨🍴🏪🎭❄️🚌🚗🎵 ▸▸ *pp412-416*

### Ins and outs

**Getting there** A Coruña is connected with Madrid, Barcelona and Bilbao by air, as well as London Heathrow (Iberia), Paris and Lisbon. There's a direct bus service to the international airport at Santiago. It's a major railhead and bus terminus, well connected with the rest of Northern Spain. ▸▸ *See also Transport, page 416.*

**Getting around** Most of A Coruña is easily explorable on foot. The coastal *paseo* around the headland is a long one, but a tram covers the route half-hourly; a beautiful ride. The bus and train stations are a 20- to 30-minute walk south from the centre of town. City bus No 1 runs from the main road between the bus and train stations into town.

**Tourist information** A Coruña's **tourist office** ① *Av de la Marina, T981 216 161, Mon-Fri 1000-1345, 1700-1845, Sat and Sun 1000-1345*, is by the leisure harbour. Nearby is the **regional office** ① *T981 221 822, oficina.turismo.coruna@xunta.es, Mon-Fri 0900-1400, 1630-1830 (1700-1900 summer), Sat 1030-1300*, is on the marina.

### Background

Such a fine natural harbour as Coruña's was pounced upon early; it was used by the Celts and Phoenicians before becoming an important Roman port, Ardobicum Coronium. It was said that the foundations were laid by Hercules himself. The city remained, and remains, a significant port; it was the westernmost member of the Hermandad de las Marismas, a trading league formed in 1296 along Hanseatic lines.

Coruña's northward orientation is historically linked with Britain, whose sailors referred to it as 'the Groyne'. British pilgrims used to disembark here en route to the tomb of Saint James. This *Camino Inglés* was the easiest of the pilgrim routes to Santiago, at least when the Bay of Biscay was in clement mood.

In 1386 John of Gaunt, son of Edward III decided to avenge the murder of his father-in-law, Pedro I, and landed here with an army. After a farcical progress through Galicia, a peace was finally brokered whereby John's daughter would marry the heir to the Castilian throne. The Castilian king compensated him for the expenses occurred in the invasion and he went home, honour satisfied.

When John's great-grandaughter, the Catholic monarch Isabel, died, Philip the Fair of Flanders landed here in 1506 to meet with Fernando and claim the Castilian throne. His grandson Philip II had plenty to do with Coruña too; while still a prince, he embarked from here to England, where he married Mary at Winchester. Some 34 years later he assembled his Armada, whose 130 ships put out from the harbour here with 30,000 men. In 1507 Francis Drake had also sailed here and set fire to the town but was thwarted by the town's heroine María Pita, who saved Coruña by seizing the British standard and rallying the townsfolk to repel the buccaneers.

In 1809 a dispirited and undisciplined British army were relentlessly pursued by the Napoleonic forces of Marshal Soult. Having abandoned all their baggage and gold, the army made for Coruña where a fleet was stationed, but Soult was hard on their heels. To save as many men as possible, the Scottish general, Sir John Moore, faced the French with a small force while 15,000 troops embarked on to the ships. Moore was killed and the force defeated, but the majority of the army got away thanks to the sacrifice. Compared to other Spanish cities, Coruña thrived in the 19th and 20th centuries; its close ties to northern Europe and its flourishing port seemed to save it from stagnation.

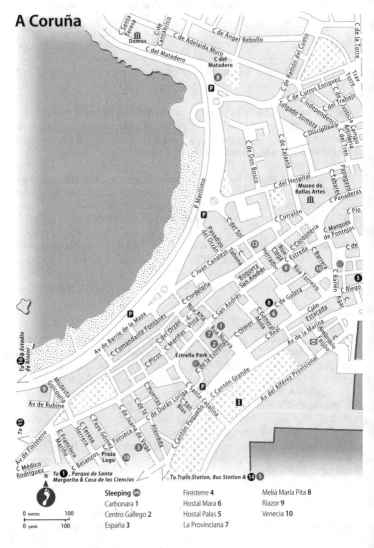

# A Coruña

0 metres 100
0 yards 100

**Sleeping**
Carbonara 1
Centro Gallego 2
España 3
Finisterre 4
Hostal Mara 6
Hostal Palas 5
La Provinciana 7
Meliá María Pita 8
Riazor 9
Venecia 10

To , Parque de Santa
Margarita & Casa de las Ciencias

To Train Station, Bus Station &

# Sights

One of the best ways to take in A Coruña's sights is a walk starting in the old town by the port and continuing anticlockwise around the headland. It's a long stroll, but you can hop on the tram that circles the route about every half-hour.

## Avenida de la Marina and around

The Avenida de la Marina is a good place to start. It's a very elegant boulevard lined with attractive old houses with trademark *galerías* or *miradores*, windowed balconies that look out over the water. Off here is the **Praza María Pita**, named after the city's heroine. The arcaded square is centred on a statue of María herself, defiantly brandishing a spear with a couple of Drake's mercenaries dead at her feet. She is commemorated with an eternal flame and faces the **Ayuntamiento**, a Galician *Modernista* building.

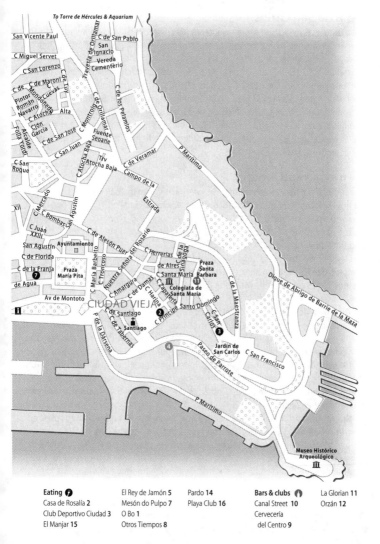

**Eating** 🍴
Casa de Rosalía **2**
Club Deportivo Ciudad **3**
El Manjar **15**

El Rey de Jamón **5**
Mesón do Pulpo **7**
O Bo **1**
Otros Tiempos **8**

Pardo **14**
Playa Club **16**

**Bars & clubs** 🍸
Canal Street **10**
Cervecería
 del Centro **9**

La Glorian **11**
Orzán **12**

A few block north of Avenida de la Marina is the modern **Museo de Bellas Artes** ① *Av Zalaeta s/n, Tue-Fri 1000-2000, Sat 1000-1400, 1630-2000, Sun 1000-1400, €2*, an excellent space that incorporates part of a former monastery and has a reasonable collection of European art, including some Goya sketches and some works by Rubens, as well as lesser-known but worthwhile Galician artists.

## Ciudad Vieja

East from the Praza María Pita is a very attractive network of old town streets, Ciudad Vieja, a quiet place with some fine houses, squares and churches. The **Colegiata de Santa María** is a wide Romanesque building with solid barrel vaulting and a small **museum** ① *Tue-Fri 0900-1400, 1700-1900, Sat 1000-1300, free*, of religious art. The 13th-century portal is a good work, as is the later rose window. In the eaves, a curious carved pattern looks like dripping wax. The side portal also features elegant Romanesque stonework.

## Jardín de San Carlos

"Not a drum was heard, nor a funeral note, as his corse to the ramparts we hurried". The small and evocative Jardín de San Carlos is the final resting place of General Sir John Moore, the Scot who turned "like a lion at bay" to engage the superior French forces of Marshal Soult to give his dispirited army time to embark on the waiting ships. He was killed by a cannonball and hurriedly buried "by the struggling moonbeam's misty light". The soldier's grave was later marked with a granite monument; in Spain, the Peninsular War is named the War of Independence, and British involvement fondly remembered, although the redcoats' behaviour and discipline was frequently atrocious. Poems by Charles Wolfe and Rosalía de Castro commemorate Moore, and fresh flowers often appear on the grave.

## The marina and around

Descending from here to the marina, the fort that juts into the bay was built by Felipe II and now houses the **Museo Histórico Arqueológico** ① *Sep-Jun Tue-Sat 1000-1900, Sun 1000-1500, Jul and Aug Tue-Sat 1000-2100, Sun 1000-1500, €2*, the highlight of which is a number of pieces of Celtic jewellery including distinctive torcs and the famous 'helmet of Leiro'.

East of here, the massive glass **cuboids** of the port authority's control tower cut an impressive figure. From here, you might want to get the tram around to the Torre de Hércules, as it's a 20-minute walk with little of interest (apart from the great waterfront views, that is).

The **Torre de Hércules** ① *Oct-Mar 1000-1745, Apr-Jun, Sep 1000-1845, Jul and Aug 1000-2045 (2345 Fri and Sat), €2*, stands very proud at the northern tip of Coruña's peninsula. It was originally built in the second century AD by the Romans, and claims to be the oldest lighthouse still operational. Its current exterior dates from an 18th-century reformation and, in truth, there's not much Roman left of it, apart from a central core and some foundations, visible in a low-ceilinged space before you ascend. It's worth climbing the 234 steps to the top, where there's a good view of A Coruña and the coast.

Not far beyond the lighthouse is the new **aquarium** ① *daily 1000-1900 (1000-2200 in Jul and Aug), €7 (€9 for combined ticket to here, Casa de Ciencias and Domus)*. It's that building you thought was a sewage plant when you were up the top of the tower. It's a good one, with a large variety of Atlantic fish (useful for those restaurant menus), and some decent displays and temporary exhibitions.

● *"She belongs more to the sea than to the stony mass of mainland behind her" is how Dutch*
● *writer Cees Nooteboom has described A Coruña; this is very much the case.*

## Shipwrecks and smugglers

The indentations and rocks that abound on Galicia's coastline provide some spectacular scenery but also have a darker side. It is a sobering fact that in the last century some 140 ships have gone down with the loss of over 500 lives. The scandalously mismanaged *Prestige* oil disaster (see page 410) of late 2002 is just one of a long series of shipping incidents on this coast.

Local legend attributes many of these wrecks to the activities of *raqueiros* (wreckers), who would lure ships onto the rocks by attaching lights to the horns of cattle. More likely though, it is the combination of sea-surges and savage rocks that make this coast so hazardous.

The natural features of the coast which make it so dangerous for shipping have made it a haven for smugglers down the years. In recent years, Galicia's smugglers have moved away from more traditional products towards drugs. A large proportion of Europe's cocaine arrives through Galicia, usually being left well offshore by a smugglers' ship, then picked up by one of the coast's fishing fleet. This has had the predictable effect of increasing problems of corruption and violence. The town of O Grove saw its former mayor facing drugs related charges and in Vilagarcía, which experienced a sudden and highly suspicious boost in wealth in the nineties, the local Chamber of Commerce Director was the victim of a professional hit. Recently heavy police activity has seen some of this trade move to other locations.

The ark-like **Domus** ① *daily 1000-1900 (1100-2100 in Jul and Aug), €2 (€4 including IMAX projection; combined ticket with aquarium and Casa de las Ciencias €9)*, looks like the hull of a boat and has become something of a city emblem since famed Japanese architect Arata Isozaki created it. There's a very strange statue of a tubby Roman soldier out the front, but inside it's an entertaining modern museum of humankind, dealing in all aspects of how we function physically and mentally. It's interactive and fun for young and old and there's a good café and restaurant.

### Beyond the old town

The curve of the city's excellent beach sweeps around the bay. It's a top stretch of sand, slightly marred by poor waterfront architecture. Although there's plenty of space, in summer it can be packed out. At its far end is the **Estadio de Riazor**. The city's football team, *Deportivo La Coruña*, tiny by European standards, rose to the top division in 1991 after decades of second- and third-division obscurity.

In the Santa Margarita park, the **Casa de las Ciencias** ① *daily 1000-1900 (1100-2100 Jul and Aug), €2, planetarium €2 (combined ticket with aquarium and Domus €9)*, has good displays on biology and mechanics as well as a planetarium, which can be dogged by lengthy queues.

# Around A Coruña ●● » pp412-416

### Betanzos

The town of Betanzos makes a good day-trip from A Coruña. The site of a Celtic settlement, and a significant Roman port, it's an attractive, if slightly faded town that was dealt a bitter blow in the 17th and 18th centuries when the port silted up and Betanzos gradually became an inland town, although it's still a junction of the two pretty rivers that are to blame for the fiasco. In summer you can take a boat trip on them.

## ⁝ Nunca Maís

In late 2002, the future of Galicia's coastline and fishing industry was put in serious jeopardy by the rupturing and subsequent sinking of the single-hulled oil tanker *Prestige*. The Spanish and Galician governments acted with culpable indecision – in an apparent effort to wash their hands of the matter, they insisted on towing the stricken vessel out to international waters, thus ensuring the oil slick spread over a larger area. The *Prestige* was carrying 70,000 tonnes of oil, over 70% of which was spilled, washing up along the Galician and Asturian coasts, reaching France and Portgual. Massive volunteer cleaning operations ensued, and the Gallego slogan *Nunca Maís* (Never Again) became a catchcry across the nation. A billion euros later and thanks to the expertise of environmental organizations and the energies of the volunteers, the long-term damage to the Galician fisheries and environment has not to be as devastating as first feared. However, until sterner worldwide controls of unseaworthy vessels are applied, *Nunca Maís* remains a hope rather than a reality.

Betanzos' main attraction is its steep streets lined with trademark Galician housing. There are a couple of nice plazas and four churches, of which the absolute highlight is the **Iglesia de San Francisco**, a monastery church built in the 14th century. It was paid for by the count Fernán de Andrade, lord over most of this region, and dubbed 'O Bóo', or the good; it's not clear by whom, probably himself. He had the church built with his own soul in mind: he intended to rest in peace in it, but wasn't prepared to compromise. His earthly love was boarhunting, and the number of carved boars both outside and in the church is noteworthy. The top attraction, however, is his tomb (although he's not actually in it). It's carved with excellent hunting scenes, all dogs, horns, and tally-ho's, and is mounted on the back of a large stone boar and a rather brainless-looking bear. There are many other tombs of lords and ladies, as well as some representations of saints. The apse is big and light and holds a simple sculpture of Saint Francis and the Crucifixion behind the altar. The vaulting is elaborate, but the pigs still pull focus.

The **Iglesia de Santa María del Azogue** dates from the 14th century and has a pleasant spacious interior with some slightly skewed columns with good carved capitals. The *retablo* is dark and is centred on an icon of the Virgin. The façade features the elders of the Apocalypse around a scene of the Adoration on the tympanum. Strange animals adorn the capitals.

The **Iglesia de Santiago** ① *1000-1400, 1700-2100, €1*, dates from the 15th century and has a very fine carved portal of Santiago Matamoros and the Pantocrator. The capitals on either side of the door are carved with frightening beasts. The interior is simple, with a triple nave. In the **Praza Constitución** there's a small museum devoted to modern prints. There are six buses a day between Betanzos and Coruña, and a couple to Santiago. The buses stop on the road across the river from the old town. The **tourist office** is behind the church on the plaza on the main road thorough town.

---

# Costa da Morte ☺🚲⛰🚌 ▸▸ *pp412-416*

## Malpica → *Colour map 1, A2.*
The first stop of interest along from A Coruña is Malpica, a lively, unadulterated fishing town ruled by a pack of large and brazen Atlantic seagulls. There's an offshore nesting sanctuary for less forceful seabirds on the **Islas Sisargas** opposite.

There's no scheduled boat service to visit the islands, but on a fine day, you can usually find a boatowner who'll be happy to take you out for a fee. Malpica also has a good beach, which can get pretty good surf.

## Corme

There are some good wild beaches west of here. The town of Corme is reached via a side road, and sits on a nice bay used to cultivate shellfish. The port is backed by narrow streets tightly packed with the houses of fishing families. Bypass the town beach and head for **Praia Ermida**, 1 km or so further around the bay. The town doesn't give too much away; it was known as a nest of anti-Franco guerrilla activity during the Civil War, and anybody prying into the coming and going of boats in the middle of the night these days might end up sleeping with the shellfish; suffice it to say that most of Europe's cocaine arrives through Galicia.

## Ponteceso and around

Ponteceso has a bridge of medieval origins that crosses the marshy river. If it's beaches you want, stop at **Laxe**, which has a top strand of white sand, and an even better one to the west; peaceful **Praia Traba**. The town itself isn't great, but we can't really complain.

## Camariñas

The coast continues to be impressive; Camariñas, the next worthwhile place from Ponteceso, makes a good place to stop. It's famous throughout Spain for its lace; if that's not your thing, it also enjoys a privileged location, on a pretty inlet stocked with pines and eucalypts. It looks across the *ría* to Muxía on the other side. The port is small but serious, with some biggish boats heading far out to sea. There's a summer-only **tourist office** on the *ría*-side *paseo*.

The **Museo do Encaixo** ① *T981 736 340, Fri and Sat 1100-1400, 1700-2000, Sun 1100-1400, 1600-1930, otherwise call first, €1.30*, details the history and practice of lacemaking; they make it bobbin-style here. It is famous throughout Spain, and can be bought at several outlets in the village; on a nice day you may even see some elderly lacemakers at work in the sun outside their houses.

The best thing to do in Camariñas is explore the **headland** to the north. There's a series of dirt roads that are just about driveable, but it's nicer on foot with the smell of pine in your nostrils. **Cabo Vilán** is about an hour's walk, a dramatic spot with a big lighthouse building and high, modern windmills, which work pretty hard here. Further east, there are a small **beaches** and an English cemetery, with the graves of some of the dead of a British navy vessel wrecked on the coast in 1890, at a cost of 170 lives.

## Muxía

The counterpart of Camariñas on the other side of the *ría*, Muxía is a tightly packed fishing town that makes up for in authenticity what it lacks in postcardy charm. It's worth visiting, though, to see the **Santuario de Nuestra Señora de la Barca** on a headland just past the town. With the waves beating the rocks to a pulp around the chapel, it's a hugely atmospheric place; it's not hard to see why fisherfolk who brave the stormy seas have a healthy religious and superstitious streak around here. The spot was originally venerated to commemorate an impressive navigational feat in the early first century AD; the Virgin Mary sailed from Palestine to this very spot in a stone boat. If you don't believe it, take a look inside the church: various fragments of the vessel are set around the sloping interior. Now, fishermen pray for the safety of their own boats, often leaving small models as ex-voto offerings.

● *On the first Sunday after 8 September, there's an important romería to the sanctuary in Muxía; part of the ritual is a claustrophobic crawl under a huge rock. It's one of the most atmospheric and meaningful of Galicia's fiestas.*

At the foot of the Finisterre peninsula, the fishing ports of Corcubión and Cée have grown into each other, stretching around the bay. It's a fairly serious fishing spot, but the old port in Corcubión is nice, and there are plenty of hotels and restaurants. Cée has a small ship-wrecking industry, a fairly tough business, but nothing compared to what confronts you a little further around the bay; a giant alloys plant that manages to effectively recreate Hell on the Galician coast. Pity the workers.

# Towards the end of the world 🖥🍴 ⟩⟩ pp412-416

## Fisterra and Cabo Finisterre

Further west from Cée, the town of Fisterra makes a better place to drop anchor for the night. It's an attractive if slightly wind-bitten fishing port, and there are plenty of facilities catering to the passing tourists heading for Cabo Finisterre a couple of kilometres beyond. There's the remains of a small fort and good views across the bay.

The most westerly point in mainland Europe is not Cabo Finisterre. It's in Portugal, and the most westerly point in Spain is a little further up the coast, but Finisterre has won the audience vote. Part of its appeal comes from its name, literally derived from the Latin for 'end of the earth', part from its dramatic location: a small finger of land jutting into the mighty Atlantic. Gazing westwards from the rocks around its scruffy lighthouse is a magical enough experience, particularly at sunset; imagine what it would have been like if you believed the world literally ended out there, dropping off into a void. The cape is 2 km uphill from Fisterra, accessible by road. There's a small bar at the top, and you can stay at the *pousada* here.

## Carnota

Moving south again towards the Rías Baixas, the village of Carnota is set 1 km back from a magnificent and wild beach 7 km long and rolling with enormous dunes. Carnota itself has a **tourist office** at the top of town and a hotel. It also boasts the longest *hórreo* (raised granary, very typical of the region) in Galicia, for what it's worth. The ridiculous 18th-century structure is 35 m long. You'll find it tucked away in a back street on the western side of the main road.

## ⬤ Sleeping

**A Coruña** *p405, map p406*

A Coruña has a large number of good-quality budget accommodation options, concentrated in the tapas zone a couple of streets back from Av de la Marina. All choices are notably cheaper outside Jul and Aug.

**LL Hotel Hesperia Finisterre**, Paseo del Parrote 22, T981 205 400, www.hesperia-hoteles.com. Superbly located on the headland, this is the nicest place to stay in A Coruña. Recently renovated, the rooms are smallish but bright, furnished with style, and many have superb views over the harbour and sea. There are all the facilities you could ask for, and an excellent restaurant.

**L Meliá María Pita**, Av Pedro Barrié de la Maza 1, T981 205 000, www.solmelia.com.

While no doubt erected to recall the glass-fronted traditional buildings round the harbour, this hotel's appearance is somewhat brash. Nevertheless, it has an excellent location on the city beach. Catering to business travellers, it has an impersonal feel and good facilities; best of all, there are often significant discounts offered, as well as weekend specials.

**AL Hotel Riazor**, Av de Pedro Barrié de la Maza 29, T981 253 400, www.riazor hotel.com. This is a big but pleasant beachfront hotel near the stadium. Recently renovated, it has rooms with excellent bathrooms and great views – make sure you specify that you want one when reserving.

**B Hotel España**, Rúa Juana de Vega 7, T981 224 506, www.hotelspa.com. This is a good, bright, clean hotel handy for both beach and harbour. Rooms have internet socket, TV and phone, and there's also a restaurant.

**D Hostal Mara**, C Galera 49, T981 221 802, www.hostalmara.com. In tapas bar heartland, this is a reliable option with good, clean en suite doubles at the quiet end of the street. They're sound people running it, and there's a decent cheap restaurant. Good value off-season.

**D La Provinciana**, Rúa Nueva 7, T981 220 400, ww.laprovinciana.com. An excellent spot to stay off-season, as the rooms are good and drop to a very low price. The rooms are heated and there's parking available; it's a good deal although it's not exactly charismatic and can be a little noisy.

**D-E Carbonara**, Rúa Nueva 16, T981 225 251, luiscarbonara@yahoo.es. One of the better choices, this is a very good central spot with friendly management and decent rooms with bathrooms in a typically attractive Coruña house.

**D-E Centro Gallego**, C Estrella 2, T981 222 236. This is a very good option above a friendly café, with excellent modern bathrooms in the rooms. It's remarkably good value considering its proximity to water, tourist office, bars and octopus taverns.

**E Hostal Palas**, C Marqués de Amboage 21, T981 247 400. This is a good option if you arrive late or are leaving early; it's right next to the bus station and just across the overpass from the train station. It's run by cheerful old folk and is modern and clean as a whistle; the rooms are quiet and spacious with cable TV and heating (make sure it's on!). They're used to people coming and going at odd hours.

**E-F Venecia**, Praza Lugo 22, T981 222 420. A very cheap option on a square a couple of blocks from the main bar zones. Rooms with or without bath available in this old but character-packed building. Great value.

**Around A Coruña** *p409*

**C Hotel Los Angeles**, C Angeles 11, Betanzos, T981 771 511, ht-los-angeles@hotmail.com. A dull, modern choice with parking but something of an attitude problem.

**E Hostal Barreiro**, C Rollo 6, Betanzos, T981 772 259. The best option and with a friendly restaurant.

**Camping**

**El Rasoares** is a campsite near Betanzos.

**Malpica** *p410*

**D Hostal JB**, C Playa 3, T981 721 906. A good bet, with appealing rooms overlooking the beach.

**D Panchito**, Praza Villar Amigo 6, T981 720 307. With snug rooms and nice folk on the convivial square in the centre of town.

**Ponteceso and around** *p411*

**D Hostal Bahía**, Av Generalísimo 24, Laxe, T981 728 207. A clean and decent year-round option if you're staying – the beach is the main reason to hang out in this town.

**Camariñas** *p411*

There are several accommodation options in Camariñas, which gets a fair few tourists in summer. Most of them are simple, family-run *pensiones* and *hostales*; there's nothing in the luxury class.

**E Hostal Dársena**, Rúa Alcalde Noguera Patiño 21, T981 736 263. Perched above the far end of the harbour, this is another decent option.

**E-F Hostal Scala**, Tras Playa 6, T981 737 109, www.hostal-scala.com, is the sort of building that planning permission was invented to stop, but the structure craning to get a glimpse of the water has clean light, and airy rooms; there's a choice of en suite or simpler pads with shared bathroom.

**Muxía** *p411*

**C Hotel La Cruz**, Av López Abente 44, T/F981 742 084. A big building with more than adequate modern comfort and little character. The best option in Muxía itself.

**D A Barca**, Chorente s/n, T981 742 525, www.a-barca.s5.com. A peaceful rural hotel set in an utterly rustic hamlet 3 km from Muxía. Heading back on the road towards Camariñas, Chorente is signposted on the left. It's a good spot for rambling around the headland.

**A Pousada O Semáforo**, Estrada do Faro s/n, Cabo Finisterre, T981 725 869, osemaforo@msn.com, Right on the headland, this is an unbeatable spot to stay. Situated in a former observatory and telegraph station, it offers considerable comfort and excellent meals (although not to the public unless previously arranged) above the wild and endless sea.

**C Dugium**, T981 740 780, F981 740 795, www.dugium.com. In the middle of the Finisterre headland, the village of San Salvador harbours this small and peaceful rural hotel with excellent rooms, a tranquil garden and a good restaurant.

**E Cabo Finisterre**, Rúa Santa Catalina 1, Fisterra, T981 740 000. This is one of several decent *hostales* in Fisterra, and the 6 rooms are, crucially, heated – so make sure they turn it on.

**Carnota** *p412*

**D Hotel Miramar**, Plaza de Galicia 2, T981 857 016. Just off the main road in the centre of town, this is a convenient and comfortable place to stay. The rooms are well equipped and warm, with a slightly run-down beach-hotel feel, and there's a decent restaurant.

## ⊕ Eating

**A Coruña** *p405, map p406*

A Coruña has a superb tapas scene, with octopus (*pulpo*) the excellent local speciality. It's usually served boiled, simply garnished with paprika, olive oil and salt, and accompanied by *cachelos* (boiled spuds). If you don't mind the slimy texture, it's superb.

Most locals eat in this way, ordering *raciones*; hence, there are comparatively few traditional restaurants.

**Ⓣ Pardo**, C Novoa Santos 15, T981 280 021. Coruña's finest restaurant treats its fish just right and is far from overpriced. It also does delicious partridge in season and good salads too. The seafood croquettes are justly famed.

**Ⓣ Casa de Rosalía**, C del Príncipe 3, T981 214 243. This restaurant is beautifully set in an old-town house once lived in by Rosalía de Castro. Recommended is the rich, homemade duck liver *foie*, or the scrambled eggs with sea-urchin roe. The fish is good too. Recommended.

**Ⓣ El Manjar**, C Alfredo Vicenti 29, T981 251 885. A cosy restaurant with excellent old-time decor near the Riazor Stadium. They do a great *zarzuela de pescado* (fish stew) and succulent *chipirones*.

**Ⓣ O Bo**, C Menéndez Pelayo 18, T981 927 237. A traditional type of place, this sticks to what the Galicians know best; all the recipes have been handed down for generations. The *cocido gallego* is a guaranteed winter warmer, while the *pulpo* is delicious and the *tortilla* famous throughout the city. Recommended.

**Tapas bars and pulperías**

The best zone for *tapas* is the long stretch of C Franja, C Galera and C Olmos heading westwards from Praza María Pita. There's little purpose to a lengthy list of recommendations; just wend your way along that route and pick a place you like. They're nearly all good; the more locals inside, the better.

**Ⓣ El Rey de Jamón**, C de la Franja 45. The thousand (or thereabouts...) hams hanging on the ceiling here will do your heart good. There are several different grades available in *raciones* or *bocadillos*.

**Ⓣ Mesón do Pulpo**, C de la Franja 11, T981 202 444. The name says it all; on the street of octopus, this place does some of the best; just follow the locals. There are several choices of our 8-legged friend, and also a good selection of other seafood.

**Ⓣ Otros Tiempos**, C Galera 54, T981 229 398. A friendly bar deservedly popular for its generous and delicious *raciones*. Sit at the homely wooden tables and enjoy, but go for tapas portions if you're not seriously hungry.

**Cafés**

**Club Deportivo Ciudad**, Rúa Tinajas 14, T981 212 302. A good, sleek, modern café near the Jardín de San Carlos. Ideal for morning coffees or for watching *Deportivo* games among fans.

**Playa Club**, Andén Riazor s/n, T981 250 063. An airy café with a superb location and views down the beach. Serves a good range of *platos combinados* and tapas. There's also an upmarket restaurant, also with unbeatable views.

**Around A Coruña** *p409*
The bars with outdoor seats on the big Plaza Mayor do decent tapas.
†† **Os Arcos**, in Hostal Barreiro, see Sleeping, above. A friendly restaurant; try the swordfish or king crab (*buey*).

**Ponteceso and around** *p411*
†† **Casa do Arco**, Praza Ramón Juega 1, Laxe, T981 706 904. Has a good seafood restaurant.

**Camariñas** *p411*
There are several cafés and seafood restaurants in Camariñas.
†† **Gaviota**, C Río 20, T981 737 032. Worthwhile seafood restaurant where you just have to eat whatever's fresh and finny that day.

**Muxía** *p411*
†† **A Pedra do Abalar**, Rúa Marina 35. A typically dependable seafood place with warmhearted old-style service.

**Fisterra and Cabo Finisterre** *p412*
There are some excellent restaurants in Fisterra.
††††-†† **O Centolo**, Paseo del Puerto s/n, T981 740 452. The classiest of Fisterra's restaurants, O Centolo, serves an excellent range of fish and seafood in a spacious light dining room, and also organizes dinner cruises on the bay in summer. You can eat here fairly cheaply or throw away the purse-strings on the finest crustaceans.
†† **Casa Velay**, Paseo da Ribeira s/n, T981 740 127. Seafood and a terrace by the beach.
† **O Tres Golpes**, Rúa das Hortas 2, T981 740 047. 'The three blows', has a distinctly nautical feel and specializes in good fish stews.

## ⚫ Bars and clubs

**A Coruña** *p405, map p406*
After tapas time is over, folk tend to move on to 1 of 2 areas. A smarter scene goes on in the streets around **Praza España** and the **Museo de Bellas Artes**. A more alternative crowd hangs out in the bars and clubs around **C del Sol** and **C Juan Canalejo de Corralón** between the tapas zone and the beach.

At weekends it's as lively as anywhere in Northern Spain.
**Canal Street**, C Barrera 5. A lively long bar with different sections. There's fashionably low and moody lighting, while a representation of the Statue of Liberty overlooks a smart young Galician clientele to the beat of dance music and the chink of G&Ts.
**Cervecería del Centro**, Rúa Torreiro 19. Popular with the young during the evening for its good cheap beer and cheap snacks, this large brick and stone space turns a little more upmarket after midnight, when the lights go down and the music cranks up. Not signed, but look for the oil drums at the door.
**La Glorian**, C Don Francisco 12. A very individual, different and intimate bar in the old town with a relaxed vibe and fishing-fleet-meets-Indian-bazaar-style decor.
**Orzán**, C/Orzán. A good, cosy bar that has a cheerful and late scene. One of many top options in this area.

## ⚫ Entertainment

**A Coruña** *p405, map p406*
**Centro Rosales**, Rosales, T981 128 092. A very big cinema complex in a shopping centre.
**Cine Equitativa**, Av Emilia Pardo Bazán s/n, T981 120 153.
**Palacio de la Opera**, T902 434 443. As well as being an opera venue, this is the home ground of the Galician symphony orchestra. Tickets are extremely cheap, ranging from €9-€26.

## ⚫ Festivals and events

**A Coruña** *p405*
**Aug** Coruña's main festival is in honour of **María Pita** and lasts the whole month, with all sorts of cultural events and a mock naval battle. The main week, **Semana Grande**, is in the middle of the Aug.

## ⚫ Shopping

**A Coruña** *p405, map p406*
C del Real, one street back from Av de la Marina, is the handiest shopping street.

▲▲ **Activities and tours**

**Camariñas** *p411*
**Horse riding**
If you fancy a gallop, there's a small horse riding operation outside town, T981 737 279.

**Sport**
The city's football team, Deportivo La Coruña, T902 434 443, www.canaldeportivo.com, play their home games at the Riazor stadium, right by the sea. It's one of the best places in Spain to watch a game, and the team are notoriously difficult to beat on their home patch. Games are normally on a Sunday evening; tickets are available from the taquilla a couple of hours before the match; you can also book by phone or Internet if you speak Spanish. Tickets booked this way must be picked up from a branch of Caixa Galicia bank.

⊜ **Transport**

**A Coruña** *p405, map p406*
**Air**
A Coruña's airport (LCG) lies to the south of the city. There are international flights to **Lisbon**, London Heathrow, and **Paris** as well as national ones to **Madrid**, **Barcelona**, and **Bilbao**. Buses run regularly from Puerta Real to the airport (€1.15). There's also a daily bus (leaving at 1030) from the Hotel Atlántico, Jardines Méndez Núñez, to the international airport at Santiago.

**Bicycle hire**
There's a municipal bike rental shed on Paseo de la Dársena by the leisure harbour. Open 0900-2100 summer; 0900-1400, 1600-2100 winter. A 2-hr rental is €6; a whole day costs €21.

**Bus**
**Local** The bus station is to the south of town, on C de Caballeros. Frequent buses (No 1) connect it with the city centre. Within Galicia, **Ourense** is served 8 times daily, **Lugo** 11 times, **Santiago** hourly (€4.15; via motorway 45 mins, via road 1 hr 20 mins), **Pontevedra** and **Vigo** 9 times, **Betanzos** 6 times, and **Ferrol** hourly. 5 buses daily go down the **Costa da Morte** to **Camariñas**.

**Long distance** Destinations outside Galicia include **Gijón/Oviedo** (4 a day, 4½-5 hrs, €22.46) , **Bilbao** (2 daily, 11 hrs, €40.96) via **Santander** and proceeding to **San Sebastián**; **Madrid** (6-7 daily, 7 hrs, €35.16); **Salamanca** 3 times, **León** (2 daily, 5 hrs, €18.90) and **Zaragoza/Barcelona** once. On Fri and Sun a bus leaves at 1400 bound for **Porto** and **Lisbon** in Portugal.

**Train**
The train station is just across the main road, and up the hill from the bus station. **Santiago** (1 hr 10 mins, from €3.40) and **Vigo** (3 hrs, from €8.50) are serviced roughly hourly. There are also trains to **Lugo** (3-4 daily, 1 hr 40 mins, from €5.75), **Ourense** (3 daily, 2 hrs 15 mins, €17-20), **Madrid** (2 daily, 9 hrs, €43), **Barcelona** (1-2 daily, 16 hrs, €47-60), and **Ferrol** (3 daily, 1 hr 10 mins, €3.40).

**Costa da Morte** *p410*
**Bus**
The excellent **Arriva** bus service, T902 277 482, www.arriva.es, covers the Costa da Morte thoroughly. There are at least 5 buses daily to every destination mentioned on this stretch of coastline. Services run from these towns both ways; ie to both **A Coruña** and **Santiago**.

❶ **Directory**

**A Coruña** *p405, map p406*
**Internet** There are a couple of booths in an unnamed copyshop at R Angel 19. **Estrella Park**, C Estrella 12, is a games arcade which has coin-op machines where €1 gets you 40 mins. **Laundry** Express, C de San Andrés; **Clean and Clean**, C Juan Florez; self service, Paseo Marítimo s/n, where the big glass control tower is. **Medical services** Hospital Juan Canalejo T981 178 000. **Police and emergency** Police 092, General emergency 112; **Post office** The main post office is on Av de la Marina opposite the tourist office. **Telephone** The sweet shop at C Estrella 14 has a couple of booths and some excellent international rates.

# Rías Baixas → *Colour map 2, B1.*

*The Rías Baixas are a succession of large and beautiful inlets extending down the west coast of Galicia almost as far as Portugal. The sheltered waters are used to farm much of Spain's supply of shellfish, and the towns still harbour important fishing fleets. It's one of Galicia's prime visitor destinations, a fact which has spawned a few myths that are worth clearing up. Firstly, the rías are not 'fjord-like' – the coast is mostly low hills, and the inlets mostly fairly shallow, retreating over mudflats at low tide. They bear more resemblance to eastern Scottish firths than Norway's dramatic serrations. Secondly, while there are some decent beaches here, they are generally not as good as those of the Costa da Morte or north coast. Lastly, they are not remote; much of the coast is a continuous ribbon of strip development. That said, there are many spots worth visiting and much good wine and seafood to be consumed! And there are several villages and peaceful spots that merit exploration; Muros and Cambados are the most appealing bases.* ▸▸ *For Sleeping, Eating and other listings, see pages 420-422.*

## Muros

The small town of Muros sits on the north coast of the northernmost *ría* of the Rías Baixas, which is named after it and Noia, its counterpart across the water. Muros has considerable charm, with a small but atmospheric old town, and a large fishing harbour. The Gothic church contains a Christ crucified that has a head of real hair; there's a lovely market reached by a double staircase, and a curious stone reptile slithering over a fountain. Apart from that, it's just strolling the seafront and watching boats come and go; very pleasant indeed. There's a **tourist kiosk** on the waterfront promenade.

## Noia

On the other side and further up the estuary, Noia isn't as attractive a place as Muros, being a busier centre for the area. It's claimed that the town's name derives from that of Noah, because this was the spot the dove found the olive branch; the ark came to rest on a nearby hill. Folk here believe it too, and the event features on the coat of arms of the town. The Gothic **Iglesia de San Martín** is the town's highlight. Fronted by a fine *cruceiro*, it's got an excellent carved portal featuring the *Apostles and the Elders of the Apocalypse*, and a beautiful rose window above. Another church, the **Iglesia de Santa María** ① *Mon-Sat 1000-1400, 1800-2000*, is full of the tombstones that were salvaged from a recent tidy-up of the graveyard. Rough slabs of granite dating from the 10th to 17th centuries, they are carved with simple symbols and figures that seem to fall into four distinct types: marks of profession, rebuses of family names, heraldic motifs and full figures of the deceased. It's a fascinating collection. Noia's **tourist kiosk** ① *Mon-Fri 1030-1300, Sat and Sun 1200-1300 (extended opening in Jul and Aug)*, is opposite the town hall, built around a small, attractive atrium. A tough place to work with those demanding opening hours.

## South of Noia

Continuing south, the coast is a pretty one, with some decent, if sometimes wild-watered, beaches. One of the better ones is **Ornanda**, just short of the decent village of **Portosín**. At **Baroña** there is a Celtic *castro*, a fort-cum-village well situated on an exposed point. A couple of kilometres from the town of Axeitos down a peaceful country lane is one of the nicer of Galicia's many **dolmens**; it sits in a dappled glade among pine cones. Near here a winding road leads up to a mirador, **La Curota**. If the day is good, the view is absolutely breathtaking, taking in all the *rías*, with their shellfish platforms looking like squadrons of U-boats in harbour. You can see north to Finisterre and south to Baiona, just short of Portugal.

## ⁑ Cela vida

Camilo José Cela was a hard-living author who was known in Spain as much for his flamboyant lifestyle as for his novels. Awarded the Nobel prize in 1989, Cela was a friend of Hemingway and the two shared a robust masculine approach to both life and literature.

Cela's first novel *La Familia de Pascual Duarte* (The Family of Pascual Duarte) had to be published in Argentina in 1942 because its was consided too violent and crude for the the Spain of the time. The story of a murderer, its uncompromising language was unlike anything else that was being produced in Spain. The book inspired many imitations and is said to be the most popular Spanish novel since Cervantes. Cela published over 70 works including *La Colmena* (The Hive),

a novel about the denizens of 1950s Madrid cafés and their lives and loves. The Nobel citation praised his work for its "rich and intensive prose" and its "restrained compassion."

Although he fought for the nationalists in the Civil war, Cela later published an anti-Franco magazine which became a forum for opposition to the Spanish dictator. His success as an author enabled him to pursue a colourful lifestyle which among other things saw him touring his native land in a vintage Rolls Royce. He died in 2002. The Spanish-based Irish literary historian Ian Gibson published a fairly critical biography of him in 2003 but, while undoubtedly a difficult man with a dark side to his character, his contribution to Spanish literature was a very significant one.

**Santa Uxía de Ribeira** (often just called Ribeira) is the main town in this region, an important fishing port that's a fine enough place but has no real allure. This is the beginning of the next inlet, the **Ría de Arousa**, the largest of this coast. **Cambados** is the most attractive place to stay on this *ría*.

## Padrón

A busy road junction, Padrón at first glance seems unappealing, but it's got several interesting associations. It was a Roman town, and tradition has it that the followers of Saint James landed here after bringing his body back from Palestine. The parish church by the bridge over the river displays the mooring-stone (*el pedrón*) under the altar.

Padrón is also famous for its peppers, which have DO (denominación de origen) status; the small, green *Pimientos de Padrón* are mild, slightly sweet and are seen all over Spain. They are typically cooked in hot oil. Although most are harmless, the odd one is famously fiery; the Spaniards have a saying: 'O los pimientos de Padrón: unos pican, y otros no' (Oh, the peppers of Padrón: some of them bite and some of them don't).

Padrón also has a strong literary connection. It was the long-time home of Galicia's favourite poet, Rosalía de Castro (see box, page 465). Her pretty gardened house has been turned into a museum, the **Casa Museo de Rosalía** ① *Tue-Sat 1000-1330, 1600-1900 (2000 in summer), Sun 1000-1330, €1.20*, opposite the station. In it are various personal possessions and biographical notes. Padrón's other writer was the Nobel prizewinning novelist Camilo José Cela (see page 418), born on the town's outskirts. A former **canon's residence** has been turned into a museum displaying various manuscripts of his work and personal possessions, including a yellowing newspaper collection. Across the road is the collegiate **Iglesia de Santa María de Iria Flavia**, where the writer was baptized; it claims to have been the first church dedicated to Mary in the world (and therefore marks the beginning of Spanish polytheism). There's a small **tourist kiosk** on the main road.

## Vilagarcía de Arousa and around

Vilagarcía de Arousa is one of the wealthier towns on this stretch of coast, with its fair share of urbanizations and brash modern villas. It's an important fishing port, but the cash here wasn't just the result of a bumper prawn harvest; seafood of a more lucrative, Colombian variety finds its way ashore around here in scandalous quantities.

It's a cheerful, uncomplicated sort of town, filled with holidaymakers in summer and doesn't make a bad base for a relaxed exploration of the coast. There's a **tourist office** ① *T986 501 008, Mon-Sat 1000-1300, 1630-1830 (2000 summer), Sun summer only 1000-1400*, on the waterfront promenade where the buses stop.

A quieter and more appealing option can be found just to the north in **O Carril**, a pretty fishing harbour with several top-quality restaurants; there's also an excellent beach nearby, **Praia Compostela**, although you won't have it to yourself in summer.

## Illa de Arousa

South of Vilagarcía, Illa de Arousa is an island linked to the mainland by a long modern bridge. It's relatively unspoiled, although not especially scenic. The main town, Illa de Arousa, is a small fishing port (that also reputedly pulls in more cocaine than crustaceans from its lobster pots). The beaches are sheltered and pleasant enough, although they're not blessed with acres of white sand. The southern half of the island also preserves some important waterbird habitats.

## Cambados

This noble old town is by far the nicest place to stay on this *ría*, and indeed perhaps on the whole of the Rías Baixas. The highlight is the huge granite-paved square, flanked by impressive buildings and a noble archway, and only slightly marred by the cars zipping across it. Other attractive houses line the narrow lanes of the town. The crumbling **Iglesia de Santa Mariña de Dozo** is now used only as a cemetery; its 12th-century ruins are an atmospheric place.

Cambados is also the centre of the Rías Baixas wine region, which has DO (denominación de origen) status. Most of the land under vines is given over to the Albariño grape, which produces highly aromatic whites, fruity and flowery but crisp-finished, somewhat reminiscent of dry German or Alsatian wines; indeed one theory of the variety's origin is that Benedictine monks brought it to the region from the Rhine. It tends to be made in small quantities, and is fairly pricey. Of several *bodegas* in the area, one of the finest is **Martín Códax** ① *5 km east of town, T986 524 499; it's open for visits by prior appointment Mon-Fri 1100-1300, 1600-2000.* **Expo Salnés** is a tourist board-style exhibition about this area of the Rías Baixas.

## O Grove and A Toxa

The resort town of O Grove enjoys an excellent natural setting at the tip of a peninsula at the southern mouth of the *ría*. No doubt it was once a charming fishing port, but is fairly developed these days. Still, it's a very cheerful and likeable place and could make a good venue for a relaxed waterside family holiday, with its large number of hotels, outdoor activities and seafood eateries.

The most interesting sight in the area is **Acquariumgalicia** ① *T986 731 515, www.acquarium galicia.com, winter Mon-Fri 1000-1900, Sat and Sun 1000-2000, summer daily 1000-2100, €9,* 5 km to the west near the village of **Reboredo**. It's a large and excellent display; of most interest for its detailed coverage of the sealife of the *rías* and North Atlantic, although perennial favourites like piranhas and angelfish are also to be seen. There are some 15,000 creatures spread among the 20 large tanks. From here, you can also sally forth in a glass-bottomed boat to see fish and shellfish at liberty, although the visibility can be a little murky.

The area around O Grove is also good for watching waterbirds; many species can be seen patrolling the muddy edges of the *ría*. The main focus for life in the town is the

**Galicia** Rías Baixas

waterfront promenade. **Acquavisión** ① *T986 731 246*, and **Pelegrín** ① *T986 730 032*, also run hourly glass-bottomed boat excursions from here in summer. The trips take about an hour-and-a-half and cost around €15 per head. There's most to be seen on and around the shellfish-breeding platforms, and the trip includes a tasting.

It's a sobering thought that A Toxa was described by Georges Pillement in 1964 as "an earthly paradise". A lover of getting off the beaten track, the French travel writer would be appalled at his little island now. It's linked to O Grove by a short bridge, and although it's still attractively wooded, most of the atmosphere has been removed by the construction of several no-holds-barred luxury hotels, ugly apartments and a casino. If you can dodge the old women selling seashells, stroll around the western half of the island, which is still undeveloped and fragrant with pine. Otherwise, while the hotels lack no comforts, the island reeks of people with more money than sense; in their paranoid wish to keep the rest of society at a healthy distance, they've even installed an armed security guard at the bridge to the outside world.

## Praia A Lanzada

The best beach around this region is Praia A Lanzada, on the seaward side of the narrow neck of the peninsula. Its an excellent sandy stretch whose waters are said to boost female fertility. There's a small chapel at the southern end of the beach; a prayer and a dip are the traditional alternative to IVF in these parts. It's most effective on the night of the 23 June, with the moon shining. The swim must last exactly nine waves.

## Sanxenxo

The resort of Sanxenxo lies on the northern edge of the Ría de Pontevedra and is something of a focus for the area's nightlife. The nicest bit of it is its high headland, while the waterfront is packed with cafés and bars. It's also a watersports centre, and makes a cheerful seaside base conveniently close to the cities of Pontevedra and Vigo.

---

## ● Sleeping

**Muros** *p417*
There are several options on the waterfront, often still referred to as Av Calvo Sotelo.
**B Hotel Muradana**, Av Castelao 99, T981 826 885, www.hotelmuradana.com. The town's smartest option is unremarkable but well equipped. The rooms are spacious and have TV and phone; some are equipped for the disabled. There's also a decent restaurant.
**C Ría de Muros**, Av Castelao 53, T981 823 776, F981 823 133. The most likeable place in town with a guest lounge facing the water. The best bedroom, also at the front, has a curious bedroom/bathroom annexe and is worth nabbing. Good value off season.
**E Hospedería A Vianda**, Av Castelao 49, T981 826 322. Cheap but serviceable rooms above a café/bar, which is also a great place for a cheap *ración* or *menú del día*.

**Noia** *p417*
**D Elisardo**, Costa do Ferrador 15, T981 820 130. Near the shallows of the *ría* with good, clean rooms with bathroom. It's modern in

feel and welcoming in style and offers decent value, even in summer, when you should book, as there are only a handful of rooms.

**Padrón** *p418*
**D Hotel Jardín**, Rúa Salgado Araujo 3, T981 810 950. This is a great little spot to stay, which offers excellent value in a big old house by the Jardín Botánico.

**Vilagarcía de Arousa and around** *p419*
**A Pazo O Rial**, El Rial 1, T986 507 011, www.pazorial.com. Just south of Vilagarcía, on the shoulder of a ridge, this hillside *pazo* (country mansion) in a walled garden off the main road is one of the best places on this coast. It's well priced with attentive service and atmosphere, and it's even got a long *hórreo* and its own *cruceiro*. Recommended.
**C Playa Compostela**, Av Rosalía de Castro 134, O Carril, T986 504 010, playacompostela@ hotmail.com. A modern hotel replete with facilities. Rooms are bright and clean, and it's not bad value year round. Free wifi access.

### Illa da Arousa p419
**E Hotel Benalúa**, Rúa Méndez Núñez s/n, T986 551 332, is a good-value option, with very acceptable rooms with en suite.

### Camping
**Salinas**, T986 527 444. The campsite with the most facilities. Open Jun-Sep.

### Cambados p419
**L Parador de Cambados**, Paseo de Cervantes s/n, T986 542 250, www.parador.es. In the heart of town, this is a good place, set in a traditional Galician *pazo* (country mansion), with a good garden and recently renovated rooms. There's a pool, tennis court, and pretty central patio.
**C Casa Mariñeira Lourdes**, Av A Pastora 95, T/F 986 543 985, www.cmlourdes.net. The nicest of several *casas rurales*, this one has big bedrooms that feel very homely and offer more than decent value. Some rooms share a bathroom and are significantly cheaper. The same owners also have apartments for rental in the village.
**E Hostal Pazos Feijóo**, Rúa Curros Enríquez 1, T986 542 810. A decent and centrally located *hostal* in the southern part of town; there's a cybercafé, **Cyber Guay**, at the same address.

### O Grove and A Toxa p419
There are so many hotels that getting a room is never a problem, even in summer, although finding a bargain is trickier.
**LL Gran Hotel La Toja**, Isla de la Toxa, T986 730 025, www.granhotelhesperia-latoja.com. The top hotel in the area, on the secluded enclave of A Toxa. It's got the lot, including a golf course, swimming pools, gym and sauna, and anything else you care to name.
**B Hotel Maruxia**, Prolongación Luis Casais, T986 732 795, www.hotelmaruxia.com. This is a reasonable choice and open all year-round – out of season its clean and proper double rooms come down substantially in value, but it's not badly priced for the zone in summer either.
**D Hostal Aguiño**, Rúa de Pablo Iglesias 26, T986 731 187. This is a friendly option offering better value than most, a couple of streets back from the main part of the action. Open summer only.

### Praia A Lanzada p420
**B Hotel Nuevo La Lanzada**, T986 743 232. This is a more than decent beachfront hotel with fine clean and bright rooms, some with balcony and views; there's also a restaurant. Open Easter-Sep; there's a minimum 3-night stay in high summer.

### Camping
**Cachadelos**, T986 745 592. The best equipped of 3 summer campsites, with a pool and bungalows. Open Apr-Sep.

### Sanxenxo p420
There are dozens of hotels here.
**L Hotel Sanxenxo**, Paseo de Silgar 3, T986 691 111, www.hotel-sanxenxo.com. This large spa hotel has excellent facilities, and pleasing rooms, nearly all with sea views. There are good off-season rates, and various packages combining your stay with meals, spa treatments, etc. There's also an outdoor pool. A minimum stay applies in summer.
**D Casa Román**, Rúa Carlos Casas 2, T/F986 720 031. A more moderately priced alternative, with comfortably simple en suite rooms that are pretty good value for this coastline.

---

## 🍴 Eating

### Muros p417
**Don Bodegón**, Rúa de Rosalía de Castro 22, T981 827 802. This reliable choice has a good range of seafood and a good atmosphere. It's definitely worth booking in summer. As well as the watery creatures, they also do a more than decent charcoal-grilled steak.
**A Dársena**, Av Castelao 11, T981 826 864, is a bright and friendly spot that does decent pizzas and good *raciones* of *pulpo* and other seafood.

### Cafés
**Café Theatre**, in the old Mercedes theatre on the plaza. A decent café and bar.
**Camelot**, C del Castillo s/n. Built cave-like into bedrock and with comfy seats to enjoy a drink or 2.

### Noia p417
**Mesón Senra**, Rúa Escultor Ferreiro 18, T981 820 084. A characterful restaurant that relies on its typical Galician decor and

sterling service and food. The excellent *zamburiñas* (mini scallops) will satisfy parts other seafoods don't reach, while the sardines (*xoubas* in Galicia) are also bursting with flavour.

### Padrón *p418*

There's little competition for Padrón's golden chef's hat.

**Chef Rivera**, Enlace Parque 7, T981 810 523. The finest spot in town. When the restaurant is named after the chef, you tend to have high expectations; this doesn't disappoint, and uses the finest of Galician ingredients. The lampreys are great, the octopus sublime and the wine list mighty impressive.

**O Pementeiro**, C del Castro s/n. Cheaper and homelier, this is a good spot to try the peppers when in season (summer). There's also a candid *menú del día* for €7.

### Vilagarcía de Arousa and around *p419*

**Loliña**, Praza Muelle s/n, O Carril, T986 501 281. The best place to eat hereabouts, this restaurant is a superb ivy-swathed place with characterful *gallego* decor. The house speciality is monkfish/anglerfish (*rape*).

**Casa Bóveda**, Paseo La Mariña 2, O Carril, T986 511 204. This is similarly good, again dealing in the fruits of the sea. They do a delicious *arroz con bogavante*, a rice dish bursting with taste and sizzling away, with pieces of lobster on top.

### Cambados *p419*

**María José**, Paseo de Cervantes s/n, T986 542 281. A very loveable 1st-floor restaurant opposite the *parador* – the quality of the food is above and beyond what you'd expect for this price, as long as you follow the staff recommendations!

**Posta do Sol**, Ribeira de Fefiñans s/n, T986 542 285. A good seafood restaurant housed in a traditional former bar.

### O Grove and A Toxa *p419*

**Beiramar**, Paseo Marítimo 28, T986 731 081. One of the better of the many seafood restaurants on the waterfront (closed Nov).

**Finisterre**, Praza Corgo 2, T986 730 748. This one treats its fish (and customers) with all the respect they deserve (closed Feb).

## ⊖ Transport

### Muros *p417*

**Bus** There are 3 daily buses to **A Coruña**. From just by the tourist office, buses leave almost hourly for **Santiago via Noia**.

### Noia *p417*

**Bus** There are hourly buses to **Santiago** and **Muros**.

### Padrón *p418*

**Bus and train** There are regular connections with **Santiago**.

### Vilagarcía de Arousa and around *p419*

**Bus** There are buses hourly from **Santiago** and **Pontevedra** to Vilagarcía de Arousa.

### Illa da Arousa *p419*

**Bus** Buses from **Pontevedra** visit the island a couple of times a day, otherwise it's not too far to walk across to the mainland, where buses along the main road are frequent.

# Pontevedra, Vigo and south to Portugal → *Phone code: 986 Colour map 1, B2*

*It's hard to imagine two more contrasting cities than Pontevedra and Vigo, yet both are enchanting. The former is a petite, genteel sort of place, with a picturesque old town studded with gorgeous plazas, while the latter is a big heart-on-sleeve blue-collar sprawl, a fishing city par excellence, situated on a spectacular bay. South of here, Baiona is one of Galicia's most appealing seaside towns, and the Celtic settlement above A Guarda stares across the Miño at Portugal, stone foundations still growling defiantly.* ⟩⟩ *For Sleeping, Eating and other listings, see pages 428-432.*

# Pontevedra 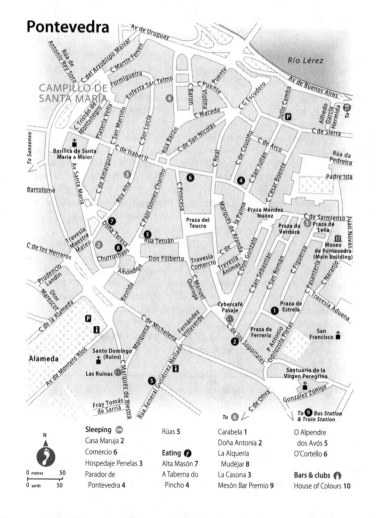 ⟩⟩ *pp428-432.*

**→** *Population: 79,372*

In contrast to its overdeveloped *ría*, Pontevedra is a very charming place; its beautiful old town and relaxed street life make it a top town to visit. It's the most attractive spot to base yourself in to explore the Rías Baixas; its good bus and train connections make daytrips an easy prospect. Its only downside is the occasionally nostril-searing odour from the massive paper mill a couple of kilometres down the *ría*.

## Ins and outs

**Getting there and around** Pontevedra's bus station is a 20-minute walk southeast of the town centre on Rúa da Peregrina. There are frequent connections within Galicia and regular long-distance services. The train station is next door. ⟩⟩ *See also Transport, page 431.*

**Tourist information** Pontevedra's **tourist office** ① *Rúa Xeneral Gutiérrez Mellado 3, T986 850 814, Mon-Fri 0945-1400, 1630-1830, Sat 1030-1230,* is just outside the old

### Pontevedra

**Galicia** Pontevedra, Vigo & south to Portugal

**N**

0 metres 50
0 yards 50

**Sleeping** 🛏
Casa Maruja **2**
Comercio **6**
Hospedaje Penelas **3**
Parador de
Pontevedra **4**

Rúas **5**

**Eating** 🍴
Alta Masón **7**
A Taberna do
Pincho **4**

Carabela **1**
Doña Antonia **2**
La Alquería
Mudéjar **8**
La Casona **3**
Mesón Bar Premio **9**

O Alpendre
dos Avós **5**
O'Cortello **6**

**Bars & clubs** 🎵
House of Colours **10**

town. There's also an **information kiosk** ① *Alameda, Mon-Sat 1030-1330, 1700-1900, Sun 1030-1330*. **Guided tours** of the town leave from the tourist office in summer at 1100 and 1800 (€1.50).

## Background

Like several inland Galician towns, Pontevedra was formerly an important seaport but was left stranded by its river, which deposited large quantities of silt into the *ría*, handing Vigo the initiative for maritime activity. It's said that Pontevedra was founded by Trojan colonists that left the Mediterranean after the defeat by the Greeks; though there's little evidence, it's not the most unlikely of the tall stories along this coast. Pontevedra declined in the 17th and 18th centuries, but on being appointed capital of this economically important Galician province a measure of wealth returned, and it's now a fairly prosperous administrative centre. Its proximity to Vigo means that many people commute between the two cities.

## Sights

Pontevedra's endearing old town is built mostly of granite, and preserves a real medieval feel around its network of postcard-pretty plazas. Perhaps the nicest of the squares is the small, irregular **Praza da Leña**, ringed by attractive houses. Like many of the plazas, it contains a *cruceiro*. The bigger **Praza da Verdura** nearby is another good space with arcades and coats of arms on some of the grander buildings.

Around the large, social **Praza da Ferrería** are two churches, the curiously rounded, domed **Santuario de la Virgen Peregrina**, where pilgrims on their way to Santiago on the *Camino Portugués* traditionally drop in; and the larger **Igrexa de San Francisco**, with some attractive stained glass, carved tombs of goggle-eyed nobles and a fine rose window, as well as an array of saints, pleasingly including some of the less-commonly venerated stalwarts of the church.

The **Basílica de Santa María a Maior** is Pontevedra's finest church, which looks especially attractive when bathed in the evening sun. Dating mostly from the 16th century, it has particularly elaborate ribbed vaulting, late Gothic arches, a dark *retablo* that predates the church, and a sloping floor. The fine Plateresque façade is the work of a Flemish master and depicts scenes from the life of the Virgin Mary. In the gardens on the old town side of the church is a stone marking the location of the old Jewish cemetery.

The **Museo de Pontevedra** ① *winter Mon-Fri 1000-1400, 1600-1900, Sat 1000-1330, 1630-2000, Sun 1100-1400, summer Tue-Sat 1000-1415, 1700-2045, free to EU passport holders, otherwise €1.20 (they don't tend to check)*, covers five separate buildings, with the main one on Praza da Leña. It's one of the better such museums in Spain's north; the Celtic jewellery is a definite highlight; there's also a large 19th-century silverware collection and a replica of a 19th-century Spanish frigate admiral's onboard quarters. Some good paintings are present, including works by Goya and Zurbarán among many Galician, Aragonese and Catalan artists. One of the museum's buildings is the atmospheric, ruined **Iglesia de Santo Domingo** by the Alameda; it contains a number of tombstones from different historical periods.

# Pontevedra to Vigo ● » pp428-432.

Moving southwards along the coast from Pontevedra, the reeking paper mill makes the first few kilometres unattractive, although the cheery maritime murals on the factory are at least a token effort. There's a large naval academy at the small port of Marín, and near Mogor some important Celtic stone carvings. The town of **Bueu** is the point of departure for summer excursions to the peaceful Isla de Ons in a glass-bottommed boat (**Naviera Illa de Ons**, T986 320 048, www.isladeons.net). One of the of Pontevedra and Vigo; it's 1 km from the main road. Its church has a Romanesque portal, but the highlight is its *cruceiro* out the front, an intricate work carved almost wholly from a single block of granite. At the top is a Crucifixion of some emotion, below is a scene of Mary helping sinners in Purgatory, while Adam and Eve stand bashfully underneath. An angel watches the scenes from another pillar nearby. It's one of the finest *cruceiros* of Galicia, although certainly not the oldest, being sculpted in 1872. There's a small tourist information kiosk nearby. The village itself is pleasant spot, and there are some very good beaches around the headland.

**Cangas** is a busy little seaside resort and satellite of Vigo, with some good bars on the waterfront as well as a pretty little chapel. There's a regular ferry across to Vigo used by commuters; it's the smart option, as the traffic between here and there is terrible. It was a hotbed of witchcraft in the 17th century, at least according to those loveable knockabout chaps of the Inquisition. Much of the unorthodox behaviour that caused concern could be attributed to post-traumatic symptoms; the town was viciously sacked by Barbary corsairs shortly before, leaving much of the population dead. If you prefer to stay here to Vigo, see Sleeping, page 428. Moaña, a little closer to Vigo, also has a ferry service, and is a bit quieter.

# Vigo 🔵🔵🔵🔵🔵 ⇒ *pp428-432.*

→ *Phone code: 986. Colour map 1, C2. Population: 293,725.*

Vigo is Galicia's largest city (and the fourth-largest in Northern Spain) and still a very important Spanish fishing, commercial and industrial port that supplies huge quantities of sardines, among other things, to the whole of Europe. With a beautiful location spread along its wide bay, it's a curiously divided place. The old part of town is a working port and wholly down-to-earth. Traffic problems, urban decay and poverty are all present and evident, but it still recalls its golden days as an important steamer port bustling with passengers bound for London, Portugal and South America. Faded but proud old buildings line the streets descending to the harbour, and the fresh seafood on offer here is as good as anywhere in Europe. By contrast, the newer zone around the marina is full of trendy cafés and waterfront promenades. If you're looking for a quiet, restful stop you may hate Vigo; if you're the sort of person who finds busy ports and earthy sailors' bars a little romantic it's an intriguing and likeable place.

*Vigo is the world's largest fishing port by volume after Toyko.*

## Ins and outs

**Getting there**  Vigo's airport is east of the centre and connected with the city by bus. There are daily flights to several Spanish cities and one to Paris. The bus station is a good distance south of the city centre, serviced by city buses from Praza Puerta del Sol (No 12 or No 7). There are dozens of local buses within Galicia and regular connections to cities throughout Spain. Some buses to Pontevedra arrive and leave from the Arenal, which is much more convenient for the centre. Vigo's train station at the eastern end of town and is well served. ⇒ *See also Transport, page 431.*

**Tourist information**  Vigo's new **tourist office** ① *Rúa Cánovas del Castillo, Mon-Fri 0930-1400, 1630-1830, Sat 1000-1200,* is opposite the passenger terminal at the heart of the waterfront.

## Background

Vigo's top natural harbour was used by the Phoenicians and Celts before the city as we know it was founded by the Romans, who named it Vicus Spacorum. Vigo's curse was often its pretty offshore islands, the Islas Cíes, which were used throughout history as cover and a supply base for a series of swashbucklers, raiders, and pirates, including Vikings, Corsairs and Britons; Sir Francis Drake spent a couple of years menacing Vigo on and off. In 1702 a passing British fleet of only 25 ships heard that the treasure fleet from South America was in the port with a French escort. Their surprise attack was a success; they sank 20 and captured 11 of the fleet. The gold and silver was still on board because at that time only Cádiz had official permission to unload bullion from the colonies. Rumour has it that most of it was dumped into the sea; numerous diving expeditions have been mounted over the last couple of centuries, but no success had been reported. In the late 19th century, as the golden age of the steamer began, Vigo grew massively and became prosperous on the back of this and increasingly efficient fishing methods; nearly all its public buildings date from 1860 to 1890. Decline set in in the 20th century, particularly during the stultifying Franco years, when Spain lagged far behind other European powers, but more recently large manufacturing plants, such as the huge Citröen operation, have brought much employment to the city. Pontevedra's status as provincial capital continues to annoy Vigo (until the new standardized numberplates came in, locals used to travel to far-away Vitoria so their car would bear the 'VI'); there has never been much love lost between the two cities, and locals feel their city doesn't get a fair slice of the pie from the provincial administration. Nevertheless, the local administration is making a big effort at urban renewal, including installing a fine series of modern sculpture all around town, and little by little Vigo is beginning to recover the sparkle that its superb natural setting deserves.

## Sights

Vigo's main sight is its busy **waterfront**. There are kilometres of it to wander if you're so inclined, and even the commercial docks are mostly easily accessible. Right in the centre is the passenger terminal where steamers used to dock; next to it is where the ferries leave for the ports of **Cangas** and **Moaña** across the bay, as well as the **Islas**

| Sleeping | Eating | El Mosquito 7 | La Cueva del |
| --- | --- | --- | --- |
| Bahía de Vigo 1 | Bitácora 1 | La Trucha 8 | Ermitaño 10 |
| Compostela 2 | Café Laxe 2 | | Pedramola 11 |
| Hostal Puerta del Sol 3 | Don Gregorio 4 | Bars & clubs | Pérgola 12 |
| La Nueva | Don Quijote 5 | Edra 9 | |
| Colegiata 5 | El Corral 6 | Iguana Club 3 | |

**Cíes** in summer. The terminal still gets the odd cruise ship in, and many a yacht still puts in at the marina just to the east, which is backed with all manner of trendy bars and restaurants.

To the west, it's worth having a look at the fishing port, where boats of all sizes and nationalities drop in on their way to and from the Atlantic fisheries. Further round are repair docks and shipwrecking yards, and the **Puerto de Bouzas** beyond is the customs-bonded dock where commercial goods are unloaded. When the fishing boats come in at dawn, *marisqueiras* (typically the wives of the fishermen) still sell fresh shellfish (the oysters – delicious) around the streets; for a bigger selection, head for the market on **Rúa da Pescadería** near the marina.

The main attraction in the town itself is the elegant architecture on the streets leading back from the passenger terminal, very faded but a poignant reminder of golden days. Just to the west, the narrow streets are the oldest part of the town; it's known as **Berbés**, and is full of little watering-holes and eateries. It has its vaguely seedy side but is on the up again. At weekends when dozens of bars seem to mushroom from nowhere; it's as lively and hard-drinking a scene as you'd expect.

The new **Museo do Mar de Galicia** ① *Tue-Sun 1000-2100*, is on the waterfront a fair way west of the centre. It's an interesting display of Spanish maritime history and includes an exhibition on the treasure fleet disaster of 1702 and the importance of trade with the New World colonies.

The **Museo Municipal Quiñones de León** ① *Tue-Fri 1000-2000, Sat 1700-2000, Sun 1000-1330*, is a museum in an old Galician mansion in the Parque de Castrelos south of the centre; it has period furniture and a decent collection of Galician paintings and makes a peaceful retreat from Vigo's working centre. In an adjacent annex is a reasonable archaeological collection.

The offshore **Islas Cíes** are a complete contrast to Vigo and the overdeveloped *rías*; an unspoiled natural paradise of excellent beaches and quiet coves, and an old pirates' haunt. In the height of summer the campsite has a pretty lively social scene. In summer (mid-June to mid-September), ferries run to the islands from the passenger dock; you'll have to return the same day unless you simultaneously purchase a voucher for the islands' campsite (T986 438 358), which has a shop and bar/restaurant. There are four boats a day, and a return ticket is €12.

# South of Vigo ●●●● ›› *pp428-432.*

## Baiona and around → *Colour map 1, B2.*
Heading south, the elegant port and resort of Baiona is the main destination of interest. On the way, **Playa América** is a long, narrow, popular and adequate beach with a well-equipped campsite (see Sleeping, below).

Baiona is a beautiful spot, built behind a large, walled fort on the headland, now a *parador* (an admission charge of €0.60 is haphazardly levied). It was mostly built by the counts of Andrade, who bossed most of Galicia in their day, but before that the headland was inhabited by Celts, Phoenicians and Romans. Take the 3-km stroll around the impressive walls, reinforced with cannon, and have a drink at the terraced bar; it's a superb spot, even if you can't afford to stay in the *parador* itself.

Baiona was agog in 1493, when the *Pinta*, of Columbus' small fleet, appeared at the port entrance with confirmation that the Atlantic could be, and just had been, crossed. There's a replica of the staggeringly small **Pinta** ① *Wed-Mon 1000-1930, €0.75*, in the port here, enlivened by a dummy crew.

On the hill above town is a giant and tasteless statue of the Virgin; you can, however, climb it for good views of the town and coast. Baiona has a small **tourist office** ① *Mon-Fri 1030-1430 (extended hours in summer)*, which is located by the entrance to the *parador*.

South of Baiona, the tiny village of **Oia** is a fairly untouched little fishing port. The licheny Baroque monastery is in a poor way. The monks here knew about Oliver Cromwell's advice to "put your trust in God but keep your powder dry"; they once repelled a Turkish pirate fleet with a volley of cannon fire. If you want to stay in this peaceful place, see Sleeping, below.

## A Guarda

The last Spanish town on the Atlantic coast is A Guarda, a fairly uninspiring spot but worth visiting for the **Monte Santa Trega** ① €0.70, high above town. Occupying the headland between the sea and the mouth of the Miño that marks the border with Portugal, it's a long but worthwhile climb (or drive). As well as great views over the town, rivermouth and out to sea, you can pace the impossibly narrow streets of the ruins of a large Celtic town. One of the round stone dwellings has been reconstructed; the *palloza*, its direct descendant, was still a feature of many Galician villages until fairly recently. At the top, there's a chapel and a small museum with some finds from the site.

## ● Sleeping

**Pontevedra** *p423, map p423*
**L Parador de Pontevedra**, Rúa Barón 19, T986 855 800, pontevedra@parador.es, www.parador.es. This lovely *parador* is in the heart of the old town, set in a *palacio* on a pretty square. There's a beautiful garden and terrace, and the rooms are decorated with plenty of style and comfort.
**C Hotel Ruas**, Rúa Padre Sarmiento 37, T986 846 416, hotelruas@terra.es. You can't beat the location of this hotel, in the liveliest area of the beautiful centre, set right between 2 of the prettiest plazas. The rooms have large comfortable beds and are very good for the price; the showers are gloriously powerful. There's a café downstairs and a warm welcome. It's much cheaper off-season.
**C-D Hotel Comercio**, Rúa González Besada 3, T986 851 217, www.hcomercio.com. This smart modern hotel isn't going to win any design awards but is fairly central, in the new town not far from Praza Herrerías. The rooms have a/c and good bathrooms.
**E-F Casa Maruja**, Av Santa María 2, T986 854 901. Good cheap rooms, clean and with TV; some en suite. Well located in the old town.
**F Hospedaje Penelas**, R Alta 17, T986 855 705. A lovely budget option in the old town, clean and comfy. There won't be much cat-swinging, but it's friendly and very cheap.

**Pontevedra to Vigo** *p424*
**C Hotel Airiños**, Rúa da Marina s/n, Cangas, T986 340 000, www.airinos.com, is a decent option on the boulevard. Rooms are comfortably spacious if darkish. It's worth

paying a little extra for larger ones with a sea view and lounge area. Free Internet terminal.
**C Hostal Playa**, Av de Ourense 78, Cangas. T986 303 674, www.hotel-playa.com. Slightly cheaper than the **Airiños** and a short way east of the main bustle. Rooms are clean and bright.

**Vigo** *p425, map p426*
There's plenty of accommodation for all budgets in Vigo.
**AL Bahía de Vigo**, Av Cánovas del Castillo s/n, T986 226 700, www.husa.es. This large sprawling hotel is no coquettish beauty, but is perfectly placed on the harbour. The reason for being here is the views, so make sure your room has got one. The rooms are spacious and well equipped, some seem a little more worn than others.
**B Compostela**, Rúa García Olloqui 5, T986 225 528, www.hcompostela.com. A quality mid-range hotel near the harbour, spruce and comfortable. It's got underground parking, an important factor in Vigo.
**C Hostal Puerta del Sol**, Puerta del Sol 14, T/F986 222 364, www.alojamientosvigo.com. Can be a bit noisy, but this is a good, well-looked after place at the top of the old town, with plenty of house plants and comfy rooms.
**F Don Quijote**, C Laxe 4, T986 229 346. This good restaurant (see below) has some decent, cheap, heated rooms available.
**F La Nueva Colegiata**, Plaza de la Iglesia 3, T986 220 952. A decent, cheap option in the old town with modernized facilities and more than adequate heated rooms that are a snip at this price.

**Baiona** *p427*

**L Parador de Baiona**, Monterreal s/n, Baiona, T986 355 000, www.parador.es. One of the chain's finest, superbly set in grassy gardens within the impressively walled fort on the headland. Comfortable rooms; many have great views out to sea. Highly recommended.

**AL Pazo de Mendoza**, C Elduayen 1, Baiona, T986 385 014, www.pazodemendoza.es. In the old dean's house in the centre of town, this is a classy option and very good value for money. Rooms are equipped with modern conveniences but haven't lost the charm of this noble old edifice.

**D Casa Puertas**, Rúa Vicente López 7, Oia, T986 362 144, www.casapuertas.com. A charming *casa rural* in a stone house in the narrow streets near the monastery. Rooms are simply furnished but comfortable, and offer great value in this peaceful village.

**D Hostal Caís**, Rúa Alférez Barreiro 3, Baiona, T986 355 643. This friendliest of places is an unbeatable budget hangout. Right by the water, it has spacious rooms with TV and phone, and even a small swimming pool.

**F Hospedaje Kin**, Rúa Ventura Misa 27, Baiona, T986 355 695. Small rooms in a good location on the main pedestrian street, focus for tapas and restaurants.

### Camping

**Camping Baiona Playa**, Praia Ladeira, T986 350 035. A year-round campsite with cabins, a pool and all the trimmings on a long beach east of the town.

**Playa América**, Playa América, T986 365 404. Campsite with bungalows and a swimming pool; it's open mid-Mar to mid-Oct.

### A Guarda *p428*

**B Convento de San Benito**, Praza San Benito s/n, T986 611 166, www.hotelsanbenito.com. This is an enchanting and peaceful place to stay, in a lovingly restored monastery with a pretty cloister. Have a look at a few rooms, as they are all quite different and have distinct charms; some are more expensive (**A**) and have hydromassage showers. Recommended.

## ● Eating

**Pontevedra** *p423*, *map p423*
It's very difficult to find a place to eat on Sun evenings in Pontevedra.

**¶¶¶ Casa Solla**, Av Sineiro 7, San Salvador de Poyo, T986 873 198. An excellent seafood restaurant with innovative dishes, 5 km west of Pontevedra on the way to Sanxenxo. The setting in a noble mansion surrounded by garden, matches the high quality of the food.

**¶¶¶ Doña Antonia**, Soportales de la Ferrería 4, T986 847 274. Excellent gourmet dishes, including game in season, can be found at this upstairs restaurant in the old centre. Courteous service and lip-smacking desserts.

**¶¶ Alta Masón**, Rúa Alta 4, T986 896 610. The best aspect of this homely resturant is its secluded little tree-shaded terrace near the basilica. The food's good too, though; they do a tasty steak, and the *zamburiñas* are full of flavour. There's a *menú del día* on weekdays for €7.

**¶¶ La Casona**, Rúa Tetúan 10, T986 847 038. A friendly, stylish restaurant that makes an excellent choice. The food is generally traditional Galician fare prepared with style; the *lenguado al albariño* is a good dish of sole cooked in the aromatic local white wine.

**¶¶ Mesón Bar Premio**, Rúa da Peregrina 29, T986 103 528. This atmospheric spot is a godsend if you are lugging heavy bags from the bus station into the old town on a hot day. A tapa of the delicious ham and a glass of something cold and you'll be on your way again with renewed vigour. It's also a great spot to sit down and eat and decorated in the traditional manner with venerable wine bottles and hanging *charcutería*.

**¶ A Taberna do Pincho**, Praza Méndez Núñez 15, T986 857 840. A popular meeting point in the heart of Pontevedra. You'll get a small free snack with your drink, and there's also a wide choice of nibbles or more substantial fare such as *revueltos*, which you can eat at the downstairs tables.

**¶ La Alquería Mudéjar**, Rúa Churruchaos 2, T986 851 258. With wooden tables, yellow lighting and a convivial buzz, this is a place to lift the spirits. There's a fine selection of wines and plenty of simple *raciones* and dishes. The *tortilla* is great, as are the brochettes; this is a real enclave of genuine hospitality. Recommended.

**¶ O Alpendre dos Avós**, C Gutiérrez Mellado 6, T986 896 228. A fairly traditional scene at this spacious and busy café, tapas bar and restaurant apart from the dishes on offer, which include tapas of kangaroo and ostrich.

¶ **O'Cortello**, Rúa Isabel II 36, T986 840 443. One of Pontevedra's best tapas options for typical *gallego* dishes like *xoubas* (sardines). Cheerful and popular. The *menú del día* is good value at €7 as well.

### Cafés
**Carabela**, Praza da Estrela s/n. A café with a relaxing outdoor terrace on the largest square, where you can watch Pontevedra's children feeding the pigeons.

### Vigo *p425, map p426*
Despite the comic restaurant war between 2 *marisquerías* on the waterfront of **Berbés**, better value can be found around **C de Carral** a little further east, opposite the passenger terminal. There's also excellent cheap seafood to be found on **Rúa Pescadería** by the fish market. More upmarket choices are clustered in the streets behind the marina.

¶¶¶ **El Mosquito**, Praza da Pedra 2, T986 224 411. This upmarket but down-to-earth and cheery restaurant in the old-town streets above the port has a deserved reputation for its seafood. Whatever you choose here is bound to be good; the octopus has an excellent reputation, as do the oysters and the *lenguado* (sole).

¶¶ **La Trucha**, Rúa de Luis Taboada 2. A corner eatery very popular with a wealthy set for a small selection of good fish and seafood.

¶¶ **Restaurante Bitácora**, Rúa Carral 26. Good *raciones* of seafood in this smartish tapas bar and restaurant. You'll struggle to pass by without entering, the sizzling smells are so enticing. The *zamburiñas* in garlic are especially tasty. They also do a great seafood paella at €19.75 each.

¶¶ **Restaurante Don Quijote**, C Laxe 4, T986 229 346. This restaurant on a steep street above the passenger terminal is excellent, particularly its wooden outdoor tables. There's a full restaurant menu or excellent *raciones* and tapas; the *mejillones* (mussels) are particularly good. Recommended.

¶ **El Corral**, R García Ollaqui 36. If you fancy a change from seafood, head here for some delicious *raciones* of ham.

### Cafés
**Café Laxe**, C Laxe 11, T986 225 081. Very tempting pastries and coffees at this popular workers' café.

**Don Gregorio**, Plaza Puerta del Sol s/n. A popular café with a big terrace at the top of the old town. Free snacks with your drinks.

### Baiona *p427*
¶¶¶ **Moscón**, Rúa Alférez Barreiro 2, T986 355 008. This has a massive reputation for the superb quality of its seafood. It's always packed in summer; you'll need to book or be prepared to wait a long while.

¶¶ **Abeiro**, R Ventura Misa 30, T986 358 375. A smart modern restaurant with excellent *pulpo* (octopus) and a good *menú del día* for €10. Closed Nov.

¶¶ **Mosquito**, Rúa Elduayen 3. The sister restaurant of **Moscón** with a homely feel, lower prices but a similarly reliable quality.

¶ **Entre Redes**, C Lorenzo de la Carrera 11. Smart seafood *raciones*.

¶ **Jaqueyvi**, Rúa Xogo da Bola 1, T986 356 157. A great spot for ham and cheese tapas accompanied by local wine.

---

## ⑪ Bars and clubs

### Pontevedra *p423, map p423*
Praza del Teucro is the old-town centre for evening drinking. After hours the *marcha* moves out a little; many people head for Sanxenxo in summer, or the town of Arcade, 5 km south, which has, as well as a phalanx of *marisquerías*, several bars and *discotecas* along its main street, **C Castelao**.

**House of Colours**, C Italia 3. Probably the most happening *discoteca* in Pontevedra itself, this is located in the modern barrio of Monteporreiro, a couple of kilometres northeast of the centre along the riverbank.

### Vigo *p425*
The bars of **Berbés** around **Rúa Real** are seedy but interesting; however, they only really get going at weekends. The classier joints around the marina see more mid-week action, but are very pricey, particularly on the terrace. Most *discotecas* are near the train station.

**Edra**, Praza de los Pescadores 6. A no-frills little bar tucked in the old town, where locals come to sit outside on the wall and drink beer.

**La Cueva del Ermitaño**, off C Victoria. A bar with an outdoor terrace located in a side alley that's the entrance to a church. Good beer.

**Pedramola**, Rúa Real 25. A good bar if you like your music loud, dark and metallic.

**Pergola**, C Pablo Morillo 7. One of the cheaper and better bars, decorated with orange and Dionysiac wallpaintings.
**Iguana Club**, C Churruca 14. One of the legendary live music venues of Northern Spain, with local and international rock bands on regularly. It's also a good spot for a drink, with 2 levels and a warehouse-like feel.

## ⊙ Entertainment

**Pontevedra** *p423, map p423*
Pontevedra has a good cultural programme; look for the monthly guide *BIPO*.
**Teatro Principal**, R Charino 6, T986 851 932. The adjacent cinema complexes **ABC**, T986 860 392, and **Multicines Pontevedra**, T986 860 392 are on Rúa Barco Porto.

**Vigo** *p425, map p426*
**Multicines Centro**, C María Berdiales 7, T986 226 366. Vigo's main central cinema.

## ⊙ Shopping

**Pontevedra** *p423, map p423*
**La Navarra**, R Princesa 13. A no-frills place to buy a good selection of Galician wines.

## ▲ Activities and tours

**Vigo** *p425, map p426*
**Football** Vigo's have-a-go football team, **Celta**, T986 214 585, www.celtavigo.net, have done well in the Spanish league and Europe in recent years, despite a brief sojourn in the *Segunda* in 2004/5. They don their sky-blue tops at Balaídos, to the southwest of town, normally on a Sun evening. Tickets are available at the stadium for a couple of days before; the booth's also open a couple of hours before the game.

## ⊖ Transport

**Pontevedra** *p423, map p423*
**Bus**
**Local** Within Galicia, **Ourense** is served 8 times a day, **A Coruña** about 10 times, and **Santiago** (€4.85, 50 mins) even more often. There are hourly buses to **O Grove**, and even more to **Sanxenxo**. 10 a day go to **Cangas** and buses leave every ½ hr or so for **Vigo** (some to the bus station, some to the

waterfront, €2.25, 25 mins). 2 a day go to **Padrón** and **Noia**, and 4 to **Tui** and **Valença** (Portugal). Hourly buses head north to **Vilagarcía**, some taking in the island of **Illa Arousa**, and 8 go to **Cambados**. 6 buses cross Galicia to **Lugo** every day.

**Long distance** To **Madrid**, 2 to **Bilbao** (12 hrs, €48.30) via Oviedo or Burgosvente, 1 or 2 to **Barcelona** and **Zaragoza**, 1 to **Salamanca**, **Gijón**, and **Valladolid**. There are many more routes from nearby Vigo. On Fri and Sun there's a bus to **Lisbon** at 1600.

**Train**
There a frequent connections to **Vigo** (25 mins, from €1.75) and **A Coruña** (2 hrs, from €7.55) via **Santiago**.

**Vigo** *p425, map p426*
**Air**
There are daily flights to several Spanish cities, mostly operated by **Spanair**. There are European flights to **Frankfurt**, **Copenhagen**, **Paris** and **Stockholm**, and intercontinental ones to **Buenos Aires** and **Washington**.

**Bus**
**Local** There are frequent buses to **Pontevedra**, leaving both from the bus station and also from C Arenal 52 (€2.25, 25 mins). Buses to **Santiago** leave every ½ hr, and there are about 10 daily to **Ourense**. Buses leave ½-hourly for **Baiona** and for **Tui** and **A Guarda**. There are about 5 daily buses to **Lugo** (4 hrs, €14.88).

**Long distance** Among many long distance interurban services, there are 6 buses to **Madrid**, 2 to **Bilbao**, 1 or 2 to **Barcelona** and **Zaragoza**, 1 to **Salamanca**, **Gijón**, and **Valladolid**. 2 daily buses at 0900 and 1830 leave for **Porto**, **Lisbon** and the **Algarve**.

**Ferry**
Vigo's days as a passenger port are just about over, but there are still ferries hourly to **Moaña** and ½-hourly to **Cangas**, across the bay. In summer boats go to the **Islas Cíes**, see page 427.

**Train**
Galician destinations include **A Coruña** almost hourly (2½-3 hrs, from €8.50),

**Ourense** 7 times daily (2 hrs from €6.80), and **Santiago** (1 hr 20 mins, from €5.20) via Pontevedra about 15 times a day. There are good long-distance connections. There is a Barcelona sleeper, a day train to **San Sebastián** and the French border, and a day and night train to **Madrid**. There are 2 trains daily to **Porto** (Portugal), and 4 a day to **León**.

**Baiona** *p427*
**Bus** Buses run to/from **Vigo** every 30 mins.

**A Guarda** *p428*
**Bus** Buses leave for **Vigo** and Tui ½-hourly (fewer at weekends). There's a ferry across the Miño to **Portugal** and another crossing further east in Goián. The first bridge is at Tui.

## ⊕ Directory

**Pontevedra** *p423, map p423*
**Internet** Cybercafé Pasaje, Rúa dos Soportais 6. Coin-op machines 40 mins/€. Also **Las Ruinas**, C Marqués de Riestra 21.
**Medical services** The Clínica San Sebastián is a medical centre on Rúa Benito Corbal 24, T986 867 890, with 24-hr attendance. **Telephone** There are cheap *locutorios* on the edge of the old town at C de la Marquesa 1 and C Marqués de Riestra 21.

**Vigo** *p425, map p426*
**Internet** There's a café on Rúa Principe just above the old town. **Post office** The central post office is on Rúa da Victoria.

# Miño Valley

*Rising northeast of Lugo, the Miño sweeps through much of Galicia in a southwesterly direction and forms part of the border between Spain and Portugal before it meets the Atlantic near A Guarda. Its lower sections run through a little-explored region of vineyards, monasteries and hidden valleys, watering the pleasant provincial capital of Ourense on the way. ▸▸ For Sleeping, Eating and other listings, see pages 436-438.*

## Tui/Tuy 🍴🏨🚌 ▸▸ *pp436-438.*

→ *Colour map1, C2.*
Perched on a rocky hill high above the north bank of the Miño, Tui doesn't have the scurvy feel of most border towns. It's an attractive ancient Galician town that has exchanged growls through history with its counterpart fortress town Valença, across the water in Portugal. A former Celtic settlement, it was inhabited by Romans, then Sueves and Visigoths, briefly serving as capital of the boy-king Wittiza in the early eighth century. It was mentioned by Ptolemy, who named it Toudai and attributed its founding to Diomedes, son of Tydeus.

### Sights

Tui has a solid assembly of attractive historical buildings, of which the highlight is the **cathedral**, which doubled as a fortress for so long. This function influenced the building's architecture, which has a military simplicity. It was started in the early 12th century and has both Romanesque and later Gothic features. There's a door of each type; the Romanesque portal has a simple geometric pattern, while the Gothic door and porch features an excellent sculptured *Adoration*, an early work with traces of colour remaining. It's flanked by later statues of the Elders of the Apocalypse. Inside are striking wooden beams; the church has a lean and has had to be reinforced over the years, especially after the 1755 Lisbon earthquake. The tomb of San Pedro González is here; he was a local Dominican who lived in the 13th century and cared for sick sailors, who dubbed him San Telmo after their patron. There's also an attractive cloister with a walkway above it that gives excellent views, as does the tower. There's a small **museum** ① *0930-1330, 1600-1900, cloister, tower and museum €1.80.*

There are several other churches in town and plenty of narrow lanes and fine old **433**
houses. It's a popular place with visiting Portuguese, and the town is well stocked with
bars. There's a narrow, attractive road bridge from Spain to Portugal 1 km below the
town; it was built by Gustave Eiffel in 1884. Although there's a depressing little border-
bargain shopping area nearby, the town of **Valença** itself has several pretty corners,
well worth ducking across to see.

---

# Ourense/Orense ⬤❷❶⊕⊟❶ ‣ *pp436-438.*

➔ *Phone code: 988. Colour map 1, C3. Population: 108,358.*
Little-visited Ourense is the capital of Galicia's inland province, a rural zone criss-
crossed by rocky hills and pastured valleys where much wheat is farmed and cheese
and wine are made. The town itself is a prosperous centre with heavy traffic and active
streetlife. Once you get away from the busy roads and into the pedestrianized old town,
it's a pleasant place indeed, with several beautiful plazas, and well worth a visit.

## Ins and outs
**Getting there and around**  The train station is across the river to the north of town
(20 minutes' walk); from Parque San Lázaro dozens of city buses go in this direction.
The bus station is further in the same direction; buses No 6 and No 12 make it out there.

**Tourist information**  There are two useful tourist offices in Ourense. The **regional
office** ① *T988 372 020, Mon-Fri 0900-1400, 1630-1830 (1700-2100 summer), Sat
1000-1400*, has just moved to new premises at the southern (city) end of the Ponte
Maior Roman bridge. The **municipal office** ① *Rúa As Burgas 12, T988 366 064,
Mon-Fri 1000-1400, 1700-1900, Sat/Sun 1200-1400*, is by the As Burgas hot springs.

## Background
Although tradition claims that the city's name derives from *ouro*, meaning gold, it
actually comes from the hot springs; the Roman town was named *Aquae Urentes*
(warm waters). It was later an important city of the Suevish kingdom, and later of the
Visigoths. As an important linking point between Galicia and the rest of Spain,
Ourense flourished after its repopulation during the Reconquista. Following the
decline that seemed to affect almost every city in Spain at some point, it is now a
prosperous palace, thriving as capital of this significant agricultural province.

## Sights
The **Catedral de San Martiño** was started in the 12th century; most of its features are
Transitional in style (ie late Romanesque/early Gothic). The most impressive of the
portals is intricately carved with scalloping and 12 good apostles below a headless
Christ. The interior is long and gloomy, with many tombs of prelates carved into the
walls; the attractive galleried cupola is a later early Renaissance
work. There's an impressive version of Santiago's *Pórtico de la
Gloria*, preserving much of its bright paintwork. The chief object of
veneration is the *Santísimo Cristo*, a similar spooky Christ to the
one in Burgos' cathedral. Made of fabric, the figure has real hair
and a purple and gold skirt. It's located in a chapel that's an amazingly bright Baroque
fantasy in gold. Off the cloister is the **cathedral museum** ① *1130-1300, 1630-1900, €1.*

The **Praza Maior** is just by here, a very appealing arcaded space. It's overlooked
by the **Museo Arqueolóxico**, the provincial museum, very attractively set in the former
bishops' palace. It contains many Roman and Celtic finds as well as some sculpture
and paintings from churches in the province. At time of this update, it was still closed
for major reforms, but should be open by the time of publication.

*The Casco Vello, Ourense's old quarter, is its most interesting, and an intriguing place to wander.*

Galicia Miño Valley

The pretty little linked **Praza da Magdalena** is off the main square and has beautiful overhanging buildings and roses. It's dominated by the cathedral and the **Iglesia de Santa María Madre**, an attractive Baroque church built from the ruins of the 11th-century original; some Romanesque columns and capitals are preserved.

The main pedestrian streets to stroll down of an evening are the **Calle Santo Domingo** and the **Rúa do Paseo**. Fans of cream and brown should check out the latter; at No 30 the **Edificio Viacambre** looks like a Chinese puzzle-box gone horribly wrong! The cloister of **Iglesia de San Francisco** is a beautifully harmonious Transitional piece of stonework, although each side has a different number of arches. The double columns are carved with capitals, many vegetal, but some featuring an array of strange beasts.

# Ourense

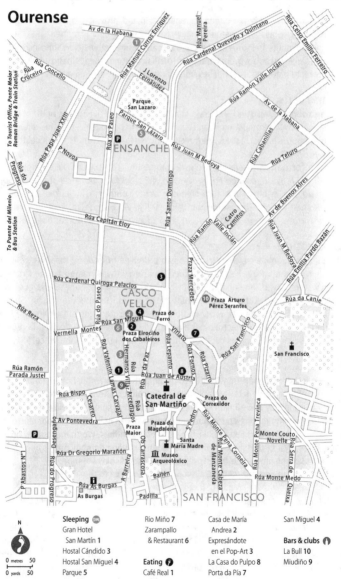

## As Burgas

Below the old town, As Burgas is the hot spring that attracted the Romans. The water streams out at a healthy 65°C. The mineral composition of the water is engraved on a plaque by the fount. Nearby is the food market, with plenty of outdoor stalls where farmers sell their produce. The Romans built a high bridge over the flood-prone Miño; it was rebuilt in medieval times and is still in use (Ponte Maior); it's worth the walk to see its elegant lines. Further along the river is the writhing metallic **Puente del Milenio**, a recent construction that's particularly impressive when floodlit.

---

# Around Ourense ☺🚲☺ ⟩⟩ pp436-438.

## Ribadavia → Colour map 1, B3.

An excellent day trip from Ourense is to head down the Miño to Ribadavia, an attractive small town that is the centre of the **Ribeiro wine region**. Ribeiro wines come both in a crisp white and a slightly effervescent red; both resemble northern Portuguese wines and are produced from the same grape varieties.The white *ribeiro* is the most common and is drunk all over Galicia out of distinctive white ceramic crucibles. The area was also notable for having been a profitable tin-mining zone.

Ribadavia is famous for having maintained a sizeable Jewish population from the 12th to 16th century, even after the expulsion order of 1492. There are still some traces of the **Jewish quarter**; the old synagogue preserves many features despite its conversion into a church and the narrow streets remain, although nearly all the buildings postdate the era. A few Hebrew inscriptions and a Jewish pastry shop evince the town's pride in this part of their history.

*♣ In early May, there's a wine festival in the town.*

The 12th-century **Iglesia de San Xuán** ① *Mon-Sat 0930- 1430, 1600-1830, Sun 1030-1500*, has a Romanesque apse and curious portal of Mozarabic influence. The nearby Plaza Mayor is a fantastic long space, which harbours the tourist office.  The massive **Convento de Santo Domingo** ① *1000-1300, 1700-2000*, was once lived in by kings; the Gothic church and cloister is worth a look. The **Museo do Ribeiro** is a fairly unenlightening display on the region's winemaking.

## North of Ourense

The **Monasterio de Santa María la Real de Oseira** ① *Mon-Sat 0930-1230, 1500-1730 (1830 summer), Sun 1230 only, €1.20, guided tour only*, is often dubbed the 'Escorial de Galicia' for its immense size and harmonious Renaissance lines. Sitting solitary in a valley, it was founded in the 12th century and still houses a community of Cistercian monks in archtectural splendour. The façade, from the early 18th century, is of monumental Churrigueresque style; the Virgin Mary occupies pride of place underneath a figure of Hope. Below is Saint Bernard, founder of the Cistercian order. The most interesting thing inside is the Claustro de los Medallones, carved with quirky depictions of historical figures. The austere church belies its Baroque façade and is of little joy apart from some colourful 17th-century wallpaintings. Worth the journey on its own, however, is the Sala Capitular, with beautiful vaulting flamboyantly issuing from the twisted barbers-pole columns; it's like a fireworks display in stone.

## East of Ourense

Off the main road east of Ourense is a beautiful gorge, the **Gargantas do Sil**, running up a tributary of the Miño. It's worth exploring by car or on foot; viney terraces soon give way to rocky slopes dropping steeply into the river.

The **Monasterio de Santo Estevo de Ribas de Sil** stands out like a beacon with its pale walls and brick-red roof against the wooded valley. Apart from the setting, the monastery isn't especially interesting, although there are three cloisters, one of them huge; another still preserves some Romanesque arching.

Galicia Miño Valley

From near the monastery, the GR56 long-distance trail is a good way to explore some remote areas of Ourense province. It heads along the gorge and takes in another couple of monasteries along its 100-km route, before finally ascending steeply to the mountain village of **Manzaneda**, a small ski resort.

The N120 continues León-wards and bids farewell to the Miño just before the town of **Monforte de Lemos**. Even if you've got a car, it's worth making a return train journey from Ourense to here, as the route is spectacular, running along the river and cutting into the Sil gorge for a short while. Monforte is dominated by a hilltop monastery (now a *parador*) and medieval tower that used to be part of a castle. If you're in the mood for lunch, try the O Grelo (see Sleeping, page 437)

Near Monforte are the amusingly named wine towns **Sober** and **Canabal**. Beyond Monforte, there are several ruinous castles in the valley, including the **Castelo de Torrenovaes** looming over the road near **Quiroga**. There's a Roman tunnel near the road at Monferado. The last major settlement in Galicia is **O Barco**, a friendly but uninteresting town whose primary industry is the manufacture of *orujo*, a grape spirit better flavoured or in coffee than neat.

## South of Ourense

To Ourense's south, **Celanova** is well worth a visit. Known as the 'hidden city' for the reticence of its inhabitants, it's only a village really, dominated by the **Monastery of San Salvador** ① *Mon-Sat 1100, 1200, 1300, 1700, 1800 (also 1000, 1600, 1900 in summer), €1.20, guided tour only*, on a huge square. While the façade could be called over-ornate, the cloisters are a gem, dating from the 16th century. The Gothic wooden choir is also attractive. Around the back of the monastery is a Mozarabic chapel, San Miguel, a well-preserved 10th-century structure.

Twenty five kilometres further south, the Visigothic church of **Santa Comba de Bande** is set above a long *embalse* (reservoir). It's a noble little structure with a small tower and square apse.

East of here, Verín makes a good place to explore and stay. It's an attractive walled winemaking town set in a valley, with an attractive church, and featuring a castle complex in the neighbouring village of Monterrei which was used in aggressions and defences against the Portuguese. There's a *parador* next to it.

## ● Sleeping

**Tui** *p432*
**AL Parador de San Telmo**, Av de Portugal s/n, T986 600 309, www.parador.es. Below the town, in a modern replica of a Galician *pazo*, the San Telmo offers good views of the town and river. It's a good place to relax, with a pool and tennis court among its conveniences.
**F Hostal Generosa**, Av Calvo Sotelo 37, T986 600 055. A simple choice; shared bathrooms, clean, comfortable but without luxury.

**Ourense** *p433, map p434*
**L Gran Hotel San Martín**, Curros Enríquez 1, T988 371 811, www.gh-hoteles.com. Looming over the park, this huge hotel may seem like some 1970s airport horror from the outside, but is much better within. It has comfortable and well-equipped modern rooms, many of them with good views of the town.

**D Hotel Parque**, Parque de San Lázaro 24, T988 233 611, F988 239 636. A clean and proper Spanish hotel, not particularly memorable, but a comfortable spot overlooking the park. It's run by friendly people, has good-value rooms with decent bathroom, and is close to the old centre. A decent breakfast (extra) is served in an adjacent bar.
**D Hotel Zarampallo**, R San Miguel 9, T988 220 053. An attractive central modernized option above a good restaurant. The rooms are well equipped; there's a small price difference between those with a shower and those with a bathtub as well.
**E Hotel Río Miño**, Rúa Juan XXIII 4, T988 215 252. This curious place offers remarkably good value. The rooms are hotel standard, with small but modern bathroom, telephone

and TV. The exterior rooms are a little lighter but have some noise; if there's nobody at reception, ask in the café.

**E Hostal Cándido**, Rúa Hermanos Villar 25, T988 229 607. This has a good central location on a quiet square. The en suite rooms are large and have big windows and balconies; the furnishings are modest but comfortable enough.

**F Hostal San Miguel**, Rúa San Miguel 14, T988 239 203, F988 242 749. Set above a good restaurant (see below), this offers cheap but adequate rooms with or without small bathroom. It's right in the heart of things, in a quiet corner of the old town.

### Ribadavia *p435*

**E Hostal Plaza**, Praza Maior 15, T988 470 576. By far the nicest place to stay in Ribadavia, this hostal is a clean, modern choice right on the beautiful main square, which some of the en suite rooms overlook.

### South of Ourense *p436*

**AL Parador de Verín**, Verín, T988 410 075, www.parador.es, verin@parador.es. Opposite the castle in Monterrei, which more or less merges with Verín itself, this *parador* occupies a well-restored traditional rural Galician mansion (*pazo*). It's a good place for families, with plenty of space, gardens, a swimming pool and a lovely rose-edged patio. The rooms are great for the price, and several boast super views over the fertile valley.

## ❼ Eating

### Tui *p432*

**❢❢ O Cabalo Furado**, Praza Generalísimo s/n, T986 601 215. One of the better restaurants, with cheerful and generous Galician *cocina de siempre*. The lampreys from the river are delicious when in season; there are also cheap (**F**-grade) but reasonable rooms with shared bathroom.

### Ourense *p433, map p434*

The Casco Vello is the centre for tapas-going and restaurants, particularly around **Praza do Ferro**, **Rúa San Miguel**, **Rúa Viriato** and **Rúa Fornos**.

**❢❢❢ Porta da Pía**, Rúa da Lúa 3, T988 251 882. This attractive place occupies a noble old building in the old quarter that's blessed with a beautiful garden terrace. Accessible from either of 2 sides, it specializes in high-quality seafood, which can be eaten by the large windows. Specials change daily, but perennial favourites include *arroz con bogavante* (rice with lobster), or *zarzuela de pescado* (spicy fish stew). Service is very good and there's a *menú del día* for €12. Closed Mon.

**❢❢❢ San Miguel**, Rúa San Miguel 12, T988 221 245. An excellent choice for seafood, with superb sardines and a good wine list. They often have locally caught things from the Miño too, such as *lampreas* (lampreys) or the fearsomely expensive *angulas* (elvers). In the café, a *menú del día* is served for €10; you won't get much better at this price if you take the waitress' recommendation.

**❢❢ Casa de María Andrea**, Praza Eirociño dos Cabaleiros 1. An excellent option with a great location overlooking a pretty little square. The interior is modern and stylish; the upstairs dining area is arrayed around the central atrium and there's an excellent *menú del día* for €9, as well as filling *raciones* (€4-11) and a range of daily specials. Recommended.

**❢❢ Zarampallo**, R San Miguel 9, T988 220 053. One of Ourense's better choices for a meal, with smart Galician fish and stews and a set *menú del día* for €9. Attractively modern interior.

**❢ La Casa do Pulpo**, Rúa Don Juan de Austria 15, T988 221 005. This friendly eatery is tucked away behind the cathedral. As the name suggests, it's specialty is octopus, which can be eaten out the back. The bar has a selection of *pinchos* and little rolls; the calamari ones are particularly tasty. There's also a good selection of Galician wine to taste.

### Cafés

**Café Real**, R Coronel Ceano Vivas 3. An elegant, old-style café, very spruce and traditional with its polished wood and seriously impressive glass chandelier. 2 levels of seating and occasional live jazz.

**Expresándote en el Pop-Art**, C Santo Domingo 15. The name means 'expressing yourself through pop-art'. It's a flamboyant but relaxed café/ bar popular with students.

### East of Ourense *p435*

**❢❢ O Grelo**, Rúa Chantada 16, Monforte de Lemos, T982 404 701. An excellent spot with traditional food cooked with a sure touch.

† **Mesón O Candil**, Estrada 31, in the hamlet of Pazos, on the road between the *parador* in Monterrei and the town of Verín. The homely, is an excellent choice for lunch or dinner. It's simple in style, with a range of *parrilladas* (mixed grills of meat or fish), all of which are delicious, especially when washed down with the house red, which they make themselves. There's a pleasant veranda to eat on in good weather too.

## ◑ Bars and clubs

**Ourense** *p433, map p434*
There are many good modern bars in Ourense, but the 'CLUB' signs in the southern end of the old town indicate brothels. Most of the bar action is around **Rúa Viriato**, **Rúa Pizarro**, **La Unión**, **Praza do Correxidor** and the **Jardines de Mercedes**, where the *discoteca* **La Bull** goes loud and late.
**Miudiño** Rúa Arcediagos 13, T988 245 536. This harmonious and low-lit stone and wood pub is just down the hill from the back of the cathedral. It's a very popular place for the first *copa* of the evening, and has Guinness on tap.

## ◉ Entertainment

**Ourense** *p433, map p434*
**Teatro Principal**, R da Paz 11, has regular theatre and occasional arthouse cinema. Tickets are cheap.

## ◉ Transport

**Tui** *p432*
**Bus** There are ½-hourly buses from Tui to **Vigo** and **A Guarda**, and some across the river to **Valença**. From A Guarda, the road follows the north bank of the Miño to Tui, and the first bridge into Portugal.

**Train** The station, north of the centre, has 2 trains a day to **Vigo** and to **Porto**; it's easier to walk across to **Valença**, where there are more trains. Guillarei station, ½ hr to the east, has connections inland to **Ribadavia** and **Ourense**; a lovely trip.

**Ourense** *p433, map p434*
**Bus** Ourense's bus station, T988 216 027, is beyond the train station across the Miño

from the old town (see Ins and outs, p433). From Rúa Progreso, buses No 6 and No 12 go there. There are 6-7 daily services to all the Galician cities: **Lugo** (€6.80, 2 hrs), **A Coruña**, **Santiago**, **Pontevedra**, and about 10 services to **Vigo**.

**Around Ourense** *p435*
**Bus** Buses run very regularly to **Ribadavia** (20 mins) and 2 daily to **Celanova**. There are several buses to **Verín** and the Portuguese border at **Feces**, and 1 daily to **Porto**.
    Buses run eastwards to **León** 4 times daily (5 hrs, €15.63, may require a change in Ponferrada), **Burgos** 3 times daily, **Madrid** 5-6 times (6 hrs 20 mins, €25.36), **Zamora** (2 daily, 4 hrs, €13.26) and **Salamanca** (2 daily, 4 hrs 30 mins, €16.17), as well as other cities.

**Train** A few trains daily head east to **León** (3-4 daily, 4-5 hrs, €14.15), **Madrid** (2 daily, 6-7 hrs, €35.50), and nore distant destinations. Several go to **Vigo** (7 daily, 2 hrs, from €6.80-15.00) via Ribadavia and **A Coruña** (3 daily, 3 hrs, €20) via Santiago. These trains tend to be inconveniently timetabled; the bus is a better bet.

**Ribadavia** *p435*
**Bus** There are frequent buses and trains to and from **Ourense** (20 mins).

**East of Ourense** *p435*
**Bus** There are 4-5 daily trains between Monforte de Lemos and **Ourense** (40 mins, €2.80-9.00). It's very possible to do a lunch day-trip to appreciate the scenery. There are also regular buses on this route.

**South of Ourense** *p436*
**Bus** Several buses a day head to **Ourense** and south to the Portuguese border. Verín's position near the main Vigo-Madrid motorway mean that there are several buses stopping going in both directions on this route.

## ◉ Directory

**Ourense** *p433, map p434*
**Internet** Servipost, Rúa do Progreso 36; CiberNetrix, C Mercado 54, €1.85 per hr, Mon-Thu 0900-midnight, Fri and Sat 0900-0200, Sun 1100-2400. **Laundry** Lava Express, Rúa Marañón 17.

**Background**

**⁝ Footprint features**

# History

## Hominids

While Northern Spain was a stamping ground for dinosaurs (literally; footprints are found all over the region), it was a species of hominid, *Homo heidelbergensis*, who first walked upright in the region. A valley just east of Burgos has yielded these remains, which are incredibly around 400,000 years old. *Homo heidelbergensis* is seen as the ancestor of the Neanderthals, of whom extensive remains have been found. Many caves in the north of Spain bear evidence of their presence; tools and remains of occupation stretching back around 60,000 years until their extinction around 27,000 years ago.

## The Upper Palaeolithic period

Some of the same caves and others, particularly in Cantabria and Asturias, have produced the first signs of *homo sapiens sapiens* in the peninsula. Dating from the Upper Palaeolithic (18,000 BC onwards), these hunter-gatherers produced fairly sophisticated stone and bone tools including arrows and spears. They also experimented with art, and found it to their liking; primitive whittling of deer bones and outlines of hands on cave walls suddenly gave way to the sensitive, imaginative and colourful bison, deer and horses found in several locations but most famously at Altamira in Cantabria, where the work is of amazing artistic quality. This so-called Magdalenian culture seemed to extend across northern Spain and into southern France, where related paintings have been found at places such as Lascaux.

A more settled existence probably began to emerge around 4000 BC. The most striking archaeological remnants are a great number of dolmens, large stone burial chambers, common across much of northern Europe at the time. These are mostly found along the north coast, particularly in the Basque lands and Galicia. There are also other remnants, such as standing stones and simpler pit burials.

## Early inhabitants

The principal inhabitants of the region are known as Iberians by default, but little is known of their origins apart from the fact that they spoke languages that are not from the Indo-European group that unites the vast majority of European and western Asian languages under its umbrella. The Basques, too, seem to have been around in those days. Their language isn't Indo-European either, but no convincing evidence has been found that can link them and the Iberians (or anyone else for that matter). Certain genetic peculiarities in the Basque population have led to theories that they are directly descended from the Palaeolithic inhabitants of the region. This ties in nicely with their own opinion that they are a very old people; they like to say God created Adam from old bones he found in a Basque cemetery.

The third important group were the Celts, who descended from the north in waves in the late second millennium BC. They spoke an Indo-European tongue and settled mostly in the north and west of the peninsula. Their influence is very apparent in place names, language and culture. There are still very close parallels between European areas settled by Celts; sitting over a cider while listening to bagpipes in Asturias you might want to ponder just how old these traditions are. The principal architectural remnant of the early Celts is the *castro*, a fortified hilltop fort and trading compound of which there are very many in Asturias and Galicia.

## Celtiberians

While the mountainous terrain of the north meant that distinct groups developed separately in remote valleys, the flatter lands of the centre encouraged contact. The

Celts and Iberians seemed to mingle in the centre of Northern Spain and form a single culture, rather unimaginatively labelled Celtiberian. This was a time of much cultural interaction; the Phoenicians, master sailors and merchants from the ports of the Near East, set up many trading stations. These were mostly on the southern coasts of Spain, but they had plenty of contact with the north, and may have established a few ports on the Atlantic coast. There was also cultural contact with the Greeks.

## The Phoenicians and Carthaginians

The heirs and descendants of the Phoenicians, the Carthaginians, came to Spain in the third century BC and settled widely in the south. While there was contact with the north, and Hannibal campaigned in western Castilla, the biggest effect was a direct consequence of his disputes with Rome. Bent on ending Carthaginian power in the Mediterranean, the Romans accurately realized that Spain was a 'second Carthage', and set out to change that. Once they realized the potential wealth in the peninsula, they set out to conquer it entirely.

## The Roman conquest

The Romans were given a tough time in the north, which it took them two centuries to subdue. The Celtiberian towns resisted the legions in a very spirited manner. Numancia, near Soria, resisted Roman sieges for many years, and was the centre of resistance that lost Rome tens of thousands of troops. Problems with the Cantabrians and Asturians lasted until Augustus and Agrippa finally did for them in the late years of the first century BC. The Romans gave up trying to impose their culture on the northern fringes; the Basques and Galicians were very resistant to it, and a 'live and let live' stance was eventually adopted in those areas.

*It is the Romans who first created the idea of Spain, Hispania, as a single geographical entity.*

While the south of Spain became a real Roman heartland, the north was always viewed as borderland of a sort. While vast quantities of gold and silver were mined in the northwest, and wine and oil poured from the Ebro and Duero valleys, few towns were founded in the north, and few wealthy Romans seemed to settle here; a couple of noble villas near Palencia notwithstanding.

Christianity spread comparatively rapidly into Spain. The diocese of Zaragoza was founded as early as the first century AD, while León and Burgo de Osma were other important early Christian centres. Christianity was certainly spread out to fit over existing religious frameworks; the Basques had few problems with the Virgin Mary considering their own earthmother figure was named Mari, and here as elsewhere the Christian calendar was moulded around pagan festivals.

## The Visigoths

As the Roman order tottered, the barbarian hordes streamed across the Pyrenees and created havoc. Alans, Vandals and Sueves capitalized on the lack of control in the early fifth century AD to such an extent that the Romans enlisted the Visigoths to restore order on their behalf. This they succeeded in doing, but the Sueves hung around and established themselves in the northwest of the peninsula. They established a capital at Astorga but the Visigoths came back as they lost control of their French territories and finally put an end to their small kingdom. After a period of much destruction and chaos, a fairly tenuous Visigothic control ensued. A beacon amidst the maelstrom was San Isidoro, writing in Sevilla, see box, page 442. Comparatively little is known

*The Visigoth regime didn't have the wherewithal to deal with the Muslims who had carried Mohammed's message so fast across North Africa.*

about the couple of centuries that followed. A handful of Visigothic churches still exist in Northern Spain; these draw on Roman architectural models but add local features, and iconography from the Visigoths' German roots. Visigothic rulers were beset by civil strife, and they never really gained control over the northern reaches of the peninsula.

## ¡ San Isidoro

*"No one can gain a full understanding of Spain without a knowledge of Saint Isidore"* Richard Ford

Born in 560, Isidoro succeeded his brother Leander as Bishop of Seville. Without doubt one of the most important intellectual figures of the Middle Ages, his prolific writings cover all subjects and were still popular at the time of the Renaissance . His *Etymologiae* was one of the first secular books in print when it appeared in 1472; it was the first encyclopedia written in the Christian west and became the primary source for the 154 classical authors that Isidoro quoted. He also wrote on music, law, history and jurisprudence as well as doctrinal matters.

Isidoro is also recognized as an important church reformer and was responsible for the production of the so called Mozarabic rite which is still practised in Toledo Cathedral today. His writings were an attempt to restore vigour and direction to a church that was in decline following the Visigothic invasions. His emphasis on educational reforms was to put the church in Spain on foundations that were to last centuries. This was recognized by contemporaries when the Council of Toledo in 653 called him "the

extraordinary doctor, the most learned man of the latter ages, always to be named with reverence, Isidore".

Another important element to Isidoro's writings was his prophecies, which were based both on the Bible and classical references. These writings appealed greatly to later generations living in the shadow of the Muslim conquests and were the source of many stories and legends, as well as expectations of a Christian deliverance. Following the expulsion of the Moors it seemed to some that an ancient prophecy was about to be fulfilled: Fernando was the hidden king of legend that was to save Christendom. The Ponce de León wrote in 1486: "There will be nothing able to resist his might because God has reserved total victory and all glory to the rod, that is to say the Bat, because Fernando is the *encubierto* (hidden one)… he will be Monarch of all the world".

Isidoro died in Sevilla in 636 and his writings continued to inspire Spain for the next 900 years. His body is now in León, moved there by Fernando I of Castilla who repatriated it from Muslim control around 1060. This act of national piety was carried out with the help of a mystic whose skill revealed the previously lost location of the saint's remains.

## The Moors

Arriving across the Straits of Gibraltar in 711, the Moors had taken most of Spain before the prophet had even been dead for a century. Under Arab leadership, most of the invaders were native North African Berbers, but there was a substantial mercenary element, many of them from eastern Europe. The state created was named

¡ *The Moors swept the Visigoths aside in a couple of years, establishing control over all but the northern fringes.*

*Al-Andalus*, and the Moors swept on into France, where they were stopped by the Franks at Poitiers.

Geography breaks Spain into distinct regions, which have tended to persist through time, and it was one of these, Asturias, that the Moors had some trouble with. They were defeated in what was presumably a minor skirmish at

Covadonga, in the far northern mountains, in 717. While they weren't too bothered by this at the time, Spain views it today as an event of immense significance, a victory against all odds and a sort of mystical event where God proved himself to be on the Christian side. Think the deliverance from Egypt meets *Die Hard* and that's something like the picture. It was hardly a crippling blow to the Moors, who were on the *autoroutes* of southern France before too long, but it probably sowed the seeds of what became the Asturian monarchy.

A curious development in many ways, this line of kings emerged unconquered from the shadowy northern hills and forests. Whether they were a last bastion of Visigothic resistance, or whether they were just local folk ready to defend their lands, they established an organized monarchy of sorts with a capital that shifted about but settled on Oviedo in 808. Their most lasting legacy has been a number of churches and royal halls; beautifully proportioned stone buildings that show some Visigothic characteristics but are also very original in style – far more graceful than the name it has been saddled with, Asturian Pre-Romanesque.

Although turned back in France, they Moors remained strong enough to repulse Charlemagne in northeast Spain in 778. After failing to take Zaragoza, he returned huffily to France but had his rearguard ambushed by Basques in the Navarran pass of Roncesvalles. The Basques were infuriated that he'd taken down the walls of Pamplona on his way through; the defeat suffered in the pass became the basis for the fanciful epic poem *Chanson de Roland*, which attributes the attack to Muslims.

‡ *The Moors established a fairly tolerant rule over most of Christian Spain.*

Although the southern portion of *Al-Andalus* was a flourishing cultural centre, the Moors couldn't establish complete control in the northlands, and several cities changed hands numerous times in skirmishing and raids in the ninth century. Life in Muslim Spain was relatively good for Christians and Jews, though. Many converted to Islam; those Christians that didn't became known as Mozárabes.

While the Covadonga defeat was insignificant, the Asturian kingdom began to grow in strength and the long process of the Reconquista, the Christian reconquest of the peninsula, began. The northmen took advantage of cultural interchange with the south, which remained significant throughout the period despite the militarized zone in between, and were soon strong enough to begin pushing back. The loose Moorish authority in these lands certainly helped; the northern zone was more or less administered by warlords who were only partially controlled by the amirs in Córdoba (who became caliphs in 929). Galicia and much of the north coast was reclaimed and in 914 the Asturian King Ordoño II reconquered León; the capital shortly moved to here, and the line of kings took on the name of that town.

Asturias/León wasn't the only Christian power to develop during this period. The Basques had been quietly pushing outwards, too, and the small mountain kingdom of Navarra emerged and grew rapidly. Aragón emerged too, and gained power and size via a dynastic union with Catalunya. The entity that came to dominate Spain, Castilla, was also born at this time. In the middle of the 10th century a Burgos noble, Fernán González, declared independence from the Kingdom of León and began to rally disparate Christian groups in the region. He was so successful in this endeavour that it wasn't too long before his successors labelled themselves kings.

‡ *As the Christians moved south, they resettled in many towns and villages that had lain in ruins since Roman times.*

The Moors weren't finished by any means. A formidable bloke named **Al-Manzur** managed to sack almost every Christian city in Northern Spain within a couple of decades (see box, page 444); surely one of the greatest military feats of the Middle Ages. Both sides were made painfully aware of their vulnerability and constructed a series of massive fortresses that faced each other across the central plains. The Muslim fortresses were particularly formidable; high eyries with commanding positions, accurately named the 'front teeth' of *Al-Andalus*. There are around 3000 fortresses and castles in various states of repair in Spain; a huge number of them are to be found in this area.

## ❖ Al-Manzur in Northern Spain

Ibn-abu-amir was born to a poor family in Córdoba around 950. Known to later generations as Al-Manzur or 'Victor of God', he is one of the most remarkable figures of the Middle Ages, representing both the strength of Muslim Spain and its ultimate failure. A lawyer, he succeeded in reforming the administration of the Caliphate and in modernizing its army. Nominally a regent, he was content to let formal power reside with the Sultan, but by 996 had assumed the title King.

With his power consolidated, he launched a series of lightening raids across the North of Spain. His army, made up of mercenary Slavs, Christian renegades and North African Berbers, sacked Zamora and Simancas in 981, Barcelona in 985 and León in 987. The Leonese king Bermudo had broken an agreement to pay tribute and was forced to flee to the Asturian mountains. The only opposition to a total takeover of Spain now lay in Asturias and remote Galicia.

Al-Manzur was not however a bloodthirsty tyrant. Under his guidance a university was established in Córdoba, he enlarged the noble Mezquita, and he was a great patron of the arts and science. On his many military campaigns both in Spain and North Africa he took a library of books. Respected and feared by his enemies, he was merciful to those he defeated.

In 997 he embarked on his final campaign to extinguish Christian opposition. He took Coruña and the holy city of Santiago whence he removed the bells of the cathedral to the mosque of Córdoba. On encountering a lone priest protecting the shrine of St James, he is said to have ordered his men to spare him and to leave the holy relics of the city untouched.

After an inconclusive battle in 1002 at Calatañazor in Castilla, Al-Manzur died of natural causes. The relief of the Christians was immense. A commentator wrote "In 1002 died Al-Manzur, and was buried in Hell". With his death the Caliphate fragmented to a number of small warring states, allowing the Christians to regroup. Never again were the Moors to be so united; his death marked a significant turning point in the history of Spain.

Background History

It was just after Al-Manzur's death that things began to go pomegranate-shaped for the Moors, as kinstrife and civil war over succession fatally weakened the Caliphate while the Christian kingdoms were gaining strength and unity. The king of Navarra Sancho III (the Great) managed to unite almost the whole of Northern Spain in the early 11th century; although this inevitably dissolved, the rival kingdoms at least had a common goal. The caliphate disintegrated in 1031, to be replaced by a series of city-states, or *taifas*. Pitted against each other as well as the north, they were in no state to resist, and were forced to pay protection money to the Christian armies, enriching the new kingdoms. The big beneficiary was Castilla; King Alfonso VI, with the help of his on-off mercenary **El Cid**, see box page 268, conquered swathes of Muslim territory, reaching Toledo in 1085.

Alfonso must have dreamed of reconquering the whole peninsula at that point, but he was stopped dead by the Almoravids, a by-the-book Islamic dynasty that quickly crossed from Morocco to re-establish the caliphate along stricter lines. They soon lapsed into softer ways though, and much of modern Andalucía was lost before a similar group, the Almohads, crossed the straits and took control back.

The nature of the Reconquista was very similar to that of the Crusades; a holy war against the enemies of the faith that at the same time conveniently offered numerous opportunities for pillage, plunder and seizure of land. Younger sons, not in line for any inheritance under customs of the time, could fight for the glory of God and appropriate lands and wealth for themselves at the same time. Knightly orders similar to those of the Crusades were founded; the Knights of Calatrava, Alcántara and Santiago.

**Santiago** (Saint James), although he had been dead for a millennium or so, played a major role in the Reconquista. The spurious discovery of his tomb at Compostela in the ninth century had sparked ongoing pilgrimage; it effectively replaced the inaccessible Holy Land as a destination for the devout and the penitent. The discovery came in time to resemble some sort of sign from God, and Saint James took on the role of *Matamoros*, Moor-slayer, and is depicted crunching hapless *Andalusi* under the hooves of his white charger in countless sculptures and paintings – quite a career-change for the first-century fisherman. With an apostle risen from the dead onside, it's little wonder that Christians flocked to the Reconquista banners. Another factor in the success of the Reconquista was the organization of Christian Spanish society, in which the first-born son, meek or not, inherited the earth and the rest were left to fend for themselves. The 'Holy War' against the Moors was a way for younger sons, as well as those of poorer birth, to gain wealth, prestige and above all the land that was up for grabs.

By the mid-12th century Northern Spain was effectively secured under Christian rule. For largely geographical reasons, it had been the fledgling kingdom of Castilla that ended up with the biggest slice of the pie, and Spain's most powerful political entity. It had already been frequently united with the Leonese kingdom by dynastic marriages and this was confirmed in 1230, when Fernando (Ferdinand) III inherited both crowns (a fact still lamented in León!).

While Navarra was still going, up in the mountains, it was Aragón which was the other main beneficiary from the reconquest. Uniting with Catalunya in 1150, it began looking eastwards to that great trading forum, the Mediterranean. After the famous battle of the **Navas de Tolosa** in 1212, the Moors lost Córdoba in 1236 and Seville in 1248 and were reduced to an area around their third great city, Granada, where they held out for another two-and-a-half centuries.

## The post-war years

With the flush of war fading from faces, the north settled down to a period of prosperity. Castilla became a significant producer of wool and wheat, and the towns of the north coast established important trading links with northern Europe to distribute it. In 1296 the **Hermandad de las Marismas**, an export alliance of four major ports (A Coruña, Santander, Laredo and San Sebastián) was formed to consolidate this. The Basques were doing very nicely at this time. Demand for Vizcayan iron was high, and Basque sailors explored the whole Atlantic, almost certainly reaching north America a century or more before Columbus sailed.

Places like Burgos and Medina del Campo became powerful centres controlling the distribution of goods to the coastal ports. Guilds and societies became more and more important in the flourishing urban centres. Meanwhile the Castilian kings still pursued military aims. Becoming an increasing anachronism in an increasingly urban society, these crusading kings came to rely heavily on the towns for political and financial support. In order to keep them onside, they began to grant *fueros*, or exemptions from certain taxation and conscription duties. The towns stubbornly defended their *fueros*, and proto-democratic assemblies, the *cortes*, began to assemble to keep the kings honest.

*The peace and wealth of this period provided a platform for important advances in art and architecture.*

Background History

## ‡ A cavalier visit

In the year 1623, a surprising visitor crossed the Pyrenees into Northern Spain. Calling himself Mr Smith and disguised as a travelling salesman, it was actually the Prince of Wales, the future Charles I. This was no regular visit; Charles wanted to travel incognito as he was searching for a bride. His target was the Infanta of Spain and Charles had the idea to size up his potential wife first rather than enter a marriage with someone known only from a flattering portrait who might not please his connoisseur's eye.

After arriving at the house of an astonished British Ambassador it soon became apparent that the prince's noble intentions could not be realized without the risk of a diplomatic incident, poisoning relations between the two counties to the point of war. In view of the breach of normal protocol, it was therefore agreed that a surprise meeting should take place the next day when the prince would fortuitously bump into a mildly surprised king of Spain in the Royal Park. The two were then formally introduced and an official meeting with the princess arranged . However it soon became apparent that *realpolitik* would put an end to the prince's romantic dreams. Hell was likely to freeze over before the king of Spain would

allow his daughter to marry a Protestant heretic.

Nevertheless there was still the formality of mutual back-slapping and one-upmanship to go through, with an exchange of gifts designed to show the status of both host and guest. Charles, a well known lover of the arts, was delighted to receive paintings by Titian, three sedan chairs, some Barbary horses, a collection of weapons and a golden basin so heavy that it required two men to carry it. In addition, the Spanish monarch, perhaps as a chastisement to Charles, gifted him 18 wildcats with no instructions on how to care for the beasts.

Thoughtfully, however, he provided an elephant as a means to transport the gifts up to the Cantabrian port of Laredo and back to England. The elephant and its four keepers did come with instructions; it was to receive a gallon of wine daily from April to September. In October it was believed to go for a very long sleep.

On returning to England from his disastrous visit Charles was met by a rejoicing populace. Tables were set out in the streets groaning under all manner of food with whole hogsheads of wine and butts of sack whilst every street corner had its bonfire. As a contemporary poet aptly observed, "even the elements rejoiced". It rained for nine hours.

Towns spent vast sums in constructing soaring cathedrals, symbols of faith in new architectural principles as much as Christianity. But already in Castilla's time of prosperity the seeds of decline were sprouting. Cities that had forged the Reconquista, Oviedo and León, became insignificant country towns as populations moved southwards in the war's wake. The massive numbers of sheep being grazed in migratory patterns across the land caused large-scale degradation and erosion of the soil; in many ways, the 'war on trees' was to prove as significant as any that had been waged against Moors. The barren landscapes of today's Castilla are a direct result of these post-reconquest years. The *fueros* that were so indiscriminately handed out meant that later kings were barely able to govern the towns, which understandably were reluctant to concede their privileges. The glory of the soldiering years rubbed off on Castilian attitudes too. Sons of minor nobles (*hidalgos*, from *hijos d'algo*, 'sons of something') yearned for the smell of battle, and scorned the dull attractions of work and education, an attitude that has cost Spain dear over the centuries and was memorably satirized in Cervantes' *Don Quijote*. The church, too, was in a poor state. Bled of funds by successive crusading kings, it developed a hoarding mentality and was in no condition to act as a moral light for the young Christian kingdoms. Furthermore, it was far from being a peaceful pastoral and urban golden age. The nuggety walled towns of the Reconquista battle lines provided perfect bases for power-hungry nobles; civil strife was exacerbated by the fact that most kings openly kept mistresses outside their arranged dynastic marriages, and illegitimate children were a dime-a-dozen.

## The 14th century

Spain was drawn into the **Hundred Years War** as the bastard Henry of Trastámara waged war with French help on his English-backed brother Pedro I (the Cruel). After Pedro was murdered, his son-in-law John of Gaunt, Duke of Lancaster, claimed the Castilian throne. Landing in Galicia, he waged an inconclusive war with Henry before agreeing to marry his daughter to the king's son. He returned to England happy enough with this outcome and with a substantial retirement package from Castilian funds.

Such conjugal ties were of vital political importance, and it was one, in 1469, that was to have a massive impact throughout the world. The heir to the Aragonese throne, Fernando, married Isabel, heiress of Castilla, in a top-secret ceremony in Valladolid. The implications were enormous. Aragón was still a power in the Mediterranean (Fernando was also king of Sicily), and Castilla's domain covered much of the peninsula. The unification under the *Reyes Católicos*, as the monarchs became known, marked the beginnings of Spain as we know it today. Things didn't go smoothly at first, however. There were plenty of opponents to the union and forces in support of Juana, Isabel's elder (but assumed illegitimate) sister waged wars across Castilla.

## Religious persecution

The reign of the Catholic monarchs was full of incident, particularly in the year 1492, when Columbus sailed the Atlantic under their patronage, they completed the Reconquista by taking Granada, and thought they would celebrate the triumph by kicking the Jews out of Spain. Spain's Jewish population had been hugely significant since the 12th century, heavily involved in commerce, shipping and literature throughout the peninsula, but hatred against them had begun to grow in the 14th century and there had been many a pogrom. Many converted during these years to escape the murderous climate; they became known as *conversos*. The decision to expel those who hadn't converted was far more that of the pious Isabel than the pragmatic Fernando and has to be seen in the light of the paranoid Christianizing climate. The Jews were given four months to leave the kingdom, and even the *conversos* soon found themselves under the Inquisition's iron hammer (see box page 237). The kingdom's Muslim population was tolerated for another decade, when they too were given the choice of baptism or expulsion. The ridiculous doctrine of *limpieza de sangre* (purity of blood) became all-important; the enduring popularity of ham and pig meat surely owes something to these days, when openly eating these foods proved that one wasn't a pork-eschewing Muslim or Jew. But the lack of cultural diversity led to long-term stagnation and the area has not recovered from the self-inflicted purge of the majority of its intellectual, commercial and professional talent.

## Conquest of the Americas

The treaty of Tordesillas in 1494 partitioned the Atlantic between Spain and Portugal, and led to the era of Spanish colonization of the Americas. In many ways, this was an extension of the Reconquista as young men hardened on the Castilian *meseta* crossed the seas with zeal for conquest, riches and land.

Under the Habsburg monarchy, Carlos V and Felipe II relied on the income from the colonies to pursue wars (often unwillingly) on several European fronts. It couldn't last; Spain's Golden Age has been likened by Spanish historian Felipe Fernández-Armesto to a dog walking on hind legs. Although over the centuries many *indianos* returned from the colonies to their native Navarra, Galicia and Asturias with newfound wealth, the American expansion sounded a grim bell for northern Castilla. The sheer weight of administration required forced the previously itinerant monarchy to choose a capital, and Felipe II set himself up in Madrid. With Sevilla and Cádiz now the focus for the all-important trade with the colonies, Castilla had turned southwards, and its northern provinces rapidly declined, hastened by a drain of their citizens to the New World across the sea.

## Regional discontent

The *comunero* revolt of the early 16th century expressed the frustrations of a region that was once the focus of optimistic Christian conquest and agricultural wealth, but had now become peripheral to the designs of a 'foreign' monarchy. Resentment was exacerbated by the fact that the king still found it difficult to extract taxes from the *cortes* of Aragón or Catalunya, so Castilla bankrolled a disproportionate amount of the crippling costs of the day-to-day running of a worldwide empire. A plague in the early 17th century didn't help matters, wiping out about a tenth of the Castilian population. Burgos' population in the middle of that century was a quarter of what it had been at the beginning of it; the same was true throughout the region.

Meanwhile, as an important focus of Spanish naval and maritime power, the north coast continued in a better vein. Much of the shipbuilding for exploration, trade and war took place here, and many of the ships were crewed by Basques and Galicians. **Elkano**, a Basque from Getaria, and his crew, became the first to circumnavigate the world after the death of the expedition's leader, Magellan, half-way round. The ill-fated Spanish Armada sailed from Galicia in 130 ships built on this coast.

Aragón, meanwhile, had become a backwater since civil strife in the 15th century had deprived it of Catalunya and therefore much of its Mediterranean trade. Above all regions, it suffered most from the loss of the Muslims and Jews; many of its cities had thrived on the cultural mixture. The union with Castilla had eventually deprived it of political significance too, and it retreated behind its *fueros*, stubbornly avoiding taxes and conscriptions, and maintaining a largely feudal system of land ownership, with all-powerful lords free to do as they pleased. This situation was changed partly after Felipe II put down a revolt in the late 16th century, but the province continued to be a minor player, especially compared to its thriving Catalan neighbour. After supporting the wrong side in the war of Spanish succession in the early 18th century Aragón was deprived of its *fueros* and laws and brought to heel, a minor region now in peninsular life. Navarra, meanwhile, had been conquered by Fernando earlier in the century and this, as well as the Basque lands, were under Castilian control.

## The decline of the empire

The struggle of the Spanish monarchy to control the spread of Protestantism was a major factor in the decline of the empire. Felipe II fought expensive and ultimately unwinnable wars in Flanders that bankrupted the state; meanwhile, within the country, the absolute ban on the works of 'heretical' philosophers, scientists and theologists left Spain behind in Renaissance Europe. In the 18th century, for example, the so-called 'Age of Enlightenment' in western Europe, theologists at the noble old University of Salamanca debated what language the angels spoke; that Castilian was proposed as an answer is certain. The decline of the monarchy paralleled a physical decline in the monarchs, as the inbred Habsburgs became more and more deformed and weak; the last of them, Carlos II – a tragic victim of contorted genetics – died childless and plunged the nation into a war of succession. "*Castilla has made Spain,*

# Jovellanos

Gaspar Melchor de Jovellanos (1744-1811) was a true Enlightenment figure who combined careers in politics, social reform and the law. In addition he was a major literary figure who made important contributions to educational theory.

Born in Asturias in 1744 he initially trained as a priest but moved to the law and started a his career as a magistrate in Sevilla. His reputation as a man of letters is based on his multi-faceted personality which allowed him to develop a variety of writing styles. His literary works published under the name Jovino have secured his place in the history of Spanish letters. His best known work *Epistola de Fabio a Anfriso* (letter from Fabio to Anfriso) is a fairly philosophical reflection on life, while his play *El si de las niñas* introduced melodrama to the Spanish stage.

Jovellanos' wide ranging interests brought him to the attention of the liberal Carlos III who, unusually for a Spanish monarch, saw Spain's forward progress as a practical matter rather than one to be based on a renewal of faith. He was commissioned to report on the condition of agricultural workers and on prisons. Both these works are consided models of their type and were the inspiration for other social reformers. His concern was the application of Enlightenment principles of reason and justice as part of a strategy for bringing Spain into the modern age.

His first political career ended with the death of Carlos in 1788 and the increasing reaction which followed the French Revolution forced him to return to Asturias where he investigated conditions in the coalmining industry. This was where he started keeping his famous diary and founded the Real Instituto Asturiano, an important carrier of the Enlightenment message to this industrial part of Spain. Much to his surprise he was appointed Minister of Justice in 1797, a post he held until 1799 when the changing political climate sawhim removed from office.

In 1802 he was arrested on the instigation of the Inquisition and held in Mallorca until 1808. While in exile he continued writing and was especially concerned with education. In 1808 with the French invasion he found himself once again in the field of action as a member of the Supreme National Junta, leading resistance against Napoleon. He was declared a *Padre de la Patria* by the Cortes of Cádiz as the French were closing in. Forced to flee by ship to his native Asturias he became ill during the voyage and died shortly after landing at Puerto de Vega.

*and Castilla has destroyed it*", commented Ortega y Gasset. Despite these misfortunes, the 17th century had been a time of much inspiration in the arts; Spanish Baroque was a cheerful façade on a gloomy building, and painters such as Velásquez, Zurbarán and Murillo hit the heights of expression.

The war of the Spanish succession didn't have a massive impact on the north, apart from Aragón (see above), but the headlong decline continued throughout the 18th century. The Catholic Church was in a poor state intellectually, and came to rely more and more on cults and *fiestas* to keep up the interest of the populace; a dogmatic tradition that is still very strong today. The Jesuits, an order that had its origins with the Basques, and a more enlightened lot than most, were expelled in 1767. They were allowed to take with them only their religious clothing and a supply of chocolate, a commodity that was extraordinarily popular at this time in Spain. After decentralization of trade with the New World, it was the Basques who established a monopoly over the import of the stuff, and for a brief time brought prosperity to their lands as a result.

Napoleon took advantage of the weak King Carlos IV's domestic problems to install his own brother Joseph (known among Spaniards as *Pepe Botellas* because of his heavy drinking) on the throne. Spain revolted against this arrogant gesture, and Napoleon sent in the troops in late 1808. The ensuing few years are known in Spain as the Guerra de Independencia (War of Independence). Combined Spanish, British and Portuguese forces clashed with the French all across the north, firstly disastrously as General Moore was forced to retreat across Galicia to a Dunkirk-like embarkation at A Coruña, then more successfully as the Duke of Wellington won important battles at Ciudad Rodrigo, Vitoria and San Sebastián. The behaviour of both sides was brutal both on the battlefield and off. Marshal Soult's long retreat across the region saw him loot town after town; his men robbed tombs and burned priceless archives. The allied forces were no better; Wellington described his own men as "scum of the earth", who sacked the towns they conquered with similar destructiveness.

Significant numbers of Spaniards had been in favour of the French invasion, and were opposed to the liberal republican movements that sprang up in its wake. The 19th century was to see clash after clash of liberals against conservatives, progressive cities against reactionary countryside, restrictive centre against outward-looking periphery. Spain finally lost its empire, as the strife-torn homeland could do little against the independence movements of Latin America. In 1823 the French put down a democratic revolution and restored the king (Fernando VII) to the throne. When he died, another war of succession broke out between supporters of his brother Don Carlos and his infant daughter Isabella.

> ✷ Despite all the troubles, industrialization finally began to reach Spain, and several of the ports of the north coast thrived.

The so-called Carlist Wars of 1833 to 1839, 1847 to 1849 (often not counted as one) and 1872 to 1976 were politically complex. Don Carlos represented conservatism, and his support was drawn from a number of different sources. Wealthy landowners, the church and the reactionary peasantry, with significant French support, lined up against the loyalist army, the liberals and the urban middle and working classes. The Carlist stronghold was Navarra and the rural Basque region; liberal reforms were threatening the two pillars of Basque country life: the church and their age-old *fueros*. In between and during the wars, a series of *pronunciamientos* (coups d'état) plagued the monarchy. During the third Carlist War, the king abdicated and the short-lived First Spanish Republic was proclaimed, ended by a military-led restoration a year later. The Carlists were defeated but remained strong, and played a prominent part in the Spanish Civil War. There's still a Carlist party in Navarra and a pretender to the throne.

Vigo, A Coruña and Santander all flourished; Bilbao, on the back of its iron ore exports, grew into a major industrial and banking centre, and Asturias mined quantities of poor-quality coal. Basque nationalism as it is known today was born in the late 19th century. Spain lost its last overseas possessions, Cuba, Puerto Rico and the Phillippines, in the 'Disaster' of 1898. The introspective turmoil caused by this event gave the name to the **'Generación de 98'** (1898 Generation), a forward thinking movement of artists, philosophers and poets, among whom were numbered the Basques Unamuno and Zuloaga and the poet Antonio Machado. It was a time of discontent and strikes began to occur more and more regularly in the towns and cities of the north, particularly in Asturias, although Spanish industry profited from its neutrality in the First World War.

> ✷ If the slow torpor of the 17th and 18th centuries damaged Northern Spain, the 19th century was worse, an almost continuous period of brutal wars and political strife.

After the Second Republic had been established in 1931, a series of petty struggles between conservatives, liberals and socialists undermined the potential value of the democratic process. Unlike the rest of the left, the Asturian miners were fairly united, with anarchists, socialists and trade unionists prepared to cooperate; they went on strike in protest against the entry of the right-wing CEDA into the vacillating centrist government. Proclaiming a socialist republic, they seized the civil buildings of the province. The arms factories worked 24-hour shifts to arm the workers; the army and Civil Guard were still holding out in Oviedo. The government response was harsh. Sending in the feared Foreign Legion and Moroccan troops under Generals Goded and a certain Franco, they swiftly relieved the garrison, defeated the insurrection and embarked on a brutal spree of retribution for which they are rightly unforgiven in Asturias.

## The Spanish Civil War

In July 1936 a military conspiracy saw garrisons throughout Spain rise against the government and try to seize control of their towns and provinces. Within a few days battlelines were clearly drawn between the Republican (government) and the Nationalists, a coalition of military, Carlists, fascists and the Christian right. Most of Northern Spain was rapidly under Nationalist control, although frightening numbers of civilians were shot 'behind the lines'. The major resistance in the north was in Asturias – where the miners came out fighting once again – Cantabria and the Basque provinces. These latter were in a difficult position; the Basques were democratic in outlook but very Catholic, and the Catholic church was on the Nationalist side for its own protection from the anticlerical Republic. A 1927 catechism had claimed that it was a mortal sin for a Catholic to vote for a liberal candidate. Carlist-oriented Navarra sided with the Nationalists, as did Alava, but the majority of Euskadi came out fighting on the side of democracy.

There was long fighting on fronts in Aragón, but the prize, Zaragoza, stayed in rebel hands throughout the war. Meanwhile, the Republican government approved a statute of autonomy for the Basques, and a Basque government was sworn in under the oak tree in **Gernika**, long a symbol of Basque government and *fueros*. The young and able leader, **José María Aguirre**, assured the Republic that "until Fascism is defeated, Basque nationalism will remain at its post". It did, with Basques fighting Nazi forces right through the Second World War, but the government was forced into exile when Bilbao fell in June 1937. This came in the wake of the appalling civilian bombings of Durango and Gernika, when German and Italian planes rained bombs on the defenceless country towns, killing almost 2,000.

✱ *Franco claimed that the devastation of Gernika and Durango was perpetrated by the Basques as a publicity gesture.*

**Franco**'s *junta*, after being formed at Salamanca, had set up base appropriately in deeply conservative Burgos; Castilla was a heartland for Nationalist support and the venue for many brutal reprisals against civilians perceived as leftist, unionist, democratic or owning a fertile little piece of land on the edge of the village. Republican atrocities were equally appalling, but an important difference is that they were rarely sanctioned or perpetrated by the government.

Separated from the rest of the Republic, Asturian and Cantabrian resistance was whittled away; Santander fell in August 1937, Asturias in October. Franco never forgave the Basques or Asturians, and the regions were treated harshly during his oppressive rule. Development was curtailed and use of the Euskara language was banned (as was Gallego, although Franco himself was Galician). Navarra and Castilla, on the other hand, were rewarded for their roles, if being blessed with a series of concrete crimes against architecture in the name of progress can be called a reward.

The Basques held out high hopes as the Second World War reached its end. Their government-in-exile was officially recognized by the Allies, and many hoped that

Franco would soon be deposed and an independent Basque state be established. Their hopes were dashed when the USA decided that the new enemy was communism. If Franco was anything, he was anti-communist, and the Americans under Eisenhower granted Spain a massive aid package and resumed diplomatic relations. This betrayal of the Basques, followed by that of Britain and France, was a bitter pill to swallow.

## Transition to democracy

**ETA**, had their most popular moment when they assassinated Franco's right-hand man, Admiral **Carrero Blanco** in 1973. The ageing dictator died two years later and his appointed successor, King Juan Carlos II, supervised a return to democracy; *La Transición*. The north of Spain has largely flowered since the first elections in 1977. Autonomous status was granted to Euskadi and Galicia, and then to Asturias, Cantabria, Navarra, La Rioja, Aragón and Castilla y León, which operate with varying degrees of freedom from the central government. The new constitution, however, specified that no further devolution could occur; Spain was 'indissoluble'.

In 1982, the Socialist government of **Felipe González** was elected. They held power for 14 years and oversaw Spain's entry into the EEC (now EU), from which it has benefited immeasurably, although rural areas remain poor by western European standards. González was disgraced, however, when he was implicated in having commissioned 'death squads' with the aim of terrorizing the Basques into renouncing terrorism, which few of them supported in any case. In 1996 the rightist PP (*Partido Popular*) formed a government under young ex-tax inspector **José María Aznar**, who was re-elected in 2000. Economically conservative, Aznar strengthened Spain's ties with Europe and set a platform for strong financial performance. ▸▸ *See also ETA box, page 454, for further details.*

## Political repression and cultural rejuvenation

Aznar then turned to ETA, using the prevailing international climate to take strong action. In 2002, the democratically elected party, Batasuna, widely seen as linked to the terrorist group, were banned by the courts after a purpose-built bill was resoundingly passed in parliament. The governing Basque Nationalist Party (PNV), wholly against terrorism, denounced the move against their political opponents as 'undemocratic' and 'authoritarian', which it undoubtedly was. Nevertheless, things quietened down and the move, backed by a massive police operation resulting in many arrests, seemed to have paid off.

In late 2002, two events combined to severely dent Aznar's popularity. The *Prestige* disaster (see box, page 410) was a direct result of the government's refusal to see the bigger picture, and then Aznar took Spain to war in Iraq against the wishes of a massive majority of the population. The extraordinary demonstrations – in some cities well over half the population was on the street – were arrogantly ignored and an angry Spain seemed determined to oust the PP in 2004.

However, in the intervening time Aznar clawed back his popularity and, a week before the polls in March 2004, a victory for the PP candidate Mariano Rajoy (Aznar's designated successor) looked on the cards. Then all the chickens came home to roost. On 11 March 2004, three days before the general election, a series of 10 bombs exploded in four commuter trains approaching Madrid's Atocha station, killing 191 people. The government was quick to blame ETA for the attack despite that group's denial and substantial evidence for involvement by Islamic extremists. The electorate was outraged at what was perceived as a vote-minded cover-up and elected the PSOE to government. The new prime minister, 43 year-old **José Luis Rodríguez Zapatero**, from León, immediately pledged to withdraw the troops and re-align Spain with 'old Europe'. Both objectives were soon achieved, and he has proceeded on a campaign of liberal reforms, legalizing gay marriage, openly debating the status of Catalunya, and pursuing peace via dialogue in the Basque country. These steps have outraged

the conservative half of Spain and, at time of writing, Zapatero, for all his good 453
qualities, was looking unlikely to win another term.

The region is still divided along political lines. The Basques have their PNV, and rural Asturias remains firmly leftist in orientation. On the other side, Navarra is still conservative, Galicia hasn't shaken off its Francoist tendencies, and one suspects plenty in parts of Castilla y León would vote for the man himself if he were still alive (and in democratic mood). The Franco era is rarely discussed; neither is the Civil War, which remains a sensitive issue with combatants and war-criminals still alive and sipping wine in the corner of local bars. No judicial investigation of events of the war or the dictatorship has ever been undertaken; there's a sort of consensus to let sleeping dogs lie, understandable, given the turbulent history of the 19th and 20th centuries.

Most of the cities of Northern Spain have shaken off the torpor of the Franco era and the preceding centuries of decline and are today prosperous, attractive places once more, best symbolized by Bilbao's astonishing urban renewal. EU funding has helped to rejuvenate their superb architectural heritage, and the lively social life remains a marvel of European society. In some rural areas, though, particularly Castilla and Galicia, depopulation is a serious issue. Many villages are inhabited only by pensioners, if at all, as the young seek employment and fulfilment in urban centres.

On a more positive note, the years since the return to democracy have seen a remarkable and accelerated reflowering of regional culture. The banned languages Gallego and Euskara are ever-more in use, and local artists, writers and poets are being keenly promoted by the regional governments. Museums are mostly free, not so much to lure tourists away from the beaches of the south as to encourage their own population to visit and learn. Salamanca's enthusiastic year as European Capital of Culture in 2002 is an example of this spirit; the great university town of the Middle Ages was back in the spotlight; whether the angels speak Castilian or Euskara these days is of little importance.

*In most urban areas, Francoist street names have been changed and statues and memorials pulled down.*

# Contemporary Northern Spain

With over 40% of the country's area, but just a quarter of its population, Northern Spain is still feeling the historical effects of the Reconquista as well as a more recent drain to Madrid and Barcelona. The difference within the region is even more striking, with the coastal provinces more than four times more densely populated than the inland regions of Castilla y León, Aragón and Navarra.

Entry to the EEC/EU in 1986 has provided a massive boost both economically and mentally; the region is looking outwards for the first time since the loss of the empire and funding from the community has been a godsend for the architectural heritage of the area, has spruced up its urban areas and finally brought a degree of modernization to an ailing agricultural sector. Apart from the EU, the single, most important step was the creation of the **comunidades autónomas,** or semi-autonomous regional governments, a modern solution to Spain's age-old problems in administering its diverse parts. Without the deadening effect of centralization, the regions have largely flourished and are in a much better position to care for their diverse natural environments and promote cultural growth. That said, some have benefited more than others. The striking success story is undoubtedly Euskadi. Badly repressed during the dictatorship, the industrious Basques have forged ahead on the back of their strong and ancient cultural unity, their significant industrial and commercial centres and their high levels of education. Optimism in the region is high, although

*After the sleepwalking decades of the Franco dictatorship, the region has been belatedly saved with the return to democracy.*

## ‧ ETA and Basque nationalism

Although many Spaniards refuse to distinguish between the two, Basque nationalism and ETA are two very different things. The vast majority of Basque nationalists, ie those who want more autonomy for the region, are firmly committed to a peaceful and democratic path. ETA, on the other hand, have traditionally been pessimistic about the possibility of achieving these aims in this manner, and have sought by planned violent action to force the issue.

To probe the wrongs, rights and history of the issue would require volumes. Viewed in the context of the changing Europe, Basques have a strong case for independence, being culturally and ethnically distinct to Spaniards. The issue is muddied by the large number of Spaniards in the region, but the real sticking point is that Spain has no intention of giving up such a profitable part of the nation. Economics don't permit it, old-fashioned Spanish honour doesn't permit it and, cleverly, the constitution doesn't permit it. It isn't going to happen, and most Basques know it. From this frustration a small percentage of extremism has developed.

The nationalist movement as we know it today was born in the late 19th century, fathered by Sabino Arana, a perceptive but unpleasant bigot who was a master of propaganda. He devised the *ikurriña* (the Basque flag), coined terms such as *Euskadi*, and published manifestos for independence, peppered with dubious historical interpretations.

The tragically short-lived break through came with the Civil War. The sundered

Republic granted the Basques extensive self-government, and José Antonio Aguirre was installed as *lehendakari* (leader) at Gernika on October 7, 1936. A young, intelligent, and noble figure, Aguirre pledged Basque support to the struggle against Fascism. The government was forced into exile a few months later when the Nationalists took Bilbao, but Basques fought on in Spain and later in France against the Nazis.

The birth of ETA can be directly linked to the betrayal of the Basque government by the western democracies. At the end of the Second World War, supporters of the Republic had hoped that a liberating invasion of Spain might ensue. It didn't, but Franco's government was ostracized by the USA and Europe. The Basque government in exile was recognized as legitimate by the western powers. However, with the Cold War chilling up, the USA began to see the value of the anti-communist Franco, and granted a massive aid package to him. Following suit, France and Britain shamefully recognized the fascist government and withdrew support from the horrified Basques, as well as from the Republican government-in-exile.

ETA was founded as ATA by angry Basque youth shortly after this sordid political turnabout. Its original goal was simply to promote Basque culture in repressive Spain, but it soon took on a violent edge. In 1959 it adopted the name ETA (after realizing that *ata* meant 'duck' in a dialect of Euskara), which stands for Euskadi Ta Askatasuna,

outside perceptions of the area continue to be clouded by the ETA issue (see box, page 454). While the governing party, the PNV, seeks full independence from Spain, it is committed to achieving it by political means, although they face an uphill task, as the Spanish constitution doesn't allow for discussion of such an issue. Legally, Spain is 'indissoluble'.

Asturias has had a similarly go-ahead approach after it too suffered under Franco. Far from well-off, it has the region's highest unemployment, yet an enlightened environmental programme has secured protection for its superb natural mountains and forests, while putting in place an impressive and ecologically sound structure for tourism.

The Basque Country and Freedom. They conducted their first assassination in 1968, and since then have been responsible for over 800 deaths, mostly planned targets such as right-wing politicians, Basque 'collaborators' and police. The organization is primarily youthful, and uses extortion and donations to fund its activities. Their demands are autonomy for the Basque region, the union of Navarra with the region and the transfer of all Basque prisoners to prisons within the region (this last is a goal desired by most Basques – Basque prisoners have been appallingly treated and routinely tortured in Guardia Civil jails – and posters calling for this, with the appeal 'Euskal Presoak Euskal Herrira' are visible everywhere).

Despite the slogans, there's nothing noble or honourable about ETA's normal modus operandi. In many cases it seems that the central leadership has little control over its trigger-happy thugs, and many targets have been people with families with little or no power within the régime. The attitude of the international public has turned sharply against ETA since their glory-days; in 1973, when Franco's right-hand man Admiral Carrero Blanco was sent sky-high by an ETA car bomb (the car was sent over a six-storey building and into its patio), the terrorist group were liberationist heroes to many. Now, in more cuddly times, such actions are seen as appalling.

For many years, the government and police were in a vicious and self-defeating cycle of violence with ETA. Whenever the terrorist group struck, their support dropped dramatically in Euskadi. A few days later, when a mystery retaliatory killing of Basques occurred, anti-government feeling would rise again. The Socialist government of the early 1990s was scandalously found to have been funding a 'death squad' aimed at scaring Basques out of supporting nationalism and ETA.

The escalationist attitude of the Madrid government continued in 2002, when the parliament overwhelmingly passed legislation specifically designed to ban Batasuna, the political party often (and probably accurately) linked with ETA. The party was then banned by the courts; this alarmingly undemocratic and heavy-handed step outraged Basques and their governing PNV (no friends of Batasuna) as well as many international observers. During the same period, the police embarked on a massive operation, with many high-profile arrests and discovery of arms caches. This significantly impacted the group, as did changing attitudes in the wake of 9/11 and the Madrid train bombings. The election of José Luis Rodríguez Zapatero as prime minister was a step in the right direction for peace, which he has been keen to achieve by dialogue. An uneasy on-again, off-again ceasefire ensued, but the opposition PP have, at time of writing, done their best to under-mine the peace process, castigating the Zapatero government for countenancing 'negotiations with terrorists'.

Castilla y León is a different entity, still politically very conservative. It's the largest administrative region n the EU and lacks the vibrancy of the coastal areas. Rural depopulation continues to be a problem; villages that were once important stops between cities are now bypassed by traffic and young people flood to the provincial capitals, leaving the agricultural zone undermanned. Travelling across the frighteningly dry *meseta*, it's a sobering thought that the region used to be forested; a committed environmental policy must be a priority for the early 21st century. One bright spot is the growing reputation of the region's wines; Ribera del Duero reds now enjoy a stellar reputation and the nearby white wine district of Rueda has achieved excellent results.

In contrast to rural areas, the cities of Castilla y León are generally thriving, many for the first time since the Middle Ages. Broadened horizons and administrative responsibilities have transformed previously moribund cities like León and Valladolid into prospering European towns. Recent facelifts to many of the huge numbers of monuments in the region have increased civic pride and have are rightly being used as the focus of tourism campaigns; the renewed popularity of the Camino de Santiago has been a valuable boost too, as has the growth of the budget flight sector.

La Rioja and Cantabria have benefited from not being attached to the mass of Castilla y León and are relatively prosperous. León itself has a good case for autonomous status of its own; historically distinct, its northern and western regions are mountainous and forested, but remote from the thoughts of the Castilian parliament. Further changes to the autonomous structure are, however, unlikely.

Increases in tourism to the Pyrenees has helped the regions of Aragón and Navarra. The former, once one of the poorest areas in Spain, is now one of Northern Spain's healthiest, although it faces the same problems in rural areas as Castilla. The upcoming Expo in Zaragoza will boost both the coffers and the profile of Aragón.

Galicia is the poorest region of the north, with half the GDP per capita of the Basque lands. Although its ports still supply huge quantities of fish and seafood, Atlantic fisheries aren't what they used to be and EU action to preserve declining species will probably be a necessary but no less painful blow. While most of the cities are relatively prosperous, the region's interior is still poor. Land ownership has followed a different pattern here to the rest of the peninsula; most agricultural land is in the form of *minifundios*, very small plots that barely sustain the families farming them. This has made large-scale mechanization difficult. Galicia's conservative politics, dogged by nepotism and corruption, haven't helped matters. Galicia is known as Europe's major gateway for Colombian cocaine; in many cases the authorities appear partially complicit in the smuggling. As the expansion of the EU proceeds, Galicia will have to come to terms with the loss of some of the agricultural subsidy it receives from the union. Spain was for years the second largest recipient of money from this kitty but is having to rebudget as large sums are earmarked for the newer members of the community these days. Galicia, too, has a significant separatist movement but many *galegos* doubt whether the region has the commercial or industrial resources to make independence a realistic or sensible goal.

> ❧ *Regionalism is the key feature of modern Northern Spain, as it has been for centuries.*

While through history the Spanish government has struggled to control its outlying areas, the opposite action of granting them autonomy has largely been a significant success and one that has been noted by other nations with similar issues. Spain can only be stronger as a looser alliance of flourishing regions; given freedom of expression (under Franco, for example, many regional fiestas were banned), cultural differences become a healthy source of celebration and pride rather than festering resentment. While surely the people of Euskadi should be allowed to secede (or at least given the constitutional right to vote on secession) if they so wish, it is understandable that Madrid is anxious not to lose such a valuable part of the nation. While it won't happen, you have only to visit Bilbao, A Coruña or Gijón to see the optimism and renewal that are the overpoweringly positive aspect of regional autonomy and European involvement.

# Economy

For many centuries, it seems, Spain has been 'catching up' with the rest of western Europe and it seems that finally is has made up much of the ground. In many aspects the Spanish economy is outperforming that of neighbouring France, and there is a perceptible shift in economic power towards the Iberian nation. Nevertheless,

## ⦂ Fact file

| | |
|---|---|
| **Area** Spain: 504,783 sq km; Northern Spain: 209,847 sq km. | **Female**: 83. |
| | **Literacy** 98%. |
| **Government** Parliamentary monarchy made up of 19 autonomous communities, 8 in the north. | **Population** Spain: 40,847,371; Northern Spain: 11,200,420. |
| | **Population growth** 0.13% |
| **Life expectancy** Male: 76; | **Unemployment** 9% |

despite the long-lasting boom in the country's economy, Spain's salary levels remain low - the legal minimum monthly salary is less than half that of France or the USA. Soaring property prices have led to banks offering mortgages of up to 50 years, and people are devoting a large proportion of their income towards meeting the repayments, leaving them vulnerable to interest rate hikes, and adversely affecting the traditionally lively social interaction.

Spain's main products are textiles, machinery and automobiles, while tourism remains a vital sector; Spain receives more annual visitors than any other European country. The story in the north is a mixed one. Euskadi, an industrial powerhouse, is prosperous by any European standards, while Aragón is also strong, at least in urban areas. Galicia and Asturias are poorer; both have unemployment rates close to 20%, and Galicia's GDP per head isn't much more than half that of Euskadi.

The north still has a very important fishing industry, while the wine trade is also significant among agricultural products. Manufacturing, particularly in the Basque lands, is strong and there's still a shipbuilding industry, although declining. Euskadi and Asturias still produce steel and coal respectively, but the boom years are long gone in that sector. Bilbao and Santander continue to be important banking centres.

One interesting case in Euskadi is the Mondragón co-operative, based in a small town near San Sebastián. Formed by five workers in the 1950s, who were influenced by the social teachings of the local priest, the MCC is now one of Spain's leading companies, with over 20,000 members involved in many types of manufacturing. It's Spain's leader in the production of domestic appliances and also runs a major supermarket chain. Easily the world's most successful attempt at this enlightened form of business, the MCC has served as a model for much sociological study. One of the keys to the co-operative's success was the creation of their own bank, the Caja Laboral, with branches throughout the region.

# Culture

## Architecture

Throughout Northern Spain, the pattern of rapid growth in the wake of the Reconquista was followed by a long decline. Although not an ideal situation for a region to be in, it has had a good effect. The building sprees of the Middle Ages were succeeded by periods where there was hardly any money to fund new construction; the result is a land which has an incredibly rich architectural heritage. Nowhere in Europe has such a wealth of Romanesque and Gothic churches, while the relationships with Islamic civilization spawned some fascinating styles unique to Spain. Today, Spain has shaken off the ponderous monumentalism of the Franco era and become a powerhouse of modern architecture, with the Basque lands jostling Valencia at the front of the pack.

**Neolithic period**

There are some very early stone structures in the peninsula, with the greatest concentration in Alava and in Galicia. Dolmens, menhirs and standing stone circles are the most common remnants of the Neolithic (late Stone Age) era. The first two mostly had a funerary function, while the latter are the subject of numerous theories; some sort of religious/astrological purpose seems likely, but an accurate explanation is unlikely to emerge. The dwellings of the period were less permanent structures, of which little evidence remains.

## First millennium BC

The first millennium BC saw the construction of sturdier settlements, usually on hilltops. The sizeable Iberian town of Numancia, though razed after a Roman siege, remains an interesting example and many of the cities of Northern Spain were originally founded during this period. The Celts, too, favoured hilly locations for the construction of *castros*. These fort/villages were typically walled compounds containing a large building, presumably the residence of the chieftain and hall for administration and trading, surrounded by smaller, circular houses and narrow lanes. These dwellings were probably built from mudbrick/adobe on a stone foundation with a thatched roof. The Galician *palloza*, still widely seen in villages well into the 20th century, had probably changed little since these times. There are many well-preserved *castros* in Northern Spain, principally in Galicia and western Asturias.

Phoenician and Carthaginian remains are few in Northern Spain. The Carthaginians were based mostly in the south; their ancestors, the Phoenicians, were so adept at spotting natural harbours that nearly all have been in continual use ever since, leaving only the odd foundations or breakwaters. Greek presence has left a similarly scant architectural legacy in the north.

## Roman legacy

The Roman occupation of Hispania was largely administered from the south and east and the majority of architectural remains are in that region. Nevertheless, the Roman legacy is of great interest in the north also. They founded and took over a great number of towns; most of the provincial capitals of the region sit on Roman foundations. Zaragoza, Pamplona, Palencia and Lugo were all important Roman centres, while the abandoned settlements of Clunia and Numancia have extensive, if unspectacular remains.

The Roman remains near Palencia are the finest villas of the north; something of an exception, as the presence in this region seems to have been largely of a military/ exploitative nature. The Seventh Legion was based at León to administer the mines of the Bierzo region, while the Duero and Ebro valleys produced large quantities of wine; but the majority of the peninsula's wealthy Roman settlements were further south. Although shored up over the years, the walls of Lugo are an impressive sight indeed.

## Visigoths

Although the post-Roman period is often characterized as a time of lawless barbarism, the Visigoths added Germanic elements to Roman and local traditions and built widely; in particular the kings of the period commissioned many churches. Most of these were heavily modified or destroyed in succeeding periods, but a few excellent examples remain; the best are San Juan de Baños (near Palencia), Quintanilla de las Viñas (near Burgos) and San Pedro de la Nave (near Zamora). All these date from the seventh century and are broadly similar. Sturdy yet not unelegant, these churches are built around a triple nave with short transepts and square apses. Friezes on the outside depict birds, fruit and flowers with some skill. The interiors are particularly attractive, with treble arches, frequently horseshoe-shaped and altarstones. These altarstones are found in many other churches of later date and are interesting for their iconography; early Christian symbols heavily borrowed from pagan traditions. Depictions of the sun, moon and crops are often accompanied by Celtic-like circles with arched spokes.

## Pre-Romanesque

In the eighth century, the style known as pre-Romanesque emerged in the Christian redoubt of Asturias. While there are clear similarities to the Visigothic style, the Asturians added some elements and created a series of buildings of striking beauty, many of which are well preserved today. The style progressed considerably in a fairly short period. There are both churches and royal halls extant. The buildings are generally tripartite, with triple naves (or nave and two aisles) and arches (some exterior) resting on elegantly carved pillars. The small windows reflect this in miniature, often divided by a bonsai column. The floor plan is rectangular or in the shape of a cross, with wide transepts; the altar area is often raised and backed by three small apses, divided from the rest of the interior by a triple arch. Small domes were used in later examples. Narrow exterior buttresses line up with the interior arches. Mural painting is well preserved in many of the buildings; the Asturian (Latin) cross is a frequent motif. The capitals of the pillars are in some cases finely carved, often with motifs presumably influenced by contact with Moorish and Byzantine civilization: palm leaves, flowers and curious beasts.

## Mozarabic

During the Muslim occupation of Northern Spain a distinctly Moorish style was used by Christian masons, particularly in church construction. These traditions persisted even after reconquest and were strengthened by the arrival of Christians who had lived in the Muslim south. Known as Mozarabic, it is characterized above all by its horseshoe arches but in some cases also by exuberant fan vaulting and ornate ribbed ceilings; some of the churches feel far more Muslim than Christian. The style persisted, and even some of the most sober of later cathedrals and churches have the odd arch or two that bends a little further in. Fresco-work is present in some Mozarabic buildings too, and in some cases, such as the Ermita de San Baudelio (Berlanga de Duero), presents a fusion of scenes; some from orthodox Christian iconography and some influenced by time spent in Moorish company, with elephants, camels and palm trees.

## Romanesque

The style that spread across the whole of Northern Spain in the 11th and 12th centuries and is most dear to many visitors' hearts is the Romanesque or *románico*. Although there are some examples of the 'Catalan' style, derived from contact with Italy, and of which the Lombard arch (exterior decoration in the shape of fingers) is a primary characteristic, most of Northern Spain's Romanesque can be traced back to French influences. Many monks from France arrived in the north of the peninsula in the 11th century and built monasteries along the same lines as the ones of their home country, but the biggest single factor in the spread of the style was the Santiago pilgrimage. News of what was being built in the rest of Europe was spread across Northern Spain and it is fitting that the portal of the cathedral at Santiago is widely considered to be the pinnacle of Spanish Romanesque.

> ❧ *The purest examples are often in the middle of nowhere; places where someone had the money to build a stone church in the 11th century, and no one's had the cash to meddle with it since.*

The typical features of Romanesque churches are barrel-vaulted ceilings (stone roofs considerably reduced the number of churches that burned down) with semicircular arches; these also appear on the door and window openings. The apse is also round. Geometric decoration is common, such as the chessboard patterning known as *ajedrezado jaqués*, first seen in the Pyrenean town of Jaca, from where it spread along the length of the pilgrim route. Fine carvings, once painted, are often

Background Culture

present on capitals and portals; the cloisters of Santo Domingo de Silos and San Juan de la Peña as well as the church of San Martín in Frómista are excellent examples. The carvings depict a huge variety of subjects: biblical scenes are present and vegetal motifs recurring, but scenes of everyday life from the sublime to the ridiculous, the mundane to the erotic, are common (and often dryly labelled 'allegorical' in church pamphlets), as are strange beasts and scenes from mythology. This is part of the style's charm, as is the beautifully homely appearance of the buildings, often built from golden stone. Some of the towns with an excellent assembly of the Romanesque are Soria and Zamora, as well as those all along the Camino de Santiago.

## Gothic

Austerity in monastic life ushered in the change to elegant remote purity. The whimsical carved capitals disappeared, and the voluptuous curves were squared off as the church authorities began to exert more control over buildings within their dioceses. It seems unbelievable that the word Gothic was originally a pejorative term, applied to the pointed style during the Baroque period to mean 'barbarous'. Spanish Gothic architecture also owed much to French influence, although German masons and master builders did much work, particularly in and around Burgos. Advances in engineering allowed lighter, higher structures than their Romanesque forebears, and the wealth and optimism of the rapidly progressing Reconquista saw ever more imaginative structures raised. The cathedrals of León and Burgos are soaringly beautiful examples of this.

*♣ Gothic architecture changed over time from its rather restrained 13th-century beginnings to an extroverted style known as Flamboyant, but many basic features remained constant.*

The basic unit of Gothic is the pointed arch, symbolic of the general enthusiasm for 'more space, less stone' that pervaded the whole endeavour. The same desire was behind the flying buttress, an elegant means of supporting the building from the exterior, thus reducing the amount of interior masonry. Large windows increased the amount of light; the rose window is a characteristic feature of many Gothic façades, while the amount of stained glass in León seems to defy physics (to the concern of engineers). Elaborate vaulting graced the ceilings. The groundplan was often borrowed from French churches; as the style progressed more and more side chapels were added, particularly around the ambulatory.

A feature of many Spanish Gothic churches, and unique to the country, is the enclosed *coro* (choir, or chancel) in the middle of the nave, a seemingly self-defeating placement that robs the building of much of the sense of space and light otherwise striven for. Nevertheless, the choirstalls are often one of the finest features of Gothic architecture, superbly carved in wood. Ornate carved decoration is common on the exteriors of Gothic buildings too. Narrow pinnacles sprout like stone shoots, and the façades are often topped by gables. Portals often feature piers and tympanums carved with biblical figures and scenes, circled by elaborate archivolts.

## Mudéjar

As the Reconquista took town after town from the Muslims, Moorish architects and those who worked with them began to meld their Islamic tradition with the northern influences of Romanesque and Gothic. The result is distinctive and pleasing, typified by the decorative use of brick and coloured tiles, with the tall elegant belltowers a particular highlight. The style became popular nationwide; in certain areas, *mudéjar* remained a constant feature for over 500 years of building. Aragón, which had a strong Moorish population, has a fine collection of *mudéjar* architecture; the Duero Valley and Sahagún are also well stocked.

*♣ A style of architecture that evolved in Christian Spain, and particularly Aragón, from around the 12th century.*

## Plateresque

The 16th century was a high point in Spanish power and wealth, when it expanded across the Atlantic, tapping riches that must have seemed limitless for a while. Spanish Renaissance architecture reflected this, leading from the ornate 'Isabelline' late Gothic style into the elaborate peninsular style known as Plateresque. Although the style originally relied heavily on Italian models, it soon took on specifically Spanish features. The word refers particularly to the façades of civil and religious buildings, characterized by decoration of shields and other heraldic motifs, as well as geometric and naturalistic patterns such as shells. The term comes from the word for silversmith, *platero*, as the level of intricacy of the stonework approached that of jewellery. Arches went back to the rounded, and columns and piers became a riot of foliage and 'grotesque' scenes.

*❖ The massive façade of San Marcos in León is an excellent example of the style, as is the university at Salamanca.*

A classical revival put an end to much of the elaboration, as Renaissance architects concentrated on purity. Classical Greek features such as fluted columns and pediments were added to by large Italianate cupolas and domes. Spanish architects were apprenticed to Italian masters and returned with their ideas. Elegant interior patios in *palacios* are an attractive feature of the style, found across the north, particularly in Salamanca, as well as Valladolid and smaller places such as Medina del Campo.

## Spanish Baroque

The fairly pure lines of this Renaissance classicism were soon to be permed into a new style: Spanish Baroque, and its most extreme form, Churrigueresque. Perhaps the finest Baroque structures in Northern Spain are to be found in Galicia, where masons had to contend with granite and hence dedicated themselves to overall appearances rather than intricacy. The façade of the cathedral at Santiago, with its soaring lines, is one of the best of many examples. Compared to granite, sandstone can be carved as easily as Play-Doh, and architects in the rest of Northern Spain playfully explored the reaches of their imaginations; a strong reaction against the sober preceding style. Churches became ever larger – in part to justify the huge façades – and nobles indulged in one-upmanship, building ever-grander *palacios*. The façades themselves are typified by such features as pilasters (narrow piers descending to a point) and niches to hold statues. On a private residence, large sculptured coats-of-arms were de rigueur.

*❖ The Baroque was a time of great genius in architecture as in the other arts in Spain.*

## Churrigueresque

Named after the Churriguera brothers who took Spanish Baroque to an extreme of ornamentation in the late 17th and early 18th centuries, the result of this style can be hideously overelaborate, but on occasion transcendentally beautiful, like Salamanca's superb Plaza Mayor. Vine tendrils decorate the façades, which seem intent on breaking every classical norm, twisting here, upside-down there, treading a fine line between levity and conceit.

## Neoclassicism

Neoclassicism again resorted to the cleaner lines of antiquity, which were used this time for public spaces as well as civic and religious buildings. Many plazas and town halls in the north of Spain are in this style, which tended to flourish in the cities that were thriving in the late 18th and 19th centuries, such as Bilbao and A Coruña. The best examples use symmetry to achieve beauty and elegance.

Modernismo

The late 19th century saw Catalán *modernista* architecture break the moulds in a startling way. Apart from a small enclave in Comillas on the Cantabrian coast, there are few examples of the school in Northern Spain, but more restrained fin de siècle architecture can be seen in the fashionable towns of San Sebastián, Santander and A Coruña, as well as the industrial powerhouses of Gijón and Bilbao.

## Art nouveau and Art deco

At roughly the same time, and equally a break with the academicism of the 19th century, art nouveau aimed to bring art back to life and back to the everyday. Using a variety of naturalistic motifs to create whimsical façades and *objets*, the best art nouveau works manage to combine elegance with fancy. Art deco developed between the World Wars and was based on geometric forms, using new materials and colour combinations to create a recognizable and popular style. San Sebastián is almost a temple to art nouveau, while both it and Bilbao have many good examples of deco, as do many other cities, particularly in old cinemas and theatres.

## Avant-garde

Elegance and whimsy never seemed to play much part in Fascist architecture, and during the Franco era Spain was subjected to an appalling series of ponderous concrete monoliths, all in the name of progress. A few avant-garde buildings managed to escape the drudgery from the 1950s on – the Basque monastery of Arantzazu is a spectacular example. The Guggenheim museum is the obvious example of the flowering that has taken place in the last few years in Northern Spain, but it is only one of many. San Sebastián's Kursaal and Vitoria's shining Artium are both excellent examples of modern Spanish works, while the much-admired Valencian, Santiago Calatrava, has done much work in the region too. Zamora is also noteworthy as a city that has managed to combine sensitive modern design with the Romanesque heritage of its old town, but in many parts of the region modern architecture is functional. Vast suburbs of unimaginative apartment blocks gird every city in the region, and in coastal areas, the concrete curse strikes where lax planning laws are taken full advantage of.

❧ *It was the dictator's death in 1975 followed by EEC membership in 1986 that really provided the impetus for change.*

## Regional traditions

Other architectural traditions worth mentioning are in Euskadi, where *baserriak* are large stone farmhouses with sloping roofs, built to last by the heads of families; many are very old. Their presence in the green Basque hills gives the place a distinctly non-Spanish air. The square wooden *hórreos* of Asturias and their elongated stone counterparts in Galicia are trademarks of the region and have been used over the centuries as granaries and drying sheds, although those in Galicia are of a less practical design and were to some extent status symbols also. *Cruceiros* in Galicia are large stone crosses, most frequently carved with a scene of the Crucifixion. Mostly made from the 17th to the 19th centuries, they stand outside churches and along roads.

# Arts and crafts

Spain's artistic traditions go back a long way; right to the Palaeolithic, when cave artists along the north coast produced art that ranged from simple outlines of hands to the beautiful and sophisticated bison herds of Altamira.

The Iberians and the Celts produced fine jewellery from gold and silver, and some good sculpture. The Romans' artistic legacy was not as strong in Spain's north as in the south, although there are some fine pieces, including mosaic floors. Good bronze, silver and gold pieces are also known from the period of the Visigoths.

Monks of the Middle Ages produced some illustrated manuscripts of stunning beauty, particularly copies of the works of **Beatus of Liébana**. Wallpaintings in Asturian pre-Romanesque and in Mozarabic churches are also early examples of medieval art.

Most of Spanish sculpture through the centuries has been in the religious sphere. The Romanesque master masons responsible for such gems as the cloisters of San Juan de la Peña and Santo Domingo de Silos are not known by name, but arguably the finest of them all is **Master Mateo**, whose tour de force was the Pórtico de la Gloria entrance to the Cathedral of Santiago.

## The Gothic period

The ornate development of the Gothic style culminated in the superlative technical mastery of the works of the northern Europeans resident in Castilla, Simón de **Colonia** and Gil and Diego de **Siloé**, whose stunning *retablos* and tombs are mostly in and around Burgos. Damián Forment was a busy late Gothic sculptor who left his native Aragón to train in Italy, then returned and executed a fine series of *retablos* in his homeland. Saints and Virgins in polychrome (ie with applied colour) wood continued to be popular, and there are some fine examples from the period.

As well as sculptors, there were many foreign painters working in the Gothic period in Northern Spain. As well as *retablos*, painted panels on gold backgrounds were popular, often in the form of triptychs. Frequently illustrating the lives of saints, many of these are excellent pieces, combining well-rendered expression with a lively imagination, particularly when depicting demons, subjects where the artist had a freer rein. Some of the better painters from this period are Fernando Gallego, whose paintings grace Salamanca, **Jorge Inglés**, resident in Valladolid

❧ *Over time, Gothic sculpture achieved more naturalism in rendering than in earlier periods.*

and presumably an Englishman named George, **Juan de Flandes** (Salamanca; Flanders), and **Nicolás Francés** (León; France). These painters drew on influences from the Italian and Flemish schools of the time, but created a distinctive and entertaining Spanish style.

## The Renaissance

The transitional painter **Pedro Berruguete** hailed from near Palencia and studied in Italy. His works are executed in the Gothic manner but have a Renaissance fluidity that was mastered by his son, Alonso, who learned under Michelangelo and was court painter to Carlos V. His finest work is sculptural; he created saints of remarkable power and expression in marble and in wood. Juan de Juni, who lived in Valladolid, is also notable for his sensitive sculptures of religious themes.

As the Renaissance progressed, naturalism in painting increased, culminating in the portraits of **Velásquez** and the religious scenes of Murillo in the 17th century.

This was the finest period of Spanish painting; one of its early figures was the 16th-century Riojan painter **Juan Fernández Navarrete**, many of whose works are in the Escorial. He studied in Venice and his style earned him the nickname of the Spanish Titian; his paintings have a grace of expression denied him in speech by his

❧ *Like Gothic, the Renaissance in Spain drew heavily on the Italian.*

dumbness. A fine portraitist, overshadowed by his contemporary Velásquez, was the Asturian noble Juan Carreño de Miranda (1614-1685). Late in life he became court painter and is noted for his depictions of the unfortunate inbred King Carlos II. Although not from the region, several works by the remarkable **Francisco Zurbarán** hang in Northern Spain; his idiosyncratic style often focuses on superbly rendered white garments on a dark, brooding background, a metaphor for the subjects themselves, who were frequently priests. The religious atmosphere of imperial Spain continued to dominate in art; landscapes and *joie de vivre* are in comparatively short supply.

**Gregorio Hernández** was a fine naturalistic sculptor working in Valladolid at this time. *Retablos* became more ornate, commissioned by nobles to gain favour with the church and improve their chances in the afterlife. As Baroque progressed, this was taken to extremes. Some of the altarpieces and canopies are immense and overgilded, clashing with the Gothic lines of the churches they were placed in; while supremely competent in execution, they can seem gaudy and ostentatious to modern eyes.

## The 18th-19th centuries

Tapestry production increased markedly but never scaled the heights of the earlier Flemish masterpieces, many of which can be seen in Northern Spain. The appropriately

❗ *The early 18th century saw fairly characterless art produced under the new dynasty of Bourbon kings.*

enough named Francisco Bayeu produced pictures for tapestries ('cartoons'), as did the master of 19th-century art, **Francisco Goya**. Goya, see box page 161, was a remarkable figure whose finest works included both paintings and etchings; his fresco work in northern Spanish churches never scaled these heights. His

depiction of the vain Bourbon royals is brutally accurate; he was no fan of the royal family, and as court painter got away with murder. His etchings of the horrors of the Napoleonic Wars are another facet of his uncompromising depictions.

After Goya, the 19th century produced few works of note as Northern Spain tore itself apart in a series of brutal wars and conflicts. The rebirth came at the end of the period with the '1898 Generation', see Literature below. One of their number was the Basque painter **Ignacio Zuloaga** (1870-1945), a likeable painter with a love of Spain and a clear eye for its tragic aspects. His best work is portraiture, often set against a brooding Castilian landscape.

## The 20th century

Figures such as **Picasso**, **Miró** and **Dalí** raised the art of the peninsula to worldwide heights in the 20th century, but the Civil War was to have a serious effect, as a

❗ *While the early 20th century saw the rise of Spanish modernism and surrealism, it was mostly driven from Catalunya.*

majority of artists sided with the Republic and fled Spain with its defeat. Franco was far from an enlightened patron of the arts, and his occupancy was a monotonous time. The main light in this period came from the Basque lands in the 1950s. Painters such as Nestor Barretxea, and the sculptors **Eduardo Chillida** and **Jorge Oteiza** (see box, page 66) were part of a revival; all

three are represented at the tradition-defying monastery of Arantzazu. Chillida (who died in 2002) and Oteiza (2004) continued to be at the forefront of modern sculpture, and their works are widespread through Northern Spain and Europe. Other sculptors such as the Zaragozans **Pablo Serrano** and **Pablo Gargallo** are also prominent. The provincial governments of Northern Spain are extremely supportive of local artists these days, and the museums in each provincial capital usually have a good collection of modern works, among which female artists are finally being adequately represented; even more than in other nations, the history of Spanish art is a male one.

# Literature

The peninsula's earliest known writers lived under the Roman occupation. Martial was born near modern Calatayud and wrote of his native land, while the poet Prudentius was from Calahorra in the Rioja region. After the Roman period, San Isidoro was a significant figure in Spain's literary history, see box page 442.

Tucked away in his monastery in the Picos de Europa, the monk **Beatus de Liébana** wrote commentaries on the Apocalypse which became a popular monastery staple for centuries, see box page 339. In the 10th century another monk made notes in Castilian in the margins of a text at San Millán, in La Rioja; this is the earliest known appearance

# ⁝ Rosalía de Castro (1837-1885)

*"I do not know what I am seeking, but it is something that I lost I know not when".*

Born in Santiago, poet and novelist Rosalía de Castro grew up in Padrón. Although officially an orphan her mother was, in fact, an unmarried Galician aristocrat and her father a priest. The publication of her *Cantres Gallegos* (Galician songs) in 1863 is seen as marking the highwater- mark of the Galician *rexurdimento* (renewal) movement that sought to express liberal ideas through the medium of the Galician language.

Her marriage in 1858 to historian and Galician nationalist Manuel Murgula brought her into contact with other writers who were using the Galician language to express political ideas. Her main achievement was to express traditional Galician tales through complex, innovative metre and in her refreshing use of pastoral imagery. Many of her poems are redolent with *morriña*, a particularly Galician word that refers to a melancholy longing; a feature common to several Celtic cultures.

Her marriage was not a happy one and for the last years of her life she struggled with chronic illness. Her ability to find a distinctive voice against such a difficult background has meant a new interest in her work from feminist critics. She continues to be a source of inspiration to many Spanish authors and in Galicia she has become something of a national icon. Her works have been translated into many languages and are widely available in English.

of the language in writing. In the 12th century, *El Cantar de Mío Cid* was an anonymous epic poem recounting the glorious deeds of the northern Spanish mercenary annd strongman, **El Cid**; it's the earliest known work in Castilian. Another early author was the Riojan poet **Gonzalo de Berceo**, who wrote popular religious verses.

An important 13th-century figure was King Alfonso X. Dubbed *El Sabio* (the wise), he changed the official language of the kingdom from Latin (much bastardized by this time) to Castilian. He was also a poet, and wrote verses in *Galego* (Galician). It wasn't unusual for the nobility to take up the pen and the 15th century saw the **Marqués de Santillana** dashing off verse, including the first Spanish sonnets. The popular form of the period was the romantic ballad, dealing in damsels and knights, Christians and Moors.

One of the finest Spanish poets of any period was the theologian **Fray Luis de León**, see box, page 259, whose 16th-century works include moving personal reflections on religion; the poems *A Cristo Crucificado* and *En la Ascensión* are noteworthy. *Lazarillo de Tormes*, an anonymous work, appeared in 1554. One of the first of the genre known as picaresque (after the Spanish *pícaro*, a rogue), it dealt with a journey across Northern Spain by a blind man's guide. It's frequently described as the first Spanish novel. The extraordinary life of **Miguel de Cervantes** (1547-1616) marks the start of a rich period of Spanish literature. *Don Quijote* came out in serial form in 1606 and is rightly considered one of the finest novels ever written; it's certainly the widest-read Spanish work. Cervantes spent a portion of his eventful life in Valladolid. The royal archives are another frequently overlooked source of interest, particularly those of Felipe II. A fascinating glimpse of the period can be had from reading his tenderly written letters to family as well as his policy decisions that affected half the world.

The opening of public theatres in the 17th century saw the rise of the great dramatists **Lope de Vega** and **Calderón de la Barca** (who was expelled from Salamanca University for defaulting on his college fees). In the 18th century the Basque **Felix María Samaniego** penned popular childlike fables. Meanwhile the Galician priest **Benito Feijóo**, a major Enlightenment figure, wrote important essays from his Oviedo base, and the later Asturian Gaspar Melchior de Jovellanos wrote significant historical-political and sociological works; both were pestered by the Inquisition for their liberal outlook.

Several of the 19th century's major writers emerged from the north. Born in Valladolid, **José Zorrilla** spent much of his life in Mexico; he's famous for his poems and a play about Don Juan, *Don Juan Tenorio*. The playwright Echegaray was of Basque descent, while **Leopoldo Alas**, known as *Clarín*, set his novel *La Regenta* in the fictional city of Vetusta, clearly his native Oviedo. It's a fantastic depiction of Spanish provincial life of the time, seen through the eyes of its heroine. At the same time, Galicia's favourite poet, **Rosalía de Castro**, was writing her soulful verses in Spanish and Gallego (see box, page 465).

A watershed in Basque writing came in the late 19th century with the fiery works of **Sabino Arana**. Littered with inaccuracies and untruths, much of his writing reads more like propaganda than literature or non-fiction, but it created modern Basque nationalism; since then it has been difficult for Basque writings to avoid the issue.

At the end of the 19th century, Spain lost the last of its colonial possessions after revolts and a war with the USA. This event, known as the 'Disaster', had a profound impact on the nation and its date, 1898, gave its name to a generation of writers and artists who sought to express what Spain was and had been, and achieve new perspectives for the 20th century. One of the foremost was the scholarly Basque **Miguel de Unamuno**, see box page 96, whose massive corpus of writing ranged from philosophy to poetry and novels, but also included much journalism. His novel *A Tragic Sense of Life* is an anguished an honest attempt to come to terms with his faith and inevitable death. The slightly later novels of **Pío Baroja** often deeply reflect Basque rural life. **Blas de Otero**, who had a complex love for his native Bilbao, spent most of his writing life overseas.

Another of the Generación de '98 was the poet Antonio Machado, see box page 222. His work reflects his profound feelings for the landscape of his homelands of Andalucía and Castilla; he lived for many years in Soria. Along with Federíco García Lorca, he is considered the greatest of Spanish 20th-century poets; Machado and Lorca, Republicans both, were lost in the Civil War. Another notable member was the essayist, historian and critic **José Ortega y Gasset**, who spent time in Bilbao.

Two writers that stand out in post-Civil War Spanish literature are from Northern Spain. **Miguel Delibes** (1920-) is from Valladolid and his works range from biting satire to evocative descriptions of the Castilian landscape. **Camilo José Cela** (1916-2002), was a Galician realist who won the Nobel Prize for Literature in 1989, see box page 418. Although the latter fought on the Nationalist side in the Civil War, both battled censors in post-war Spain as editors of anti-Francoist newspapers.

**Bernardo Atxaga** is a talented contemporary Basque writer whose best-known work is the anecdotal *Obabakoak*; Julián Ríos is an award-winning Galician writer whose most acclaimed work is the novel *Amores que flotan*.

# Language

Spanish is, of course, the major language. Known as *español* or *castellano*, the constitution states that all citizens have a duty to know it. Nearly all do, although if you get right off the beaten track in Galicia, Aragón or Asturias you'll find the occasional elderly person who doesn't. Languages and dialects are always thorny political issues, and Northern Spain has its fair share.

## Castellano
With Castile playing a major role in the Reconquista the language spread rapidly and was adopted as the official one of the kingdom of Alfonso X, which encompassed most of northwest Spain. The fact that it is now spoken by some 360 million people

worldwide is perhaps more than an accident of history; its accessibility and comparatively simple grammar may have aided its spread in the first place. In Spain, the most respected institution dealing with it is the *Real Academia Española*, a hoary old body whose remit is "to purify, clarify, and give splendour" to the language.

There are many regional accents of *castellano*. Many words are purely local; olives are called *aceitunas* in some places and *olivas* in others; ordering *buey* in Castilla will get you an ox steak, in Galicia a large crab. Similarly, slang differs widely from city to city. One entertaining story about Castilian is that the /th/ sound used for the letters *z* and *c* came about because courtiers were anxious not to offend a lisping Habsburg king. It's almost certainly not true – linguists point to the fact that not all /s/ sounds are converted to /th/ – but it's often used to poke fun at mainland Spain by Latin Americans, who don't do it (neither do Andalucíans).

## Gallego
Of the regional languages, the one with the most speakers is *Galego* (Gallego), with some three million in Spain. It's related to Portuguese and the two are mutually intelligible. Although banned under Franco (who was himself Galician), it remained strong and is now taught in schools again. It's similar enough to Castellano not to cause visitors too much concern. ▸ *See Footnotes, page 478, for further details of regional dialects.*

## Euskara
Although the first known document written in the Basque (Euskara; also known as Euskera) language dates from the same time as Castilian, it's a far older tongue whose origins are as obscure as the Basques themselves. It's a difficult language with no known relatives. Like Finnish, it is agglutinative, meaning roughly that distinct bits are joined on to words for each element of meaning. Some 800,000 people speak Basque in Spain, and the number is rapidly rising.

## Bable
The Asturian tongue, known as Bable, is similar enough to Castilian to be labelled a dialect. In truth, though, it's probably more accurate to put it the other way, as Castilian is thought to be largely derived from the tongue spoken in the Christian mountain kingdom. It's still widely spoken in Asturias, unlike Leonese, which is similar, but spoken by few people in that province (although sporadic efforts are made to revive it).

## Aragonese
Aragonese is a word with two meanings; it refers to the version of Castilian spoken in Aragón and to the native language of the region, more similar to Catalán than anything else and still used, especially in the more remote mountain regions.

# Music

## Musical traditions
Based on folk traditions the post-Franco years have seen a rapid evolution of traditional forms and their incorporation into the mainstream of musical life. The music is mostly performed during festivals, some of which were banned during the Franco period. There has also developed a strong musical infrastructure incorporating festivals, CD production and distribution, and a network of venues for live events. Oviedo has an internationally famous folk festival and León has a small-scale Celtic music festival in October. As well as showcasing traditional music these festivals offer an opportunity for musicians to experiment in a variety of different styles.

‡ *The differing musical traditions of Northern Spain are one of the most obvious ways in which identity is expressed.*

Background Culture

468

## The gaita

The *gaita* is the Asturian and Galician bagpipe, often a surprising sight for visitors in the many processions and festivals. It's a simpler instrument than its Scottish cousin, normally having only one pipe. The bag is traditionally made from goatskin.

The sound produced is clear and slightly cheerier than the Scottish version, and is the basis for much modern Celtic music. The Museo de Gaitas in Gijón is a good exhibition on the history and nature of bagpipes around the world.

The northwestern provinces of Galicia and Asturias derive their musical traditions from Celtic origins. Traditional instruments include bagpipes, accordions, fiddles and tin whistles. There are a variety of different vocal styles in each province. Industrial Asturias has a tradition of male voice choirs similar to that of Wales. The unaccompanied choirs sing traditional Asturian songs and of the industrial struggles of the 20th century.

The Galician group **Leilía** have produced two albums of these haunting traditional ballads (*Leilía* and *E Verdade le mentira*). The songs are preformed with the traditional *pandereta* (tambourine), an instrument associated with women players in Galician culture. Other traditional Galician instruments include the *caneveira*, a kind of split cane used for making clapping sounds, and the *zanfona*, a Galician hurdy gurdy. The group *Habas Verdes* have used these on their recording *En el jardín de la yerba buena*.

*In Galicia songs have emerged from the largely agricultural sector many of them sung exclusively by women.*

Galician immigrant history has meant that some musicians have incorporated Latin rhythms into traditional Galician songs. **Noitebregos** from Ourense are one such group. They are part of a group of young musicians trying to move traditional Galician music in a more experimental direction. Bagpiper **Carlos Nuñez** was probably the first to develop this trend. A veteran of the European circuit, he has collaborated with a variety of musicians, including Ry Cooder. Other recommended Galician bands are **Na Lúa** (In the moon), **Fia Na Roca** and **Dhais**. For Asturian music **Llan de Cubel** are an interesting starting point, while **Hevia** is one of the region's best traditionally based musicians.

Traditional Basque music is mostly associated with the accordion, or *trikitrixa*. Musicians associated with this include **Josepa Tapia** and **Kepa Junkera**. The tensions inherent in Basque culture are reflected in both the lyrical content and the forms which are performed. Songs are therefore an important part of Basque musicians' repertoire. On the other hand there is the desire to innovate within the traditional form in order to ensure that it remains a living tradition rather than one of concern only to musicologists.

**Benito Lertxundi** is the Basques' most revered singer/songwriter and has been an inspiration to musicians for a generation. The first Basque band were **Ez doz Amairu** (It's not 13) who were part of the **Kantaldi Garaia** (Its time to sing movement). The aim of this movement was to give Basque culture a modern appeal and its effects continue to this day. Independence-minded Basques have frequently found musical expression in anti-establishment hard rock and punk music; some other important bands include Kortatu, Negu Gorriak and Soziedad Alkohólika.

*Traditional songs are an important part of Basque culture.*

**Hemendik At!** have produced three albums of Basque language dance music. Their lyrics are concerned with the problems of young Basque people rather than on a romanticizing of history. However the identification of dance music with the Spanish cultural mainstream has meant that producing music in this form has been difficult. Their 2001 album *Etorkizun* expresses a more relationship-centred Basqueness which has not always been widely welcomed by more politically minded musicians.

By far the most popular form of music is pop, with the reality-TV show *Operación Triunfo* having created a production line of stars who are adored by the younger public. Every summer is marked by a handful of *canciones de verano*, modish (and usually awful) hits that are played continuously until autumn comes and then forgotten.

The Spanish passion for dancing is carried out to this and also to the sounds of *bacalao*, a happy Spanish techno, which is widely popular and an essential background track to any Spanish visit. Groups are by definition ephemeral.

Rock music in Spain was a symbol of the *Transición* – the return to democracy, and is still enthusiastically embraced by that and younger generations. Groups of that era, such as León's **Los Cardiacos**, still evoke all the frenetic passion of those years when played in bars. Younger rock groups play to packed houses, particularly in more working class cities such as Vigo, Gijón, Bilbao or Ponferrada.

> **⁑** There are many opportunities to listen to all kinds of music at live venues.

Jazz, soul and R&B are represented in nearly all of the larger towns, most of which have at least one bar or venue devoted to the style. Live appearances of local musicians are common, while internationally renowned artists mainly play Madrid and Barcelona only, with perhaps a concert in Vigo, Bilbao, Zaragoza, or Gijón thrown in.

# Dance

If a broad definition of dance is that it is ritualized movement, then a strong case can be made for saying that dance is at the very core of Spanish society. What else is the *paseo* but an enormous communal dance where each participant has their allotted role and which tradition guides from beginning to end.

Local fiestas and weddings showcase traditional regional dancing, but it is during *la marcha* that Spain's living dance culture comes into its own. Come 0200 the whole of Spain seems to be engaged in an enormous Bacchic celebration of hip-swinging, hand-waving dancing that goes on till the last person leaves.

Although modern in approach Spain's dance culture has deep roots. In the north, each region has its own traditional dances. Mostly seen at fiestas these dances reflect the historical background of each region. Thus in Galicia and Asturias the dances are Celtic in origin and are similar to Scottish dances, following the basic reel pattern.

Many of the Basque dances are extremely physical as may be judged by their names, for example *Bolant Dantza* (flying dance). Perhaps the most famous of all Basque dances are the *Espatas* (sword dances). Performed using interlocking swords these dances reflect their martial origins although in contempary Basque culture they are preformed more to impress than intimidate. Less exclusive are the Basque social dances where men and women dance together in a circle linked by either holding hands or handkerchiefs. At the fiestas of northern Castilla a recent innovation has seen the importation of

> **⁑** The dances of the Basque country are more complicated although the difficult parts are usually left to the dantzari, or experts.

Eastern European dance companies to lead the party. With a less developed dance history, the Castilians are certainly no slouches when it comes to reinvigorating local traditions. These itinerant troupes can be seen all over Castilla in the summer months inspiring the partying locals to add the *polka* and *mazurka* to their repertoire.

Northern Spain has a variety of both ballet and modern dance companies that perform all over Spain and abroad. Drawing on local traditions these groups are very much part of the European mainstream and a number of innovative dancers have come from them. They are, however, very much at the top of the dance pecking order. It is much more important to emphasize that dance in Spain is entirely democratic in spirit.

# Cinema

The history of cinema in Northern Spain is inevitably linked to the history of Spanish cinema generally. With the infrastructure of the industry located historically in Madrid, Barcelona and Andulucía, it has only been the patronage of the regional governments and TV companies that have enabled a regional film culture to evolve at all. That said, there are well established film production facilities in the Basque country – with the internationally important San Sebastián film festival attracting worldwide attention – and to a lesser extent in Galicia. Valladolid also has an important film festival in October of each year attracting over 80,000 visitors. Technicians, directors and actors from Northern Spain have played an important role in Spanish film generally although northern themes have necessarily been subservient to national ones.

One of the early pioneers of cinema was the Aroganese film maker **Segundo de Chomón** who was hired by the French film company Pathé in order for them to compete against the great Georges Melies. He was an innovator in trick photography and made one of the earliest colour films *Le scarabée d'or* (*The Golden Beetle*). However, it was indicative of the weakness of Spain in general at that time that he had to work outside his homeland. A shortage of capital and an underdeveloped home market meant that it was extremely difficult to develop any indigenous production facilities. Demand was mostly met by imported American films.

Another artist who did most of his work outside Spain was **Luis Buñuel**, who was a pioneer of surrealism in cinema. Although his work was largely seen by a middle-class élite, it was to influence generations of directors. His collaboration with Salvador Dalí on *Un Chien Andalou* produced images that are still iconic. Buñuel left Spain in the 1930s but he returned shortly before his death to work on a number of collaborations.

The beginnings of a native Spanish film industry came during the 1930s with the help of the Republican government. Locally produced films such as *Paloma Fair* (1935) and *Clara the Brunette* (1936) proved to be immensely popular and produced the first Spanish-language star, the unlikely named Imperio Argentina. Another important development in this period was the move to dub imported films into Spanish, a practice which continues to this day and has given employment to thousands of Spanish actors.

The establishment of the Franco dictatorship saw the end of progress and development in the Spanish film industry. For the next forty years cinema was to be made subservient to the goals of the state and all film production had to be approved. The emphasis was on films with a unifying message. Historical epics, inoffensive comedies and chaste romances were the order of the day. Regional differences were not encouraged and the use of Basque and Galician was forbidden.

Despite this, some filmmakers managed to put their message across. The most important of these was **Antonio Bardem**. His films, especially *Death of a Cyclist* (1956) suggested that it was possible to introduce some critical elements into film making. He founded the film magazine *Objectivo* in 1953 which for the 15 issues that it was allowed to operate became a rallying point for critics of the Franco regime. Bardém was arrested on numerous occasions and it became increasingly difficult for him to produce in Spain.

Since the end of the Franco era Spanish cinema has witnessed the transformation mirrored in other cultural activities. There are around 80 films produced by Spanish companies each year and Spanish films make up around 15% of the Spanish market. Spain records one of the highest number of cinema visits per head of population at around five a year. The director Pedro Almodóvar has enjoyed international success with his quirky, slightly seedy style while Penélope Cruz and Antonio Banderas have made the move from Spanish films to international stardom. Cinema in Northern Spain has undergone a similar if slightly less dramatic transformation.

At the end of September the film world turns its attention to San Sebastián and over 200,000 visitors come to view the enormous number of both Spanish and international films on offer. As well as awarding internationally prestigious prizes the festival focuses attention on regional Spanish cinema and tries to ensure that it is seen outside the limited area of its production. Recently there has been a recognition that although there is a basic production infrastructure in the North of Spain, especially in the Basque country, there is a need to develop skills in marketing and promotion if the films are ever to be seen outside the area in which they were produced. The establishment of a national film school in Ponferrada, and the recent successes of Galician-set films such as *Mar Adentro* (The Sea Inside) and *Los Lunes al Sol* (Mondays in the Sun) indicate that success is being delivered.

# Religion

In a land where *Radio María* gets plenty of listeners, religion is bound to be a significant factor. The history of Spain and the history of the Spanish Catholic church are barely separable but in 1978, Article 16 of the new constitution declared that Spain was now a nation without an official religion; less than a decade after Franco's right hand, Admiral Luis Carrero Blanco, had declared that "Spain is Catholic or she is nothing".

From the sixth-century writings of San Isidoro onwards, the destiny of Spain was a specifically Catholic one. The Reconquista was a territorial war inspired by holy zeal, Jews and Moors were expelled in the quest for pure Catholic blood, the Inquisition demonstrated the young nation's religious insecurities and paranoias, and Felipe II bled Spain dry pursuing futile wars in a vain attempt to protect his beloved Church from the spread of Protestantism. Much of the strife of the 1800s was caused by groups attempting to end or defend the power of the Church, while in the 20th century the fall of the Second Republic and the Civil War were engendered to a large extent by the provocatively anti-clerical actions of the leftists.

> ♥ *Faced with a recent census form, a massive 94% of Spaniards claim to be Catholics, but less than a third cut regular figures in their parish church.*

Although regular church-going is increasingly confined to an aged (mostly female) segment of society, and seminaries struggle to produce enough priests, it's not the whole picture. *Romerías* (religious processions to rural chapels) and religious fiestas are well attended, and places of popular pilgrimage such as Santiago, Zaragoza, Loiola and Covadonga are flooded with Spanish visitors during the summer. Very few weddings are conducted away from the Church's bosom, and at Easter a huge percentage of the male population of some towns participates in solemn processions of religious *cofradías* (brotherhoods). Although not involved to the same degree in education as it once was, the Church runs some 15% of Spanish schools and several universities. The Church and the right wing remain closely connected in Spain; the opposition Partido Popular is implicitly largely a Catholic party, and allegations of Opus Dei involvement are frequent (see box page 176).

One curious aspect of Spanish Catholicism is its Marian aspect. Worship and veneration of the Virgin seem to far outstrip that of Christ himself, who is often relegated to a side chapel; María is still by far the most common name in Spain (even being used for boys in combination with another name, eg José María), and the majority of girls are named after one incarnation of the Virgin or another (eg Carmen, Pilar, Mercedes, Esperanza, Concepción, Begoña).

The practice of Catholicism in Spain is far more devotional than liturgical. The devotions of the *Via Crucis*, or Stations of the Cross (which arose in the 17th century), the *Sacred Heart* (which became popular in the 16th), and the *Rosary* are the focus of a sentimental and far from robust approach to the religion; the Bible itself has historically not been widely available to, or read by, the people. Encouraging the performance of these ritualistic elements was a way for the church to keep a superstitious populace in regular attendance; indulgences were traditionally offered as a carrot. The number of *fiestas* in Spain, which are nearly all religious in origin, historically had a similar aim.

Background Culture

# Land and environment

## Geography

Spain's area of 500,000 sq km makes it the fourth largest country in Europe and second largest in the EU after France. It's also high; the average altitude is second only to Switzerland. Geographically, Spain is divided into very distinct areas; to a large degree these have corresponded with cultural and political boundaries over time.

Although if you arrive over the Pyrenees it may not seem it, Spain's central plateau, the *meseta*, is high, with an average elevation of some 600-700 m. It covers most of Castilla y León as well as extending further to the south. It's bounded by mountains; the Pyrenees to the northeast, the Cordillera Cantábrica to the north and the Montes de León in the northwest. In itself, it's not particularly flat either.

While Spain's highest peak is in the south, in the Sierra Nevada, it's the Pyrenees that are its biggest and most rugged, straddling the northern border like a hardman bouncer. The highest summit of the Pyrenees is Aneto (3,404 m), one of many that top the 10,000 ft mark. The Cantábrica is basically a westwards extension of it, and includes the Picos de Europa in its westwards run along the coast. Further west still, at the corner of Spain, Galicia is fairly hilly with a wild coast indented with sheltered inlets (*rías*).

The two great rivers of Northern Spain are the Ebro, rising in Cantabria and flowing eastwards to its Mediterranean destiny, and the Duero, flowing west right across the *meseta* and into Portugal, where it becomes the Douro. Galicia's Miño is another major river; it forms a long section of the border with Portugal. The scarcity of water on the *meseta* has dictated settlement patterns; most towns and villages are on or near rivers.

## Climate

The green hills of the north coast are that way for a reason: it rains a hell of a lot. Parts of Galicia get 2 m of rain a year, more than 10 times the precipitation of some towns in Castilla. It's a typically maritime climate, with mild summers and winters, and the rain fairly constant through the year; up to 150 rainy days per annum.

The high *meseta* has a continental climate with very low rainfall, scorching summers and freezing winters. Adding to the winter discomfort is the biting wind, which 'can kill a man but can't blow out a candle' according to locals. The climate in places like Burgos and León is popularly characterized as *nueve meses de invierno, tres meses de infierno* (nine months of winter, three months of hell).

The mountains, too, receive high rainfall, particularly the coastal Cordillera Cantábrica. Snow is usually there to stay from January on, and many of the higher passes can still be snowbound as late as June or July.

## Wildlife

The best havens for wildlife in the peninsula are the mountainous parts of Asturias and the Pyrenees, where conservation is most advanced and the habitats less accessible. While the *meseta* can be good for birdwatching, deforestation and the Spanish passion for hunting have made most four-legged creatures larger than a mouse fairly scarce.

## :: Storks

One of Castilla's most distinctive summer sights is a bevy of graceful white storks, *cigueñas*, circling their massive nests in the setting evening sun. Most of them arrive in June from Africa and southern Spain and busy themselves with spring-cleaning their nests, feeding on insects and fish from around the *meseta*'s wetlands and raising young. Their distinctive clacking call is an eerie sound when it comes from high in the eaves of a deserted rural church.

Their sheer numbers can be something of a problem, often overwhelming small villages entirely. Councils have taken to moving their nests in some places, as churches and cathedrals struggled to withstand the impact of a hundred or so of the heavy birds. The diminishing natural wetlands of Castilla have meant that the storks have to forage elsewhere for food; they are often to be seen on the edges of town looking for morsels in rubbish dumps or scouring farmers' fields. They normally leave Castilla in late August, although increasing numbers are spending the whole year in Northern Spain.

In the mountains, a common sight are chamois or isard (*rebeco* or *sarrío*), a type of agile antelope that like the high altitudes. Also common are *jabalí* (wild boar), but being nocturnal, they're harder to see. Extensively hunted, they tend to be extra-wary when people are about. Still present, but in smaller numbers, are brown bears, subject to an Asturian conservation programme, which will hopefully ensure their survival in the wild, and wolves, which still howl in the Galician hills. A variety of deer are present both in the mountains and on the plains, where their heads make popular trophies.

Smaller mammals include the stoat/ermine, which changes colour in winter, the fox, pine marten, red squirrels and several species of bat. Wildcats are also present, although interbreeding with feral domestic cats has created a debased population.

Other creatures you might spot are salamanders, brightly coloured in yellow and black, and many species of lizard and snake in the dustier lands of Castilla. Few of the snakes are poisonous, although there are a couple of species of viper. Frogs can create deafening noise around some of Castilla's rivers.

Northern Spain is a popular destination for watching flocks of migrating species, with plentiful birdlife, see Sport and special interest, page 49. Largest of all are the plentiful storks of Castilla in the summer months, see box page 473. One of the most dramatic species is the lammergeyer, or bearded vulture. Known as 'bone-breaker' (*quebrantahuesos*) in Spanish for its habit of dropping bones on rocks to shatter them and get at the marrow, it's a superb sight, drifting up valleys on its massive wings. Smaller but far more plentiful is the endemic common or griffon vulture (*buitre*). Golden eagles (*águila real*) can also be spotted in the Pyrenees. Numerous other birds of prey are common sights both in the mountains or circling the the endless horizons of the *meseta*. The rivers of Northern Spain have always been full of trout and salmon, yet overfishing and hydroelectric projects have reduced their numbers in many areas.

Rare sights in the mountains include capercaillie (*urogallo*) and wallcreepers; woodpeckers, choughs and owls are more common. On the plains, larks, doves and grouse are common sights, as are two species of bustard. Coastal areas are home to a wide variety of waterbirds, as are some inland lakes; Galicia, Navarra and La Rioja are good areas for these species. There are many species of interesting butterflies and moths; clouds of them grace the Pyrenees and the Picos in early summer.

**Background** Land & environment

# Vegetation

The war on trees conducted in Castilla through the centuries is over, with the sinister trunked creatures successfully eliminated. Most of the arid plains of the *meseta* were once covered with Mediterranean forest, but systematic deforestation, combined with overgrazing and war, have left it barren and bare; some of it barely able to support the sparse, scrubby *matorral* that covers the land deemed unfit for agriculture.

Reforestation schemes in Castilla have primarily been for logging purposes, and the region needs a more enlightened environmental programme such as that of Asturias, which preserves some superb stretches of ancient forest.

The forest cover of the northern Spanish coast and mountains is impressive in many parts, with chestnut, beech and holm oak at lower levels, and Scots pine and silver fir higher up, among other species. South of Burgos, one of Castilla's few forested areas is Europe's largest expanse of juniper trees.

In spring, the wildflowers of the Pyrenees and the Cordillera Cantábrica are superb, with myriad colourful species. The *meseta*, too, can be attractive at this time, with fields of poppies and cultivated sunflowers bright under the big sky.

# National parks

Spain has several *parques nacionales* (national parks); the first, established in 1918, were Covadonga (now part of the Parque Nacional Picos de Europa) and Ordesa, in the Aragonese Pyrenees. These remain the only two in the region covered by this book. Far more numerous, and covering a larger area, are *parques naturales* (natural parks) administered by the autonomous communities. Although protection for the species within these areas in some cases isn't absolute, it is significant, and crucial in many cases for survival. Asturias has the best-administered parks, with several in its forested hills and valleys: Muniellos and Somiedo are two of the finest. Galicia's Illas Ciés islands are another especially worth noting, as are many in the Pyrenees. *Reservas de caza* are protected areas that also have significant coverage but for less noble reasons; so that there'll be plenty of animals to shoot when the hunting season comes around.

# Books

## Food and drink

**Barrenechea, T** *The Basque Table* (1998), Harvard Common Press. A cookbook with traditional Basque recipes.
**Read, J** *Wines of Spain* (2001), Mitchell Beazley. Updated edition of this good in-depth guide to Spain's wines and wineries.

## History and politics

**Brenan, G** *The Spanish Labyrinth* (1943), Billings & Sons. A good explanation of the background to the Spanish Civil War.

**Carr, R** (ed) *Spain: A History* (2000), Oxford University Press. An interesting compilation of recent writing on Spanish history, with entertaining and myth-dispelling contributions from leading academics.
**Elliott, J** *Imperial Spain* (1963), Edward Arnold. History as it should be, precise, sympathetic and very readable.
Gibson, I *Ligero de Equipaje* (2006). A moving biography of poet Antonio Machado by excellent Spanish-based Irishman Ian Gibson. Hopefully it will appear in English before too long.

**Kurlansky, M** *The Basque History of the World* (1999), Vintage Press. A likeable introduction to what makes the Basques tick, what they eat, what they've done and what they're like. Informal, fireside style.

Rankin, N Telegram from Guernica (2003), Faber & Faber. This biography of the fascinating war correspondent George Steer has more on his Ethiopian experiences than the Guernica events, but is still a decent read that evokes the frenzy of the Civil War.

**Ross, C** *Contemporary Spain*: A Handbook (1997), Arnold Press. Slightly dry but useful overview of Spain's politics and economy.

**Steer, G** *The Tree of Guernica* (1938), Hodder & Stoughton. Written by a pro-Republican reporter who was an eyewitness to the atrocity of the bombing, this is of most interest for an evocative description of the event itself.

**Thomas, H** *The Spanish Civil War* (1961/77), Penguin. The first unbiased account of the war read by many Spaniards in the censored Franco years, this is large but always readable. A superbly researched work.

**Zulaika, J** *Basque Violence: Metaphor and Sacrament* (2000), University of Nevada Press. An academic but intriguing exploration of the roots of Basque nationalist feeling, and the progression to violence.

## Literature, art and reportage

**Atxaga, B** *Obabakoak* (1994), Vintage Books. A dreamlike series of anecdotes making up a novel by a well-respected contemporary Basque author. Drawn from Basque heritage rather than about Basque culture. Individual and profound.

**Alas, L (Clarín)** *La Regenta* (1885). Good novel about small-town prejudices in Spain, set in mythical Vetusta, heavily based on Oviedo.

**Baroja, P** *The Tree of Knowledge* (1911). While mostly set in Madrid and Valencia, this is the best introduction to this powerful Basque novelist.

**Burns, J** *Spain: A Literary Companion* (1995); John Murray. Good anthology of Spanish writers.

**Cela, C** *La Familia de Pascual Duarte* (1942). Nobel-prize-winning writer's first and best novel, a grimly realistic novel about post-war Spain. *La Colmena* is another good one that has been translated into English.

**Cervantes Saavedra, M de** *Don Quijote* (1605/1615). Don Quixote is an obvious choice and a superbly entertaining read.

**Cohen, J (ed)** *The Penguin Book of Spanish Verse* (1988), Penguin. Excellent collection of Spanish poetry through the ages, with original versions and transcriptions.

**Hemingway, E** *Death in the Afternoon* (1939), Jonathan Cape. Superb book on bullfighting by a man who fell heavily for it.

**Hemingway, E** *Fiesta/The Sun Also Rises* (1927), Jonathan Cape. One of Hemingway's greatest works, an evocative description of the Pamplona *fiestas* and trout-fishing in the Pyrenees.

**Hooper, J** *The New Spaniards* (1995), Penguin. An excellent account of modern Spain and the issues affecting peoples' lives.

**Orwell, G** *Homage to Catalonia* (1938), Secker & Warburg. About Orwell's experience of the Spanish Civil War, and characteristically incisive and poignant.

**Pérez-Reverte, A** *The Dumas Club* (1993), Harvill Press (Eng version). Not from the north, but a very popular light-reading novelist; this is his best work.

**Unamuno, M** *Tragic Sense of Life* (1913), Dover Publications (1990). The anguished and heroically honest attempt by the great Basque and Salamantine philosopher to come to terms with faith and death.

## Travelogues

**Borrow, G** *The Bible in Spain* (1842), John Murray Press. Amusing account of another remarkable 19th-century traveller who travelled widely through Spain trying to distribute Bibles during the first Carlist War.

**Brenan, G** *The Face of Spain* (1950), Turnstile Press. Although set in the south, this is worth a read for Brenan's insights into the people he lived among for many years.

**Ford, R** *A Hand-Book for Travellers in Spain* (1845), John Murray Press. Difficult to get hold of (there have been several editions) but worth it; comprehensive and entertaining guide written by a 19th-century British gentleman who spent 5 years in Spain.

**Ford, R** *Gatherings from Spain* (1846), John Murray Press. Superb and sweeping overview of Spanish culture and customs; Richard Ford was something of a genius and has been surpassed by few if any travel writers since.

**Jacobs, M** *The Road to Santiago*, Pallas Athene Publishers. One of the best guides to the architecture of the pilgrim route, full of knowledgeable insight but happily piety-free.

**Lee, L** *As I Walked Out One Midsummer Morning* (1969), Penguin. A poignant account of a romantic walk across pre-Civil War Spain.

**Morris, J** *Spain* (1960), Penguin. Morris didn't know Spain that well, and that is the book's strength; it's a good collection of insightful first impressions.

**Morton, H** *A Stranger in Spain* (1955), Methuen. Not one of Morton's best; he was fastidiously unwilling to adapt to Spanish culture, but still very readable.

**Nooteboom, C** *Roads to Santiago* (1992), The Harvill Press. An offbeat travelogue that never fails to entertain. One of the best travel books around, soulful, literary and moving, by a Dutch writer with a deep love of Romanesque architecture.

**Pillement, G** *Unknown Spain* (1964), Johnson Press. Likeable and useful (if not hugely entertaining) book describing various routes discovering the architecture of Northern Spain.

## Other

**Arias Páramo, L** *Guía del Arte Prerrománico Asturiano* (1994), Trea. The best book around on Asturian pre-Romanesque architecture. Spanish, but with an English summary.

**Ball, P** *¡Morbo!* (2001) Excellent overview of Spanish football and its rivalries.

**Farino, T and Grunfeld, F** *Wild Spain*, Sheldrake Press. Knowledgeable book on Spain's wildlife and the quiet corners where you find it.

# Footnotes

# Basic Spanish for travellers

Learning Spanish is a useful part of the preparation for a trip to Spain and no volumes of dictionaries, phrase books or word lists will provide the same enjoyment as being able to communicate directly with the people of the country you are visiting. It is a good idea to make an effort to grasp the basics before you go. As you travel you will pick up more of the language and the more you know, the more you will benefit from your stay.

## Vowels

| | |
|---|---|
| a | as in English *cat* |
| e | as in English *best* |
| i | as the *ee* in English *feet* |
| o | as in English *shop* |
| u | as the *oo* in English *food* |
| ai | as the *i* in English *ride* |
| ei | as *ey* in English *they* |
| oi | as *oy* in English *toy* |

## Consonants

Most consonants can be pronounced more or less as they are in English. The exceptions are:

| | |
|---|---|
| g | before *e* or *i* is the same as *j* |
| h | is always silent (except in *ch* as in *chair*) |
| j | as the *ch* in Scottish *loch* |
| ll | as the *y* in *yellow* |
| ñ | as the *ni* in English *onion* |
| rr | trilled much more than in English |
| x | depending on its location, pronounced x, s, sh or j |

---

# Spanish words and phrases

## Greetings, courtesies

| | |
|---|---|
| hello | *hola* |
| good morning | *buenos días* |
| good afternoon-evening/night | *buenas tardes/noches* |
| goodbye | *adiós/hasta luego* |
| pleased to meet you | *encantado/encantada* |
| how are you? | *¿cómo estás?* |
| I'm fine, thanks | *muy bien, gracias* |
| I'm called... | *me llamo...* |
| what is your name? | *¿cómo te llamas?* |
| yes/no | *sí/no* |
| please | *por favor* |
| thank you (very much) | *(muchas) gracias* |
| I speak a little Spanish | *hablo un poco de español* |
| I don't speak Spanish | *no hablo español* |
| do you speak English? | *¿hablas inglés?* |
| I don't understand | *no entiendo* |
| please speak slowly | *habla despacio por favor* |
| I am very sorry | *lo siento mucho/discúlpame* |
| what do you want? | *¿qué quieres?* |
| I want/would like | *quiero/quería* |
| I don't want it | *no lo quiero* |
| good/bad | *bueno/malo* |

## Basic questions and requests

| | |
|---|---|
| have you got a room for two people? | *¿tienes una habitación para dos personas?* |
| how do I get to_? | *¿cómo llego a_?* |
| how much does it cost? | *¿cuánto cuesta? ¿cuánto es?* |
| is VAT included? | *¿el IVA está incluido?* |
| when does the bus leave (arrive)? | *¿a qué hora sale (llega) el autobús?* |
| when? | *¿cuándo?* |
| where is_? | *¿dónde está_?* |
| where can I buy? | *¿dónde puedo comprar...?* |
| where is the nearest petrol station? | *¿dónde está la gasolinera más cercana?* |
| why? | *¿por qué?* |

## Basic words and phrases

| | |
|---|---|
| bank | *el banco* |
| bathroom/toilet | *el baño* |
| to be | *ser, estar* |
| bill | *la factura/la cuenta* |
| cash | *efectivo* |
| cheap | *barato/a* |
| credit card | *la tarjeta de crédito* |
| exchange rate | *el tipo de cambio* |
| expensive | *caro/a* |
| to go | *ir* |
| to have | *tener, haber* |
| market | *el mercado* |
| note/coin | *el billete/la moneda* |
| police (policeman) | *la policía (el policía)* |
| post office | *el correo* |
| public telephone | *el teléfono público* |
| shop | *la tienda* |
| supermarket | *el supermercado* |
| there is/are | *hay* |
| there isn't/aren't | *no hay* |
| ticket office | *la taquilla* |
| travellers' cheques | *los cheques de viaje* |

## Getting around

| | |
|---|---|
| aeroplane | *el avión* |
| airport | *el aeropuerto* |
| arrival/departure | *la llegada/salida* |
| avenue | *la avenida* |
| border | *la frontera* |
| bus station | *la estación de autobuses* |
| bus | *el bus/el autobús/el camión* |
| corner | *la esquina* |
| customs | *la aduana* |
| left/right | *izquierda/derecha* |
| ticket | *el billete* |
| empty/full | *vacío/lleno* |
| highway, main road | *la carretera* |
| insurance | *el seguro* |

| | |
|---|---|
| insured person | *el asegurado/la asegurada* |
| luggage | *el equipaje* |
| motorway, freeway | *el autopista/autovía* |
| north, south, west, east | *el norte, el sur, el oeste, el este* |
| oil | *el aceite* |
| to park | *aparcar* |
| passport | *el pasaporte* |
| petrol/gasoline | *la gasolina* |
| puncture | *el pinchazo* |
| street | *la calle* |
| that way | *por allí* |
| this way | *por aquí* |
| tyre | *el neumático* |
| unleaded | *sin plomo* |
| waiting room | *la sala de espera* |
| to walk | *caminar/andar* |

## Accommodation

| | |
|---|---|
| air conditioning | *el aire acondicionado* |
| all-inclusive | *todo incluido* |
| bathroom, private | *el baño privado* |
| bed, double | *la cama matrimonial* |
| blankets | *las mantas* |
| to clean | *limpiar* |
| dining room | *el comedor* |
| hotel | *el hotel* |
| noisy | *ruidoso* |
| pillows | *las almohadas* |
| restaurant | *el restaurante* |
| room/bedroom | *la habitación* |
| sheets | *las sábanas* |
| shower | *la ducha* |
| soap | *el jabón* |
| toilet | *el inódoro* |
| toilet paper | *el papel higiénico* |
| towels, clean/dirty | *las toallas limpias/sucias* |
| water, hot/cold | *el agua caliente/fría* |

## Health

| | |
|---|---|
| aspirin | *la aspirina* |
| blood | *la sangre* |
| chemist | *la farmacia* |
| condoms | *los preservativos, los condones* |
| contact lenses | *los lentes de contacto* |
| contraceptives | *los anticonceptivos* |
| contraceptive pill | *la píldora anticonceptiva* |
| diarrhoea | *la diarrea* |
| doctor | *el médico* |
| fever/sweat | *la fiebre/el sudor* |
| pain | *el dolor* |
| head | *la cabeza* |
| period/sanitary towels | *la regla/las toallas femininas* |
| stomach | *el estómago* |

## Family

| | |
|---|---|
| family | *la familia* |
| brother/sister | *el hermano/la hermana* |
| daughter/son | *la hija/el hijo* |
| father/mother | *el padre/la madre* |
| husband/wife | *el esposo (marido)/la mujer* |
| boyfriend/girlfriend | *el novio/la novia* |
| friend | *el amigo/la amiga* |
| married | *casado/a* |
| single/unmarried | *soltero/a* |

## Months, days and time

| | |
|---|---|
| January | *enero* |
| February | *febrero* |
| March | *marzo* |
| April | *abril* |
| May | *mayo* |
| June | *junio* |
| July | *julio* |
| August | *agosto* |
| September | *septiembre* |
| October | *octubre* |
| November | *noviembre* |
| December | *diciembre* |
| | |
| Monday | *lunes* |
| Tuesday | *martes* |
| Wednesday | *miércoles* |
| Thursday | *jueves* |
| Friday | *viernes* |
| Saturday | *sábado* |
| Sunday | *domingo* |
| at one o'clock | *a la una* |
| at half past two | *a las dos y media* |
| at a quarter to three | *a las tres menos cuarto* |
| it's one o'clock | *es la una* |
| it's seven o'clock | *son las siete* |
| it's six twenty | *son las seis y veinte* |
| it's five to nine | *son las nueve menos cinco* |
| in ten minutes | *en diez minutos* |
| five hours | *cinco horas* |
| does it take long? | *¿tarda mucho?* |

## Numbers

| | |
|---|---|
| one | *uno* |
| two | *dos* |
| three | *tres* |
| four | *cuatro* |
| five | *cinco* |
| six | *seis* |
| seven | *siete* |
| eight | *ocho* |
| nine | *nueve* |
| ten | *diez* |

| eleven | *once* |
| twelve | *doce* |
| thirteen | *trece* |
| fourteen | *catorce* |
| fifteen | *quince* |
| sixteen | *dieciséis* |
| seventeen | *diecisiete* |
| eighteen | *dieciocho* |
| nineteen | *diecinueve* |
| twenty | *veinte* |
| twenty-one | *veintiuno* |
| thirty | *treinta* |
| forty | *cuarenta* |
| fifty | *cincuenta* |
| sixty | *sesenta* |
| seventy | *setenta* |
| eighty | *ochenta* |
| ninety | *noventa* |
| hundred | *cien/ciento* |
| thousand | *mil* |

## Regional languages

**El País Vasco** Spanish is the main language of the Basque lands, and spoken by everyone. The Basque language, Euskara/Euskera, is an ancient and difficult language with no known relatives. After decades of hiding under Franco, the Euskara has come back with a bang. An evergrowing number of people are learning and using it. You'll see it everywhere: on road signs, in bars, on posters. Place names are often written in both Euskara and Spanish. Some of the regional towns use only Euskara. In some cases the Basque version is more common (eg Hondarribia over Fuenterrabia), in others the Spanish takes precedence (Bilbao/Bilbo). A regularly used compromise is to use both in a double-barrelled arrangement, thus Vitoria-Gasteiz. Basque words you'll hear regularly are *eskerrik asko* (thank you), and *agur* (goodbye).

**Asturias** Bable is broadly very similar to Spanish. The main difference you'll notice is that words tend to end in *u* where they would end in *o* in Spanish, thus *Asturianu*. You'll see many signposts where Gijón has been changed to Xixón with a spraycan.

**Galicia** *Galego* (Gallego) is the language of *Galiza* (Galicia). It is more similar to Portuguese than Spanish. Though most people in cities use *castellano* in everyday speech, *Galego* is commonly heard in rural areas and seen on signs. *Galego* place names have mostly replaced their Spanish counterparts, and are used in this text.
▸▸ *See also Language, page 466.*

# Food glossary

It is impossible to be definitive about terms used; different regions often have numerous variants.

For meats, *poco hecho* is rare, *al punto* is medium rare, *regular* is medium, *muy hecho* is well-done.

## A

**aceite** oil; *aceite de oliva* is olive oil

**aceitunas** olives, also sometimes called *olivas*; the best kind are *manzanilla*, particularly when stuffed with anchovy, *rellenas con anchoas*

**agua** water

**aguacate** avocado

**ahumado** smoked; *tabla de ahumados* is a mixed plate of smoked fish

**ajo** garlic, *ajetes* are young garlic shoots

**ajo arriero** a simple sauce of garlic, paprika, and parsley

**albóndigas** meatballs

**alcachofa** artichoke

**alcaparras** capers

**alioli** a tasty sauce made from raw garlic blended with oil and egg yolk; also called *ajoaceite*

**almejas** name applied to various species of small clams

**alubias** beans

**anchoa** preserved anchovy

**angulas** baby eels, a delicacy that has become scarce and expensive; far more common are *gulas*, false *angulas* made from putting processed fish through a spaghetti machine; squid ink is used to apply authentic colouring

**añejo** aged (of cheeses, rums, etc)

**anís** aniseed, commonly used to flavour biscuits and liqueurs

**arroz** rice; *arroz con leche* is a sweet rice pudding

**asado** roast; an *asador* is a restaurant specializing in charcoal-roasted meat and fish

**atún** blue-fin tuna

**azúcar** sugar

## B

**bacalao** salted cod, an emblematic Basque food; an acquired taste, it is worth trying *al pil-pil* (a light yellow sauce made from oil garlic, and the natural gelatin of the cod, very difficult to make, and Bilbao's trademark dish); *al ajo arriero* is mashed with garlic, parsley, and paprika

**berberechos** cockles

**berenjena** aubergine/eggplant

**besugo** red bream

**bistek** cheap steak

**bizcocho** sponge cake or biscuit

**bocadillo/bocata** a crusty filled roll

**bogavante** lobster

**bonito** Atlantic bonito, a small tasty tuna fish

**boquerones** fresh anchovies, often served filleted in garlic and oil

**botella** bottle

**brasa (a la)** cooked on a griddle over coals, sometimes you do it yourself at the table; excellent

**buey** ox, or in Galicia, a large crab

## C

**cabracho** scorpionfish

**cabrales** a delicious Asturian cheese similar to Roquefort

**cabrito** young goat, usually roasted (*asado*)

**cacahuetes** peanuts

**cachelos** boiled young potatoes, traditionally served with *pulpo* (octopus) in Galicia

**café** coffee; *solo* is black, served espresso-style; *cortado* adds a dash of milk, *con leche* more; *americano* is a long black

**calamares** squid

**caldereta** a stew of meat or fish; the broth may be served separate, like with a *cocido*

**caldo** a thickish soup

**callos** tripe

**caña** a draught beer

**cangrejo** crab; occasionally river crayfish

**caramelos** sweets, popular with young and old

**carne** meat

**carta** menu

**castañas** chestnuts

**cava** sparkling wine, mostly produced in Catalunya

**cazuela** a stew, often of fish or seafood

**cebolla** onion

**cecina** cured beef like a leathery ham; a speciality of León province

**cena** dinner

**centollo** spider crab

**cerdo** pork

**cerveza** beer; if you want draught beer, ask for a *caña*

**champiñon** mushroom

**chipirones** small squid, often served *en su tinta*, in its own ink, deliciously mixed with butter and garlic

**chocolate** a popular afternoon drink (and evening smokable)

**chorizo** a red sausage, versatile and not too hot

**chuleta/chuletilla** chop

**chuletón** massive T-bone steak, often sold by weight

**churrasco** barbecued meat, often ribs with a spicy sauce

**churro** a fried dough-stick usually eaten with hot chocolate (*chocolate con churros*)

**cigalas** The 4WD of the prawn world, with pincers; Dublin Bay prawns in English

**cochinillo/lechón/ tostón** sucking pig

**cocido** a heavy stew, usually of meat and chickpeas/beans, typical of the mountains; *sopa de cocido* is the broth

**codorniz** quail

**cogollo** lettuce heart

**comida** lunch

**conejo** rabbit

**congrio** conger-eel

**cordero** lamb

**costillas** ribs

**crema catalana** a lemony *crème brûlée*

**croquetas** deep-fried crumbed balls of meat, béchamel, seafood, or vegetables

**cuajada** junket, a thin natural yoghurt eaten with honey

**cuchara** spoon

**cuchillo** knife

**cuenta (la)** the bill

## D

**desayuno** breakfast

**dorada** a species of bream (gilthead)

**dulce** sweet

## E

**embutido** any salami-type sausage

**empanada** a savoury pie, either pasty-like or in large flat tins and sold by the slice; *bonito* is a common filling, as is ham, mince or seafood

**ensalada** salad; *mixta* is usually a large serve of a bit of everything; excellent option

**ensaladilla rusa** Russian salad, potato, peas and carrots in mayonnaise

**entrecot** A juicy, fatty cut of steak, often from ox

**erizos/ericios** sea urchins; definitely an acquired taste, but strangely addictive

**escabeche** pickled in wine and vinegar

**espárragos** asparagus, white and usually canned

**estofado** braised, often in stew form

## F

**fabada** the most famous of Asturian dishes, a hearty stew of beans, chorizo, and *morcilla*

**fideuá** a bit like a *paella* but with noodles

**filete** a cheap cut of steak

**flan** the ubiquitous *crème caramel*, great when home-made (*casero*), awful out of a plastic cup

**foie** fattened gooseliver Often made into a thick gravy-like sauce

**frambuesas** raspberries

**fresas** strawberries

**frito/a** fried

**fruta** fruit

## G

**galletas** biscuits

**gambas** prawns

**garbanzo** chickpea

**granizado** popular summer drink, like a frappé fruit milkshake

**guisado** stewed, or a stew

**guisantes** peas

## H

**habas** broad beans

**harina** flour

**helado** icecream

**hígado** liver

**hojaldre** puff pastry

**horno (al)** oven (baked)

**huevo** egg

## I

**ibérico** See *jamón*; the term can also refer to other pork products

**idiazábal** the Basque sheepmilk cheese, a speciality that sometimes comes smoked

## J

**jabalí** wild boar, usually found in autumn

**jamón** ham; *jamón de York* is cooked British-style ham, but much better is the cured *serrano*; *ibérico* refers to ham from a breed of pigs that graze wild in western Spain and are fed partly on acorns (*bellotas*) Particular regions and villages are known for their hams, which can get mighty expensive

**judías verdes** green beans

## K

**kokotxas** pieces of hake cheek and throat, cooked in a rich sauce; don't be put off, they are usually delicious, if a little fatty

## L

**lacón con grelos** Galician stew of pork and potatoes
**langosta** crayfish
**langostinos** king prawns
**lechazo** milk-fed lamb
**leche** milk
**lechuga** lettuce
**lenguado** sole
**lentejas** lentils
**limón** lemon
**lomo** loin, usually sliced pork
**longaniza** a long sausage, specialty of Aragón
**lubina** sea bass

## M

**macedonia de frutas** fruit salad, usually tinned
**magret de pato** fattened duck breast
**manchego** Spain's national cheese; hard, whitish, and made from ewe's milk
**mantequilla** butter
**manzana** apple
**manzanilla** a word referring to the nicest type of olive; also camomile; and a dry wine similar to sherry
**marisco** shellfish
**matanza (la)** early Nov is pig-killing time, scene of much feasting and many pork products
**mejillones** mussels
**melocotón** peach, usually canned and served in *almibar* (syrup)
**membrillo** quince jelly, usually eaten with cheese
**menestra** a vegetable stew, usually served like a minestrone without the liquid; vegetarians will be annoyed to find that it's often seeded with ham and bits of pork

**menú** a set meal, usually consisting of three or more courses, bread and wine or water
**merluza** hake is to Spain as rice is to southeast Asia
**miel** honey
**mollejas** sweetbreads; ie the pancreas or neck glands of a calf or lamb
**migas** breadcrumbs, fried and often mixed with lard and meat to form a delicious peasant dish of the same name
**morcilla** blood sausage, either solid or semi-liquid; a specialty of León and Burgos
**morro** cheek, pork or lamb
**mostaza** mustard
**mosto** grape juice, a common option in bars

## N

**naranja** orange
**nata** sweet whipped cream
**navajas** razor-shells
**natillas** rich custard dessert
**nécora** small sea crab, sometimes called a velvet crab
**nueces** walnuts

## O

**orejas** ears, usually of a pig
**orujo** a fiery grape spirit, often brought to add to coffee if the waiter likes you
**ostra** oyster

## P

**pan** bread
**parrilla** grill; a *parrillada* is a mixed grill
**pastel** cake/pastry
**patatas** potatoes; often chips (*patatas fritas*); *bravas* are with spicy sauce; *a la*

Riojana is with paprika and chorizo
**pato** duck
**patxarán** the sloe-berry, but usually the liqueur made from it, often flavoured with *anis*; some are fairly medicinal, most light, fruity and delicious
**pechuga** breast (usually chicken)
**perdiz** partridge
**percebes** goose-neck barnacles, a curious specialty of Galicia; salty and tasty, but tough to open
**pescado** fish
**picadillo** a dish of spicy mincemeat
**picante** hot, ie spicy
**pichón** squab
**pimienta** pepper
**pimientos** peppers; there are many kinds; *piquillos* are the trademark thin Basque red pepper; Padrón produces sweet green mini ones; Bierzo loves theirs stuffed *rellenos*
**pintxo/pincho** the reason you put on weight in the Basque country; bartop snack
**pipas** Sunflower seeds, a common snack
**plancha (a la)** grilled on a hot iron
**plátano** banana
**pochas** young haricot beans, a Riojan speciality
**pollo** chicken
**postre** dessert
**puerros** leeks
**pulga** a colloquial word for the tiny submarine-shaped rolls that feature atop bars in the Basque lands; the word actually means 'flea'
**pulpo** octopus, particularly delicious *a la gallega*, boiled Galician style and garnished with olive oil, salt, and paprika

**queimada** a potent Galician ritual drink of *orujo* mixed with coffee and then heated over a fire

**queso** cheese

## R

**rabas** crumbed calamari strips, often eaten at weekends

**rabo de buey** oxtail

**ración** a portion of food served in cafés and bars; check the size and order a half (*media*) if you want less

**rana** frog; *ancas de rana* is frogs' legs

**rape** monkfish/anglerfish

**relleno/a** stuffed

**reserva, gran reserva, crianza, cosechero** terms relating to the age of wines; see page 45

**revuelto** scrambled eggs, usually with mushrooms or seafood; often a speciality

**riñones** kidneys

**rodaballo** turbot; pricey and delicious

**romana (*a la*)** fried in batter

## S

**sagardotegi** cider house in the Basque country

**sal** salt

**salchichón** a salami-like sausage

**salmón** salmon

**salpicón** a seafood salad with plenty of onion and vinegar

**San Jacobo** a steak cooked with ham and cheese

**sardiñas** sardines, delicious grilled

**seco** dry

**sepia** cuttlefish

**serrano** see *jamón*

**setas** wild mushrooms, often superb

**sidra** cider

**solomillo** beef fillet steak cut from the sirloin bone

**sopa** soup

## T

**tarta** tart or cake

**té** tea

**tenedor** fork

**ternera** veal or young beef

**tocino** pork fat; *tocinillo del cielo* is an excellent caramelized egg dessert

**tomate** tomato

**tortilla** a Spanish omelette, with potato, egg, olive oil and optional onion

**trucha** trout; *a la Navarra* comes with bacon or ham

**toro** a traditional Basque fish stew or soup

**txaka/chaka** a mixture of mayonnaise and chopped seafood, featuring heavily in *pintxos*

**txakolí** slightly effervescent Basque wine produced from underripe grapes

**txangurro** spider crab, superb

## U

**uva** grape

## V

**vaso** glass

**verduras** vegetables

**vermut** vermouth; delicious when it's the bar's own. Traditionally drunk at weekends before lunch – *la hora de vermut*.

**vieiras** scallops, also called *veneras*

**vino** wine; *blanco* is white, *rosado* or *clarete* is rosé, *tinto* is red

**vizcaína (a la)** in the style of Vizcaya, Bilbao's province; usually based on onions and dried peppers

## X

**xoubas** sardines in Galicia

## Z

**zamburiñas** a type of small scallop, delicious

**zanahoria** carrot

**zumo** fruit juice, usually bottled and pricey

**zurito** a short beer in the Basque country, useful for tapas-hopping; varies in size from a splash to a quarter-pint

# Index

# Map index

# Complete title listing

Footprint publishes travel guides to over 150 destinations worldwide. Each guide is packed with practical, concise and colourful information for everybody from first-time travellers to travel aficionados. The list is growing fast and current titles are noted below.

(P) denotes pocket guide

### Latin America & Caribbean
Antigua & Leeward Islands (P)
Argentina
Barbados (P)
Bolivia
Brazil
Caribbean Islands
Chile
Costa Rica
Cuba
Cuzco & the Inca heartland
Discover Belize, Guatemala & Southern Mexico
Discover Patagonia
Discover Peru, Bolivia & Ecuador
Dominican Republic (P)
Ecuador & Galápagos
Mexico & Central America
Nicaragua
Peru
South American Handbook

### North America
Discover Western Canada
Vancouver (P)

### Africa
Cape Town (P)
Egypt
Kenya
Morocco
Namibia
South Africa
Tanzania

### Middle East
Dubai (P)
Jordan

### Australasia
Australia
Discover East Coast Australia
New Zealand
Sydney (P)

**Footprint guides are available from all good bookshops and online at www.footprintbooks.com**

# Acknowledgements

As well as large debts of gratitude from previous editions, I owe some particular thanks for this update. David Jackson, Menchu Hevia, and Oscar Jackson Hevia always have a notebook handy on their travels around the north and unearth many interesting places. Edgar Reina knows every restaurant in Bilbao before they even open, and Begoña García, my parents, Ian Johnston, and Mike Burren have been excellent companions on further research trips. As ever, copious thanks to the readers who took the time to write in with their invaluable comments and suggestions, and to the team at Footprint, especially editor Nicola Jones.

# Credits

**Editor**: Nicola Gibbs
**Map editor**: Sarah Sorensen
**Picture editor**: Robert Lunn

**Publisher**: Patrick Dawson
**Editorial**: Sophie Blacksell, Felicity
Laughton, Alan Murphy, Jo Williams
**Cartography**: Kevin Feeney, Robert Lunn,
John Higgins
**Sales and marketing**: Andy Riddle
**Advertising**: Debbie Wylde
**Finance and administration**:
Elizabeth Taylor

## Photography credits

**Front cover**: Age fotostock/SuperStock
**Back cover**: Age fotostock/SuperStock
**Inside colour section**: Age fotostock/
SuperStock, José Fuste Raga/SuperStock,
Juan Carlos Muñoz/SuperStock, Gonzalo
Azumendi/SuperStock, Nature Picture
Library/Alamy

## Print

Manufactured in Italy by LegoPrint
Pulp from sustainable forests

## Footprint feedback

We try as hard as we can to make each
Footprint guide as up to date as possible
but, of course, things always change.
If you want to let us know about your
experiences – good, bad or ugly – then don't
delay, go to www.footprintbooks.com
and send in your comments.
   Hotel and restaurant price codes
should only be taken as a guide to
the prices and facilities offered by the
establishment. It is at the discretion of
the owners to vary them from time to time.

## Publishing information

Footprint Northern Spain
3rd edition
© Footprint Handbooks Ltd
April 2007

ISBN: 978 1 904 777 81 6
CIP DATA: A catalogue record for this
book is available from the British Library

® Footprint Handbooks and the Footprint
mark are a registered trademark of
Footprint Handbooks Ltd

## Published by Footprint

6 Riverside Court
Lower Bristol Road
Bath BA2 3DZ, UK
T +44 (0)1225 469141
F +44 (0)1225 469461
discover@footprintbooks.com
www.footprintbooks.com

# Northern Spain

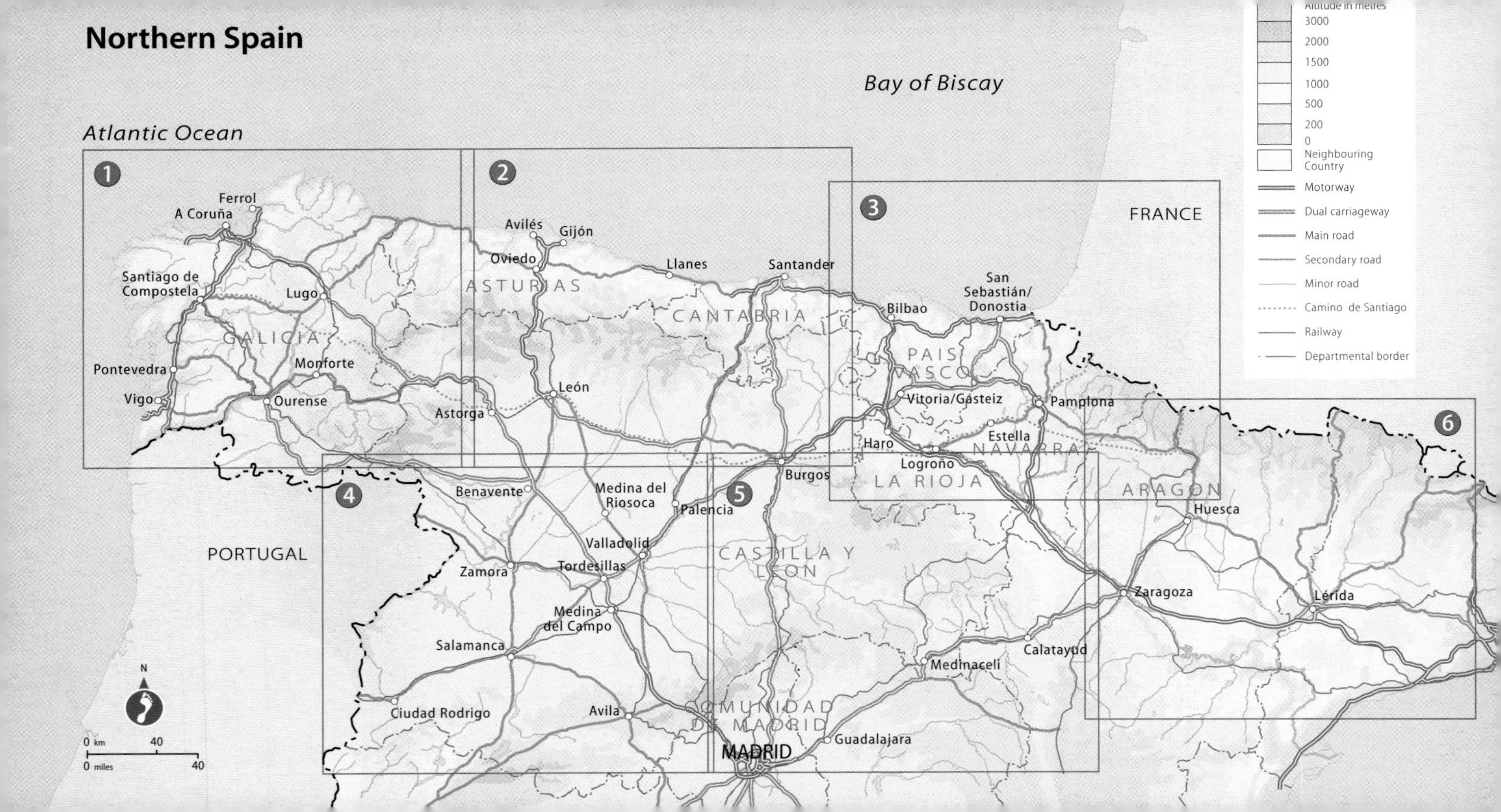

**Altitude in metres**

| | |
|---|---|
| | 3000 |
| | 2000 |
| | 1500 |
| | 1000 |
| | 500 |
| | 200 |
| | 0 |

- Neighbouring Country
- Motorway
- Dual carriageway
- Main road
- Secondary road
- Minor road
- Camino de Santiago
- Railway
- Departmental border

Atlantic Ocean

Bay of Biscay

FRANCE

PORTUGAL

**1** **2** **3** **4** **5** **6**

Ferrol
A Coruña
Santiago de Compostela
Pontevedra
Vigo
Lugo
Monforte
Ourense
GALICIA

Avilés
Gijón
Oviedo
Llanes
Santander
ASTURIAS
CANTABRIA

León
Astorga
Benavente
Zamora
Salamanca
Ciudad Rodrigo
Ávila

Bilbao
San Sebastián/Donostia
PAÍS VASCO
Vitoria/Gasteiz
Pamplona
NAVARRA
Estella
Logroño
Haro
LA RIOJA

Huesca
ARAGÓN
Zaragoza
Lérida
Calatayud
Medinaceli
Guadalajara

Burgos
Palencia
Medina del Ríoseco
Valladolid
Tordesillas
Medina del Campo
CASTILLA Y LEÓN
COMUNIDAD DE MADRID
MADRID

N

0 km 40
0 miles 40

# Map 1

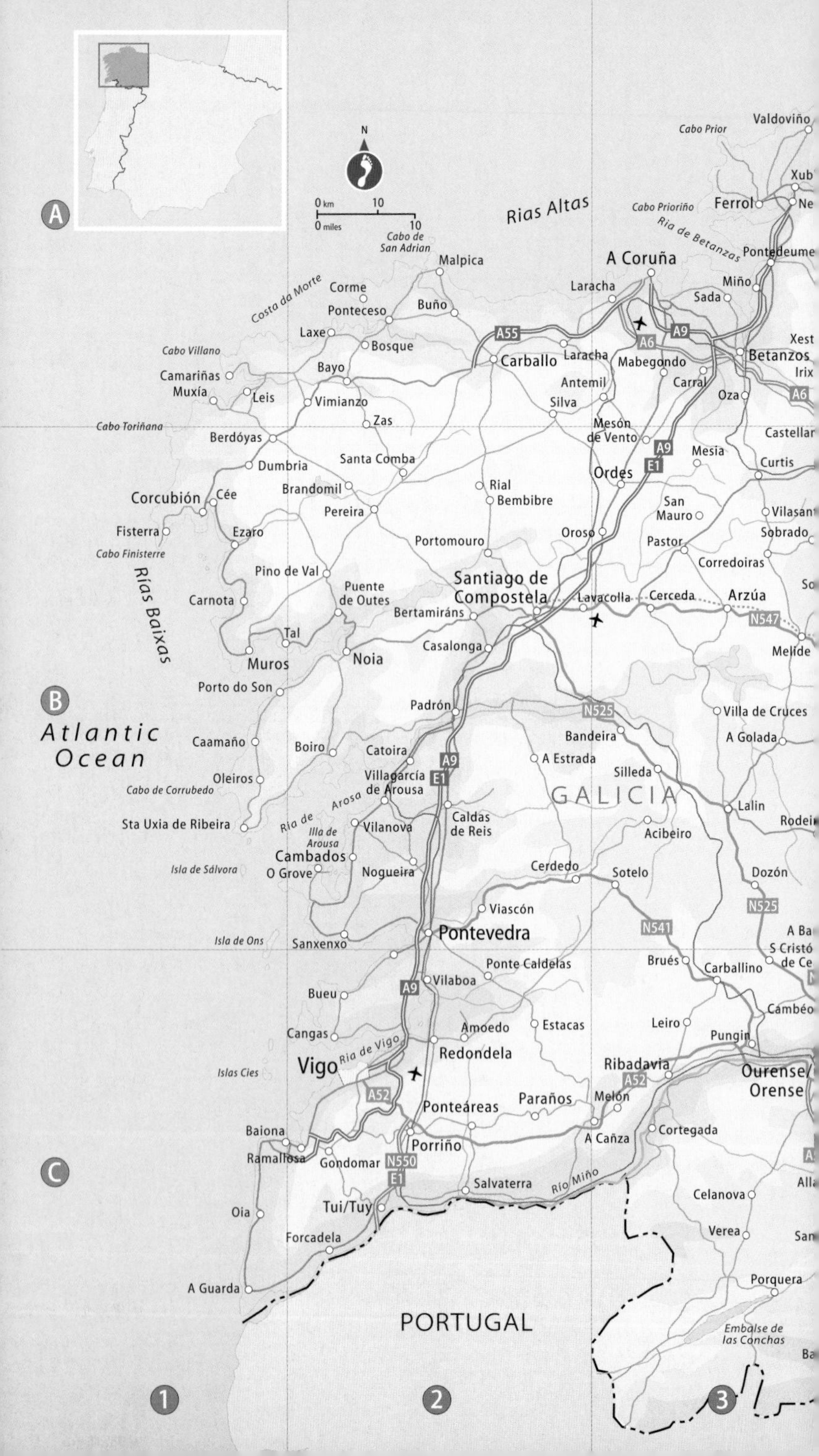

N

0 km 10
0 miles 10

Cabo de San Adrian

Rias Altas

Costa da Morte

Cabo Prior
Valdoviño
Xub
Ne
Ferrol
Cabo Priorño
Ria de Betanzas
Pontedeume

A Coruña
Malpica
Laracha
Miño
Sada

Corme
Ponteceso
Buño
Mabegondo
Carral
Oza
Xest
Irix
Betanzos
A6

Laxe
Bosque
Carballo
Laracha
Antemil
Silva

Cabo Villano
Bayo
Castellar

Camariñas
Muxía
Leis
Vimianzo
Zas
Mesón de Vento
A9
E1
Ordes
Mesia
Curtis

Cabo Toriñana
Berdóyas
Santa Comba
Rial
Bembibre
Oroso
San Mauro
Pastor
Vilasán
Sobrado

Dumbria
Brandomil
Pereira

Corcubión
Cée
Corredoiras

Fisterra
Ezaro
Portomouro
Santiago de Compostela
Lavacolla
Cerceda
Arzúa
N547

Cabo Finisterre
Pino de Val
Puente de Outes
Bertamiráns
Melide

Rias Baixas
Carnota
Casalonga

Tal
Noia
Padrón
N525
Villa de Cruces
A Golada

Muros
Porto do Son
Catoira
Bandeira
Silleda

Atlantic Ocean
Caamaño
Boiro
Villagarcía de Arousa
A Estrada
GALICIA
Lalin
Rodei

Cabo de Corrubedo
Oleiros
Vilanová
Caldas de Reis
Acibeiro
Dozón

Sta Uxia de Ribeira
Ria de Arosa
Illa de Arousa
Cambados
Nogueira
Cerdedo
Sotelo
N525

Isla de Sálvora
O Grove
Cerdedo
A Ba
S Cristó de Ce

Isla de Ons
Sanxenxo
Viascón
Pontevedra
N541
Brués
Carballino
Cambéo

Bueu
Vilaboa
Ponte Caldelas
Leiro
Pungin

Cangas
A9
Amoedo
Estacas
Ribadavia
Ourense/Orense

Islas Cies
Vigo
Ria de Vigo
Redondela
A52
Melón
Cortegada

Baiona
Ponteáreas
Paraños
A Caña
Celanova
Alla

Ramallosa
Gondomar
N550
Porriño
Salvaterra
Río Miño
Verea
San

Oia
Tui/Tuy
E1
Forcadela
Porquera

A Guarda
PORTUGAL
Embalse de las Conchas
Ba

A
B
C
1
2
3

# Map 2

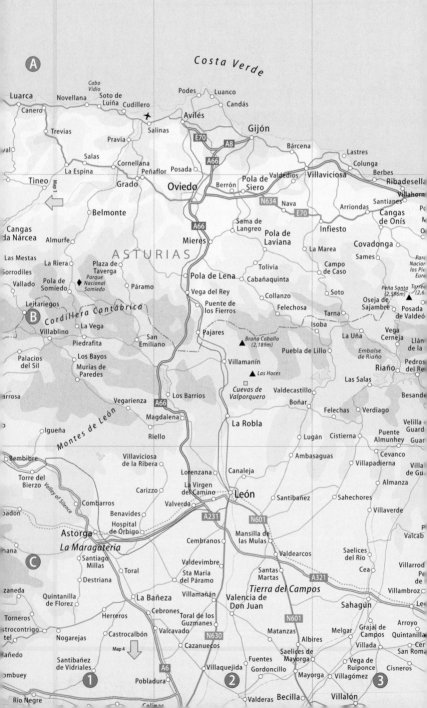

Costa Verde

Luarca · Novellana · Soto de Luiña · Cudillero · Podes · Luanco · Candás

Cabo Vidío

Canero · Trevias · Pravia · Salinas · Avilés · Gijón · Bárcena · Lastres

Salas · Cornellana · Peñaflor · Posada · Berrón · Pola de Siero · Valdedios · Villaviciosa · Berbes · Colunga · Ribadesella

La Espina · Grado · Oviedo

Tineo · Belmonte · N634 · Nava · Arriondas · Santianes · Villahorn

Cangas de Nárcea · Almurfe · Mieres · Sama de Langreo · Pola de Laviana · La Marea · Infiesto · Cangas de Onís · Covadonga

ASTURIAS

Las Mestas · La Riera · Plaza de Taverga · Pola de Somiedo · Páramo · Pola de Lena · Tolivia · Cabañaquinta · Campo de Caso · Sames · Parc Nacion los Pic Euro

Sorrodiles · Parque Nacional Somiedo

Vallado · Vega del Rey · Collanzo · Soto · Felechosa · Tarna · Oseja de Sajambre · Peña Santa (2,596m) · Torre (2,6 · Posada de Valdeó

Lejtariegos · Puente de los Fierros

Cordillera Cantábrica

Villablino · La Vega · Pajares · Braña Caballo (2,189m) · Isoba · La Uña · Vega Cerneja · Llán de la

Piedrafita · San Emiliano · Puebla de Lillo · Embalse de Riaño · Pedros del Re

Palacios del Sil · Los Bayos · Villamanín · Las Hoces · Riaño

Murias de Paredes · Cuevas de Valporquero · Valdecastillo · Boñar · Las Salas · Besande

rrosa · Vegarienza · A66 · Los Barrios · La Robla · Felechas · Verdiago

Igueña · Magdalena · Riello · Lugán · Cistierna · Puente Almunhey · Velilla Guard · Guar

Montes de León

Bembibre · Villaviciosa de la Ribera · Lorenzana · Canaleja · Ambasaguas · Villapadierna · Cevanco · Villa de Gu

Torre del Bierzo · La Virgen del Camino · León · Santibañez · Sahechores · Almanza

adon · Valley of Silence · Combarros · Carizzo · Valverda · A231 · N601 · Villaverde

Astorga · Benavides · Hospital de Órbigo · Mansilla de las Mulas · Saelices del Río · Valcab

La Maragatería · Cembranos · Valdearcos · Cea · Villarrod · Pe · Villambroz

hana · Santiago Millas · Toral · Valdevimbre · Sta Maria del Páramo · Santas Martas · A321 · Le

zaneda · Destriana · Villamañán · Valencia de Don Juan · Tierra del Campos · Sahagún

Torneros · Quintanilla de Florez · La Bañeza · Cebrones · Toral de los Guzmanes · Matanzas · Melgar · Grajal de Campos · Arroyo · Quintanilla

stocontrigo · tel · Herreros · Valcavado · N630 · Albires · Villada · Cér San Roma

lañedo · Nogarejas · Castrocalbón · Cazanuecos · Saelices de Mayorga · Vega de Ruiponce · Cisneros

mbuey · Santibañez de Vidriales · Villaquejida · Fuentes · Gordoncillo · Mayorga · Villagómez

Pobladura · Valderas · Becilla · Villalón

Rio Negro

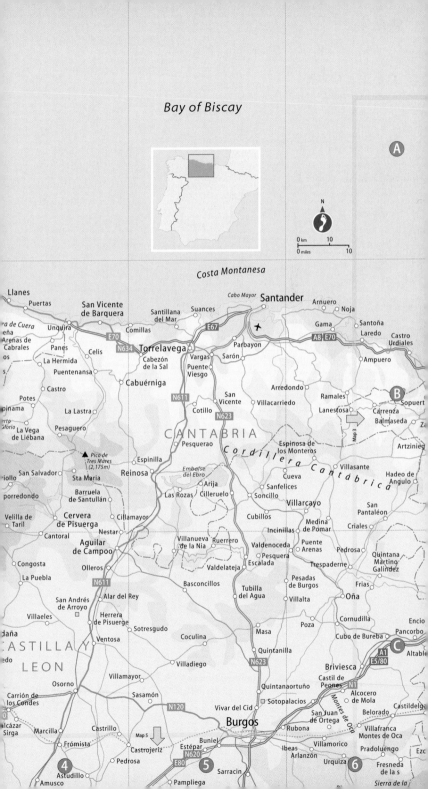

Bay of Biscay

*Costa Montanesa*

**A**

N

| 0 km | 10 |
| 0 miles | 10 |

*Cabo Mayor* Santander

Llanes
Puertas
San Vicente
de Barquera
Santillana
del Mar
Suances
Arnuero
Noja

ra de Cuera
eña
Arenas de
Cabrales
os
Unquira
Comillas
E67
Gama
Santoña

Panes
Celis
Torrelavega
Parbayon
A8 E70
Laredo
Castro
Urdiales

La Hermida
Puentenansa
Cabezón
de la Sal
Vargas
Sarón
Ampuero

Potes
Castro
Cabuérniga
Puente
Viesgo

pinama
La Lastra
N611
San
Vicente
Arredondo
Ramales
**B**
Sopuert

rto
sforio
La Vega
de Liébana
Pesaguero
Cotillo
Villacarriedo
Lanestosa
Carrenza
Balmaseda
Za

s.
CANTABRIA
N623
Espinosa de
los Monteros
Artzinieg

▲ Pico de
Tres Mares
(2,175m)
Pesquerao
Cordillera
Villasante
Hadeo de
Angulo

riollo
San Salvador
Espinilla
Cantábrica

Sta Maria
Reinosa
Embalse
del Ebro
Arija
Cueva
Sanfelices
Villacayo
San
Pantaléon

porredondo
Barruela
de Santullán
Las Rozas
Cilleruelo
Soncillo
Criales

Velilla de
Taril
Cervera
de Pisuerga
Cillamayor
Nestar
Cubillos
Medina
de Pomar

Congosta
Aguilar
de Campoo
Villanueva
de la Nia
Ruerrero
Incinillas
Puente
Arenas
Pedrosa
Quintana
Martino
Galindez

La Puebla
Olleros
Valdenoceda
Pesquera
Escalada
Trespaderne
Frias

daña
N611
San Andrés
de Arroyo
Alar del Rey
Valdelateja
Tubilla
del Agua
Pesadas
de Burgos
Oña

Villaeles
Herrera
de Pisuerge
Basconcillos
Villalta
Cornudilla

CASTILLA Y
LEON
Ventosa
Sotresgudo
Coculina
Masa
Poza
Cubo de Bureba
Encio
Pancorbo
**C**

edo
Osorno
Villadiego
Quintanilla
A1
E5/80
Altabe

Carrión de
los Condes
Villamayor
Sasamón
N120
N623
Briviesca
N1

lcázar
Sirga
Marcilla
Castrillo
Map 5
Vivar del Cid
Quintanaortuño
Sotopalacios
Castil de
Peones
Alcocero
de Mola
Castildelg

Frómista
Pedrosa
Castrojeriz
Estépar
E80
N620
Burgos
Rubona
San Juan
de Ortega
Villafranca
Montes de Oca
Belorado

**4**
Astudillo
Amusco
Buniel
Ibeas
Arlanzón
Villamorico
Pradoluengo
Ezc

**5**
Sarracin
Urquiza
**6**
Fresneda
de la s

Pampliega
*Sierra de la*

**Map 3**

*Bay of Biscay*

**A**

**B**

**C**

**PAIS VASCO**

**LA RIOJA**

Santoña
Noja
Laredo
Castro-Urdiales
Plencia
Bakio
Bermeo
Elantxobe
Ampuero
Santura
Getxo
Mundaka
Lekeitio
Ramales
Portugalete
Mungia
Arteaga
Ondarroa
San Sebastián/
Donostia
Carrenza
Sópuerta
Barakaldo
Bilbao
Gernika
Zumaia
Getaria
Zarautz
Lanestosa
Basauri
Markina-
Xemein
Deba
Zestoa
Usurbil
Balmaseda
Zalla
Sodupe
Galdakao
Amorebieta
Berriz
Eibar
Azpeitia
Errezil
Villabona
Andoain
Artziniega
Llodio
Ceberio
Durango
Bergara
Loiola
Tolosa
Villasante
Menagaray
Castillo y
Elejabeitia
Elorrio
Legazoi
Zumárraga
Lizartza
Hadeo de
Angulo
Amurrio
Arrasate-
Mondragon
Oñati
Bessain
Betelú
Lecunberri
San
Pantaléon
Orduña
Corbesa
Arantzazu
Echarri-
Aranaz
Altsasu-
Alsasua
Irur
Criales
Berberana
Murgia
Legutiano
Zalduondo
Huarte-
Araquil
Pedrosa
Osma
Salvatierra
Equilaz
Olazagutia
Trespaderne
Espejo
Salinas
de Añana
Larraona
Zudair
Ech
Frias
Quintana
Martino
Galindez
Bergüenda
Vitoria/Gasteiz
Gaceo
Alqiza
Oña
Cornudilla
Encío
Miranda
de Ebro
Arraia
Maeztu
Santa Kurutze
Kanzepu
Bernedo
Acado
Abarzuza
Estella
(Lizarra)
Cubo de B
Pancorbo
Ameyugo
Peñacerrada
Monasterio
de Irache
Pue
la Re
Grauquri
Mendigorria
Briñas
Altable
Elvillar
Oteiza
Briviesca
Castil de
Peones
Casalarreina
Haro
Laguardia
(Biazteri)
Elciego
Los Arcos
Allo
Larraga
Belorado
Castildelgado
Santo Domingo
de la Calzada
San Asensio
Oyon
Viana
Torres del Rio
Mendavia
Sesma
Lerin
Miran
de Ar
Pradoluengo
Ezcaray
Cenicero
Logroño
Lodosa
Urquiza
Nájera
Nizo
Navarrete
Andosilla
Fresneda
de la s
San Millán
de la Cogolla
Baños
Río Tobía
Islallana
Ribaflecha
Ausejo
Cárcar
Persal
Pineda de la
Sierra Tirón
Anguiano
Torrecilla
en Cameros
San Román
de Cameros
El Villar
Calahorra
Barbadillo
de Pez
Canales
San Lorenzo
(2,271m)
Embalse
de Glacara
Arnedillo
Arnedo
Aldeaunueva
Barbadillo
de Herreros
Mansilla
Villavelay
Autol
Salas de
los Infantes
Neila
Montenegro
Enciso
Turruncun
Pajares
Yanquas

**1** **2** **3**

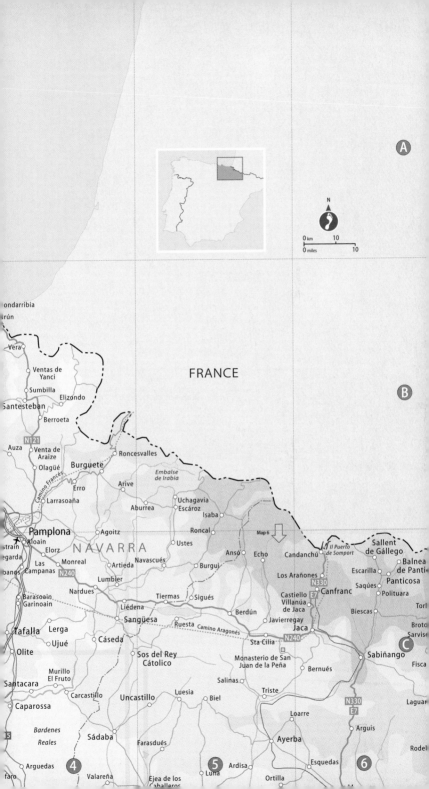

# Map 4

PORTUGAL

N

0 km    10
0 miles    10

rei erin

Vilardevo

El Cañizo

A. Mezquita

Map 1

Puebla de Sanabria

Rioconejos

Jusfei

Nogarejas

Castrocalbo

Espadañedo

Santibañez de Vidriale

A52

Asturianos

Mombuey

Sandin

Sitrama

Rio Negre

Villardeciervos    Camarzana

Coli

Cional

Otero de Bodas

Mahide

Sierra de la Culebra

Sarraci de A

San Vitero

N122

E82

Alcañices

Ceadea

Vide de Alba

Fonfria

Montamarta

Pino

Ricobayo

Roales

Zamora

Morale del Vi

Pereruela

La Tuda

Fadón

Bermillo de Sayago

Fermoselle

Villar del Buey

Corral

N6

Peleas

Almeida

Tamame

El Cuba de Tierra del Vin

Viñuela

Pereña

Trabanca

Embalse de Almendra

Almendra

Aldeadávila

La Zarza

Monteras

Villaseco de los Reyes

Moraleja

Barruecopardo

Sanchón

Villasbuenos

Vitigudino

Villar de Peralonso

Ledesma

Calzada de Valdunciel

Fregeneda

Peralejos

Villaseco

Valverdón

Lumbrales

Traguntia

Sando

Golpejas

Castellan

Doñinos

San Felices de los Gallegos

Villavieja

Cabeza de D Gomez

Salamanca

Retortillo

La Fuente

Aldehuela de la Bóveda

Boadilla

Robliza

Rad

N620

E80

N6

Villar de la Yegua

Castillejo de Martin Viejo

Sta Olalla

Cabrillas

Vecinos

N8

Sancti Spiritus

Fuentes de Oñoro

N620

Ciudad-Rodrigo

Peña de Cabra

Beleñ

Tamames

Fresno Alhándi

El Bodón

Pastores

Serradillo

Aldeanueva

Sierra de Peña de Francia

El Cabaco

Sequeros

Frades de la Sierra

Monsagro

La Albergueria

Fuenteguinaldo

Martiago

Endrinal

Guijuelo

La Alberca

Casillas de Flores

Robledo

Las Mestas

Cristóbal

Navastrlas

Villasrubias

Sierra de Gata

Robjedillo de Gata

Pino Franqueado

Vegas de Coria

Nava de B

El Payo

La Calzada

Valverde del Fresno

Hovos

Cadalso

Casar de Palomera

Mohedas

Granadilla

Baños de Montemayor

Puerto

Bejar

El Bard de Avi

Cilleros

Perales del Puerto

Pozuelo de Zarzon

Ahigal

Albadia

Puerto Castilla

La Navalongui

Jerte

Tornavacas

Moraleja

Santibañez

1    2    3

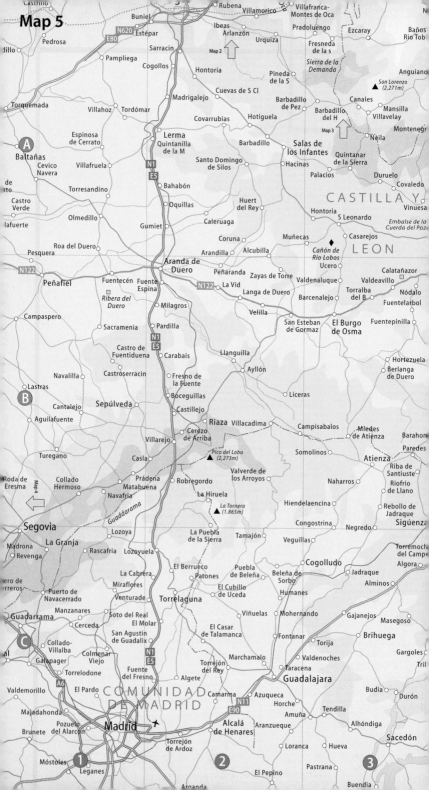

# Map 6

Roncal
Ansó
Echo
Candanchú
Puerto de Somport
Sallent de Gállego
Escarilla
Balneario de Panticosa
Panticosa
Polituara
Saqués
Monte Perdido (3,355m)
Parzán
Torla
Ordesa
Bielsa
Parque Nacional Ordesa y Monte Perdido

Burgui
Navascués
Los Arañones
Canfranc
Castiello
Villanúa de Jaca
Biescas
Broto
Sarvisé
Salinas
Hospital
Escalona

Tiermas
Sigüés
Berdún
Javierregay
Jaca
Sabiñánigo
Fiscal

Ruesta
Sta Cilia
Monasterio de San Juan de la Peña
Bernués
Laguarta
Boltaña
Aínsa
Arro
Embalse de Mediano

Sos del Rey Católico

Luesia
Biel
Salinas
Triste
Loarre
Arguis
Rodellar
Abizanda
Sta Liestra y San Quile
Embalse de El Grado

Farasdués
Ardisa
Esquedas
Parque Natural de los Cañones de Sierra de Guara
Map 3
Alquézar
Naval
Graus
Torreciudad

Ejea de los Caballeros
Erla
Luna
Ortilla
Huesca
Abiego
El Grado
Embalse Barasor

Sierra de Luna
Embalse de la Sotonera
Tormos
Almudévar
Angüés
Estada
Barbastro
Fonz

Gúrrea de Gallego
Castejón de Valdejasa
Tardienta
Grañén
Berbegal
Monzón

Esteban (744m)
Zuera
Robres
Poleñino
Ballerias
Tamar
Binéfar

Villanueva de Gallego
Leciñena
Alcubierre
Sariñena
Sena
Alcolea de Cincal
Almacell

Remolinos
Villamayor
Farlete
Lanaja
Palleruelos de Monegros
Ontiñena
Chalamera

Alagón
Zaragoza
Villafranca de Ebro
Monegrillo
Los Monegros

Maria del Huerve
Osera
La Almolda
Fraga

Muel
Mediana de Aragón
Fuentes de Ebro
Pina de Ebro
Bujaraloz
Candasnos
Sere

Embalse de Mezaloche
Quinto
Gelsa
Embalse de Mequinenza
Mequinenza

Villanueva de Huerva
Fuendetodos
Embalse de Riba-roja

Embalse de La Torcas
Belchite
Azaila
Río Ebra
Fayón

Azuara
Escatrón
Pantà de Riba-ro

Herrera
Lécera
Samper de Calanda
Caspe
Embalse de Caspe

Bádenas
Hijar
Maella
Batea

Albalate del Arzobispo
Desierto de Calanda
Alcañiz
Mazaleón
Caseres
Gandes

Fonfria
Muniesa
Valdetormo
Calaceite
El Pin

uerta (92m)
Embalse de Cueva Foradada
Oliete
Alloza
Andorra
Horta de Sant Joan
Prat d Comte

Seguro de los Baños
Vivel del Rio Martin
Embalse de Escuriza
Calanda
La Fresneda

Utrillas
Montalbán
Gargallo
Alcorisa
Embalse de Calanda

Pancrudo
Mas de las Maias

ARAGON

Pyrenees

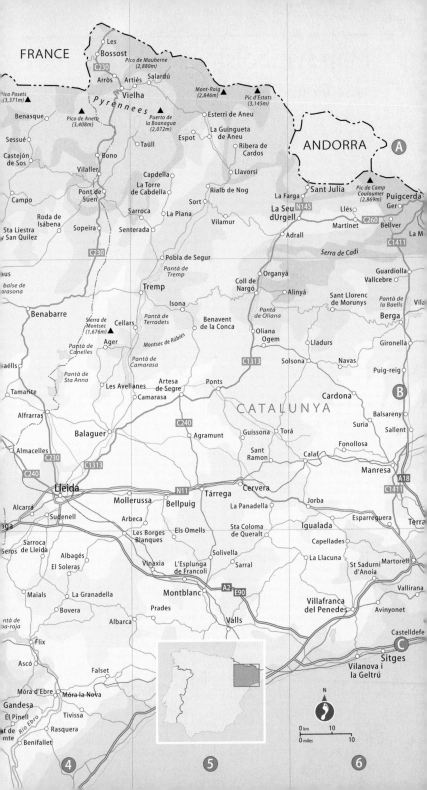

# Map symbols

## Administration

□ Capital city
○ Other city, town
≈ International border
≈ Regional border
≈ Disputed border

## Roads and travel

═ Motorway
— Main road (National highway)
— Minor road
---- Track
······ Footpath
+━ Railway with station
✈ Airport
🚌 Bus station
Ⓜ Metro station
---- Cable car
++++ Funicular
⛴ Ferry

## Water features

≋ River, canal
◯ Lake, ocean
ᵛᵛᵛ Seasonal marshland
▦ Beach, sandbank
💧 Waterfall
⌒ Reef

## Topographical features

◎ Contours (approx)
▲ Mountain, volcano
⇌ Mountain pass
⊔⊔⊔ Escarpment
▦ Gorge
▦ Glacier
▦ Salt flat
▦ Rocks

## Cities and towns

═ Main through route
═ Main street

═ Minor street
═ Pedestrianized street
)⊂ Tunnel
→ One way-street
▥▥ Steps
⇄ Bridge
▀▀▀ Fortified wall
▦ Park, garden, stadium
● Sleeping
❷ Eating
❶ Bars & clubs
▦ Building
▫ Sight
✝ ✝ Cathedral, church
🏮 Chinese temple
🛕 Hindu temple
🕯 Meru
🕌 Mosque
⌂ Stupa
✡ Synagogue
ℹ Tourist office
🏛 Museum
✉ Post office
Ⓟ Police
Ⓢ Bank
@ Internet
☏ Telephone
🏪 Market
➕ Medical services
🅿 Parking
⛽ Petrol
⛳ Golf
Ⓐ Detail map
◁Ⓐ Related map

## Other symbols

∴ Archaeological site
♦ National park, wildlife reserve
❀ Viewing point
Ⓐ Campsite
⌂ Refuge, lodge
🏰 Castle, fort
🤿 Diving
🌳🌲🌴 Deciduous, coniferous, palm trees
⌂ Hide
🍇 Vineyard, winery
⚗ Distillery
🚢 Shipwreck
⚔ Historic battlefield